Emperor's Chambermaids

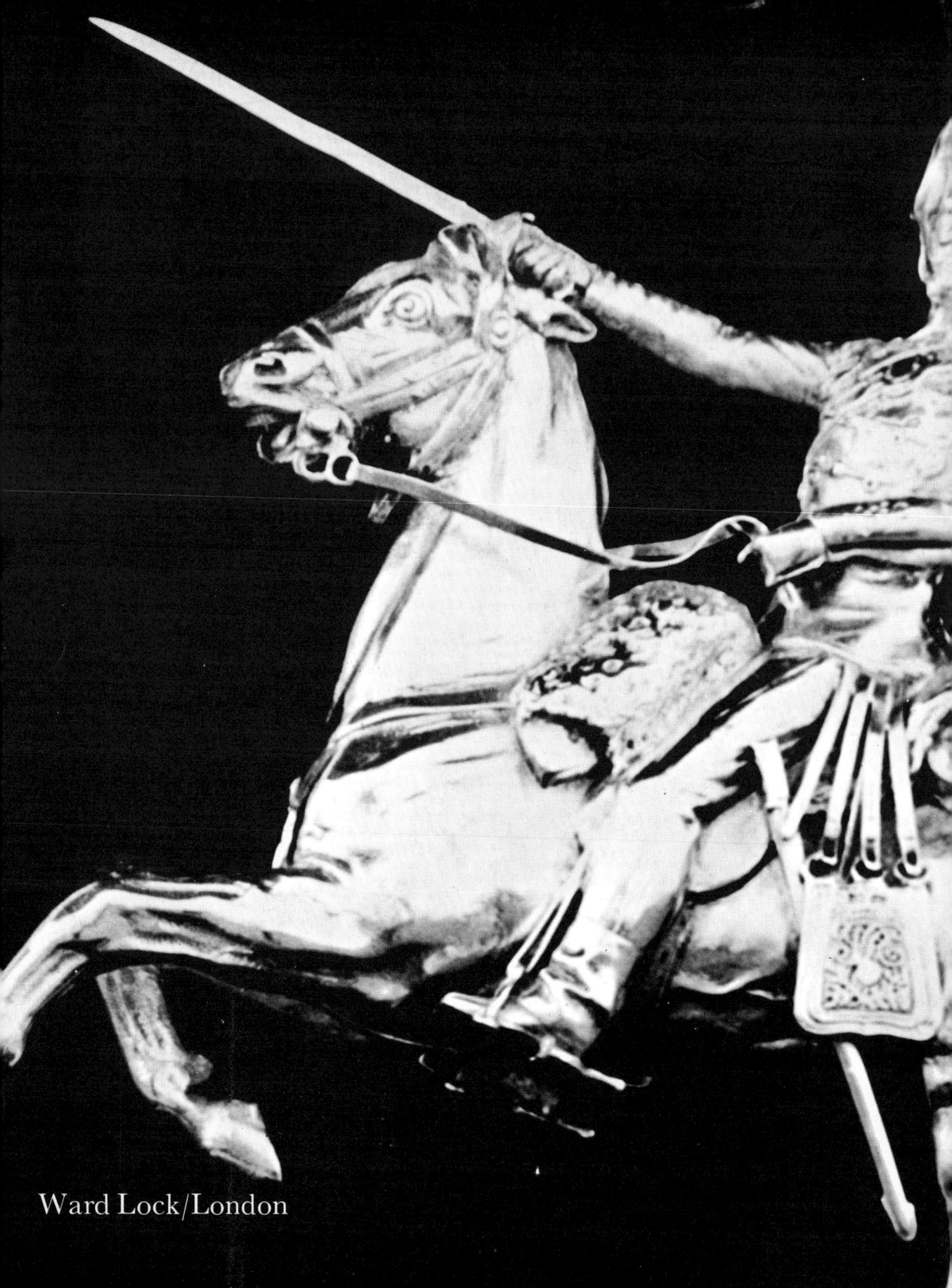

Ward Lock/London

Foreword by M. R. D. Foot

Emperor's Chambermaids

The story of the 14th/20th King's Hussars

Lt.-Colonel L. B. Oatts, DSO

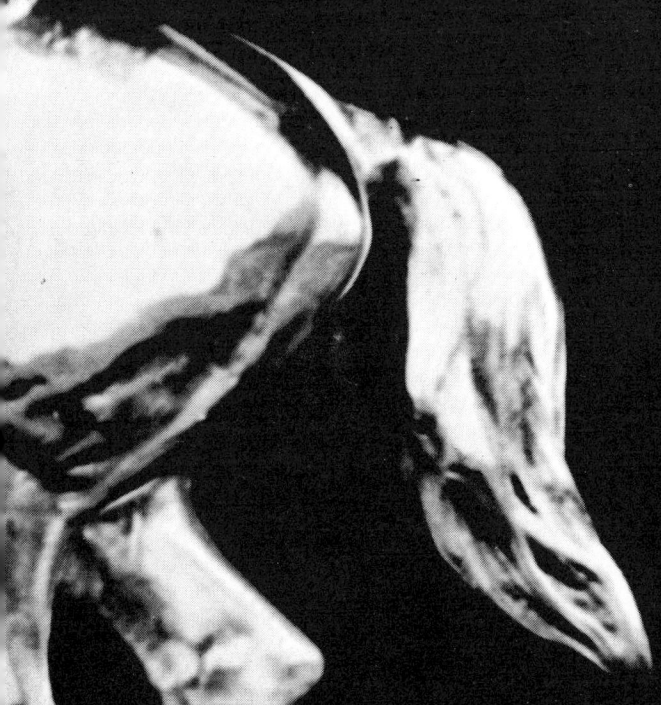

Design   David Roberts

All Rights Reserved. No part of this publication may be reproduced, stored in a retrieval system, or transmitted, in any form or by any means, electronic, mechanical, photocopying, recording or otherwise, without prior permission of the Copyright owner.

Ward Lock Limited, 116 Baker Street, London W1M 2BB

Copyright © 1973 14th/20th King's Hussars
Regimental Endowment Fund
Filmset by Keyspools Ltd, Golborne, Lancs.
Printed in Spain by Editorial fher s.a.

ISBN 706310012

Preface

THIS story was commissioned in order to combine in one volume the Histories of the 14th King's Hussars, the 20th Hussars and their offspring, the 14th/20th King's Hussars.

The basic material came from the very detailed volumes 1 and 2 of the 14th King's Hussars, which spans the years 1715–1922, and The Great War History of the 20th Hussars. The last few chapters bring the history up to date with the record of the 14th/20th King's Hussars from 1922–1969.

By using the political climate as a framework for the deeds of the Regiment, the Author has produced a light and readable story, not only of the Regiment but also of the times which required its services.

R.J.S.

Acknowledgements

I was commissioned to write this history by Colonel R. J. Stephen when he was Colonel of the Regiment, and I would like to thank him and his successors, Colonel B. B. N. Woodd and Colonel R. P. D. F. Allen for their assistance and interest.

I am also indebted to the following for accounts of their personal experiences: Lieutenant-Colonel W. D'Arcy Hall, late 20th Hussars, who was able to describe the first encounters with the enemy in August 1914; the late Brigadier J. G. Browne, who served with the Army of Occupation after the First World War; Colonel the Rev. H. A. R. Tilney who led the Regiment at Medicina in April 1945; and Colonel B. C. L. Tayleur who served with the Regiment throughout the Second World War.

I am also grateful to Professor M. R. D. Foot of Manchester University for reading through the text and making many helpful comments.

The work put in by Major M. A. Urban-Smith and his secretary, Mrs K. M. Kay, at Home Headquarters has been considerable, including maps, captions, appendices and proof-reading.

Finally, I must mention the invaluable technical assistance given by Mr A. A. Shipton, Managing Director of Ward Lock Limited, who served with the Regiment as a young National Service officer. He has given much time to the preparation of the book, and the black-and-white photographs of pictures in the possession of the Officers' Mess were all taken by him personally.

L. B. O.

Foreword

It is at once a pleasure and an honour for a historian in a Lancashire university to be asked to introduce this history of what has quite recently become a local regiment. Here the reader will see, deftly intertwined, the stories of two light cavalry regiments, the 14th and the 20th Light Dragoons, which were eventually amalgamated, after the Great War, into the 14th/20th King's Hussars, and now recruit primarily from this county.

Neither the regiment nor its constituent parts claim ever to have been that one outstanding, heroic unit, upon the action of which the fate of continents has turned on some stricken field; though the 14th still remember their victorious charge at Ramnuggur in the Sikh war of 1848 (one Englishman who took part was still alive in 1932), and the 20th know that they fired the first British shot in anger in 1914, and delivered the last effective British cavalry charge as late as 1920. All through their history four interwoven strands can be observed; gallantry, patience, discipline, and skill. What has made this regiment so distinguished, even among its distinguished light cavalry fellows, has been that its members have always put themselves out to make sure that they are particularly good at their job. All through their career, men in this regiment have excelled at horsemanship, swordsmanship, marksmanship; three principal military skills which they have mastered.

And, being light cavalrymen, they have always kept an eye

open for any opportunities of distinction or of enjoyment that might offer.

It is a nice example of this spirit that makes the most treasured possession of the mess the silver chamberpot belonging to Napoleon's brother Joseph which the 14th captured from his coach when the French army broke at Vittoria in 1813. Yet, though they could and did take part in victories, charges, skirmishes, reconnaissances without number, the officers and men who served in the campaigns described below nevertheless found themselves waiting, most of the time, for something more exciting to do. It is a mark of the skill of their regimental historian that he never keeps his reader waiting for some more exciting page, but maintains a steady level of informed interest.

It is because the army has so regularly had in it people who are prepared to put up with boredom, hunger, dirt, thirst, and danger not simply for hours or days, but for months and years on end, that this country has been able to exist so long uninvaded. It is on such regiments as the 14th/20th that the honour and safety of the country now largely depend; and we have here, in all its fascination, the story of how the regiment grew from small beginnings, nearer three than two centuries ago, to what it is today.

Manchester University   M. R. D. Foot.
22nd May, 1971

Contents

	Preface	page 5
	Foreword	7
1	Early Days	15
2	Cavalry and Dragoons	27
3	War with Revolutionary France	41
4	The West Indies	53
5	Various Small Adventures	65
6	The Start of the Peninsular War	79
7	The Talavera Campaign	91
8	French Invasion of Portugal	109
9	The French Evicted from Portugal	123
10	1812	137
11	Salamanca	151
12	Vittoria	165
13	The Final Advance	181
14	Sideshows	191
15	Riots and Small Wars	205

16	Ramnuggur	219
17	The Indian Mutiny	231
18	Central India, South Africa and the Sudan	243
19	Outbreak of the South African War	257
20	The Advance to Pretoria	273
21	Operations in the Transvaal	291
22	End of the South African War	305
23	Outbreak of the First World War	317
24	Mons, the Marne, the first Ypres	327
25	Start of the Mesopotamian Campaign	343
26	The Western Front 1915–1916	359
27	Mesopotamia and the Western Front 1916–1917	371
28	The Last Twelve Months	393
29	Aftermath	409
30	The Second World War	431
31	The End of the War and Aftermath	457
	Appendix: Maps, Regimental data, etc.	490
	Index	513

Illustrations

Dragoon uniforms	*facing page*	24
Lieutenant-General Louis Dejean		27
Officer of the 14th Dragoons 1740		36
A 14th Light Dragoon 1776		41
General Charles Fitzroy, Lord Southampton		50
Recruiting poster, Napoleonic War		53
H.R.H. Princess Frederica		62
Lieutenant-Colonel Hawker		65
Officer of the 14th Light Dragoons, period 1796–1812		76
Lieutenant-Colonel Charles Taylor		79
Uniform 14th Light Dragoons, 1798–1812		91
Duke of Wellington on *Copenhagen*		102
General John Egerton, Earl of Bridgewater		109
14th Light Dragoons, Guidon c. 1832		123
The flag of truce		137
Uniforms between 1715 and 1900		148

	facing page	
Capture of Joseph Bonaparte's coach		148
Officer of the 14th Light Dragoons, period 1812–1819		151
Officer and trooper 20th Light Dragoons, 1814		162
Capture of the silver chamber-pot ('The Emperor')		165
The silver chamber-pot known as 'The Emperor'		169
Colonel John Townsend		178
The Reception of Princess Frederica of Prussia		202
14th Light Dragoons, full dress 1819		205
King William IV		208
Lieutenant-Colonel William Havelock		219
Lieutenant-Colonel (later Major-General) Herbert Gall		231
The engagement at Ranode, 1858		243
The 20th Hussars arriving at Suakin, 1885		254
14th King's Hussars, review order 1880 (full dress)		257
Silver statuette of *Sanfoin*		260
Officer of the 14th King's Hussars, 1902		273
14th King's Hussars, 1900		291
Colonel E. D. Browne-Synge-Hutchinson		305
14th King's Hussars silver cross-belt pouch		317
Tigris river-steamer		343
Lieutenant-Colonel R. W. Hewitt		356
Men of the 20th Hussars at Bailleul		359
Clearing out snipers at Khazimain		371
On the track of the Turk		371
British cavalry, 1917		390
14th Hussars at Ramadi		393
Farrier-Sergeant Hayward rescuing Lieutenant Hamer		393
Men and horses of the 14th/20th		409
Annual dismounted inspection		409
Medals of Troop-Sergeant-Major Stratford		425
Mounted officer and dismounted trooper, 1936		427
Secunderabad, 1939		428
Tank of the 14th/20th		431
Gendarme reporting to tank crew		431

Scout cars of the Reconnaissance Troop	*facing page*	434
The entry into Kermanshah		440
Trumpetters in Berlin		457
Guidon parade Catterick Camp		457
The Regimental Shooting Team of 1952		468
Presentation of the Guidon, 1961		475
Field-Marshal Sir Gerald Templer reviewing the Regiment		475
The Guidon on parade		476
'C' Squadron patrol in Cyprus		476
H.R.H. The Princess Anne		482
Chieftain Tank in B.A.O.R.		499
General Sir Richard L. McCreery		500
Major-General Sir Henry W. Hodgson		503
General Sir George De S. Barrow		503
Brigadier F. B. Hurndall		503
Lieutenant-Colonel R. J. Stephen		503
Lieutenant-Colonel B. B. N. Woodd		503
Lieutenant-Colonel R. P. D. F. Allen		503
The Regimental Medal		511

Regimental Armour, 1938–1970 pages 485–88, 498

Colour Illustrations

Lieutenant General James Dormer	*facing page*	17
Colonel Sir Felton Bathurst Hervey Bart		17
The 14th Light Dragoons seizing the coach of King Joseph Bonaparte		32
14th Light Dragoons Guidon c. 1830		225
The Battle of Ramnuggur		225
A camp scene, 1858, during the Indian Mutiny		240
Colonel E. D. Browne-Synge-Hutchingson, VC, CB		321
The capture of Medicina		336
The Guidon of the 14th/20th King's Hussars 1961		465
Regimental Silver		465
Her Royal Highness The Princess Anne		480

July 1715 Raising of the 14th Dragoons
November 1715 Battle of Preston
May 1717 The 14th leave for Ireland
1742 Outbreak of the War of the Austrian Succession
July 1745 Landing of Prince Charles Edward
September 1745 The 'Canter of Coltbridge' and Battle of Prestonpans

1713

Early Days

1

In 1713 the long war of the Spanish Succession was ended with the signature of the Treaty of Utrecht, by which vast overseas territories as well as trading rights were secured by Great Britain, which now became a Great Power.

The Duke of Marlborough, whose military and political genius had brought this about, had fallen into disgrace and been dismissed from his offices before the end of the war, with the result that there was no-one in a position to exercise any restraint over the British Government as it carried out its usual policy at the end of hostilities of a wholesale disbandment of the armed forces. By 1715 the British Army had consequently been reduced to a total of 22,000 men, of whom two-thirds were stationed in Flanders and the colonies. This left a ludicrously small number for the maintenance of law and order in the United Kingdom, at a time when there was every reason for expecting trouble.

The death of Queen Anne and the accession of the Elector of Hanover as King George I in 1714 resulted in the return of Marlborough to his old appointment of Captain-General. Further disbandments in the Army were then checked, and various improvements in training, equipment and conditions of service were instigated. Before they could become effective, however, an attempt was made by the exiled son of King James II to

1715

regain the throne of the United Kingdom. Backed by France, and with the hope of support from the English and Welsh Jacobites, the Stuart standard was raised in Scotland by the Earl of Mar, and soon after, James Stuart himself, the 'Old Pretender', arrived in the Highlands.

With so few troops available to deal with it, the rebellion of 'the 'fifteen' caused considerable panic in government circles, and twenty-one new regiments were hastily raised, of which thirteen were dragoons and the rest foot.

At this time cavalry as such – soldiers, that is to say, who fought on horseback – was still in the state of eclipse dating from the days of musketeers and pikemen, whose close formations and firepower made it impossible for cavalry to charge them. Horse had therefore given place to dragoons on the eighteenth-century battlefield, and no new regiments of horse were raised.

Dragoons, who took their name from the *dragon*, a short musket, were theoretically mounted infantry. They were organised by companies, after the manner of infantry, were mounted on 'inferior horses', and drilled by drum instead of trumpet. They were intended to dismount out of range and, leaving a horseholder in charge of every ten horses, attack in infantry formations on foot. This at least, was the original theory. In practice, owing to constant changes in tactics, dragoons tended to engage mounted, and to fire from the saddle which, against infantry, actually placed them at a disadvantage. In the end they became cavalry again, but at this time they were still neither one thing nor the other.

The 14th, or Dormer's Dragoons, later the 14th Light Dragoons and finally the 14th Hussars, was raised in the southern counties in July 1715 by Brigadier-General James Dormer. Owing to the situation in Scotland, it had to be raised in considerable haste, and the majority of the original officers and men had almost certainly served before in regiments disbanded after the Treaty of Utrecht. Although a Dragoon regiment, which should have been organised into companies like the infantry, it was in fact organised into six troops which were led respectively by the Colonel (whose troop was commanded by Lieut. J. Stevens as Captain-Lieutenant), Lt.-Col. H. Killegrew, Major Sol Rapin, and Captains H. Pelham, W. Boyle and Beverly Newcomin.

The regiment marched north at the end of October 1715, at a total strength of 231 all-ranks. This was about half the regular establishment at that time, but it had been unable in three months to complete itself in men, horses, arms, uniforms and equipment, which is scarcely to be wondered at. Because of the

Lieutenant-General James Dormer. Founder of the 14th, 22nd July 1715. Colonel of the Regiment 1715–1720 during which time the Regiment was known as Dormer's Dragoons.

Colonel Sir Felton Bathurst Hervey, Bart. A distinguished young officer who commanded the 14th during the greater part of the Peninsular War after losing an arm during the crossing of the Douro in 1809. He served on the staff of the Duke of Wellington at Waterloo.

haste in which the regiment was raised, no more definite location of origin can be given to it than the 'southern counties'. The senior officers and captains would each have been responsible for raising their own troops, with the help of their subalterns and, while doing so, would have ridden considerable distances over the countryside attempting to attract recruits in competition with the officers of the other newly-raised regiments. Many of the original recruits to the 14th appear to have been Irishmen, probably discharged cavalrymen unable to find employment and too poor to get home. This led to Ireland being named as the country of origin of the 14th in the regimental records, which were commenced some forty years later, but it seems reasonably certain that this was an error. The first uniforms issued were scarlet, with lemon-yellow facings and white, red and green mixed lace, but it seems unlikely that the regiment could have obtained them in time to wear them for the march north, so that the first appearance of the 14th Dragoons on the line of march could scarcely have been very impressive – although the Dragoons themselves were fine men.

In Scotland the Earl of Mar had speedily raised an army of about 12,000 men, which was sufficient to overrun the whole country and evict all the Hanoverian troops, had it been properly handled. Mar, however, made no pretence of being a military leader, and had no idea as to how to plan a campaign. He had come over in advance of the Old Pretender in order to raise troops, and was expecting his master to follow him and take charge. When the Old Pretender failed to arrive, Mar was obliged to start operations without him. One or two abortive thrusts towards Perth and Edinburgh were easily frustrated by the Duke of Argyll who, at the head of about 6,000 Government troops, then faced the Jacobite army at Sheriffmuir, near Stirling on the 12th November. The battle was indecisive, with both armies retiring, but meanwhile a Jacobite force of about 1,500 men had marched into England west of the Pennines, hoping to collect English and Welsh recruits. On the 8th November this force occupied Preston, and General Wills, at Manchester, thereupon marched against it with such Government troops as he had available. These were the 9th, 11th, 13th and 14th Dragoons, Pitt's Regiment of Horse and three regiments of foot. The Dragoon regiments afterwards became the 9th Lancers, and the 11th, 13th and 14th Hussars, while Pitt's Horse – like all regiments of horse outside the Household Brigade – was turned into Dragoons and became the 2nd Dragoon Guards (Queen's Bays).

1716

The Jacobite leaders, who had been busy beating up for recruits – with a certain amount of success – had not known that Wills had so many troops at Manchester, and were taken by surprise. Their position in fact was hopeless, and all they could do was to secure the bridge over the Ribble, and all other roads into Preston. They were mostly farm labourers from the Borders, who had been obliged to follow their lords, and the only men among them capable of engaging regular troops on equal terms were a few hundred Highlanders of the Clan Mackintosh, led by Mackintosh of Borlum, known as 'Old Borlum', who was an experienced soldier and had seen much service under the French.

Marching through Wigan, General Wills arrived before Preston on the morning of the 12th November and, finding the Jacobites defending the approaches, dismounted the Dragoons – for an attack on a defended town was not a cavalry affair. The bridge over the Ribble was defended by a hundred Mackintoshes led by Farquarson of Invercauld, while another important locality was held by Lord George Murray – another experienced soldier – with some more of Borlum's men. Borlum himself defended what was known as the Windmill Barrier. The 14th, dismounted, attacked Lord George Murray's position. Although they advanced twice with great resolution, and succeeded in carrying the barricades, they were driven back on each occasion by a murderous fire from the adjoining houses.

All other attacks met with the same fate, and General Wills then changed his tactics and commenced methodically to set fire to the houses which covered the Jacobite sharpshooters. The arrival of Government reinforcements under General Carpenter at last convinced the Border lords that their cause was hopeless and they surrendered 'at discretion' on the 14th November. Altogether, 1,468 prisoners were taken and housed in various gaols. One batch was escorted by the 14th Dragoons to Lancaster gaol, and the regiment remained in the vicinity for the next six months. During this time the Old Pretender made a belated appearance in Scotland, but by that time the clans had dispersed and the Duke of Argyll had regained control. James Stuart accordingly returned to France, taking with him a number of Jacobite lords. After a fairly moderate number of prisoners had been hanged, drawn and quartered as an example, the rebellion of the 'fifteen' came officially to an end.

In 1716 the 14th marched from Lancaster to Lincoln, and were quartered in that area until May 1717, when the regiment moved to Ireland and remained there for the next twenty-five years.

Apart from another attempt at rebellion in the Highlands in

1719, there now ensued a period of peace longer than Great Britain had previously enjoyed in history. It was ushered in by further cuts in the establishment of the Army which the 14th, by serving in Ireland, were fortunate to escape. Even during times of quiet, troops in that country had always to be on the alert, as well as being almost continually on the move, so that – at any rate to a certain extent – the 14th were also unaffected by the neglect and collapse of discipline experienced by the regiments in the United Kingdom; and which was so evident that soldiers were not always sober when furnishing royal guards and escorts. Although in fact, in the United Kingdom as in Ireland, the Army provided the only means of maintaining law and order, it was allowed to sink into a state in which it was incapable of doing so among its own rank and file, in spite of the most savage punishments. Fortunately, however, the country was experiencing an unexampled prosperity so that, although it was a fine time for highwaymen and smugglers, the authorities were not threatened by any disaffection or industrial troubles.

George II, who had served under Marlborough and had a fair knowledge of military matters, succeeded to the throne in 1727 and immediately endeavoured to restore discipline and efficiency in the Army. His method of doing so was to dress the soldiers better, with a view to giving them self-respect as well as to attract recruits. Hair was ordered to be tied back in pigtails, pomaded and powdered; officers being ordered to abandon the peruke and, if they did not wear their own hair, to adopt the powdered tie-wig with side-curls. Enormous jackboots were provided for the cavalry and white gaiters for the infantry, while all arms wore laced tricorn hats. The appearance of the regiments of Horse and Dragoons was also enhanced by painted or embroidered saddle-housings and holster-caps, but spoiled at the same time by the practice of docking the tails of the horses – although this was in accordance with contemporary fashion, so that long-tailed horses became difficult to come by.

Everyone, especially a monarch, who attempts to improve the appearance of the Army, is automatically subjected to criticism and ridicule, and King George was no exception. Nevertheless it seems that his efforts did have the desired result of restoring the confidence and self-respect of the officers and men. The standard of training, especially in the cavalry, was still, however, nothing to be proud of. All the lessons so hardly learnt under the Duke of Marlborough appear to have been forgotten, and the cavalry to have been ignorant of the most elementary principles and practices of field operations. So long of course as their duties were

1743

confined to escorting royal carriages and chasing highwaymen this did not matter much, but the time soon came when something had to be done about it.

Relations with Spain had been worsening for some years when, in 1729, an English smuggler, Captain Jenkins, lost an ear in a fracas with Spanish coastguards on the shores of South America. This incident brought to a head the grievance under which English captains were suffering by not being allowed to trade in those parts. The war which resulted had barely petered out before the War of the Austrian Succession started in 1742 by a French invasion of King George's Electorate of Hanover and subsequent threats to Austria and Belgium. This was no frivolous matter like the loss of an ear. With one short interval of peace, it was to plunge most of Europe into a war lasting eleven years.

The 14th, who had been for so long leading an uneventful life in Ireland, were recalled to England on the outbreak of war. There is no record of where the regiment was stationed, but it was no doubt as widely dispersed over the country as it had been in Ireland. This wide dispersal, which often led to troops of cavalry being divided by having to provide numerous detachments commanded by corporals, was necessary in order to keep the peace, but it prevented a regiment from reaching even the lowest standards of efficiency for it could never carry out any training. Apart from its subjection to these adverse conditions the regiment on arrival in England would have had to part with all or most of its trained soldiers to those regiments under orders for the Continent. As usual, the establishments of all regiments had been greatly increased on the outbreak of war; a cavalry regiment being increased from four to six troops, and the strength of each troop doubled. While in Ireland, the 14th had been kept at little more than a cadre strength, and although it had retained six troops it is unlikely that there were more than 25 men in each; yet, in 1743, just after parting with its trained men, its establishment was increased to 59 a troop. To all intents and purposes, the regiment had therefore to start life again, but whereas in 1715 it had been able to enlist veteran discharged soldiers, in 1743 there were none but raw countrymen available and young unbroken horses. At the same time the regiment lost its Colonel, Archibald Hamilton, who was promoted to Major-General, and was commanded by the Lieutenant-Colonel, William Wright.

The outbreak of war had given fresh hope to the Jacobites, who could now count upon the active support of France, whose interests would be greatly forwarded by a rebellion in England. An expedition under Marshal Saxe, and accompanied by Prince

1745

Charles Edward, the 'Young Pretender', set sail in the autumn of 1743, but was dispersed by storms when off Dungeness. The threat caused considerable alarm to the British Government, and all available troops, including the 14th Dragoons, were sent to Scotland and northern England.

After the failure of the expedition, Prince Charlie had returned disconsolate to Paris, where his attempts to enlist further French support met with no success. Although warned by his British adherents that his cause would be hopeless unless he could bring at least six thousand men, he finally determined to try his fortune alone, and in 1745, encouraged by the British defeat at Fontenoy, he landed on the west coast of Scotland on the 25th July, accompanied by only seven followers.

It was officially estimated at that time that the Highland clans could put 32,000 men into the field, and this number, which was certainly an under-estimate, would have been more than sufficient to put the Stuarts back on the throne. The clan chiefs, however, would never combine in any common cause, being of different political complexions and madly jealous of one another. Even such men as Montrose and Dundee had never succeeded in gathering much more than 10,000 Highlanders at a time, and these they had the greatest difficulty in keeping together. The chiefs, however, were well-aware that they had little future under a Whig Government, and were in general ready enough to call out their clans in the Stuart cause if there was a reasonable hope of victory.

Bonnie Prince Charlie, when he landed near Moidart off a French brig with his seven men, brought no such hope, and was but ill-received by the MacDonalds of Keppoch and Glengarry, whose territory this was. He was in fact only saved from the necessity of re-embarking by the opportune arrival of Clan Cameron, under its revered chief, 'the Gentle Lochiel', who succeeded in persuading the MacDonalds to take a chance and call out their men. Lochiel could parade about 800 Highlanders, Glencarry 500, and Keppoch 300, and, with this meagre force of under two thousand men, and without any artillery, cavalry or transport, Prince Charlie set out to win back the throne of his forefathers.

Although General Sir John Cope, the Commander-in-Chief in Scotland, had heard rumours of Prince Charlie's arrival, the Prince had been in Scotland for a week before these rumours were confirmed. Cope was in a very awkward position, for he had only about three thousand men at his disposal, most of whom were raw recruits indifferently armed. Not unnaturally he was inclined to

1745

remain on the defensive and await reinforcements, but the Lords Justices in Edinburgh, who were in a state of considerable apprehension, ordered him north, and he set out accordingly for Fort Augustus. After narrowly escaping being exterminated by Prince Charlie's Highlanders, he ended up in Inverness where, not liking the idea of retreating through the Highlands, he sent for ships to take him back to Edinburgh.

After entering Perth on the 4th September and collecting many useful adherents, Prince Charlie marched by Stirling, crossed the Forth and on the 15th arrived within eight miles of Edinburgh whose regular troops – apart from the garrison of the Castle – were the newly-arrived 13th and 14th Dragoons, both of which regiments were wholly composed of young English recruits who were in mortal fear of the Highlanders as, indeed, were the citizens of Edinburgh.

Although irregular troops, the Highlanders were far from being undisciplined mobs. They owed, and willingly gave, implicit obedience to their chiefs, most of whom were educated and cultured men with military experience. In the field, the clans were organised into regiments, under the leadership of their officers who were mostly kinsmen of the chief. They were dressed in long tartan plaids, which they wore belted round the waist, in such a manner that they could carry their rations and essentials in the folds, and draw the ends over their heads in rough weather or while sleeping. Their basic arms were a broadsword, dirk and target, or round leather shield, but a fair number carried muskets or pikes – sometimes scythe-blades fixed to poles, which were useful against horsemen. Their normal method of attack was to draw up in two lines, preferably up-hill of the enemy. After a pause to work themselves up into the *mir cath* – 'the desperate frenzy of battle' – they would advance within range at a stately walk, then halt, fire a volley and throw away their muskets, draw their swords and dirks, and charge at great speed. Given reasonable conditions, they could always break a line of regulars in this way. They had acquired a high – indeed terrifying – reputation in the rank and file of the British Army, but although this was fully deserved, it was more than off-set by their traditional and temperamental peculiarities, not least among which was their hubristic standard of honour, which in battle made them prefer to stand up and be shot at like a man, rather than skulk under cover and await a favourable opportunity for getting the better of the enemy.

As for the Dragoons, they were armed with heavy curved cavalry swords, but also carried infantry muskets and bayonets for, as previously mentioned, they were in theory expected to fight on foot. In actual fact, they usually fired a volley from the saddle after which, as it was impossible to load a musket on horseback, they were left encumbered with a useless firearm, which prevented them from either drawing swords or controlling their horses, so that, to such men as Prince Charlie's Highlanders, they were easy meat.

The 13th Dragoons, under Colonel Gardiner, had been retiring before Prince Charlie's army since it had crossed the Forth, and their gallopers had apprised the authorities in Edinburgh of its arrival at Corstorphin. The news threw the city into confusion and the 14th Dragoons, who had just arrived, were sent out at once to reinforce Gardiner, accompanied by a party of the town-guard, who were not much better than armed watchmen. On the morning of the 16th the two Dragoon regiments and the town-guard were drawn up at Coltbridge. They appear to have been dismounted behind a line of mounted picquets. They were too close to the Highlanders for comfort, and the sound of Lochiel's war-pipes caused the town-guard to bolt back to Edinburgh, while the untrained horses of the Dragoons, sensing the atmosphere, became restive. When the order was given to mount, both regiments were already in some disorder. At this time Prince Charlie had no cavalry, but he had managed to collect 'some gentlemen on horseback' who acted as his vanguard. These gentlemen now made their appearance and, on sighting the line of picquets, rode at them firing off their pistols and succeeded in bolting the lot. The picquets, coming back at full gallop through the two regiments, bolted them also, for the young soldiers, encumbered by their heavy muskets, could not hold their horses. What became dubbed as 'the Canter of Coltbridge' then ensued and, in spite of the oaths and entreaties of their officers, it became impossible to halt either regiment until darkness.

Arriving at the West Port at dusk, the Camerons tricked the town-guard into opening it for them, which enabled Prince Charlie to capture the city – except the castle – by daybreak without striking a blow and with most of the inhabitants unaware of what had happened. Riding in the next morning, one of the citizens was staggered to find Highlanders on guard at the gate. 'Where the devil is the guard?' he asked. 'She was relieved,' replied the sentry, with a sly grin.

On the same day 'Johnny Cope' disembarked his troops at Dunbar, and on the 19th, having collected the 13th and 14th Dragoons, began to march up the coast towards Edinburgh.

1745

Prince Charlie had been warned of his arrival and, leaving Edinburgh, had taken up a position on Carberry Hill overlooking the coast road. As usual, the Highlanders made no attempt to hide themselves, and Johnny Cope got a severe shock when he saw them, quietly waiting in his rear. He immediately took up a strong position at Prestonpans, with his rear on the sea, his right on a marsh, and his left protected by some high walls. Thereupon the Highlanders came down from the hill and formed up across the marsh, causing Johnny Cope to change front to that direction. Deeming the marsh impassable, he posted no picquets along his front, but the Highlanders crossed it during the night with the help of local guides, and shortly before daybreak on the morning of the 21st September, Cope discovered them formed up for attack only two hundred yards to his front. Hastily beating to arms, he formed his infantry in line facing the Highlanders, with the 13th Dragoons on the right and the 14th on the left, both regiments mounted. His artillery, which consisted of a few naval guns manned by seamen, was in front of the infantry, presumably because there was no time to get it into a more secure position.

Prince Charlie, who was in command in person, had some difficulty in forming line of battle in the dim light of the September dawn, just after negotiating a marsh, but once his men were ready he lost no time in giving the signal for attack. Firing a volley, the Highlanders drew their swords and advanced at a steady trot, gradually increasing their speed until, with wild howls, they flung themselves on the gunners and rushed in among the Dragoons, cutting at the noses of the horses. Although the infantry made a show of resistance, they were no match for the Highlanders, and the whole affair was over in a few minutes, with Cope's army broken and in flight.

Johnny Cope could probably have put up a better performance than this, had he not been taken by surprise, and left with no time to make any proper plan. It was, however, inexcusable to use the Dragoons as cavalry and yet not order them to charge, for cavalry when halted was always more vulnerable than infantry. The result of the battle naturally gave great encouragement to the Jacobites, and their jokes at the expense of Johnny Cope and his men – particularly the Dragoons – have resulted in posterity regarding their conduct in the worst possible light. In actual fact, the Dragoons did their best in a perfectly impossible position and many of them, especially their officers, fought gallantly. Colonel Gardiner of the 13th was killed and his Lieutenant-Colonel, Whitney, badly wounded, while Major Bowles of the 14th and several of his troops put up a spirited fight during which Bowles

1745

had his horse killed under him and received eleven wounds, being saved from being hacked to pieces by the intervention of one of the officers of Clan Cameron. The battlefield presented an even more horrible appearance than usual, for no fewer than four hundred of Cope's men had been cut down by the Highland broadswords, and their remains were an alarming reminder to the thousand and more prisoners of the fate from which they had been spared by the clemency of the clan chiefs.

After the battle the 13th and 14th Dragoons, with the hundred or so other survivors, assembled at Berwick-on-Tweed and later joined a force under General Wade at Newcastle, which was preparing to defend the southern routes through Northumberland.

Dragoon uniform: *left* 1742, *right* 1715. These were the first uniforms worn by the 14th. Facings were yellow. Dragoons were in theory expected to ride to the battle and then fight on foot, dressed in high boots and spurs and armed with swords, muskets and bayonets.

Lieut.-General Louis Dejean, Colonel 14th Dragoons 1752–57. He served originally in 1st Troop, Horse Grenadier Guards, part of the Household Cavalry. During his Colonelcy the 14th carried out internal security duties in Ireland where British troops were widely deployed.

January 1746 Battle of Falkirk
1747 The 14th return to Ireland
1756 Outbreak of the Seven Years' War
Beginnings of Light Cavalry
1759 Raising of the 20th Light Dragoons
Music and Muster-Rolls
Dress, Guidons, Equipment and Horses

1745

2

Cavalry and Dragoons

After Prestonpans many new adherents joined Prince Charlie. His force increased to about 6,000, and some French officers, bringing money and arms – including artillery – came over from France. Owing, however, to the temporary desertion of many of his Highlanders – who had taken home their battlefield loot – and to divided counsels among his chiefs and advisers, he was unable to follow up his success, and was delayed in Edinburgh until November.

Meanwhile urgent steps were being taken by the Government to deal with the rebellion. The Duke of Cumberland and all British forces on the Continent were recalled, and new regiments raised at home. Until they could all be assembled however, the only effective opposition to a Jacobite invasion of England rested in Field-Marshal Wade's formation at Newcastle. Wade himself was old and infirm, and his troops young and unreliable. Prince Charlie was accordingly strongly tempted to march against him, but was persuaded to take the old route west of the Pennines, which was unguarded and offered more chance of obtaining active supporters. The Highlanders, however, were far from enthusiastic at the idea of invading England without the certainty of a welcome from at least some of the inhabitants and after they had marched as far as Derby without any signs of such,

1746

the Prince was prevailed upon to abandon the venture and withdraw back to Scotland.

The Jacobites retraced their steps accordingly and, having got the better of Cumberland's vanguards, arrived back in Scotland in very good order. Prince Charlie's next objective was Stirling Castle, but while he was besieging it, General Hawley, who had relieved Field-Marshal Wade, crossed the Border and began preparations for marching north. His advanced guard, consisting of the 14th Dragoons and some infantry, arrived at Linlithgow on the 13th January, 1746, and ran into a Jacobite force under Lord George Murray who, in a letter to his wife dated the 15th January, described the encounter as follows:

'On Monday morning (13th) I marched to Lithgow with five Batalions & some horse in order to see what provisions were got there for our enemys, & resolv'd to return at night. In the fornoon we see'd a Reg: of Dragouns & gave them chasse for an houre, but could not come up with them. We returned & dined; then just as we were comming out of town to return, their Dragouns, four Regiments of Regular foot, & some Militia came closs up to us. It was too great a venture for us to have atact them, since it was risquing the whole cause, tho' we had the fairest prospect imaginable to have cutt them off. Locheall's Regement, which should also have been with us, had, to my great concern, been ordered over to Alloa two days before; Had that not hapned, we would have had it so sure that nothing would have prevented us from atacting them. They followed us to the bridge on this side of Lithgow; we were very near, but not a shott.

'The whole of their Armie is now come from Edr & I believe incamp't twixt this and Lithgow, so we expect a Batle in a day or two. They are 12 Regs foot, 2 Dragouns, besides two thousand Militia, & it is said another of horse & two of foot will join them from Ingland very soon.'

Lord George Murray's information was extremely accurate. The '2 Dragouns' were, of course, the 13th and 14th, while the other regiment of horse which he mentions as being on its way north was the 9th Dragoons. The Duke of Cumberland, after relieving Carlisle, had been recalled to the south to prepare for a threatened French invasion of the southern coast.

General Hawley's army was far from being in good shape. The Militia was practically useless; only two or three of the infantry regiments were experienced and reliable, and the 13th and 14th Dragoons were still suffering from the effects of their unhappy experience at Prestonpans. It seems likely indeed that their descriptions of the prowess and ferocity of the Highlanders at close quarters – which would have lost nothing in the telling – had had an adverse effect on morale generally, and that by this time the rank and file regarded Prince Charlie's men with a kind of superstitious awe. It is, of course, not at all unusual for the morale of an army to be lowered in this manner, and it is the business of a commander to prevent it happening in the first place or immediately to rectify it if it does. The Duke of Cumberland had studied the reasons for the defeat at Prestonpans, and had designed a special formation for receiving and defeating the Highland charge, while at the same time he went to great lengths to counter the fear with which the Highlander had come to be regarded throughout the Army. Nothing of this sort, however, had been done by General Hawley, although he owed to Cumberland his appointment as Commander-in-Chief in Scotland. Like Cumberland, he was a brutal disciplinarian, but he did not have the imagination to attempt to restore morale other than with the lash. Still, he was an efficient soldier who at least understood the principle that cavalry must not receive an attack mounted but must either dismount or, preferably, advance and charge.

On the 16th January Prince Charlie, hearing of Hawley's march on Falkirk, raised the siege of Stirling Castle and formed up on Falkirk Muir, south of the English camp. Hawley had gone off to have a drink with Lady Kilmarnock (whose husband was in the Jacobite army) at Callendar House and General Huske, who had been left in charge, was apparently taken by surprise. As the drums beat to quarters a galloper was sent for Hawley, who soon came tearing into camp without his hat. The 9th Dragoons had arrived and the General took the three regiments, 9th, 13th and 14th, at a gallop through a storm of driving sleet, in an attempt to gain the summit of Falkirk Muir before the Highlanders who, however, were too quick for him.

Hawley then formed line of battle on the lower ground, with his left on a morass, and the three regiments of Dragoons in front of it. Prince Charlie's left, with the MacDonalds in front, supported by the Athol Highlanders, was facing Hawley's centre. Both armies were about nine thousand strong. As soon as he was ready, Hawley sent forward the Dragoons to charge the MacDonalds. The ground, however, was so rough, besides being uphill, that the Dragoons were unable to get up speed and arrived in front of the Highlanders in a ragged line at a stumbling trot. The sleet drove straight into their faces, so that they were barely able to see the steady line of their redoubtable opponents who, with

1746

their bagpipes playing, awaited them with the utmost confidence.

The MacDonalds held their fire until the very last moment, firing a devastating volley at a range of no more than ten yards. Throwing down their muskets they then drew swords and fell upon the Dragoons, slashing at the horses' heads as at Prestonpans. This soon bolted the 13th and 14th Dragoons who were in the lead but the 9th, who were in support, came on in somewhat better order – but with no better success for when ridden down, their hardy, agile antagonists disappeared among the horses' legs and dirked them in the belly. This treatment disposed of the 9th Dragoons and while Hawley's foot were thus unsteadied by the rout of his horse, they were set upon by the Camerons, Macphersons and Appin Stewarts. All of them except the two regiments on the right – who were not charged – turned and fled, with the Highlanders making havoc among them.

'My heart is broke,' wrote Hawley. The only part of his force that he was able to rally immediately consisted of the 9th Dragoons and the 4th and 48th Regiments of Foot which had come off unscathed, but he soon collected the remainder and was able to report that discipline had been recovered. An odd feature of his report on the affair, was that while he severely castigated the foot for 'scandalous cowardice' his only mention of the Dragoons was that thirty-one of Hamilton's (the 14th) were to be hanged for 'deserting to the rebels'. This is hard to understand, and it can only be supposed that these unfortunates had surrendered to the Highlanders after being unhorsed. As the Jacobite army had no means of dealing with prisoners – unless they were men of standing and importance – they were no doubt turned loose later, picked up by Hawley, and hanged as an example. Thirty-two of the foot were shot for 'cowardice' which probably meant that they threw away their muskets when they ran for it, and so could not claim that they thought an order had been given to retire.

After his defeat at Falkirk, Hawley concentrated his force at Linlithgow where he hanged, shot and flogged it into good order. Cumberland, having decided that there was no longer any danger of a French invasion in the south, hastened to Edinburgh to take over.

By the time he arrived there, Hawley had restored morale and was preparing to march again on Stirling. Prince Charlie then moved on Inverness, with Cumberland on his heels and, after a period of manoeuvring and small skirmishes, the two armies eventually faced one another on Culloden Moor on the 16th April. Here the Highlanders met with their first and decisive

1748

defeat, and the rebellion was crushed. Neither the 13th nor the 14th Dragoons took part, being employed patrolling the roads to the west. Their losses in officers and non-commissioned officers had been heavy, and it is evident that neither regiment had recovered from the series of disastrous experiences suffered at the hands of Prince Charlie's Highlanders.

Thus ended a black period in the history of the British Army in general, and the 14th Dragoons in particular, for which there is no parallel. Neither the King nor the Duke of Cumberland held anyone to blame for the conduct of the troops in Scotland, or attempted to find a scapegoat. They were only too well-aware that this conduct was the inevitable result of years of neglect, which had led to the necessity, in a major national emergency, of filling the ranks with idle vagabonds and indifferent horseflesh and sending them into battle undisciplined and only about a quarter trained. The regimental officers were also for the most part inexperienced, but unlike their men, they were good material, and in action did not hesitate to risk their lives in attempts to keep order.

The example provided by the rebellion of the 'forty-five' of the folly of neglecting the armed forces was not lost on the British Government and, although the armed forces have continued to be a political plaything to the present day, and subject to all manner of extraordinary treatment in the cause of parliamentary expediency and vote-catching, they have never been allowed to sink to quite so low a level of efficiency as that reached in the mid-eighteenth century. Prince Charlie had also other lessons to teach the British Army – although in the eyes of posterity he is only allowed to take the blame for failure, and receives no credit for his successes. The remarkable mobility of the Highland army, its admirable tactics and use of ground, and its bold manoeuvres in action all received close attention from the Duke of Cumberland and his officers, and may well have contributed to the unrivalled reputation which the British Army henceforward acquired on the battlefields of the world.

The War of the Austrian Succession came to an end in 1748, with the signature of the Treaty of Aix-la-Chapelle, under which France restored her conquests. Throughout the war she had had the advantages of unity and superior numbers, as well as an outstanding commander in Marshal Saxe. The fact that she was obliged, under these circumstances, to concede what amounted to a draw, appears to have been due to the state of the French armed forces, which was even worse than that of the British. This had also prevented France from mounting an invasion of Great

1748

Britain in support of Prince Charlie, losing her an opportunity of disposing of her great trade rival which was never to recur. The peace treaty, however, merely brought to an end the war in Europe. The struggle for colonial advantage between the two powers continued in India and North America with gradually increasing intensity. In accordance with their usual practice, the British politicians turned a blind eye to this fact as long as possible, pretending that the country was at peace, and giving armed support to the British colonies and trading companies only when forced to do so as a last alternative. The British Army therefore continued to be subjected to a never-ending series of alterations in establishment as the demands for its services waxed or waned, which made the business of training it for war one of some difficulty.

Before leaving the period of the Jacobite rebellions, attention must be drawn to the fact that the affair at Preston, in 1715, was, besides being the first action fought by the 14th Dragoons, the only occasion in the history of the regiment on which it was actually used as Dragoons; that is to say, dismounted and formed as a battalion of infantry before getting to close quarters. During the later rebellion of the 'forty-five, the idea of the regiment dismounting and fighting as infantry never seems to have occurred to anyone. The same can be said of all the other Dragoon regiments at the time, although when the Duke of Cumberland took charge and followed the Highland army to Inverness, he endeavoured to put his 'Corps of Dragoons' in its place, reminding the regiments that 'they are still Dragoons and not Horse, that they are to March and attack on foot, if there is occasion when dismounted. Therefore the mens' boots are not to be encumbered with great spur-leathers and chains, to hinder them from getting over a hedge, ditch or works, when they are ordered to attack, and when ever they are ordered on such service, they are to sling their swords over their shoulders.'

'Butcher' Cumberland was a most formidable character. Disregard for his orders and wishes was unwise, to say the least of it. Yet, as far as can be ascertained, his Dragoons paid no attention to these directions whatsoever. The trouble arose from the method of first forming regiments of Dragoons in the British Army. Instead of raising them from scratch, some of the old regiments of Horse were converted and, to make up for what was officially recognised as a 'denegration' these regiments were given the title of Dragoon Guards, as a sop to their injured pride. Very naturally, the implication that they were inferior to the Horse was not accepted by the Dragoons, who continued to regard themselves

The 14th Light Dragoons seizing the coach of King Joseph Bonaparte after the Battle of Vittoria, 21st June 1813.

Oil painting by R. Hillingford, R.I.

as cavalry, going out of their way to prove themselves so on every possible occasion. The official reaction was eventually to convert all regiments of Horse into Dragoons with the exception of the Household regiments; presumably in the hope that if there was no cavalry, the temptation for Dragoons to pretend to be cavalry would disappear. By the time this measure was completed, however, the need for cavalry on the battlefield had returned, and Dragoons ceased to be regarded as mounted infantry who were supposed only to fight on foot. The scheme in fact never worked in the British Army, and it is not at all clear why it was ever attempted, except that originally a regiment of Dragoons cost less than a regiment of Horse – the pay being less and the horses of inferior quality. Experience in later wars, at any rate, tended to show that, whenever the circumstances in any particular campaign demanded the use of mounted infantry, it was better to mount the infantry rather than 'denegrate' the cavalry. This after all, is commonsense, and so might well have been thought of in the first place. An infantryman, while only too glad to save his feet on the line of march by riding a horse – and the more spiritless the animal the better – has no desire to continue in the saddle when he comes under fire, but instinctively prefers to have both his feet – and his stomach for that matter – on the ground. A cavalryman on the other hand, who has been trained to ride the enemy down, feels only half a soldier on foot and is therefore reluctant to dismount under fire – whether from a horse or an armoured vehicle.

In 1747, the 14th Dragoons returned to Ireland and remained in that country for the next forty-eight years. The regiment just escaped being disbanded at the end of the War of the Austrian Succession, when it became the junior cavalry regiment in the British Army, after all below it had been paid off. The Irish establishment at that time consisted of no fewer than thirty-seven regiments, horse and foot, but they were kept at a very low strength, that of a cavalry regiment being about 200 men, divided into six troops which were usually widely dispersed.

Great Britain was not long at peace. In spite of the Treaty of Aix-la-Chapelle, the clash of British and French trading interests led to continued engagements between the armed forces of the two countries in North America, and it soon became evident that France was contemplating some form of military operation nearer home. Concentrations of troops in the Atlantic ports seemed to point to an invasion of England, but in 1756 the island of Minorca was attacked and captured in a combined operation launched from Toulon. Thereupon the British Government

1759

declared war on France, and the Seven Years' War began, with Great Britain, Hanover and Prussia on the one side and France, Austria, Saxony, Sweden and Russia on the other. Apart from the loss of Minorca, it started badly with set-backs in India and Canada. In a panic the British government, under the Duke of Newcastle, sent for Hanoverian troops to defend the country, and shot Admiral Byng for failing to prevent the capture of Minorca. The Newcastle administration nevertheless fell and William Pitt came into power, causing the King of Prussia (among many others) to heave a sigh of relief. 'England,' he said, 'has been long in labour; at last she has produced a man.'

On the outbreak of war the establishment of all regiments in the United Kingdom was greatly increased, and many useful though belated reforms were carried out in the organisation and administration of the Army. An interesting innovation was the introduction of Light Troops into the Dragoon regiments. These Light Troops, eight in number, were then brigaded to form a Light Cavalry Brigade, which took part in a large-scale raid on the Continent around St Malo. The value of Light Cavalry being proved in this manner, several regiments of Light Dragoons were raised as such, and the British cavalry became more or less officially divided into three parts – the Heavies, represented by the Household regiments, which were the equivalent of the continental Cuirassiers, the Medium Cavalry, represented by the Dragoons, and the Light Cavalry or Light Dragoons. Taken at its face value, 'Light Dragoon' is a contradiction in terms, especially when he is further described as a Light Cavalryman, after the authorities had been patiently trying to explain to the Dragoons for fifty years that they were not cavalry at all. The advent of the Light Dragoon at least put an end to this notion, and finally proved that the Dragoons had been right in maintaining that they were cavalry, and the authorities quite wrong.

The regiments in Ireland, like the 14th, were not affected by the increase in establishments and the other reforms, but in 1759 the 20th Regiment of Light Dragoons was raised by the town of Inniskilling as a contribution to the war effort. The regiment was known as the 20th Inniskilling Light Dragoons. Its establishment was 12 officers and 232 rank and file, organised into four troops. The uniform was scarlet with yellow facings, and it was commanded by Lieut.-Colonel Sir James Caldwell, Bt. It was, of course, composed entirely of Irishmen, but so also was the 14th and most of the other regiments on the Irish establishment. There was never any lack of recruits in Ireland and, outside their native land and away from politics, they gave excellent service. At home, their value as soldiers was somewhat uncertain even in the defence of their own country, for they might well take it into their heads to welcome an invading enemy as friends and fight one another instead. Neither the 14th Dragoons, nor the 20th (Inniskilling) Light Dragoons (not to be confused with the 6th (Inniskilling) Dragoons) had any trouble or excitement during their long years in Ireland. There was a certain amount of trouble going on, as usual in that country, and in 1765 the Irish regiments in Dublin appear to have mutinied, but the 14th and 20th marched endlessly all over Ireland without having to do anything more than arrest a few trouble-makers from time to time. When the war ended in 1763, the 20th were disbanded, but they came to life again in due course after it had been discovered that the declaration of the Treaty of Paris that 'there shall be a Christian, universal and perpetual peace and a sincere and constant friendship' between the warring nations, was easier to make than to carry out.

Although there was no honour or glory to be had, some aspects of the service of the 14th Dragoons in Ireland are of interest. When the regiment first arrived in the country, it still retained the peculiarities of Dragoons as opposed to cavalry proper. It had no trumpeters for example, but drummers and 'hautboys' or flute-players, like the infantry. In those days, trumpets for the cavalry and drums for the infantry were essential, for the troops were drilled by the various calls and beats, by which they were controlled in action.

A side drum was an awkward thing to carry on horseback, and useless for giving signals in a mounted regiment. It was sometimes beaten at the head of the troop on the line of march at the walk, accompanied by the hautboy, and on ceremonial occasions all the drummers and hautboys combined to make 'musik' at the head of the regiment. Otherwise, they could only be used for beating to arms before mounting, after which orders had to be given verbally. It is said that in many regiments neither drummers nor hautboys existed other than as names on the muster roll, which enabled the Captains to draw their pay *in absentia*.

This kind of fiddling with accounts was not regarded as dishonest in those days of widespread corruption in official circles; it had existed in England since the days of William III but was eventually got more or less under control under George III and by 1782 'the Muster-Rolls, one for each troop, were most accurately kept, and were rendered quarterly.' They had by that time to be signed by all the officers and sworn-to as being correct in front of a magistrate, which finally put an end to the practice of

1763

filling the rolls with the names of soldiers who had been dead or discharged for many years.

Although, prior to this date, the muster rolls had been suspect in relation to the rank and file, the officers had to be more accurately accounted for, and several details are disclosed concerning the commissioned ranks which make odd reading today, although they excited no comment at the time. The Chaplain for example, the Rev. Peter Vatass, who drew a salary of £120 a year, was shown as being on leave of absence for 52 years on the authority of the commanding-officer. He never in fact reported for duty after his appointment in 1745 until he was superannuated in 1797 at the age of 75. It seems possible that he may have established a record as regards a period of leave, but this sort of thing was nothing out of the way in the eighteenth century. Another possible record – although again, it was nothing out of the way – was established by Thomas Erle, who was appointed Lieutenant-Colonel of the 14th in 1754. His commission as Cornet of Horse dated from 1707 – the year of his birth – and he was promoted Lieutenant (by purchase) on his fifteenth birthday. He commanded the 14th for 19 years, until his retirement at the age of 66.

At the commencement of their service in Ireland, the 14th Dragoons were dressed in long scarlet coats with lemon-yellow linings, scarlet cloaks with lemon-yellow capes, tricorn hats bound with silver lace, and the heavy boots of jacked leather with spurs and chains which had so annoyed the Duke of Cumberland. Their horse-furnishings were also of lemon-coloured cloth. Besides his sword and pair of pistols, each Dragoon was armed with an infantry musket and socket-bayonet. He was also issued with a pair of infantry-pattern spatterdashes, or long gaiters which buttoned up over the knee for 'dismounted duties'. After the regiment had been in Ireland for some years, these spatterdashes appear to have been worn both mounted and dismounted, even during inspections, and it seems that during the Seven Years' War there was some difficulty in replacing boots and other worn-out articles of clothing, so that the actual appearance of the regiment may not have been so impressive as the current clothing regulations would lead one to believe.

Like the other Dragoon regiments, the 14th carried three Guidons. In the old regiments of Horse, each troop had carried its own standard, upon which it dressed in line and to which it rallied in action. During Marlborough's campaigns, however, the practice of cavalry engaging with troops in line gave way to the formations of squadrons in line, which then became the estab-

Silver statuette depicting an officer of the 14th Dragoons in 1740. The uniform of the period included high boots and spurs.

lished custom. A squadron usually consisted of two troops which required only one standard between them, upon which they dressed to right and left. The 14th had six troops at this time, and therefore three Guidons.

In marching-order, the cavalryman and Dragoon had to carry a phenomenal amount of kit, most of which he had to jettison before engaging the enemy, in order to ease his horse. Even if the day ended in victory, it was not always possible to collect it again, for there was nearly always a civilian element hanging about in the vicinity of the battlefield, awaiting a favourable chance of enriching itself at the expense of the soldiers. The weight carried by the troop horse in marching order, was, however, very considerable, and it was essential to ease it whenever possible before closing the enemy, in order that it should not 'be brought blown to the charge'. The modern cavalryman, before mechanisation, rode at about twenty stone in marching order, although a great deal of thought had gone into the matter of his saddlery and equipment with a view to easing the burden on his horse. The man himself was also shorter than his eighteenth-century predecessor who, in the 14th Dragoons, measured between five feet eight inches and six feet. Taking into consideration the heavy uniform and jacked boots of the period, the ponderous saddle of black leather with brass studs mounted on a wooden tree with iron clamps, the leather valise, heavy cloak, pair of long horse-pistols in holsters, musket, picquetting-pole and sword, to say nothing of the bayonet, canteen, ammunition, haversack and nosebag – usually containing three days' rations for man and horse – spare horseshoes and the like, it is difficult to see how the cavalryman of the day could have ridden at much under twenty-five stone. Yet it was not unusual for extraneous burdens to be carried, such as bundles of fascines for filling in ditches and even, for a mile or two, a fully armed infantryman.

The horses stood at about $15\frac{1}{2}$ hands, and were generally black, a colour which has seldom been seen in English and Irish horses for the past century. Even two hundred years ago it was evidently dying out, for the cavalry began to change to bays. Most horses at this time had been docked as foals; a very odd and pointless fashion, except possibly in the case of carriage-horses whose docked tails were not so liable to foul the reins. It was not popular in the cavalry, which was always on the lookout for long-tailed horses, even though the fact of parading with both long- and short-tailed horses must have rather spoilt the appearance of a cavalry regiment. The horses, not surprisingly, received the close attention of inspecting officers, and the number with long tails was always noted in their reports. The size and condition of the horses was also reported on, as well as their manners and performance in the ranks. Those of the 14th were regularly described as 'nimble', in reference to their light mouths and ability to change legs properly at the gallop. The drill movements also required them to respond correctly when reined back, and to passage to right and left. Very little time was given to their schooling in those days, but there seems no doubt that they learnt the 'paces of the manege' in a much shorter time than is required nowadays; for the fact is, that in that tough age both man and horse had to learn quickly on pain of suffering extremely rough treatment – the cat o' nine tails, the whip and spur were all freely used as a matter of course without any inhibitions about cruelty.

A regular criticism levelled against the cavalry by Commanders-in-Chief, such as the Duke of Cumberland, was that they rode too long. This is very mysterious for the type of saddle then in use forced the cavalryman to sit bolt upright with his legs straight down, taking much of his weight on the stirrups. It is difficult to see how he could possibly have ridden short. Nor is it clear why it should have been thought wrong to ride with straight legs. Most men whose lives are spent in the saddle, such as ranchers and cowboys, do so to this day, and still use much the same type of saddle as the cavalry of the eighteenth century for, by riding long, a horseman does not tire so easily. The modern seat, with knees slightly bent, did not come in until the mid-nineteenth century, but by then the whole art of horsemanship had greatly changed, and jumping horses over obstacles – which was seldom done in the old days – had become a skill which every horseman had to learn.

1776

A 14th Light Dragoon of 1776, in which year the 14th were converted to Light Dragoons. Muskets were replaced by carbines and cocked hats by crested leather helmets. Horses were selected for speed and nimbleness as befitted light cavalry.

1776 The 14th become Light Dragoons
1779 Return of the 20th and
1784 Disbandment
1789 Outbreak of French Revolution
1791 20th Light Dragoons raised again
1792 The 20th sail for the West Indies
1794–1795 Adventures of a squadron of the 14th on the Continent

1776

War with Revolutionary France

3

THE British victory in the Seven Years' War gained for the United Kingdom a great Empire which it was necessary not merely to exploit, but also to administer and defend. These last responsibilities were not at first appreciated by the British Government, which was no longer headed by Pitt. He had been thrown aside as soon as the international situation improved sufficiently for it to be safe to dispense with the services of that outstanding war leader. In North America, Canada was ceded by France to Great Britain, and all colonial territories down to the Mississippi recognised as British Imperial possessions. The colonists, however, had long objected to paying taxes to their home country and, now that they were secure from the threat of French domination and the Red Indians more or less under control, they decided to revolt and fight for their independence.

The opening shots in the War of American Independence were fired in April, 1775, and a fratricidal struggle ensued which lasted for eight years. Its effects, as far as the British Army was concerned, were to point to the need for light and mobile troops. The 14th Dragoons, who were still in Ireland, were consequently turned into the 14th Light Dragoons in 1776. The conversion took about two years, during which all arms, equipment and saddlery were changed to lighter patterns and hats were replaced

41

1779

by brass helmets. The height standard for recruits was reduced. So, also, was that of the horses which came down to an average of 15 hands. The simultaneous reduction in the heights of both men and horses would appear at first sight to cancel one another out and leave the mobility of the regiment unchanged. In fact, however, the horses were a lighter type, selected for their speed and 'nimbleness'. All of them had long tails and, with arms and uniforms all brand-new, the regiment must have presented a very creditable appearance after its conversion to a 'Light Corps'. Once it had achieved this perfection it never afterwards lost it except under the rigours of active service when, like all light regiments, it made up in swagger what it lost from shreds and patches.

The 20th Light Dragoons were resuscitated in 1779. The new regiment was raised at Bury St Edmunds from the Light Troops of the 3rd Dragoon Guards, 1st Royal Dragoons, 6th Inniskilling Dragoons, and the 11th Dragoons. It thus bore no relationship to its predecessor, from whom it inherited nothing, except the number. This second incarnation of the regiment passed most of its service chasing smugglers along the coasts of Norfolk and Suffolk; a traditional employment for Dragoons on the home establishment, and one which made them exceedingly unpopular among the residents of coastal districts, large numbers of whom benefited in one way or another from the activities of the 'Free-traders'. It was nevertheless essential for coastal patrols to be maintained in such troublous times, for it was not only contraband which was being surreptitiously landed, but also enemy agents and other undesirables. Following the British surrender at Saratoga in 1777, France had thrown in her lot on the side of the American rebels and was soon joined by Spain. Great Britain again became exceedingly hard-pressed and, with most of the army overseas and few ships of the line in home waters, was casting anxious eyes across the Channel. The smugglers and their accomplices had no interest in the war other than in the opportunity which the preoccupation of the Royal Navy gave them for slipping in lucrative cargoes – and even more lucrative passengers and mail, concerning which they asked no questions, so long as they were well paid:

> Brandy for the parson, baccy for the clerk,
> Laces for the lady; *letters for the spy....*

A combined Franco-Spanish expedition re-took Minorca, and another laid siege to Gibraltar which, however, managed to hold out for over three years until the Treaty of Versailles ended the war in 1783. Although the American Colonies and one or two others were lost, Great Britain – thanks to the Army and Navy – did not come off too badly, but in fact emerged from a most perilous experience in a much better position than either France or Spain – or the Americans, for that matter. Nevertheless, with France, Spain and Holland remaining jealous of Great Britain's world influence and success in trade, only such incurable optimists as the British Cabinet could envisage any lengthy period of peace. Retrenchments and cuts in the fighting services were immediately put into effect, and the 20th Light Dragoons were once again disbanded.

In 1784 the 14th Light Dragoons, then stationed at Clonmel, changed their uniforms from scarlet to dark blue, in accordance with the general orders for light cavalry. The regiment continued its endless peregrinations round Ireland, seldom staying more than a year in one place. It seems at least possible that the policy of keeping light cavalry regiments continually on the move was to enable the officers to avoid the matrimonial entanglements in which, especially in Ireland, a Light Dragoon was constantly in danger of becoming involved. At about this time, Lord St Vincent expressed the opinion that when a naval officer married he was 'damned for the Service', and there is no doubt that the same precept held good for the Army.

While the 14th were trying on their new uniforms, the Whig government fell and William Pitt the younger came into power – not a moment too soon. Although he was definitely a man of peace, with little or no understanding of military matters, he had quite sufficient commonsense to be appalled at the condition into which the defences of the United Kingdom had been allowed to fall, with a bare 7,000 fighting men left in the country. Among the various reforms which he instigated, was the transfer to the War Department, from the Colonels of regiments, of the responsibility for the pay, clothing and equipment of their units. This must have been a great relief to General Warde, the Colonel of the 14th, who was faced with the provision of a complete set of new uniforms to the regiment.

In 1789 the French economy collapsed, resulting in the overthrow of the monarchy and the outbreak of the French Revolution. A Republic was proclaimed in 1791 which forthwith declared war on all the monarchies of Europe, following it up by pouring hordes of armed and undisciplined revolutionaries across the frontier of the Austrian Netherlands. As all French officers in the cavalry and infantry had been aristocrats, and consequently either guillotined or hanged on lampposts, the actual military potential of the French revolutionary army was

1790

at that time small. The danger lay in the possibility of the revolutionary plague spreading over Europe – and beyond – and all civilised nations became exceedingly alarmed. Pitt, however, was determined if possible, to avoid any military entanglement in Europe. He decided instead, to support the nations in defending their territories against the revolution by financial subsidies, while the British Navy cut off the French overseas possessions and protected British commerce. As an economist and something of a financial expert (though not in regard to his own affairs) he was confident that France could soon be brought to her knees by economic sanctions, without the necessity for marching a British army against her. This attractive method of bringing down an opponent is still practised by successors of Pitt, and with the same results. In 1789, however, the policy of attempting to wage an economic war was a particularly unfortunate one, for the failure to crush the militant French Republic at the outset brought about, in due course, the rise of Napoleon and the deaths of millions; and the war against France lasted no less than twenty-five years.

Nevertheless, it must be acknowledged that in 1789 it was impossible for Great Britain to fight the French on the Continent, for there was no army available with which to do it. Furthermore, in 1790 a strange situation arose in the West Indies which forced the British government to take action against the islands in French possession: the fact that it happened to be her declared policy to do so being coincidental.

The Declaration of the Rights of Man by the French National Assembly led to unrest among the blacks and mulattos in the French West Indies; especially in St Domingo, the most important of them. This unrest was actually encouraged by the revolutionaries in Paris, first of all by a society known as the Negro's Friends, which asserted the equality of coloured men with whites, and then by the Assembly itself, which made this assertion a matter of law. The Negroes and mulattos rose in revolt, chaos ensued and the small garrisons of French troops were soon in extremity and were forced to appeal to the Governor of Jamaica for help. He sent over some arms and ammunition, and appealed to the government for military reinforcements to maintain law and order in Jamaica, where it was feared that the Negroes might also rise in sympathy with their fellows in the neighbouring island. The British government agreed to send a cavalry regiment and two additional battalions of infantry – provided the planters would pay for them, which, with an understandably bad grace, they eventually agreed to do. As there was no cavalry regiment which could be spared from the United Kingdom, it was necessary to raise one. Early in 1791 a letter of service was issued to Lieut.-Colonel H. Farrington Gardiner of the 16th Light Dragoons, authorising him to raise a regiment of Light Dragoons, 300 strong, and with four troops, for service in Jamaica. In this manner the 20th Light Dragoons was resurrected for the third time.

Colonel Farrington Gardiner was apparently only able to get three recruits for the regiment, and one mysterious character picked up in Ireland, who is shown on the muster-rolls as 'a deserter from the 19th Light Dragoons in India'. The remainder of the rank and file were obtained by transfer from the five regiments of Light Dragoons then in England, and the six regiments in Ireland, including the 14th, which sent sixteen men. The N.C.O.s and trumpeters all came from the 15th and 16th Light Dragoons. The Colonel was Lieut.-General Sir Charles Grey, who had been appointed Commander in the West Indies. This had become an appointment of considerable importance, for since the government had grudgingly agreed to reinforce Jamaica with the 20th and two battalions, the situation in the West Indies generally had become so serious that by 1792 no fewer than nineteen battalions were either there or on their way.

Apart from the Colonel, Lieut.-Colonel, and the Major, George Sandford from the Greys (then known as the Royal North British Dragoons), the officers appointed to the 20th were a somewhat mixed lot. Two of them were infantrymen from the 3rd Foot, a Sergeant-Major from the 29th Foot was Adjutant, and two cavalry Quartermasters and one private gentleman were made Cornets. One of the Lieutenants, however, was George Anson from the 10th Light Dragoons, who afterwards commanded a cavalry brigade on the Peninsula and ended his career as General Sir George Anson. On the whole they were not an impressive collection, and when it is considered that the men were all drafted from different regiments which, as usual, would have taken the opportunity of getting rid of their worst scoundrels and trouble-makers, it seems surprising that the 20th Light Dragoons ever managed to get themselves to Jamaica intact.

The regiment sailed for Jamaica in two wings, from Falmouth and Portsmouth, during the summer of 1792, and was eventually concentrated in Spanish Town in November. On its arrival the Governor of Jamaica was ordered by the British government to announce to the House of Assembly the fact that its wishes for reinforcements had been met; a cavalry regiment having actually arrived, while two additional infantry regiments were on their

1792

way from Nova Scotia. The House of Assembly, after pondering over this announcement, replied to the Governor confirming its agreement to meet the expense of the 20th Light Dragoons so long as it was necessary to keep it on the island for internal security, but added a representation to the effect 'that this House consider that as they already contribute their full proportion to the support of the Empire, they are entitled to efficient protection from the British Government adequate to their local situation and circumstances, without being compelled to purchase the same for the protection of their lives and property.'

It is difficult not to feel some sympathy for the unfortunate planters in the Jamaican Assembly who, in fact, contributed very considerably in one way and another to the British Exchequer, and might reasonably have expected full protection in return. The government, however, still adhered to the principle that British colonies had to be self-supporting and a source of revenue, not of expense. In 1789, trouble with the East India Company over the cost of giving it armed support had resulted in the Declaratory Bill, which laid down that 'the expense of raising, transporting and maintaining such troops as may be judged necessary for the security of the British Territories and Possessions in the East Indies, should be defrayed out of the revenues arising out of the said Territories and Possessions.'

The East India Company could of course well-afford to accept such expense, but in the smaller colonies, such as the West Indies, it was a different matter. In the case of the 20th Light Dragoons therefore, the British Government agreed to raise the regiment and transport it to Jamaica free of charge. It arrived in Jamaica, however, with its pay in arrears and without either horses or transport. Besides the cost of its pay and upkeep, which amounted to something like £27,000 a year, the Colonial Government had to meet innumerable other charges, such as:

Purchase of 32 Negro slaves at £70
,,   ,, 300 troop horses at £45
,,   ,, 24 cart horses at £45
,,   ,, 300 sets of horse-furniture at £5 16s d
etcetera.

Under the circumstances, with their lives and possessions in grave danger, the planters had no option but to pay up; but they would have done so with a better grace had they felt that they were getting their money's worth. The regiment, however, arrived at an effective strength of under 150 men, and within six months the commanding-officer and thirty-two rank and file were dead from yellow fever: half the remaining officers were on sick leave, and forty-seven rank and file were in hospital. The initial contribution to the defence of Jamaica made by the 20th was therefore not impressive, but fortunately its services did not have to be called upon before it had had time to get into shape.

The situation in Europe had meanwhile obliged the British Government to show the flag along the frontiers of Belgium, in order to put some heart into the Austrians and Dutch, who were showing small enthusiasm for halting the march of the French revolutionaries. An expeditionary force was hurriedly scraped together and sent over to the Continent early in 1793, under the command of the Duke of York. It consisted of twenty squadrons of cavalry and two brigades of infantry; a very meagre assembly by Continental standards, but it was hoped that it would be sufficient, with the assistance of the King's Hanoverian troops and Hessian mercenaries, to enable the allies to capture Valenciennes and open the way to Paris.

The strong fortress of Valenciennes was in fact taken and, in accordance with orders, the Duke of York then laid siege to Dunkirk. Faced by immensely superior numbers he was, however, obliged to withdraw on his base at Ostend, and the spring of 1794 found the British and Austrians, with some half-hearted support from the Dutch, still engaged along the Franco-Netherlands border with nothing much achieved so far. Like the Dutch, the Austrians remained un-cooperative and, although the British and Austrian cavalry fought several successful actions, this led to a French victory at Tourcoing followed by an Austrian withdrawal to the Rhine, leaving the Duke of York, with 40,000 men, facing 150,000 Frenchmen.

Stirred into activity by these untoward events, and in particular by the threat which had developed to Ostend, the British Government sent over about 10,000 reinforcements, consisting of the garrisons of the Isle of Wight and the Channel Islands, three infantry regiments from Ireland, and numbers of newly-enlisted recruits. This force, commanded by Major-General the Earl of Moira, was joined at Ostend on the 25th June by a squadron of the 14th Light Dragoons and the 33rd Foot from Ireland. The latter regiment was commanded by Colonel Arthur Wellesley, then aged twenty-five, whose relatives had purchased his various steps in rank, and who was not particularly well thought of at that time: 'An impecunious younger son, with no experience or qualifications other than some skill in playing the violin,' was the description given by Lord Moira of the future Duke of Wellington.

The usual dissensions among the Allies, which had formerly so plagued the Duke of Marlborough, had resulted in all initiative

1794

passing to the French who fortunately, owing to the constant interference by the revolutionary leaders with their field commanders, were unable to exploit it to the full. Nevertheless, they were advancing steadily, with orders to secure the Channel Ports as a first step towards the invasion of England. Lord Moira, who was under orders to defend Ostend at all costs found, when he arrived, that the French advanced guards were within four miles of it, and that the port itself was militarily indefensible. He therefore marched out of it, and took up a defensive position on ground of his own choosing. 'The defences are so detestable,' he wrote, 'that I shall go into the open field if we must come to blows.' As the Allies continued to retreat, however, while Moira was in receipt of contradictory orders from the Government, the Duke of York, and the Austrians, he abandoned the idea of defending Ostend on his own initiative and marched to Ghent, just in time to avoid an encircling movement which the French launched to cut him off. On the 5th July, he left Ghent and joined the Duke of York at Alost.

The squadron of the 14th, which was brigaded with the 1st Dragoon Guards and 8th Light Dragoons under the command of Colonel Vyse, had not so far come under fire, and suffered only from hardship, which was considerable. A complete failure of the administrative services resulted in the Duke of York's army being left without clothing, pay or food, so that it had to live off the country, which was not so easy when most of the inhabitants had fled and the enemy was pressing on hard. By the end of August the Allies had been driven out of Belgium, and the Duke of York had taken up a position inside Holland, with his right at Bois-le-Duc and his left on an area of marshy ground known as the Peel. His advanced posts were at Bokstel on the Dommel river, and these were attacked and over-run on the 14th September. The Duke immediately sent forward General Abercromby with ten squadrons and ten battalions to recapture Bokstel and the river line. One of the squadrons was the 14th Light Dragoons, and one of the battalions the 33rd Foot, so that the 14th and Colonel Wellesley both went into action for the first time in the campaign on the same day, in what proved to be an abortive counter-attack.

As Abercromby's force advanced, the cavalry soon came into contact with the French, but in a manner which they had not expected, for the enemy turned out to be 'Citizen-General' Pichegru's main army, advancing to the east. Abercromby fortunately realised the situation in time to withdraw before getting seriously involved, though not without a sharp fight in which he lost about ninety men, two of them from the 14th. The Duke was then obliged to retire across the Maas, after which he took up a position along the north bank.

Without the co-operation of the Dutch, which was not forthcoming in spite of heavy bribes sent over by the British Government as an inducement to fight for their own country, it was impossible for the Duke of York to deny the passage of the Maas along a seventy mile front to the overwhelming numbers of French. After they had crossed the river in October and threatened his left flank, he withdrew behind the Waal, with his headquarters at Arnhem, sending the majority of the cavalry into winter quarters across the Yssel. The squadron of the 14th, however, appears to have been retained at Arnhem with one or two others, for patrol duty. By this time, the cavalry horses were in very poor shape, but those of the 14th were still capable of getting up speed if pressed in an emergency. The soldiers themselves were in far worse case, starving and in rags. Winter had set in with such exceptional severity that even the bigger rivers, such as the Maas and Waal were frozen hard enough to bear the weight of artillery. Yet only a few men had greatcoats and these, which had been provided by public subscription a year previously, were now worn out. The officers, who were generally better off, not being dependent on the Government for their campaign equipment, were considerably distressed by the miserable condition of their men, and clubbed together to purchase a supply of flannel waistcoats which not only provided them with some measure of warmth but also of decency, for large numbers of them had very little else in the way of clothing. There was also a great shortage of ammunition, for many regiments had taken the field with only nine rounds of cartridge a man. As for pay, King George's 1s. 9d. a day was rather better than was offered by his descendant Queen Victoria, but whereas the soldier did at least receive his emoluments under the Queen, it was all too seldom that the King could be persuaded to settle.

Under such conditions the Duke of York's army would certainly have disintegrated, had there not been plenty of plunder to be had in the wealthy Netherlands, to which the soldier had no compunction to helping himself, both from sheer necessity and an intense dislike of the Dutch, who let him down in every action fought in the defence of their country, from refusal to co-operate, incompetence or plain cowardice. Plundering, which was said to disgrace the British Army, nevertheless kept it alive and in the field. If disgrace there was, it adhered to the members of the Government, from Pitt downwards, who, with a staggering lack

1794

of imagination or of feeling for the sufferings of the soldiers, sent them off to fight the war which they had blundered into without the barest necessities for enabling them to win it.

By the end of November, over half the 21,000 infantry in the Duke's army were sick from typhus, exposure and under-nourishment. In December, however, when a French column raided across the frozen Maas and Waal, putting the Dutch to flight and threatening the British flank, a British counter-attack, in which the squadron of the 14th was one of six taking part in the action, easily routed the enemy and drove them back across the Waal.

On the 4th January, the French again crossed the frozen Waal and attacked Tuil, driving off the Dutch defenders. When, however, the enemy advanced westward along the north bank, they were set upon by three British regiments of foot, and again routed with considerable loss. Although the 14th, as well as the 8th Light Dragoons to which they were now attached, were present on this occasion they were kept in reserve owing to the poor condition of their horses and the difficult country.

Four days later the 14th and 8th Light Dragoons with three infantry regiments were in action before Geldermalsen, driving the French back upon the Waal, but large reinforcements crossed the river and overcame the Austrians on the allied left. On the 14th January they attacked along the whole line from Arnhem to Reenen and, although they were repulsed with heavy casualties the Hanoverian General Walmoden who was in command (the Duke of York had been summoned to England to report some time previously) decided that he could not hold out any longer and ordered a general retreat.

The retreat to the Yssel which followed, carried out in the depth of winter across barren wastes deep in snow, was probably the most disastrous in the history of the British Army. It is doubtful if many of the original squadron of the 14th survived to tell the tale. Lack of supplies forced a continuance of the retreat beyond the Yssel, along the banks of which sick and wounded British soldiers were abandoned to die in their thousands. The remnants of the British force were finally evacuated from Bremen in March and April, but the cavalry was left behind. The squadron of the 14th – or what remained of it – was, however, officially incorporated with the 8th Light Dragoons at the end of the campaign, so that its further adventures form no part of the history of the 14th/20th Hussars.

General Charles Fitzroy, Lord Southampton, Colonel 14th Dragoons 1765–72. His early service was with the 1st (Grenadier) Foot Guards. He served as ADC to Prince Ferdinand of Brunswick at the Battle of Minden in 1759.

1801

THE 14th LIGHT DRAGOONS OR DUCHESS OF YORK'S OWN

A HORSE! A HORSE! MY KINGDOM FOR A HORSE!

Now my lads, for the 14th Light Dragoons or the Duchess of York's Own. All you who are kicking your heels behind a solitary desk with too little wages and a pinch-gut master—all you with too much wife, or perplexed with obstinate, unfeeling parents, may apply to:—

Sergeant Hammond, Rose and Crown, Whitechapel.

You are quartered in the fertile county of Kent, where you have provisions remarkably cheap; luxurious living to the brave, ambitious mind, is but a secondary object, else thousands would repair to the standard of the gallant 14th could they obtain the honour of being received. Those of address and education are sure of preferment, your comforts in this service surpass all clerks and mechanics an hospitable table and capacious bowl of punch that will float or sink the little Corsican Chief.

N.B.—Four farriers are wanted, and a master for the Band.

1793 The Negro Revolt in St Domingo and the Maroon Revolt in Jamaica
1795 The 20th in Jamaica and the 14th in St Domingo
1797 Capture of Le Mirebalais
1797 The 14th return home
1798 The 14th become the Duchess of York's Own
1802 The 20th return home

1793

The West Indies

4

THE disgraceful ending of the campaign in the Netherlands, during which the lives of thousands of British soldiers were thrown away to no purpose, other than to demonstrate to the world the ineptitude of the British Government and its positively staggering incapacity in the waging of war, was followed by an even darker episode although, having regard to the conditions during the retreat to the Yssel and the subsequent evacuation of the British Expeditionary Force, this would scarcely seem possible.

The policy of Pitt, of bringing Republican France to her knees by cutting her off from her overseas possessions and disrupting her trade, has already been mentioned. The Negro insurrection on St Domingo and the consequent peril to the French garrisons on that and neighbouring islands in the West Indies appeared to offer an opportunity for the furtherance of this policy, although it was not for that reason that the 20th Light Dragoons were sent to reinforce Jamaica.

British intervention in St Domingo was, however, primarily taken not by the home government but by the Governor of Jamaica in response to the appeals for help made by the French colonists; but his initiative was supported by the home government which diverted further reinforcements to Jamaica to enable a force to be organised for the occupation of St Domingo.

◁ A typical recruiting poster of the Napoleonic War period. Recruiting sergeants usually based themselves on public houses. The West Country and the Midlands were fertile recruiting areas but records show that in one year (1775) the regiment was almost entirely Irish.

1793

It seems that neither the Governor of Jamaica nor the home government properly understood the situation in St Domingo, but were misled by the French emissaries, who were endeavouring to exploit it for their own ends. Being no longer subject to the ties of patriotism, and acknowledging no allegiance to the republican government, they had no concern other than the security of their lives, property and position. Their action in appealing to the Governor of Jamaica, to whom they in fact surrendered their garrison and ceded the French territory in St Domingo, was of course repudiated by the republican government, which sent out deputies who proceeded to restore order by arming the Negroes and using them to put down the colonists. This resulted in complete chaos, with Negroes, half-whites and whites all fighting one another. It was into this inferno that the British Government committed a small British force, with no very clear directions as to what it was expected to do.

The expedition sailed from Jamaica and landed in St Domingo in September 1793, hoisted the British flag and formally annexed the French-held part of the island, which extended to the borders of Haiti, then held by Spain. The British force consisted only of the 13th Foot, the flank companies of the 49th, and a few guns – a total of not more than seven hundred men. The 20th Light Dragoons remained in Jamaica, except for Lieut. Rollo Gillespie, who had just joined from the Carabiniers. This officer presumably volunteered to sail with the expedition, being the type of soldier that it is impossible to hold back when action is pending. When in Ireland with the Carabiniers, he had acquired a certain notoriety as a result of a duel, in which he acted as second to a brother officer. The principals having exchanged shots twice 'without effect', an attempt was made to settle the matter amicably. This aroused Gillespie's scorn to such an extent that the affair ended with himself and the other principal, a youth of the name of Barrington, exchanging shots across a handkerchief. Barrington was killed, and Gillespie tried for murder. The adverse summing-up by the judge had no effect upon an Irish jury in such a case, especially as it was mostly composed of officers on half-pay. A verdict of 'Justifiable Homicide' was returned, and Gillispie was duly discharged, not exactly without a stain on his character, but certainly without any adverse effect on his career. As might be expected, he greatly distinguished himself on this perilous adventure, and soon obtained his Captaincy in the 20th.

The situation on St Domingo rapidly worsened and got beyond control with the whites, both British and French, in great danger. At the same time, the Negro revolt spread to the Windward

Islands, while in Jamaica itself the Maroons, a class of ex-slaves, were being stirred up by French republican propaganda. The British Government, though still unable to visualise the true state of affairs and the danger facing the lives and property of the whites, began collecting troops from all quarters with the object of taking over all French possessions in the West Indies. Troops, however, were very hard to come by, and for a long time there were none to spare to reinforce the hard-pressed garrison in St Domingo. The 14th Light Dragoons, and several other cavalry and infantry regiments in Ireland, were placed under orders for the West Indies during the summer of 1793, but owing to lack of shipping most of them did not reach their destination for well over a year. The 14th, without their horses, sailed from Ireland in June, but the regiment then appears to have been left at Bristol awaiting embarkation until the spring of 1795. The regiment was then embarked in merchant ships, laden with cargoes for Jamaica. The fact appears to be that, ridiculous as it may seem, although the Government wished to send the regiment to St Domingo these merchantmen were under charter to sail to Jamaica and nowhere else, so that the 14th Light Dragoons were in due course put ashore at Port Royal, as were all the other reinforcements for St Domingo, whether they or the Government liked it or not.

How long the 14th were held up in Jamaica is uncertain. The collection of ships to take them and the other reinforcements to St Domingo seems to have taken only a few weeks, but during this period the attitude of the Maroons became so threatening that the Governor, Lord Balcarres, appears to have temporarily retained at any rate some of the reinforcements for the internal security of Jamaica.

The focal point of the Maroon revolt was Montego Bay, and Lord Balcarres decided on an attempt to encircle the area with cavalry, and then send in infantry to mop them up. About 130 men of the 18th and 20th Light Dragoons, under the command of Colonel Sandford of the 20th, were ordered accordingly to ride against Montego Bay, which lay on the other side of the island from Spanish Town, through extremely difficult and close country. The 83rd Regiment followed on foot, accompanied by the island militia. On the 12th August Colonel Sandford, who was riding ahead with a detachment of the 18th and 20th Light Dragoons and some horse militia, was ambushed by the Maroons in bush country. He and fourteen dragoons were killed, and by the time the remainder of his party had deployed and attacked, the enemy had faded away into the jungle. Thereafter Lord Balcarres proceeded with caution, and the Maroons were gradu-

1795

ally hemmed in and forced to surrender; though not before they had succeeded in inflicting considerable casualties on the British forces, by means of the guerrilla tactics of firing from cover and then withdrawing before they could be caught. The cavalry found this type of warfare particularly trying for they were, of course, especially vulnerable and out of their element. The 20th relieved their feelings by cursing Lord Balcarres, whom they held responsible for their casualties and discomfort. He certainly made some mistakes but, nevertheless, succeeded in getting the better of the Maroons without any undue waste of time.

The same could not be said for his predecessor in office, Sir Adam Williamson, who had taken charge of affairs in St Domingo. The problems facing Williamson, however, were not such as could be solved in a matter of weeks, even by some man of genius. In his efforts to pacify the island he was faced by French regular troops as well as the Negroes. The latter swarmed all over the country in armed bands, sometimes fighting each other, and sometimes taking sides with either the French or British. The French planters, most of whom were royalists, aided the British, but were uncertain allies. The cession of Haiti from Spain to France at first appeared to be advantageous to the British forces, for the Spanish planters hated the French and were prepared to assist the British rather than pass under French domination. They proved, however, to be as unreliable as the French royalists, and the situation became further confused with British, French republicans, French royalists and Spaniards all trying to enlist the support of the Negroes in order to fight one another and gain control of the island.

The British troops, most of whom were raw recruits straight out from England, were meanwhile being decimated by yellow fever, which also spread to the West Indies fleet. Although Pitt was relying on the British sea power in these operations against the French possessions, the Royal Navy was considerably outnumbered by the French in these waters at that time, and was often unable to protect the British supply ships.

The 14th Light Dragoons appear to have landed in St Domingo early in July, 1795, and were mounted on horses brought over from South America. The regiment was one of seven British Light Cavalry regiments landed on the island, and there were also two foreign cavalry regiments which had been brought over from the Continent: Hompesch's and Irving's Hussars. There was some difficulty, however, in mounting what added up to a total of 4,000 horsemen, so some regiments, including the foreigners, were ordered to transform themselves into light infantry. This caused considerable umbrage among the cavalrymen, especially the foreigners, and the matter was gradually put right. The dislike of even heavy dragoons to fighting on foot has already been mentioned. Among the light dragoons the idea was too absurd to be considered. It was, it seems, not so much a matter of distaste for using one's legs, as the arrogance common among the cavalry, who tended to regard the foot soldier as a very low sort of fellow with whom they preferred not to be too closely associated.

The country in St Domingo and Haiti was rough, mountainous and forested, and therefore unsuitable for cavalry, so that it may seem odd that nine regiments should have been sent there. It did in fact seem odd to the regiments concerned, who expressed their opinions on the matter with some force. It was, however, their potential mobility which made them valuable in such operations, but this attribute was largely negatived by their dislike of going into action on foot, although mounted action was nearly always impossible.

For over a year, the 14th spent their time on outpost and patrol duties, varied by treks across the island escorting supply trains. Their potential mobility could seldom be taken advantage of, and it was not unusual for the 14th and the other regiments of light cavalry to take twenty-four hours over covering a dozen miles. The reason was that their pace was restricted to that of their black pioneers, who had to lead the way in order to cut paths through the dense tangles of prickly pear with which the country was covered, and which were impassable to infantry as well as cavalry. The black pioneers, incidentally, were slaves brought over from Jamaica, similar to those brought by the 20th at £70 apiece. It seems strange, but there is no record of any of the slaves belonging to the British regiments in St Domingo escaping and joining the rebels. They were doubtless as well looked after as the situation of the soldiers allowed, but probably they also acquired a sentimental attachment for their regiments, as well as pride in the privilege of wearing their insignia. Free Negroes had served as trumpeters, drummers and bandsmen in the British Army for a century at least, and it mattered little in those days whether they were freemen or slaves; most of them were quite happy either way unless, like the rebels, they had been terrorised into supporting some power-hungry revolutionary.

Although these operations were exceedingly frustrating for the soldiers, they were not without effect. Gradually the rebels were isolated and cordoned off, and some measure of order restored to the island. Toussaint L'Ouverture, leader of the ex-slaves, was

1797

forced into Haiti which, until Spain ceded it to France, had been left alone by the British. In March, 1797, when it appeared that the Spanish settlers might be persuaded to join the British if assured of armed support, a detachment of troops was sent into the former Spanish colony. It was immediately surrounded by Toussaint L'Ouverture, who also secured Le Mirebalais and closed in on Port-au-Prince. A small British force was then landed at Port-au-Prince and drove the Negroes off. Shortly after, a light cavalry Brigade, composed of the 14th, 18th and 21st Light Dragoons and commanded by Brigadier Churchill, was sent to recapture Le Mirebalais and arrived before it on the 30th May. Although termed a Brigade, and certainly consisting of three regiments, this force was probably little more than four hundred strong, for the casualties from yellow fever had been shocking. This disease, a form of malignant malaria carried by mosquitoes, was not invariably fatal – or there would have been no soldiers left – but on those who recovered it had a depressive effect which, combined with the misery and boredom resulting from years of frustrating operations in a dreadful climate, without comforts or civilised amenities of any kind, lowered the morale of the troops to a dangerous degree. This was manifested by bad discipline in all the regiments, so that opportunities of destroying several bands of Negroes which were encountered were not taken advantage of. Although therefore the towns of Le Mirebalais and Grand Bois were recaptured at the cost of a couple of Dragoons wounded, the pursuit was ineffectual. Brigadier Churchill's despatch referred to an easy victory, in which the Negroes decamped as soon as they saw his force approaching, leaving him in possession of the fort and six guns. Although, however, the 14th, 18th and 21st Light Dragoons 'pursued them with that alacrity and spirit which has ever distinguished him' (Colonel Arthur Carter of the 14th who commanded the cavalry) 'he could only come up with a very few.'

After this affair conditions in the island again lapsed into chaos, with Negroes, mulattos, French republicans, French royalists and the British all struggling to gain control. 'What are a handful of worn-out British soldiers to do against six thousand disciplined blacks, backed by the French?' wrote General Whyte. In the end Toussaint L'Ouverture, who was as skilled a politician as he was a guerrilla leader, turned against the French and came to terms with the British, who evacuated the island and left him in charge. Thus Pitt's adventures against the French West Indies ended in evacuation like his half-hearted efforts in supporting his allies in Europe. His policy for the conduct of the war had collapsed.

1797

The 14th Light Dragoons did not remain in the West Indies to see the end of this dreary affair. The regiment arrived back in England in October, 1797, at a strength of twenty-five all-ranks, and was stationed at Chelmsford. As was customary, when a regiment serving abroad was ordered home, the rank and file were given the opportunity of volunteering for transfer to other regiments remaining overseas. There was usually a good response for places like India, where the conditions were at least tolerable, but the West Indies had so bad a reputation that regiments embarked at Portsmouth or the Cove of Cork for that destination had to be specially guarded in port, to avoid wholesale desertions, or even suicides. It seems improbable, therefore, that many of the 14th would have voluntarily transferred to other regiments. Accepting the fact that some of them were reluctant to say goodbye to the dusky beauties with whom they had become enamoured, and that others were 'Sergeant-Major's Volunteers', who had been forceably persuaded to remain behind in order to make up the quota, it still seems that the 14th must have left over three hundred dead behind it, when it sailed for home. No records of casualties were kept, but for a regiment to lose about this number in dead during the dark episode of St Domingo was the common fate. The 13th Light Dragoons, for example, are known to have lost 287. Very few of these casualties were incurred in action; they were nearly all the result of excessive hardship or disease.

The 20th Light Dragoons still remained quartered in Spanish Town, Jamaica, being brought up to strength in 1797 by drafts from the regiments sent home from St Domingo. Many of the men in these drafts, which included some from the 14th, had originally belonged to the 20th and had either volunteered or been compulsorily drafted to St Domingo. Apart from such men, the 20th had also been represented in the operations in St Domingo by its commanding-officer, Lieut.-Colonel Churchill who, as mentioned, was in command at the capture of Le Mirebalais. His Brigade-Major was Rollo Gillespie, who had greatly distinguished himself, both at Le Mirebalais and in many other smaller affrays during the operations. In 1797, Churchill was promoted Major-General and handed over command of the 20th to Gillespie who was then a Major and retained that rank until 1799, when the Jamaican Assembly informed the Governor that:

'If His Majesty should graciously be pleased to appoint a second Lieutenant-Colonel to the 20th or Jamaica Light Dragoons, this House will provide for the expense thereof and ... being sensible of the care and attention of Major Gillespie to the health and discipline of the regiment since it has been

1797

under his command, contemplate with satisfaction the probability of an officer, who has served with such distinguished credit in various high situations, being advanced in professional rank...'

As the expenses of the 20th Light Dragoons were a burden on the Jamaica Treasury which the House of Assembly had felt to be unjustified from the beginning, and were a continued source of grievance, the kindly gesture by which the House voluntarily added to the expenses those to be incurred by Gillespie's and other officers' promotions was remarkable. It would be difficult indeed to find a parallel. Two years later, however, by which time the Royal Navy had become fully capable of protecting the British West Indies against invasion, the House asked that the regiment should be withdrawn, as its services were no longer required.

On this request being acceded to, the House went to some trouble over making it clear that their desire to be quit of the 20th Light Dragoons was based on the expense of the regiment only, and had nothing to do with its conduct. A deputation was accordingly sent to the Governor 'ordered by this House to wait upon your Honour, and to express to your Honour the high sense they entertain of the merits and uniform good conduct of Lieutenant-Colonel Gillespie, the officers, non-commissioned officers, and privates of the 20th or Jamaica Light Dragoons, during their long service in this Island.' At the same time they voted Gillespie a hundred guineas, 'to be by him expended in the purchase of a sword, as a testimony of the high esteem in which his conduct is held by this House.' Gillespie replied that he was highly flattered by such a mark of approbation as the gift of a sword which 'I should be at all times ready to draw in defence of so esteemed and respectable a colony.'

In view of his services in the West Indies, and in Jamaica particularly, it is odd that in 1802, immediately after the regiment had returned home, Gillespie was court-martialled at the instigation of Major Cameron, a brother-officer and brother-Scot, on charges of faking the muster-rolls while in Jamaica, and thereby drawing allowances to which he was not entitled. He appears to have been accused in fact, of the old game of drawing pay for dead men. He was 'most honourably acquitted' of the charges, on the grounds that he 'acted entirely for the good of the service, from long-established custom, and, in the instance of the regiment which he commanded, with the sanction of the Commander of the Island and the States thereof.' His accuser, Major Cameron, was informed that 'His Majesty has no further occasion for his services.' Gillespie did, it seems, sign false returns in order to draw more cash than he was entitled to receive, but he was able to show that he had not pocketed any of it, but had used it for legitimate expenses which there was no other way of meeting. As already mentioned, this was a normal procedure in the United Kingdom until the late eighteenth century, and it was evidently accepted as a good defence that in Jamaica the accuracy of muster-rolls did not, as at home, have to be sworn to before a magistrate.

While the 14th and 20th Light Dragoons were away in the 'Sugar Islands' the war against Revolutionary France was being carried on, for the most part by a series of raids directed both against the mainland of Europe and islands of strategic importance, such as Malta and Minorca. Usually undertaken with inadequate and ill-equipped forces tied to the political apron-strings of Pitt's deplorable government, they seldom achieved any useful purpose, and there were but few opportunities for the forces engaged in carrying out these feeble tactics to gain laurels. Death, wounds and discomfiture were their usual reward, and so ineffectual did Great Britain's prosecution of the war appear to the French that in '97 they even had the impertinence to land a raiding party in Wales. This was gathered up by the Pembroke Yeomanry, and there were some other creditable affairs carried out by the combined services in situations where they succeeded in avoiding political control. Gibraltar was held for three years against the might of France and Spain, and the Cape of Good Hope, Ceylon and Malaya were seized from the Dutch who, their country being under French occupation, were treated as enemies.

These years saw the rise of Napoleon, who first came to notice when his tactical efficiency obliged the British to evacuate the French naval base at Toulon. Nelson came upon the scene at about the same time and, when Napoleon landed an army in Egypt in '98, caused the future Emperor considerable embarrassment by destroying the French fleet when it was at anchor in Aboukir Bay. The stranded French army, abandoned by Napoleon, was eventually obliged to surrender to a greatly inferior British force.

Wellington, the third of the great military triumvirate with which this period is associated, was still, at the turn of the century, a jumped-up Colonel of Foot, serving in the operations against Tippoo Sahib in Southern India. Impatient of authority, impetuous and immature, he had a few more years to go before the genius within him developed and became unmistakable.

1798

On its return home in 1798 the 14th Light Dragoons was stationed at Chelmsford and, as there was a great wave of patriotism sweeping the country at the time, soon raised its meagre numbers to six hundred, which were organised in eight troops.

In the same year the regiment had the honour of receiving H.R.H. the Princess Frederica, daughter of King Frederick William II, Princess Royal of Prussia and wife of Frederick, Duke of York and Albany, the second son of George III and the only one with whom he was on speaking terms. The marriage had taken place in 1791. The regiment escorted her to London, and as a mark of royal favour in consequence was re-designated the 14th (Duchess of York's Own) Regiment of Light Dragoons. The honorary appointment of Colonel-in-Chief of a regiment was not conferred at that time, but the Duchess was designated 'Royal Patroness' of the 14th Light Dragoons who were then granted the Prussian Eagle as a badge, and changed their facings from lemon-yellow to orange which was the livery colour of the Prussian royal house. On the insistence of the King, the Duke of York had just been appointed Commander-in-Chief of the Army and charged with the task of rectifying the shortcomings in its training, organisation and administration which the operations in Flanders had brought to light. He carried out this duty with energy, devotion and competence, paying much attention to the welfare of the soldiers with whom – and with the people of England in general – he became extremely popular. Among the many reforms for which he was responsible was the production of an excellent manual on cavalry training – the first of its kind – and the inclusion in the establishment of each cavalry regiment of a veterinary surgeon, armourer and saddlers. He also regularised the transport system, improved the medical service and started the Chaplain-General's Department – an innovation which would certainly have dismayed the Reverend Peter Vatass, absentee chaplain of the 14th.

Unfortunately, although her portraits show her to have been an attractive woman, the Royal Patroness of the 14th was unable to retain the affections of the Duke, and the marriage, which was childless, ended in separation. The Duke's private amours, after being regarded with tolerance by the British public for many years, finally caused a national scandal owing to the indiscretion of one of his mistresses, Mary Anne Clarke, who was suspected of influencing the Duke in a matter of military appointments. Although she was probably as good a judge of a soldier's capabilities as the Duke, the trouble was that she did not give her services

1802

for nothing, and although the Duke was cleared of the suspicion of sharing in the proceeds he was obliged to resign his appointment as Commander-in-Chief, which was a great blow to the Army. But by that time he had done his work in the creation of an Army which proved itself capable of beating all others whatever the odds, from the Muslim hordes of southern India to the devoted armies of Napoleon.

Napoleon's set-back in Egypt had so small an effect on his prestige in France that, on his return, he was able to get himself elected First Consul, so becoming the virtual dictator of the country. In this august position, he was able to manipulate peace overtures to the British, with a view to gaining time to prepare fresh plans and reorganise his army, whose Egyptian Expeditionary Force had been allowed to go home under the terms of its capitulation. In his anxiety to end the war, Pitt agreed to the return of all conquered territory, except Trinidad and Ceylon. The Treaty of Amiens was then signed in March 1802, and Great Britain, optimistically regarding it as a lasting settlement, made haste to disarm and return to shopkeeping which Napoleon, not without justification, regarded as the national pursuit.

When the peace treaty was signed, the 14th were at Romford and Hornchurch, and the 20th at Ipswich. The establishment of the 14th was immediately cut by two troops, and two more were taken away later. The regiment, however, had ten troops at the time, with a total strength of nearly a thousand all-ranks, so there was no question of it being reduced to a cadre, as was usually the case at the end of a war. The 20th suffered no reductions, for it had not had time to complete to establishment after returning from the West Indies.

H.R.H. Princess Frederica (Princess Royal of Prussia), Duchess of York, 'Royal Patroness' of the Regiment in 1798.

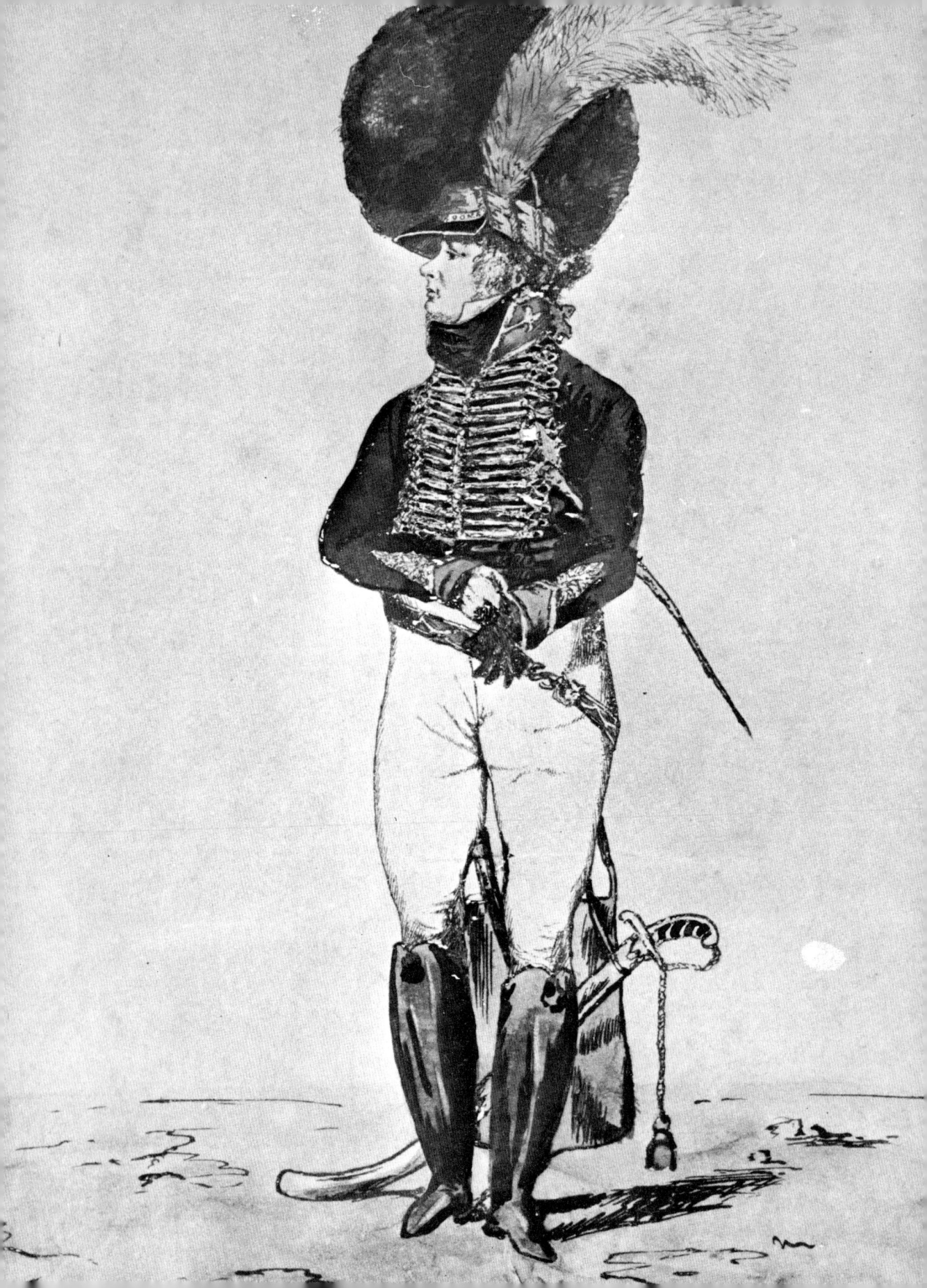

1805 The 20th sail for the Mediterranean
1805 Two squadrons of the 20th in South Africa and the Argentine
1808 The 20th sail for Lisbon

1803

Various Small Adventures

5

ALTHOUGH there was, as always, a 'lunatic fringe' in the House of Commons which insisted that the Treaty of Amiens had introduced a period of 'perfect tranquillity' and that there was accordingly no sense in throwing away money on the armed forces, the majority, fortunately, was not so sure. Napoleon in fact, never bothered to hide his hostile designs against Great Britain, being apparently, like many others in his position at one time or another, misled by the prominence given to the activities of the peace party in the United Kingdom. He showed no signs at any rate, of putting up his sword, but marched about Europe, sent off an expedition to St Domingo, and renewed the French attempts to get the British out of India.

In these circumstances the British Government halted its measures of disarmament, and refused to evacuate Malta as stipulated in the Treaty, until Napoleon showed some signs of keeping to his part of the bargain. The first Consul was, or professed to be, shocked beyond measure at this example of the perfidy of the British, and his conduct thereafter became so impossible that Great Britain, after innumerable efforts to come to an understanding, was at last obliged, on the 16th May, 1803, to declare war on him. The 'perfect tranquillity' had come to an abrupt end, not to return again until Napoleon had been finally cornered at Waterloo, twelve years ahead.

◁ Caricature of Lieut.-Colonel (later General Sir Samuel) Hawker. He served originally in the 16th Light Dragoons in the Netherlands, commanded the 14th during the early days of the Peninsular War, and returned to England after being severely wounded at Talavera, 1809.

1804

On the renewed outbreak of war, the 14th were at Chelmsford, moving later to Hythe, and the 20th at Colchester. The establishment of both regiments, after being subjected to several variations, was fixed at ten troops of ninety men apiece, but it seems doubtful if either of them actually reached this high figure. It is certain that neither of them could be classed as efficient. Nor could any other British cavalry regiment in the United Kingdom at this time; but this was not surprising, for they were all lacking in experience, and had little or no idea of what would be required of them in a theatre of war. The Duke of York's training manual had introduced a somewhat complicated method of manoeuvring by threes, controlled by trumpet-signals, with the sole object of getting a cavalry regiment deployed with squadrons in line, in a favourable position to charge. No instructions were given at this time on such normal cavalry tasks as scouting, reconnaissance and protection, and dismounted action was completely ignored. Apart from this, the cavalry – and infantry – regiments at home were always widely dispersed owing to accommodation problems, so that they could seldom train together as formed units. Not that this mattered much in the case of a cavalry regiment, for there were very few areas in the United Kingdom where it was possible for it to train anyway. 'Is there', asked General Money, an experienced cavalryman who had learnt his trade from the French, 'between London and Ipswich any ground on which three squadrons of horse can form without being in reach of musketeers from the hedgerows in their front and flank? Of what use then, in God's name, is cavalry when they cannot form to charge? For if they cannot form they cannot charge.' He recommended a return to the old notion of Dragoons, able to dismount and engage the 'musketeers' on equal terms, but in advocating this retrograde step he had allowed himself to become unduly influenced by the peculiar nature of the English countryside, with its maze of small fields, surrounded by hedges and ditches; whereas the cavalry were not in fact, destined to fight in any such country but:

> 'Over the hills and over the main,
> In Flanders, Portugal and Spain,'

all of them countries in which they could, and did in due course, form and charge.

Their lack of training facilities, however, meant that the cavalry had to learn their trade on the battlefield, a place, as Napoleon remarked 'where one learns quickly'. Provided the soldier succeeds in remaining alive long enough to learn and to make use of his knowledge, this of course is quite true, but there were certain traditions in the British cavalry, reaching back to the days of Prince Rupert and his cavaliers, which no amount of battlefield experience succeeded in breaking. The most important of these was the instinct to charge any enemy on sight and leave the consequence to Fortune. There were two usual consequences: if the enemy was strong and steadfast, he stood firm, and a mêlée developed: if he was weak and nervous, he was either ridden through or ran for it. In the latter case, the attacking cavalry should have pulled up and rallied, but the British cavalry was never trained in this essential manoeuvre and only too often galloped away out of sight, becoming an easy prey to a counter-attack as well as depriving the Commander of its services, sometimes at a critical moment. This bad habit resulted in the British cavalry being subjected to severe criticism, but nevertheless, its almost invariably gallant use of shock tactics caused it to be generally feared on the battlefields of two centuries; an achievement which certainly merits forgiveness for its occasional lapses.

A man who would certainly have understood and appreciated the predilection of the cavalry for *l'arme blanche* was Nelson, whose basic idea was, on sighting an enemy, to trust in God and lay close aboard. This tactic had brought him success even against the shore batteries at Copenhagen, and he was resting on the laurels gained in that victory when, in the spring of 1803 when war had become a certainty, he sailed to take command in the Mediterranean. Napoleon had made it clear, even before war broke out, that he regarded the invasion of England as his first priority, and his troop movements soon showed that he was not bluffing. Before he could launch a large-scale invasion he had, however, to gain control of the Channel. As this was impossible without a very lengthy period of manoeuvring, he began by concentrating all his efforts against British trade hoping, by denying Great Britain access to European ports, to break her economy. As, owing to the activities of the Royal Navy, he could not blockade these ports from the sea, he was obliged to occupy them with soldiers and therefore to conquer the countries which owned them. While thus employed he did not abandon his first priority, assembling a vast army on the coast, and personally directing the movements of his admirals in attempts to keep the Royal Navy out of the Channel long enough for him to get his troops across. The bulk of the French and Spanish fleets were in Mediterranean ports; especially the naval base at Toulon, and it therefore fell to Nelson to keep an eye on them and stop them getting into the Atlantic. This was a very hard and frustrating task, especially for a man of Nelson's disposition, who was always longing for close

1805

action. As the vagaries of wind and weather made it impossible for him to keep permanently within sight of the ports, there was always the chance of the enemy slipping out to sea unnoticed with a favourable wind, and this at last happened at the end of March, 1805, when he found that the French fleet had left Toulon. He did not at first dare to leave his station in the Mediterranean, for the French might well have sailed eastwards as they had before. In May however, he received the news that a large British convoy with 5,000 troops on board was heading for the Straits of Gibraltar. His duty of ensuring that this convoy did not fall into the hands of the French at once determined him to leave the Mediterranean and escort it through the dangerous waters past the south coast of Portugal. He was greatly hampered by his lack of frigates, 'the eyes of the fleet', and, in much anxiety and doubt as to what to do next, hove-to with six sail of the line off Cape St Vincent. It was here that three squadrons of the 20th Light Dragoons sighted him on the morning of the 11th May, 1805. It is pretty certain that while those soldiers who were not sea-sick were staring across the waters at the British squadron, with H.M.S. *Victory* prominent in the middle of it, Nelson was staring back at them through his telescope, thankful that at least their expedition was safely past the French. He had just heard that the French fleet under Admiral Villeneuve was steering for the West Indies (as part of a Napoleonic ruse to get Nelson out of home waters) and, before the convoy was out of sight, he was clapping on sail to follow.

Having thus lured Nelson away from the Channel in accordance with Napoleon's orders, Villeneuve turned about and made back towards the French coast, but he was intercepted by Admiral Calder off Cape Finisterre, lost his nerve and took refuge in Cadiz, where he was joined by the Spanish fleet. Nelson, who was hot on his heels, was soon outside Cadiz, lying off-and-on, and Napoleon, recognising that his plans for gaining temporary control of the Channel had failed owing to the pusillanimity of his Admiral, struck his camp at Boulogne and relieved his feelings by trouncing the Russians and Austrians at Austerlitz. Before marching, he ordered Villeneuve to put to sea and fight. On the 21st October, 1805, the combined fleets of France and Spain were intercepted by Nelson, and decisively defeated off Cape Trafalgar. This victory gained for Great Britain the complete mastery of the seas and, secure from invasion, she was now able to release the Army for more active employment.

For nearly two years there had been nothing for the British Army to do except prepare for an invasion, and furnish troops for various small and usually abortive combined operations in the western Mediterranean. It was on one of these that the three squadrons of the 20th had been proceeding, when they sighted Nelson off St Vincent. A British force under Sir James Craig had been despatched for the protection of the Kingdom of Naples, which included Sicily. As usual, it was quite insufficient for the task allotted, and when Napoleon started to take over Italy, reinforcements totalling somewhat over 4,000 men, of which the three squadrons of the 20th were the only cavalry, were sent out. By the time they arrived in the Mediterranean, Sir James Craig had retired to Sicily, where he was joined by the Neapolitan Court, and the reinforcements were landed at Malta. The 20th had embarked without their horses, which was the usual practice at this time. The transport of large numbers of horses by sea was a troublesome business for any voyage likely to last longer than a week; for they were difficult to embark and disembark, took up a lot of room and, as may be imagined, their condition rapidly deteriorated on board. On this particular voyage, it was certainly as well that no horses were carried, for it turned out to be inordinately long. Before he sighted Nelson's fleet, the Commodore had been so nervous of falling in with the French, whom he knew to be at large, that he had kept very close inshore, and on one occasion had run for the Tagus. The troops were then disembarked at Gibraltar, where they waited for orders from Sir James Craig until the end of June. After landing at Malta there was a further delay of five months, 'busily passed in drills and inspections', while Craig made plans with the Russians for an allied landing at Naples – and at the same time tried to get horses for the 20th and the three batteries of artillery which had accompanied the expedition, from Sicily and Sardinia, 'without much success.' The troops finally re-embarked at the end of October and, 'after tacking about for ten days within sight of Malta,' at last landed at Castellemare, while the Russians landed at Naples.

Like nearly all the expeditions launched by the British Government at this time, the one to Naples was planned with an incompetence amounting almost to imbecility. This was in no way the fault of the soldiers or their commanders, but was simply due to the fact that the Government had no understanding of the business of war; nor was it possible for its military advisers to advise it, for its policy was continually being changed at short notice, in accordance with the political situation in Europe which was so confused that it required someone with considerably more strength of mind than was possessed by any of the Ministers of State to determine and carry out the best course of action.

1805

The remaining two squadrons of the 20th Light Dragoons, whose officers and men had felt very sore at being left behind, were destined however, to take part in a rather more successful affair. Holland being under the thrall of Napoleon, and consequently nominally at war with Great Britain, her overseas possessions, like those of the French, were legitimate targets for attack. The Cape of Good Hope, lying athwart the trade route to India, was one in particular which could not be allowed to remain in enemy hands, and an expedition under Sir David Baird was sent to capture it.

The two squadrons of the 20th, in company with seven regiments of foot and three batteries of artillery, had embarked without their horses at Portsmouth in May, 1805, and sailed for the Cove of Cork. None of the soldiers had any idea as to whither they were bound, or upon what mission, but they were apparently all in high spirits with the hope of any sort of action which 'the wretched appearance of the boatmen and people on shore' at Cork, did nothing to damp. The expedition had, as usual, been hurriedly scraped together and bundled into transports during a moment of governmental panic, caused on this occasion by Nelson's report that the French fleet had escaped him and was heading for the West Indies. The troops were in fact intended to reinforce the West Indies, but before the convoy had time to sail, a dispatch arrived from Admiral Calder reporting that he had met the French returning from the West Indies, and had chased them into Cadiz. Sir David Baird was accordingly told not to bother assembling another expedition for the Cape, but to take the troops already on shipboard in the Cove of Cork.

The convoy sailed from the Cove on the 31st August and, with a gentle breeze astern which lasted the whole way, arrived off Madeira on the 28th September. It was composed of sixty-one transports, escorted by nine men-of-war commanded by Commodore Sir Home Popham, an officer with considerable experience of combined operations, but with a deserved reputation of caring more for prize-money than for the mere tactical success of any venture in which he might be engaged. This characteristic had, not unnaturally, made him much beloved by his sailors, but it had led him into several somewhat questionable undertakings, and was shortly to lead him into yet another. He was a great friend of General Sir David Baird, the commander of the troops, who had won renown during the wars against Tippoo Sahib in Southern India. He had spent some years in captivity in the dungeons of Seringapatam, where the prisoners were chained together in pairs. 'God help the lad,' said his mother, with much feeling, when she heard of his fate, 'wha's chained to oor Davie.' In the final siege and capture of Seringapatam in '99, Baird had claimed the leadership of the stormers, to enable him 'to pay off old scores,' and had made 'the Tiger of Mysore' pay with his life for the previous indignities to which Baird had been subjected. He had also secured a considerable sum in prize-money, and was no more averse than Popham to the undertaking of the more profitable military adventures in order to make adequate provision for his old age should he, as seemed unlikely, be spared to end his days in retirement and not suddenly with his boots on.

On the 10th November, the fleet put into San Salvador (now Bahia) in Brazil, in order to purchase horses for the 20th and the artillery. This took some weeks, and when the voyage was resumed a contrary wind wrecked one of the transports and a storeship, which were driven ashore. Only three men were drowned, but one of them was the artillery commander, Brigadier Yorke. 'Nor would these have perished,' wrote Sergeant Landsheit of the 20th, who witnessed the disaster, 'but for the intemperance of two, and the misguided and fatal avarice of the third.' In other words, the two soldiers were drunk, and Brigadier Yorke 'had so loaded himself with doubloons, that falling short of his leap from the bowsprit to the rock, he sank like a stone, and never rose again.' Sergeant Landsheit appears to indicate that the Brigadier had come by his doubloons in some unorthodox manner. This may well have been the case, but gives no excuse for Landsheit's sanctimonious strictures, for if he had not himself contrived to pocket a few doubloons while on shore in a place like San Salvador, he would have been a most unusual Sergeant of Light Dragoons.

The fleet made its landfall in the neighbourhood of Table Bay on the morning of the 4th January, 1806. The landing was delayed owing to a gale, and this gave the 'Boors' time to form up along some heights known as the Blueberg, guarding the approach to Capetown. Although they appeared to be in sufficient numbers to merit the deployment of his whole force, Baird entered with the Highland Brigade only (71st, 72nd and 93rd), giving his cavalry, English and Irish regiments nothing to do. 'Such proceedings long have been, and still are, far too common among our Scottish generals,' comments Sir John Fortescue, with some asperity.

The Highland Brigade, however, succeeded in chasing off the 'Boors' without any difficulty and when the 20th, which had been landed at Saldanha Bay and ordered to march on Capetown, arrived at their destination they found that the Dutch had

1806

capitulated. This was an extremely aggravating discovery after a long and difficult march. Their horses were 'in a wretched condition' after the voyage, although it had only lasted ten days, for their cramped conditions and the unaccustomed motion had put them off their feed. The gun-horses collapsed almost at once, so that for most of the way the guns had to be drawn by hand, while most of the cavalrymen had to use their own feet.

There was, however, at least the satisfaction of knowing that the mission had been successfully accomplished. Unfortunately neither Baird nor Popham appear to have been given any instructions as to what they were to do next; possibly because the British Government had become so accustomed to failure that so easy a success as this had not been taken into consideration. The General and Commodore were both men of action, unaccustomed to resting tamely on their laurels, and once the final capitulation had been signed under which Cape Colony passed under British rule, lost no time in casting about for fresh fields to conquer.

Sir Home Popham had more than once tried to interest the Government in supporting a revolutionary movement in South America against the Spaniards; being chiefly, it is to be feared, influenced in this idea by the thought of the rich financial pickings to be gathered in those parts. The Government had not fallen to his blandishments but now, being within easy sailing distance of the Argentine, he decided, with the help of Sir David Baird, to try his luck on his own. The result was the unauthorised expedition against Buenos Aires by the 71st Highlanders, of which regiment Sir David Baird was Colonel, accompanied by an officer and six men of the 20th Light Dragoons, and four guns. This expedition, after a long and tiresome voyage, landed in the Argentine in June, overcame the opposition without difficulty, and occupied Buenos Aires. About 1,100,000 dollars in coin and specie was collected out of the Argentinian treasury which, when eventually divided up, enriched Sir David Baird (who had never left the Cape) by £30,000, Sir Home Popham by £6,000, and each soldier by £18 6s. This was of course, highly satisfactory, but unfortunately the Argentinians took a different view and, when they discovered that they had been put to flight and had abandoned their capital city through an attack by little more than 1,600 men, their feeling of shame roused the whole country, and the small British force commanded by General Beresford was soon surrounded and hard-pressed.

The 20th Light Dragoons had meanwhile been ordered home, and had just handed over their horses to the 21st, who had come to relieve them, when one of Popham's frigates arrived in Capetown with despatches from Beresford, asking for reinforcements. General Baird thereupon embarked the 20th, without their horses, and two troops of the 21st with their horses, and sent them off to join Beresford, accompanied by the 38th and 47th regiments a company of the 54th, and some guns. Another frigate, with despatches from Popham, had sailed for home, carrying the gold – or some of it – looted from the Argentine Treasury, which the Commodore hoped would induce the Government to take a more tolerant view of his activities. The Government was in fact, very glad to get the gold, which was useful for propaganda purposes at a time when everything was going wrong and the tonic effect of Trafalgar had died down. Nevertheless, to have been committed in this manner to a mad adventure in South America was a considerable embarrassment, and although a couple of thousand men under Sir Samuel Auchmuty were sent out as immediate reinforcements, orders were given to Beresford and Popham to withdraw and return home if there was any danger that they could not maintain their position.

The Indiamen carrying the 20th reached the Rio Plate in October, to find that Beresford had already been forced to surrender. Colonel Backhouse, commanding the reinforcements, thereupon decided to land at Maldonado, at the mouth of the River Plate. There was however, a considerable delay before a landing became practicable, for the voyage had been a stormy one and the transports scattered. The 20th, who were the first troops to arrive, had therefore to remain on board in the estuary, watching Sir Home Popham bombarding Monte Video. As his fleet was mostly composed of schooners and other small ships, with only two of the line with 64 guns apiece, he could do little damage until a 74, on her way home from India, was fortuitously blown into the estuary and immediately taken under Popham's command on the grounds that she was in too bad a condition to continue her voyage.

The landing was eventually made on the 29th October, covered by the guns of the line-of-battle ships and with each boat carrying troops armed with a carronade in the bows. Under this fire, the Argentinians fell back out of sight and the 38th regiment was able to form up with its grenadier company on the right and the 20th, acting as light infantry, on the left. The mounted squadron of the 21st was held back in reserve, as were a couple of small guns dragged by seamen. The line was echeloned back from the grenadiers, who therefore were the first to come within range of the enemy and suffered severely. As each successive company

1806

advanced and fired a volley, the enemy disintegrated and on being charged by the 21st, took to their heels and were chased into and through Maldonado. The town was then sacked by the British troops who, according to Sergeant Landsheit, had been given 'three hours' licence' by Colonel Backhouse. It is most unlikely that he did any such thing, especially as he knew himself to be in danger of a counter-attack. The troops, having their blood up, and being enraged by the losses suffered by their grenadiers, probably got out of hand and ran riot. This often happened in those days, when the non-commissioned officers did not have the same standing and authority among the soldiers as they have now, so that the officers had to restore discipline unaided. Landsheit describes them rushing round the town, hauling the troops away from the liquor supplies, and breaking open casks and smashing bottles to try and keep their men sober. The whole scene filled him with disgust, but it never seems to have occurred to him that it was his duty to assist his officers in stopping it. 'I kept quiet,' he says,' but no sooner was discipline restored, than I determined to see whether the wholesale plunderers had left any gleanings behind, such as might satisfy my moderate desires.' He was obviously in fact, a greater rogue than any of his comrades whom he was accustomed to denounce so self-righteously. By distributing among the women of the regiment various items of feminine underwear which he had looted, he 'soon won their hearts,' and, no doubt, suitable rewards. There is no record of how many of these women had accompanied the two squadrons of the 20th from England, but the average number was six per hundred men with of course, their children. Only the toughest survived the hardships of following the drum, so that there were seldom more than one or two children per woman.

Sergeant Landsheit had helped himself only just in time, for once discipline had been restored it was firmly maintained by the Provost-Marshal, who patrolled the streets with an armed guard and 'soon became the only successful marauder in the place; for . . . if he caught a poor devil laden with booty, he eased him of his burden forthwith, tied him up, and gave him five-and-twenty lashes.'

The Argentinians fortunately made no moves towards recapturing the town, but contented themselves with keeping it under observation from about ten miles off. Backhouse was therefore given time to consolidate, and also to obtain horses for the 20th Light Dragoons. During the next three months, while this small force was left on its own, precariously holding on to a corner of a vast and hostile land, the cavalry, sometimes supported by a company of infantry, were continually out on foraging expeditions, collecting beef both for the garrison of Maldonado and the fleet. This beef had almost always to be fought for, and it would appear that the 20th were far more efficient than the bulk of British cavalry at this time, and able to manoeuvre in conjunction with the infantry with considerable success. The position however, began to deteriorate as the Argentinians were stung into active retaliation, and it was with great relief that the garrison greeted the sight of the topsails of Auchmuty's ships heading in towards the Plate on the 5th January, 1807.

Sir Samuel Auchmuty brought with him about 4,000 men which, with the 2,000 in Maldanado, he considered to be sufficient for an attempt to regain the initiative. After consultation with Admiral Stirling, who had come out to relieve Popham, he decided that Buenos Aires was too tough a proposition; but that the capture of Monte Video would be a reasonable venture to undertake as an alternative. All troops were accordingly embarked at Maldonado on the 13th January, and landed in a small bay nine miles below Monte Video three days later. The whole affair was carried out 'without beat of drum,' and it was not until the Spaniards saw the force disembarking that they were aware of it. Although they formed up in front of Monte Video, they were deterred by the guns of the fleet from attempting an attack, and Auchmuty was able to establish himself on shore unopposed. He advanced on the 19th, led by the cavalry, which consisted of the 20th and 21st Light Dragoons, and some of the 9th and 17th, which were newly-arrived and not fully mounted. They came under heavy artillery fire from an enemy force of about 4,000 men drawn up along some heights before the city, and were then halted until Auchmuty galloped up and ordered them forward to charge the guns. His horse lost a leg from a cannon-ball while he was doing so but, like most generals of that time, he appeared quite indifferent to such occupational mishaps, mounted a spare charger immediately, and personally directed the cavalry against certain guns which seemed likely to 'annoy the infantry as they come up.' The 20th then charged and took three guns, cutting down all their crews, after which, on the 95th regiment arriving, the Spaniards fled into the city, pursued up to the gates by the cavalry.

Monte Video was then closely invested by Auchmuty, who had some heavy guns brought ashore from the fleet. The Spaniards then made a sortie with about six thousand men who, according to Sergeant Landsheit, were all drunk. They were repulsed at all

1807

events with great slaughter, and thereafter made no further attempts to interfere with the siege. This did not last long; the city being taken by storm on the 3rd February, when about eight hundred Spaniards were killed, at the cost of one hundred British. Monte Video was not sacked after the manner of Maldonado, for Auchmuty had his men well in hand. He was one of those commanders indeed, who manage to secure from the rank and file a respect amounting to devotion, so that they carried out his orders without question – even when they were unpopular orders, such as those forbidding looting and rape.

It was very unfortunate that Auchmuty was not reinforced and left in command of the operations on the Plate, but the British Government, being in some doubt and confusion regarding the position in South America, decided to send out General Whitelock, with orders to capture Buenos Aires. With so few troops available, this was a very tall order to give any General, and Whitelock was of no more than average capability and was cursed with a hectoring manner which led to him being generally disliked in the army. However, he did his best but was frustrated in the end by the determined resistance which the Spaniards put up, street by street, in Buenos Aires itself, in which the lay-out and construction of the houses greatly assisted the defenders. Finding that the place could not be taken except at the cost of heavier casualties than he was prepared to accept, Whitelock finally came to terms with the enemy and, after all prisoners had been exchanged, evacuated his forces. Monte Video was retained for three months while the exchanges were being carried out, being finally handed over in September, 1807 when the 20th, which had not taken part in the operations against Buenos Aires, returned home. There is no record of the exact number of casualties suffered by the two squadrons in South America, but only about half of the original number actually landed back in the United Kingdom at the end of the year. It appears that the two squadrons sailed in two different ships, and that one of these was wrecked off the Needles, in which case it is doubtful if there was more than a handful of survivors – if any.

The remnants of the two squadrons were sent to Guildford to recruit. They were apparently ordered to recruit up to regimental strength, ignoring their three squadrons still in the Mediterranean. The regiment, at any rate, commanded by Colonel Taylor who had returned from the Mediterranean, sailed from Portsmouth for Cork and Lisbon in July, 1808, with six troops.

Silver statuette of an officer of the 14th Light Dragoons. The uniform is of the period 1796–1812. The sword is of the pattern introduced for Light Cavalry in 1796 and used throughout the Napoleonic War.

1807 A squadron of the 20th in Egypt
May 1807 The action at El Hamid
August 1807 The 20th land in Portugal and march on Lisbon
21st August 1807 The Battle of Vimiera

1806

The Start of the Peninsular War

6

WHILE the left wing of the 20th were adventuring in South America, the right wing was continuing to participate in Sir James Craig's operations in the Mediterranean, where their experiences were equally strange and untoward. After landing at Castlemere, and being mounted on an odd collection of animals collected locally, the three squadrons had marched for the Neapolitan frontier. Scarcely had they reached it, when news came that 30,000 Frenchmen were marching south through Italy and, after a council of war had been held between the British and Russian commanders, a retirement was ordered, as it was evident that the defence of the frontier against so numerous an enemy was impracticable. The Russian contingent was then thrown into further depression by the news of Austerlitz, which caused the Tsar to order it to abandon Naples and proceed to Corfu. This left the British no alternative but to evacuate the kingdom also, and in January, 1806, the British troops were transferred to Sicily, where they were later joined by the Neapolitan court. The French then advanced to the northern shores of the Straits of Messina, and were only deterred from crossing into Sicily by the presence of the British contingent, facing them across the Straits.

General Stuart, who relieved Sir James Craig, noted that the

◁ Lieut.-Colonel Charles Taylor, a popular commanding officer of the 20th Light Dragoons (1803–8). He was slain at the head of his regiment during the Battle of Vimiera, 1808, and buried on the battlefield. Wellington specially praised the 20th for 'valour and discipline'.

1806

French, though superior to him in numbers, were widely scattered over Calabria, and he therefore decided, in collaboration with Admiral Sir Sidney Smith, the Commander-in-Chief in the Mediterranean, to make an attack across the Straits. Such an attack could only be launched in the nature of a raid, without any prospects of permanent results, but both Stuart and Smith were adventurous types, rather like Sir Home Popham, who were always on the lookout for chances to enhance their reputations with a little honour and glory. Although they have been much criticised on this account, it is, after all, a commander's business to seek for opportunities for engaging the enemy, and raids with limited objectives are better than no action at all. The expedition sailed from Sicily on the 26th June but as, most unfortunately, Stuart was so short of transports that he was unable to take many horses, only sixteen of the 20th went with it, and there were no other cavalry, which proved a grave disadvantage. General Reynier, the French commander, was taken completely by surprise, but managed to concentrate about six thousand men near San Pietro di Maida where Stuart, with about the same numbers but no cavalry except the 16 men of the 20th, managed to beat him on the 4th July.

The remainder of the 20th must have felt very sore at missing this engagement, at which their presence could scarcely have failed to turn the French defeat into a complete disaster. As it was, the French lost half their men in a singularly bloody encounter. The other half could not have escaped, had there been even three squadrons of British cavalry in the field. Other work, however, was pending for the 20th Light Dragoons.

By the end of 1806, Napoleon had made himself master of Europe, and of the former allies of Great Britain only Russia remained. Russia was always a difficult ally, and at this moment, just after the collapse of Prussia, the Tsar contrived to become embroiled with Turkey, his hereditary enemy, which had been trying to keep out of the struggle so far. Napoleon was quick to seize the opportunity for putting various strategic measures in train, with the object of separating Russia from Great Britain, thereby alarming the British Government sufficiently to cause it to support Russia more actively than it might otherwise have contemplated. Eight sail of the line under Sir John Duckworth were sent up the Dardanelles to bombard Constantinople and sink the Turkish Fleet; but the mission failed owing to having no troops with it (a lesson which might profitably have been recalled by the Government of 1915).

The Government then decided to send a force back to Egypt

which, after the British had evacuated the country in 1803, had fallen into Turkish hands. It was feared that as Turkey was now, if not exactly an ally of Napoleon, at least on the same side, he might contemplate returning to Egypt himself, as a step towards India. The expedition, commanded by Major-General Fraser Mackenzie, sailed from Messina on the 7th March, 1807. It numbered about six thousand all-ranks – with 364 women and 323 children. The only cavalry with it was a squadron of the 20th of 4 officers and 74 rank and file. This force had been embarked and kept packed on the transports under highly unpleasant conditions for nearly a month before sailing, awaiting the arrival of a naval escort, which turned out to be one ship of 64 guns – a French prize in poor condition.

The day after sailing, heavy gales blew the convoy apart, and when General Fraser arrived before Alexandria on the 16th March, he had only fourteen sail of transports left out of a total of thirty-three. The Turkish garrison of Alexandria however, amounted to less than 300 men, so that Fraser commenced to land the 2,000 soldiers, who included the squadron of the 20th, that he still had with him. The landing proved very difficult owing to the increasing violence of the surf, and eventually the operation had to be suspended, after the 20th had managed to get ashore with about a thousand infantry. The Turks closed the gates of the city and opened fire with cannon and muskets, but after Fraser had surrounded it, and the missing transports had arrived, the Governor capitulated without further ado.

The capture of Alexandria completed Fraser's mission, and he was not required to do any more than to remain and defend it. He decided however, that the port was not tactically secure without the occupation of Rosetta and Rahmanieh, some forty miles distant, which were garrisoned by Albanians. A force of 1,600 all-ranks, without cavalry, was sent to occupy Rosetta on the 31st March and, having marched into the middle of it without any previous reconnaissance, was set upon by hordes of Albanians and driven out again, with a loss of nearly 500 men. A further attempt, with 2,500 men, including the 20th, was made on the 3rd April. This time the Turks were naturally on the lookout, so that the venture appeared less promising than before, but Fraser was counting on the support of the Mamelukes – mounted warriors who had ruled Egypt until defeated by the Turks, on whom they were anxious to revenge themselves.

The enemy were first encountered at El Hamid, a village about four miles south of Rosetta on a neck of land between the Nile and Lake Edko. Most of them were Albanian cavalry, who rode off

1807

after exchanging a few shots with the 20th. The village was then occupied by 300 infantry, while the main body advanced to Rosetta, a walled town with its gates shut and its walls lined with Albanian musketeers, who opened a steady fire on the British, but without much effect. As the British force brought forward its mortars and heavy guns, the Albanians attempted several sorties, but they were easily driven off by the squadron of the 20th, which was keeping an eye on the sally-ports.

One of the defenders' advanced batteries was then captured in a night attack by the 78th Highlanders, but thereafter the siege made no progress, for there was no sign of the Mamelukes, and without their help the town could not be surrounded. It was thus impossible to stop the arrival of Turkish reinforcements, and on the 19th a large body of Turkish cavalry crossed the Nile and attacked El Hamid, while at the same time a strong sortie was made by the garrison of Rosetta. The Turkish cavalry were charged by the squadron of the 20th which, however, being vastly outnumbered, became completely cut off, losing one man and six horses killed, while the squadron leader, Captain Delaney, the Surgeon and eleven men were taken prisoner. The squadron dismounted and formed square, losing fourteen horses to the enemy while doing so. A galloper, Pte. Tremble, was then sent to El Hamid for help. He had actually to hack his way through the enveloping Turks, but he got through safely and brought out a couple of infantry companies which drove off the enemy and rescued the squadron. The fact that Pte. Tremble's name should have been preserved for posterity is an indication of the particular gallantry of his exploit. There were no decorations given for gallantry in those days, and few indeed are the names of either officers or men which are still remembered, no matter what feats of valour and self-sacrifice they may have performed on innumerable battlefields of the past, which have now likewise been forgotten.

The sortie from Rosetta was also driven off, but as large enemy reinforcements began to arrive, and there was still no sign of the Mamelukes, it was decided to abandon the enterprise. This was not easy, and during a fighting withdrawal heavy casualties were suffered, and over eight hundred officers and men were cut-off at El Hamid and either killed or captured.

Thereafter the force remained at Alexandria until returning to Sicily in September by the orders of the British Government, which had come to the conclusion that it had not the resources available to keep a foot in Egypt and defend Sicily at the same time. Thus ended yet another abortive and mis-managed ex-

1807

pedition, in which the only pleasant incident was the action of the Turkish Caliph, Mahommed Ali, in returning all British prisoners in good condition and with many polite expressions of esteem and regard. The same, of course, had been done by the Spanish colonists in South America, but they had not been nearly so polite about it and, although Spain had now become an ally of Great Britain, neither she nor her colonists showed any signs of letting by-gones be by-gones.

Spain had been the ally of France since 1795, but had become increasingly restive under the iron hand of Napoleon, who exacted a heavy annual tribute without giving anything in return except preremptory orders and harsh words. At the end of 1807, becoming suspicious of her fidelity, he deposed the monarch, substituted his brother Joseph and took the country over. He then sent Marshal Junot to take over Portugal also, with a view to denying all ports of Europe to British trade. These proceedings were too much for the Spaniards and Portuguese to stomach. In May, 1808, a revolt started in Madrid and spread rapidly across Spain, being soon followed by a complementary rising in Portugal. In June, a Spanish mission arrived in London to solicit aid, and, as it had become imperative for Great Britain to halt Napoleon without any further delay, an expeditionary force commanded by Sir Arthur Wellesley was sent to Portugal to evict the French and secure Lisbon as a base for operations into Spain.

Sir Arthur Wellesley – the future Duke of Wellington – had acquired some renown in India where, with the help of the 72nd and 74th Highlanders, the 19th Light Dragoons and some Madrassi sepoys, he had defeated vast hordes of Mahrattas, led by French officers. He had had no experience of high command in continental operations, which were very different from those in India, and for the Government to match him against an experienced Marshal of France like Junot, was a surprising decision; but he had contrived to impress the Secretary for War with his views on how affairs in the Peninsula should be conducted. He had been born in the same year as Napoleon, who had left him far behind in the race to the top – Napoleon now being an Emperor who could shake the world with the lift of an eyebrow, while Wellesley was only a Major-General. Napoleon contemptuously described him as a 'Sepoy General' and although seven years hence the Emperor was made to eat his words, this was not an unfair estimate of Wellesley's capabilities at that time.

Wellesley's expedition, consisting of nearly eleven thousand men, sailed from the Cove of Cork on the 13th July. It included the 20th Light Dragoons, who embarked at a strength of 13

1808

officers, 368 rank and file, and 215 horses. The regiment had left two troops behind to form a depot squadron at Maidstone. This was customary in both cavalry and infantry regiments when they went overseas, and was necessary for the provision of reinforcements. The depot squadrons and companies did not necessarily stay in the same place, but moved about as occasion demanded, in order to recruit. With four troops in Sicily and two at Maidstone, the regiment would have embarked four troops only, which had evidently been brought up to war establishment at the expense of those in Maidstone.

The 20th had spent the time since returning from South America 'in training recruits, breaking young horses, and discharging the common duties of home service,' but had not carried out anything much in the way of training. It had been issued with new arms – swords, carbines and pistols – and new uniforms. The latter consisted of the blue, frogged jacket, associated with Horse Artillery and Hussars to the present day, white breeches and black knee-length boots, peaked leather helmets with bearskin crests and red and white plumes. The four troops, as they rode down to Portsmouth from Guildford to embark for the Cove, must have presented a very fine spectacle, and they were fortunate in a fair-weather voyage, with a moderate wind astern, so that they were able to disembark in Mondego Bay in good heart, and with their magnificent appearance little diminished except for several individuals, who fell into the sea while landing. The landing was carried out in what, in the jargon of modern times, would be called 'Horse Landing Craft' which were rectangular boats with flat bottoms, in which the horses stood in pairs with their heads towards the beach, saddled and bridled and with their riders beside them. The riders were ordered, in the case of a boat overturning, to spring into the saddle, 'a judicious precaution which proved in two or three instances eminently useful.'

Shortly after the force had landed, it was joined by General Spencer, with 5,000 men from Gibraltar, bringing Wellesley up to 15,000 men, with whom he marched on Lisbon on the 10th August. He moved by the coastal road, in order to keep in touch with the fleet, and on the way the 20th were joined by about a hundred officers and men of the Lisbon Mounted Police, who came in by twos and threes until they were able to form a squadron of their own, which was then attached to the regiment under command.

The 20th were kept a day's march ahead of the main body, reconnoitring towards Leira, supported by the 60th Rifles and the Rifle Brigade, but no enemy were encountered before

1808

Alcabaca, which the 20th reached on the 12th August to find some French cavalry just pulling out. These were the rear elements of a force under General Delaborde, whom Junot, on hearing of Wellesley's arrival, had pushed forward to cover his concentration. Delaborde was not looking for a fight until he had found a good defensive position, and so fell back to some rocky slopes by the village of Rolica leaving a rearguard at Obidos covered by an outpost line through Brilos. The 20th did not apparently discover the outpost line, and their first sight of the enemy was at Brilos, where the French retired without firing a shot. The two rifle battalions meanwhile attacked the outpost line and drove it back, but suffered heavy casualties from pressing forward too closely.

Arriving at Obidos on 21st August 1808, Wellesley climbed the church tower and examined Delaborde's position, as a result of which he sent a Portuguese Brigade round the enemy's left flank and led a frontal attack with the rest of his force, preceded by the 20th who, however, had to dismount and take cover when they got within range, for the enemy position was unrideable. Wellesley, who outnumbered Delaborde by four to one, eased him out of his position using only one brigade but Delaborde then carried out an extremely skilful retreat, which Wellesley was unable to turn to any advantage. It was of course, followed up by the 20th, which was the only British cavalry regiment present, but the retirement was covered by French cavalry in such numbers that no opportunity presented itself for a charge – which was about the only warlike manoeuvre properly understood by the 20th at that time. The regiment accordingly formed in single rank and marched at a walk, keeping the French on the move, until ordered to halt, when it bivouacked in a village.

On the following morning Wellesley heard that two brigades of reinforcements had arrived in the fleet, which was still lying offshore. Giving orders for them to land at the mouth of the River Maceira, he took up a position at Vimiera to cover the disembarkation. Information then reached him that Junot's advanced guard was at Torres Vedras, with the French army concentrating behind it. He immediately gave orders to march, with the idea of turning Junot's position before he could form up, but at this moment Sir Harry Burrard, a general senior to him, arrived in Maceira Bay in the frigate *Brazen*. Not wanting him ashore – for Wellesley always disliked being ordered about – he hastened on board to greet him. Burrard, after hearing his report, ordered him not to march from Vimiera until the arrival of Sir John Moore with reinforcements from England. This was the sort of inter-

1808

ference with his plans that Wellesley had been expecting, and it left him greatly disgruntled. Experience however, inclined Burrard to caution. It was a policy for which Wellesley had no use at that period, but he possessed an inspired genius on the actual battlefield which enabled him to escape from the 'confounded scrapes' into which his impetuosity led him from time to time, whereas ordinary generals were obliged by their limitations to be more orthodox.

The 20th Light Dragoons were still with the 60th and Rifle Brigade, forming a light brigade, commanded by Brigadier John Fane, which, with another infantry brigade, bivouacked on Vimiera Hill. Wellesley had not taken up any defensive position as, until stopped by Burrard, he had intended to march against Junot and not wait for him. The precautions against surprise were however, very thorough, and the 20th had to send out mounted patrols in the direction of Torres Vedras throughout the night. One of these, led by Sergeant Landsheit, discovered the French army on the march towards Vimiera, and returned immediately to report. The patrol was of course challenged by the vedettes, and the noise awoke the Brigadier who, Landsheit noted, had pitched his tent in front of the outposts. Landsheit told him his news, and was ordered to gallop immediately to Wellesley's headquarters, which he reached about midnight, finding Wellesley 'with a large Staff, all of them seated on a long table in the hall, back to back, and swinging their legs to and fro, like men on whose minds not a shadow of anxiety rested.'

After listening to his report, Wellesley told Landsheit that he had done well, and sent him below stairs to get a meal. As he left the hall, he heard the orders being given to rouse up the soldiers without beat of drum and get them quietly under arms; to 'desire all the outposts to be on the alert.' He found his own regiment under arms on his return, when it was moved down into the valley, with the village of Vimiera on its right front. This village lies across the road from Torres Vedras. To the south is Vimiera Hill, which was held by Fane's and Anstruther's brigades, and to the north, the rest of the British force was disposed along two long, low ridges. Wellesley kept his troops out of sight along the reverse slopes, so that Junot, when he arrived at about 7 a.m. on the 21st August, got very little information out of his reconnaissance, and evidently came to the conclusion that the bulk of the British force was on Vimiera Hill. He led off by sending General Brennier with a regiment of Dragoons and an infantry brigade against the eastern ridge intending to attack Vimiera Hill as soon as Brennier was on his objective. Wellesley reorganised to meet this threat, and his movements were spotted by Junot, who became alarmed, and sent another brigade to support Brennier. These brigades lost direction, and eventually went into action independently, while Junot, getting impatient, launched a major attack against Vimiera Hill.

The French advanced in close columns, protected by screens of skirmishers, and with their cavalry hanging about on the flanks, watching for an opportunity to charge. The British received them in lines, which were kept under cover until the last moment, behind a screen of picquets. When the enemy had driven back the picquets, the lines advanced in three ranks and halted within close musket shot. The front ranks then knelt and held their fire, while the rear ranks fired a volley at about one hundred yards range, hastily reloading under cover of the front ranks. When the enemy appeared to be sufficiently softened up by this treatment, they went in with the bayonet, but the moment for this required very nice judgement, and the whole manoeuvre was, in fact, not nearly as easy to execute as it sounds. While advancing, the British lines were very vulnerable to cavalry, but the drill of any seasoned regiment was so excellent that it could form square quickly and without confusion, and in this formation was able to withstand very heavy cavalry charges.

The 20th Light Dragoons, with their Portuguese squadron, spent the morning sitting along the side of the Torres Vedras road, holding their reins and listening to the sound of battle on either side, but unable to see anything of what was happening. They were still under the orders of Brigadier Fane, and their commanding-officer, Colonel Taylor, was continually riding off to Vimiera Hill to ask to be allowed to do something. It looked to him as if the British on the Hill were getting decidedly the worst of it, and that a charge by the 20th was long overdue. Fane, however, was treating the whole affair in the unperturbed, and indeed nonchalant, manner typical of the British officer of that period – and all other periods, for that matter – and refused to allow his battle to be messed about by cavalry. At length, when Taylor was in despair, a charge by the 43rd Regiment near the entrance to the village routed the French Grenadiers, and the Brigadier called at last, 'Now we want you, 20th! Forward and charge, and show them what you are made of!'

The 20th were in the saddle before Taylor had time to give the order. 'Threes about and forward! Trot.' As the regiment came up the slope, into view of the British infantry, it was given a rousing reception. Having been plagued all day by the French cavalry galloping about, the infantry had been wondering where

1808

their own was, rather as the modern British soldier in battle wonders what has happened to his own aircraft. It was with their cheers ringing in their ears that the 20th formed column of half-squadrons and, with a troop of Portuguese policemen on either flank, bore down upon the French infantry, some of whom were broken and disorganised, some retreating in good order, and others still standing fast but beginning to look over their shoulders. Among them were the French cavalry under General Margaron, which were still in formation, trying to cover the retreat. They had gone into battle about two thousand strong, and there was probably about a thousand of them on the Hill at this stage, against whom Taylor directed his attack. The 20th galloped through the French infantry without trouble, increasing speed until, when they reached the cavalry, they were going 'as fast as the body can bear, in good order.' The French Chasseurs and Dragoons, besides being in some confusion and disorder, had no time to get up any speed in order to meet the attack by the 20th, who therefore rode through them 'cutting and hacking, and upsetting men and horses in the most extraordinary manner possible, till they broke and fled in every direction.'

Beyond the French cavalry were some columns of infantry retiring, who faced about as the 20th, now scattered and out of control, galloped across the field towards them. First to reach them was Colonel Taylor, riding a hot thoroughbred with its bit between its teeth. He was shot dead by a French corporal, but his fate was not noticed by any of his men at the time, for they were too busy laying about them 'till our white leather breeches, our hands, arms and swords, were all besmeared with blood'. There was so much smoke and dust about, that none of them could see more than a few yards, and so their horses carried them over a low fence, lined with enemy grenadiers, who thrust their bayonets into the bellies of the horses as they jumped, but these brave fellows were cut down to a man as the 20th, finding that there was no way out of the field into which they had jumped, at last pulled up. They were then in some difficulty, for the French infantry surrounded the field, outside of which Corporal Marshall of the 20th could be seen fighting off four French dragoons. A powerful man himself, he was mounted on an equally powerful and spirited stallion, which did not leave all the fighting to his master, but lashed out in all directions with both fore and hind feet, 'screaming all the time.' Marshall clove one enemy to the teeth, and with a back stroke took another across the face, and 'sent him from his saddle,' and at that moment the 50th Regiment arrived at the 'double quick' and got the French on the move again, greatly to

1808

the relief of the 20th, who looked like being all killed or taken prisoner.

The French being now in full retreat, and the day won, the 20th marched out of action and dismounted on the Torres Vedras road. The Portuguese policemen, who had pulled up before the charge and refused to engage, were waiting for them 'formed up like troops on parade, and quite bloodless.' Not unnaturally they were given a somewhat chilly greeting by the 20th. On the roll being called, the commanding-officer, one captain, and fifty-three rank and file failed to answer to their names. Twenty of these were afterwards found to have been killed, and twenty-four wounded. The others were missing, and some later rejoined. Thirty horses had been killed and ten wounded.

A party was immediately sent out to look for Colonel Taylor, who was found among the dead and wounded which covered the slopes of the Hill and the plain beyond. He was stripped to the drawers, for the Portuguese peasants, 'together with women from our own army' had already got to work, plundering the fallen. Taylor, who had been greatly liked and respected by his men, was buried on the field.

The 20th Light Dragoons were among eleven regiments specially mentioned in his despatches by Sir Arthur Wellesley for their particular 'valour and discipline'. In addition to this tribute their efforts acquired for the 14th/20th King's Hussars the first battle-honour borne on the guidon:

VIMIERA

14th Light Dragoons, uniform of the period 1798–1812, blue with orange facings. The Prussian Eagle badge was worn on the side of the helmet. In 1812 the helmet was replaced by a shako.

December 1808 The 14th sail for the Peninsula
1809 Operations against Oporto
June 1809 The advance from Abrantes
July 1809 The Combat of Salinas
28th July 1809 The Battle of Talavera
Withdrawal to Portugal

The Talavera Campaign

Sir Arthur Wellesley was not allowed to follow up his victory, for Burrard took over control immediately after it, being then joined by Sir Hew Dalrymple, who was again senior to him. While the three generals were conferring a squadron of French dragoons arrived, escorting General Kellermann with a flag of truce. Negotiations were opened which led to the signing of the Convention of Cintra, under which the French evacuated Portugal and were taken home in British ships. The British army marched into Lisbon in September, and in the same month Sir John Moore arrived with reinforcements which brought it up to about 40,000 men.

On hearing of Junot's defeat, Napoleon marched into Spain with 150,000 men, and the Spaniards again asked for assistance. The British government, which was not best pleased about the Convention of Cintra – which had caused a public outcry – recalled the three signatories, Wellesley, Burrard and Dalrymple, and confirmed Sir John Moore as commander-in-chief in Portugal. Misled by false intelligence regarding the position in Spain, Moore marched into that country only to find that the Emperor had given the Spanish regular army such a thrashing that it had temporarily ceased to exist. Being thus unsupported, with the Emperor on one side of him and Soult on the other,

1808

Moore had no option but to make for Corunna across the mountains in the depth of winter, hard-pressed by Soult the whole way. On arrival at Corunna he was obliged to stand and fight before it was possible to embark and, although he got the better of Soult and the army was safely evacuated, he was himself killed in action. Hastily buried under the ramparts of Corunna, it was left to Soult to erect a monument over his grave, to 'John Moore. Leader of the English Armies. Killed in Battle.'

Although the Corunna campaign was regarded as a grievous reverse in Great Britain, it was not so in fact. A tactical incident in the desperate gamble of war, it had the effect of drawing the French away to the north-west, giving the Spaniards a chance to rally, and, by drawing French attention to the weakness of their lines of communication, along 'the great road' to Bayonne, made them very sensitive to threats in this direction. It was a weakness of which Wellington was to take full advantage in due course.

Wellington – or Wellesley, as he still was – succeeded in clearing himself of the opprobrium attached to the convention of Cintra, by representing that he had only signed it under orders. In March, 1809, he was again appointed to the chief command in Portugal where the army, under Sir James Cradock, had been brought up to a strength of 26,000 all-ranks. Among the reinforcements sent out were the 14th Light Dragoons, who sailed from Falmouth in December 1808, and landed at Lisbon on the 23rd of the month.

Since 1804, the 14th had been greatly dispersed, with its headquarters at either Guildford or Hounslow, and its troops in detachments all over the place. A specially picked detachment of a Captain, 9 Sergeants and 34 Corporals was stationed at Kensington for duties in connection with the royal household, but many of the other troops were called upon for escorting the royal carriages and other similar employments. Although such duties were not merely ceremonial, but were necessary for the actual protection of the King and others of the Royal family during those troublous times, they were not, of course, of much use in training the regiment for war. The only training carried out in fact was that of the recruits and remounts, for the regiment could never get together, and its detachments were always out on patrol for the maintenance of law and order. It was still on the high establishment of ten troops, with 54 Sergeants, 10 Trumpeters, 50 Corporals, and 950 Private Men, but it is doubtful if it was ever fully up to strength. At about this time, it had 640 troop horses, out of an establishment of 1,064, and probably the rank and file numbered about 700.

1808

Although the actual voyage lasted only about three weeks, the 14th spent well over a month cooped up on board ship. The transports carried little in the way of ballast – packed with men and horses, there was no room for any – and in the rough seas running at that time of year the horses had a very poor time of it, going off their feed and getting badly out of condition. Normally they would soon have picked up again after landing, but the 14th found that there was no forage available in Lisbon, so that when their horses recovered their appetites there was nothing to give them and, before long, they barely had the strength to walk on to parade. It was not a promising commencement to an arduous campaign, but the French were fortunately too occupied in Spain to be able to give any attention to Portugal for the moment, so that a respite was secured.

Wellesley landed in Lisbon on the 22nd April and took over from Cradock two days later. The Army in Portugal then amounted to about 28,000 men, apart from 15,000 Portuguese, led by British officers and commanded by General Beresford. He was faced by the same frustrations that had hampered Cradock; there was a dearth of everything essential for a campaign; horses, mules, supplies and money. Of the latter commodity he had only £10,000 in cash, so that he was unable to pay the soldiers – which was nothing new – and had to get everything on credit. His obvious determination to advance however, commended him to the Portuguese, who did what they could to smooth his path, and, considering the extraordinary difficulties with which he was faced, he was able to get the army more or less fit for active service in a remarkably short space of time.

In the Order of Battle of the Army in Portugal, the Light Cavalry Brigade, commanded by Major-General Stapleton Cotton, was composed as follows:

14th Light Dragoons, less one squadron detached to the Portuguese Army, and with one troop of the 3rd Hussars, King's German Legion attached.
16th Light Dragoons.
20th Light Dragoons, less two squadrons in Sicily.

This brigade was the only cavalry available to cover Wellesley's advance. There were two British heavy cavalry regiments in Portugal, the 3rd Dragoon Guards and 4th Dragoons, but he had to leave these behind for the defence of Lisbon – and also because of forage difficulties.

At the end of March, Soult had arrived before Oporto and taken it by storm; a disaster which had greatly shaken both the British and Portuguese governments. Wellesley's first objective

1809

was to retake the port and clear Soult out of Portugal, and on the 27th April he gave orders for the Light Cavalry Brigade and eight infantry brigades to concentrate at Coimbra, inland from Mondego Bay and about half-way between Oporto and Lisbon.

In planning his operations against Oporto, Wellesley had been counting on the presence of the Portuguese levies in Soult's rear, but when these levies under General Silveira, having been rash enough to try conclusions with the Marshal on their own, were heavily defeated, he had to think of some other way of distracting Soult's attention. General Beresford with six thousand Portuguese, supported by a British infantry brigade and a squadron of the 14th, was directed to march by Vizeu, collect Silveira's levies at Lamego, and thereafter prevent Soult from crossing the Douro, which Wellesley expected him to attempt after he had been driven out of Oporto: but, 'Remember', he warned Beresford, 'that you are a commander-in-chief, and must not be beaten; therefore do not undertake anything with your troops unless you have some strong hope of success.' This was Wellesley's established formula for the guidance of commanders-in-chief, although the conduct of some of his operations seems to indicate that he did not always follow it himself.

On the 7th May, the British advanced guard left Coimbra and marched upon Oporto. It consisted of the 14th Light Dragoons, less one squadron with Beresford, a field-battery, and an infantry brigade. It marched by the coast road through Aveiro, in order to cover the embarkation of two infantry brigades which had been ordered to land at Ovar and support the Light Cavalry Brigade, which was advancing along the main road ahead of the main body, as soon as the cavalry reached the French outposts. The plan of operations, which had many other aspects to it besides these, was undoubtedly complicated, as the Duke of Wellington's plans often were in spite of the fact that he insisted that he never made any, but was 'guided by circumstance.' It is very unusual for complicated plans to work out exactly in war, and this one was no exception. Wellington presumably never expected them to, being content with bamboozling the enemy by the intricacy of his movements: in this he usually succeeded.

The French were known to be holding the bridge across the Vouga River, and the first task given to the cavalry was to drive them from the river and seize the bridge. When the cavalry arrived, however, they were found to have withdrawn and when the cavalry came up with them they were too strongly posted to be attacked by other than infantry, so that Cotton was obliged to halt the brigade. The country was in any case difficult for cavalry, being rocky and enclosed, so that the brigade became road-bound and, once the infantry had gone through, could not get ahead of them again until a halt was called at Oliviera. A squadron each from the 16th and 20th, under the command of Major Blake of the 20th, were then sent forward to Feira to link up with the force landed at Ovar. The leading brigade of this force, however, had met with opposition and was forced to await the arrival of the second brigade, which used the same boats.

The two squadrons therefore rode on towards Grijo, being obliged to keep in file owing to the narrowness of the track and the nature of the country on either side. They were just about to emerge from a wood before Grijo, being then in single file, when they were halted by a staff officer and told to retire, as the rocky ground ahead was strongly held by French infantry and it was impossible for cavalry to attack. Blake passed the order down and the leading squadron had turned about, when another staff officer arrived in the rear and commenced shouting orders to go forward. The two squadrons were thus facing one another in single file on a narrow track, within musket shot of the enemy, and with a staff officer at each end giving directly contradictory orders. This situation, which would have been comical if lives had not been at stake, was not improved by the fact that the unfortunate Blake was unable to leave the track in order to find out what was happening and take control. Nor was inter-regimental rivalry, which was very strong at that time, especially in the cavalry, a help in a situation in which the two squadrons came from different regiments. It seems probable indeed that the squadron of the 16th, which was leading, was inclined to resent Blake's authority.

However, as might be expected with British troops, when one voice is calling 'Back!' and another 'Forward!' they did not long hesitate before obeying the latter; filing out of the wood in full view of the French and galloping forward in very ragged formation with their swords out. The French, of whom there were about three thousand, fortunately commenced to retire as soon as they saw them, imagining that infantry would be close behind and not wishing to be pinned down in that locality.

The two squadrons were therefore able to do considerable execution amongst them and captured about a hundred prisoners. The large number of prisoners appears to have been due to the fact that the dragoons could not bring themselves to cut down men on the run, for they had not been long enough in the field to understand that it was the business of cavalry to spread terror and havoc among the enemy whenever he showed signs of weakening

1809

and that quarter should only be given to those who had thrown down their arms. Large numbers of Frenchmen escaped on this occasion to fight another day owing to this repugnance for cutting them down, while the casualties suffered by the 16th and 20th were very heavy; 2 officers and 19 men killed, and 6 officers and 63 men wounded – at least half the strength of the two squadrons engaged.

After this affair the French withdrew across the Douro and Soult, awaking to his danger, burnt the bridge behind them and began making preparations for retreat through Tras-os-Montes. He was expecting the British to bring up the boats from which they had landed at Ovar, but Wellesley in fact got his infantry across the river in some barges which the French had neglected to destroy. At the same time he sent General Murray, with the 14th Light Dragoons, two guns and two battalions of the King's German Legion, to cross by the ferry at Avintas, about three miles up-river.

The unexpected infantry attack on Oporto demoralised the French, who streamed along the road to Vallonga out of control. Murray was waiting for them on the flank, but apparently lost either his head or his nerve, and gave no orders to advance. Wellesley then sent General Stewart at the gallop to order Murray forward. On arrival, Stewart took over command, ordered Murray's infantry to deploy and advance, and personally led the 14th forward. The French by this time had almost got clear, but General Delaborde, who was in command, had seen the 14th in his rear and turned his rear guard about. He had little time to take up a position, for the 14th were coming on at the gallop, but he managed to line with sharpshooters the low walls on either side of the road, while the infantry of the rear guard stood in close column with bayonets fixed.

The two squadrons of the 14th, commanded by Majors F. B. Hervey and the Hon. Charles Butler, and led by General Stewart, were in column of threes, being unable to form line in the narrow walled road with trees and buildings on either side. Thus they suffered heavily from the sharpshooters. Of the officers only Butler came through unscathed. Hervey lost his right arm, Captain Hawker and Lieutenants Knipe and Dormer were also wounded. Twelve of the rank and file were killed, and nineteen wounded. The French infantry, however, would not face the charge, but broke just as the leading files reached them. The 14th wrought havoc among them, cutting down great numbers including General Foy, unhorsing General Delaborde, and taking about three hundred prisoners.

1809

In his despatches, Wellesley commended 'the bravery of the two squadrons of the 14th Light Dragoons under command of Major Hervey, and led by Brigadier General the Honourable Charles Stewart.' The conduct of the regiment was in fact admirable, and helped in no small way in the decisive defeat of the French, which is commemorated on the guidon by the second battle honour – DOURO. Generals Murray and Stewart, however, have been censured by historians for their activities on the Douro; the first for missing an opportunity, and the second – who was Wellesley's Adjutant-General and responsible for discipline rather than the conduct of operations – for interfering with another general on the battlefield, and galloping away with his cavalry without so much as a by-your-leave. It was Stewart, as a matter of fact, who had been responsible for chasing the two squadrons of the 16th and 20th into action before Grijo, at a time when a General-Staff officer was trying to hold them back. In both cases the ground was highly unsuitable for cavalry, and the only excuse for taking them in was that the infantry were not up. Nevertheless, the results were impressive, and appear fully to justify the risks involved in such unorthodox tactics.

After the taking of Oporto, Wellesley moved north on Braga, while Murray marched on the parallel road to Guimaraes. Meanwhile Beresford with the Portuguese – and the detached squadron of the 14th – had crossed the Douro at Lamego as planned, and was driving the French up the road to Chaves. His presence in the west was a severe shock to Soult, who realised that he had been completely out-generalled and that his army was in danger of destruction. He had now no option but to destroy all his artillery and baggage, and beat a retreat into the bleak mountains of Galicia. The British army followed up hard, and some of the 14th caught up his rear guard beyond Braga. While shots were being exchanged, Wellesley brought up the Guards Brigade and some guns, causing the French once again to fall back in disorder. On the 19th May, he finally called off the pursuit, having run completely out of supplies, so that his men were on starvation rations and many of them barefooted. The cavalry horses were bags of bones, many of them shoeless like the infantry, and unable to get up more than a shambling trot. They kept going, however, and the squadron of the 14th with Beresford got as far as Ginjo, well into Galicia, before a halt was called and Wellesley returned to the Tagus.

While Soult was being chased out of Portugal into Galicia in this ruthless and efficient manner, his brother Marshal, Victor, had been making a tentative advance up to the Tagus, along the

1809

Portuguese frontier with Estremadura. Supply problems finally obliged him to retire up-river to Talavera, but he remained a threat to Lisbon, and so had to be dealt with. Although not of the same stature as Soult, his defeat posed some far bigger problems than had faced Wellesley on the Douro, for he had his back to Madrid, and could count on the active support of Napoleon's brother, King Joseph. Wellesley was also faced with administrative difficulties of the first magnitude. His military organisation and the British Government were to all intents and purposes bankrupt. His troops' pay was two months in arrears, and he had no money to hire transport or purchase supplies. His campaign against Soult had been reluctantly financed by the city of Oporto, but he could no longer get any loans in Portugal where he owed money all over the country, and so had to apply to Cadiz, which only sent him funds after a lot of haggling, during which he was unable to march.

The army for the Talavera campaign was concentrated round Abrantes. It consisted of a cavalry division and four infantry divisions. The cavalry division, commanded by Major-General William Payne, was organised into one heavy and two light brigades, led by Brigadiers Fane, Cotton and Anson. In Fane's brigade were the 3rd Dragoon Guards and 4th Dragoons; Cotton had the 14th and 16th Light Dragoons, and Anson the 1st and 23rd Light Dragoons and the King's German Legion. Under orders from the Horse Guards (War office) the 20th Light Dragoons, after being relieved by the 23rd in June, had left for Sicily to join the other squadrons of the regiment, taking with them the 3rd Hussars of the King's German Legion.

In planning his march against Victor at Talavera, Wellesley was counting on the support of General Cuesta and his Spanish regulars, who had agreed to cross the Tagus and join him at Oropesa. He was also reckoning on Soult, Mortier and Ney being unable to march down from the north in time to support Victor. Finally, not having the transport to carry supplies with him, he was expecting to be able to feed his army off the country to a certain extent, being under the impression that this should not be difficult in the rich valley of the Tagus. By accepting these provisos with such readiness, he was taking an enormous risk. The Spaniards were not really trustworthy, and there was no knowing how commanders of the calibre of Soult and Ney would react.

Leaving Beresford and the Portuguese to keep an eye open for Soult and Ney, and having sent his civilian Commissaries forward in advance to arrange supplies, Wellesley marched from Abrantes on the 27th June, with 23,000 men. His army was not in the best shape, having had neither the time nor the means nor the opportunity to recover from the arduous operations on the Douro. The cavalry horses had certainly not had time to pick up condition and, although some drafts of remounts had arrived from England, many cavalrymen were mounted on transport animals. Almost the only transport available for the army's needs was provided by pack mules, of which each cavalry regiment was allotted one for each troop and six for its headquarters; to be used for the chests of the surgeon, veterinary surgeon, armourer and saddler, one for entrenching tools and one for the paymaster's books which, as all the soldiers were permanently in credit, were not without importance – the sight of the paymaster writing up their credits no doubt had a certain cheering effect on the soldiers, even if he had no money to give them.

The 14th were now seasoned cavalrymen, nearly all of whom had blooded their swords. It is probable however, that they were still lacking in knowledge of much of the work of cavalry in the field, for in the Douro campaign the nature of the country had forced them to operate on very narrow fronts. They had never been able to put out any form of screen in front of the infantry, or to manoeuvre with squadrons in line. Nor, when leading the advanced guard, had it even been possible for them to put out the 'side patrols' which were so essential when moving through enemy country. In the Talavera campaign they were also gravely hampered by the poor condition of their horses, and the weight which each had to carry; normally about twenty stone, but now increased by the weight of three days' rations for horse and man, and a good deal of equipment which should have been in the transport wagons – had there been any. It was by no means an auspicious start to a campaign and Wellesley, as he sat on his horse by the side of the road watching the army on the line of march, could scarcely have felt any great confidence in the outcome. But he gave no sign of any doubts or fears which he may have had, and while it was never his practice to attempt to hearten his troops with verbal addresses, he well understood the value of a personal appearance, quietly but impeccably turned-out, and wearing an expression of stern serenity. Like that of Napoleon, the aura of his personality had an effect equal in value to the physical appearance of thousands of reinforcements in a moment of emergency; of this he was well aware, and was always ready to use this attribute to advantage whenever necessary.

The army commenced the march in two columns, moving north and south of the Tagus, but before crossing into Spain the columns joined at Castelo Branco, after which the march was resumed towards Plasencia. Wellesley soon found out that he had been over-optimistic regarding supplies, for his Commissaries were inefficient and venal, the Spaniards un-cooperative, and the French had been over the ground first, wasting the country and even building their bivouacs out of ripe wheat. He also discovered that the Spanish regular army was nothing but an undisciplined rabble, and that its commander, Cuesta, was old and surly, and suffering from rheumatism and kindred afflictions of the aged. News from Beresford and captured French despatches also caused him anxiety about his left flank, which Cuesta had agreed to protect by holding the mountain passes of Perales and Banos, through which roads fit for artillery ran through to Plasencia. He began seriously to consider the advisability of withdrawing to the frontier; but such a move would have had the most serious political repercussions. Then, while he was hesitating, news came that Victor had fallen back behind the Alberche, with Cuesta in pursuit. On the 23rd July, he proposed to Cuesta that a joint attack should be made on the new French positions, but Cuesta refused and, when the French again withdrew, followed them up as before. Beginning to smell powder in the air, Wellesley became increasingly anxious, and sent the cavalry division and two infantry divisions, commanded by Generals Sherbrooke and Mackenzie, forward to support the Spaniards. Sherbrooke, incidentally, was in such desperation for something with which to feed his starving troops that he had just threatened to hang his Commissary if he did not produce supplies immediately. The Commissary complained to Wellesley, who raised his eyebrows and strongly advised him to make every effort to comply, 'otherwise, from my knowledge of General Sherbrooke, I fear that you will most certainly be hanged.'

As Wellesley was expecting, Marshal Victor was reinforced by King Joseph from Madrid, and then turned on Cuesta and routed him on the 26th July. The Spaniards made no bones about running for it, and a very serious situation would certainly have developed had it not been for the cavalry and the two infantry divisions, whose presence checked the French pursuit, and gave cover for the Spaniards to reform.

Wellesley had meanwhile been reconnoitring for a defensive position, in the choice of which he was always exceptionally sound. Resting his right on the town of Talavera, which was easy to defend and protected by the Tagus, he carried his line northward along the Portina rivulet, which ran through a valley of increasing steepness until it reached the heights of the Cerro de Medellin. These heights were separated from the mountain ridge of the Sierra de Montalban by a rugged valley. Wellesley's right was thus covered by the Tagus, and his left by the mountain ridges. The Spaniards were allotted the defence of Talavera itself, while the British drew up behind the Portina, in two lines of infantry. Anson's and Fane's cavalry brigades, with a Spanish cavalry brigade, were drawn up behind the British left, in the rugged valley already mentioned, while Cotton's Light Brigade took post in the rear of Sherbrooke's division, which was holding some high ground in the centre of the British line.

While taking up this position on the 27th July, Wellesley left Mackenzie's Division, with Anson's and Cotton's cavalry brigades, at Cazalegas, some six miles in front, in case the French renewed their advance before he was ready for them. They did in fact advance about mid-day, whereupon the British division withdrew somewhat, and halted behind a wood with a ruined house, known as the Casa de Salinas, in its rear. It is not clear where the cavalry were at this moment, but it would seem that they were behind the Casa, and had just arrived. The 14th, at any rate, were sent forward to the Alberche River, where the ford and both banks were obscured by a dense cloud of smoke, blowing across from a burning French encampment, which Mackenzie's Division had fired before falling back. The leading French division had already crossed the ford under cover of this smoke screen. This was unobserved by the 14th, who crossed to the far side and deployed on a wide front to engage the lines of French skirmishers whom they found advancing in front of Victor's main columns.

The leading French division had meanwhile worked through the wood and opened fire on the rear British brigade, which was taken by surprise. Its two Irish regiments, the 87th and 88th, whose discipline had been none too good during the Douro campaign, and was now far worse owing to excessive fatigue and empty stomachs, retired in disorder, followed by the French sharpshooters who surrounded the Casa. On an open turret of the house was Wellesley himself, who had come forward on reconnaissance. He had only his orderly with him, who was at the foot of the turret holding his horse. Fortunately, he managed to get to his horse, gallop through the French, and take charge of Mackenzie's division, which he withdrew in good order covered by the cavalry. The 14th were ordered back across the Alberche, but remained out until nightfall, engaging the leading enemy division, commanded by General Lapisse. Although the French Horse Artillery had come forward and was shelling Mackenzie's division, the French cavalry were over on the right flank, no doubt looking for the Spaniards, so that the 14th had only the sharpshooters to contend with. These were difficult targets for cavalry, and it is surprising that the losses of the regiment were not higher than they were. At the end of the day, these amounted to nine horses killed and an officer and soldier wounded, whose horses had bolted and been taken by the French. The British infantry losses during the 'Combat of Salinas' as this affair was called, were very heavy, amounting to about 450 all-ranks, killed, wounded and missing – a grim and depressing introduction to the great battle of the following day.

While Wellesley was engaged in the Combat of Salinas, the British Army was taking up its positions in some confusion and uncertainty, for none of the commanders was sure about his intentions. It was sometime, however, before he could be found, for as soon as he got back from Salinas he galloped away to Talavera to stop the Spaniards from bolting – being apparently aware that they were about to do so by the instinct which never failed him in an emergency. The situation was extremely grave, and there is no doubt that if he had not been sufficiently agile to escape from the Casa and remain at large to dominate the battlefield by his personality, the Spaniards would have quitted Talavera and the British would have been outflanked and destroyed.

Marshal Victor, elated at having first defeated the Spaniards and then driven back Mackenzie's Division, gave no orders to halt at nightfall, but pressed on hard and had to be evicted from several key positions by local counter-attacks. No-one in the British and Spanish armies therefore got any rest that night. Wellesley himself spent it sitting on the ground among his staff, constantly asking the time, for he well knew that the French would be upon him at dawn. It was probably the only occasion in his career when he was unable to hide his anxiety. The rumbling of enemy gun-wheels, and even the cracking of whips, could be heard quite distinctly during the hours of darkness, and when the moon rose the French columns could actually be seen moving into position against the British centre and left, along the Cerro de Medellin.

The 14th, with the rest of Cotton's brigade, passed the night lying or sitting in front of their horses, with their reins in their hands. During the preceding twenty-four hours the horses may have been given a handful or two of grain, and the men may have chewed pieces of half-cooked horseflesh, carried in their haversacks. The horses may have been given a chance to snatch a drink from the Portina, but the water was far too foul for men to drink out of it, so that the soldiers were dependent on the odd bottle of

Silver statuette of the Duke of Wellington riding his favourite horse Copenhagen. He is depicted wearing a plain blue frock coat and a Mameluke sword which later became regulation issue to General officers.

wine bought or looted on the line of march. Both men and horses were weary to the point of exhaustion, but they had become so accustomed to this condition that they had quite forgotten what it was like to feel otherwise.

In the British infantry lines there was almost as much noise and activity throughout the night as there was among the French, but the cavalry, being some distance in the rear, were able to doze off occasionally. Even so, conditions were far from restful, and the sound of the infantry drums beating to arms at dawn was greeted with relief. The same sound got Wellesley to horse, and when the sky lightened he was on the Cerro de Medellin, knowing that it was here the danger lay. This being a defensive battle, there was no immediate employment for the cavalry, who were consequently held in reserve ready to counter any outflanking movement or breakthrough by the enemy; to get them on the run if they fell back; or to cover an infantry withdrawal if things went wrong. It was not in fact until well after midday that the 14th mounted.

The French forces were now under the command of King Joseph, who had marched from Madrid with his Chief of Staff, Marshal Jourdan, to support Victor. From the French point of view, the situation offered an excellent opportunity for the complete destruction of the British army, for they not only knew that the Spaniards were demoralised, but also that Soult was on his way to Plasencia through the Pass of Banos which was not held by the Spaniards as Wellesley thought. Furthermore the British soldier was not very highly regarded by the French at this time, for he had been given little chance of showing his mettle so far. Although Jourdan, being of a more cautious nature, did his best to restrain the monarch's impetuosity, King Joseph nevertheless insisted on launching a full-scale attack against the British left and centre, without either making a previous reconnaissance or bringing up his reserves. This was no way to get the better of a man like Wellesley, and after a few hours of desperate fighting the French fell back discomfited and a sort of unofficial truce ensued, during which the infantry of both sides peacefully slaked their raging thirsts in the Portina, which by then was full of corpses in addition to the usual debris thrown into it by the peasants.

At about 2 p.m. King Joseph launched a turning movement round the left flank, which was frustrated by Payne's and Anson's cavalry brigades. A renewed attack against the centre also failed, but when Sherbrooke's division followed up, it was counter-attacked and driven back in disorder. This resulted in a dangerous gap in the British line, but Wellesley had anticipated the event the moment he saw that Sherbrooke had advanced too far. He had therefore reorganised in time to meet the danger and turn the situation to his advantage, counter-attacking at just the right moment so that the French, in their turn, were flung back in disorder.

Now at last, it was time for the Light Cavalry Brigade to enter. Led by Stapleton Cotton, the 14th and 16th Light Dragoons crossed the Portina, formed line and charged Lapisse's division, cutting their way right through it and turning its retreat into a rout. The charge, however, was not the dashing affair commonly associated with light cavalry. The unfortunate horses could only be urged into a shambling gallop by a very liberal use of the spur, and they soon pulled up, no longer able to put one leg in front of the other. None of the cavalry was able to carry out a pursuit for the same reason, but they had nevertheless played a decisive part in the battle. The French had had enough, and by the next day were back across the Alberche.

In the charge at Talavera, the 14th Light Dragoons lost three men killed and five officers and six men wounded. Twenty-one horses were killed, and another sixteen wounded or missing. The regiment was lucky to get off so lightly in such an engagement as this. The battlefield was a shocking sight, covered by the bodies of something like 12,000 killed and wounded men and, as if the sufferings of the wounded were not already sufficient, the grass caught fire in the intense heat and the fire spread rapidly, burning large numbers to death and cruelly scorching many others.

This great battle, in which the British soldiers, though weak from semi-starvation, met and defeated continued assaults by more than double their numbers, secured for both them and their commander a reputation in Europe which they never afterwards lost. In future the French treated them with considerably more respect, and were a great deal more cautious in their operations against them. But Wellesley was by no means elated by his victory, the aftermath of which seemed to bring home to him the true conditions under which the mismanagement and parsimony of his government forced him to fight. Unable to move for want of supplies, and unable to relieve the sufferings of the wounded, either British or French, he wrote:

'It is positively a fact, that during the last seven days the British army have not received one third of their provisions, and that at this moment there are nearly 4,000 wounded soldiers dying in hospital from want of common assistance and necessities, which any other country in the world would have given, even to its enemies. I positively will not move – nay, more, I will disperse my

1809

army – till I am supplied with provisions and transport, as I ought to be.'

The answer of the British Government was to have him created the Viscount Wellington which, though agreeable no doubt, was of no help to him in his predicament, even had the news of it reached him in time. Soult however got there first, and when Wellington heard that the Spaniards had sold the Pass of Banos, he realised that move he must, with or without supplies. Soult being in the neighbourhood of Plasentia, directly in his rear, he marched from Talavera on the 3rd August intending to attack him and clear his lines of communication through Alcantara, but when he arrived at Oropesa, he learnt from captured enemy despatches that Ney and Mortier were also in the Tagus valley under Soult's command, and that the bridge of Almaraz, one of his lines across the Tagus, was in enemy hands. Information reached him at the same time that King Joseph was again advancing and that Cuesta had consequently abandoned Talavera.

In this dangerous situation, Wellington had no option but to put the Tagus between himself and the French without delay and endeavour to reach the main road from Merida to Lisbon before the enemy headed him off. The army therefore crossed the river by the bridge of Arzobispo and marched by Deleytosa to Jaracejo and along the road to Merida. Crauford's division, followed by Cuesta, was detached to Almaraz for flank protection.

Having reached Jaracejo safely, and thus escaped from the enemy trap, Wellington halted for a while, with Crauford still at Almaraz and Cuesta at Arzobispo. Soult marched against Cuesta and defeated him, while Ney marched against Crauford but could find no ford across the river by which to outflank him. Finally, the supplies which he had collected at Jaracejo becoming exhausted by the 20th August, Wellington withdrew Crauford and retired by Merida to Badajoz. Here he remained until the end of 1809 with the troops camped in the Guadiana valley between Badajoz, Elvas and Campo Mayor, where they suffered heavily from typhus. In December, a Spanish defeat in the north endangered the other route into Portugal by Ciudad Rodrigo, so that Wellington had to move his army to the Agueda, between Almeida and the fortress of Ciudad Rodrigo. Realising the hopeless condition of the Spanish army, and anticipating an invasion of Portugal which his own forces were scarcely strong enough to resist, he gave orders, in the utmost secrecy, for the commencement of the Lines of Torres Vedras, a series of fortifications constructed along high ground of great natural strength in the country around Lisbon.

1809

Thus ended the campaign of TALAVERA, commemorated by the third battle honour on the guidon. It had been one of quite exceptional hardship, during which the 14th, like all the other cavalry regiments engaged, lost nearly half their horses, which had foundered from starvation along the road back. Both officers and men were also in poor shape from disease, exposure and malnutrition, and in December the regiment was moved back to Santarem, some fifty miles to the north of Lisbon, to recuperate. Here it was brigaded with the Royal Dragoons, who had just arrived from England, the brigade being commanded by General Slade.

1809 The 20th in the Mediterranean
July 1810 The 14th in the affair at Villa de Puerco
July 1810 The 14th on the Coa
27th September 1810 The Battle of Busaco
The retirement to Torres Vedras

1809

French Invasion of Portugal

8

Wellington's campaigns in Portugal and Spain were not the only major events of 1809. Other spheres of operations included the West Indies; the Scheldt (the mismanaged Walcheren Expedition) and the Mediterranean. In the latter the bold British Admiral, Collingwood, was constantly urging a more aggressive policy on the hesitant British General, Sir John Stuart. The French, under Murat, still held Italy in thrall, but there were the beginnings of a resistance movement among the Italians, similar to that on the Peninsula, and Collingwood was doing his best to encourage it by landing raiding parties at various points along the coast. 'All our frigate captains are great generals,' he wrote, 'and some in the brigs are good brigadiers.' A local raid by the ship's company of a frigate was, however, a very simple operation compared with that of a military force of all arms, which, once committed, could not simply cut a few throats and sail away again. Nevertheless, Stuart was well aware that with a force of fifteen thousand men at his disposal and supported by Collingwood, who definitely ruled the waves in the Mediterranean, he ought to be able to cause the French some discomfiture. His trouble was, that he could not make up his mind as to what objective to make for, and this indecision led to constant changes in his plans, sometimes after the

◁ General John Egerton, Earl of Bridgewater. He served originally in the 7th Light Dragoons and later, as a General, had the 14th under his command at Chelmsford where he re-organised the regiment after its heavy losses in St Domingo. Colonel of the Regiment 1797–1823.

1809

troops had embarked. His senior officers gradually left him on one pretext or another, and the others became insubordinate to a degree which affected the rank and file, so that a danger actually arose of open mutiny. Driven to desperation, Stuart finally decided to occupy the island of Ischia in the Bay of Naples, as an adventure which, with the command of the sea, could scarcely go wrong. He put to sea from Milazzo in North East Sicily on the 11th June, with about 13,000 men, who included a thousand cavalry consisting of 300 of the 20th Light Dragoons and 700 Neapolitans.

Owing to the light airs and frequent calms, it took the fleet thirteen days to cover the two hundred miles from Sicily to Ischia. Water ran short and the heat was severe, so that the horses in particular suffered severely. It is not indeed clear why cavalry were considered necessary in the conquest of a small island which was, in fact, captured by a couple of light infantry regiments, the first troops to land.

The neighbouring island of Procida was captured in a like manner, and reinforcements sent over by Murat from Naples were intercepted at sea. Collingwood then discovered that a French fleet was fitting out at Toulon, and advised Stuart to evacuate the islands as, in the event of contrary winds, he might not be able to protect the fleet of transports lying off Ischia. Stuart was only too glad to fall in with this advice, as he was worried about the safety of Sicily, although a British raiding party had already captured all the guns which Murat had collected for an invasion, and had thrown them into the sea. However, the expedition re-embarked on the 26th July, and having favourable winds this time, reached Milazzo three days later.

Although this adventure seemed a ridiculous waste of time, it did in fact yield some positive results. The two islands were disarmed, numbers of ships and prisoners had been taken, and Murat had been given a bad fright. Stuart was able to rest on his laurels for a couple of months, until Collingwood bullied him into capturing the islands of Zante and Cephallonia in the Adriatic, as the Admiral wanted them to harbour those of his ships watching Corfu. One troop of the 20th sailed on this expedition without their horses. It was carried out during October and succeeded in its objectives without trouble. Garrisons were retained in the islands, and those of Ithaca and Santa Maura were also occupied during the following few months.

The ousting of the French from four of the Ionian Islands made a great impression on Turkey, where French influence began to wane. Stuart was accordingly urged to seize Corfu as well;

followed by the remainder of the Seven Islands Republic. Stuart, however, felt unable to comply, for he was still worried about the possibility of an invasion of Sicily, renewed preparations for which were again visible across the Straits of Messina. He was also plagued by the machinations of the Queen of Naples, who was supposed to be on his side but who seemed constantly to be working against him. She was in fact, trying to keep a foot in both camps, and the marriage of Napoleon to a relative of hers, the Archduchess Marie Louise of Austria, inclined her so far towards the French that it soon became obvious that she was on no account to be trusted. Stuart therefore for once had some justification for staying where he was, and the 20th Light Dragoons – less their troop in Zante – stayed with him, being quartered in Messina and joined, in September, 1809, by the rest of the regiment from Portugal.

After Napoleon's brilliant defeat of the Austrians at Wagram, on the 6th July, 1809, he had again turned his attention to the Peninsula, pouring troops into it until they reached the staggering total – for those days – of 366,000 men. They were organised into three armies: *The Army of the South*, commanded by Marshal Soult, and comprising the corps of Victor, Mortier, and Sebastiani, had over-run Andalusia and was besieging Cadiz; *The Army of the Centre*, commanded by King Joseph, was in and around Madrid; and *The Army of Portugal*, composed of the corps of Ney, Reynier, and Junot, with Montbrun's cavalry corps, and commanded by Marshal Massena, was spread out between Salamanca and the French frontier. Ney, Junot and Montbrun were around Salamanca, and Reynier in the valley of the Tagus, near Alcantara. *The Army of Portugal*, as its name implies, was intended for the invasion of that country. Its commander, Massena, 'the old fox', was one of the Emperor's most experienced Marshals, but he had another nickname, 'the spoiled child of victory', which suited him better than the other, for he was becoming lethargic with increasing years, and felt that it was high time he was left in peace to enjoy the wealth and honours gained through an unbroken series of successes in the field. It was out of the question of course for any servant of Napoleon to question his orders, but Massena accepted his assignment with secret reluctance, took his mistress to war with him, and otherwise made himself as comfortable as he could.

Wellington had spent the winter and spring of 1810 in organising Portugal for defence, and increasing the number of Portuguese under arms until they reached a strength of 30,000 regulars under British officers, and 30,000 militia. The British army, about

1810

25,000 men, he kept under his own immediate command at Viseu, Celorico, Guarda, and Pinhel, with the cavalry in the Mondego Valley, and his headquarters at Viseu. Crauford's Light Division had been pushed out between the rivers Coa and Agueda, watching Ciudad Rodrigo which was garrisoned, as was the other frontier fortress of Badajoz, by Spaniards. The Portuguese regulars were kept at Thomar as a reserve, and the militia north of the Douro. Supply dumps had been formed all over the country, and the work on the Lines of Torres Vedras – carried out by Portuguese peasants under British engineers – was hastened.

The retirement from Talavera, the mismanaged Walcheren Expedition, and the series of bungling adventures in the Mediterranean, had had a depressive effect on the British Government and public, resulting in the formation of a strong body of opinion to the effect that further operations in the Peninsula should be abandoned. Wellington, however, could not countenance any such course of action, for he had pledged his word to both Spaniards and Portuguese that Great Britain would continue to give them active support in the field until the French had been expelled. At the same time he warned the Government that for the time being he would have to stand on the defensive. His views were accepted by the Government, though with some uneasiness and probing questions as to the readiness of the Portuguese ports to handle a large-scale evacuation.

The French plans for the invasion of Portugal had been worked out by the Emperor himself. Massena was to advance from Salamanca and Soult, after taking Badajoz and Elvas, was to move on Lisbon up the Tagus. There was nothing original about these plans, and Wellington was well aware that something of the sort was in his adversary's mind. Although threatened by vastly superior forces, the fact that the enemy had to operate in countries bitterly hostile to him, whereas Wellington, in Portugal at least, could count on every possible support, gave him a tremendous advantage, which was increased by the jealousy and lack of cooperation current among the French Marshals. Nevertheless, he could not afford to make any mistakes.

The 14th Light Dragoons had wintered at Santarem, where they had been brought up to strength by drafts of men and horses from England. On the 14th March, 1810, they marched to join Sir Rowland Hill, whose division of about 10,000 men, half of whom were Portuguese, was in the area of Abrantes and Portalegre, watching the road from Badajoz. The regiment was quartered at Arronches, with posts along the Spanish frontier to Elvas. There was, however, no immediate threat from Soult, but in the north Massena opened the campaign at the end of April by sending Ney across the Agueda to invest Ciudad Rodrigo, while Reynier got on the move in an attempt to draw Wellington's attention away from Ney.

As Ney advanced, Crauford with the Light Division fell back towards the Coa, in accordance with orders. Wellington moved his headquarters to Celorico, taking Spencer's division with him, and ordered Hill to send Slade's cavalry brigade of the Royals and 14th to Guarda. Crauford had meanwhile discovered that the French forces which had arrived before Ciudad Rodrigo numbered only about four thousand men, and Wellington had some difficulty in restraining him from attacking them. In fact, Ney had prematurely disclosed his intentions by sending forward a force insufficient for its task, and Wellington, now that he knew for certain what was coming, had no intention of becoming embroiled over Ciudad Rodrigo, whose eventual capture he would be unable to prevent.

Ney himself arrived before Ciudad Rodrigo on the 30th May, with his whole corps and a reserve division of cavalry. Besides investing the fortress, he bridged the Agueda River in two places and sent over a light cavalry brigade and one-and-a-half divisions of infantry, which drove in Crauford's outposts. When this happened, the 14th Light Dragoons were sent forward to Almeida where they joined their old friends, the 16th Light Dragoons and the Hussars of the King's German Legion, under Stapleton Cotton.

The Light Division, with both its flanks threatened and an enemy force in front of it which Wellington reckoned at 50,000 men, was in a somewhat awkward position, but nevertheless maintained an offensive posture in the hope of distracting the French operations against Ciudad Rodrigo. An outpost line was established along the Azava River, almost within musket shot of the French, while the cavalry established officers' picquets between the posts, watching possible crossing-places. A certain amount of minor skirmishing went on, while the French siege batteries roared away in the background, until Massena at last became apprehensive about the activities of the Light Division and on the 4th July sent a reconnaissance in force over the Azava, driving back two squadrons of the 16th, which were picquetting the crossing. Crauford, however, had already concentrated his infantry at Gallegos, and fell back towards Almeida, covered by the cavalry and a troop of Horse Artillery.

To a man such as Crauford, a retirement in the face of the enemy without first coming to blows was altogether too much to

1810

bear. Having been obliged to fall back, under the direct orders of Wellington delivered personally, he started immediately to look for some opportunity for relieving his feelings – for his temper when crossed was ungovernable, and if he could not find someone to give a lesson to, he became quite unbalanced. An opportunity appeared to offer itself on the night of the 10th July, at almost the same time, when, unknown to him, Ciudad Rodrigo surrendered. During the day, he had observed numerous French foraging parties among the villages to the east of the Dos Casas and, with a view to catching them at daybreak, crossed the Dos Casas with three squadrons of the 14th, two of the 16th, one of the German Hussars, some infantry and two guns. Arriving at Villa de Puerco during the night, this force took cover until dawn, when a troop of French Dragoons was seen on the horizon. Crauford at once mounted the cavalry and led them forward in column of half-troops, with the Germans leading, followed by the 16th, and the 14th in rear.

The half-troop formation, with a front of about twenty men, was the normal one for cavalry on open ground, for it enabled them to form line quickly in any direction. In an attempt to cut off the enemy Dragoons, however, Crauford led the brigade at a trot through a narrow rocky defile, which broke up its formation. On emerging from it the Germans saw infantry ahead, and were at once ordered to charge without being given time to form line. Half of them did so, and found the enemy in square, so that they lost a dozen men and horses to no purpose. Before the others could follow, they were sent to chase the French Dragoons, being automatically followed by the 16th. The Dragoons were duly rounded up, but when the 14th arrived, Crauford ordered the leading squadron to charge the infantry square without waiting for the rest of the regiment. The leading squadron was led by the commanding-officer, Lieut.-Colonel Neil Talbot, who had to form line on the move. Even then, the distance was too short to get up full speed, and after receiving a volley the charge was broken on the bayonets of the square. Talbot, a warrant-officer, and eleven men were killed and twenty-three others wounded. They did some execution among the French, of course, but nothing like enough to atone for their own heavy casualties.

The other two squadrons were sent off by Crauford on a fool's errand, in pursuit of a body of Horse who turned out to be friends, and while they were away, the French infantry seized the chance to escape into a wood. Altogether, the affair could scarcely have been worse mismanaged, and it seems that Crauford must have been in one of his unbalanced moods. Not unnaturally, the 14th were exceedingly sore about it, especially as it had led to the death of a commanding officer who was greatly respected in the regiment. Cotton unfortunately was on leave, and it seems that there was no-one in actual command of the light cavalry brigade, whose regiments were subject to direct orders from the divisional commander. In those days, however, the 'chain of command' was never strictly adhered to, especially in action when it was common practice for general officers, from Wellington downwards, to give direct orders to a regiment in a formation commanded by a subordinate, without considering it necessary to give him any explanation or make an apology. This, as happened on the Douro, occasionally led to confusion owing to regiments and formations being given contrary orders by several different superiors at the same time. That such a practice could be tolerated was due to the fact that the orders were given verbally and on the spot, and that the officer giving them was able to enforce them by the use of his personality as well as his seniority.

Colonel Talbot's body was recovered under a flag of truce, as was customary in the case of senior officers and those killed under especially gallant circumstances. He was buried with military honours, and his place taken by Major F. B. Hervey, who proved to be a commanding officer of exceptional ability. Colonel Talbot was described by a brother officer as 'a noble-looking fellow' but 'singular and eccentric, particularly in his dress'. When he was killed, he was wearing 'nankeen pantaloons' which appear to have excited a certain amount of comment. He was by no means the only eccentric in Wellington's army in which, among the senior ranks, there were some very odd characters indeed. Eccentricity in manners and dress is, however, a common device employed by commanders to the present day, in order to attract the attention of the rank and file, giving them the impression that they are being led by someone out of the ordinary. It is likely, therefore, that Crauford's hysteria, Picton's top hat and frock coat, and Talbot's nankeen pantaloons, were all assumed with this end in view. Characteristically, Wellington's own method of asserting himself was to appear quietly but impeccably dressed at all times, to ride blood horses of exceptional quality and spirit, and to preserve the calm, unruffled manner traditional to the English aristocrat. This was the most successful of all: the troops regarded Crauford with surly admiration, laughed at Picton and loved Talbot; but no-one laughed at or loved Wellington, who inspired all ranks with a salutary and wholesome awe.

On the fall of Ciudad Rodrigo, Wellington expressed himself

1810

as being 'not desirous of engaging in an affair beyond the Coa', and warned Crauford several times not to get involved, but without giving him direct orders to retire. As usual, Crauford could not bring himself to withdraw without a fight, but when Ney arrived before his outpost line on the 21st July, he fell back reluctantly to the south of Almeida, after blowing up Fort Conception – and Talbot's body, which had been buried on the glacis of the fort. Captain T. W. Brotherton of the 14th, whose squadron's line of picquets had been driven in upon the fort by a mass of French cavalry galloping forward to secure it before it could be destroyed, not only lost several of his men and horses in the explosion, but actually saw the body of his late commanding-officer blown into the air. Having succeeded in delaying the French just long enough to enable the sappers to blow the fort, he was too closely engaged to recover the body a second time, and had to gallop clear.

In spite of Wellington's directives, Crauford did not continue his retreat across the Coa, but drew up the Light Division along the Almeida ridge, with the river in his rear, impassable except by a single bridge. Marshal Ney, when he came forward to reconnoitre, could hardly believe his eyes when he saw the Light Division still on the wrong side of the river and his for the taking. His cavalry attacked at dawn on the 24th July. The vedettes of the 14th, on seeing them coming, galloped back to their posts to report, and the news was quickly passed back to Crauford, who belatedly awoke to his danger and ordered the cavalry, guns and supply wagons back across the bridge. By that time, however, the cavalry were in close action with vast numbers of Frenchmen, and had to fight their way back. The combat being an open one, sword versus sword, the 14th escaped with few casualties and in good order, but Cornet Blackford was 'hit by a fragment of a shell in the posterior'. His squadron leader, Brotherton, gave him scant sympathy 'as he was rather a soft sort of fellow, I thought, at first, that he made too great a fuss about it,' but poor Blackford had been mortally wounded, and died slung face downwards across a troop horse, jammed in a chaos of traffic crossing the bridge.

Crauford having completely lost both his head and all control of the situation, the Colonels of his light infantry regiments were left to get out of this mess as best they could, and as their men were of very high quality, they succeeded in driving back about ten times their number of Frenchmen and eventually getting back across the Coa with a loss of 330 men. Ney was so furious at their escape that he lost his head in his turn, making a series of reckless attacks on the bridge, which eventually cost him about double the number of casualties which he had inflicted on the British.

While the infantry were holding the main bridge, the cavalry were sent to watch the fords of Castello Bom six miles to the south, in case Ney should have the sense to cross the river there and so cut off the Light Division from the main army. Fortunately he was too enraged to be capable of thinking of this possibility, and the Light Division was able to continue its retreat to Pinhel. Stapleton Cotton then returned and took command of the cavalry which was established in a line of outposts in touch with Almeida. As Massena made no advance against the fortress and Wellington became anxious about the Marshal's intentions, he withdrew the whole of his army to the valley of the Mondego on the 27th July. He was extremely annoyed with Crauford, but took no action against him. 'If I am to be hanged for it,' he wrote, 'I cannot accuse a man who, I believe, has meant well.' He was surprisingly forbearing towards his subordinates, and when he did lose his temper with them it often appears to have been on occasions when they had done nothing to deserve it. This fact illustrates the difficulty of making a correct appreciation after an event, the true significance of which could only be comprehended by one who was actually present and on the spot. This especially applies to events in the field, which are impossible to understand fully, and judge accurately, in cold blood.

On the 15th August, Ney commenced the siege of Almeida, which was garrisoned by Portuguese commanded by Brigadier Cox. Wellington then moved Picton's and Crauford's divisions forward to keep in touch and to prevent the French from foraging. He reckoned on Almeida holding out for a couple of months, but on the 26th August its magazine blew up, and Cox was forced to capitulate. This misadventure gravely upset Wellington's plans, and he was in an anxious situation owing to the development of a flanking movement by Reynier through Sabugal. On the 28th August, the enemy attacked the cavalry outposts at Frexadas. One of them, consisting of a squadron of the Royals and another of the 14th, under the command of Major Dorville of the Royals, advanced and charged a greatly superior enemy force of cavalry and infantry, driving them back with many casualties. The British army then commenced a gradual withdrawal towards Lisbon, where a panic had been caused by the news of the fall of Almeida – and also, apparently, by highly-coloured accounts of the masses of Frenchmen whom they had to deal with, given by Wellington's general and other officers. Besides adding to his political difficulties, such defeatism did not

1810

help the morale of Wellington's army. 'There is a system of croaking in the army,' he wrote, 'which is highly injurious to the public service, and which I must devise some means of putting an end to, or it will put an end to us.'

On the 21st September, Wellington rode up to the convent on the ridge of Busaco, which had been prepared as his headquarters. 'We have a most excellent position here,' he remarked, 'where I am strongly tempted to give battle.' His whole army, at the time, was within a few hours' march with the exception of Hill's division, which was a day behind schedule. The cavalry had their line of posts astride the road at Mortagoa, supported by the Light Division. Here they remained while Wellington formed up on the Serra do Busaco, but they were attacked on the 24th September. Wellington then ordered the Light Division back, covered by the light cavalry brigade, in which a charge made by a squadron of the 14th killed thirty Frenchmen.

In the face of the belligerence of the light cavalry brigade the French checked and drew back, whereupon Crauford doubled the Light Division forward from the heights above Mortagoa down into the plain below in order to get at the French. When on the following day Reynier appeared with his whole corps, Crauford still waited in the plain, and the Light Division was soon heavily involved. Wellington was obliged to intervene in person, sending in the 14th and Royals to cover a withdrawal on to the Serra, which required all his skill to execute. The 14th had six casualties and lost a dozen horses while galloping about with the French Dragoons and charging odd parties of infantry which exposed themselves.

In the Battle of Busaco, which was fought on the 27th September, 1810, the cavalry were positioned before Milheada, behind Wellington's left flank. To his front the country was intersected by watercourses and deep ravines, so that cavalry could not operate. It was therefore held in reserve and took no part in the battle, although had things gone wrong, its presence on the left flank could have been vital. It was now in division, commanded by Stapleton Cotton, and the 14th were again brigaded with the Royals under Slade. Nothing went wrong in the battle – except for the French – and Wellington's judgment of a good defensive position was once again proved sound. He had no tactical reason for fighting a major action at this moment, for he was not being unduly pressed by Massena, who was content to shepherd him gently along to Lisbon and into his transports. He had decided, however, that it was essential to beat the French before withdrawing behind the Lines, in order to dispel both at home and on the Peninsula the despondency which a series of retreats had brought about.

Having been repulsed at Busaco with losses of over 5,000 men, Massena marched on Coimbra, crossing the Boyalva Pass which was supposed to be held by Portuguese; but they did not get there in time. Wellington was thus outflanked, and so retired through Coimbra, Pombal and Leiria, behind the Lines of Torres Vedras. In covering this final withdrawal, the cavalry were in action almost daily, and 'the Fourteenth had frequent opportunities of proving their valour,' as Captain Brotherton put it. He himself gave frequent examples of the chivalry with which warfare was generally still conducted in those days between civilised foes, examples which provide the strangest contrast to the fierce brutality with which engagements were fought. He was absolutely horror struck, for instance, when during Busaco he caught a German staff officer hiding behind a rock with a rifle and 'picking off French officers and soldiers by way of amusement!' He 'remonstrated with him on his barbarous conduct, and shamed him out of it.' Again, when he was leading his squadron through Sobral, looking out for a favourable spot on which to engage the French Hussars who were close on his tail, twenty nuns ran out of their convent and grabbed his reins, imploring him to save them from the French. Although 'they were neither young nor handsome, but old and sallow,' he gallantly mounted them behind twenty of his dragoons, and brought them safely behind the Lines. This exploit earned him an invitation to dinner from Wellington, who 'complimented me on my chivalrous affair, and laughed heartily about it.'

During the operations in Spain, when Brotherton was at Medina, 'patrolling through the streets in search of the enemy,' he was approached by a priest, who begged him to carry off the immensely valuable Murillo altar-piece in the church, in order to keep it out of the hands of the French. Brotherton agreed, and after taking down the large picture rolled it up carefully and carried it off, laid across the valises behind the saddles of two of his dragoons. When he heard, however, that the French never entered Medina, he became so anxious in case his action should be misconstrued that he took the picture back again, having to ride a considerable distance in order to do so, and hung it up once more behind the altar. He was then greatly chagrined to hear that Soult got hold of it and kept it among the enormous collection of treasures acquired during his campaigns. Had Brotherton been caught with it in his possession the consequences might indeed have been embarrassing, for Wellington was so set against

1810

1810

plunder that his officers never dared to be seen carrying a scrawny chicken or a few potatoes, even when they were supposed to be living off the country, but it was a pity that Brotherton did not get a written authority from the priest and take his chance on this occasion.

The final stages of the withdrawal into the lines began on the 1st October, when the outposts were brought in from the heights of Coimbra. A squadron of the 14th under Major the Hon. Charles Butler provided the cavalry of the rearguard, while the rest of the cavalry division was deployed along the Mondego, watching the fords. It seems in fact that the enemy were first engaged on their side of the river, and that the British cavalry, in the face of overwhelming numbers, got across with much difficulty, and that a good deal of sword-play went on in the water.

In the early morning of the 5th October the cavalry division was again engaged with the French cavalry near Pombal. The French entered about 36 squadrons against the British ten, belonging to the 14th, 16th, Royals and German Hussars. The French came on as the British were leaving their outposts, and had to be halted by several charges, during which the 14th lost 6 killed and 8 wounded. On the 8th October, they had another brush with the enemy at Alcoentre, where a Horse Artillery troop had been left owing to an oversight by Cotton's staff. It had to be rescued by a squadron of the 16th which lost 18 men in the process, but in the general skirmishing the 14th lost 13 men.

On the 10th October, the British cavalry entered the Lines of Torres Vedras. 'On every occasion,' reported Wellington, 'their superiority has been so great that the enemy does not use his cavalry except when supported and protected by his infantry.' This was very high praise from a man like Wellington, but every word of it was thoroughly deserved. The efforts of the cavalry division did in fact save the infantry from a very severe mauling, for their discipline had broken and they left the ranks in large numbers to plunder the towns and villages. Wellington used every possible method of restoring order, and the sight of British infantrymen swinging from hastily erected gallows became quite familiar to the cavalry. It also brought it home to them perhaps that it was advisable to keep their ranks, for they were no more resistant to temptation than the infantry, of whom indeed they had the advantage of horses on which to load their loot, instead of having to carry it themselves. Disciplinary measures were, however, hampered by the chaos prevailing along the march route, which was flooded by refugees.

1810

However, once within the Lines order was soon restored, and Wellington could face the future with some confidence. He was in an impregnable position, and no longer had any supply problem with the port of Lisbon at his disposal. Far other was the case of the French, accustomed to living off the country, for Wellington had seen to it that there was not a blade of grass left standing, so that Massena had but two grim alternatives; to let his army starve to death or to retire back into Spain, through country which was bitterly hostile, and with an enemy which he now recognised as possessing a fighting capacity never before encountered, pressing him from the rear.

The 14th took over a part of the Lines in the vicinity of Sobral. The French advanced guards had been putting in abortive attacks in this area since their cavalry had discovered the defences on the 11th October. On the 14th Massena himself came forward to see what was holding him up, and arrived at Sobral while Junot was superintending an engagement against a line of picquets held by the 71st H.L.I. The 71st held their ground without difficulty, and Junot suggested that Massena should organise a major assault in the Sobral area. Wellington was half-expecting such an attempt, and the troops in the locality were therefore on their guard and looking forward to it with lively anticipation. But Massena, having learnt a lesson at Busaco, made a careful reconnaissance first, and in chagrin and despair realised that Wellington had lured him to destruction, and that there was nothing whatever he could do about it.

1798.

Guidon of the 14th (Duchess of York's own) Regiment of Light Dragoons – 1798. The 'field' is orange.

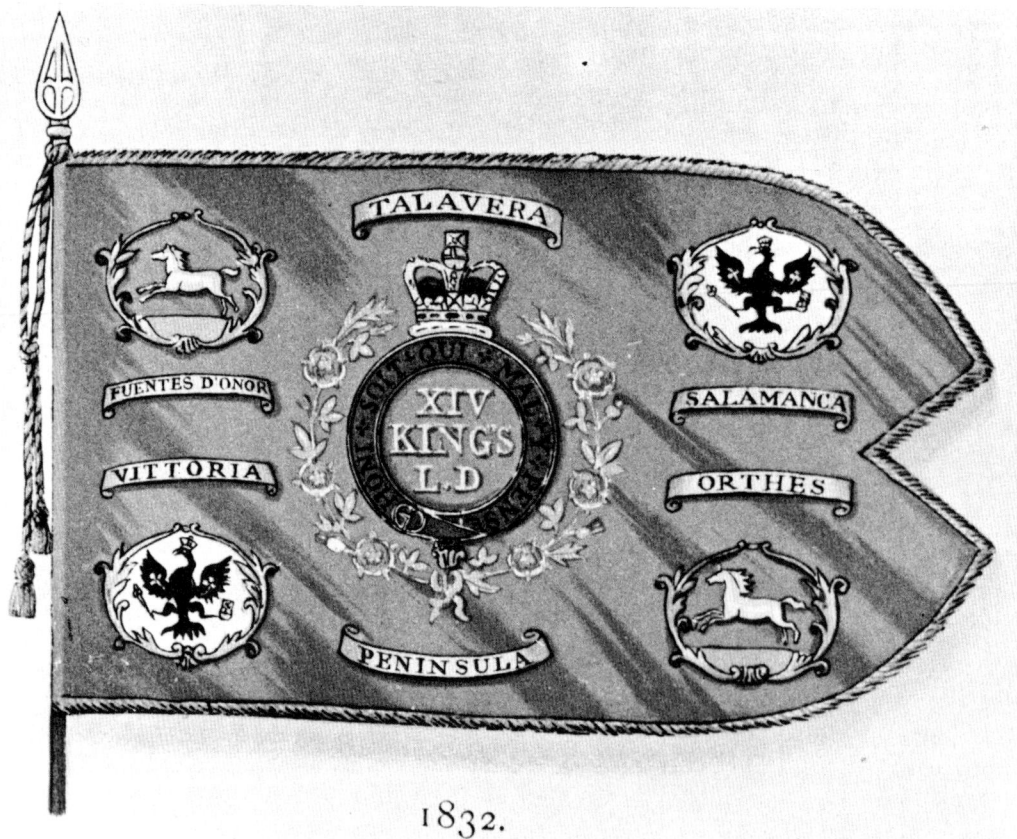

1832.

King's (or First) Guidon of the 14th or the King's Regiment of Light Dragoons – 1832. The 'field' is crimson.

1810 The 14th at Sobral
March 1811 The French retirement from Torres Vedras
2nd May 1811 The 14th in the pursuit, Brotherton loses his trousers
May 1811 The action at Gallegos
3rd–8th May 1811 The Battle of Fuentes D'Onor

The French Evicted from Portugal

9

1810

Realising that the launching of a major attack against the Lines was out of the question, Massena placed his army in position around them, with his Eighth Corps entrenched before Sobral, and composed himself to await help from the Emperor, to whom General Foy had been sent with his despatches. His army, however, began rapidly to break up under the pangs of hunger. Hundreds of deserters came over to the British lines begging for food, and so many of the others were dispersed over the countryside looking for something to eat that Wellington, who often came up to the Sobral position to see what the French were up to, was heard to exclaim, 'By God! I've a damned good mind to attack 'em!' Any general would have been similarly tempted under the circumstances, but Wellington realised the folly of impatience, and that he had only to wait a while and let famine do his work for him. 'I could lick those fellows any day,' said he, 'but it would cost me 10,000 men, and as this is the last army England has, we must take care of it.'

At Sobral, the close proximity of the French, and the frequent visits by Wellington, meant that the 14th were unable to relax to anything like the same extent enjoyed by most other regiments within the Lines of Torres Vedras. Their patrols were also very restricted in their movements, and seldom had any excitement,

123

1810

such as chasing enemy foraging parties, which was a frequent diversion for the cavalry in other posts. The officers no doubt, could get an occasional day with the pack of hounds which Wellington had sent for from England, and they could also go on leave to Lisbon; but for forty-eight hours only, the longest period, in Wellington's opinion, 'that any reasonable man would wish to remain in bed with the same woman.' The rank and file, when not on duty, ate, drank, played football and held sing-songs. On the quiet, they also fraternised with the French, who had nothing to eat but seemed to have plenty of brandy. With the British troops it was the other way round, so that friendly intercourse with the enemy resulted in mutual benefits. The utmost discretion was, however, essential, for if a soldier was caught in such trafficking, and Wellington heard of it, he might well have been hanged – the only remedy for bad discipline that the commander-in-chief ever seemed to have heard of.

The long Napoleonic wars gradually established the principle of the Officers' Mess. Previously, officers had made their own domestic arrangements, both in peace and war; sometimes asking a friend or two to share their dinner in their lodgings or bivouacs. It had now become the general custom for all the officers of a regiment or headquarters to mess together, in a building if one was available, but otherwise round a bivouac fire. Captain Brotherton, when recalling his adventures in later life, described an argument he had with a mule, which was carrying him back from a dinner to which he had been invited by the officers of another regiment. At a road-junction near Sobral the mule flatly refused to go in the direction required. Brotherton finally gave in, and was safely delivered at his bivouac. Had he been allowed to go the way he had wanted, he would have walked straight into the French outposts. It would seem that the reason the 14th were posted to so lively a part of the Lines as Sobral was that they had entered at that point after covering the infantry of the rearguard. Brotherton's squadron, in fact, had not reached safety when Junot's advanced guard attacked the 71st on the 14th October. He described the action as a 'sharp affair' in which the 71st, the Rifles, the 14th and the French were 'literally intermixed'. Noticing another officer, Perceval, on the ground 'pierced by two balls', he dismounted and helped him on to his own charger, afterwards dismounting one of the Dragoons and taking his horse for himself. 'As in action,' he explained, 'the presence and exertions of an officer are more valuable than those of a private, it is not only justifiable, but it is incumbent on an officer, sooner than leave the field, to dismount a private and take his horse.' Unfortunately, this particular private chanced to be the orderly of General Sir Denis Pack, 'a warm-hearted but very passionate man', who galloped up and, ignoring the presence of the 71st, the Rifles and the French, expressed his opinion of Brotherton in no uncertain terms. Brotherton agreed that 'it is essential for a General to have his orderly in action,' and offered his profound apologies. His recollections, though interesting, are, like those of most elderly men, confused and incomplete. He did not, for example, say what he had done with the nuns, and whether they too were mixed up with the others in this affair.

On receipt of Massena's pleas for help, Napoleon had sent orders to Soult, who was investing Cadiz, to march to his support by way of Badajoz. Leaving Victor to continue the blockade of Cadiz, Soult marched on Badajoz accordingly and captured it on the 10th March, after a siege of only six weeks. Before he could join Massena, however, news came that Victor had been defeated at Barrosa by the Spanish guerrillas, under La Pena, supported by 4,000 British troops commanded by Sir Thomas Graham. This gave him an excuse to abandon Massena, with whom he was on no friendly terms. It seems that the Emperor had not fully grasped the extent of the ill-feeling among his Marshals in Spain. In fact, only his personal presence could have induced them effectively to combine, and he could not be everywhere at once. Massena, who had been hanging on before the Lines of Torres Vedras in daily expectation of news from Soult, was finally obliged to withdraw on the 5th March, the same day as Barossa. That he had been able to hold out so long was because Wellington's orders for the destruction of crops and livestock had not been fully carried out by the Portuguese peasantry. Long before the 5th March, however, the resources of the countryside had come to an end, and when the retreat was at last ordered, 'without beat of drum', the French were indeed in sorry case.

Massena retired in two columns. Junot's corps, accompanied by Montbrun's cavalry and followed by Ney's corps, marched by Thomar and Leiria for Pombal and Coimbra. A flanking force marched by Thomar and Espinhal on Murcella, and the rearguards were controlled by Ney, who was a master of delaying tactics. Before following the main body, the rearguards had to remain behind long enough to destroy the French stores and guns, which could not be moved for lack of horses.

Wellington set off in pursuit with some caution, for he did not of course know of the victory at Barossa, and he was uneasy about the intentions of Soult, whom he knew to be besieging Badajoz. Although therefore it was found on the morning of the 6th March

1811

that the French had retired, orders for the British army to advance were not given for another twenty-four hours, and not until the 8th March were the Lines of Torres Vedras finally abandoned.

The 14th, who had held the outpost line before Sobral all winter, were still there when the advance started, and so naturally marched with the advance guard to the main body, following Ney through Thomar and Leiria to Pombal. The French had gained a lead of nearly four days, so that the British cavalry had to ride hard to get up with them. It was a nightmarish sort of ride, such as the most hardened of its survivors could scarcely have forgotten to his dying day. The French soldiers, mutinous, starving and in rags, were set upon by the Portuguese guerrillas, who captured stragglers and small parties and burned or buried them alive. In a fury of bitterness and exasperation, the French retaliated in kind against men, women and children, so that the march route was littered, not only by the normal debris of war, but with the evidence of vengeance too horrible to contemplate. This naturally infuriated the British troops, so that whenever they came to the sword-point, the fighting was even more savage than usual, and conducted with a complete absence of that mutual respect and consideration which soldiers of civilised nations normally give to one another.

On the 8th March, Wellington reached Thomar, with an advance guard of Slade's and Anson's cavalry brigades and two infantry divisions. The cavalry pressed on towards Leiria, which had been reported clear of the enemy, but the 14th came up with four squadrons of French dragoons at Venta de Serra. The 14th were led by Babington's squadron which after some preliminary manoeuvring, charged the enemy just as they were starting to withdraw, and captured fourteen of them with their horses. The information thus gained enabled Wellington to deduce Massena's intentions with some accuracy; in particular, that he was heading for the frontier as fast as he could go under cover of Ney's rearguards. He thereupon sent Beresford with two divisions to Badajoz, in the hope of saving it from Soult, while he himself pushed on to Pombal.

Marching from Leiria at dawn on the 10th March, the 14th came up with the French cavalry at Machados after only a couple of hours' march. Cavalry skirmishing went on all morning until the Light Division arrived, when the enemy fell back and the march was resumed to Pombal, which was found to be strongly held. Becoming anxious, Wellington recalled one of Beresford's divisions although, had he known it, Massena was just as anxious as he was, and had some sort of disagreement with Ney, which resulted in the latter pulling out of Pombal without orders.

When the advance was resumed, on the morning of the 12th March, the Royals and German Hussars took over from the 14th as advance-guard cavalry with the Light Division. When, however, the advance guard caught up with Ney before Redinha, the 14th and 16th Light Dragoons attacked in line with the Light Division; the cavalry moving at a trot, and the Light Infantry in double time. A major engagement ensued during which the third and fourth divisions came up into line, outflanking Ney on both sides and obliging him to pull out. He did so with such skill, however, as to thwart all efforts by the British cavalry to engage, and got clear away in good order. Knowing that Ney must turn west at Condeixa, as the Portuguese held Coimbra to the north, Wellington kept close on his tail and sent Picton through Fonte Cuberta to head him off. This caused Ney to burn Condeixa and fall back hastily to Casal Novo, without informing Massena, who was surprised at Fonte Cuberta by the German Hussars leading Picton's division. The Marshal was having a picnic dinner at the time, and saved his skin only by the use of his legs in a far from dignified scramble. This incident further enraged him against Ney, who was contemptuously declining either to carry out his orders or to keep him informed. Nevertheless, he reinforced Ney with two divisions, and on the 14th March the British cavalry came up against a very strong rearguard position at Casal Novo.

The 14th, bivouacked beyond Condeixa, most of which was still in flames throughout the night, rode out at dawn with the Royals ahead of the Light Division. The morning was both dark and foggy; the French outposts were stumbled upon without warning, and before long the whole Light Division and the cavalry were in close action in a position which, when the fog lifted, was seen to be a highly unpleasant one. Wellington, however, had already sent Picton round the enemy's left flank, so that Ney was soon again obliged to pull out; but again he did so with such skill as to present no opportunities to the cavalry and Light Division, who were in action the whole day with little to show for it except casualties and exhaustion.

Nevertheless the discipline in the French army was now on the verge of complete collapse, owing to the intense sufferings of the rank and file, and Massena felt obliged to hasten the retreat, giving orders to destroy all baggage, vehicles and worn-out animals. This resulted in the horrors of the march route becoming even worse than before, for the French did not waste their ammunition on their horses and mules, but merely hamstrung them and left them suffering along the roads, where they were often ridden down by the British cavalry and guns.

The fog persisted as Ney retreated across the Ceira and took up a position along the heights of Foz d'Arouce. Through some mistake or misunderstanding of orders, two divisions and a cavalry brigade were left on the wrong side of the river, where they were found by the cavalry during the afternoon of the 15th March. It was so late in the day when Picton's and the Light Division arrived, that a halt was called and the troops started to bivouac. On seeing this, the exhausted Frenchmen followed suit, imagining themselves safe for the night, but when Wellington rode up to the front he saw the opportunity and ordered an attack at once. Taken by surprise, the French centre panicked, and a scene of the utmost confusion ensued, during which the French divisions narrowly escaped extermination. It is difficult indeed to see how they did escape, except that the confusion was as great on the British side as on the French. However, they managed to get across the solitary bridge and to blow it up behind them under cover of the night, with a loss of about four hundred men. Although the 14th were engaged in this action, it is doubtful whether they could have found much to do, and they suffered no casualties.

Having halted for a day at Foz d'Arouce while the bridge was repaired, Wellington resumed his advance on the 17th March, but on reaching Moita was again obliged to halt, having outrun his supplies. This enabled Massena to get safely back to Celorico and Guarda, and gave him a breathing space in which to concoct fresh plans. Completely ignoring the condition of his troops, who were not only starving but also in rags and marching in bare feet, he determined to move by Sabugal into the valley of the Tagus, and to endeavour to unite with Soult or Joseph. Ney, who thought that the retreat should be continued to Almeida, then became so insubordinate that Massena was obliged to relieve him of his command, thereby losing the services of his most capable though disloyal subordinate.

While the British were halted at Moita, the cavalry were sent forward to keep an eye on the French, whom their reports indicated to be strongly posted at Guarda. Resuming his advance after a halt of five days, Wellington manoeuvred them out of this position on the 29th March, after which Massena retired across the Coa and took up a position with his entire army round Sabugal. Wellington thereupon concentrated his own army at Adao, and issued orders for an attack on Sabugal to be carried out on the 3rd April. His plans as usual were for a wide turning movement. While his main force threatened a frontal attack, the Third and Light Divisions were to cross the river by fords west of the French positions and threaten their line of retreat. Hawker's cavalry brigade, consisting of the Royals and 14th, was ordered to cross the Coa higher up, and take post above the village of Torre, to reach which they had to march right round the French flank.

By this time only Reynier's corps remained before Sabugal, Massena having withdrawn his main forces to Alfaiates. Wellington had therefore a good chance of routing Reynier completely, had everything gone as planned. Success depended, however, on accurate timing and close co-ordination, both of which turned out to be lacking. The Royals and 14th, who were under the command of Sir William Erskine of the Light Division, crossed the Coa by the ford of Quadrazaes early on the foggy morning of the 3rd April. They were accompanied by Erskine himself, and instead of halting at Torres as ordered, rode on to the road between Souto and Alfaiates and attacked some French batteries on the line of march. The French drivers cut their traces and galloped back to report, which put Reynier on the alert. Meanwhile the Light Division, in the absence of its commander, was in some doubt as to his intentions, and one brigade crossed the river prematurely, running into the French in the fog and causing general chaos. Finding his flank turned, Reynier took immediate action to pull out, but before he could get clear, some very fierce fighting developed, first with the Light Division and then with Picton's Third Division. Once he realised that Reynier had got clear, Wellington halted the pursuit and let him go, but not before the cavalry, far out on the right flank, had captured his personal baggage and caused his men to step out a little faster.

Wellington's supplies had again run out, so that on the 4th April he followed up the French with the Third and Light Divisions only, preceded by the Royals and 14th who, after one or two cavalry skirmishes, crossed the Spanish frontier to Alamedilla, which was the first inhabited village they had seen for nearly two years. Having thus driven the French out of Portugal, Wellington invested Almeida and cantoned his troops along the Coa. Reckoning that Massena, having suffered losses during his retreat of about 45,000 men, was finished for the time being, he then went off to reconnoitre Badajoz, and draw up instructions for Beresford, who had been ordered to besiege it.

While Wellington was away, Stapleton Cotton returned from England and resumed command of the cavalry, and also of the outpost line along the Agueda. This was fortunate, for Slade who had been acting for him, was not up to the task. The cavalry division, owing to some regiments being with Beresford and with other detached forces, was at this time at a very low strength compared with the vast numbers of cavalry disposed by the enemy. Slade's Brigade consisted of the Royals (388 all-ranks) and the 14th (378). Arentschild's Brigade had the 16th (362) and the 1st Hussars, King's German Legion (414). Barbacena's Brigade had the 4th and 10th Portuguese Cavalry, whose combined strength was only 312. Thus the whole cavalry division mustered but 1,854 men, mounted on horses which, after marching right across Portugal on scanty rations and with little rest, were certainly not in the best condition. There was nothing wrong with the men however. The first part of a soldier to go wrong – at least in those days – was his feet, and as the cavalry did not have to use them over much, the cavalrymen were generally in better shape than the infantry. Their horses' feet, on the other hand, were always a source of great anxiety during any prolonged campaign, but the farriers seem to have been very efficient, and the horse management was usually good.

Shortly after his return, Cotton received information that the French were on the march from Salamanca towards Ciudad Rodrigo. On the 1st May the 14th, who were on outpost along the left bank of the Agueda, at Villa del Agueda, were ordered to send out a fighting patrol, and Captain Brotherton led out his squadron towards San Felice, an important road-junction with forks towards Ledesma, Salamanca and Ciudad Rodrigo. After searching all day without result, he sent his squadron back but remained out himself, with a patrol of twelve men. At nightfall he brought this patrol back to San Felice, where he put up at the house of a priest, his men and horses in the back yard and himself, after undressing, in the best bed. He was awakened by the priest in the middle of the night, with the news that the French cavalry were riding through the town. Going to the window, he saw that this was indeed the case. In the light of a bright moon the French were 'very composedly' knocking at doors to find billets. While hastily dressing, he heard a loud knocking at the priest's door, whereupon he jumped out of the back window without his breeches, roused his men and escaped. Reluctant, however, to report back to the regiment in his shirt tails, he later returned for his breeches and, finding that the French had left, had a hearty laugh with the priest over his adventure. It is indeed extraordinary that so seasoned a campaigner should have gone to bed under such circumstances without even posting a sentry, but it is an interesting example of the casual behaviour of British officers in the field which, though reprehensible in some respects, is not without its effect with regard to morale.

Having reckoned on Massena being unable to mount any major operation for several months, Wellington was taken aback when he heard that the French were on the march. Immediately divining that their objective was the relief of Almeida, and that it was essential to stop them, he hastened back from his conference with Beresford and decided to give battle at Fuentes D'Onor. It was not a good defensive position, but it was the only one at which the French march on Almeida could be blocked. His position extended for over five miles, along a broad tableland, with the Dos Casas River in front and the rivers Turones and Coa in rear. The right was at the village of Fuentes D'Onor where the plateau ended in a level plain, and the left at Fort Conception, on the road from Ciudad Rodrigo to Almeida. The French outnumbered him by about 10,000 men, and, as already mentioned, he was very weak in cavalry.

The cavalry were sent out to cover the concentration, and Stapleton Cotton moved his headquarters to Gallegos, on the Ciudad Rodrigo road, and placed his outposts along the Azava River, which was swollen and provided quite a formidable obstacle. The Light Division was on the right of the cavalry, before Espeja.

Neither the cavalry nor the Light Division was in a position to prevent the French crossing the Azava, nor were they expected to. Advancing in two columns, the leading French corps drove in the British picquets on the morning of the 3rd May, and the cavalry and Light Division retired slowly towards Fuentes D'Onor. The picquets of the 14th were commanded by Lieutenant John Townsend, who had to retire under heavy artillery fire. The rest of the regiment got involved with masses of French cavalry behind Gallegos, but contrived to fall back on the Dos Casas in good order.

Massena, who had come up to the front to reconnoitre, soon perceived that the key to Wellington's position was the village of Fuentes D'Onor, the possession of which would enable his flank to be turned. Making a feint attack to the north, he therefore threw his whole strength against the British right. He made the mistake, however, of not concentrating first, but sent in his divisions as they came up. Wellington therefore divined his intention at once, and strengthened and prolonged his right, calling over the cavalry division to take post in the right rear and watch the flank. The Seventh Division was sent to Poco Velho, to prevent a crossing of the Dos Casas River, and Brotherton's

1811

squadron apparently scouted ahead of it, for it was reported to have had a 'sharp skirmish' in that area during the 3rd May.

The first assault on Fuentes D'Onor commenced in mid-afternoon on the 3rd May, and the fiercest possible struggle developed for possession of the village, with both sides throwing in reinforcements until 10 a.m. on the following morning, when 'by mutual consent' the combatants stopped for a rest and to succour the wounded, who, with the dead, were lying two and three deep along the village streets, making it difficult for the sound men to get close enough to one another to use their bayonets. As usual, the moment the drums beat out the order to cease firing and rally, all were friends again. French and British worked together to clear the streets, and exchanged brandy, tobacco and compliments. This cordiality was enlivened by the music of the French regimental bands, which came down to their side of the river to play cheerful or sentimental airs.

Massena had meanwhile come to the conclusion that he had made a blunder in attacking the village, and that he should have gone wide round the flank, which cavalry reconnaissance had discovered to be open – except, presumably, for Brotherton. On the 5th May, he therefore made only a holding attack upon Fuentes D'Onor, and sent most of his cavalry, supported by an infantry division, round the flank. Wellington at once ordered the Cavalry and Light Divisions with a Horse Artillery Battery to hasten to the assistance of the Seventh Division; and the First and Third Divisions were also ordered to take ground to the right.

The 14th, less Brotherton's squadron detached, moving at an extended trot in troop column, arrived at Nave d'Aver just in time to witness some Portuguese guerrillas doing a bolt in front of a French cavalry brigade. The regiment formed squadrons in line, and 'showed a bold front', but were overwhelmed by the masses of Frenchmen and were pushed back, cutting away for their lives, upon the picquet line of the Seventh Division at Poco Velho, where their enemies had to run for it in the face of a series of musket volleys. This was only the start to a long, desperate, and critical action, during which both sides put their whole hearts into the business of getting the better of one another at the sword and bayonet point. Montbrun, the French cavalry leader, brought up his whole division and ordered a general charge, which was met only by the Royals and 14th. The leading French squadrons being disorganised and out of control, could be halted by counter-charges, but a fantastic mêlée developed, during which a Horse Artillery battery of two guns, commanded by Captain Norman Ramsay, was swallowed up by the French.

Ramsay formed his gunners in line, ahead of the guns, and getting up top speed, crashed through the enemy cavalry, presenting a more than stirring sight as he broke out, 'his horses, breathing fire, stretched like greyhounds along the plain.' The Royals and 14th had both rallied, when Stewart, the Adjutant-General, galloped up and led them in a charge which overwhelmed the French and resulted in the capture of Lamotte, one of the French cavalry brigadiers.

In the face of these massive French cavalry assaults, the Light Division had had to form squares, but the Seventh Division was very strongly posted in rocky ground and behind stone walls, where the volleys from its foremost battalions kept the enemy at a distance. The British cavalry had meanwhile been brought back behind the infantry to rest and reform. For a time there was a lull in the fighting, caused, it seems, from a reluctance on the part of Montbrun to attack round the British right flank without the support of the infantry, whereas Marchand, the leading French divisional commander, hesitated to advance across an open plain without the close support of the cavalry. Nevertheless, the Light and Seventh Divisions were now cut off from the rest of the British army, so that the flank was in fact turned, and the position one of grave danger. Wellington therefore ordered the Seventh Division back across the Turones River towards Frenada covered by the Light and Cavalry Divisions, thus denying his flank. It was a most difficult movement to execute when in close action, and more so in the face of a Marshal of France. It would in fact have been impossible, had it not been for the skill and gallantry of the Light and Cavalry Divisions.

The retirement, first of the Seventh and then of the Light Divisions, was covered by the British cavalry, with the Royals and 14th particularly distinguishing themselves. A great spirit of warm comradeship had been generated in this battle between the British cavalrymen and infantry owing to each arm having to rely on the other, turn and turn about, for the protection of its soldiers' lives. Thus, when the Royals and 14th were ordered out from the security of the infantry line to cover its retirement, every Dragoon put his heart into the matter.

As the two regiments came out into the open at the trot and with squadrons in line, to face the ragged squadrons of the enemy (it was believed that many of their men were drunk), a battery of French artillery came forward at the gallop, unlimbered and opened fire at a couple of hundred yards range. It was very difficult for cavalry to deal with this kind of situation, for to make a frontal attack on guns in action was always regarded as suicidal.

However, the leading squadron of the 14th, led by Captain Knipe, advanced in order to cover the retirement of the others, and the charge was sounded at a distance of a little under a hundred yards. Knipe himself was killed, and the squadron was rallied and brought back by Lieutenant John Townsend, after temporarily silencing the guns and imposing further caution on the French. According to Brotherton, an argument had developed among the officers as they sat round the watch fire the night before, during which Knipe had maintained that it was perfectly possible and correct for cavalry to charge guns from the front. The others all disagreed, but Knipe continued obstinate to his last breath, insisting as he lay dying that his charge had been justified. The fact is, of course, that although it was undoubtedly foolish to charge guns from the front when it could be avoided, occasions did arise in battle when the risk had to be accepted. Such was the case in this desperate engagement, and Knipe's brave charge was probably fully justified. It did, after all, silence the guns at a small cost and with considerable effect.

The Royals and 14th had then to cover the retirement of the Light Division which was carried out in squares, or in close columns of companies which enabled squares to be formed at a moment's notice. Montbrun sent all his cavalry against them, but they could make no impression and offered good targets for the British cavalry as they cantered about disorganised round the infantry squares.

So the new front was formed and the flank denied, but the Royals and 14th had no sooner dismounted to the rear of it, when a squadron from each regiment was mounted again and led off at a weary gallop to rescue some skirmishers of the Guards Brigade, who had been charged and captured by some French Hussars. In the final charge of the day, two squadrons rode down the Hussars and took twenty-five of them prisoner, at the same time releasing some of the Guardsmen.

In addition to this outflanking movement, Massena made the most desperate renewed attempts to take Fuentes D'Onor, but was steadily repulsed. On the three days following the battle he made no major attack, and Wellington was able to strengthen his defences. Then on the 8th May, after several fruitless reconnaissances, Massena acknowledged his defeat, and marched back to Salamanca.

For Wellington the Battle of Fuentes D'Onor was one of the many 'damned, close-run things' and 'confounded scrapes', which he experienced during his remarkable career. 'If Boney had been there,' he remarked, 'I'd have been damnably licked.'

It could not be said on this occasion that the day was saved by his own skill and the heroic steadfastness of the British infantry, for those were two factors constant in all his battles. What did stand out on the field of Fuentes D'Onor was the conduct of the handful of British cavalry, and in particular of the Royals and the 14th Light Dragoons, which contributed so materially to the frustration of the enemy's attempts against the right flank and to the success of the day. The gallantry and skill with which they beat off ten times their number and the manner in which they were able to reform and charge again each time they were galloped through and overwhelmed, was quite out of the ordinary. One of the most honourable affairs in which the 14th were ever engaged, the Battle of Fuentes D'Onor proved beyond doubt that the British cavalryman, like the British infantryman, was the best of his kind in Europe.

The losses of the regiment on the field of Fuentes D'Onor were Captain Knipe, 4 Dragoons, and 6 horses killed; Lieut.-Colonel Hervey, Captain Milles, Lieutenants Townsend, Gwynne, Badcock, Ellis, 13 Sergeants, 28 Dragoons and 23 horses wounded; and three men and four horses missing.

An outpost of the 14th Light Dragoons parleying with the French on the River Coa. Such meetings occurred frequently during the Peninsular Campaign.

25th September 1811 The skirmish at Carpio
January 1812 The capture of Ciudad Rodrigo
March–April 1812 The Siege of Badajoz
11th April 1812 The engagement at Llerena
June 1812 The advance to Salamanca
The skirmish on the Valmusa and the cavalry fight on the Guarena

1811

1812

10

After Wellington had left Beresford in April, 1811, to halt Massena's march on Almeida, Beresford had opened *The First English Siege of Badajoz*. He was, however, pounced upon by Soult, whom he just managed to get the better of at Albuera, on the 16th May, in one of the fiercest battles of the war. Having thus failed to relieve Badajoz, Soult retired towards Seville, upon which Wellington returned and opened *The Second English Siege of Badajoz* in person.

The Emperor then relieved Massena by Marmont, sending with him another 50,000 soldiers into Spain, and giving every indication of taking the field himself in order to expel the British from Portugal. As he was, for the moment, at peace with all the great powers except Great Britain, this seemed to be a more than likely course of action.

On arriving at Salamanca, Marmont, no doubt on the Emperor's orders, marched south and joined Soult, when the pair made a joint advance against Wellington, who, in the face of such strength, was obliged to raise the siege and withdraw towards Elvas. He was fully expecting the two Marshals to follow him up, and for the Emperor to arrive on the scene with another army; he therefore made urgent preparations for another retreat through Portugal, including the strengthening of the Lines of

137

1811

Torres Vedras. Fortunately the French were forced to separate, owing to provisioning difficulties. Marmont returned to Salamanca, and Soult to Seville, but the former then moved into the valley of the Tagus, strengthening the Pass of Banos, and keeping in touch with the French south of the river by a bridge of boats at Almaraz.

In August, Wellington returned to the Agueda, cantoned the army along both banks, and blockaded Ciudad Rodrigo, hoping either to starve it into surrender or to attract French forces to its relief so that he could trap them. Slade's cavalry brigade, still containing the Royals and 14th Light Dragoons, maintained an outpost line west of the river, from Villa del Egua, through Gallegos to Espeja. It was a front with which they were intimately acquainted. While Wellington was away in Estremadura, the Royals, with a squadron of the 14th, covered the withdrawal of the Light Division from Gallegos to Nave d'Aver, in the face of a large enemy expedition escorting a convoy to Ciudad Rodrigo. Two separate charges were delivered against the French cavalry during this movement, and each was highly successful in the face of the usual long odds. Their efforts received a commendation in General Sir Brent Spencer's report to the commander-in-chief, '. . . being all that were employed in covering the front from Villa del Egua to Espeja, were assembled at Gallegos, and retreated from thence agreeably to my directions, and notwithstanding all the efforts of General Montbrun, who commanded the French cavalry, to outflank the British, pressing them at the same time in front with eight pieces of cannon. Their retreat to Nave d'Aver merits the highest commendation.'

Following this episode, which took place in June, Marmont endeavoured to tempt Wellington forward, in the hope of being able to get behind him, sever his communications, and relieve Ciudad Rodrigo. As Wellington made no move, he was obliged once again to advance himself and introduce another convoy into the fortress. This time, however, his arrangements were on a fantastic scale, for he hoped to drive Wellington back and so relieve Ciudad Rodrigo, instead of merely breaking the blockade. For the protection of an immense convoy of sheep, oxen and wagons, he assembled no fewer than 6,000 cavalry, over 50,000 infantry, and 100 guns; and to cover the advance of this host upon Ciudad Rodrigo, he ordered diversionary movements along both banks of the Tagus.

Wellington could not prevent a convoy on such a scale from reaching Ciudad Rodrigo but, nevertheless, he concentrated his forces closer to the fortress, along heights on the left bank of the

Agueda. His centre was near El Bodon, and the Light Division was posted on the right bank of the Agueda, south of Ciudad Rodrigo. The cavalry outposts were on the Azava watching the left flank, the 14th Light Dragoons having their headquarters at Espeja, with advanced posts at Carpio and Marialva.

The French arrived before Ciudad Rodrigo on the 24th September and, after driving back the British covering forces, pushed a large number of cavalry to the west of the fortress and sent in the convoy. Instead of retiring, however, as Wellington had expected, they then commenced an outflanking movement towards Espeja. At daybreak on the 25th September, the cavalry outposts at Carpio had to withdraw in the face of some fourteen squadrons of the Imperial Guard which, after leaving six squadrons at Carpio, crossed the Azava and followed the retreating British. Another four French squadrons were then halted near the river. This left only four for the pursuit, which was insufficient odds to get the better of the squadron of the 14th and another of the 16th, which were falling back in front of them. The 14th and 16th halted and formed line at a suitable distance in front of a wood, through which the French squadrons – two of Lancers and two of Hussars – were riding. As soon as they emerged from the wood at a slow pace in extended column, they were charged by the 14th and chased back into the wood in disorder. The light companies from three British regiments then came up at the double, and when the French rallied and advanced again, they were met with three volleys which disorganised them. The 14th and 16th had meanwhile formed line with four squadrons on the flank, and at the right moment made a controlled charge, gradually increasing pace from the walk, trot and gallop. This finished the French, who were chased through the wood and for a couple of miles beyond. Apart from those shot by the infantry, about ten were cut down by the cavalry and another thirty captured. Among the latter was their Chef d'Escadron, who turned out to be an Irishman, named O'Flyn, and who was shot as a traitor by one of the Irishmen in the 16th. Lieutenant Hall, two dragoons and five horses of the 14th were wounded by lance-thrusts in this affair, which ended in the re-occupation of Carpio.

In spite of this initial success, Wellington was still in a very awkward position, for his 35,000 men were extended over some twenty miles, and the Light Division was separated from the rest by the Agueda River. Fortunately, Marmont was unaware of this, and advanced with caution. A violent action took place at El Bodon, where Marmont hurled masses of cavalry against

1811

Wellington's centre, but they were repelled by the British infantry in squares, and Wellington was enabled to establish another position on the ridge of Fuente Guinaldo, which he held until the Light Division joined him. Meanwhile the 14th had again to evacuate Carpio and fall back, fighting hard and making several charges against the French Hussars and Lancers at Carpio, El Bodon, Aldea Ponte and Espeja. It was during this fighting that the well-known incident occurred, when a French officer making a cut at Colonel Bathhurst Hervey of the 14th, noticed in time that his opponent had lost an arm, and was unable to defend himself. Checking his cut, the Frenchman brought his sword to the salute and rode on. Hervey was a particularly gallant officer, who had been wounded many times; the last at Fuentes D'Onor, when an eight-pound shot hit his sabretache and passed through his horse, bruising the Colonel's right leg which 'immediately swelled to an immense size', and he was also rolled on by the dying horse. Nevertheless, he refused to leave the field, but continued in command of the 14th, sitting under a tree. It was said that he would certainly have lost his right leg, had he not been carrying a heavy book in his sabretache, which checked the cannon-ball.

At Espeja, on the 26th September, when the 14th were temporarily brigaded under Count Arentschild of the German Hussars, Montbrun's Lancers of Berg came up and halted on some rising ground in front. Arentschild rode up to Colonel Hervey and ordered: 'Sir, you will charge them'. The 14th advanced accordingly with squadrons in line, but although they saw them coming, the enemy lancers made no move other than to lower their points, and the 14th galloped through them without difficulty, cutting down about sixty. It was not unusual for French lancers to meet an attack halted, in this manner. They seemed to have had a mistaken confidence in the defensive power of the lance, which could however easily be struck aside with a sword, unless it had the force of a galloping horse behind it. The British cavalry were trained never to meet an attack halted, but to meet charge with charge. It is surprising that the French cavalry had not also been trained in this elementary principle.

On the 28th September, having run out of supplies, Marmont withdrew to the valley of the Tagus, leaving Wellington to canton his army along the Coa. Thus the campaign of 1811 came to an end. The French were still in possession of the important fortresses of Badajoz and Ciudad Rodrigo, but the British were in possession of Almeida and Elvas, and had defeated all the French efforts to re-enter and hold Portugal. The campaign proved to be the last of the purely defensive operations against Napoleon, and marked the limits of his conquests; for never again would a French army invade Portugal.

Wellington was also plagued by the problem of feeding – and paying – his army: 'The pay of the army was three months in arrear, the supplies were very scanty, half and quarter rations were often served; often there was no bread for three days consecutively, and the men's clothing was so patched that scarcely a regiment could be known by its uniform. Chopped straw, the only forage, was very scarce; the regimental animals were dying of hunger; corn was rarely distributed save to the generals and staff.' Apart from this, the British army was very sickly, suffering from some form of dysentery brought on by drink and rotten fruit – two commodities which appear to have been fairly plentiful, and in which the soldiers therefore naturally over-indulged themselves. Reinforcements, both of cavalry and infantry, came out from home during the winter, but at the same time the cavalry regiments already in the field were reduced in strength from eight to six troops, owing to a shortage of horses and the difficulty of feeding them. Considering this situation it seems odd, to say the least of it, that the cavalry regiments should have been given an increment to their establishments of a schoolmaster-sergeant. The idea, presumably, was that a schoolmaster would be able to occupy the minds of the soldiers with his lessons, and so alleviate the boredom leading to drink; but in so tough an army as that on the Peninsula, it seems most improbable that such a scheme could have met with much success.

In spite of the condition of his army, Wellington planned to carry an offensive into Spain, in the campaign of 1812, with the fortresses of Ciudad Rodrigo and Badajoz as his first objectives. The first was stormed and captured by the Third and Light Divisions on the 19th January, after a siege of only twelve days. As it was uninterrupted by the French, the cavalry, who were on the lookout for them, had nothing to do. Marmont did not hear about the siege until the 15th January, when he hastily marched to relieve it; but by the time he arrived the place was garrisoned by Spaniards, and Wellington had retired back to the Coa. As the breaches had been repaired and Marmont had no siege train (as Wellington knew) there was nothing he could do about it, and he also withdrew, dispersing his army in order that it could continue to support itself off the country. He himself, with the bulk of the 'Army of Portugal' went to Salamanca on the orders of the Emperor, who thought that Wellington was likely to march into Spain by that route.

1812

Napoleon was, of course, perfectly correct in his appreciation of the likely course of Wellington's future moves into Spain; but Wellington was not yet in any position to undertake any major operations through a country so densely populated by Frenchmen, and he had still to capture the other key fortress of Badajoz, before he could advance with the feeling that the frontier of Portugal was secure.

Badajoz was a far more formidable proposition than Ciudad Rodrigo. Standing upon an eminence on the left bank of the Guadiana River, it was encircled by a curtain wall twenty feet high, and covered by numerous demi-lunes and bastions. Before the curtain was a fosse thirty feet deep and of great breadth. Either the Guadiana or the Roillas stream flowed close to the walls on three sides, while the fourth, the only vulnerable side, was defended by a fort and two lunettes. The garrison was 5,000 strong, well-armed and supplied, and commanded by Phillipon, who was well-known for his courage, energy and resource. With his large siege-train, whose movements he had been carefully hiding from the enemy, Wellington had no doubts about being able to capture the place, given time. The problem was that he had to hammer his way into it before Soult arrived. Although, as a result of his reconnaissance, he believed this to be possible, he could not be sure, and he was therefore obliged to take practically the whole of his army to cover the siege, leaving Ciudad Rodrigo and Almeida to look after themselves. Calculating that the risk was worth accepting, he put in train various ruses to deceive the French, sent Sir Rowland Hill with 30,000 men up the Guadiana River to watch the road from Almaraz, and marched against Badajoz with about 25,000 men at the end of February, 1812.

On the 9th and 10th March, the army crossed the Tagus by a bridge of boats at Vilha Velha, and marched south in appalling weather, with the rain coming down in torrents and enforcing a delay which Wellington could ill-afford, in the execution of so formidable a project as the capture of Badajoz, under the nose of the enemy. He would not be deterred, however, and the fortress was fully invested by the 17th, with the unfortunate infantry, sappers and gunners labouring up to their knees in mud and water in the construction of parallels, zig-zags and batteries. The cavalry were spared these arduous duties, being fairly comfortably billeted in various surrounding villages, close enough for the officers to ride over to Badajoz and watch the progress of the siege. The 14th, who were brigaded with the 12th and 16th Light Dragoons under Major-General Anson, shared the town of Villa Vicosa with the 16th. In the far-off days of peace and monarchy, this had been the summer residence of the Portuguese court. Although ravaged by years of war, it was still a pleasant place enough, with a park still stocked with deer. Strictly speaking, no-one was allowed to shoot the deer without Wellington's permission, for which no-one would dare ask him. It may be taken, however, that the officers and men of the 14th and 16th did not go hungry during their stay in Villa Vicosa. There was also forage available, so that their horses soon began to pick up in condition, like the men. The 14th had, however, to keep one squadron in the vicinity of Badajoz in case of a sortie by the garrison. A sortie was, in fact, made during the afternoon of the 19th March, by a force of forty cavalry and eleven hundred infantry. It took the British soldiers by surprise, and they were driven from some of the trenches where they had been working up to their waists in water. The enemy were soon counter-attacked and retired back to the fortress after losing nearly two hundred men. The squadron of the 14th had two men wounded in this affair, and it was afterwards kept in a constant state of immediate readiness, with one troop always mounted and the other standing by its horses. As may be imagined, this was an extremely trying business, and in one way the infantry were better off, having hard work to occupy their minds. The 14th were not relieved of this duty until the 28th March.

Wellington's sudden descent on Badajoz had taken the French by surprise, as he had intended. Not until the 23rd March did Soult leave Madrid and commence the assembly of a relieving force at Seville. He could not concentrate sufficient numbers to defeat the British army besieging Badajoz, so Wellington was not particularly worried about his movements, except with regard to the necessity for keeping him at a distance until Badajoz had fallen. Sir Rowland Hill was guarding the road from Almaraz, and Sir Thomas Graham was deployed before Llerena. Both commanders were ordered to fall back as Soult advanced, Hill to Merida and Graham to Villa Franca and Zafra, thus bringing the French within Wellington's reach, so that he might fall upon them as soon as Badajoz had been taken. Although these plans were upset by Marmont's movements in the north, they did in fact enable the siege to be successfully completed.

Anson's cavalry brigade marched to cover Graham's withdrawal on the 29th March. On the 31st, the brigade halted for three days at Olivenza, where Stapleton Cotton and most of the cavalry division had already arrived. It was a good place to halt, having escaped the attention of the French hitherto. It was full of Spanish refugees from Badajoz, who joined with the inhabitants

1812

in offering hospitality to the British cavalry, whose officers were invited to a ball every night during the halt. These functions were gay and romantic affairs, in which the dim light caused by a scarcity of candles and lamp-oil was kind to the patched and faded uniforms, and the makeshift gowns of the ladies. Almost drowning the music, the continual roar of Wellington's guns at Badajoz had no effect on the spirits of the senoritas, happy in the company of such fine young men. 'Ah!' they would exclaim from time to time, 'I wonder if they have hit our poor house yet!' Little did they know of the hell which was approaching its climax in their home town, or the fate awaiting their friends and relatives who were still there. Beneath the walls of Badajoz but a few miles away, the scaling ladders were being lashed together, and below the tumbling masonry of the breaches the stormers and forlorn hopes were assembling. On the night of the 6th April Badajoz would be taken by direct assault in the teeth of five thousand gallant and determined Frenchmen with a ferocious heroism which beggars description. Driven clean out of their wits by the horrors through which they had passed, and mad for vengeance, the British soldiers would then get out of control and sack the town, sparing no-one.

The sound of the cannonade had intensified by the 5th April, as an all-out effort was made to get the breaches practicable, for Wellington was becoming anxious. On this day the cavalry left Olivenza, for Soult's advanced guards had reached Bienvenida, and Graham was starting to fall back. As the cavalry rode forward, they met his infantry, guns and transport on the line of march for Albuera, and the 14th Light Dragoons entered Villa Franca just as Graham himself was leaving with his staff. There was a certain amount of apprehension in their air, for most soldiers were aware that things were touch and go at that moment. Everything changed, however, with the arrival of the news of the fall of Badajoz, which reached Soult on the 8th, and so upset him that he rushed round his lodging, breaking every piece of crockery he could lay his hands on. Having relieved his feelings in this manner, he halted his advance and prepared to fall back on Llerena and further if necessary, for he had far too much respect for Wellington to meet him under adverse circumstances.

With the news of the fall of Badajoz, orders came for Stapleton Cotton to press hard on Soult's rearguards, with the object of making him think that Wellington intended chasing him into Andalusia. On the 11th April, therefore, Anson's Brigade was ordered forward, with Slade's and Le Marchant's Brigades in support. Anson himself was on leave at this time, and his brigade was commanded by General Ponsonby. Cotton rode out to Bienvenida and climbed the church steeple, from which he was able to see that the French were still in Llerena, covered by a large force of cavalry which was bivouacked in a wood. Ponsonby, with the 12th and 14th Light Dragoons, was in the town, waiting while the General made his reconnaissance, at the end of which Cotton ran down from the church and sent Ponsonby off to Usagre with orders to engage the French cavalry. At the same time he sent for his other two brigades. When these arrived, it occurred to him that if he had not sent Ponsonby off on his own, he could have surrounded the French with the three brigades and caught the lot. A galloper was immediately sent to recall Ponsonby, but reached him too late, for he had already sent a squadron of the 14th and another of the 12th to drive in the French picquets. Having carried out this task, the two squadrons chased the French through Villagarcia, but ran into the main body of the enemy cavalry which was formed up beyond. 'Threes about!' and back they came at the gallop, whereupon Ponsonby attacked with the remainder of the 12th and 14th – about six hundred men. Cotton had meanwhile arrived with his other two brigades and, sending word to Ponsonby to 'skirmish' and fall back, he deployed on the flanks. The French Cavalry General, Lallemand, seeing only the 12th and 14th in front of him, was easily trapped and, when Ponsonby withdrew the two regiments into a ravine between some stone walls, followed them up with his whole force. He was then charged from both flanks; the 16th jumping a wall in line, in order to get at him. A charge by the 5th Dragoon Guards, carried out on blown horses, was repulsed, but the 5th rallied at once and charged again. The French then broke and fled, pursued by the whole British cavalry division. Cotton, however, kept the division in hand, for Wellington was always furious whenever cavalry regiments cut loose after a successful charge – as they often did – and 'went hunting'. By halting the division in order to re-form, he allowed the French to reach the cover of their infantry, escaping with losses of about two hundred, mostly prisoners, instead of being cut to pieces. This brilliantly-conducted action therefore resulted in much ill-temper among the officers, who blamed Cotton for halting the pursuit, while Cotton blamed Ponsonby for not carrying out his orders correctly – it is hard to say on what grounds. The British losses were about fifty, in killed, wounded and missing. During the following night, a troop of the 14th led by Lieutenant Pellew surrounded one of the French cavalry picquets and took twenty-two of them prisoner after a little sword-play.

1812

The sufferings of the wounded in these actions were very great. The medical arrangements were rudimentary, and those who were too severely wounded to be able to ride or walk were not infrequently abandoned and left to die, after being stripped by the peasants. In cavalry engagements, the majority of wounds were caused by the heavy, curved cutting swords, which seldom killed a man outright, but inflicted terrible injuries. 'The prisoners,' wrote Captain Tomkinson, of the 16th Light Dragoons, after this particular action, 'were dreadfully cut, and some will not recover. A French dragoon had his head nearer cut off than ever I saw before; it was by a sabre cut at the back of the neck.' The wounded prisoners on both sides were given the same attention and treatment as those of the wounded among their captors, but they would, of course, be the first to be abandoned if they were unable to march and if there was no room for them in the transport. Few soldiers of this period ever forgot the harrowing experience of marching away from a battlefield, and trying to ignore the cries of the wounded, many of whom may have been their own friends and comrades. It had to be accepted, however, as part of the business of war, and of the soldier's life; but with such constant evidence of the likely fate which awaited them sooner or later, unless they were uncommonly lucky, the courage with which the soldiers faced such dangers should be appreciated.

After the Badajoz operations, a temporary lull set in while the opponents re-grouped and rested. The 14th marched north and bivouacked along the Agueda, within easy march of Ciudad Rodrigo. The initiative now lay with Wellington, who had determined to march against Marmont, with a view to threatening the French communications through Valladolid and Bayonne; thus forcing Soult to leave Andalusia for the defence of Madrid, and so freeing the south of Spain. As a preliminary to his offensive, Wellington sent Sir Rowland Hill to capture Almaraz, and so interrupt the communications between Marmont and King Joseph with Soult. This was successfully accomplished during May, and on the 13th June, 1812, Wellington left the Agueda and marched against Salamanca.

The army marched by three roads, with the right column, commanded by Sir Thomas Graham, heading towards Los Santos. It consisted of the 14th Light Dragoons, and the 1st, 6th and 7th Infantry Divisions. The 1st (German) Hussars led the centre column, followed by the Light Division and the 12th and 16th Light Dragoons, and the 11th Light Dragoons led the left-hand column, followed by Le Marchant's Heavy Cavalry Brigade.

1812

The first contact with the enemy was made on the 16th June, when the German Hussars engaged some French cavalry on the Valmusa rivulet about six miles – 'two leagues' – in front of Salamanca, and drove them back one league. Then the 11th Light Dragoons came up on the left and the 14th on the right. A skirmish followed, in which Brotherton's squadron had a sergeant and trumpeter killed with four privates and five horses wounded. It was quite a lively affair, and ended with the enemy retreating across the Tormes. Brotherton had been looking for a ford across the Tormes – which he seemed to think was the Douro – when the French caught him, and chased him back over the river. His unfortunate trumpeter had been shot through the body, and 'kept howling aloud', which greatly irritated him. Coming back with his whole squadron, but having no trumpeter, his signal to gallop was a *view holloa*, which 'so astonished' the French, that 'they went back rapidly'. By a strange chance, they turned out to be the 14th Chasseurs, who wore orange facings, like the 14th Light Dragoons. During the subsequent skirmish, Brotherton engaged a young French officer, with whom he kept up a friendly conversation during a deadly exchange of sword-play. The Frenchman aimed his cuts at Brotherton's reins, and eventually wounded his bridle-hand, which much annoyed Brotherton, as it stopped him from playing the fiddle with which he was accustomed to entertain his comrades round the watch-fires. He retaliated with a savage thrust through the body, on which his opponent rode off. Feeling anxious about him, Brotherton sent a flag of truce to enquire after his welfare, and was much distressed to hear that he had died, as he had taken a great liking to the young man.

A more serious affair took place along the Guarena River, beyond Salamanca, on the 18th July, when Victor Alten's cavalry brigade, consisting only of the German Hussars and the 14th, engaged a French cavalry brigade supported by infantry. Alten's Brigade was at first heavily outnumbered, and was very hard put to it to hold the field. The arrival of British and Portuguese infantry then turned the scale, and the French were driven off, pursued by the German Hussars and 14th, who had suffered heavy losses during many charges and counter-charges. Eighteen men and twenty horses were killed, and thirty-four men and eighteen horses wounded. Three officers were wounded, including Captain Brotherton, who was run through the right side of his body, the sword-point reaching his navel. He was always so scornful of the fuss made by others over their trumpery wounds, that it is satisfactory to record that he did in fact practise what he

1812

preached, and treated his affliction with a gentlemanly nonchalance. Although unable to ride, he refused to leave the field, and was present throughout the Battle of Salamanca. The long thrusting sword carried by the French Heavies, from which he had received his wound was, he observed, a far more efficient weapon than the curved cutting sword carried by the Light Cavalry.

Dragoons, Light Dragoons, and Hussars, showing changes in uniform ▷ between 1715 and 1900. *Centre*, the 14th Light Dragoons capture the coach of Joseph Bonaparte at Vittoria, 21 June 1813. The coach contained the silver chamber-pot which became the Regiment's prized trophy.

Silver statuette of an officer of the 14th Light Dragoons in full dress of the period 1812–19.

22nd July 1812 The Battle of Salamanca
26th July 1812 Cpl. Hanley at Blasco Sancho
12th August 1812 Wellington enters Madrid
October and November 1812 The retreat from Burgos
May and June 1813 The advance to Vittoria

Salamanca

ALWAYS apprehensive of a threat to his communications through Salamanca, Marmont had strengthened its defences with a number of forts, the capture of which took Wellington ten days, and cost him 600 men. While he was thus held up, Marmont concentrated his army behind the Douro. On the 8th July, after blowing up the forts, Wellington followed him and drew up his line with his left on the Guarena and his right at Rueda. The armies thus faced one another for several days, for Wellington would not undertake an opposed crossing in the face of Marmont's host so strongly posted. He was thus in an awkward position, and although he did make plans to force a crossing if necessary, he was hoping to be saved the trouble by Marmont having to withdraw owing to lack of supplies. Instead of retiring, however, Marmont took the offensive by suddenly moving to Toro and making a crossing at that point, thus threatening Wellington's left flank. On the 17th July, Marmont then made a forced march back along the right bank of the Douro and crossed it at Pollos and Tordisillas. By nightfall, he had concentrated his whole army at Nava del Rey, after some of his troops had marched fifty miles without a halt.

Wellington's object, in the face of the offensive now developing, was to cover the town of Salamanca and the road to Ciudad

1812

Rodrigo. He therefore ordered a withdrawal behind the Guarena. It was an attempt by Marmont to force a passage of this river which had been defeated on the 18th July as described in the last chapter. After this set-back, Marmont marched rapidly up the right bank, crossed unopposed, and moved round Wellington's right towards the Tormes River. Should he succeed in crossing this river, he could cut Wellington's communications with Ciudad Rodrigo. Wellington was under no apprehension, for the fords at Huerta and Alba were held by the Spaniards. He did not know what Marmont knew; that the Spaniards had decamped. Nevertheless he was very keenly on guard, and watching Marmont's movements with the closest attention. A series of remarkable manoeuvres followed, with each commander doing his utmost to outwit the other. Having tried and failed to get across the French line of march at Cantalpina, Wellington made a right-wheel and accompanied Marmont to the Tormes, the two armies marching parallel to one another within shouting distance – a fact of which the soldiers of both sides made full use. On the 21st July, both armies crossed the Tormes; Wellington by the fords of Santa Marta and Aldea Lengua, and Marmont by those of Huerta and Alba. During a very wet and stormy night, Wellington then learnt that large French cavalry reinforcements were approaching, and that King Joseph was also on the line of march from Madrid. He therefore decided to fall back on the Portuguese frontier but the officer riding with his dispatches was captured by the French, and Marmont, thus being made aware of his intention, determined to prevent him.

As may be imagined, during these complicated manoeuvres, carried out by long columns of tired infantry, sweating along within close musket-shot of one another and accompanied by their guns and transport, both British and French cavalry were riding about in a positive frenzy of impatience, seeking opportunities to charge – for to a cavalryman, the world offered few pleasanter sights than that of the enemy infantry and guns on the line of march in rideable country. They succeeded, however, in keeping one another away from the infantry, by constant vigilance and skirmishing during which the British cavalry, being as usual, outnumbered, had to ride a great deal harder than the French. The 14th, still with the German Hussars in Alten's Light Brigade, engaged the enemy several times during the three days of these manoeuvres.

At dawn on the 22nd July, 1812, with the sky clear of clouds and the visibility sharp after the storm of the night before, Marmont was soon to horse, and galloping eagerly up the heights of the Calvarrassa de Arriba, along which his army lay. He was expecting to see the beginning of Wellington's retreat to Ciudad Rodrigo, and what he did see apparently confirmed his expectations. To his front, a single British division was in position across his line of advance, while in the distance, what he took to be the escort to Wellington's baggage train was moving up the hill of Aldea Tejada. No other enemy were visible, except Wellington himself and some staff officers, who were sitting their horses on the summit of a range of hills opposite. The main British army, with its Portuguese and Spanish allies, was out of sight along the reverse slopes. On Marmont's left were the twin hills of the Arapiles, between which the road passed through the village of Los Arapiles and round the British right. The two opposing commanders appreciated the tactical importance of these features simultaneously, and a race took place which ended with honours even; Wellington securing the northern, or Lesser Arapil, and Marmont the southern, or Greater Arapil. All was then ready for the Battle of Salamanca. All that remained was for one commander to make a false move, and for the other to profit by it.

Marmont's advance on the Arapiles made it clear to Wellington that the French were about to march round his right flank. He therefore re-formed, so that his line faced south instead of east. At the same time he occupied Los Arapiles with the light companies of the Guards, and sent the Third Division to Aldea Tejada, some three miles to the north. As Picton was on leave, the 'Fighting Division' was commanded by the Hon. Edward Pakenham, Wellington's brother-in-law.

These movements appeared to Marmont to confirm that the British were about to retreat, and he hastened to intercept them, not realising that Wellington had changed front, for the main British army was still under cover. The military game of chess still continued, however, with the two masters making cautious moves and counter-moves, and observing each other with the greatest attention. It was not until near noon that Marmont's attention was distracted by a cloud of dust in the distance, which he assumed indicated that Wellington was still passing troops to his rear, and that the British retreat was in progress. In great hurry and confusion, he set his army in motion, marching south of the Arapiles. His leading division, commanded by General Thomiere, was directed towards the Ciudad Rodrigo road, and with the remainder he attacked Los Arapiles, expecting to be able to destroy that part of Wellington's army which had not commenced the retreat. As he advanced, a considerable gap

1812

developed between his left wing, which was in the lead, and the remainder of his force. After a series of admirable, indeed brilliant, moves he thus at last made a mistake.

Wellington, who was having his lunch on the top of the Lesser Arapil, left his meal immediately. 'Marmont is lost', he exclaimed. Ordering four divisions forward, he mounted and galloped at top speed to Aldea Tejada, where the Fighting Division was drawn up under arms behind a hill. 'Ned!' he shouted, 'move on with the Third Division; take the heights to your front, and drive everything before you!'

Pakenham got on the move immediately, being already in formation. He advanced in four columns. On the right was Alten's Light Cavalry Brigade, commanded by Arentschild on this day, and consisting of the 14th Light Dragoons, the 1st German Hussars, and D'Urban's Portuguese Horse. To their left was Wallace's Brigade of the 45th, 74th and 88th Regiments; in the centre a Portuguese Brigade, and next to that Campbell's Brigade of the 5th, 83rd and 94th Regiments. To get to close quarters, the Fighting Division and the cavalry brigade had to cover a distance of about two miles and a half, for most of which the troops were hidden from the French by the intervening hills, and Thomières never suspected their presence until they were almost upon him.

The first into action were D'Urban's Portuguese Horse, who charged the leading French battalion, supported by the 14th. The charge broke and scattered the French, but also alerted Thomières to his danger. His division was very strung out, and to cover its concentration he deployed a screen of skirmishers supported by twenty guns, and sent six squadrons of light horse round Pakenham's right flank. Arentschild, who was riding with the German Hussars, saw the six squadrons on the other side of a deep ravine, and, without hesitation, filed the regiment across the ravine, formed line on the farther side and charged. The 14th were meanwhile galloping up in support, and had just formed line across the ravine when the Germans came back in disorder, having broken the enemy first line but been overwhelmed in the mêlée. Arentschild rallied them behind the 14th and charged with the whole brigade, led by the 14th. This attack was entirely successful and the French cavalry were scattered and pursued, many prisoners being taken.

Wallace's Brigade then entered, moving at a very brisk pace, with Pakenham riding among them, trying to hold them back in line. The commanding-officer of the 88th was shot and dragged across the front of his regiment with his foot caught in a stirrup.

The sight infuriated his Irishmen, who broke forward with wild howls of rage. Pakenham shouted, 'All right! Let them go then!' and the battle was joined.

As soon as he saw that Pakenham was in action, Wellington attacked the French centre. Marmont had been wounded and the French command had passed to General Clausel, who had no time to assert his authority before things got beyond his control. Nevertheless, with his left broken, his centre in peril, and the normal confusion of a great battle at close quarters intensified by the long grass catching fire, he did manage to launch a counter-attack which, although it was repulsed, enabled him to draw back upon the Tormes and eventually retreat across the ford at Alba. For a major engagement, the Battle of Salamanca was over in record time; 'Forty thousand Frenchmen beaten in forty minutes,' and the 14th had not returned from their pursuit of the light cavalry on the right wing before it was all over – a brilliant victory in which the French were saved from extermination only by the skill of General Clausel.

The casualties at Salamanca amounted to about 6,000 British and allies, and 15,000 French. They included many senior officers on both sides, Wellington himself being slightly wounded by a spent bullet. The 14th came off lightly with four killed and six wounded, among whom Captain Brotherton made an unofficial seventh. Having been threatened with arrest by Colonel Hervey if he did not stay in bed until recovered from his sword-thrust, he had ridden out in 'undress' to look on. Knowing that Hervey was far away on the right wing, and seeing some Portuguese cavalry riding against the Greater Arapil, he joined them and received another wound when their attack was repulsed.

Four days after the battle when Arentschild's Brigade was still in pursuit of the enemy, a patrol led by Corporal William Hanley of the 14th and consisting of three dragoons of the 14th and four German Hussars, caught up with a troop of French dragoons at Blasco Sancho and, by presenting a bold front, got them to surrender, thus capturing 2 officers, 2 NCO's, 27 dragoons and a private servant, with their horses and baggage. It was a good effort by eight men, and when Wellington heard of it he gave Lieut.-Colonel Hervey a 'pecuniary reward', for distribution among the members of the patrol; a kindly gesture which shows that he was not unappreciative of his soldiers' efforts as his frequent criticisms of their behaviour might lead one to suppose. Corporal Hanley received a silver medal presented by his officers, in recognition of his courage and resource.

As the defeated French army fell back through Aravelo,

1812

Wellington followed up closely and reached Valladolid on the 30th July. Large reinforcements of cavalry had been sent to Clausel's assistance from the Army of the North, and now covered his retreat, making things very difficult for the exhausted British cavalry, who had lost Stapleton Cotton, wounded, and Le Marchant killed. Command of the cavalry passed to General Bock, who crossed the Tormes on the 23rd and engaged the French rearguards, breaking three battalion squares with the Heavies, while the 14th charged and took many French cavalry prisoners near Penarada. Arentschild's Brigade thereafter led the advance, passing through Arevalo and up the main road to Valladolid, collecting many French wounded and stragglers on the way, and occasionally sighting the enemy rearguards, but making no attempts to bring them to action. There seems to have been some good deal of grumbling among the cavalry officers over the opportunities missed by these cautious tactics, but the brigadiers were evidently acting under Wellington's orders. Looking upon warfare as an art, in which the primary object is to outwit the enemy, he was always adverse to minor engagements undertaken purely for the sake of honour and glory, and in this view he was not infrequently at variance with his dashing cavalrymen who were always seeking opportunities for coming to blows, whatever the tactical situation might be. However, his genius and his soldiers' spirit made an unbeatable combination, as he sometimes acknowledged himself, on the rare occasions when he thought about it.

While Wellington was marching on Valladolid, King Joseph, who had left Madrid to join Clausel, arrived at Blasco Sancho, so that Wellington's communications with Ciudad Rodrigo were again threatened. Wellington had therefore to leave Valladolid and march against Joseph, who hastily withdrew, first to Madrid and then southwards to Toledo. Following up, Wellington reached Madrid on the 12th August, and made a triumphant entry into the city among the loud acclamations of the populace. He immediately besieged and soon captured the small fortress known as the Retiro, in which a couple of thousand Frenchmen had been left to guard Madrid. This final blow to French arms, following on the defeat of Marmont and the retreat of Joseph, obliged Soult finally to raise the siege of Cadiz, evacuate Andalusia and march north. As the Army of the North, under Clausel, had begun to reassemble on the Douro, Wellington could not risk waiting for Soult. On the 1st September he left Madrid, returned to Valladolid and, when Clausel retired before him, followed up and laid siege to the castle of Burgos.

1812

The 14th Light Dragoons had not entered Madrid, having been sent off with the German Hussars to watch the pass at Escurial, across the Sierra Guadarama. Here they remained in bivouac, with a screen of outposts, until the third week of October. Wellington had meanwhile failed to take Burgos after five separate assaults. As Soult, Clausel and Joseph were now in combination against him, he was in one of those awkward positions which he described as 'damnable scrapes', and was forced to raise the siege and commence the retreat from Burgos. This began in great secrecy during the night of the 21st October, and was carried out under conditions of the greatest hardship and danger, such as usually attended major withdrawals in the face of the enemy.

Arentschild's Brigade was at this time under the orders of Sir Rowland Hill who, when Soult evacuated Andalusia, had been freed from his watch over Badajoz and the Alemtejo, and had taken up a position covering Madrid from the south. He was now ordered to join Wellington at Salamanca, and so withdrew through Madrid towards Arevalo. The 14th and German Hussars were called in to Madrid to cover his withdrawal, which they did all the way to San Christoval near Salamanca, marching by way of Arevalo and Alba de Tormes, closely followed by the French, with whom they had frequent skirmishes.

Wellington arrived at San Christoval on the 6th November, and the retreat was then continued to Ciudad Rodrigo, which was reached on the 18th, the 14th Light Dragoons being still with the rearguard. As usual during a major retreat, the infantry discipline (though not its morale) broke down, and the cavalry were almost as much occupied in rounding up stragglers as they were in fighting off the French. The stragglers were those who had left the ranks to look for something to eat, and there was a certain amount of excuse for them as they were not issued with any rations for, as usual, the civilian commissariat broke down. The country through which they marched was covered by a vast forest, in which roamed great herds of swine, pursued by numbers of famished British soldiers with muskets. Wellington did his best to restore order by his usual method of hanging a few of them, but as the troops felt themselves to be dying of starvation, they had little fear of the rope.

During the retreat the 14th were constantly in action, notably on the 16th November, when the rearguard was attacked by seventeen squadrons of French Lancers, who drove back the German Hussars but were checked by the infantry light companies and a battery of Horse Artillery firing grape. They were

1812

then charged by the 14th, led by Colonel Hervey (now Sir F. B. Hervey, Bart.) and driven back, although in very superior numbers. Several prisoners were taken by the regiment in this affair, in which it lost a corporal and two horses killed, one man wounded and one missing. Hervey, having only one arm, was nearly taken, becoming surrounded by enemy lancers and unable to fight his way through. He was saved by his orderly, who cut a path for him and then remained behind to cover his retreat, becoming the one man missing in the regiment. Hervey was naturally anxious to find out what became of him if possible, and Brotherton went over to the French outposts, *en parlementaire*, as he put it, to make enquiries. He was accompanied by a German trumpeter whom he ordered to sound the *parlementaire* when he saw the French advancing. The German, however, for some reason or other sounded the charge instead, upon which the French 'precipitately retired', and Brotherton was obliged to gallop after them through the forest for a considerable distance before he caught them up. This, like many other of Brotherton's stories, told in his London club in his declining years, may perhaps be found difficult entirely to believe by present-day readers. It should be remembered, therefore, that it never occurred to his listeners at the time to doubt his word, nor did his stories seem anything out of the way a century ago when life itself, let alone the conduct of war, was a vastly different matter, so that proven facts are often as difficult to believe and understand as Brotherton's yarns.

At the end of November, Wellington cantoned the army along the Coa and Agueda rivers, and the French also dispersed in search of supplies. The campaign of 1812 thus came to an end, with the 14th Light Dragoons at Fundao, and their horses out at grass. According to Brotherton, they did not altogether relish being left at liberty to fend for themselves, and paraded every morning in the town square without orders, apparently expecting to be groomed and fed. 'Considering the work they have done,' wrote Tomkinson of the 16th, 'both men and horses are by no means in bad order.' This seems to have been the case in the army generally, although Wellington was far from satisfied. From his headquarters at Freneda on the 28th November, he addressed a long directive to divisional and brigade commanders on the training and administration to be carried out during the winter, in which he commented with much severity on the state of discipline: 'I am concerned to have to observe that the Army under my command has fallen off in this respect in the late campaign to a greater degree than any Army with which I have ever served or of which I have ever read. Yet this Army has met with no disasters, it has suffered no privations which but trifling attention on the part of the Officers could have prevented, and for which there existed no reason whatever in the nature of the service; nor has it suffered any hardship excepting those resulting from the necessity of being exposed to the inclemency of the weather at the moment when it was most severe.' He was certainly hard to please, and it is difficult to realise that he was referring to an army which, in one year, had expelled the French from Portugal, captured Ciudad Rodrigo and Badajoz, won a decisive victory at Salamanca and entered Madrid, and finally extricated Wellington from a 'confounded scrape', by a fighting retreat from Burgos, carried out under appalling conditions without any pay or rations. However, he always believed in keeping everyone up to the mark.

Napoleon's disastrous campaign in Russia, and the destruction of his army, had resulted in a wave of optimism sweeping the United Kingdom, and in the government deciding at last to give Wellington every possible support to enable him to drive the French from Spain in 1813. Considerable reinforcements were sent out, and the army was reorganised and re-equipped. In Spain itself, the guerrillas increased their activities and banded together into more-or-less organised armies, causing the French more trouble than ever before, especially as Napoleon had been obliged to withdraw many thousands of men across the Pyrenees to prop up his tottering imperial throne.

At the beginning of 1813, Wellington, who was now in supreme command of all allied forces in the Peninsula, including the Spaniards, had 44,000 British troops, with 6,000 cavalry and 90 guns, along the Coa. With the British were 30,000 Portuguese and part of a large Spanish force under Castanos. The total number of troops at his disposal now, for the first time, approximated to the French total of about 190,000 men, and he had the advantage of being concentrated, whereas the French were widely scattered besides being disheartened by a long series of defeats, and with no confidence in their nominal commander-in-chief, King Joseph.

Under the circumstances, Joseph and his Marshals well knew that they would have to oppose an invasion of Spain in the spring of 1813, and, assuming that Wellington would march by Salamanca as before, prepared to defend the line of the Douro, and to the last man if necessary. Wellington's plans, however, were a good deal more subtle. Having reconnoitred the Tras os Montes, north of the Douro in Portuguese territory, he decided that though difficult, the country was passable for troops and

1813

guns, while, by sending a force through it, he could turn the French left flank on the Douro. He therefore advanced in three columns, sending the main force under Sir Thomas Graham through the Tras os Montes to join with the Spaniards in Galicia and march on Zamorra; the centre column under his personal command towards Salamanca, while the right, under Sir Rowland Hill, marched also on Salamanca by a southern route through Tamames and Matilla.

The army marched in the middle of May, 1813, and on the 26th, the 14th Light Dragoons, leading the centre column, made contact with the enemy before Salamanca, which they found to be occupied and barricaded, with a French force in position along the heights above the ford of Santa Marta. This turned out to be General Villatte's division which, with about 300 cavalry, was awaiting Wellington's advance in the hope of gaining some information regarding his plans. This was a dangerous thing to attempt under Wellington's very nose, and resulted in the French having to make a precipitous retreat to avoid being cut off by ten times their number. Riding through Salamanca, the 14th were delayed by the barricades which, although the enemy had left, they had to remove to let the Horse Artillery through. By the time they got forward, Wellington had halted the pursuit, for Villatte had conducted his retirement with great skill and avoided destruction, although he lost about five hundred men and a great quantity of stores and transport.

The British advance then continued exactly in accordance with Wellington's plans. Graham, having linked up with the Spaniards in Galicia, turned the French flank along the Esla, and joined Wellington across the Douro. King Joseph drew back on Burgos, followed by Wellington in what appeared to be a leisurely manner; but in fact, he was merely stepping short to allow Graham to get forward on the left, thus easing the French off one position after another by constantly threatening their right flank. 'The army,' said Wellington, 'is in better shape than I have ever known them. God knows how long this will last.' It was unusual for him to say anything nice about his soldiers, and it is not clear what prompted him to do so at this time, for large numbers of them were on the verge of mutiny caused by a hunger approaching starvation – for the supplies had again given out, and there was no plunder to be had in the wake of the retreating French. This position was to be eased as soon as the enemy left Santander, where Wellington's store ships from Corunna were lying off-and-on, waiting to come in to port and open a base; but meanwhile the troops had to tighten their belts and keep on the move – not for the first, nor the last time, during the Peninsular War.

King Joseph now abandoned all hope of holding Burgos, and started to send his artillery and ammunition wagons back to Vittoria, where he intended to accept battle. Being in great difficulties from lack of horses, it was imperative for him to delay Wellington's advance as long as possible, and his retirement was covered by strong rearguards, with which the 14th were continually coming in contact. The most important of these was that commanded by General Reille before Burgos, who held so strong a position that Wellington sent forward all his cavalry against it, supported by the Light Division and some of Hill's infantry. Reille fell back when the British cavalry got round his right flank, and withdrew in good order towards Burgos by the bridge of Villa de Buniel before the British could get at him. Captain Milles' squadron of the 14th, however, managed to put in a charge against the French rear on the near side of the bridge, supported by Gardiner's troop of Horse Artillery, and captured several prisoners and a gun, at a cost of one man and a horse killed, and another man and five horses wounded.

After this affair, which took place on the 12th June, the French evacuated Burgos and blew up the castle, in such haste that a hundred and twenty of their dragoons, with their horses, were unable to get clear and were blown up with it. As may be imagined, this disaster further impaired the morale of the French cavalry, which was already none too good, and far below that of their infantry.

The morale of the French High Command, in particular that of Joseph and his chief of staff, Marshal Jourdan, was also at a low ebb, for they were unable to anticipate any of Wellington's moves, or to agree upon the best course to pursue. They could probably have been hustled out of Spain in disorder without any major engagement, had not Joseph been more frightened of Napoleon than he was of Wellington. This fear drove him to assert himself and to over-rule the defeatist advice of his Marshals, insisting upon giving battle at Vittoria as the last chance of securing his communications through the Pyrenees. The retirement therefore continued towards that end, under close pressure by the British cavalry. The 14th crossed the Ebro by the bridge of Frias on the 15th June, and engaged the enemy near Pancorba, but they fell back quickly. Wellington had by then concentrated his entire army, and on the 17th June Graham took the lead along the main road to Vittoria, with Wellington following close behind and Hill bringing up the rear. The army did not of course march only along the 'Great Road' but on a wide front, using various

1813

tracks and byways which were so primitive that the French had thought them impassable. It was indeed hard going, through barren, rocky and mountainous country devoid of inhabitants, food or forage; but the British army continued 'in good shape', and pressed on in spite – though not regardless – of hardship, hunger and fatigue, with all of which it was only too familiar.

On the 20th June the cavalry arrived in sight of the French positions in the basin of Vittoria, and the 14th had a skirmish with some French cavalry near the village of Huarte. Wellington, whose army was strung out in various columns, all hastening forward by forced march, rode up to the front to reconnoitre and make his plans. All day he galloped from one vantage point to another, examining the French positions through his telescope and sending officers back with orders to the columns closing up behind him. All his commanders knew what action they had to take – though not the general plan – by the time the bivouac fires were lighted and the sun set, on the eve of the Battle of Vittoria.

Officer and Trooper 20th Light Dragoons 1814.
Uniform: Blue with orange facings, the same colour as the 14th
Light Dragoons at that time. Water colour by Stadden.

1813

After the Battle of Vittoria, 21 June 1813, the 14th Light Dragoons help themselves to the contents of King Joseph Bonaparte's coach, including the famous silver chamber-pot which became known in the Regiment as 'The Emperor'. (King Joseph was the Emperor Napoleon's brother.)

21st June 1813 The Battle of Vittoria
November and December 1813 The pursuit to
Pampluna, the 14th in the Pyrenees, the 'Ragged Brigade',
the 14th on the Nivelle and at the crossing of the Nive
13th December 1813 The Battle of St Pierre;
Brotherton's adventure at Hasparren

1813

Vittoria

12

In the spring of 1813 the allied army, British, Portuguese and Spaniards, numbering about 70,000 men, with 90 guns, bivouacked along the River Bayas. Opposite lay the French army, of about the same strength but with 150 guns, bivouacked along the River Zadorra. By the direction of his advance, Wellington had now forced the French to evacuate Santander, where his store ships were already alongside. Having turned the Ebro and brought the French to bay, he now intended to drive in their right and cut them off from the Bayonne road – their main line of communication with France.

The French were well-aware of Wellington's intentions – though not how he planned to carry them out. Their positions along the Zadorra in front of Vittoria ran almost parallel to the Bayonne road. Their left, under General Gazan, rested on the Heights of Puebla, then extending past the village of Arinez to the Zadorra near Margarita. A second line under General D'Erlon supported Gazan's right, between Arinez and Hermandad. The right, under General Reille, was in position north of Vittoria watching the passage of the Zadorra by the Bilbao road. The French cavalry corps was in position between the two flanks, and all high ground and villages of tactical importance were strongly held.

165

1813

After having a good look at these dispositions during the 20th June, Wellington decided to attack in four columns – the right, the right and left centres, and the left. The right, commanded by Sir Rowland Hill, was directed against the Heights of Puebla. The two centre columns were to act under Wellington's personal command, and the left, under Graham, was to attack along the Bilbao road and secure the bridges north of Vittoria – which the French had left intact.

The battle opened at 10 o'clock on the morning of the 21st June, 1813, when the sound of Graham's guns on the Bilbao road turned all French eyes in that direction. At the same moment, Hill advanced against the Puebla Heights. All of Wellington's movements were carried out with astonishing precision, and such set-backs as inevitably occurred during a general engagement so fiercely contested were immediately rectified by a combination of Wellington's genius and the valour of his troops. The only matter for criticism on his conduct of the operations is the lack of clear orders to the cavalry, who were distributed between the four columns with no other directions than to support the infantry. In fact, they were allowed to do much as they liked, riding about, seeking opportunities to charge, and in the end getting so mixed up that their pursuit of the beaten enemy was not as effective as it should have been.

The 14th were in Victor Alten's Light Brigade, consisting of themselves, and the 1st and 2nd Hussars of the King's German Legion. The Brigade was under Hill's command on the right flank, and, having crossed the Zadorra at Puebla de Arganzon and secured the Puebla Pass, stayed in position astride the road to Vittoria while Hill's infantry – the 71st H.L.I., 50th and 92nd Highlanders – battled for the possession of the Heights. When these had been secured, after some very hard fighting, Hill moved through the Pass and captured the village of Subijana de Alava on the far side, while Alten's Brigade advanced on his left. A French counter-attack on the village failed, but they came on again several times, until the field was covered with their fallen and the visibility obscured by a dense pall of smoke from the black powder, so that no-one knew how the day went. The ground was too rough and broken to be suitable for cavalry, and the 14th, although in the thick of the fighting, were never able to form line or get out of a trot. As Hill's column began to work round the enemy flank, and the French drew back on Vittoria, the cavalry followed up however, and the 14th eventually became mixed-up with the Household Cavalry and Ponsonby's Brigade in the centre columns.

By early afternoon all of Wellington's army was across the Zadorra and the French were beaten. They made a desperate stand round Arinez, but Wellington was there in person to throw them back, just as Reille had commenced to retreat before Graham's attack on the French right. The end came at about six o'clock when Hill attacked the last enemy position on the high ground between Armentia and Ali, about a mile to the west of Vittoria. After fighting gallantly in this last stand, the French at last fled in disorder, leaving all their guns and baggage on the field, and the 14th, with several other light cavalry regiments, rode through Vittoria and chased them up the road to Pampluna.

As already mentioned, the cavalry pursuit was unco-ordinated and the British regiments were in almost as much disorder as those of the French. The French baggage-train, consisting of thousands of carriages filled with women, children, looted art treasures and Spanish doubloons, had been formed up on the road beyond Vittoria but had not had time to get on the move. It had become held up in the fantastic traffic-jams caused by thousands of vehicles of all descriptions trying to force their way through the masses of soldiers, civilians, camp followers and animals which blocked the roads leading out of the town. The leading elements of the British Army then arrived on the scene, both cavalry and infantry, and in a state of disorganisation not much better than the French. It seems that a part of the 18th Hussars rode against the royal escort, which was the only formed body of enemy in sight, and one of them fired a pistol through the carriage window. The King jumped out and mounted his horse, escaping in the turmoil with his dragoons. There was then some attempt made by the British soldiers to ransack the carriage, for a corporal of the 18th fought a drummer of the 87th for the possession of the King's baton. Discipline, however, must have then been restored, for the King's possessions, documents and looted works of art were secured and safely handed over to General Headquarters, including the baton which, after being repaired, was sent home with Wellington's despatches for presentation to the Prince Regent. A notable exception was the King's silver chamber-pot, engraved with his coat of arms, which was secured by a patrol of the 14th. Because, no doubt, the sight of this particular domestic utensil usually causes some amusement, especially under such circumstances as these, no objections seem to have been raised to its retention by the 14th. As it was believed to have been a present to his brother by the Emperor Napoleon it was known as 'the Emperor', and so, in the Peninsular Army the 14th, as its custodians, became known as 'the

1813

'The Emperor' – the silver chamber-pot which came into the possession of the 14th Light Dragoons after the Battle of Vittoria. As its custodians the 14th thus became known by the nickname of 'the Emperor's Chambermaids'.

Emperor's Chambermaids', a nickname which apparently gave much pleasure to the regiment at that time. Actually, it was probably the carriage itself which was the imperial gift, and of which the chamber-pot formed one of the regular fittings – a *pot de voiture*, as the French would call it. During the century and a half since the Battle of Vittoria it has accompanied the regiment wherever it has gone, together with its original linen napkin, becoming a kind of mascot, and used as a loving-cup on special occasions in the officers' mess.

The value of the artistic treasures, pictures, gold and silver plate, and specie captured after the battle was enormous, and its honest application would have greatly eased Wellington's financial problems in the conduct of war, besides benefiting all ranks of the army. Before he could get his hands on it in a proper manner, however, it had nearly all been looted. This put him into a frenzy of rage, during which he described his soldiers as 'the scum of the earth'. Very few of his fighting men had in fact managed to fill their pockets. While they were following up the French, the treasures were looted by the followers, such as the commissaries and other non-combatants, and the Spanish peasants. In the cavalry regiments it was the farriers who were the rogues. They were well-known to be such, for, according to Brotherton, it was their usual practice when the regiment was passing through a village or township to hang behind and see what they could pick up, under the pretence of shoeing horses. They carried their loot in the 'churns', or leather buckets fixed to their saddle-bows, in which they were supposed to keep their tools and medicaments. In the 14th they were caught out on this occasion, for shortly after the regiment had off-saddled at Pampluna, Colonel Hervey suddenly ordered the *Rouse and Assembly* to be sounded, and when the regiment had paraded, formed it in a square and ordered the farriers to dismount in the middle, much to the jubilation of the assembled troops. A search of their churns then revealed a great quantity of jewellery and other portable items of value, all of which was later sold by auction and the proceeds fairly divided throughout the regiment. It did not apparently occur even to Hervey that it ought to have been handed in to Army Headquarters, but anyway his soldiers certainly deserved some reward after all their efforts, especially as they had had no pay for several months. The plunder was apparently nearly all sold at regimental auctions throughout the army, and the proceeds shared among the members of the regiments which had captured it. Normally, all such legitimate plunder captured after a victory was disposed of centrally or sent home for Treasury valuation, after which prize-money was shared out according to rank. It is surprising that Wellington did not insist on this being carried out, although his failure to do so profited the lower ranks at the expense of the generals, who would otherwise have found themselves the richer by many thousands of pounds.

After the brief halt necessary to secure the chamber-pot, the 14th did not again draw rein until they caught up with the French rear-guard on the 24th June, about six miles from Pampluna. The regiment attacked, supported by two troops of Horse Artillery led by Major Ross, RHA, and a charge was made by Brotherton's squadron capturing an ammunition tumbril which the French, who had lost nearly all their reserves of ammunition at Vittoria,

1813

could very ill-spare. The pursuit was then halted at Pampluna, where the 14th billeted with their horses too worn-out to go further, while the French continued along the main road and entered the Pyrenees by the Pass of Roncesvalles. In Pampluna was one of their fortresses which, with those of Santona and San Sebastian, would have to be reduced before Wellington would be able to establish himself along the frontier and carry the war into France.

In a campaign so ably conducted as that of Vittoria, few criticisms are possible. Almost the only one made by military critics is on Wellington's use of the cavalry which should, had it been given sounder directions, have cut out General Gazan's division and stopped it from reaching the Pampluna road.

It is certainly undeniable that the cavalry was not effectively used. The reason given in Wellington's despatch is that 'the nature of the ground did not allow of the cavalry being generally engaged.' The ground was in fact very rough and rocky, and covered with woods, vineyards and streams, so that the cavalry would have been at a grave disadvantage against the enemy infantry had they been put in too early. This, however, was quite a usual aspect of any attack against a prepared position, and it was the general practice under such circumstances to hold the cavalry in reserve or for the protection of the flanks. That this was not done at Vittoria was no doubt due to the exceptional length of the frontage, so that Wellington was only able to keep personal control of the centre and was obliged to divide the cavalry up between the four separate columns to enable each commander to act independently as opportunity offered.

Having retired across the Pyrenees, King Joseph re-formed his army along the Bidassoa, where he was joined by other French forces, including those of General Foy who, after making a stand at Tolosa, was attacked by Graham and forced to retreat through San Sebastian. General Clausel, who had marched on Vittoria from Logrono too late to enter the battle, was also driven off through Saragossa, escaping across the Pyrenees with the loss of all his artillery. The only French forces then remaining in Spain were those of Marshal Suchet, and the garrisons of San Sebastian and Pampluna. The siege of the former fortress was commenced on the 9th July, while the latter was blockaded. An expedition including the 20th Light Dragoons under Sir John Murray having failed to take Tarragona, the blockade of Pampluna was liable to be broken at any moment by Suchet marching to its relief, but this possibility was accepted by Wellington, who proceeded with his plans for carrying the war into France.

1813

Dealing with Generals Foy and Clausel temporarily diverted Wellington from keeping up pressure on King Joseph, but on the 3rd July he arrived at Pampluna and sent Sir Rowland Hill's corps forward to drive the French from the valley of Bastan, with a view to securing the Pass of Maya, the possession of which was essential for an invasion of France. On the 4th July, the 14th, riding ahead of Hill's leading brigade, fell in with the French at Almandoz, but they offered little resistance and withdrew through Aniz to Ciga. They proved to belong to General Gazan's corps, and Gazan was in exceedingly low spirits after his trouncing at Vittoria, where his wife had been captured. (She was returned to him immediately, under a flag of truce.) However, he showed more spirit after Hill's advanced guard had arrived at Ciga, which he re-took with a counter-attack and established a strong position covering it. Hill brought up another brigade, and Wellington himself arrived on the 5th July, while the patrols of the 14th were reconnoitring. Wellington, who never had any scruples about interfering in the conduct of operations by one of his subordinates, soon had the French on the run by developing threats against their flanks, and although Gazan had expressed his determination to defend the Pass of Maya to the last man if necessary, he was again outflanked and obliged to retire across the frontier at Ainhoa, leaving Wellington in possession of the Pass on the 8th July. He had achieved his object by manoeuvring rather than fighting, and the British casualties amounted only to one hundred and twenty-nine, while Gazan lost three hundred and forty-four.

On learning of the French defeat at Vittoria, Napoleon, who was at Dresden, ordered Marshal Soult, who was with him, to travel with all haste to King Joseph's headquarters at Bayonne, take over supreme command and 're-establish the Imperial business in Spain, and save Pancorbo, Pampluna and San Sebastian.' Soult arrived at Bayonne at the beginning of July, and by the 15th had assumed command of the French Armies of Spain. A rough, unpleasant sort of man, he was a master of strategy, but no match for Wellington on the actual battlefield. His arrival put new heart into the French, and his offensive tactics caused some temporary inconvenience to Wellington who, when he saw how things were going, sent a warning to Hill to expect attacks on the mountain passes, especially at Maya, where the 14th were holding the outpost line and 'posts of correspondence'.

The 14th were now brigaded with their old comrades of the 'forty-five rebellion, the 13th Light Dragoons, under Major-

1813

General Long. The two regiments were so battle-worn that they were known in the army as 'the Ragged Brigade', but they were of very different stuff from their unfortunate predecessors, who had been given such a rough time by Prince Charlie's Highlanders. To merit such a soubriquet in the Peninsular Army, which was far from fastidious over its attire, implies that their appearance at this time must have been ruffianly in the extreme, but they were disciplined and experienced fighting men, hard and fit, only, like their horses, showing more bones than flesh. There was no grazing to be had on the heights of Maya, and all forage had to be sent up in ox-wagons like the men's rations, which meant that both men and horses were almost permanently on a starvation diet and ready to eat anything. Brotherton's Arab mare, Fatima, developed a taste for raw beef and caused much ill-feeling by stealing from the soldiers' meagre supplies, which they had to hang up in trees out of her reach – she was too much of an aristocrat to endure being tied up. She was never picquetted in bivouac, but slept beside her master, whom she was always careful not to disturb, Brotherton recalling that she would look to see if he was asleep or not before deciding that it was safe to turn over or stand up.

Soult's plan was to force Wellington's right by making simultaneous attacks through the passes at Roncesvalles and Maya; then relieving the besieged fortresses of San Sebastian and Pampluna. On the 22nd July, Wellington learned that he had arrived at St Jean-Pied-de-Port with two divisions, which were evidently to attack the passes, but he judged that this action was a feint to draw attention from the French right, and so awaited further developments before making any major move.

On the arrival of Reille's French division at Maya on the 25th July, the 14th were brought back into reserve, for the ground was impossible for cavalry action. A desperate and bloody infantry battle then ensued, lasting two days, during which the 14th were employed in taking the wounded to the rear, slung across their horses and suffering extremely. The Pass of Maya was held by two weak British brigades without any central direction – for the divisional commander had not expected an attack, and had gone elsewhere. They were eventually opposed by three whole French divisions and were withdrawn by the order of Sir Rowland Hill, after their ammunition had run out and they had been reduced to rolling boulders down on the enemy.

Roncesvalles was likewise abandoned, and Soult advanced on Pampluna, but he was out-manoeuvred and defeated by Wellington at Sorauren on the 30th July. The 14th who had been in close action covering Wellington's movements, were again used for bringing the wounded out of action on this day, but a charge was made by Brotherton's squadron during an attack on a French post at Arestegui. After the battle Soult retired through Lisasso through the pass of Dona Maria to Santesteban, closely pressed by Wellington endeavouring to head him off. The French army fell into confusion and part of it was severely mauled in the Baztan valley during the 1st and 2nd August. Wellington, however, who had arrived at Santesteban, was nervous of becoming too closely engaged in the valley, as he knew that General Foy's corps was somewhere on his right. It appeared in fact, that Foy did send reconnoitring parties towards the valley, and decided not to commit himself after seeing British cavalry moving towards Maya. The British cavalry observed included, of course, the 14th, who, after taking part in the rout of the demoralised French along the Bidassoa, reached the Pass of Maya on the 5th August, and took up their former outpost line. Here the regiment remained until November, suffering great privations from the increasingly cold weather, while Wellington completed the reduction of San Sebastian and Pampluna and moved his army across the Bidassoa. By this time, the mountain passes were knee-deep in snow and the troops holding them reduced to a very low scale of rations indeed. It is doubtful if any beefsteaks were available during this period for Fatima to steal, and it cannot be imagined that she would have taken kindly to horseflesh like the soldiers. She would therefore have been reduced to occasional handfuls of grain and a chew at her saddlery and blanket, which was the usual fare of the humble troop horses.

The army was short, not only of food, but of every other commodity including clothing and ammunition. It is astonishing in fact, that it held together, for its condition was undoubtedly far worse than that of the French. Wellington has been criticised for not following Soult into France immediately, once he had got him on the run, but the reason, of course, was that he had run out of supplies and that his starving soldiers were becoming difficult to hold. They were deserting in quite large numbers in search of food and warmth, and had he led them forward before he had managed to get them fed, they might well have deserted *en masse* as soon as they arrived in the fertile lands of southern France. Plundering, desertion and other acts of indiscipline are subjects which are not generally mentioned in regimental records, and their prevalence can only be deduced from Wellington's continual fulminations about them. It is as well to remember, however, that they were a constant feature of all wars and in all

1813

armies up to and including that of the Crimea, after which the administrative services of an army received as much attention as its tactical efficiency and skill at arms. In 1813 that stage had not been reached, and the hardships of a British soldier's life in the Pyrenees were every bit as bad as those suffered by his descendants in the trenches before Sebastopol.

By the middle of October, the supply problem had been overcome, but it had been overtaken by that of the weather. Hill's corps along the summit of the Pyrenees could not move because of the snow, and the rest of the army was bogged down in continually heavy rain which, wrote Wellington, 'will destroy us if it lasts much longer'. His first objective was to turn the French positions along the Nivelle, and Hill, having been relieved of his responsibilities at Roncesvalles, had concentrated around Maya preliminary to attacking towards Ainhoa. After several cancellations the advance commenced on the 10th November when Hill's corps descended from the Pyrenees before daybreak with Beresford's corps, to which a squadron of the 14th was attached, on the left. Soult, who had been expecting an attack for some weeks, was ready for it when it came, and the most desperate fighting ensued, lasting the whole day. The British soldiers were even fiercer in action than usual, for they were still hungry and knew very well that in victory lay their only hope of a square meal. Defeat, and a retreat up the grisly heights of Maya, was simply not to be thought of. Nevertheless, they had their work cut out to prevail over the French, who launched a counter-offensive which in some places brought them round the British rear, where they fell upon the baggage-train. The 14th in fact, actually saw their carts being ransacked without being able to get to their assistance. The regimental baggage was in the charge of an un-named Troop Sergeant-Major, who had been given this unpopular duty because of his nervousness in action. It was with some surprise, therefore, that the regiment watched him fight to the last in the most valiant manner, defending his charge against a whole battalion of *voltigeurs*; his death witnessed by his comrades with admiration, coupled with sorrow that they had so misjudged him.

The day ended with the French driven from their positions, and Wellington advancing down both sides of the Nivelle, while the 14th, with their detached squadron rejoined, moved on to Espelette. The chief sufferers from the loss of the baggage were the officers, who had lost everything they possessed, but all the regimental records, with the paymaster's and adjutant's books had disappeared which was a serious matter, although the soldiers, who never had any possessions other than those carried on their horses, were probably more amused than upset by the disaster. There were, no doubt, some regimental women and children with the baggage. No mention was made regarding their fate, so that presumably they survived and rejoined in due course.

After the battle on the Nivelle, Soult fell back upon Bayonne, leaving Generals Foy and D'Erlon guarding the approaches south of the River Nive, and General Paris north of the river near Mount Ursouia. Heavy and continuous rain brought operations almost to a halt. The 14th, who were on outpost duty around Espelette, were sent forward on the 12th November as cavalry of the advanced guard to Hill's corps, which had been ordered to demonstrate towards Ustaritz and Cambo, but the demonstration discovered nothing, except that any general advance was impossible until the weather cleared. The 14th had to struggle through mud which was up to their horses' knees, and sometimes up to the girths, while the fords at Cambo, where the regiment tried to cross the river, were running swift and deep. Two men and their horses were drowned, and the advanced guard was then recalled. But Wellington was anxious about the possibility of a surprise attack against his right from the direction of Cambo, and Hill had to make another attempt. This time the 14th made for the town bridge, but the French blew it when they saw them coming.

At this time Wellington was having trouble with the Spaniards, and to a lesser extent with the Portuguese, to say nothing of his own government, which would send him no money, give him no help, and seemed almost to have disassociated itself from his activities. However, he was never afraid of anyone, and never shrank from taking the sternest measures when necessary. After he sent the entire Spanish army, except one division, back into Spain and resigned his command of it, all three governments pulled themselves together and the crisis passed, but not until it had seriously disrupted Wellington's plans by delaying his advance and giving the French time to consolidate their defences.

The delay landed Wellington in an awkward tactical position, with his army cooped up between the Nive and Nivelle. He could not take the whole of it across the Nive without first taking Bayonne, which was impracticable at that stage; whereas if he only took part across, he would divide his forces and give Soult the advantage of interior lines. This, however, was the only alternative to withdrawing back across the Nivelle to avoid being attacked on unfavourable ground. He therefore accepted the risk entailed by a partial crossing and, having distracted Soult's

1813

attention by a feint towards Bayonne on the left bank of the Nive, made a crossing between Cambo and Ustaritz.

The 13th and 14th Light Dragoons were patrolling the left bank of the Nive near Cambo, when orders came to prepare to cross at dawn on the 9th December. The 14th were saddled up and sitting down in front of their horses, holding the reins, when the light from a signal beacon was observed just before dawn. The order came to mount and the regiment moved off with squadrons in file, plunging into the icy waters of the Nive at various known fords, where the river was running so deep from the incessant rain as to come well over the saddles. Vivian's Brigade was followed by Victor Alten's German Hussars and Ross's troop of horse artillery. While the cavalry were driving in the French picquets, Stewart's 2nd Infantry Division crossed the fords at Cambo, led by Cadogan's Brigade of the 50th, 71st H.L.I., and 92nd Highlanders. In support of Hill, Beresford crossed at the same time with the 3rd and 6th Divisions by pontoon bridges near Ustaritz, but the country was so waterlogged that progress was slow. While the cavalry moved westerly to watch the flank, the infantry fought their way to the Bayonne road and eventually took up a position between Lourbintoua and Ustaritz, in thick fog.

Although the passage of the Nive had thus been accomplished, and every possible effort had been made to keep the design secret, Soult had not been taken by surprise. His spies had kept him well informed of Wellington's intentions, and he had ordered a withdrawal on his left, being content to get his opponents divided on either side of the river, when he had every confidence of his ability to get the better of them under such favourable conditions. 'It seems to me,' he now wrote, 'that the enemy by extending his troops has lost the advantage of his numerical superiority, and I have resolved to attack him in the false position which he has taken up.' Having withdrawn his troops opposing Hill on the right bank of the Nive, he opened a major attack against the British forces remaining on the left flank. This, after heavy fighting during the 10th and 11th December was thrown back, so on the 12th December he made an attempt against Hill on the right bank. Wellington reinforced Hill with a division from the left bank, but during the night the bridge near Villefranque was swept away by the flooded river, so that further communication between the two halves of his army was impeded at a very critical moment.

Hill's Light Cavalry Brigade, consisting of the 13th and 14th Light Dragoons, and now commanded by Colonel Hussey Vivian of the 7th Hussars, who had taken it over from Colquhoun Grant on the 24th November, was still over on the right flank, in the neighbourhood of Hasparren. On the 11th December, Brotherton's squadron had fallen in with an enemy convoy on the Bayonne road, near Mendione, about five miles to the south of Hasparren, and had driven off the escort, capturing four men and their horses in addition to the convoy which was carrying corn, wine and salt; the first two items at least, being a very welcome prize for cavalrymen. On the 12th Soult's Light Cavalry Division, supported by an infantry division, arrived at Hasparren on a reconnaissance in force. Vivian's Brigade fell back on Urcuray, where a Spanish division, reinforced by a British brigade, turned the French back on Hasparren. On the following morning, Soult made an attack along the right bank of the Nive, hoping to finish off Hill before Wellington could get reinforcements across the river.

The engagement which took place along the right bank of the Nive on the 13th December, 1813, is known as the Battle of St Pierre. Sir Rowland Hill, with 14,000 men, was faced in front by 35,000 Frenchmen. In his rear, the French Light Cavalry Division and General Paris's infantry division were being engaged before Hasparren by Vivian's Light Cavalry Brigade and Morillo's Spanish Division. Wellington, at Villefranque on the south bank of the Nive, was personally superintending the repair of the bridge, so that he could get three divisions across to the support of Hill. He was able to lead the 6th Division across shortly after mid-day, by which time Hill, after throwing in the last of his reserves into the bloodiest battle of the war, had won the day on his own. 'I'll be damned,' said Wellington, as he looked over the battlefield, 'if I have ever seen so many dead men before.'

Over in the west, the 13th and 14th Light Dragoons were almost as heavily outnumbered before Hasparren as were Hill's infantry at St Pierre. It is doubtful if the two regiments together numbered as many as seven hundred men, but they acted on the offensive nevertheless, and eventually succeeded in driving the enemy out of Hasparren. As was to be expected, Brotherton's squadron was well to the front during this desperate fighting. He was a great friend of Sir Hussey Vivian, the Brigadier, who demonstrated his friendship on this occasion by ordering Brotherton to charge the village in order to give him a chance to distinguish himself. 'A sort of forlorn hope,' was how Brotherton described his mission. It seems that he advanced in column of half squadrons, and discovered the 13th Chasseurs and Hussars of Chamboran posted behind a narrow bridge at the entrance to the village, upon which he ordered his trumpeter to sound the charge 'so that those behind who were to support should advance at the same time.' It is difficult to imagine what those in front could have made of the trumpet-call, for the bridge was too narrow to admit more than one horseman at a time, so that only Brotherton and his orderly, followed by Lieutenant Southwell ('a distinguished officer, who I had chosen to accompany me') were able to get across. Southwell's horse was shot under him, and the orderly had his bridle hand 'nearly chopped off' and was run through the body, leaving Brotherton to fight it out with the two French regiments all by himself. He was 'beloaboured with cuts and thrusts from all sides', but saved from being hacked to pieces by a buffalo hide cuirass of his own invention. After being wounded in the neck, thigh, right side and 'in the bottom', he felt that he had had enough, but as he had tied his sword to his wrist he had difficulty in intimating that he wished to surrender. Finally, after a blow on his helmet had nearly broken his nose, and 'a fellow cocked his pistol and put it to my head to blow out my brains', he remembered enough French to gasp out '*Je me rends!*' and was trussed up and galloped off to the rear. He was greatly assisted throughout this unequal combat by the mare Fatima, who did not leave all the fighting to her master, but used all four hooves to great advantage. Although the French had his wounds attended to, and treated him with kindness and respect, they took Fatima away to a stud-farm and he never saw her again. Also, according to Brotherton, they refused to release him in exchange for a captured French Major sent over by Vivian under a flag of truce.

While Brotherton was fighting for his life, Vivian brought up the brigade at a gallop and got into the village at various points, but the French decamped before he could rescue his friend. Why they should have retreated so precipitously is not clear, and it can only be supposed that they had received orders from Soult. They were followed up by Vivian's Brigade until they had crossed the Adour at Urt, after which the 13th and 14th Light Dragoons established posts along the left bank of the Joyeuse. Soult's new positions ran from Bayonne along the right bank of the Adour, and then south along the Bidouse river to St Palais. Wellington concentrated his forces before Bayonne, and along the Adour as far as Urt. The Joyeuse was left for the light cavalry to protect, and he made no attempt at this stage to gain contact with the enemy on the Bidouse. The campaign of 1813 thus ended.

179 Colonel John Townsend, commanding officer of the 14th Light Dragoons, 1829–45. He served throughout the Peninsular War mainly as a troop commander until he was taken prisoner near Pau in southern France. He took part in the attack on New Orleans, December 1814–January 1815.

The Peninsular and South of France 1808/1814

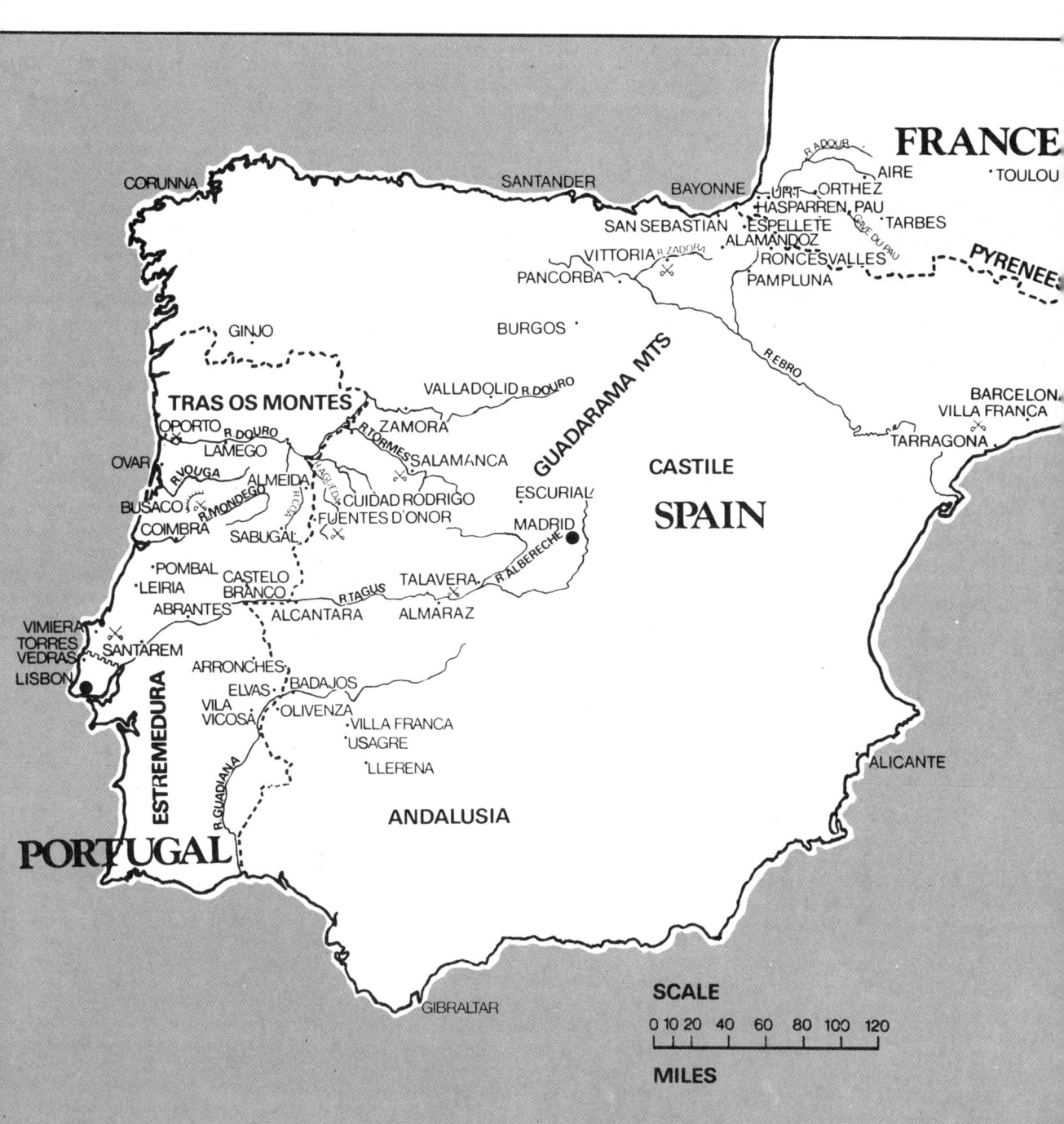

January and February 1814 The Passage of the Gaves
27th February 1814 The Battle of Orthez
March and April 1814 The advance to Toulouse
18th August 1814 End of the War

The Final Advance

13

1814

The campaign of 1814 opened with Wellington far outnumbering Soult, for Napoleon, who was now in sore straits, had withdrawn large numbers of Soult's old soldiers and replaced them with young conscripts, most of whom had promptly deserted. After spending January reconnoitring the defences of Bayonne, Wellington had concluded that any direct assault would be too costly, and that he must endeavour to pass between the city and the coast by bridging the Adour below the city. In order to distract Soult's attention from this bold project, he commenced the outflanking movement known as the Passage of the Gaves, in which Beresford's and Hill's corps worked round the extreme French left, along the base of the Pyrenees and across the rivers Joyeuse and Bidouse, and the Gaves de Mauleon, d'Oleron and de Pau.

The weather during January was exceptionally severe, and the light cavalry along the Joyeuse had a most miserable time, bivouacked in deep mud and cold, drenching rain and sleet, and deficient, as usual, in clothing, food and forage. Brushes with the French were frequent, for the forage had to be cut under their noses. It consisted chiefly of furze, which was 'cut and pounded, and made into a sort of paste'. More than ever before, was the soubriquet of the 'Ragged Brigade' justified. In appearance, both

1814

officers and men were nothing more than a collection of bearded ragamuffins, mounted on horses which looked like something out of the Apocalypse. They did, however, occasionally get a day or two under cover in Urt or one of the other villages, and there was the great consolation of the fact that, this being French territory, there always seemed to be plenty of good brandy about, even though there was no food. Once at least, they were visited by Wellington himself, immaculate and magnificently mounted as usual. He 'saw for himself the state of affairs', but appears to have made no comment. Obviously they must all have been sober at the time, or he would certainly have had one of his outbursts.

In such villainous weather operations were out of the question, but the moment it showed signs of clearing at the beginning of February, the army moved into position, ready to advance. On the left, Hope's corps closed up to the south west of Bayonne. In the centre Beresford deployed between the Nive and Adour, facing towards Bayonne with his right at Urt; while Hill assembled behind the Joyeuse, with an advanced guard formed at La Bastide Clairance. 'The Ragged Brigade', still consisting of the 13th and 14th, was sent out along the St Palais road to cover these preparations.

On the 14th February, Hill advanced his right and drove the French back on St Palais, and then across the Bidouse to Sauveterre. This involved heavy fighting which all fell on the infantry, for the country was impossible for cavalry operations and the Light Brigade was kept in the neighbourhood of St Palais in order to disrupt the French communications with St Jean-Pied-de-Port. It was, however, brought into action on the 17th, against its old opponents of Pierre Soult's cavalry division, but as the French were too numerous for Fane's brigade to charge in the open, and they made no attempt to charge themselves, the affair developed into a duel between the opposing horse artillery, during which the 14th and 13th, stationed on open ground with squadrons in column, were 'for some time much exposed' to the enemy cannon-balls, which whistled past from every direction. It was customary on the battlefields of the day to profess an indifference to cannon-balls, for there was in fact little that could be done about them and no regiment, cavalry or infantry, could afford to change its formation or take cover while in close proximity to the enemy, merely on account of a few round-shot ploughing through its ranks, although their effect, observed at close quarters, must have been very unnerving. The horses in general stood the fire with the same stoicism as their masters, although Wellington said that his own charger, Copenhagen, 'winced and leaned over' when a round-shot passed close by. 'Which only goes to show,' added the Duke, 'what damned fools horses are, for of course, when one hears the shot, the danger is past.'

On the 18th February, Wellington commenced to swing round his centre and right, pivoting on Urt, where Beresford started to build a bridge of boats. Hill's Corps then concentrated between the Saisson, or Gave de Mauleon, and the Gave d'Oleron. At this time Soult changed his headquarters from Bayonne to Orthez, being worried about Wellington's movements among the Gaves. He appears to have arrived at Orthez just as Wellington, satisfied with the progress of his enveloping movement, returned to St Jean-de-Luz to direct the operations against Bayonne, leaving Hill in charge on the right. The naval squadron, however, on whose help he was dependent for getting across the mouth of the Adour, had had to stand out to sea in order to ride out the winter gales. He therefore decided to leave Bayonne alone for the moment, and hastened back to his right. All this galloping to-and-fro greatly confused Soult, who seems to have been keeping Wellington under very close observation.

Wellington crossed the Gave D'Oleron on the 24th February, by making various feints along the 24 mile front, which enabled the light cavalry brigade to splash through the icy fords at Villenave and head towards Orthez, followed by most of Hill's corps. The French fell back before it, for Soult was completely bewildered. He had opposed the crossing of the Gave at all the wrong places and, in fact, fell in so well with Wellington's plans that he might almost have been acting under his orders. The light cavalry bivouacked that night along the barren slopes between Loubieng and Castentner, with the 13th on the right and the 14th on the left. It was a clear night, with the whole countryside covered in a mantle of snow and ice. Behind a screen of picquets and vedettes, the cavalrymen huddled round their watch-fires or stamped up and down, too cold and hungry to sleep. Forage parties went out but came back empty-handed, and a welcome diversion was afforded by Captain Townsend of the 14th, when he rode in with his troop escorting a French officer whom he had captured during the day, while out with the vanguard.

Dawn came as a relief, when the cavalry mounted and moved on, hoping that the day would bring them something to eat, but after an hour's ride they found themselves looking down across the Gave de Pau upon the town of Orthez, and upon thousands of French troops moving along both sides of the Gave. The order came to dismount, after which picquets were detailed and patrols sent out, and there they waited for the time being, saddled-up and expecting action at any moment. During the day the whole of Hill's corps arrived, headed by a Portuguese Brigade, whose guns unlimbered and opened fire on the defences before the bridge at Orthez, while a couple of their battalions moved down to the Gave. Soult had destroyed all bridges except the main one at Orthez, and apparently thought that the Gave was therefore impassable, but Beresford's infantry forded it at various places during the day, and some pontoon bridges were built. The French then concentrated around Orthez, where Wellington attacked them on the 27th February.

The Battle of Orthez opened by an attack against the French right, while Hill engaged the defenders of the main bridge, at the same time sending the cavalry up-river to look for a crossing. The opposing armies were about equal in number, but whereas Soult had his concentrated and strongly posted, Wellington's was widely deployed and divided by the Gave. The opening attack failed, and defeat was only averted by Wellington's surpassing skill on the battlefield. Even so, it is doubtful if he could have managed to turn it into victory had not the Ragged Brigade found a ford at Souars, which enabled Hill to turn the French left. This movement threatened Soult's line of retreat at St Sever, and caused him to break off the engagement. The 13th and 14th Light Dragoons galloped forward in an effort to reach the bridge of Soult de Navailles and so stop the retreating French from crossing the Luy de Bearn, but they could not get much speed out of their starved and exhausted horses, and when they came in sight of the bridge they found the French already in possession of it, with their artillery posted on the heights across the river. The round-shot knocked over a number of men and horses, and the brigade had to be withdrawn under cover, but continued the pursuit on the following day, riding about twenty miles and taking many prisoners. The 14th reached the Adour on the 1st March, and crossed it by a ford, but the pursuit was called off after they had ridden about three miles, and they eventually bivouacked in pouring rain along the south bank of the river. Soult continued his retreat and eventually took up a position near Aire, across the road to Toulouse and covering those to Bordeaux and Pau. Bayonne had to be left to its fate, for on the day before Orthez, a combined operation had put Wellington's men across the Adour on the seaward side of the city, and it was now closely invested and beyond help.

During his retreat, Soult destroyed all bridges across the

numerous streams and rivers in his rear. This, combined with the exceptionally severe weather and lack of transport in the British army, held up the pursuit. The continuous heavy rain meanwhile turned the country into a morass, across which it was impossible for cavalry to operate other than on reconnaissance and protective duties. These, of course, often brought it into close contact and the 14th had many skirmishes with the French cavalry and infantry. Generally, however, after finding the enemy positions, the British cavalry had to draw off to one side and leave the infantry to deal with the situation. This was a new experience for the cavalry, which as a rule had too much to do on the battlefield to be in a position to sit back and watch others. As there were no war-correspondents in those days, it is interesting to have an unbiased firsthand account of the conduct of Wellington's infantry, for it was against his principles ever to say anything nice about it himself. 'Our cavalry could only look on and admire their gallant conduct,' wrote an officer of the 13th, and this was the opinion generally held of the ragged and half-starved soldiers, who had carried their colours all the way from Lisbon without defeat.

On the 2nd March, the leading squadron of the 14th discovered the enemy positions before Aire and pointed them out to Hill, who had come forward with his staff, all of them digging their spurs into their horses to keep them going over the waterlogged ground. Hill brought up the infantry and turned the French right, after which they retired along both banks of the Adour towards Tarbes, abandoning all their magazines and stores. The Ragged Brigade followed up slowly, through rain, sleet and snow, arriving at Garlin, about ten miles south of Aire, on the 7th. Here they had a brush with some French cavalry who had ridden out from Conches along the parallel road to Aire on their left flank. Sir Rowland Hill came up and halted the brigade on an outpost line, supported by three infantry companies. He then brought up his whole corps, along a front between Garlin and St Mont, on the Adour, a proceeding which took three days.

Wellington was unable to press the pursuit at this time, having sent off Beresford's corps to receive the surrender of Bordeaux, which had declared for the Bourbons. This was the first major defection from the Emperor who, in the north, was being driven back on Paris by the armies of Russia, Austria and Prussia, but most of the inhabitants of southern France were now only too ready to follow Bordeaux' example. The news of these events brought Soult back on to the offensive, in a final effort to maintain Napoleon's authority, but a series of manoeuvres designed to outflank Wellington met with no success.

1814

At the same time that Beresford was sent to Bordeaux, General Fane was ordered to Pau, escorted by the 14th Light Dragoons, an infantry battalion and a couple of guns, with instructions to offer British assistance to the citizens should they decide to declare for Louis XVIII. They readily accepted this offer, and Fane withdrew, leaving Captain Townsend and his squadron in the town. Soult had meanwhile learned of Pau's intention to change sides, and sent a cavalry regiment to arrest the Mayor and Councillors. What happened then is obscure, and the only sure facts are that the French failed to arrest the Mayor and Councillors, but that they did succeed in capturing Townsend and four Dragoons. Obviously there was a fight of some kind in the centre of the town, following which the French retired without their quarry; but it seems likely that they surprised Townsend in his quarters, before he could get his boots on.

Townsend was captured on the 8th March. On the 10th, the Ragged Brigade reconnoitred towards Lembeye, and two days later fell in with vastly superior numbers of enemy cavalry on the road between Lembeye and Conches, before whom they fell back on Garlin. Supported by infantry and guns, they then drove the French back past Conches, carrying out two separate charges, in one of which Captain Babington was wounded and taken prisoner.

With Beresford returned from Bordeaux, Wellington then marched south in three columns. On the 19th an action was fought at Vic-de-Bigorre, lasting until nightfall, when the 13th and 14th Light Dragoons, very tired indeed, bivouacked in a wood in pouring rain, 'without baggage or tents'. Here they were joined, in the middle of the night, by the Royals and 3rd Dragoon Guards, forming a cavalry division under the command of General Fane. At daybreak the whole division mounted and forded the Adour, afterwards marching along the right bank upon Tarbes, led by the Ragged Brigade with the 14th in front. Most of the remainder of Hill's corps marched by the left bank.

Soult was by this time in full retreat to Toulouse, while Wellington was trying to head him off with the cavalry and so force him to stand and fight. He did not apparently realise at first that the countryside was so inundated that it was impossible for cavalry to move off the roads. Soult knew this full well, and planned his retreat accordingly behind a strong rearguard position at Tarbes. This was taken by the British infantry in an action 'short, but wonderfully fierce and violent', causing the French to continue their retreat in such haste as to fall into disorder.

1814

Wellington failed to exploit this situation, but followed up in a cautious and leisurely manner. This was partly due to the weather conditions, but chiefly to his uncertainty over the political situation following Napoleon's defeats in the north and the large French defections in the south. He was concerned in fact, that France might collapse into anarchy, and would have preferred to treat with the mighty Napoleon, rather than the ineffective Louis. The allied governments, however, insisted on the substitution of Napoleon by Louis before discussing peace, and Wellington held his hand accordingly, rather than become involved in what he felt to be a misguided policy.

After the conflict at Tarbes, the British cavalry was dispersed over a very wide front to ensure that Wellington was kept informed of all French movements, for he thought that it was not at all unlikely that Napoleon might come south in person and take over from Soult, in an attempt to form a strong front in the south of France. Fane's cavalry division continued under the command of Sir Rowland Hill, but the movements of the individual regiments are uncertain, and the 14th can only be pictured as advancing by squadrons, each with a picquet, commanded by an officer, several hundred yards in front, and all splashing along in threes through mud and water up to their hocks. They had several encounters with the French, during which they took many prisoners and had a few casualties themselves, both officers and men. A regimental memorial erected at Biarritz in 1882 gives the name of Lieutenant William Lyons and others killed at this time, but where they fell cannot be determined. Nor is it certain on what date the regiment first sighted the spires of Toulouse, and the last battlefield of the Peninsular War, but it was probably the 25th March, 1814.

Soult's defences at Toulouse were exceedingly formidable, and Wellington took his time over deciding how best to deal with them. The city lay astride the river Garonne, and the fortified suburb of St Cyprien on the left bank was covered by a line of French posts along the Touch tributary. These posts were ridden through by Hill's cavalry, which then reconnoitred south of the suburb, looking for crossing-places up-river of Toulouse. Hill then crossed the Garonne near Portet, but when Wellington found that the country was 'impracticable for the manoeuvres of an army on that side of the city,' the troops were recalled, and Hill took up a position facing St Cyprien. It is not certain whether or not his cavalry had crossed the Garonne at this time. Wellington then put Beresford's corps across to the north of Toulouse, but the pontoons went adrift and left Beresford

1814

isolated. Wellington appeared unmoved by this mishap, and as Soult made no attempt to take advantage of it, it seems that the position was not in fact as serious as it would appear to have been in theory.

The Battle of Toulouse took place on the 10th April, 1814, when, the waters of the Garonne having subsided enough to allow another bridge to be built, Wellington sent Beresford's corps on a dangerous flank march round the north of the city, while Picton made a feint attack along the right bank of the river and Hill attacked St Cyprien on the left bank. It was Hill's guns which commenced the engagement, between eight and nine o'clock, but his attack, like that of Picton's, was diversionary only and designed to draw Soult's attention away from Beresford. After driving the French before St Cyprien back under the cover of their main defences, Hill therefore held his hand in accordance with his orders. Beresford succeeded in his dangerous mission after a great deal of desperate fighting, and a lull then ensued while Wellington got up more ammunition and made arrangements for investing the city. During the night of the 11th April, however, Soult decamped, followed up by Beresford's cavalry. On the 12th April, Wellington entered Toulouse in triumph at the head of Fane's Ragged Brigade, followed by the rest of Hill's corps, being loudly cheered by the citizens, who were uncommonly glad to see the back of Soult whose undisciplined soldiers had given them a very rough time.

Although the 14th had not been given the opportunity of distinguishing themselves in any spectacular manner during the battle, the regiment had been far from idle, being in close action on the banks of the Garonne for most of the day. It is therefore not clear why the battle-honour, TOULOUSE, was not granted to the 14th, especially as their associates, the 13th, received it, but it was presumably due to some oversight, or to the failure to submit a claim in due course, as seems to have happened in the case of many other regiments in the field on that day. However, the honour of accompanying the Duke of Wellington over the 'great bridge' and into the city of Toulouse after nearly six years of fighting under his command, was a compensation which had been most fully deserved. It is a far cry from Lisbon to Toulouse, and the successful termination of the journey in the face of such mighty odds and under such adverse conditions was certainly a cause for celebration and congratulation. DOURO, TALAVERA, FUENTES D'ONOR, SALAMANCA, VITTORIA, PYRENEES, ORTHES, PENINSULA, are the honours on the guidon of the 14th/20th King's Hussars which commemorate the Peninsular War, a

1814

conflict which the consistent skill of the commander, and the valour of his troops, render outstanding in military history.

The Battle of Toulouse, fought and won at the expense of a terrible amount of bloodshed on both sides, proved to have been unnecessary. The Emperor Napoleon had already abdicated, and peace had been arranged with a provisional government in Paris, but Wellington did not learn of this until the 12th April, when emissaries arrived at his headquarters in Toulouse. The Duke sent them to inform Soult who, however, refused to believe them and continued to carry out warlike dispositions. This alarmed Wellington, who feared that his old opponent was trying to start a civil war, and he set off after him accordingly. Fortunately, just as the outposts were about to engage, Soult received orders from Napoleon's staff, and hostilities ended on the 18th April.

Three days after the Battle of Toulouse, a sortie was made by the French garrison in Bayonne, which had not accepted the decision of the inhabitants to acknowledge the Bourbons. The village of St Etienne was captured by the enemy, and although it was soon recaptured by Sir John Hope's corps, the incident no doubt increased Wellington's fears of civil war breaking out. Fane's cavalry brigade – the Ragged Brigade – of the 13th and 14th Light Dragoons, was sent off to Bayonne, instead of accompanying Sir Rowland Hill's corps in the final advance against Soult, but as all fighting ended with the official announcement of peace, the brigade was diverted to Mont-de-Marsan, and there remained before embarking at Bayonne for the United Kingdom.

The 14th, which had embarked for the Peninsula at a strength of 770 men and 720 horses, returned after five-and-a-half years in the field with 561 men and 278 horses. During the Peninsular War it had, of course, received frequent drafts of men and horses. Its total casualties during the war, from all causes, were 654 men and 1,564 horses.

1812 and 1813 The 20th land in Spain
April 1813 Action around Villena
June to September 1813 The 20th at Tarragona and in the retreat to Villa Franca
1814 The 20th land in Italy, and advance to Genoa
May 1814 They return home
December 1814 to January 1815 The 14th at New Orleans
March and May 1815 They return home

Sideshows

14

IN 1812 Wellington had become anxious about the intentions of Marshal Suchet, who commanded a French army in Valencia, and sent an urgent message to Lord William Bentinck, the commander-in-chief in Sicily and Naples, asking for a diversion to be made on the east coast of Spain, so as to stop Suchet from marching north. Bentinck had become involved in a maze of intrigue while trying to conduct his own operations in southern Italy, and was none too willing to send troops to the assistance of Wellington, with whom he was to a certain extent in professional competition. However, in accordance with directives from the British government, to the effect that Spain and not Italy was to be regarded as the main theatre of operations, he reluctantly embarked a force of about 7,000 men, including 167 of the 20th Light Dragoons, which, after a short stay in Minorca, landed at Alicante on the 9th August.

The convoy first made for Barcelona, and dropped anchor in the Bay of Blanes, just out of range of the French shore batteries. Most of Suchet's army was in the area and to the south, and the sight of the vast numbers of French troops marching about on the shore could not have been very heartening for the British soldiers in the transports, for they were, as usual, absolutely in the dark concerning the projected operations. The squadron of the

1813

20th was embarked in the 'horse landing-craft' and made for the beach, preceded by naval cutters taking soundings. No doubt to the considerable relief of the soldiers, they were then recalled as soon as they came under fire, and re-embarked in their transport. At nightfall, the convoy quietly made sail and steered for Alicante which, with a strong northerly wind, it reached in eighteen hours.

At Alicante, the landing was unopposed and General Maitland, who commanded the expedition, advanced to Elda, about eighteen miles to the north. He then heard that Soult had joined Suchet, and that one or both of them were on the march for Valencia, so he withdrew to Alicante intending to re-embark, but was stopped by Wellington. He had been joined by two Spanish divisions, which brought his force up to 18,000 men, supported by a large fleet of transports and men-of-war. His mere presence on the east coast of Spain therefore had a considerable effect on the French plans, and prevented their armies from combining against Wellington. Large forces had to be sent by Suchet to keep an eye on Maitland, who unfortunately was taken ill and in no condition to undertake any but purely defensive operations. As far as the squadron of the 20th was concerned, the remaining months of 1812 were spent mostly on outpost duty, with occasional skirmishes in only one of which, at Vicente on the 17th August, were any casualties suffered.

Under further pressure from Wellington, channelled through the British government, Lord William Bentinck then embarked two more detachments for Alicante. The first, sailing on the 14th November, included thirteen of the 20th Light Dragoons, and the second, which followed on the 5th December, the regimental headquarters and another squadron. The dispositions of the regiment in January, 1813, were then: headquarters and two squadrons (four troops) at Alicante; two troops at Palermo; two troops at Maidstone; a detachment in the Ionian Islands, and four dragoons attached to the Russian Army with Colonel Sir Robert Wilson. The colonelcy of the regiment at the beginning of 1813 passed from Lord William Bentinck to Sir Stapleton Cotton (afterwards Field-Marshal Lord Combermere), Wellington's famous cavalry commander during the Peninsular War. Stapleton Cotton had apparently been trying to get a peerage for a long time and had been nicknamed in the army 'Lion d'Or'.

The British and allied force at Alicante, after four changes of command in as many months was, in February, 1813, taken over by Sir John Murray. Up to that time it had done little in the way of fighting, for lack of supplies and trouble among the Spanish and Italian elements had rendered it unfit to take the field against Suchet, who had gone over to the defensive with an entrenched camp at Mogente and forward posts at Alcoy. Murray had little confidence in his ill-equipped force of five different nationalities – British, German, Italian, Spanish and Portuguese – but, feeling obliged to take action of some kind, advanced against Alcoy on the 3rd March, when the 20th Light Dragoons drove in the French outposts. Some desultory fighting followed, resulting in the French withdrawing from Alcoy, but Murray was too nervous to follow them up and, when he heard that Suchet had arrived in the area to take command in person, he concentrated at Castalla, leaving the Spaniards to look after Alcoy, Yecla and Elda.

In Castalla, which was an ancient Moorish fortified town, the 20th spent some weeks on fatigue duties repairing the defences – work which was normally somewhat beneath the dignity of light cavalrymen. They could not have been as 'ragged' in appearance at this time as the 14th, for they had been issued with new uniforms before leaving Sicily. These were of the blue hussar pattern, which did not show dirt and wear and tear like the old scarlet so that, even in the field, the regiment presented a reasonably smart appearance from some distance off. The change in colour appears to have excited no comment in the regiment, or in the British Army generally, which has a traditional indifference to its appearance in wartime. The French, however, who since the days of Marlborough had paid the British Army the compliment of keeping a special look-out for the activities of the redcoats on the battlefield, were irritated by so unnecessary an addition to the confusion which was already so marked a feature of military operations.

On the 11th April, Suchet decided that he would have to resume the offensive to prevent any further build-up of the British base at Alicante. He commenced by throwing the Spaniards out of Yecla, then marching against Villena, also defended by the Spaniards. Murray sent his cavalry against him, supported by an infantry brigade under Colonel Adam. The 20th got to horse at dawn on the 12th April, and rode out on what Sergeant Landsheit described as 'altogether one of the most agreeable excursions in which I had ever taken part.' The feeling of well-being which prompted this remark appears to have been derived from the fact that, for once in a way, both men and horses were fresh and well-fed, and so able to appreciate the beauty of the countryside on a glorious spring day. In fact, all thoughts of war and its horrors appear to have vanished from their minds, and

1813

the 20th were dismounted on a hill north of Vallena, enjoying an excellent picnic lunch, when the French advanced across the plain in front of them. Then came 'the sharp, stern order', the long note on the trumpet, and the 20th rode down on to the plain, accompanied by the Brunswick and 'Foreign' Hussars (commanded by Captain Jacks of the 20th, with Landsheit as his Sergeant-Major) and followed by the 27th Regiment, an Italian regiment, the Calabrian Free Corps and two companies of the King's German Legion. It was a motley sort of force with which to oppose Suchet, and its only elements which could be trusted not to run for it were the British and Germans. Adam, however, had been ordered not to engage too closely, and Suchet was also being cautious.

After the first shots had been fired, Adam withdrew slowly through Villena to the Pass of Biar, where he made a stand in order to give Murray time to form up behind him, covering Castella. The 20th, by galloping about continuously over rough ground, skirmishing and threatening the enemy flanks, had exhausted their horses and, like the Brunswick and Foreign Hussars, had to dismount during the defence of Biar. After some very hard fighting, Adam withdrew back to a position in the centre of Murray's main body, which was by that time drawn up in a strong position before Castella. The cavalry was then sent to the right flank – Murray's left flank being entrenched. Suchet advanced on the 13th April, and a general engagement ensued in which the French got the worst of it and retired in disorder. The small body of cavalry, 20th, Brunswick and Foreign Hussars, numbering not more than four hundred men, had again exhausted its horses in charges against the French left. The horses, it appears, had been neither fed nor watered for over twenty-four hours, and during the action had had to take as many jumps over ditches and fences as in the normal hunting field. They were consequently unable to take advantage of the French disordered retreat, and Suchet managed to get back to the Pass of Biar. When Murray advanced against him, however, he made no attempt to stand and fell right back to Fuente de la Aiguerra.

Shortly after the action of Castella, orders arrived from Wellington for Murray to embark ten thousand men and lay siege to the fortress of Tarragona. This must have given him something of a shock, for he was not one of the more thrusting types of soldier. However, after being heavily reinforced by Spanish regular troops, he embarked over seventeen thousand men at the end of May, including 828 cavalrymen of the 20th Light Dragoons, Brunswick and Foreign Hussars. Escorted by three ships of the line, the convoy sailed on the 31st May and dropped anchor in Salou Bay, eight miles south-west of Tarragona, on the 2nd June.

On landing, Murray sent off a brigade to occupy the pass of Balaguer, some eight miles to the south, and thus protected his operations from an advance from Tortosa. The cavalry then marched right round the fortress and established a line of picquets to the north, while the infantry and siege train commenced to dig parallels and build batteries before Fort Royal on the west. All this was capably carried out routine, but Murray was obsessed by fears of the arrival of Suchet and had apparently lost all confidence in his troops. Why this should have been so, when he had only recently beaten Suchet with the same troops, is beyond conjecture. The fact remains, that he lost his head completely, and continually interrupted the siege operations in order to concentrate to meet rumoured French advances. His nerves growing worse, he then began re-embarking the troops, only to disembark them again shortly after. This took place several times and was, as may be imagined, particularly trying for the cavalry. The cavalry brigade, which was commanded by Lord Frederick Bentinck, brother of Lord William, enjoyed a momentary excitement on the 11th June, when it was sent galloping off to support the Spaniards holding Altafulla, who had reported that ten thousand Frenchmen were descending upon them. As these Frenchmen did not turn up, however, Copons, the Spanish leader, sent the cavalry to look for them. It was then found that a French column, under General Mathieu, had in fact advanced from Barcelona, but had unaccountably turned back at Villafranca. It might have been thought that this news would have put some heart into Sir John Murray, but by that time he had made up his mind to raise the siege. The guns were then spiked and the whole army was re-embarked on the 12th June, except for the brigade at Balaguer. The commander of this brigade then reported that three thousand Frenchmen were at Bandellos on his right flank, whereupon Murray disembarked his army again and marched on Bandellos, only to find that the French had been withdrawn by Suchet. A great deal of French marching and counter-marching followed which, although it was not being carried out with that intention, reduced Murray to such a hopeless state of nerves and confusion that his subordinates persuaded him to abandon the whole enterprise. Although Lord William Bentinck arrived to take over command before Murray had started re-embarkation, he found affairs in such chaos that he could only agree to let it go forward. 'The debarkation and re-embarkation continually going on was enough to confound any operations in the world,' said Admiral Hallowell, the commander of the convoy.

The expedition against Tarragona thus ended in farce, lowering Great Britain's prestige among the allies, and making her look ridiculous. A public outcry obliged the government to suspend Sir John Murray and take steps to court-martial him, but it took so long over it that the court-martial was not held until long after the end of the war, when essential witnesses had disappeared and everyone had lost interest. By stretching the facts a bit, he was thus able to talk his way into an acquittal. He could at least claim that by keeping Suchet on the run he had done something to help Wellington's operations on the Peninsula, although he took care, no doubt, to keep well out of the Duke's way afterwards. Probably Suchet, whose blunderings were almost equally reprehensible was similarly careful to avoid a meeting with Napoleon.

At this time, it will be remembered, Soult had taken over command of the French armies facing Wellington and was disposed along the Pyrenees with the intention of resuming the offensive. Wellington, of course, had other ideas, but the plans of both commanders were affected to a certain extent by the movements of Suchet in Catalonia. Fortunately, Suchet was not anxious to get too close to Soult, for he did not wish to surrender his independence; but nevertheless, his presence in the east was an embarrassment to Wellington. It was essential that he should be closely watched and prevented from interfering in the main operations. Bentinck, therefore, as soon as his army had disembarked at Alicanté, marched it north to Valencia, with the intention of proceeding against Tarragona by land. A division was, however, sent by sea to occupy the pass of Balaguer to cover the passage of the Ebro which, as the river was three hundred yards wide, was a long and hazardous proceeding, especially for the cavalry which, at this period, seldom crossed rivers by swimming but was dependent upon such expedients as flying bridges and rafts.

Suchet, having blown up the defences of Tarragona, retired to the line of the Llobregat river, whereupon Bentinck advanced to Villa Franca and sent forward a brigade under Colonel Adam to hold the pass at Ordal, a few miles from Barcelona. On the 13th September, Suchet attacked the pass and overwhelmed Adam's brigade after some desperate fighting. Bentinck formed line of battle behind a ravine to defend Villa Franca, but when he saw Suchet coming ordered a retreat, which was covered by the 20th Light Dragoons and Brunswick Hussars under Lord Frederick

Bentinck, who seems to have been more of a fighting soldier than his brother – but he did not have the same responsibilities, of course.

Suchet, when he saw the retreat commencing, sent forward his cavalry – about two thousand strong, supported by horse artillery – to pursue, but as they were forming up to charge the infantry of Bentinck's rearguard they were charged and routed by the 20th and Brunswick Hussars. These two regiments (the 20th were at four troops) were outnumbered by the French cavalry by about three to one, and consequently had their work cut out to get the best of the encounter, especially as their horses were in poor condition. During a desperate mêlée, with everyone cutting away for all he was worth, Lord Frederick Bentinck engaged the French General-of-Brigade Meyer, and succeeded in wounding and unhorsing him in single combat. After this incident the French galloped off, but rallied on their infantry and came on again, to be stopped this time by the fire of the 10th Foot (Lincolns) and a couple of guns. Suchet then broke off the engagement and withdrew.

In this gallant affair, the 20th lost Captain Hanson, a sergeant and seven men killed; four sergeants and twenty-three men were wounded, and six men and twenty-four horses were missing. The Brunswick Hussars lost fifty-three all-ranks. There seems little doubt, that had it not been for the cavalry charge, Bentinck would have got into serious difficulties. Neither he nor Suchet emerged with any credit from this, or any of the other operations along the east coast of Spain but, as was the case with Sir John Murray, their intelligence was extraordinarily bad, and they were accordingly obliged to be cautious. In the case of the two British commanders, this was very surprising, since they were operating in what was supposed to be a friendly country, in which they might have expected to be furnished with sound information of the enemy's movements by the inhabitants. Wellington himself, however, was seldom able to rely on Spanish intelligence and had usually to make his own arrangements.

After this engagement, Bentinck retired to Tarragona, handed over command to Sir William Clinton, and sailed for Palermo, where the other four troops of the 20th had arrived. Murat had defected from the Emperor and signed an armistice both with the Austrians and Bentinck (acting on behalf of the British government) but Bentinck did not trust either Murat or the Austrians, and was in any case determined to liberate the Italians and establish a democratic government in the country, whether they liked it or not. He commenced by sending an expedition by sea to

1815

Leghorn under General Montresor, and the four troops of the 20th accompanied this force which landed at Leghorn on the 10th March, 1815. The 20th rode north, through Pisa and Lucca to Sarzana, where they found the French disposed in strength along the Magro River. At this stage of the war they were disinclined to fight, and when Montresor brought up the rest of his force, and a British squadron sailed into the Gulf of Spezia, they abandoned their positions and ran for it.

After a few days' siege, Montresor captured Fort Santa Maria, after which Bentinck arrived and ordered an advance on Genoa. The 20th took part in short engagements at Sestri on the 8th April, and Nervi on the 12th. A rather more serious affair occurred at San Martino on the 17th, during which the 20th had some jumping to do, over the walls and fences in the suburban area through which the French lines ran, but they appear to have suffered no casualties, and when the French left was turned the enemy retired precipitately into Genoa. On the 21st this city was surrendered after a parley. The French garrison marched out with the honours of war, and in May the four troops of the 20th returned to Palermo, where they were joined in December by the four troops from Tarragona. Except for two troops at Maidstone, the regiment was thus once more united.

In May, 1815, the 20th sailed for Malta, and returned to England in September, landing at Portsmouth. On the way home it left a detachment at Marseilles, presumably for the maintenance of law and order.

In 1812, the United States had declared war on Great Britain, partly in consequence of the British blockade against French possessions, which involved the stopping and searching of American ships on the high seas and partly, with Napoleon's encouragement, in the hope of conquering Canada while Great Britain was too busy elsewhere to prevent it. The Canadians, however, at that time strongly anti-American, succeeded with the help of a few British troops in turning the tables on the Americans. British reinforcements were sent, and in 1814 an expedition under General Ross defeated an American force at Bladensburg and burned down the public buildings in Washington. This offered favourable conditions for the British government to negotiate peace terms, especially as the downfall of Napoleon enabled the blockade to be lifted. Anger over the American 'stab in the back' of 1812, however, led to the dispatch of another expedition under Sir Edward Pakenham, Wellington's brother-in-law, against New Orleans, which sailed from England in August, 1814.

1814

The 14th Light Dragoons, after landing at Dover on the 17th July, 1814, were inspected by the Commander-in-Chief, the Duke of York, a few days later on Hounslow Heath. His Royal Highness, who was not an easy man to please, was much impressed by the turn-out of the regiment, and commented 'they appear as if they had never been on service', which seems to indicate that it had been issued with new uniforms, and was no longer 'ragged'. All ranks were no doubt looking forward to a spell at ease, now that Napoleon was in custody and their dangers and hardships at an end. The ceremonial parade had scarcely ended, however, before orders arrived for active service. Two troops embarked at Portsmouth on the 31st August, and two more from Plymouth on the 10th October, all four troops being united in Jamaica in November, under the command of Lieut.-Colonel C. M. Baker who had taken over from Colonel Hervey on his promotion. The four troops, with two more left behind in the United Kingdom, represented the whole resources of the regiment at this time, although its nominal establishment was eight troops. Two troops, commanded by Major T. P. Milles, sailed from Jamaica in December, with an advance contingent under General Keane, which arrived off New Orleans on the 10th December. The other two troops, with regimental headquarters, arrived on the 5th January, 1815. A third squadron, recruited in England to bring the regiment up to establishment had embarked at the beginning of January, but its sailing was cancelled following a peace treaty with the United States news of which, unfortunately, did not arrive at New Orleans in time to prevent bloodshed.

The operations in Louisiana were instigated by Admirals Cochrane, Cockburn and Malcolm of the British fleet in the Gulf of Mexico. They wanted to get at the American ships in the Mississippi, which represented a very substantial sum in prize-money, and this they could not do without the help of the Army to wipe out the land defences along the river. They had no understanding of the tactical issues involved, and cared less. The disastrous campaign in the Argentine of 1805 had, it will be remembered, been instigated in a similar manner by Commodore Sir Home Popham. The Admirals of the Royal Navy, besides being very formidable characters, usually out-ranked the officers of the Army with whom they were associated, who were seldom more than Major-Generals, and whom they were thus able to bully into undertaking unsound and ridiculous adventures against their better judgment. It was unfortunate that Pakenham himself did not arrive on the scene with the leading con-

1814

tingent for he, with his powerful connections, would have been able to stand up to the Admirals – as he certainly would have done after a reconnaissance. Keane did not stand a chance, either against the Admirals or the Americans, and could only resolve to do his best to disprove the veiled aspersions cast on his own and his soldiers' courage, efficiency and resource.

Admiral Cochrane, with the first contingent of troops, anchored off Ship Island in Mississippi Sound on the 8th December. His intention was to land the troops on the shore of Lake Borgne, at a place five miles from the Mississippi, so that they could outflank the forts defending the mouth of that river. The head of the lake was defended by several gun-boats and other craft, which the Admiral dealt with himself by sending his sailors against them in all the rowing boats he could muster from his fleet. The unfortunate sailors, after a long row and several sharp fights with cutlasses during which they captured all the American ships, had then to return for the soldiers who, including the 14th Light Dragoons dismounted, were eventually put on shore up the Bayou Bienvenu, a creek leading out of Lake Borgne, at a point about twenty miles from New Orleans. The date was the 23rd December and the rain, which had been pouring down in torrents, had given way to heavy sleet driven by a northerly gale. The sailors had been in the boats for eight days on end, and at the oars for most of the time, but they were better off than the soldiers, who had been in the boats for six days but packed so tightly that they were unable to move, reaching a depth of misery unequalled in all their previous experience in war, even in the Pyrenees.

Had Keane advanced at once, he might have taken New Orleans without much difficulty, for the American General, Jackson – 'Old Hickory' – was not aware of his presence. The condition of his troops, and his uncertainty regarding his whereabouts and those of the enemy led him to decide, however, to wait for Pakenham. A couple of American picquets were overrun and, as night fell, orders were given to bivouac. This meant that fires were lighted, around which the starving, frozen soldiers huddled to boil their kettles and get some warmth into themselves. But by this time Old Hickory had heard of their arrival, and had arranged with the American brig-of-war *Carolina* to give him covering fire, while he went for them with a couple of thousand sharpshooters. The British soldiers round the fires thus suddenly found themselves in the middle of a hail of round-shot from the *Carolina* and, just as they were taking cover, Old Hickory arrived with his sharpshooters. The British picquets, fortunately, were provided by the 95th (Rifle Brigade) whose courage and marksmanship were more than a match for the Americans, so that time was given for Keane to deploy. A chaotic battle ensued in the darkness, when it was impossible to distinguish friend from foe, while the brig *Carolina* gaily continued to dump round-shot in the middle of them. After about three hours of this, the fact that the British were disciplined and the Americans far from being so, finally established itself. The sharpshooters became a disorderly rabble, lost heart, and ran off in the direction of New Orleans. The casualties were about equal, being somewhat over two hundred killed and wounded on each side.

After this affair, Old Hickory dug himself in with his right on the Mississippi, about three miles from Keane, who made no move to interfere. On the 25th, Pakenham arrived with the remainder of the force. The gales and sleet continued, so that visibility was down to a few yards. In these conditions, one of the naval boats, packed with thirty-seven dragoons of the 14th, with Lieut. Brydges and Cornet Hammond, was surprised and captured by the enemy while the oarsmen were taking a breather in the creek.

On his arrival, Pakenham found that the manoeuvres of the Admirals had got the army into an impossible situation, hemmed in on a narrow strip of land between an enormous swamp and the Mississippi River, an entrenched enemy in front and a lake in the rear, two enemy men-of-war on his left flank and his nearest supply base eighty miles away. He commenced operations by taking on the men-of-war, erecting batteries on the river bank, with furnaces for heating the shot. On the 27th, the *Carolina* was set on fire and sunk by this means, to the great satisfaction of the soldiers of the first British contingent. The *Louisiana* managed to get up-river and lie alongside the American entrenchments, which she was then able to cover by flanking fire.

Seeing that the only hope of success lay in a frontal attack, Pakenham got up fourteen heavy guns from the fleet – an astonishing achievement by the seamen who had to bring them – and opened fire on the 1st January, 1815, in an attempt to breach the American lines. The attempt was a failure, owing to effective counter-battery work by the *Louisiana*. Several of the guns were knocked off their carriages, and had to be got away by night. Pakenham then attempted to get a brigade across the river, to enfilade the enemy lines from the right bank. This required boats from the fleet, which could only get into the Mississippi by way of a narrow canal leading across the swamp from the Bayou Bienvenu. On the night chosen for the crossing, the troops were

1815

ready, but only enough boats arrived to take four hundred men, the remainder having stuck. Nevertheless, a general assault was made at dawn on the 8th January, but failed after the most desperate and gallant efforts to scale the unbreached enemy emplacements. Only the troops on the right bank were successful, and they were too few to influence the battle. Pakenham was killed, Generals Gibb and Keane wounded, and there were nearly two thousand casualties in all. General Lambert, who took over command, sent a flag of truce to arrange for the collection of the wounded, and the period of truce was lengthened by mutual consent, for 'Old Hickory' had no intention of 'sticking his neck out'. He knew perfectly well that the British were going back to their ships, and he was not going to risk making them change their minds by attempting anything against them.

Before Lambert could retreat, he was obliged to construct some sort of passage across the morass, in order to get back to the Bayou Bienvenu. This took eight days, so that the retreat could not start before the 18th January and, even then, many soldiers were swallowed up by the morass, in front of the horrified eyes of their comrades. However, most of them got back on board, and the fleet sailed on the 5th February. As some sort of gesture of defiance, it hove-to off Mobile Bay on the 7th February, and the soldiers landed and captured Fort Bowyer at the entrance. On the 14th a sloop of war arrived with the news of peace, which had in fact been signed on the preceding 14th December. The troops remained on the Isle of Dauphine, adjoining Fort Bowyer, until the middle of March, when they sailed for home.

The Reception of Princess Frederica of Prussia by the Royal Family in 1791. The Princess had married Frederick, Duke of York, second son of King George III and Commander-in-Chief of the British Army. She was escorted by the 14th on her arrival in England and became Patroness of the Regiment. The adoption of the Prussian Eagle as the Regimental badge dates from 1798, the Regiment being styled 14th (or Duchess of York's Own) Regiment of Light Dragoons. Present on this occasion were: the Royal Princesses, King George III and Queen Charlotte, the Duke of Clarence (later William IV), Princess Frederica, the Prince of Wales (later George IV) and the Duke of York. Paintings by Richard Livesay.

14th Light Dragoons, full dress 1819. After the end of the Napoleonic War cavalry dress became more ornamental, with overalls which were blue-grey in colour and more baggy. At this time the Regiment was reduced to six troops, having had ten when it left for the Peninsular.

June 1815 Major Percy and the Waterloo Despatch
1825–1829 The 14th in England and Ireland
1831 The Bristol Riots
1841 The 14th sail for India
1846 and 1848 The Sikh Wars
The advance to Ramnuggur

1815

Riots and Small Wars

15

For their services in the unhappy affair on the Mississippi, the 14th were mentioned in General Lambert's despatches: 'The conduct of the two squadrons of the 14th Light Dragoons, latterly commanded by Lieutenant-Colonel Baker, previously by Major Milles, has been the admiration of everyone, by the cheerfulness with which they have performed all descriptions of service.' They, or rather their survivors, landed at Portsmouth in the middle of May, after a voyage of seven weeks, and rejoined the rest of the regiment at Hounslow. By that time, Napoleon, who had escaped from Elba on the 1st March, was preparing to invade Belgium while Wellington, at Brussels, was endeavouring to anticipate his movements. It was too late for the 14th to join the campaign, and the regiment thus missed the honour of fighting at Waterloo. The regiment was, however, represented at the battle by Colonel Sir Felton Bathurst Hervey, Bart., and Major the Honourable H. Percy, both of whom served on the Duke's staff.

Percy, who was the son of the Earl of Beverley, and the grandson of the Duke of Northumberland, was enjoying himself at the Duchess of Richmond's Ball in Brussels, when the drums were heard beating outside the soldiers' billets and all officers were ordered to rejoin their regiments immediately.

205

1815

'Ah! Then and there was hurrying to and fro,
And gathering tears and tremblings of distress,
And cheeks all pale that but an hour ago,
Blushed at the praise of their own loveliness.'

The young people present had all been brought up under the grim shadow of Napoleon. Most of them would have been told at one time or another of how fathers, brothers or close friends had fallen in action during a war that had gone on so long that they had no idea of what peace was like. They knew only too well what the call to arms implied.

As Percy said a hasty good-bye to his unknown partner, who was doubtless in tears like the others, she thrust into his hand her velvet sachet, a small bag in which ladies kept their handkerchiefs and the other modest necessaries of those days. Percy put it in his pocket, ran off to his lodging where he pulled his boots over his silk stockings, grabbed his sword, and mounted his horse which had been brought round by his orderly, and reported to Wellington's headquarters, still in his dress uniform.

During the battle all Wellington's Aides-de-Camp, who were used to take his orders to the formation commanders, were either killed or seriously wounded except Percy, who got off with a graze on the foot. It therefore fell to him, to take home Wellington's despatch, which the Duke gave to him personally, telling him at the same time to take two of the captured French Eagles and lay them at the feet of the Prince Regent. Percy put the despatch in the velvet sachet, which he still had in his pocket, and galloped off to Ostend in a chaise and four. There he embarked in the brig *Peruvian*, and when the wind failed some miles off Dover, continued the journey in the captain's gig, taking a hand at the oars himself. Setting off in another chaise and four, he had another triumphant gallop to London, changing horses at Canterbury, Sittingbourne and Rochester, with the Eagles sticking out of the window, the post-boys yelling and 'springing 'em' for all they were worth, and everyone along the road cheering with relief.

In London, he first called on Lord Castlereagh with the news of victory, and then set out to find the Prince Regent, whom he ran to earth at a Ball in St James's Square. Making a dramatic entry into the Ballroom in his torn and bloodstained dress uniform, with an Eagle in each hand and hardly able to stand from fatigue – he had not been to bed for nearly a week – he flung the Eagles at the Prince Regent's feet, sank to one knee and held out the despatch in the velvet sachet, gasping out 'Victory, Sire, victory!'

Reading the despatch, the Regent, when he came to the

casualty list, burst into tears. He afterwards made Percy a Commander of the Order of the Bath, and raised him to Lieut.-Colonel, but Percy did not live long to enjoy his honours, for he died eight years later, at the age of 40.

The velvet sachet is still kept at Alnwick Castle, the seat of the Duke of Northumberland and, with Percy's dress uniform worn at Waterloo, was placed on view at the Waterloo Exhibition held in London in 1965, to mark the 150th anniversary of the Battle.

The 20th Light Dragoons being at Malta at the time, also missed the battle. After returning home and being reduced to peacetime establishment, which brought its numbers down to under five hundred, the regiment was sent to Ireland in 1817, and disbanded in December of the following year.

The 14th, which was also reduced in strength to about five hundred and thirty all-ranks, was posted to Ireland in 1816. At this time, for once in a way, there was no trouble in Ireland, although there was plenty brewing up in England. After suffering annual and pointless changes in establishment, like all other regiments on home service, the 14th therefore returned to England in 1819, landing at Liverpool and marching 200 miles to Canterbury, where it arrived 'with no sore backs'.

With its headquarters at Canterbury, the regiment was then deployed along the coast, from Yarmouth to Deal, and employed 'assisting the Riding Officers' in attempting the prevention of smuggling. This was a hard, and highly unpopular duty. Much of the coastal population depended on smuggling for its living and the rest of it, including many of the gentry, depended on it for many little luxuries and so gave the 'free-traders' active support. Furthermore smugglers, when caught, were liable to be hanged at short shrift and did not therefore surrender without a hard fight. As they were tough and ruthless men, well-armed and with an intimate knowledge of the coast, capturing any of them, or their cargoes, was a far from easy job. In fact, unless they could be surprised in the act of landing their cargoes – which was seldom possible – their local knowledge enabled them to disappear with their pack-ponies among the mists of the marsh-lands, where it was almost impossible for cavalry to follow or find them. The best area for their activities was the Romney marsh, where most of the 14th were stationed during 1820, billeted in various far from friendly farms and suffering a great deal from 'ague and similar complaints' owing to the damp and unhealthy nature of the country.

It was no doubt to recover its health that the regiment was stationed at Brighton in 1821, with detachments at Hastings,

1821

Arundel and Eastbourne. The Prince Regent, who now ascended the throne as George IV, had turned Brighton into a centre of culture and fashion, so that the officers of a smart cavalry regiment would certainly not have found the place dull. They did not, however, neglect the welfare of their men. Contrary to popular belief, this has never been a fault of the officers of the British Army. The general attitudes and behaviour of all ranks – and all classes of society – has of course changed from century to century, so that an action which would be considered disgraceful today, was a perfectly normal one two hundred years ago. Punishment, for example, whether civil or military, nearly always meant the infliction of pain on the culprit; but it is more than likely that the soldier of those days thought less of a dozen lashes than his successor of today thinks of a deduction from his pay.

In 1821 the 14th had a strength of 320 rank and file, of whom 83 were married. This was a very high proportion for those days, when an infantry regiment of double the numbers seldom had more than forty wives. No special provision was made for a soldier's wife, who shared his quarters wherever and whatever they might be, and who had to earn her keep by doing washing and mending. Those of the 14th had 110 children, who in the ordinary way would have been sent out to earn a living at a very tender age. The exploitation of children was, in fact, a national scandal at this period, but the officers of the army, generally, were a good deal in advance of the civil authorities in their attempts to care for the welfare of the children of their own regiments. In the 14th a school was started in which the boys were taught trades and the girls knitting and sewing, but it is not clear where the funds came from, unless out of the pockets of the officers. Later, when regimental schools received official blessing, schoolmasters were appointed to teach not only the children, but also any illiterate soldiers, to read and write, but this advance had not yet been made when the 14th opened its school in Brighton.

The 14th spent only a year at Brighton, before moving on to Coventry, Dorchester and Exeter, and then back to Ireland in 1825. After marching all over the south of Ireland for three years, the regiment returned to an England seething with unrest, in 1829, and was stationed by troops around the industrial areas of Leeds, Birmingham and Coventry, where there was constant danger of riots. These riots were political in nature, being fomented by various agitators to demand the passage of the Reform Bill. The working classes in the industrial towns, who were having a hard time from low wages and unemployment,

King William IV, who reviewed the Regiment in 1830, the year of his accession, and was so pleased with it that he commanded it should bear the title '14th or King's Light Dragoons'. The previous title, 'Duchess of York's Own', thus lapsed.

1831

could be easily roused for any demonstration against authority, especially as drink was cheap, though bread was dear. As such demonstrations were invariably attended by the looting of shops, they were naturally popular with the masses and, in the absence of a regular police force, were most difficult to stop. The army had to be constantly called upon for the protection of life and property, and to restore and maintain law and order, although soldiers, who are men trained to arms, are not suitable for such duties and should normally only be called out in aid of the civil power as a last resort, when matters have got completely out of hand and can only be rectified by armed force.

In the suppression of rioting, the cavalry was generally more effective than the infantry, owing to its mobility, moral effect, and the use of its horses for pushing back crowds. During this period of industrial unrest, all cavalry regiments of the line were kept constantly on the move in troops and smaller detachments, and the marches and countermarches of the 14th, from Lancashire to Sussex and back again, were too varied and uninteresting to be worth recording. In 1830, when the regiment was quartered for a short time in the neighbourhoods of Paddington and Lambeth, it was inspected in Hyde Park by King William IV, who had just succeeded his brother, George IV. As an expression of his approval of the services of the regiment, His Majesty took the opportunity to command that its designation should be changed from 'the Duchess of York's Own Regiment of Light Dragoons', to 'the King's Regiment of Light Dragoons', from which its subsequent title of King's Hussars is derived. The second Badge of the Royal Cypher within the Garter dates from this time.

During 1831 the 14th sent troops in aid of the civil power to several places in England and Wales, but there appears to have been no bloodshed except at Bristol in October, where the rioting assumed serious proportions. The Recorder of Bristol, Sir Charles Wetherall, M.P., was a well-known opponent of the Reform Bill, and was consequently very unpopular with the industrial workers. When he arrived in the city on the 29th October to hold Sessions, a mob collected before the Mansion House and pelted him and his escort of special constables with mud and filth. After he had entered the Mansion House the mob increased in numbers and began breaking the windows and showing signs of forcing an entry in order to get at him. The magistrates had therefore to call for military assistance from Colonel Brereton, a half-pay recruiting officer, who had at his disposal a troop of the 14th, commanded by Captain Musgrave, and a troop of the 3rd Dragoon Guards which had just arrived after a long march.

Captain Warrington, leading the troop of the 3rd Dragoon Guards, appears to have been an easy-going type of man who exercised his humorous charm on the mob to such effect that he and his dragoons were soon sitting their horses with mugs in their hands, drinking toasts to 'the King and Reform'. Musgrave on the other hand, although in normal circumstances doubtless equally good-tempered, was smarting from the effects of a shower of bricks, with which his troop had been received on first making its appearance. When, after repeated warnings, the crowd continued its barrage, he shot one with a pistol. This in fact, did have the effect of calming them down, but their leaders went to Brereton and urged him with threats and promises to get rid of those 'bloody blues', an allusion to the 14th who, unlike the 3rd, had not gone into scarlet. Brereton then ordered both troops to leave the scene, being apparently of the opinion that the 3rd were becoming too friendly with the rioters, while the 14th were inflaming them.

After the cavalry had left, the rioters really got busy, breaking open both the Mansion House and the gaol, where they released all the prisoners, of whom sixteen were awaiting the attentions of the hangman. The unfortunate Recorder only saved his skin by escaping over the roof-tops, 'in a manner little suited to a Recorder of the City of Bristol'.

The Mansion House and several toll-houses were then burned down, accompanied by much loss of life; private houses and shops were broken into and looted, and on the Sunday morning the bishop's palace was burned down.

Colonel Brereton still made no move to recall the troops, and it seems possible that the whole city would have been destroyed, had not Major Mackworth, A.D.C. to the Commander-in-Chief, Lord Hill, arrived on the scene. Another troop of the 14th, led by Major William Beckwith, rode in at the same time, being followed later by the 52nd Light Infantry and a troop of horse artillery. Mackworth, ably supported by Beckwith, collected the three troops of cavalry – about a hundred men – and led them against the rioters with their swords out. Previously, Brereton had refused to allow them to draw, from fear that the sight of naked swords would further inflame the mobs; but, that this was a sad misjudgement, was soon proved. The three troops made several charges – at the trot, and under a hail of missiles – and used their swords without further compunction, dispersing the rioters in a very short space of time. The troop of the 3rd Dragoon Guards was then sent through the centre of the city, while Beckwith and the squadron of the 14th cleared the wharves.

1839

Order was thus restored at last, after considerable loss of life and damage to property, most of which could have been avoided had the cavalry been firmly led at the outset. The unfortunate Brereton shot himself, although the magistrates were more to blame than he, for he could only act under their orders – although Mackworth and Beckwith, men of stronger personalities, did not bother about magistrates in such an extreme emergency. It was hardly to be expected that the soldiers should have received any thanks for their efforts, and, in fact, they incurred the usual grossly unjust opprobrium consequent on the cutting down of helpless civilians. The troop-leaders indeed, were lucky to escape with only mild censure which, curiously enough, blamed Warrington of the 3rd for not being sufficiently tough, and Mackworth and Musgrave of the 14th for being too much so.

Apart from a period of royal escort duty in 1832, when the regiment was at Hounslow, the 14th spent most of its time during the next six years in assisting the civil power to keep law and order, although none of the disturbances assumed the proportions of those at Bristol. In April, 1832, the regiment, which was then at Gloucester, was called out when the Lunatic Asylum was set on fire and, for its efforts in quelling the blaze and dealing with the lunatics, was presented with a reward of £40 by the Insurance Company. This sum, which was regarded as 'very handsome' in those days, was shared out among the rank and file, who numbered about 350. Between 1833 and 1836, the regiment was in Ireland, where it also spent its time marching about and suppressing riots – mostly in connection with elections, or local assizes, and not to do with home rule. The same pattern continued after its return from Ireland in 1836, when it was sent to keep order in Scotland where, it is intriguing to note, three of its troops were required at Dalkeith in 1837, during the election of the representative peers for Scotland – an event which might have been expected to pass off quietly, without the assistance of a strong force of cavalry. The efforts of the 14th on this and other potentially explosive occasions in Scotland were greatly appreciated, as is shown in a letter from Major-General Lord Greenock, who described himself as 'Commanding in North Britain'. He concludes by expressing the opinion that the 14th was 'for all the purposes of Light Cavalry service, the most efficient corps in the British Army.'

In 1839, the 14th returned to Hounslow and another spell of royal escort duties, which were fairly onerous at that time. A troop stationed at Hampton Court put out another fire, at Bushey Farm, for which it received the thanks of the Queen Dowager who 'offered to give the men a dinner', which was presumably accepted. In 1839, the 14th had the honour, first of escorting Prince Albert into London on his arrival for his marriage to the Queen, and secondly of escorting the married couple from Buckingham Palace to Colnbrook, where they handed over their royal charges to the 2nd Life Guards. Shortly after, the regiment moved to Dorchester, with troops scattered throughout the adjoining district, but before it could settle down – not that it ever got the chance to settle down anywhere in those days – orders came for India.

The first effect of the orders for India was that the establishment was increased to 55 sergeants, 12 trumpeters, 8 farriers, 40 corporals, and 627 private men – about double the strength of its previous establishment. The troop horses numbered 701, although these were not taken to India, but had to be provided nevertheless, if only to enable the recruits to be taught to ride. The recruits were obtained through the efforts of special recruiting parties in Dorchester, Canterbury, Worcester, and their neighbourhoods. Many would have had some experience with horses, but a very high standard of horsemanship was then, as always, required in the cavalry. However, there was not much time for riding instruction for, after being inspected by the Inspector-General of Cavalry on the 20th April, the regiment was dismounted and marched to Gravesend to embark.

Before leaving Canterbury, the 14th presented their mess-table to their old comrades, the 13th Light Dragoons, who were in the same station. This mess-table is believed to have been part of the loot taken at Vittoria. It was no doubt bought by the officers at one of the official auctions held after the battle, for it is improbable that a cavalry regiment could have lifted it and carried it off in the same manner as a portable item like a chamber-pot.

The regiment embarked in two East India Company steamships, the *Repulse* and *Reliance*, both cargo ships in ballast, in which the holds had been adapted for the accommodation of troops. The result was not unlike the old slave-trading days, although the soldiers were not packed quite so tightly as had been customary with slaves. Although described as steamships, the winds were still the primary motive power, and the chief effect of the engines – which were most unreliable – was to slow the ship down, so that the voyage took some weeks longer than a good passage in one of the old East Indiamen under sail.

The *Repulse* and *Reliance* reached Bombay in September and October, 1841, each of them having been over four months at sea. The regiment then marched to Kirkee, where it was joined

1843

by 150 volunteers from the 4th Light Dragoons which regiment, having been relieved by the 14th, sailed for home. The horses of the 4th were also taken over, and another hundred men arrived from home in 1842, which brought the 14th up to establishment.

The Governor-General of India, and the Governors of the Provinces of Calcutta, Bombay and Madras, were appointed by the British government, but in practice the country was still run by the East India Company, which employed its own soldiers and administrators, and which was more concerned with trade than conquest. Having, during the Napoleonic wars, ousted the French, Portuguese and Dutch by force of arms, the Company no longer had any trade rivals, but as the paramount power it had become responsible for law and order and defence. This was no light matter in a land constantly threatened by the Afghans in the north, and peopled by innumerable different races, all at loggerheads with one another. Nor was it made any easier by the fact that the greater part of the country was still independent, and ruled by warlike princes, few of whom could be trusted an inch.

The 14th arrived in India at a time when British prestige had received a severe blow from the disasters of the First Afghan War, although they had been redeemed to some extent by an 'Avenging Army', which had gone up the Khyber, relieved a beleagured garrison at Jellalabad, and burnt Kabul. In order to get to Afghanistan, the British forces had had to march through the independent territories of the Amirs of Sind and the Sikhs of the Punjab, who reluctantly let them pass without interference. Nonetheless, the Government of British India decided to take over Sind, partly as a strategic measure and partly because the Amirs were scoundrels who grossly exploited the Baluchis in this part of India.

Sind was annexed in 1843 by General Sir Charles Napier, a strange character who bore so strong a resemblance to the Jew in *Oliver Twist* that he was known throughout the army as 'Fagin'. With only the 22nd Regiment (Cheshires) and a couple of thousand of the Company's native troops, he defeated vast hordes of Baluchis at Meeanee, and followed up by taking Hyderabad, when the Amirs surrendered.

Trouble then broke out in the Mahratta state of Gwalior, which had lapsed into a state of chaos following the death of the Maharaja, when a dispute over the succession resulted in the state forces taking over control. A British force defeated the insurgent Mahrattas at Maharajpur in December, 1843, and withdrew after law and order had thus been restored, without annexing the territory. As part of these operations, two squadrons of the 14th, numbering 15 officers and 289 rank and file, marched from Kirkee to Kholapur under the command of Major Harvey, to keep order in the south. They remained in and around Kholapur until the following year, taking part in the reduction of a couple of Mahratta strongholds, but no details of their adventures have survived.

What was known as the First Sikh War then broke out, in consequence of the Sikhs invading British territory with the object of seizing Delhi. After a hard campaign, they were finally defeated at Sobraon in February, 1846, and surrendered with a very ill grace. The Indian Government was reluctant to annex the Punjab, whose administration was more than it could comfortably cope with at that time. A Council of Regency was set up, consisting of four British officials and four Sikh chiefs, which it was hoped would be able to keep order. In 1848, however, Mulraj, the semi-independent governor of Multan, murdered two British officials and roused the south-west Punjab to revolt. A combined British and Sikh force went against him, but the Sikhs defected and the British had to withdraw to await reinforcements. This indication of weakness set the whole Punjab in flames. All Sikh warriors sprang to arms, and the Second Sikh War commenced.

The 14th had left Kirkee in November, 1845, and marched to Amballa, through Agra and Meerut. The whole journey, which included long halts at various townships, took them three months, during which they lost an officer and seventeen rank and file from cholera. Another officer, Lieutenant Herbert Gall, also caught the disease, and had reached the stage of being prepared for burial when the hospital orderly saw his lips moving and brought him round with champagne. This was not an unusual experience in regiments marching through India in those rough and ready days, and it is greatly to be feared that there were many unfortunates who did not have the same luck as Herbert Gall.

On the 5th December, 1846, the sailing ship *Duchess of Bedford* arrived at Calcutta after a five-month voyage from Deal. She was so crammed with troops that about a third of them had to 'keep watch on deck', for there was no room for them below. Among them was Private George Tookey, the son of a Warwickshire farmer, who had enlisted for the 14th. Some of his letters to his mother and relatives have fortunately survived, making it possible to get an impression of the conditions in the service from a soldier's point of view. In general, like other surviving soldiers' correspondence of the 19th century, they give the same picture of

1848

hardships – which would be thought intolerable today – borne with astonishing cheerfulness and courage. Conditions for the British soldier in India did not, in fact, change very much, and Tookey would not have noticed any great difference in them had he returned in 1946. Most discomforts had their corresponding compensations; 'we live like gentlemen here', wrote Tookey, on his arrival, and it is noticeable that, when a regiment was ordered home, there was never any lack of volunteers for transfer to another regiment remaining in the country. In contrast to the present day, in Tookey's time death was always waiting round the corner, but even this had its compensation, for the soldier, never knowing if he would live to see another sunrise, developed a comfortable philosophy of making the most of whatever time he had left, whatever the dangers and hardships.

In February, 1848, the 14th left Amballa and marched to Ferozepore, sending its left wing to Lahore. One of the squadrons at Lahore, commanded by Major King and consisting of 4 officers and 91 men (including Tookey) marched out to join the force of British and Sikhs sent against Mulraj. The British infantry in this expedition were sent up the Ravi river in boats, but King's squadron crossed the river in rafts, with the horses swimming, and joined the 7th Irregular Cavalry and 73rd Native Infantry on the far side. The enemy Sikhs in the area decamped, pursued by the squadron of the 14th, which captured about sixty of them. Some forts were blown up, and the squadron returned to Lahore.

Owing to the troubled situation, which kept the regiment continually on the alert, Tookey had difficulty in attending to his correspondence, and his mother wrote to his troop leader, Captain Clarke, who admonished him for not writing to her regularly. It seems that Clarke had even taken the trouble to visit her while he was home on sick leave and tell her how her son was doing. She told Tookey that she was sending £5 for him to Clarke, whereupon he earnestly begged her to send it to him instead by money-order, which he assured her he could cash at the local post-office just as easily as he could at home. He well knew that if his officer got hold of it, it would be grudgingly doled out to him at a rupee a time, and that he would be made to account for every anna.

The 14th took the field in the Second Sikh War in November, 1848, at a strength of 56 sergeants, 12 trumpeters, 8 farriers, 40 corporals and 627 private men. It was commanded by Lieut.-Colonel William Havelock. While the Commander-in-Chief, General Sir Hugh Gough, was assembling an army at Ferozepore, a covering force was sent across the Sutlej to guard against an enemy advance on Lahore where the 14th had left their women and children, stores and baggage, under the protection of a small rear party consisting mostly of invalids. The covering force was composed of the 3rd Light Dragoons, 14th Light Dragoons, 8th Native Cavalry, 12th Irregular Cavalry, 3 troops of horse artillery and a light field battery. It took up a covering position at Kela Dedar Singh, where it was reinforced by two infantry brigades. First under the command of General Cureton, it was taken over on the 8th November by General Sir Colin Campbell, who arrived with another brigade.

The main Sikh army lay at Ramnuggur, on the Chenab river which ran through its positions, giving an opportunity for an attack. Campbell accordingly advanced against Ramnuggur, but as soon as he did so the Sikhs withdrew across the river, leaving a line of outposts and some guns between Ramnuggur and the south bank. Campbell then encamped about eight miles from Ramnuggur and waited for Gough, who arrived on the 21st November with the rest of the army. A cavalry division of two brigades was then formed under General Cureton, of which the 1st Brigade, commanded by Brigadier White, consisted of the 3rd Light Dragoons, 14th Light Dragoons, and the 5th and 8th Native Cavalry.

Immediately on his arrival, Gough ordered Campbell to advance with the cavalry division, an infantry brigade, and three troops of horse artillery, drive the Sikhs across the Chenab, and capture any guns there might be on the south bank. Campbell marched during the night of the 21st/22nd November, and arrived at Ramnuggur at dawn, being then able to look down on the Sikh positions along the Chenab.

Lieut.-Colonel William Havelock, K.H. (in staff undress uniform). He first saw action in the Peninsular War when, at the age of 15, he carried the colours of the 43rd Light Infantry. The Spaniards nicknamed him 'El Chico Blanco' – the fair boy. He was killed while commanding the 14th at Ramnuggur.

22nd November 1848 The Battle of Ramnuggur
13th January 1849 The Battle of Chillianwalla
21st February 1849 The Battle of Gujerat
The 14th in the pursuit to the Frontier
1856 War with Persia

1848

Ramnuggur

16

BETWEEN Ramnuggur and the Chenab lay about two miles of flat ground, across which parties of Sikhs could be seen retiring towards the river. Like many Indian rivers, the Chenab consists of a very wide, sandy bed, over which the river winds its way in numerous streams of varying width and depth. The sandy approaches to such rivers are nearly always soft and deep, and often treacherous, for quicksands are not uncommon. Campbell, of course, was well aware of this fact, and that the banks of the Chenab were no place for cavalry. However, there were two miles of rideable country in front, and he therefore advanced the 3rd Light Dragoons and two troops of horse artillery to chase the retiring Sikhs and shoot them up as they crossed the river.

The enemy then sent cavalry over from the north bank to cover the retreat of their comrades, upon which the 3rd Dragoons charged and drove them back across the river. They then returned in greater numbers, whereupon Brigadier White withdrew the 3rd Dragoons, to avoid becoming involved in a mêlée on the soft surface of the river bed. One of the horse artillery guns then got stuck in the sand and had to be abandoned, upon which more enemy cavalry crossed the river to capture it. Campbell was about to send forward the infantry to save the gun, when Gough arrived and ordered in the 14th Light Dragoons.

1848

Colonel Havelock – brother of Henry Havelock – was like all his family a 'death or glory' type of soldier. As a youth he had served in the Peninsular War, and had won distinction when fighting with Spanish Irregulars by whom he was nicknamed 'El Chico Blanco' (the fair boy). On this occasion he had been awaiting the order to advance with so much impatience that, when it came at last, he was in an absolute frenzy and could think of nothing except the chance to 'win his golden spurs', as he put it. Men such as he, who are usually of a kindly and chivalrous disposition when off the battlefield, can be most useful on occasion, provided they are kept well in hand when the smell of powder is in the air. At Ramnuggur, however, he got out of control and went off at a gallop in the direction of the largest body of enemy he could see, which was the Sikh reserve of cavalry formed up on the river bed, covered by the guns and infantry fire of the main body on the north bank.

Behind Havelock rode the 14th Light Dragoons in column of troops, all mounted on powerful Arab horses which, like the Havelocks, have an inherited liking for going into action in this manner. The 5th Native Cavalry followed the 14th in support. Cureton, the cavalry commander who had once been a Private in the 14th, and Gough both saw that Havelock was heading for destruction. The former galloped out to try to head him off, but was shot through the head, while an aide-de-camp sent by Gough for the same purpose was unable to catch him up.

During their advance, the 14th were exposed to a continual hot fire from the enemy guns and hidden infantry, but owing to their speed suffered few casualties until they got to the top of the steep bank leading down to the river. Here they had to pull up and form line of squadrons, in obedience to the shouted orders of their officers and a confusion of trumpet blasts. The Sikh cavalry and infantry, in considerable numbers, were formed up along a sandy bank in the middle of the river-bed, behind a shallow stream. When, after the regiment had ridden down the steep bank, and the charge was sounded, it was found impossible to get up any speed, for the ground was so soft that many horses sank down up to their hocks. Nevertheless, they got to the sword-point and cut down the Sikhs, who fled back across the river in confusion. Havelock sounded the rally and re-formed, taking the 5th Native Cavalry under his command. He should certainly have withdrawn, but could not bring himself to do so while there were still unbroken enemy in front, even though these consisted of large numbers of infantry under cover, who could only be approached across ground so soft that it was practically a bog. The *advance* was sounded again, and followed almost immediately by the *charge*. A desperate engagement at the sword-point followed, during which the Sikhs slowly withdrew across the river, disputing every inch of ground. Havelock fell, and command was taken over by Major Doherty, assisted by Major King, who had arrived with the reserve squadron of the 14th, and the regiment with the 5th Native Cavalry was then led out of action.

Like the famous Charge of the Light Brigade, the charge at Ramnuggur was a 'blunder'. Both attacks were made against the wrong objectives. Both, however, were successful, and although neither had any immediate decisive effect on the operations, the shock to the enemy's morale was considerable. It is at least arguable that the spirit behind such 'blunders', which are not an infrequent aspect of war, may be one of the reasons for the eventual triumph of the British armed forces in nearly all the conflicts in which they have been engaged, in spite of the odds being heavily against them. At Ramnuggur at any rate neither Gough nor Campbell stressed the fact that Havelock had attacked the wrong objective. Both of them knew that such a happening was nothing out of the ordinary, and both expressed their profound admiration for the conduct of Havelock and the 14th, which did in fact contribute not a little to the eventual overthrow of the enemy. The Sikhs were natural warriors and respected above all things an opponent who did not hesitate to come to close quarters.

At Ramnuggur the 14th lost in killed their commanding-officer, Lieut.-Colonel William Havelock, K.H., Sergeant John Harwood, a corporal and 12 private men, with 37 horses. Wounded were five officers, four sergeants and 18 private men, with 15 horses. One of the wounded officers, Captain Fitzgerald, afterwards died of his wounds. Havelock's body, when recovered later, was found cut to pieces with the bodies of nine of his men around it, who had apparently died in an attempt to save him after he had been unhorsed in the mêlée. His grey charger had been killed under him.

The recollections of the survivors of this gallant affair are naturally confused, especially as the difficulties of forming line under heavy fire on such tricky ground had thrown the regiment out of alignment so that the final charge, which brought at least one squadron to the enemy guns, was quite unco-ordinated, and consisted of numerous small detachments of the 14th riding into the Sikhs and laying about them with their swords. One of the troop leaders, Captain Herbert Gall, left his troop to seize an enemy standard, followed by several of his men without orders.

1848

He was called back by the Adjutant, Captain Apthorp, who was trying to get the regiment into line, but he secured the standard after having his right hand nearly cut off. It is interesting to note the devotion of the Adjutant to his regimental duties under such dangerous and trying conditions. After carefully watching the skill with which a newly-joined subaltern, Cornet D'Urban Blyth, was using his sword, killing several Sikhs and saving the life of Captain M'Mahon, he called him over and told him that he was 'dismissed from any further sword-drill'.

After the affair at Ramnuggur, Gough made no move until the end of November while reconnaissances were made along the Chenab to find crossing-places. During the wait, he took the trouble to pay several visits to the field hospital to make sure that the sick and wounded were being tended as well as the primitive conditions allowed. Among them was George Tookey, who was suffering from inflammation of the lungs, for which he was 'bled, blistered and leeched until I could not stir without assistance'. He described Gough as 'a fine-looking old soldier . . . he comes round the hospitals and speaks to the privates as free as he would to an officer, and he gives us no small amount of praise, I can tell you.' He told Tookey to be careful to keep himself well wrapped-up and not catch cold. Gough and his brother generals were a vanishing breed of men, whose like has now completely disappeared. They continued to lead troops in action while well on in their seventies – and from the front at that. A lifetime of service seemed to have made them indestructible, and they were as physically and mentally fit as those half a century their juniors. It is not surprising that the soldiers regarded them with a respect amounting to awe, and would have followed them anywhere.

It was from Helan, beyond the Chenab river, that Tookey wrote to his mother for the last time, sending his 'kind love' to all his friends, and expressing the hope that he would be able to 'drink a glass of the Old Burton Ale with them yet'. Recovered from his illness, he wrote that 'the cavalry duties are very severe, for the 3 days before Xmas I was never off duty, consequently I had to keep in full dress the whole of that time, and the saddle on my horse's back. I have managed to enjoy myself pretty well tho' I have little time to spare as there are plenty of amusements going on as ours is a sporting regiment, and the Officers are very ready to subscribe for foot races and other games among the men and horse races etc among themselves. They had a sham fight in the mess on Xmas Day when everything was broke in the tent that was breakable, about £50 worth. The Colonel received a black eye from a plum pudding so that we have not seen him since.' Poor Tookey never got the chance of drinking a glass of Old Burton with his friends, for he was killed at Chillianwalla a couple of weeks later, dying for his Queen and country at the age of twenty-three.

At the end of November, Gough had sent a turning column, commanded by Sir Joseph Thackwell, to cross the Chenab north of Wazirabad and march against the Sikhs down the right bank. After some initial set-backs, this operation was successful. Following a somewhat half-hearted engagement at Sadullapur on the 3rd December, the Sikhs fell back from the Chenab, enabling Gough to cross the river at Ramnuggur and establish a standing camp at Helan. Here he was obliged to halt, having run out of supplies, while the Sikhs established a new line of defences along the Jhelum. It was in the camp at Helan that the commanding-officer of the 14th, Lieut.-Colonel J. W. King, who had taken over after the death of Havelock, got his black eye from the Christmas pudding.

On the 3rd January, 1849, the Sikh stronghold of Multan was stormed and captured by a force under General Whish. This greatly eased Gough's situation, but immediately afterwards came news that an Afghan army had taken Attock, and was on its way to join the Sikhs. It was imperative for Gough to march at once and defeat the Sikhs before the arrival of the Afghans, and he therefore advanced on the 9th January, reaching Dinga, some eight miles from the Sikh positions at Chillianwalla on the 12th. The cavalry division had now been reorganised, and was commanded by General Thackwell. The 14th were in the second brigade, commanded by Brigadier Pope, with the 9th Lancers and the 1st and 6th Native Cavalry.

At dawn on the 13th January, Gough advanced in line of battle, with the second cavalry brigade on the right, and the first brigade on the left. His intention was to drive off the Sikh outposts and then encamp, while he reconnoitred the main enemy defences, for it was jungle country with few points of observation, so that it was difficult to plan for a general engagement. After the enemy outposts had been disposed of, however, and Gough was about to make camp, the Sikhs advanced and he only just had time to form up before battle was joined.

The jungle, which in some parts of the field was dense, made confusion inevitable, but Gough's infantry brigades got the better of the Sikhs at close quarters in ferocious fighting during which both sides lost heavily. The first cavalry brigade on the left, commanded by White, also defeated an enemy attempt to get round the flank. The second cavalry brigade, on the right,

1849

met with disaster owing to the extraordinary incompetence of its Brigadier, Pope, who was a Lieut.-Colonel of native cavalry and so old and infirm that he had to be helped on to his horse. It appears that, apart from his infirmities, he had never actually commanded anything larger than a squadron before, and so was quite at sea with a brigade, especially in close country where he could see only a small part of it at a time. Having sent out two squadrons each of the 9th Lancers and 1st and 6th Native Cavalry to watch his right flank, he endeavoured to advance with the remainder in line without either scouts in front or reserves behind. Discovering that he was then masking the fire, both of his own horse artillery and part of the infantry brigade on his left, he then tried to take ground to the right, but got the brigade into such confusion that he had the halt sounded in order to sort things out. After a short pause, he gave the order 'threes right', but it was scarcely out of his mouth when the Sikhs charged the native cavalry who were halted between the 14th and the 9th Lancers. The order was thus translated as 'threes about' and the two British regiments, who were not engaged, and whose officers stated that they distinctly heard this order, wheeled about and retired at a walk. The whole brigade was then charged from the rear and got to the gallop, with the native cavalry routed and the British cavalry trying to keep formation in a situation in which it was impossible to rally, or in fact to do anything. The two British regiments soon pulled up to a trot and then halted, turning about and dressing their lines in time to receive Gough with swords at the *recover*, when he came over to see what had happened. The native cavalry were not seen again that day, and the horse artillery, which was not 'Royal' but 'Company's' was overrun and lost six guns, and nearly all its officers and men. The 14th lost in killed Lieut. A. J. Cureton – son of the General – and Private George Tookey, and in wounded Major C. Steuart and 14 men, of whom two died of wounds. In spite of the situation, the Sikhs by no means got everything their own way and several were cut down by the 14th in single combats. After one such combat a Sikh was seen galloping off with a troop-sergeant-major's sword sticking out from between his shoulder-blades – many of the Sikhs apparently wore chain-mail under their shirts, and this particular one was not as badly smitten as it appeared.

Chillianwalla was a particularly bloody affair, in which nearly all the fighting was at close quarters in jungle country, against preponderant numbers of ferocious Sikhs. The casualties in the infantry were very heavy – the 24th Regiment (Warwickshires) lost 21 officers and nearly 500 men in killed and wounded.

(above) 14th Light Dragoons Guidon c. 1830. The Prussian Eagle centre device was replaced by the title of the Regiment within the garter, surmounted by the crown, in 1830, as the result of the 14th becoming a Royal Regiment in that year. (below) The Battle of Ramnuggur – 22nd November 1848. Lieutenant-Colonel William Havelock leading his Regiment against the Sikhs.

Because of this – and also because Gough was on bad terms with the Governor-General, Lord Dalhousie – the battle was represented as a 'disaster', and became the subject of an outcry at home, followed by various enquiries. As was only to be expected in such circumstances, a great deal of odium became attached in the popular imagination to the 9th Lancers and 14th Light Dragoons, who were believed to have fled in panic, and although the previous and subsequent services of the two regiments showed that such a thing was highly unlikely, to say the least of it, their association with the debacle in Pope's cavalry brigade took a lot of living down.

A strange aspect of the period in British history between Waterloo and Mons, was the manner in which the public followed the fortunes of the Army in the 'Small Wars', rather as nowadays it follows the fortunes of leading football teams. Victory was always expected as a matter of course, and courage was taken for granted, but only in the Crimea did any dim impression of the sufferings and self-sacrifice of the British soldier make any impact on the public mind. Next to victory celebrations, there was nothing the citizens liked better than demanding that someone should be called to account for a 'disaster' and, in consequence, the circumstances attending the results on battlefields tended to be exaggerated and obscure. 'Triumph and disaster,' wrote Kipling, were 'two impostors,' which any sensible man should treat alike. It was extremely sound advice, but rarely followed.

Chillianwalla resulted in the Sikhs withdrawing into their entrenchments along the Jhelum at Rasul, leaving Gough master of the field. He refrained from following them until he had collected his dead and wounded. Nor did he see any point in doing so, for he knew where they had gone, and that he would not have the strength to attack them until he had been joined by reinforcements from Multan.

At Rasul Shere Singh, the Sikh commander, was joined by the army of Chattar Singh, and it is significant that in spite of this large reinforcement he made no attempt to attack Gough, but remained in his entrenchments in the barren country along the Jhelum, where lack of subsistence soon obliged him to move. On the 2nd February, leaving 10,000 men to watch Gough, he marched off to the eastward, and commenced a series of manoeuvres designed to tempt Gough into attacking him in the open. Gough bided his time until, on the 15th February, he marched to Lasuri to effect a junction with General Whish who was approaching Ramnuggur. Shere Singh had meanwhile taken up

1849

a position at Gujerat, with the intention of marching on Lahore. On the 19th, Gough, having been joined by Whish, marched to Shadiwal, thus cutting Shere Singh off from the fords across the Chenab, and so from Lahore. Having now, however, a force of 24,000 men and 96 guns with him, he was ready to deal with Shere Singh where he stood.

The cavalry division with Gough now had three brigades, and the 14th were in the 1st Brigade under Brigadier Lockwood, which consisted, besides themselves, of the 1st Bengal Light Cavalry, and detachments of the 11th and 18th Irregular Cavalry. The division was commanded by General Thackwell. The Sikhs, with about 60,000 men and 60 guns, were drawn up about a mile south of Gujerat in a crescent formation with both flanks slightly refused, and watched by their cavalry. Gough's plan was to send Lockwood's and Hearsey's cavalry brigades against their left and left centre, and then destroy their right wing by two converging attacks.

On the morning of the 21st February, 1849, the British/Indian army was drawn up in line before Gujerat, with the 1st and 2nd Cavalry brigades on the extreme right, three infantry divisions in the centre, and the 3rd Cavalry brigade on the left. With the same formality which Marlborough had employed before Blenheim, the venerable Gough rode down the line from right to left, drawing a roar of cheering from his excited troops who, no doubt because the day was fine, with a sharp nip in the air, seem to have been particularly ready to get to work although they all knew that it was the last day on earth for many of them, and that many others were going to get badly hurt.

The line advanced at 7.30 a.m., and marched resolutely forward across about two miles of open ground, until the Sikh guns opened fire prematurely as Gough had expected, giving away their positions. Halting, he sent forward his own guns, covered by skirmishers, and an artillery duel commenced which ended, after a couple of hours, in the silencing of most of the enemy batteries. Meanwhile the Sikh horse had advanced in great numbers against the 1st and 2nd cavalry brigades on Gough's right. Hearsey, who was commanding both brigades, manoeuvred with great skill to prevent them turning his flank, but in doing so, left the infantry flank exposed and had to send Lockwood's brigade back to protect it. The Sikh horsemen, who were in fact Afghans, then tried to get between the two cavalry brigades, but were foiled by the horse artillery. This cavalry work was all an affair of manoeuvre, for the Afghans persistently avoided coming to close quarters. While it was going on, the British/Indian infantry advanced and steadily overcame the Sikhs, who in the early afternoon broke and fled in all directions, throwing away their arms as they ran. It was a surprising exhibition by such staunch fighting men, and goes to show that their previous experiences in battle with the British, including Chillianwalla, had led to an abysmal lowering of morale.

The cavalry, being so busy trying to outwit one another on the flank, were at first unaware that the day had been lost and won by the infantry, but when the Afghans suddenly realised that the sounds of battle were dying away to the north, they pulled round and made off in that direction at the gallop. The British cavalry on both flanks immediately pursued, those under Hearsey on the right trying to get ahead of those under Thackwell on the left, who were riding hard to cut the fugitives off from the Jhelum. The 14th, who were naturally anxious to avenge Chillianwalla, were very unpleasant people for the fleeing enemy to have in their rear, and a rout ensued such as is seldom seen in war. Large numbers of both Sikhs and Afghans were cut down by the regiment, and an Afghan standard of red silk was captured by Corporal William Pain, after he had fought and killed the horseman who was carrying it. The cavalry pursuit of a routed enemy, although essential, is of course an extremely repugnant affair both to witness and describe. The enemy, however, is seldom deserving of pity, and the Sikhs and Afghans certainly deserved all they got. Enemy soldiers who surrender after throwing down their arms were, in fact, usually spared by British troops, but such chivalrous conduct is often dangerous as was shown in the case of Captain Scudamore of the 14th who, having spared the life of what he thought to be an unarmed Sikh, was shot by him in the back and wounded as he rode on.

On the day of the battle, the 14th did not draw rein until dark, when they were fifteen miles beyond Gujerat. The pursuit was resumed at dawn, and by the evening of the 24th the regiment reached Naurangabad. Here it was learned that what was left of the Sikh army was crossing the Jhelum, and the 1st cavalry brigade rode on to intercept, but arrived at the river on the following day too late, seeing about twenty thousand Sikhs on the opposite bank out of reach. General Sir Walter Gilbert, who was leading the pursuit with about 12,000 all arms, crossed the Jhelum on the 28th February without opposition, for the Sikhs on the other side fled when they saw him coming. Led by the 1st cavalry brigade he marched on, until by the 8th March he was within thirty miles of Rawalpindi, where Shere Singh had halted with about 16,000 men. On the same day Shere Singh

1849

surrendered, bringing with him from Rawalpindi all the British soldiers he had captured at Peshawar and Attock. Gilbert, however, marched on to Rawalpindi, where the Sikhs handed over their arms, of which there were left about twenty thousand small arms and forty-one guns.

It still remained to chase the Afghans up the Khyber, and Gilbert marched on to Attock, which he reached with the cavalry on the 17th March. The Afghans made a demonstration on the far bank of the Indus, but they cleared off as soon as they saw the British troops crossing the river. Peshawar was reached on the 21st March, when it was found that the Afghans had fled up the Khyber two days previously, and that the campaign was therefore at an end. The 14th left Peshawar on the 4th April and marched to Lahore, which was reached on the 1st May. Their losses at Gujerat had been one officer, Lieut. Lloyd, killed, and two officers and four rank and file wounded.

On the 19th January, 1851, the 14th left Lahore and marched to Meerut which they reached on the 6th March. Here they remained until 1854, when the Crimean War broke out, and orders were received in late January 'to proceed to Bombay with all despatch, preparatory to embarkation for the seat of war in Turkey.' After receiving a flattering message from the Commander-in-Chief, in which he 'congratulates the corps on its brilliant destination', the 14th set out for Bombay on the 16th January, 1855, but after only one day on the road 'orders were received from the Governor-General direct by electric telegraph for the Fourteenth to march to Kirkee'. The regiment, marching at a strength of 20 officers and 705 rank and file, accordingly made for Kirkee – 884 miles away. It may here be mentioned, as a matter of general interest, that even after the advent of railways and indeed, up to the time of the Second World War, it continued to be customary for regiments on the Indian service to change station by march route. On such occasions both cavalry and infantry regiments thought it nothing out of the way to undertake marches of many hundreds of miles, occupying weeks and even months. Although such marches often led through very unhealthy tracts of country in which, in the old days, deaths from cholera and other tropical diseases were commonplace, they were on the whole an enjoyable experience which was very beneficial to the spirit and stamina of the troops, besides being a method of 'showing the flag', and curbing lawlessness.

The 14th reached Kirkee on the 21st April, having lost two men from disease during the march. Here the regiment remained for the rest of the year and the whole of the following, suffering

1856

from the extreme frustration common to professional fighting men, of being reduced to reading about the exploits of the light cavalry in the Crimea in the newspapers, and eventually realising that the war had dragged to its close without their participation.

The reason for the cancellation of the orders for the Crimea was that trouble had arisen over a threat by Persia against the fortified city of Herat, inside the borders of Afghanistan. British relations with Afghanistan had always been strained and, as already related, the Afghans had given active support to the Sikhs during the conflicts with the British in the Punjab. It may therefore seem odd, that the British government should have been worried over the fate of a remote Afghan city far removed from any contact with civilisation. Afghanistan, however, lying across the north-west frontier of India, guarded the routes by which all previous major invasions had been launched. Violations of its borders were therefore of concern to any government of India, which could never afford to allow it to fall under the domination of another power, especially as Russia made no secret of her intention to march on India through the old invasion routes sooner or later.

In 1852 a Persian force invaded and occupied Herat, and had then formally annexed it, but had withdrawn after British representations. A dispute between Great Britain and Persia continued, however, and culminated in the withdrawal of the British mission to Tehran in December, 1855. Another Persian expedition against Herat was then organised, and some months of negotiations followed. These broke down in July, 1856, when the British government ordered the Governor-General of India to prepare an adequate force for the occupation of the island of Kharak and the city and district of Bushire in the Persian Gulf. Orders for this force to proceed followed at the end of September, and on the 1st of November the Indian government declared war on Persia.

Lieut.-Colonel (later Major-General) Herbert Gall, C.B., 14th Light Dragoons. He commanded the left wing and later the whole regiment during the Indian Mutiny. Reproduced by kind permission of Lieut.-Colonel J. B. R. Nicholson, Editor of *Tradition* magazine.

1857 The 14th in Persia
June 1857 Aurangabad
October 1857 Mandsaur
February 1858 Relief of Saugor
March 1858 The Siege of Jhansi
April 1858 Lieut. James Leith awarded the Victoria Cross
The Combat on the Betwa River

1857

17

The Indian Mutiny

THE Persian Campaign of 1857 was an uncommonly short one, which was just as well for, 'the climate is a very pestilential one'. Some details of the 14th, which travelled in sailing ships, never even had time to disembark before the war was over, and came straight back again. The expedition, commanded by Major-General Sir James Outram, consisted of two divisions; and the 14th, with Jacob's Horse, formed the cavalry of the Second Division, under Henry Havelock, brother of William Havelock, killed at Ramnuggur at the head of the regiment.

The regiment, at a strength of 25 officers and 614 rank and file, with 649 horses, embarked at Bombay in January, after marching from Kirkee by squadrons, and disembarked at Bushire at the beginning of February. Advancing with the First Division, Outram routed the Persians at Kush-ab and a month later, having formed an entrenched camp at Bushire, embarked about four thousand men and sailed for the delta of the Euphrates. Captain Prettejohn's troop of the 14th accompanied this force, which was delayed in the Shat-el-Arab by the grounding of the transports, so that rafts had to be constructed to get the men and horses ashore. No opposition was encountered until the troops arrived before Mohamra, where the Persian army was drawn up,

1857

but the enemy fled as soon as the guns of the warships opened fire, without waiting to be attacked. As they had too good a start, Outram did not attempt to pursue, but he sent three hundred British infantrymen up the Karun river in steamboats. This small force landed at Ahwaz and put to flight 10,000 Persians. Peace was signed in Paris on the 4th March, and the expedition returned to India, the 14th landing at Bombay on the 15th May. The adventure had achieved its object, in that Persia surrendered all claims to Herat and bound herself not to interfere with the internal affairs of Afghanistan; but from the soldier's point of view, no honour could be gained in conflict with such pusillanimous enemies, and it had all been a shocking waste of time – and also of life, for there had been many deaths from dysentry, including General Stalker of the First Division, and the Commodore of the Naval Squadron. The 14th, however, only lost 22 horses and no men.

The 14th had no sooner arrived back at Kirkee than they were dispersed to Ahmednagar, Poona, Satara, and other parts of the Bombay presidency. The Indian Mutiny had broken out on the 11th May with a rising at Meerut, which had been followed by the capture of Delhi by the mutineers, and the restoration of the last of the Moguls, Bahadur Shah.

Disaffection among the native units of the East India Company's Bengal Army had been growing for a considerable time, but the Indian Government was quite unprepared for any general uprising, for the latent causes behind it had not been fully appreciated, and the British officers in the native units had always strongly resented any imputations of disloyalty upon their men. Those behind the outbreak were, however, extremely powerful groups and individuals, ranging from the Brahmin priesthood, anxious to maintain its authority in the face of British inroads, to princes deprived of their kingdoms on one pretext or another. One such was the formidable Rani of Jhansi, a childless widow, who had not been allowed to adopt an heir in accordance with Hindu custom. Another was the Nana Sahib, nominal ruler of the Mahrattas but now living on a British pension at Cawnpore (where he was very popular among the British residents). All these various elements had managed to combine behind the scenes, establishing 'cells' throughout the Bengal Army whose business it was to rouse the sepoys to revolt by spreading tales among them of British attempts to destroy their caste by such subtleties as causing them to bite open cartridges greased with the fat of cows and pigs. Once the mutiny had spread, those behind it called out their own followers and subjects in support, so that the greater part of northern India was soon in a state of rebellion, which showed signs of spreading to the south.

At the time of the outbreak there were a bare forty thousand British soldiers in the whole of India, and even this meagre number had been weakened by expeditions to China, Burma and the Persian Gulf. Had not large numbers of the native regiments remained loyal, the whole sub-continent would almost certainly have sunk into a bloody chaos. Even as things were, the suppression of the Mutiny required the exercise by all British soldiers of a measure of courage, endurance, skill at arms and sheer hardihood, for the like of which one may search the annals of military history in vain.

While the 14th were deploying through the Bombay Presidency, the Indian Government was frantically collecting a force to recapture Delhi. Meanwhile, the small garrisons of various cantonments were surrounded by rebels and mutineers, and becoming hard pressed. Cawnpore and Lucknow were cut off with no hope of early relief, but Indore and Mhow, where the British residents were also in danger, were within reach of the Bombay Army. The difficulty was, in a situation of such extreme gravity, to decide on the priorities of the operations necessary, for they could not all be undertaken at the same time by the forces available, especially as the loyalty of the native units was everywhere suspect. However, on the 8th June, a column was sent out by the Governor of Bombay to secure the road to Agra and keep open the communications with Central India. It consisted of five troops of the 14th and the 25th Native Infantry, with an East India Company Horse Artillery battery. The column was ordered to march first on Mhow, but was diverted on the line of march to secure Aurangabad, where the native troops had mutinied. The 14th were fortunately in time to rescue the British women and children at this station, but the mutineers, consisting of two cavalry regiments, an infantry regiment, and a field battery, had entrenched themselves on high ground. When summoned to surrender, all except the 1st Hyderabad Cavalry did so. The 14th thereupon advanced against this regiment, with the 25th Native Infantry on the left and the horse battery in the centre. The mutinous cavalry then got to horse and galloped off, pursued by the 14th whose horses, however, were too tired to catch up.

Some rebels were taken during the following days, not only by the 14th but also by the rest of the native cavalry, who had changed their minds and decided to remain loyal. The rebels were immediately tried at the drum head, and hanged, shot, or

1857

blown away from the guns. This kind of rough justice was, of course, alien to the British character even in those days; but it was certainly no time for softness, and the hearts of all British soldiers in India had hardened after evidence of the fate meted out by the rebels to British women and children, especially at Cawnpore where, after being promised safe-conduct, they were murdered, raped, cut to pieces and thrown down a well. It was indeed, under the spur of the fury engendered by these atrocities, that the British troops during the Indian Mutiny were able to endure the most phenomenal hardships and exertions, normally far beyond the limits of human capacity.

The monsoon had started soon after the column from Bombay had begun its march on Mhow, making progress very difficult. Swimming the wide Nerbudda in its swollen state was in itself a remarkable feat for cavalry, and not one which would normally be undertaken. As a rule, when swimming rivers, the saddlery and accoutrements were sent across by raft, although this was not always practicable. The crossing was usually done with troops in line, taking the water together, with bit reins knotted and the horses guided by the bridoons. If the men were not good swimmers nearly always some were drowned. No such casualties are recorded in the 14th at the crossing of the Nerbudda, although there seems to be no doubt that the horses were saddled, and burdened with the accoutrements of marching order. The 14th, incidentally, were wearing turbans, with the pugri fringe hanging down the back after the Moslem fashion, and their tunics open at the neck without stocks. Most British regiments made similar adaptations to their dress during the Indian Mutiny, in concession to the rigours of the climate. Later on, tunics were dispensed with altogether, and the soldiers marched either in shirt-sleeves or in blouses made of pugri cloth and dyed with curry-powder – thus introducing the colour known as khaki.

After the column had reached Mhow, further operations became impossible owing to the severity of the monsoon rain, which came down in torrents. A halt had therefore to be called, although at Indore, only ten miles away, the Maharaja Holkar lay with his State forces which had all mutinied, and a large number of armed rebels. They were all Mahrattas, countrymen of the villainous Nana Sahib, and it was urgently necessary to deal with them before they dispersed to plunder and ravage the country in the old Mahratta manner. A hundred and twenty miles to the north of Indore lay Prince Feroz Shah, with the mutinous cavalry of the Gwalior State forces, and about fifteen thousand armed rebels. In Hyderabad, to the south-east, the

Nizam, 'Faithful Ally of the British Empire', had managed to keep control of his forces, and had offered their services unreservedly to the British; but nevertheless, there were a large number of rebels abroad in his dominions, and the general situation was very far from pleasant.

With the abatement of the monsoon in October, a column known as the Malwa Field Force, led by Brigadier C. S. Stuart, marched against Feroz Shah at Mandsaur. It consisted of 5 troops of the 14th, 4 companies of the 86th Regiment (Royal Irish Rifles), the 3rd Hyderabad Cavalry, 25th Native Infantry, and a couple of field batteries and a contingent of the Madras Sappers and Miners. After crossing the Chambal, this force arrived before Mandsaur on the 21st October. Feroz Shah came out against it, but was halted by Stuart's cavalry during the afternoon. On the following day Stuart launched an attack with his whole force, although he was outnumbered by at least ten to one. The ensuing action was notable for the bold handling of the cavalry, opening with a charge by the 14th which resulted in the capture of all the enemy guns, which were then turned round by the 25th Native Infantry and used against the shaken rebels. A series of cavalry charges followed, during which the 14th secured three enemy standards, and ended with the rebels retreat into the fort of Dhar. This was captured on the 31st October, after it had been abandoned by the rebels, who had dispersed and fled. However, it was found to contain a considerable quantity of treasure, and the efforts of the British troops were rewarded by a substantial sum in prize money.

After about seventy captives had been tried at the drum head and shot on the banks of the Chambal, the column advanced and camped about four miles from Mandsaur on the 21st November. The town was strongly held, but Stuart's intention was to by-pass it and relieve Neemuch, some fifty miles beyond, where the British colony was in danger. While engaged in this operation, the rebels made several sorties from Mandsaur in attempts to cut him off, but they were repulsed by innumerable charges by the 14th and Hyderabad Cavalry. The 14th suffered fairly heavy casualties at this time during several hand-to-hand engagements, but they cut down the rebels in great numbers, riding so hard that it is astonishing how their horses stood up to it. It is even more astonishing, however, how both British and Indian infantry kept going as they did upon marches of such length which included long distances covered at the double. It was these powers of rapidity of movement which in the end suppressed the Indian Mutiny.

1858

As a result of these operations both Neemuch and Mandsaur were captured, and the whole of the western district of Malwa cleared of rebels. The Malwa Field Force had therefore completed its task, and thereafter became the 1st Brigade of the Central India Field Force, commanded by General Sir Hugh Rose. Only two troops of the 14th, however, remained with the 1st Brigade. The rest of the regiment marched with the 2nd Brigade, commanded by Colonel Charles Steuart of the 14th.

The plan for what was known as the Central India Campaign was that Sir Hugh Rose should march from Mhow through Jhansi to Kalpi, keeping in touch with a column under General Whitlock which was to march from Jubbulpore upon Banda. The operations were designed to prevent rebels from Gwalior attacking the rear of Sir Colin Campbell's forces across the Jumna. In preparation for the campaign, Rose assembled the 1st Brigade at Mhow and the 2nd Brigade at Sihor. On the 16th January, 1858, he set out for Saugor with the 2nd Brigade to relieve the small British garrison there, which had been under siege for eight months. Marching by way of Bhopal and Bhilsa, the 2nd Brigade arrived on the 24th January before the fortress of Rahatgarh, which was of considerable strength. Having a siege train with him Rose, however, commenced to pound away at it. An attempt to relieve it by the Rajah of Banpore with a large force of rebels was easily defeated, and the garrison fled by night, leaving Rose to march in and dismantle the place on the 28th January. Among the booty was the charger of Lieutenant Redmayne, who had been killed in the action at Mandsaur. It had a severe wound over one eye, but was bought at auction by Rose himself who rode it during the rest of the campaign.

The sound of Rose's siege guns greatly heartened the British men, women and children besieged at Saugor, who had almost abandoned hope. As soon as his cavalry had returned from cutting down the fugitives from Rahatgarh, and he had hanged a couple of rebel chieftains over the gate of the fort, Rose marched on over 20 miles to Saugor, putting the enemy to flight and relieving it on the 3rd February. It was a great experience for the 14th to ride in among the waving handkerchiefs of the ladies of the garrison who were also, it appears, cheering lustily, although that was regarded as such unfeminine behaviour in those days that the 14th were unable to believe their ears. Loading rifles for their menfolk, and even firing them, besides defending their virtue with swords and daggers was not, curiously enough, regarded as unfeminine but only to be expected from the wives and mothers of Englishmen.

1858

After the relief of Saugor, Rose advanced immediately against the fort of Garhakota, about twenty-five miles away. The garrison decamped, pursued by two troops of the 14th, under Captains R. J. Brown and Arthur Need, with the Hyderabad Cavalry and some guns. They caught them up after a chase of twenty-five miles and cut down about a hundred, of whom five fell to the sword of Captain Need, who was renowned for his dash and swordsmanship.

During the siege of Saugor the rebels had laid waste the entire district, leaving the inhabitants starving. Sir Hugh Rose was able to relieve them out of his large stocks of captured grain, but its distribution took time and delayed his advance. Before moving on Jhansi, however, he had in any case to wait for General Whitlock to march from Jubbulpore, and also make contact with his 1st Brigade, which had left Mhow in January and was marching by a parallel route to the west. Led by a squadron of the 14th under Major Gall, the brigade had reached Goona without incident at the end of February, and arrived before the fortified town of Chanderi on the 5th March. It was strongly held by a considerable force of rebels, numbers of whom had to be chased out by the cavalry, although the country was so broken by walls and ditches that it was scarcely rideable. This fact made an effective pursuit impossible when the garrison of the fort fled after it had been stormed by the wild Irishmen of the 86th Regiment on the 17th, to the music of their band playing *St Patrick's Day*. Meanwhile, Rose had marched for Jhansi with the 2nd Brigade on the 27th February. The main road led through the pass of Marhat, which was strongly held by the Rajah of Banpur. Major Scudamore, now recovered from his wound at Gujerat, with a squadron of the 14th, some native infantry and guns, was sent to make a feint against it, while Rose himself forced the adjoining pass of Muddenpore, held by the Rajah of Shahgarh. All went according to plan, and the rebels abandoned both passes and fled. The capture of the fort of Chanderi by the 1st Brigade sent them out of the district altogether, when the Union Jack was hoisted, and the territories of the Rajah of Shahgarh formally annexed to the British Crown.

The inexorable advance of the Central India Field Force, and the dashing behaviour of its cavalry, both British and Indian, in charging anything in sight without hesitation; its ruthlessness in pursuit and summary execution of those captured in arms, had by this time scared the rebels almost out of their wits, so that they seldom waited for close quarters in spite of their great preponderance in numbers. The followers of the Rani of Jhansi, however,

1858

were still more frightened of that formidable lady than they were of Sir Hugh Rose; and indeed, her oriental methods of dealing with weaklings made ordinary execution seem quite tame. The capture of Jhansi, held by the Rani with 12,000 men and forty guns, was therefore not likely to be a walk-over. Rose, however, was not merely determined to capture it, but to make sure also that none of its garrison escaped. Before opening fire with his guns he therefore ringed it with his cavalry and horse artillery, disposed in seven 'flying camps', so that deserters from the garrison trying to slink off were nearly all captured and executed.

At the siege of Jhansi the 14th Light Dragoons were together for the first time in the campaign. Or, it would perhaps be more correct to say the whole regiment was in the one place; for it continued to operate in two independent squadrons or wings, each of three troops. The right wing was led by Major Scudamore and the left wing by Major Gall, who arrived with the 1st Brigade on the 21st March after covering the seventy miles from Chanderi in two days. The commanding officer, Colonel Charles Steuart, commanded the 2nd Brigade, and must not be confused with Colonel Charles Stuart of the Bombay Army who commanded the 1st Brigade; besides the similarity of name, both officers were temporary Brigadier-Generals.

Realising that her position was hopeless, the Rani of Jhansi sent for help to Tantia Topi, the Nana Sahib's military commander, who was besieging the fort of the Rajah of Charkari north of the Jumna with 20,000 men. Marching at once, he arrived in the vicinity of Jhansi on the 31st March, placing Rose with his small army in a perilous position.

Rose's whole force did not amount to much more than 12,000 men, of whom less than half were British, and which, on the arrival of Tantia Topi, was fully committed to the encirclement of Jhansi. Had he raised the siege in order to face Tantia Topi the Rani would certainly have fallen upon his rear, while if he continued the siege there was no doubt that Tantia would attack him while his army was dispersed. This awkward problem did not apparently worry him in the slightest. Under cover of darkness he assembled about 1,200 men by thinning out the lines before Jhansi, and sending elephants forward to bring eight field guns out of the advanced batteries. These elephants, obeying the whispered instructions of their mahouts, carried out this task so silently that the operation was unnoticed by the enemy, who were further deceived by Rose striking the tents of the 1st Brigade in order to distract their attention from his point of assembly. Shortly after midnight, Rose heard that a large enemy force was crossing the Betwa by a ford about eight miles down river. He immediately sent off Brigadier Stuart with Lieut. Giles' troop of the 14th, a squadron of native cavalry, two companies of the 86th (Royal Irish Rifles) and the 25th Bombay Native Infantry to oppose them. Meanwhile he drew up the rest of his force, of about 950 men, within hearing of the yells and jeers of Tantia Topi's main army. The only British soldiers with him were three troops of the 14th, led by Captains Need, Prettejohn and McMahon, and two companies of the 109th, at that time the 3rd Bombay European Regiment of the East India Company's Army, but later the 2nd Leinsters. His native troop consisted of 100 Hyderabad Cavalry and 300 of the 24th Infantry. This tiny force had to oppose the advance of about 1,000 horsemen, 28 guns and something like 10,000 drugged fanatics on foot.

Tantia Topi advanced at daybreak on the 1st April, and the vedettes posted by the 14th and Hyderabad Cavalry fell back. Rose ordered his infantry to lie down – an unusual procedure at the start of an action in those days – and advanced his cavalry and horse artillery on each flank, thus enfilading the enemy just as they were hesitating under the fire of the British and Indian infantry. Mounted on Redmayne's fine charger, Rose charged the enemy's left with Captain Need's troop of the 14th, while on the other flank Captain Prettejohn led two troops against their right. 'It was a glorious sight to see them thundering along,' wrote one of the N.C.O.'s, 'one minute and they were among the enemy, and all that was to be seen was a confused mass of flashing swords and bayonets, struggling men and horses, and hoarse shouts of rage.'

It was indeed, a very surprising affair, in which victory was only possible for men fired with hatred and contempt, and inspired by the remarkable qualities exhibited by Sir Hugh Rose. Above the tumult the cavalry trumpets could be heard ceaselessly sounding the charge, as the three troops of the 14th hacked their way deeper into the dense masses of rebels, who were already reeling back before the musket volleys, while ricocheting cannon-balls ploughed through their rear flanks. As their line crumpled up, the 109th advanced and charged, and in a moment Tantia Topi's entire army dissolved into groups of demoralised fugitives; but the trumpets went on sounding the charge, and the 14th continued to cut them down without mercy. 'By St Patrick,' said a soldier of the 86th, 'they couldn't spare one of the murtherers! Why should they, when they remembered the little babies and the poor ladies who were butchered in Cawnpore and Jhansi?'

1858

Nearly two thousand rebels were slain in this conflict – more in fact, than the entire British force engaged – and many more were drowned as they fled across the Betwa after abandoning all their guns. Stuart had a similar experience at the ford, where Lieut. Giles' troop charged across very bad ground, and had half-a-dozen casualties. Across the Betwa the jungle was on fire, either from bursting shells or deliberately lighted by Tantia Topi to cover his retreat. The pursuing cavalry galloped through it, getting quite a few men and horses badly burned. They rode hard for over nine miles before Rose pulled them up, by which time nearly all the rebels' elephants, ammunition and stores had been captured, all of the 28 guns, and several standards. The casualties suffered by the 14th were 5 men and 11 horses killed; 25 men and 16 horses wounded. Lieutenant James Leith was awarded the Victoria Cross: 'For conspicuous bravery at Betwa on the 1st April, 1858, in having charged alone and rescued Captain Need of the same regiment when surrounded by a large number of rebel infantry.' These two officers were dashing swordsmen of a type which was prolific in all three of the fighting arms of the British Army in this period. This is not to imply of course, that there is any lack of a similar spirit among their descendants of the present day; but there is no doubt that it was far more enlivening to sight the quarry between the ears of one's horse, than from a machine of some kind, or even beyond the point of a bayonet. Many of the mounted officers in the infantry, who were not as expert as the cavalrymen in using the swords on horseback, used to carry hogspears during the Central India Campaign with which they did not hesitate to ride down the enemy far ahead of their men. In the affair on the Betwa, it appears that Need galloped after the enemy up a rocky height and that his horse came to a standstill, unable to move, while he was in the middle of a crowd of infuriated Mahrattas cutting at him with tulwars. By the time Leith got to him, his clothing, reins and saddlery had been slashed to pieces, but he himself escaped with a few scratches.

During this combat with Tantia Topi, which took place almost under the walls of Jhansi, it might have been expected that the garrison would have made a sortie, in which case Sir Hugh Rose's position would have been desperate. He had, however, guarded against the possibility as well as he could, by sending Major Gall's squadron of the 14th with a couple of guns to make a feint attack on one of the sally ports, where the enemy were observed to be forming up. This effectually deterred them from venturing out; evidence both of a craven spirit and a lack of military knowledge among the leaders.

A camp scene, 1858, during the Indian Mutiny – Orlando Norie. While in India the 14th sometimes wore turbans with pugri cloths as head dress as they were more comfortable and serviceable than the heavy shakos.

1858

On the 3rd April, Gall's squadron again made a feint attack accompanied by the same section of field artillery. The sound of the opening shots of his guns was the signal for the stormers to leave cover and mount the breach. The storming of a fortress was not usually attempted unless the stormers had an advantage of three to one over the garrison; but at Jhansi it was the garrison which held this advantage, so that the breach was carried only after desperate fighting. It was successful owing to the low morale of the garrison following the defeat of Tantia Topi, and to the feint by Major Gall which divided the enemy at a critical moment. After fleeing from the city, many of them established themselves in the suburbs and on adjoining heights, and these were all attacked by the cavalry and dispersed with heavy losses. The Rani herself got away, galloping off with a sword in one hand and with the other holding her adopted child on her saddle-bow. She and her cavalry escort were hotly pursued by a detachment of Hyderabad cavalry. They captured her tent and belongings but she herself outdistanced her pursuers.

After the capture of Jhansi, Sir Hugh Rose remained in the vicinity for nearly three weeks, clearing the district of rebels. The 14th Light Dragoons were continuously in the saddle on this task, deployed over the countryside by troops, of which those led by Lieutenant Gowan and Cornet Beamish seem to have been the most successful, especially Beamish's troop which accounted for about three hundred rebels whom they found hidden in suburban gardens or in the surrounding cornfields.

On the 22nd April a mixed force under Major, now Brevet Lieut.-Colonel Gall, and including three troops of the regiment, marched for Calpee, which was Tantia Topi's arsenal, defended with a large force, by his nephew, the Rao Sahib. Sir Hugh Rose, with the 1st Brigade, followed on the 25th April, with the 2nd Brigade two days' march in rear.

The engagement at Ranode, 17 December 1858; one of the last operations of the Indian Mutiny; Captain Prettejohn's squadron, consisting of 'A' and 'H' troops (150 men), putting the rebels to flight.

1st May 1858 The action at Kunch
26th May 1858 The action at Calpee
16th June 1858 The assault on Morar
20th June 1858 The capture of Gwalior
2nd May 1861 The 20th Light Dragoons raised again at Muttra
1863 and 1868 The Ambeyla and Hazara Campaigns
August 1861 Light Dragoons become Hussars
1881 The 14th in South Africa
1885 and 1889 The 20th in Egypt and the Sudan

1858

18

Central India, South Africa and the Sudan

On the 1st May, Gall, with the advanced guard, arrived at Pooch, about fifty miles from Jhansi, where he learned that Tantia Topi had taken up a strong entrenched position at Kunch, fourteen miles ahead and barring the approach to Calpee. Sir Hugh Rose joined him later in the day, followed by the 1st Brigade, and ordered a halt to await the 2nd Brigade which marched in on the 5th. A halt was essential in any case, for the heat was terrific, with a burning wind blowing night and day across an arid, dusty land almost devoid of water and shade. The Central India Field Force was here joined by the right wing of the 71st Highland Light Infantry, newly arrived from Malta, where they had barely had time to recover from the ardours of the Crimea. They were dressed in loose khaki blouses, issued under regimental arrangements in Bombay, with peaked caps fitted with curtains to shade the back of the neck, but they still wore their thick tartan trousers. They were armed with the muzzle-loading Enfield rifle, an accurate weapon with a long effective range, but which was now found to be most unreliable in the great heat of the Indian plains, for the bullet could not be forced down the barrel. Also, their long, triangular bayonets were 'of little use against these desperate men', as one of them wrote. 'When it is drove into them they seize hold of it, and cut at

243

1858

you with tulwars. Some severe wounds were received this way.'

Sir Hugh Rose decided to make a holding attack with the 2nd Brigade and outflank the enemy position with the 1st Brigade, but before marching he sent Gall with his column to take Lohari fort, near Kunch. This was stormed with little ceremony, at a cost to the 14th of one man killed and five officers and thirteen men wounded.

Among the officer casualties was Gall himself, who led the stormers, but his wounds did not keep him from duty. The use of cavalrymen in the storm of a fort in this manner is probably without precedent, but his shortage of manpower forced Sir Hugh Rose into many unorthodox shifts.

On the morning of the 7th May, after a march of fourteen miles, Sir Hugh Rose arrived before Kunch and formed up on the rebel flank, sending Gall forward to reconnoitre with some of the 14th and Hyderabad cavalry.

On his approach the rebels withdrew closer to the town, leaving picquets in occupation of some wooded positions and outworks. The action commenced with an attack by the 2nd Brigade, which was brought to a halt by strong enemy resistance.

It was not intended, however, to be more than a holding attack, to enable Rose to bring in the 1st Brigade on the flank. After a period of heavy firing from both sides, the order 'Forward and charge!' was given to the 14th, who advanced accordingly, with the Hyderabad cavalry in support. The scene was well-described by a soldier of the 71st, James Watt: 'Sir H.R. ordered up the 14th Cavalry and the Hyderabads of the 1st Brigade. The enemy's cavalry being under cover, as soon as they saw ours comind down prepared to meet them. At it they went, their sabres gleaming in the sun. It was a fine sight to see, the ground being broken in front of our cavalry (and holes dug by the enemy) wavered for a moment, as it were, but then being past the broken ground their charge was irresistible, the enemy did not wait a moment longer but to the right-about they went, and off, and our fellows after them, cutting and slashing. Then came the order for us to enter, and we entered double-quick, but stand they would not, they saw the Day was lost. All of the enemy who had horses to mount got away, but those who had none were cut up. The cavalry and artillery went off in pursuit, the infantry being exhausted was ordered to halt.'

The action at Kunch was fought out in a temperature of 110° in the shade – and there was not much shade about – by troops already exhausted by long marches and lack of water. The worst sufferers, of course, were the British infantry, in which an average of a dozen men in each regiment engaged dropped dead in their tracks, but it was no picnic for the mounted men either, and Sir Hugh Rose himself fell off his horse several times from the effect of the heat, and required medical attention. The 14th, although they cut down vast numbers of rebels, did not come off unscathed, for the enemy fought fiercely at close quarters and wounded several men and horses with their bayonets and tulwars. The 14th also suffered many casualties from enfilade fire while slowed up by the broken ground.

The total losses of the regiment in this affair were 5 men killed and 2 dead from heatstroke, while an officer and 17 men were wounded. In addition nearly 150 men were prostrated as a result of prolonged and violent exertions in the intense heat. The Central India Field Force was, in fact, knocked out and temporarily unable to march. Fortunately, before becoming reduced to this state, it had given Tantia Topi so severe a hiding that he was in no position to take advantage of it.

It being imperative to keep the rebels on the run, Sir Hugh Rose allowed his men only twenty-four hours to recover, and had them on the line of march at 2 o'clock in the morning of the 9th May. They were preceded as before by Colonel Gall with the cavalry, who discovered that the rebels had ambushed the Calpee road, and were holding strong entrenched positions along it. Ordering the 2nd Brigade to continue along the road, two days' march in rear, Sir Hugh Rose thereupon made a diversion to his right with the 1st Brigade, to effect a junction with a force under Colonel Maxwell on the Jumna and then to outflank the enemy's left.

Besides Tantia Topi, the rebels at Calpee were led by the Rani of Jhansi, the Nawab of Banda, and the Rao Sahib, a villainous trio who exacted obedience from fear rather than loyalty, an authority which seldom stands up in adversity. The Central India Field Force, however, continued to suffer so terribly from the heat that it became very vulnerable on the line of march, and was only saved from extinction by the efforts of the cavalry which frustrated every attempt by the rebels to cut it off from the Jumna. On the 18th May, Rose effected a junction with Maxwell before Calpee, upon which the rebels decided not to await an attack but to make one themselves which, after swearing by the sacred waters of the Jumna not to hold their hand until the British had been totally destroyed, they launched on the 22nd. Rose was ready for them, being aware of their intentions, and had made his dispositions with great skill. The action commenced with an attack on Rose's left, led by Banda and the Rao Sahib. It was held with great difficulty, but Rose refused to reinforce the flank, being convinced that the main assault was coming against his right. He was quite correct, and thus got the better of the rebels by his tactical skill, aided, of course by the extraordinary valour of his troops who, besides being heavily outnumbered, were still suffering from the intense heat. The enemy could do nothing against them, and at last broke and fled.

The 14th, who had been in the saddle for over twelve hours, chased the enemy for eight miles along the Jhansi road, making several charges and capturing three guns, besides cutting down the rebels in hundreds. It was not, as may appear, a matter of sabring panic-stricken men on the run. Although broken and in retreat, the rebels sold their lives dearly, taking up a series of defensive positions when they heard the trumpets of the 14th and Hyderabad cavalry sounding for troops in line. Both horse and field batteries kept up with the cavalry, and each charge was preceded by an artillery bombardment. The exertions called for were indeed unique in such an inferno of heat and dust.

On returning from this pursuit, Colonel Gall reported to Sir Hugh Rose that the greater part of the rebel host had fled towards Jalaon in the north, and on the evening of the 23rd Rose accordingly sent out a 'column of observation' in this direction. The column included first one troop of the 14th, and finally the whole regiment. When it became clear that the rebels were on their way to Gwalior, Rose marched with his whole force after them although, after the capture of Calpee, he had announced that it was to be broken up, and in a farewell order thanked the troops for their good discipline and devotion to duty. The Central India Field Force had, he declared, marched over a thousand miles through jungle and across plains, over rivers and mountain passes. It had captured the strongest forts, taken a hundred guns, and had never sustained a check.

Tantia Topi with his friends the Rani of Jhansi and the Rao Sahib, arrived before Gwalior on the 30th May. The Maharaja of Gwalior, who was loyal to the British, marched out against them, but his troops had been suborned by agents of the Nana Sahib and went over to the enemy, proclaiming the Nana Sahib as Peishwa, or Chief of the Mahrattas. Sindia, the Maharaja, was then obliged to fly for his life, leaving Gwalior, one of the strongest fortresses in India, in rebel hands. On hearing the news, Sir Hugh Rose concentrated all the troops he could lay hands on and marched at once for Gwalior by forced marches in spite of the heat, meeting the rebels at Morar, three miles from Gwalior, on the 16th June.

1858

The village of Morar contained a cantonment, and this apparently inspired Sir Hugh Rose to attack without delay, in spite of the exhaustion of his men, in order to gain shelter for them before they dropped down with heat-stroke. By turning the rebels' flank, he got the better of them with little difficulty, although the infantry had some hard work with the bayonet among the nullahs in which the enemy were taking cover. As they were driven out they were charged by the 14th, who cut them down in great numbers. While they were doing so, the British infantry reached the shelter of the cantonment and collapsed exhausted inside the buildings. It became in fact, impossible to rouse them. 'When they awoke they were not able to stand on their feet,' wrote Private Watt of the 71st. 'A ruse was tried in the shape of crying "Turn out", 2 or 3 times; at last a piper started up a reel and all who could lift a leg went at it. This had the desired effect of completely arousing the sleepers, yet some had to be taken to hospital, but mostly all recovered in a few days.'

In spite of the condition of his troops, Rose lost no time in following up the rebels whom, in collaboration with a column from the Rajputana Field Force, he defeated on the 17th June at Kotah-ki-Serai, four miles south of Gwalior. A squadron of the 14th took part in this affair, which ended under the walls of Gwalior, where the Rani of Jhansi, dressed as a man, was unhorsed and killed by a charge of the 8th Hussars, who were a bit upset by the incident, for at that period women were held sacred by British soldiers, who not infrequently risked having their positions over-run in action, rather than continue firing when there was any chance of hitting women. The Rani in particular, was greatly admired by all-ranks for her romantic gallantry, which equalled that commonly displayed by British women during the horrors of Cawnpore, Lucknow, and innumerable other besieged stations during the Mutiny. Any British soldiers who had the misfortune to fall into the hands of the Rani would certainly, however, have quickly altered their opinion of her.

Gwalior fell to Sir Hugh Rose on the 20th June, after hard fighting during which a squadron of the 14th with a horse artillery troop much distinguished itself by its steadiness 'under shot and shell, and the ardour with which they afterwards fell on the guns and the retreating enemy'. Foremost among the retreating enemy was, as usual, Tantia Topi, who disappeared into the jungle. The Maharaja Scindia made a ceremonial entry into his capital, escorted by squadrons of the 8th Hussars and 14th Light Dragoons, and was received by Sir Hugh Rose and Sir Robert Hamilton, representing the Governor-General. He was not, un-

1858

naturally, delighted at the turn of events, which had fully justified his loyalty to the British, and presented to the officers and men of the Central Field Force the 'Gwalior Star', a silver medal with an orange ribbon. Authority to wear it was afterwards given by the Queen.

Following the capture of Gwalior, the Central India Field Force was broken up. For some months the 14th remained at Gwalior, with one squadron at Jhansi, but as it was essential for Tantia Topi to be hanged before law and order could be re-established in India, the regiment had to take part in the operations for hunting him down. In so vast a country, this was no easy matter, and that it should have been successful in a comparatively short space of time is almost miraculous. 'Tanti hunting', as the troops called it, involved wide sweeps across every imaginable type of country; through jungles, across rivers and over arid, dusty plains, with frequent small but very bloody battles. Tantia was finally run to earth in a jungle hide-out on the 7th April, 1859, and hanged without ceremony. A man, according to Sir John Fortescue, 'of small military talent, but with a perfect genius for running away', he had been responsible for a quite phenomenal amount of devastation and loss of life, not to mention trouble and hardship, during his brief career as a rebel-leader.

While engaged in 'Tanti-hunting', the 14th took part in many sharp engagements, of which that at Ranode on the 17th December, 1858, was typical. A squadron of the regiment, under Captain Prettejohn, had marched from Gwalior with a small column of all-arms to intercept Feroz Shah, one of Tantia Topi's chieftains, and met him at Ranode on the Scind River. The column, about 500 strong, was all mounted with the infantry, a company of the 71st H.L.I., on camels. The rebel army was several thousand strong, and when encountered was drawn up along a frontage of nearly a mile, but Sir Robert Napier, who commanded the column, nevertheless charged immediately with his whole force; the 71st on their camels trotting behind the galloping 14th. Some very brisk hand-to-hand fighting followed in the middle of the rebel host, but the enemy morale quickly collapsed and they were soon streaming off the field leaving 150 dead. They were chased by Prettejohn for a dozen miles, although he and 13 of his men had been wounded in the fight.

Order was not fully restored in India until the end of 1859, by which time the last of the rebel gangs had been dispersed. The 14th Light Dragoons were ordered to Bombay in March of that year to embark for home, but the embarkation was postponed until February, 1860, when, after about 200 men had volunteered for transfer to other cavalry regiments in India, they sailed from Bombay at a strength of 13 officers and 391 rank and file, with 19 women and 39 children. The regiment arrived in Dublin in June, and was then sent to Newbridge to recruit and purchase horses. Its losses in dead during the Central India Campaign had been 1 officer and 72 rank and file.

In 1858 the peculiar system under which a trading company had exercised direct rule over India, and enforced its decrees with its own armed forces who owned no allegiance to the Crown, came to an end with the extinction of the East India Company and the assumption of authority by the Queen as Empress of India. The Governor-General, Lord Canning, became the Queen's Viceroy, faced with the staggering task of reorganising this vast country after it had been torn apart in mutiny and rebellion. The traditional iron hand in the velvet glove was used by Canning with fair success but, as might be expected, he did not bother with the velvet glove when dealing with his own countrymen. Both he and the British Government assumed that the armed forces of the East India Company would be automatically transferred to the Crown, and this was done without consulting the soldiers concerned, who found that they had become Queen's men with a legal commitment to serve her and her heirs and successors under far worse terms than they had enjoyed under the Company. This resulted in the 'White Mutiny' of the disgruntled British soldiers in the Company's regiments. It was checked by Sir Hugh Rose, who had become Commander-in-Chief in India, before it could assume any serious proportions. After disbanding the 5th Bengal European Regiment and hanging one of its private men as an example, he offered reasonable concessions to the Company's men on becoming soldiers of the Queen, and three cavalry regiments and nine infantry regiments were transferred to the Queen's service accordingly, without further trouble. The cavalry regiments became the 19th, 20th and 21st Hussars. Thus, over forty years after their last disbandment, the 20th Light Dragoons emerged from limbo. They were formed at Muttra on the 2nd May, 1861, out of volunteers from the 2nd Bengal European Light Cavalry. Although actually raised as Light Dragoons, they were re-designated Hussars a few months afterwards.

It appears that the officers of the Bengal Light Cavalry were more ready to volunteer for the Queen's service than the men. At the beginning of 1863, when the 20th Hussars marched to Sialkot, the officers numbered 23, all from the Company's service, while the rank and file amounted only to 375, of whom a hundred were

1863

volunteers from the 14th and other cavalry regiments leaving India. The 20th had over a hundred spare horses, which was most unusual at the time, when most regiments did not have enough horses to mount all their men.

Before India had time to recover from the effects of the Mutiny, trouble broke out on the North-West Frontier, where the Pathan tribes raiding into what was then the northern Punjab but later became the North-West Frontier Province, were to prove a thorn in the side of successive British-Indian Governments. In 1863, it was fomented by a tribe of Mahommedan refugees from Bengal, and led to what was known as the Ambeyla expedition. The frontier hills were not at all the place for cavalry, but cavalry nevertheless took part in all operations on the North-West Frontier as a matter of course, being expected to ride over any sort of ground and against any sort of opposition; as, in fact, they could and did.

The 20th remained on the Frontier for seven years, participating both in the Ambeyla Campaign of 1863, and the Hazara Campaign of 1868, but they got no chance of honour and glory in either, being used for the protection of the lines of communication and in chasing the Pathans away from various tactical localities. After the Hazara Campaign, the regiment moved to Ambala, where it remained until 1872, when it was ordered to Bombay for embarkation. It was probably one of the first British regiments in the Indian service to travel by rail instead of by the usual march-route.

After arriving in the United Kingdom, the 20th were stationed first at Colchester and then at Aldershot where, in 1874, the regiment received official recognition as the legitimate descendant of the old 20th Light Dragoons, and therefore entitled to the Battle-Honour PENINSULA.

On the 17th August, 1861, a few days after the Prince of Wales (afterwards King Edward VII) had dined with the officers of the 14th in the cavalry barracks at Newbridge, the regiment became Hussars. Except for some changes in uniform and horse furnishings, the conversion from Light Dragoons made little difference, for light cavalry had the same function whatever its individual regiments might be called. The new title was the 14th (King's) Hussars, and the uniform remained blue, with yellow busby-bags and white plumes. At the same time, Colonel Scudamore, the commanding-officer, was awarded a 'good-service' pension of £100 a year, a somewhat odd gesture on the part of the authorities, for he was far from being financially embarrassed and his service was no more distinguished than that of many other officers of his rank. Furthermore, he had no intention of retiring and exchanged later in the year with Lieut.-Colonel Sir William Russell, Bart., of the 7th Hussars, who took over command of the 14th. It seems possible that His Royal Highness was particularly pleased with his dinner, unlike H.R.H. the Duke of Cambridge, when he dined with the officers at Colchester in 1875. The Duke, it appears, was so inordinately fond of pork chops, that his hosts had always to ensure that he was offered them at dinner, but the pork chops ordered by the 14th mysteriously disappeared, and were said to have been eaten by the riding-master, who shared the same taste. No good-service pension, at any rate, was awarded to Colonel F. P. Campbell, who was commanding at the time.

Following their return home after the Indian Mutiny, the 14th and 20th divided their time between England and Ireland, and were almost continually on the move, guarding against industrial troubles in England and keeping the peace at elections in Ireland, which were favourite occasions for the Irish to break one another's heads, desisting in order to throw stones at any soldiers who appeared to restore order. There was a good deal of unrest all over the United Kingdom, and also over the world in general, caused by the competition among the Great Powers in an imperialistic struggle derived from a vast increase in trade and the necessity for finding overseas markets by fair means or foul. A series of international crises developed in which Great Britain was usually involved, some of which were settled by running up the Union Jack, while others resulted in a small war. The 14th were not called upon until the outbreak of the First Boer War of 1881, while the 20th had to wait until 1885, when the regiment went out to the Sudan to take part in operations which had already been going on for years. While the regiments themselves had been on home service, however, many of their officers and men were fighting overseas in the ranks of other regiments or on the staff.

The 14th left Colchester for India early in 1876, and were quartered first at Poona and then at Bangalore. In 1878 orders were received for active service in Afghanistan. Swords were sharpened and accoutrements blackened but the orders were countermanded. Orders for active service in the Transvaal, however, were not rescinded, and the regiment sailed for South Africa at the end of February, 1881, and landed at Durban in March.

Following the defeat of their old enemies the Kaffirs on their northern borders, the Transvaal Boers began to clamour for independence, and when told that they must be satisfied with the honourable position of a British Crown Colony, first refused to

1881

pay taxes and then raised the standard of revolt in December, 1880. At that time there were only about a thousand British troops in the Transvaal, who were widely scattered in various detachments which were encircled and wiped out by the Boers. The first news of the war which the 14th received on arriving at Durban, was of the defeat and death in action of Sir George Colley, the commander-in-chief, at Majuba Hill. In all these engagements the British troops had fought bravely and skilfully, before being overwhelmed by the numbers and mobility of their opponents. They had given the Boers a severe shock, and there is little doubt that Sir Evelyn Wood and Sir Frederick Roberts (afterwards Field-Marshal Lord Roberts) who were on their way to the Transvaal with considerable reinforcements, would soon have brought the rebellion to an end had they been permitted to engage. Gladstone's Government, however, was nervous at the idea of a protracted struggle with the Boers at a time when Great Britain was on bad terms with every government in Europe, for it seemed likely that the Boers in the Orange Free State and Cape Colony would rise in support of the Transvaal. The Government therefore granted virtual independence to the Transvaal without further ado; a move which was well-meant and in accordance with its liberal doctrines. Unfortunately, being an apparent surrender to force, the decision resulted in a severe blow to British prestige, especially in South Africa where the Boers began to extend their territory under the impression that the British Government could be flouted with impunity.

The 14th did not, therefore, see any action in this war – if war it could be called. After a spell at Ladysmith, the regiment marched into Zululand, where a squadron escorted Sir Evelyn Wood on a tour of visits. At the end of 1881 it returned to India, and was stationed at Secunderabad.

In 1882, the grievous blow to British prestige resulting from the capitulation to the Transvaal Boers was a little softened by Wolesley's victory at Tel-el-Kebir, which established British control over Egypt and the Suez Canal. Gladstone, who was still Prime Minister, was strongly against these imperialistic wars, and had agreed to Wolesley's campaign only because circumstances left him no option. He had hoped that as soon as stable government had been restored to Egypt, it would be possible to withdraw and leave the country once again to its own devices, but it was in such a mess that this proved to be quite out of the question. As a result, Great Britain found herself responsible not only for the administration of Egypt but for its defence as well. Thus ensued the long series of military operations in the Sudan,

1885

whose warlike inhabitants had the strongest possible dislike for the Egyptians, who had for years regarded the Sudan as a convenient breeding-ground for slaves.

A year or two before Egypt had been taken over by the British, a *jehad*, or Holy War, had been proclaimed against her by the Mahdi, the religious leader of the Sudanese, and the Egyptian forces had been defeated several times. Having now the responsibility for the protection of Egypt against the Mahdi, Gladstone characteristically thought only of withdrawing all Egyptian garrisons from the Sudan and establishing a purely static line of defence along the border, forgetting the vital importance to Egypt of the Nile valley, which was controlled by the Sudanese.

Operations in the Sudan started with the dispatch from Khartoum of a small Egyptian force under British officers against El Obeid, which had been captured by the Mahdi. This force was surrounded and exterminated in 1883, and General Charles Gordon was then sent to Khartoum to negotiate the evacuation of the Sudan. He was soon blockaded in Khartoum by the Mahdi, but Gladstone refused to send a British column to his relief until it was too late. An expedition under Wolesley which went up the Nile in the autumn of 1884 just failed to reach Khartoum before it was overwhelmed in January, 1885, and Gordon killed. All British forces were then withdrawn to Egypt.

In February, 1885, two squadrons of the 20th Hussars embarked at Portsmouth, landed at Suakin in March, and immediately rode out into the desert on a reconnaissance in force, but without meeting any Dervishes. They were then ordered back to Suakin.

The garrison at Suakin, which included British, Australian, and Indian detachments, as well as Egyptian, was commanded by General Sir Gerald Graham, whose orders were 'to make the best arrangements he could for the destruction of the power of Osman Digna', a former Arab slave-trader who now commanded a large force of Dervishes operating in the neighbourhood of Suakin, a port used for the purchase and export of slaves. Graham's first objective was the destruction of several thousand Dervishes at Tamai. The reconnaissance in force led by the 20th Hussars discovered an enemy outpost at Hasheen, and a brisk action followed in which the Dervishes were put to flight. About 45 casualties were suffered by the British force, which then returned to Suakin, where the squadron of the 20th re-embarked and joined the rest of the regiment in Cairo.

By this time, the last Egyptian garrison at Kassala had been overwhelmed and the Sudan was abandoned to barbarism. On

1885

the Egyptian Frontier a British brigade held Aswan, with outposts at Wadi Halfa and Korosko. One troop of the 20th was stationed at each of these places from July, 1885, onwards, and the rest of the regiment arrived at Aswan in August and moved to Wadi Halfa in December. Gladstone's Liberal government fell in June of this year, and was succeeded by the Conservatives under Lord Salisbury, whom Wolseley at once pressed to abandon purely defensive measures and allow him to advance into the Sudan. Lord Salisbury refused, and in December the Dervishes formed up at Ginnis, about midway between Wadi Halfa and Dongola. The British brigade at Aswan had now been reinforced by a brigade of the Egyptian Army, which had been reorganised and was led by British officers. It was termed the Frontier Field Force, and led by General Sir Frederick Stephenson, who led it out against the Dervishes on the 30th December.

The Battle of Ginnis is notable for the fact that it was the last action fought by British soldiers in the red coat worn by the British Army for three centuries. The British tactics were as old-fashioned as the coat, but still just the thing against Dervishes, especially as the British carried long-range rifles in the use of which they were exceedingly adept, thinking nothing of opening an accurate fire at 1,500 yards and over. Otherwise, the red coats advanced in the time-honoured British Line, with the cavalry out on the flanks with troops riding in file, and the commanding-officer nearest the enemy, watching for an opportunity to wheel into line and charge. This came when the Dervishes broke under the infantry volley-firing, when the 20th charged and routed them. They left about 800 killed and wounded on the field, while the British and Egyptian losses totalled only 41. The battle was decisive, in that it put an end to the danger of an invasion of Egypt by the Dervishes.

During 1887, the 20th Hussars left Aswan and returned home in batches, leaving in Egypt one squadron which moved to Suakin at the end of 1888. Suakin, which for some obscure reason the British authorities had decided not to evacuate with the rest of the Sudan, was now besieged by Osman Digna's Dervishes, who were entrenched all round. The port now had a Military Governor in the person of Colonel Herbert Kitchener, later Field-Marshal Earl Kitchener, but at this time an Intelligence Officer whose intrigues among the Dervishes had greatly annoyed 'Chinese' Gordon of Khartoum. He had gained, however, a number of adherents in the enemy camp, and with their co-operation he made a sortie from Suakin on the 20th December, 1888, and drove the Dervishes from their entrenchments. They were then charged by the squadron of the 20th and put to flight with a loss of 500 killed and wounded against about 50 British and Egyptians. Kitchener was wounded in this affair, of which the details are obscure. In making the sortie, he was no doubt acting under the orders of Sir Francis Grenfell, the commander-in-chief, but there seems no doubt that he led it in person and thereby established the reputation which eventually brought him to the top of his profession.

The security of Suakin being now assured, the squadron of the 20th was brought back to Cairo in January, 1889. In July, a Dervish force led by the Sheik Wad-an-Nagumi, advanced against Egypt and was driven back at Argin, near Wadi Halfa. The Sheik then made for Aswan, which was reinforced by the squadron of the 20th, which sailed up the Nile in barges and landed at Toski on the 1st August. They had barely time to disembark and mount before the Dervishes arrived. 'Parading for reconnaissance', the squadron rode out against them, while Sir Frederick Grenfell formed his line of battle. The ensuing engagement lasted seven hours, and ended with the total rout of the Dervishes, who lost over a thousand men, including Wad-an-Nagumi himself whose camel was brought down in a cavalry charge delivered by the squadron of the 20th and the Egyptian cavalry.

After the Battle of Toski, the service squadron rejoined the regiment at Aldershot. The battle-honour 'Suakin 1885' was awarded for its services in Sudan, and also that of 'Vimiera', in respect of the earlier services of its predecessor, the old 20th Light Dragoons.

In March 1885 two squadrons of the 20th Hussars arrived at Suakin from England and joined the squadron which had arrived earlier to form part of the Camel Corps. *From the original painting in the possession of Colonel C. G. Mangles.*

1881

14th King's Hussars, review order 1880 (full dress). The 14th had become Hussars in 1861. The most important changes in uniform were the busby in place of the shako, and the Hussar jacket; 14th busbies had white plumes and yellow bags.

1881 to 1886 The 14th at Secunderabad
1886–1899 Home Service
December 1899 The 14th leave for South Africa
February 1900 'B' Squadron in the ride to Kimberley
27th February 1900 Paarde Berg

1881

19

Outbreak of the South African War

THE 14th had arrived at Bombay from South Africa in November and December, 1881, and marched to Secunderabad in two wings. The distance was covered by forty daily marches of about twelve miles each, and there were occasional daily halts, the whole journey taking about six weeks. This, of course, was very leisurely progress for a cavalry regiment, but the pace of units of all arms on a peacetime march through India was regulated by the transport, most of which was hired from civilian contractors, and consisted of a miscellaneous collection of bullock-wagons, mule-carts, elephants and camels which, over roads little better than dust tracks, could seldom get up to three miles an hour and often got stuck, especially at river crossings. Reveille, during these lengthy marches, was usually sounded at 3 a.m., when tents were struck, loaded, and sent on ahead, with the regiment following about an hour later. Each day's march was usually completed, and the tents up again on the new camping-ground by 9 a.m., so that there was always plenty of time for the officers to go out with their guns and rifles after snipe, duck or panther. Pigsticking was indulged in when the country was rideable, although this required the co-operation of the inhabitants to find the pigs and drive them out of covert. A somewhat curious, though undoubtedly exciting, form of sport,

257

1881

it had been a favourite with British officers at least as far back as the Maharatta wars of 1803 onwards, when Wellesley's officers marching against Scindia used to ride ahead or on the flanks with their hogspears, often bringing back useful information about enemy movements.

The 14th spent four years in Secunderabad, which was one of the larger military stations with a cavalry brigade, two infantry brigades, horse and field artillery. The temperature, even during the summer, was moderate for India, and the life led by the British soldier, officer or man, was pleasant enough although death was still a frequent visitor, and attendance at someone's funeral was almost as regular a duty as the weekly church parade. The Commanding-Officer, Colonel Knox, died of a liver complaint, two subalterns were struck dead by lightning while playing billiards, a bandsman shot himself and a soldier was killed falling down a well, while numerous all-ranks died of 'fever'. These tragedies caused only a momentary gloom, which was soon dissipated in a rousing social round of dinners, dances, flirtations, concerts and private theatricals, and by racing, paperchasing, polo, cricket and pigsticking. As far as the last was concerned, the officers certainly rode out with spears, but they may not actually have been after pig, which were not generally hunted in the Deccan, perhaps because the Nizam was a Moslem. In June, 1882, the regiment gave a luncheon party for about a hundred officers and ladies of the garrison, all of whom got to horse immediately afterwards and rode out. The intention was to have a paperchase, but a panther was 'enlarged', and hunted by the subalterns of the 14th with spears. Lieut. Broadhurst got first spear, and the animal was then killed by the others after it had nearly killed one of the native grooms. 'A capital paperchase' followed. Hunting a pig was a tough sport enough, but a panther was a very dangerous animal to spear from horseback, although it was customary for pigstickers to make the attempt should one appear while they were looking for pig. However, the favourite sport of cavalry officers at that time was steeplechasing or hurdling, and the officers of the regiment not only won many good races at Secunderabad but took their horses to the meetings at Poona and Bangalore where they were equally successful.

The Indian Mutiny was by this time a half-forgotten memory, only commemorated by the custom of British troops taking their rifles to church – for the sepoys at Meerut at the outbreak of the Mutiny had planned to take advantage of the fact that British regiments paraded unarmed for church in those days. Otherwise, an unprecedented period of peace and prosperity was being enjoyed by the whole of India up to the frontier hills, and there was no immediate call for a soldier's professional services, even for the maintenance of law and order. Nevertheless, if there was no trouble in India, there was plenty elsewhere. Jealous eyes were watching the British moves for the consolidation and security of the Empire, and the sorry ending to the First Boer War had given encouragement to the enemies of Great Britain among whom were numbered practically every major power. In such circumstances there was no feeling of frustration among British soldiers, and no temptation to let their arms rust in idleness, for they never knew when and where they might suddenly be needed. It must not be supposed therefore that the 14th, or any other British regiment, spent most of the time amusing itself. The training was exceedingly hard and thorough, and went on all the year round, with the 14th riding out on at least two 'field-days' each week. Visits by inspecting officers were a regular occurrence, and 'field manoeuvres' were carried out under the direction of General Sir Frederick Roberts (afterwards Field-Marshal Lord Roberts) himself, at that time Commander-in-Chief of the Madras Army. Not an easy man to please, he reported very favourably on the 14th, particularly with regard to scouting and patrolling. In more recent times, after the motor-car had arrived to render the cavalry horse obsolescent, a tendency arose in the cavalry to pamper their horses and concentrate on their glossy coats and rounded contours, rather than on the wind and muscle essential for active service. This was not the case in the 1880s, when horses and men had to be permanently fit to take the field at a moment's notice. The maintenance of such a standard in a cavalry regiment required many hours of hard work daily; in addition to which there was, of course, the ordinary stable routine and dismounted training with sword and rifle.

However, no alarms disturbed the pleasant life of the 14th at Secunderabad, and in 1886 the regiment sailed for home in H.M.S. *Serapis*, at a strength of 17 officers and 405 rank and file, with 3 officers' wives, 24 soldiers' wives and 58 children. After disembarkation the regiment was stationed at Shorncliffe, but thereafter changed station almost annually, moving to Aldershot, Hounslow and Brighton, and being subjected at the same time to a never-ending series of changes in establishment. The reason behind these changes, which were common throughout the army at home, is beyond conjecture, for they seem neither to have saved expense nor increased efficiency. Presumably they were in the nature of experiments; but if so, the outcome was never apparent. The last forty years of the nineteenth century

1890

were, however, a period of reform for the British Army, during which its organisation was radically altered; and it was also a period of small wars abroad and industrial unrest at home so that, in one way or another, the soldier was kept more than usually busy and with the feeling that he might find himself in the field at short notice. Training at home was as hard as that in India, but as hospitality, both in London and the country, was unprecedented in its liberality the officers had a very good time, for there was an unending demand for their presence at every possible variety of social function. The officers of the 14th were as keen on racing as ever, and Captain Sir James Miller's chestnut *Sainfoin* won the Derby of 1890 – the only time in history that this classic has been won by a serving officer. While at Brighton, which was then still a fashionable resort for society, the regiment gave three 'Grand Military Tournaments' open to the public, and also a 'Grand Full-dress Ball' at the Pavillion, which was attended by four hundred guests. State visits to England by the German Emperor, the Kaiser Wilhelm II, in 1889 and 1891, brought the 14th into contact with this singular personage, first, when they took part in a 'sham fight' laid on at Aldershot for his amusement, and later, when they provided a detachment at Windsor and a travelling escort from the Crystal Palace to Buckingham Palace. The kettle-drums were dressed in new drum-banners presented by the Adjutant, Sir James Miller, on which the Prussian Eagle was 'conspicuous', and duly noted by the Kaiser who was naturally pleased. The escort Commander, Captain L. J. Richardson, was presented with a signed photograph of the Emperor in a silver frame. Subsequently, on the outbreak of the Great War, he dashed it to the ground and trampled it to smithereens in a rage.

Threatened industrial unrest in the North-West took the regiment up to Leeds and Birmingham at the end of 1891, and it was called out in aid of the civil power many times in various parts of a large area including Wales. There was fortunately no need ever to use force to keep the peace, for the rioters in all districts dispersed at once, on the appearance of the troops. Whilst at Manchester a squadron in full dress under Major 'Ayala' Gage was called out to quell a riot at Chester. This was quelled before they got there but, as they were returning, they chanced on a Meet of the Cheshire Hunt. Gage said, 'Boys, I think we go hunting,' and trotted up to the Master with the classic greeting, 'Morning, Master – what's the Cap for a Squadron?'

In May, 1894, Queen Victoria arrived at Manchester to open the Ship Canal, and a Sovereign's Escort was provided by the 14th. Shortly afterwards the regiment embarked for Ireland. The

1890

annual inspection of this year is of interest, in that it included a 'reconnaissance', during which it was recorded that the longest march was 32 miles and the average weight carried by the troop horses was 18 stone, 8 pounds. At this time the cavalry carried light carbines rather awkwardly fitted in slings attached to the offside of the saddle. Before 1914, these had been replaced by the infantry rifle, carried in a leather bucket, with the bayonet slung from the bandolier. Although a more efficient weapon and arrangement, it considerably increased the weight on the horse.

During the nineteenth century the defence of the British Isles,

Silver statuette of *Sanfoin*, a chestnut colt that won the Derby in 1890. The horse was owned by Captain Sir James P. Miller, Bt.. who was Adjutant of the 14th Hussars. To the present day this has been the only Derby winner to have been owned by a serving officer.

1895

and the security of the vast and ever-increasing British Empire, became more than ever firmly based on the British command of the seas; with successive British governments keeping a wary eye on the size of the fleets of other powers. This was all very well but the truth was that Her Majesty's ships could not get up the Nile to chase the Sudanese, or the Irrawaddy to confront King Thibaw. Nor were they of the slightest use against the Afghans, Ashantis, Zulus, Abyssinians or Boers. all of whom urgently needed control. The fact that this control could only be exercised by soldiers was accepted by the government with the most extreme reluctance, with the consequence that the British Army was always far too small for its world-wide commitments. This led to a series of unfortunate incidents, such as the battles of Maiwand, Majuba, and Isandhlwana at which small British forces were surrounded and cut to pieces by vast numbers of opponents. Although they were only minor set-backs, which were usually avenged later, the general effect was deplorable, for it gave the world the impression that the lion's tail could be twisted with impunity anywhere out of reach of salt water. By continental standards the British Army simply did not exist, and it is noteworthy that during the state visits of the Kaiser previously mentioned, the British government had been obliged to call out the Militia, in a pathetic attempt to impress him by a show of numbers.

This expedient could not, of course, be tried in South Africa where the Boers, after their easy success of 1881 and the indifferent display put up by Lord Chelmsford against the Zulus, had written-off the 'red-necks' as something of a joke, not to be taken seriously in the field. Such misapprehension was unfortunate, to say the least.

After receiving their independence, the Boer Republics had set about extending their territories towards Bechuanaland and Zululand, being kept temporarily in check by Cecil Rhodes, the Prime Minister of Cape Colony, who founded Rhodesia. The discovery of gold and diamonds in the republics had attracted considerable numbers of foreigners, mostly British, who opened and worked the mines, furnishing most of the wealth on which the republics subsisted. Their presence was none-the-less resented by the Boers, who referred to them contemptuously as *Uitlanders* and denied to them all civic rights. They were encouraged to stand up for themselves by Rhodes, who supplied them with arms. The Administrator of Rhodesia, Dr Jameson, then went further and fixed a date for an armed insurrection which he promised to support with the Rhodesian Mounted

1899

Police. When, however, he led his force into the Transvaal, the *Uitlanders* failed to rise as expected, so that Jameson was obliged to surrender. This incident caused great jubilation among the Boers, who united under their anti-British President, Kruger, while the British Government, though embarrassed, was faced with the fact that British subjects were being treated in a manner which it was impossible to tolerate. Furthermore, the Boer Republics made no secret of their intention to take over Cape Colony and extend their domination over the whole of South Africa, afterwards treating all 'foreigners' in the same way. Natal, the only province in which the population was nearly all British, was isolated and in danger of invasion from which the British troops in South Africa were far too small in number to protect it. Representations to Kruger having been contemptuously rejected, large British reinforcements were sent out to the Cape. This led to an ultimatum by the Boer Republics to withdraw all British troops from the frontiers of Natal forthwith. When this was rejected the Boers declared war in October, 1899, and immediately invaded Natal.

Initially, the Boers were able to put into the field 60,000 mounted riflemen, who were organised into 'Commandos' of varying strength. The British troops in South Africa amounted to about one third of that number, and they consisted mostly of infantry which was fairly widely dispersed, the bulk being in Natal, with others in isolated garrisons, such as Mafeking and Kimberley, over 500 miles from Cape Town. Making full use of their mobility and superior numbers before British reinforcements could arrive, the Boers advanced at all points. By mid-December they were riding into Cape Colony; Ladysmith, Mafeking and Kimberley were beleaguered, and attempts to relieve Kimberley by Lord Methuen and Ladysmith by Sir Redvers Buller had been frustrated with heavy casualties. This was the bleak situation in South Africa found by the 14th when the regiment landed at Capetown in January, 1900.

The 14th, then stationed at Newbridge in Ireland, had been ordered to mobilise on the 9th October and, at a strength of 687 all-ranks, were prepared for immediate embarkation for the Cape. To their great disgust, an outbreak of influenza and 'pink-eye' among the horses led to the orders being cancelled, but the sympathetic authorities assured the regiment that it would be sent to Aldershot as soon as the horses were fit and that, 'in the event of more cavalry being required in South Africa', the 14th would receive favourable consideration.

The apparent existence of doubts as to whether or not more

1899

cavalry would be required for the conduct of the war is almost beyond belief, but the maxim that 'infantry is the arm which in the end wins battles', was so firmly held in the British Army that cavalry was regarded as being something of a luxury. One cavalry regiment to scout ahead of each infantry division, and whatever others happened to be available acting independently under the orders of the Commander-in-Chief to get information, was the basic idea. At the outbreak of the Boer War, the vast size of the theatre of operations and the fact that each Boer had his own horse, producing a situation which required special treatment, was certainly insufficiently appreciated.

The Boers, however, had also miscalculated. Led astray by their easy successes in '81 against isolated British units, some of whom did not even know that there was a war on, they had grossly underestimated the fighting capacity of the 'red-necks'. Although, therefore, their numbers and mobility had won them the initiative on all fronts, they had had several set-backs and fairly severe casualties. The élan with which they had taken the field had subsequently quickly evaporated, being replaced by sober doubts and fears. Certain adjustments in tactics were in fact required by both sides. This was first realised by the Boers who, after experiencing the accuracy of the British long-range volley-firing and field artillery, abandoned their practice of lining the tops of the *kopjes* and took to occupying trenches along the bottom. This enabled them to hold up Methuen on the Modder River and to decimate the Highland Brigade at Magersfontein, but it had the considerable drawback, for mounted irregulars like the Boers, that they were separated from their horses, which were held under cover on the reverse side of the *kopjes*. The adjustment made by the British was to put into the field every cavalry regiment that they could lay hands on, to raise the corps of Imperial Yeomanry and a large number of regiments of irregular horse, and to mount as many of the infantry as the available horseflesh allowed. Generally speaking, one company from each infantry battalion was mounted, and Mounted Infantry battalions were then organised which would have met with the approval of the Duke of Cumberland for, unlike the 14th and the other old dragoon regiments, they did not consider it beneath their dignity to dismount and engage the enemy on foot.

At the beginning of 1900, Field-Marshal Lord Roberts arrived at the Cape and took over command, deciding to make his main advance through Cape Colony on Bloemfontein and Pretoria, while Sir Redvers Buller made another attempt to relieve Ladysmith and drive the Boers out of Natal. Roberts' immediate task was to defeat Cronje and his men facing Lord Methuen across the Modder River and relieve Kimberley. As a preliminary he withdrew General French's Cavalry Division from Natal to the Modder River, and ordered French to break through to Kimberley.

The 14th left Aldershot for the war on the 13th December, 1899, less 'B' Squadron, which followed ten days later, and sailed from Southampton in the passenger ship *Victorian* on the same day. All ranks were apparently convinced that they would be too late to take any active part in the war, and were consequently in a far from cheerful mood, which was not improved by the wintry weather and the complete lack of any public interest in their departure. During the first months of the war, regiments had seldom left for the front without being given a fine send-off by the local civil and military dignitaries, with bands playing and crowds cheering, but no-one cheered the *Victorian* away except a few relatives and 'loafers', while the only music was provided by one of the said loafers who played *Soldiers of the Queen* on a cornet. The public in fact was also convinced that the war was over and no longer imagined that soldiers sailing for South Africa were at all likely to run into any danger. This optimism regarding the progress of the war was, of course, quite unjustified and the reason for it difficult to understand. It was probably based upon face-saving speeches by the Cabinet, allied to the proud patriotism existing at the time, which made it difficult for anyone to believe that the British Empire could long be embarrassed by the aggressiveness of such backward people as the Boers, who had not even been able to get the better of the Kaffirs without British assistance.

However, a severe jolt was administered to this complacency when General Gatacre with 3,000 men got trounced at Stormberg on the 9th December, and on the following day an attack by the Highland Brigade was repulsed at Magersfontein, with a loss of nearly a thousand all-ranks. Then, on the 15th December, Sir Redvers Buller, when attempting to cross the Tugela and relieve Ladysmith, was repulsed at Colenso, losing over a thousand men and ten out of his twelve guns. The news of 'Black Week', as the second week in December was afterwards called, was received by the 14th when their ship was lying off Las Palmas and they were hoping to be allowed on shore. Although the tidings were not exactly cheering, they had a very invigorating effect on all ranks, who got out their pistols and carbines and, for the rest of the voyage, practised shooting at bottles thrown overboard. Further-

1900

more, as there now seemed to be a possibility that they might have to go into action soon after arriving at the Cape, they got the horses out of the hold in batches and exercised them round the decks on coconut matting. Nothing like this had ever been attempted before.

The 14th disembarked at Durban on the 5th January, 1900, and travelled by rail to Estcourt, coming under the orders of Sir Redvers Buller, who was preparing for the attempt to relieve Ladysmith. 'B' Squadron, which had landed at Capetown, was sent to join French's Cavalry Division on the Modder River and, after a long journey by train and march route, arrived at Orange River Station on the 2nd February, where it was attached to the Carabiniers, who had just returned from an unsuccessful attempt to dislodge a party of Boers from the hills near Ramah. They were in a hurry to catch up with French, having heard that the Cavalry Division was about to march on Kimberley, and they set out at so brisk a pace that 'B' Squadron had difficulty in keeping up, for the horses were weak from their long voyage and subsequent train journey. A halt became necessary at Ramdam when, fortunately for 'B' Squadron, the Carabiniers were ordered to escort the Divisional Supply Column forward to the Modder River, which meant keeping to a walk.

French, however, could not advance until the supply column arrived, for at this time of the year the heat in South Africa was terrific, and every blade of grass on the open veldt had been burnt up. For some days the horses had been ridden to the limit of their endurance, without a mouthful of forage and very little water. The Carabiniers and 'B' Squadron therefore caught him up at De Keil's Drift on the Reit River, where he was waiting for the supplies to arrive before making for Klip Drift on the Modder River, twenty miles distant. They were just in time to hear him addressing his officers. 'This is the largest assembly of British cavalry in history,' he was shouting, 'and we're damned well going to relieve Kimberley even if we lose half of it in doing so!'

While the Division was being fed, the infantry were closing up behind, and Lord Roberts himself soon arrived to confer with French. The Carabiniers, with 'B' Squadron still attached, joined the 1st Cavalry Brigade with the Greys and a squadron of the Inniskillings. The Division marched at 10 o'clock on the morning of the 14th February, moving on a wide front with the 1st Brigade in the centre, the 3rd Brigade (9th and 16th Lancers) under General Gordon on the left, and the 2nd Brigade (Household Cavalry, 10th Hussars and 12th Lancers) under General Broadwood, on the right. The total strength of 'the largest assembly of British cavalry in history', was about 6,000 men, including seven batteries of Royal Horse Artillery. The enemy were known to be at Jacobsdal on the left front, and the 3rd Brigade pushed patrols out in that direction but the Boers seemed quite unconscious of the movement round their flank. Cronje, the Boer commander holding the Boer positions at Magersfontein barring the road to Kimberley, was of course soon warned of the movement but was not impressed, believing that the cavalry was merely reconnoitring.

The march was extremely arduous, for the heat of the sun was tropical in intensity and the brown, scorched grass of the veldt kept catching fire, destroying the cable which the Royal Engineers were paying out behind the column, so that communication was cut between French and Roberts. There was no water to be found, so that the horses had to be kept to a walk, and about a hundred of them foundered even then. However, Klip Drift was reached in the evening and crossed against only slight opposition, for the Boers watching it were apparently taken by surprise and fled up into the kopjes to the north. They went in such a hurry that their camp was found intact, with a large number of wagons and supplies, and food cooking on the fires, all of which was very welcome to the cavalry.

Having secured the kopjes north of the Drift, with 'B' Squadron doing its first spell of outpost duty, the Division bivouacked along the north bank of the Modder River. It was obliged to rest during the 14th, both for the sake of the horses and to await the infantry. The Boers came up again and commenced to shell the camp, but without much effect or making any attempt to mount a proper attack. During the night Lord Kitchener, Roberts' Chief of Staff, came into camp to confer with French, when it was decided that the cavalry should push on to Kimberley on the following morning.

The Cavalry Division paraded at 8.30 a.m. on the 15th February, 1900 – a date which was to prove of historical significance for British Cavalry. In front, a long valley led up through the kopjes which, during the night, had been blocked by the Boers who had erected a rudimentary wire fence across it and occupied the flanking kopjes with a thousand men and three Krupp guns besides pom-poms. Gordon's Lancers went out to reconnoitre, and a troop of 16th under Lieut. Escott, was sent to pull down the wire fence. It was a suicidal mission, which in the old days, would have been attempted by volunteers, but the practice of calling for volunteers had gone out of fashion and Escott was sent in the ordinary course of duty, his troop happening to be

1900

handy at the time. He was shot dead and most of his troop killed or wounded – but they did the job as ordered.

On receiving Gordon's report, French had to make up his mind whether to dismount and clear the kopjes or to gallop the position. Deciding on the latter he formed up the Division in mass, with four paces interval between files. Gordon's Brigade was in front, followed by 'B' Squadron which was extended in front of General French and his staff, with the 1st Brigade behind them and the 2nd Brigade in rear.

The movements necessary to form a whole cavalry division in mass, which were carried out at the trot with a certain amount of galloping, raised a huge cloud of dust which blotted the Division from sight and was as good as a smoke-screen – although very unpleasant for those inside it. Among the officers there were not a few glum faces. They had not been impressed by French's 'pep talk' at De Keil Drift and now, as it dawned upon them that he was intending to charge with the whole Division against a position held in front and flanks, they began to suspect that he had had a touch of the sun. Such tactics were not favourably regarded since the advent of the magazine rifle of high velocity and low trajectory, although the fact was that, until the Boer War the British Cavalry had not had any experience against enemies armed with this weapon. In 'the small wars', the cavalry had usually been employed in riding down tribesmen of one sort or another whose firearms had not been accurate enough to prevent their approach at the trot, canter and gallop, so that the old-fashioned *arme blanche* had been just the thing. But to try it against a civilised enemy armed with modern weapons: 'had we made a similar attack at Aldershot,' said one officer afterwards, 'we should certainly have all been put out of action, and have been looked upon as idiots.'

However, the soldier's business was still to obey orders and not argue. 'All ready, Sir,' reported French's chief staff officer. 'All right,' he replied, 'Walk march! . . . Trot!'

Once they got to the gallop there was very little that anyone in the rear of Gordon's Brigade could see of the affair, for the dust rose in a dense cloud and visibility was limited to one's horse's ears. With six thousand sets of horse-shoes 'all four round' hammering on the iron surface of the veldt; the thunder of artillery and the wheels of guns and limbers driven at their highest speed, the din was terrific. The unfortunate Boers holding the pass, about two hundred in number, got up and ran, but they were nearly all speared by the Lancers and their bodies left in the wake of the brigades following, whose horses jumped them.

S. S. M. Currie of 'B' Squadron said that his horse also jumped the body of Lieut. Escott, who had been shot through the head. The officers, peering through the dust with their eyes streaming, were continually expecting to see the whole Division collapse under a hail of lead, but when French pulled them up five miles on, it was found that they had come through at a cost of fifteen men and twenty horses killed and wounded.

Gordon's Brigade having fallen out to water at a spruit, the advance was resumed by the rest of the Division at a more moderate pace, with 'B' Squadron now in the lead. The Boers investing Kimberley were completely surprised by the arrival of the Cavalry Division and decamped without delay, with the exception of some holding a position known as the Susannah Laager who, however, followed their friends when French rode at them with the 1st Brigade. The Kimberley garrison meanwhile mounted and rode out to greet French, headed by Colonel Kekewich and Mr Cecil Rhodes. French, attended by 'B' Squadron, accompanied them back into the town, leaving the Cavalry Division to bivouac outside. After their ride of fifteen miles from Klip Drift, the horses were so done-up that any pursuit was out of the question. This caused French much anxiety and, again attended by 'B' Squadron, he mounted two brigades at 3 a.m. the following morning and led them northward, finding the Boers entrenched across the railway line at Dronfield, ten miles from Kimberley. After Lieut. Dawes' troop of 'B' Squadron in the vanguard had drawn their fire, a dismounted attack was launched which lasted until nightfall, when the Boers withdrew. S.Q.M.S. Ayres, who was hit in the knee, was the only casualty in 'B' Squadron, but the losses in some of the other regiments were fairly heavy.

French's brilliant leadership had done more than merely relieve Kimberley. Cronje at Magersfontein was roused by the arrival at his laager of the Boers who were supposed to be holding Klip Drift, but who had now become a demoralised mob of panic-stricken fugitives. His fury with them must have been impressive to watch, for, not having been at Klip Drift himself, he was at a loss to understand their 'damnable fear of the English'. The charge of six thousand horsemen was, however, a spectacle which no-one in the world had witnessed since the death of Murat, Napoleon's cavalry leader, and its effect had been quite shattering. Although he did not understand this, Cronje was quick to realise that it had put him in an impossible position, and that unless he got moving quickly he would be trapped. He therefore struck camp immediately and trekked to the east,

1900

hoping to evade Roberts and reach Bloemfontein. As he managed to cross the Modder River just before Roberts came up with his infantry, he might well have got clean away had he abandoned his immense train of ox-drawn wagons. This he would not do, so that the tired British infantry was able to keep in sight of the cloud of dust which marked its progress although they could not, of course, get ahead of it. An officer was therefore sent to Kimberley at the gallop, with orders for French to cut across to the Modder and head Cronje off. French got the message just after returning from Dronfield, but he mounted and set out at once with as many cavalrymen as he could raise with fit horses. Those which had just returned from Dronfield were not fit, although French was on the verge of taking them nonetheless. 'Weary, hungry, footsore, the horses returned to their bivouacs,' wrote one of the officers, 'and it was thought that with a few days rest and plenty of food the poor lean skeletons we saw in horses' skins would soon be filled out again. But a despatch rider came in with the news that a large body of men and convoy, believed to be Cronje's force from Magersfontein, were in full retreat and were being engaged in a rearguard action by the infantry we had left behind us at Klip Drift.' With some reluctance French led off the 10th Hussars, 12th Lancers and two squadrons of Carabiniers, who had not been to Dronfield, although they had been all day scouting in the neighbourhood of Kimberley. The rest of the Division was left to follow on later. After a thirty mile ride at the trot and canter over rough and unknown country, French with his two-and-a-half regiments headed Cronje off at Paardberg, and the Boers, not knowing how many men he had with him, went into laager along the south bank of the Modder River. The laager was attacked by the infantry when they arrived, but the attack was called off by Roberts as likely to prove too costly to drive home. A summons to surrender was declined by Cronje, who was hoping that Christian De Wet would ride to his assistance, but the arrival of the rest of the Cavalry Division on the 21st February prevented this, and Cronje was obliged to run up the white flag on the morning of the 27th. This was 'Majuba Day', the anniversary of the British defeat in 1881 which every officer and man of the British Army had since been burning to avenge. Cronje's surrender, with 4,000 horsemen and a vast quantity of wagons crammed with stores was therefore greeted with the greatest jubilation.

Although the courage and endurance displayed by the British infantry on the Modder River was quite remarkable, there is no doubt that the credit for the great success of these operations belongs to the cavalry, and to French in particular. Possibly because the 'shock tactics' used were considered out of date, and a bad example to cavalrymen generally, the relief of Kimberley and the capture of Cronje have never received the recognition they deserved, but it excited a great deal of interest in military circles at the time. Each of the nations with which Great Britain was more or less in friendly relations was allowed one military observer in the field, whose duty it was to make a report to his government on any useful lessons learned on strategy and tactics. The German observer commented on the dash to Kimberley as follows:

> 'This charge of French's cavalry division was one of the most remarkable phenomena of the war. It was the first and last occasion during the entire campaign that infantry was attacked by so large a body of cavalry, and its staggering success shows that, in future wars, a charge of great masses of cavalry will be by no means a hopeless undertaking even against troops armed with modern rifles, although it must not be forgotten that there is a difference between charging strong infantry in front and breaking through small and isolated groups of skirmishers.'

Silver statuette of an officer of the 14th King's Hussars, 1902. Officers were armed with sword and revolver. Badges of rank were affixed to the chain mail on their shoulders.

1900 The 14th on the Tugela
February 1900 Pieter's Hill
3rd March 1900 Relief of Ladysmith
13th March 1900 Bloemfontein
May 1900 Kroonstad
31st May 1900 Johannesburg
3rd June 1900 Pretoria
8th June 1900 Diamond Hill

1900

20

The Advance to Pretoria

WHILE Lord Roberts, having relieved Kimberley and captured Cronje in this forthright manner, was preparing to march on Bloemfontein, capital of the Orange Free State, Sir Redvers Buller was preparing for another attempt to relieve Ladysmith. Buller had been responsible for a number of serious setbacks, notably the defeat at Colenso during his last attempt on Ladysmith, and had shown no signs of the possession of luck, which Napoleon had always insisted was an essential quality in a General. Roberts, however, who had relieved him as commander-in-chief, had sufficient faith in his capabilities to retain his services in a vital part of the field, so that it would seem that his misfortunes were due not to incompetence but to lack of the facilities necessary for the prosecution of a successful campaign; a situation in which almost every British general invariably finds himself at the beginning of a war.

After establishing a base camp at Chieveley and reorganising his army of 20,000 men into two infantry divisions and the cavalry – or mounted troops – Buller marched for the Tugela on the 11th January, 1900. The cavalry, under Lord Dundonald, numbered about 3,000, mostly irregular horse, mounted infantry, mounted police and so on, with the Royals and 14th Hussars the only regulars; the 13th Hussars being corps troops. The 14th had

1900

reached Estcourt on the 8th January and Frere on the 13th. Here they camped on an old camping site 'very foul and full of flies', close to the railway on which lay the wreckage of the armoured train in which Mr Winston Churchill, war correspondent of the *Morning Post*, had been taken prisoner in the previous November. Having made his escape, this gentleman was now riding with the South African Horse in a combatant capacity but still sending despatches to his newspaper. He did not think much of Buller's methods of waging war: 'I watched,' he wrote, 'the almost interminable procession defile (from Chieveley). Ox waggons piled high with all kinds of packages, and drawn sometimes by ten or twelve pairs of oxen, mule waggons, Scotch carts, ambulance waggons with large Red Cross flags, ammunition carts, artillery, slaughter cattle, and last of all the naval battery with its two enormous 4.7 pieces, dragged by long strings of animals and guarded by straw-hatted khaki-clad bluejackets, passed in imposing array, with here and there a troop of cavalry to protect them or to prevent straggling. Here I must make an unpleasant digression. The vast amount of baggage this army takes with it hampers its movements and utterly precludes all possibility of surprising the enemy. I have never before seen officers accommodated with tents on active service though both the Indian Frontier and the Sudan lie under a hotter sun than South Africa but here today, within striking distance of a mobile enemy whom we wish to circumvent, every private soldier has canvas shelter, and the other arrangements are on an equally elaborate scale. The consequence is that roads are crowded, drifts blocked, marching troops are delayed, and all rapidity of movement is out of the question. Meanwhile the enemy completes the fortification of his positions, and the cost of capturing them rises.'

Buller's plan was to turn the Boer right flank across the Upper Tugela, and Dundonald's cavalry was ordered to seize the crossing at Springfield. Shortly after the march had started, however, the whole column became hopelessly bogged-down, with the transport in such complete chaos that Dundonald was unable to get forward. Eventually he succeeded in collecting some of his mounted troops and secured Springfield without difficulty, for the Boers in the area withdrew in front of him.

During these operations the 14th were split up. Regimental Headquarters with two troops of 'A' Squadron and two companies of mounted infantry under command, supported by two naval 12-pounders, defended the base camp at Chieveley. 'C' Squadron covered Estcourt, and Lieut. Hutchison's troop of 'A' Squadron rode forward to Spearman's Camp and was attached to Coke's infantry brigade. This troop took part in the battle of Spion Kop, a key position on the Boer flank which was captured but later abandoned on the arrival of Boer reinforcements. It was an infantry affair during which Hutchison patrolled round the flank, drawing fire but suffering no casualties. A general retirement was then ordered and Buller came back across the Tugela.

Meanwhile Colonel Hamilton with Regimental Headquarters and the troops mentioned patrolled up to the Tugela near Hlangwane Hill and came under shell and rifle fire from Boers along the river. This was a prelude to a reconnaissance in force to the same area which was carried out on the 23rd January. This time, the Boers were on the look-out and a patrol under Sgt. Storer came under heavy fire from Hlangwane Hill. Storer's horse bolted while he was dismounted and looking through his field-glasses, but his squadron leader, Capt. Lawrence, galloped up with a spare horse and got him away. By this time the Boers had launched a heavy counter-attack and the whole force was soon surrounded, mostly dismounted, with Boers crawling up through the rocks and bushes to within short range and others galloping round the flanks. Major O'Brien, who was in command in the absence of Colonel Hamilton, ordered a withdrawal by alternate troops, and this was successfully carried out, but at the cost of 26 casualties among the units taking part, including Capt. Dalton, Medical Officer to the 14th, who was shot through the stomach while attending a wounded man. The Boer responsible went up to him and apologised, saying that he had not noticed his brassard, but neither he nor his comrades offered any assistance and Dalton, whose patient had died, had to make his way back on his own during the night, in spite of his severe and painful wound.

The casualties suffered in this affair were rather higher than was usual in cavalry units in the Boer War, probably because the 14th were new to the game. Such actions normally commenced when the cavalry patrols drew fire. When this happened the horse artillery guns went into action immediately, and under cover of their fire the leading troops attacked dismounted, while those in support galloped out to the flanks in an attempt to get round to the rear of the enemy position. The object was to discover the strength of the opposition and not to capture or hold any particular feature, which was not the business of cavalry. Attacks were not therefore pressed home against any determined defence, but the decision as to when to withdraw required good judgement, and if delayed too long would result in sections and troops getting cut off and having to fight their way out at close

1900

range, with inevitable casualties. At Hlangwane Hill, for example, some troops had to withdraw and get mounted when the Boers were less than a hundred yards away, which was only possible owing to the accuracy of the horse artillery fire which was an outstanding feature of the whole campaign.

During the days following, 'A' and 'C' Squadrons reconnoitred towards the Tugela, exchanged shots with the Boers and rounded up their cattle, horses and sheep from the farms along the river. Meanwhile the wounded were being brought back from Spion Kop, and the detached troop of 'A' Squadron rejoined. Buller was in no way disconcerted by his failure, which had at least brought him valuable information and experience, and he made a new plan involving a feint attack towards Brakfontein and a genuine one against Vaal Krantz, a long ridge leading some miles to the east and south of the Brakfontein Hills. What was known as the 1st Natal Cavalry Brigade was formed, commanded by Brigadier-General Burn Murdoch of the Royals, and consisting of the Royal Dragoons, 13th and 14th Hussars, and 'A' Battery, R.H.A. It was told to get ready to gallop round the backs of Vaal Krantz as soon as it was taken, and head the retreating Boers away from Ladysmith. A great mass of artillery was assembled, and a subaltern sent aloft in a balloon to report the effect of its fire. He telephoned down to say that the shells were landing right on target, but when the infantry attacked the Boers were found to be unharmed and full of fight, so that the battle of Vaal Krantz ended in yet another general retirement. Burn-Murdoch's Cavalry Brigade remained out on the flank all of the first day, mounted and ready to gallop when the moment came. On the following morning the cavalry bivouac was shelled, just as the Mess-Sergeant of the 14th was superintending the preparation of the officers' breakfast. He was 'much put out' when ordered to pack it up again and get ready to move, and preferred a formal complaint to the Colonel. The Brigade, however, moved back under cover and there remained until the infantry retired, when orders and counter-orders caused a great deal of confusion. The retirement started on the 8th February and, after covering it, the 14th returned to Springfield on the 10th, thereafter going into outposts. The Boers followed up closely, and the regiment was engaged with them on several occasions, especially Major Brown's squadron which drove some of them back across the Tugela at Skiet Drift.

Having been defeated at Colenso in December, while attacking the enemy centre, and more recently at Spion Kop while trying to get round the right flank, Buller now decided to make an attempt against the left flank. The key to such an operation was Hlangwane Hill, south of the Tugela and east of Colenso, which the 14th had already reconnoitred as described. Its capture was essential before the crossing of the Tugela below Colenso could be forced. Buller advanced against it on the 12th February with the infantry and mounted infantry, while the cavalry watched the Tugela near Colenso. Contrary to expectations, the Boers made no determined effort south of the Tugela and were soon driven across it. Buller then massed his artillery on Hlangwane Hill and built a pontoon bridge about a mile east of Colenso. When the infantry crossed they ran into some very stiff opposition, but Buller was convinced that it was from Boer rearguards only and sent the cavalry across prematurely, for until the infantry advanced there was no room for them to operate. With the Boers launching several vicious counter-attacks and resisting stoutly at all points the infantry could make headway only with the greatest difficulty and at the cost of heavy casualties, including half the Irish Brigade. The cavalry were then sent back across the pontoon bridge which was being shelled by the Boers, who continued to shell the Brigade outposts and bivouacs during the days following, with everyone expecting yet another general withdrawal to start any moment. But, with a determination which he had not before exhibited, Buller kept the Boers at the bayonet-point and, after some days of desperate fighting, won a great victory with the enemy broken and on the run. The cavalry recrossed the Tugela immediately, and on the 28th February came up on the flank near Pieter's Station, where they could see the Boers in full retreat. It was a moment to draw swords and gallop, but before they could do so they were halted by Buller's personal order. He had, it appeared, lost his nerve, not of course, from fear of the enemy but owing to the outcry in the Press over the casualties suffered in this long drawn-out battle. So the Boers were left alone to fight another day, much to the fury of the cavalry for, although the pursuit of a beaten enemy was always a distasteful business, it was nonetheless a very necessary one and, in war, when the other fellow is down it never pays not to hit him. However, Buller was persuaded to allow two squadrons, one from the 13th Hussars and one from the 14th, to harass the retreating Boers as far as Elandslaagte, on the strict understanding that they incurred no casualties while doing to. This proviso naturally hampered their operations, and when they eventually came under shrapnel-fire they had first to dismount and take cover, and then to withdraw under orders from the Brigadier. The casualties during the fourteen days fighting in

1900

1900

what was known as the Battle of Pieter's Hill were, incidentally, about 2,000 all-ranks out of the 25,000 engaged which, as the 14th recorded, could hardly be described as excessive.

Ladysmith was relieved on the 3rd March, 1900, on which day the 14th led the march into the town. Buller had thus arrived at last, and only just in time, for the garrison was on the verge of starvation and, unlike that of Kimberley, 'looked very ill'. They had been reduced to such dietary expedients as blancmange made out of starch and 'Vinolia Powder', biscuits spread with dubbin, mouldy birdseed, starch and Kerosine oil.

A week after the relief of Ladysmith, Roberts, who had been obliged to halt after Paarde Berg to rest, refit and await reinforcements, resumed his advance on Bloemfontein at the head of 30,000 men. De Wet's and Delarey's Commandos, which had been heavily reinforced with men and guns from Natal and the Transvaal, were known to be in position at Poplar Grove some twenty miles east of Paarde Berg. Roberts marched one infantry division along the north bank of the Modder against the Boer right, another against their centre and the third against their left flank, which French with the Cavalry Division was ordered to turn – an operation which required a thirty-mile ride and a fight at the end of it. The Boers at Poplar Grove, however, were in a state of jumps caused by the British successes at Kimberley and Paarde Berg. As soon as they saw the immense cloud of dust kicked up by the Cavalry Division as it rode round their left, they abandoned their positions and rode off, in spite of the furious exhortations of President Kruger, who was with them. Had the cavalry been able to gallop, they would have caught the President, who was among the last to leave, but the horses were done-up after their long march over the sun-scorched veldt without water, and the Boers got clean away with their President, guns and transport. According to the German Military Attaché, the poor condition of the British cavalry horses was due as much to bad discipline as to hard conditions, for he noted that the men 'lolled about' in their saddles unchecked by their officers and N.C.O.s. There seems to have been some substance in this criticism, for the march discipline and horse-management in the British cavalry began to improve as a result of experience in the Boer War, until it finally became the best in the world. The first measure, which was introduced after Poplar Grove, was to lighten the weight carried by the horse by transferring much of the impedimenta to the first-line transport.

Roberts resumed his advance on the 10th February, marching in three columns each consisting of a cavalry brigade, a detachment of mounted infantry and an infantry division. The 1st Cavalry Brigade, to which 'B' Squadron still belonged, rode with the left column, accompanied by General French and his staff. On the previous day, 'B' Squadron had made a reconnaissance to the north of Driefontein and was fired on at long range from Abraham's Kraal, which turned out to mark the right of the Boer positions. When the 1st Cavalry Brigade came up it was shelled from this point and French, seeing that it would be suicidal for the brigade to continue its advance when the Modder river prevented a movement round the north flank, led the Brigade across the front of the army advance and took it to the head of the right column. This movement, which was carried out without any reference to Lord Roberts, threw the whole advance out of alignment and resulted in the infantry attack going in uncoordinated.

French, however, having thus collected the 1st and 3rd Cavalry Brigades on the right, led them against the Boer left and rear, expecting the enemy to pull out and run for it as before; but they stood fast this time, being well hidden among the kopjes, so that the cavalry could only keep galloping at them and retiring. In the end, the infantry got them on the move with the bayonet, but by that time the cavalry horses were too tired to pursue. It was not, in fact, one of French's better days and Roberts no doubt told him what he thought of him in private. One satisfactory feature of the affair was that the 1st and 3rd Cavalry Brigades, owing to the speed of their manoeuvres, suffered very few casualties, while their horse artillery guns made things very uncomfortable for the Boers. 'B' Squadron, although under fire all day, escaped unscathed.

Following this battle, President Kruger left Bloemfontein for the north, after empowering the mayor to surrender the city on summons, to avoid unnecessary destruction and loss of life. This decision was apparently forced on him by a large pro-British element in the city, whose cheers greatly surprised Roberts and his men when they marched in on the 13th March. Union Jacks made their appearance all over Bloemfontein, and 'B' Squadron was present when the flag was run up over the government buildings and the annexation of the Orange Free State formally proclaimed.

While 'B' Squadron was having these adventures, the rest of the regiment left Ladysmith and embarked at Durban for East London, thereafter travelling by train to Bethulie. A draft of 115 men had joined, and at Bethulie the heavy losses in horses were made up by an issue of Argentine remounts and Boer ponies,

1900

none of which were in any way up to the normal standard required by British cavalry. The Argentines were also still suffering from the effect of their long voyage from South America. The regiment marched for Bloemfontein on the 31st March, having to escort a large convoy of ox-wagons, remounts and detachments, which delayed it considerably. On arrival at the capital it joined the 4th Cavalry Brigade with the 7th Dragoon Guards and 8th Hussars, and went into camp at Donderhoek nearby. 'B' Squadron arrived shortly after, so that the 14th Hussars were once again united, for the first time since leaving England.

After their evacuation of Bloemfontein the Boers, under the personal command of their Commandant-General, Louis Botha, took up a strong position at Karree Siding, twenty miles to the north, in order to block a further British advance. Roberts got them out of it after a successful attack at the end of March, but the 4th Cavalry Brigade could take no part owing to a strange incident which left them temporarily without horses. While at Donderhoek a special effort was made to get the horses into condition, and their rations were brought up to the normal scale of 10 lb. oats and 10 lb. hay for the English horses and a bit less for the others. They were also allowed out to grass for a period each day, although the English horses did not much care for the coarse grass of the veldt. While they were out grazing one day, the 17th Lancers were seen practising various movements in line close by the brigade camp, then the whole regiment suddenly and inexplicably galloped without warning, stampeding all the horses. It took several days to round them up, and numbers were lost for good, including 53 belonging to the 14th. Furthermore their period at liberty on the high veldt living on nothing but poor grass lost them the condition which was so carefully being built up. Feeling, as may be imagined, ran very high against the unfortunate 17th, who must have been thankful to get back into action when the march started against Karree Siding.

The affair at Karree Siding introduced another change in Boer tactics. While Roberts halted to regroup and arrange for the administration of his supply line, Louis Botha developed a counter-stroke against his right flank. De Wet's and Olivier's commandos raided into the south east of the Free State – or Orange River Colony as it had now become – cutting the Bloemfontein water supply by seizing the pumping station at Sanna's Post, and bottling up a British detachment at Wepener. These and other exploits encouraged large numbers of Boer deserters to rejoin their commandos, and a grave situation quickly developed in which Roberts' convoys were being attacked and captured, the railway line blown up, the water supply interrupted and the burghers everywhere taking up arms and resuming their guerrilla activities.

Roberts' immediate concern was the recapture of Sanna's Post and the relief of Wepener – sixty miles south-east of Bloemfontein. Neither presented any great problem, but he deployed against them in force, hoping to round up the commandos at the same time. For the relief of Wepener, he detailed the 3rd and 4th Cavalry Brigades and the 9th Infantry Division, and this force marched at dawn on the 21st April. The Boers were covering the approaches to Wepener in strongly-held positions at Leeuwkop and De Wet's Dorp, and the cavalry came up against their outposts early on the 22nd, along a low ridge and kopje known as Paardekraal Hill. Owing apparently to some mistake on the part of the flank guard, the two brigades came under long-range fire while halted and in mass, which caused them a few casualties including a sergeant and four horses killed and wounded in the 14th. The infantry had meanwhile gone into action before Leeuwkop and the cavalry moved out to the flank to cooperate, while the 14th rode round to get across the enemy line of retreat; but the Boers got away too quickly to be caught. They had not, however, evacuated Paardekraal, from which they again opened fire on the 4th Cavalry Brigade on the following morning. In the subsequent action the 14th were sent against the enemy flank position on a kopje. The regiment rode against it at a gallop and had to pull up sharply when it was found that the Boers had erected a barbed-wire fence in front. It was cut without casualties and the regiment galloped through the gap under fire from two pom-poms, dismounted under cover and captured the kopje, all at the cost of one man and two horses hit. Once again, it seemed that the Boers were disconcerted by the speed at which the cavalry moved.

The Cavalry Division now marched for De Wet's Dorp, through country studded with kopjes each of which seemed to have Boers on it, either in position or hanging about on horseback. On the 24th April, while the 4th Cavalry Brigade was passing Roodekop, the 9th Lancers had to ride against some Boers on the left flank, leaving the 8th and 14th Hussars marching forward in column of troops. As they approached a high ridge running across the line of advance, a galloper arrived with orders for them to occupy it, upon which both regiments wheeled into squadron columns, galloped forward and dismounted, finally reaching the top of the ridge just before the Boers. A hot fight then developed at close range, with the 14th enfiladed and unable to

1900

advance until the 8th had made some progress on the flank, after which the Boers were driven off. Until then, 'A' Squadron in particular had a very unpleasant time, being under such heavy fire that heads had to be kept down and it was impossible to fire back. Capt. Denny, attached from the King's Dragoon Guards, who was commanding the squadron, was shot through the heart, two men were mortally wounded and seven others hit.

This opposition delayed the Cavalry Division, so that it was unable to cut off the Boers retreating from Wepener and De Wet's Dorp as Roberts had planned. Rundle's Infantry Division had just taken De Wet's Dorp when the cavalry arrived, by which time De Wet's commando had withdrawn into the mountainous country round Thabanchu, thirty miles to the north, where he was joined by Louis Botha with a large force from Wepener. French chased after them at once, trying to get behind them, but after leaving Thabanchu on the 28th April the 4th Cavalry Brigade narrowly escaped encirclement itself. 'The Boers,' reported Winston Churchill, who was an interested spectator from one of the gun positions, 'came down on our rear and flank, opening furious fire at long range, and galloping eagerly forward so that the Brigade and its guns, so far from entrapping the enemy were all but entrapped themselves.'

The 'furious fire' of the Boers, which was made from the saddle, did not cause many casualties, but the situation became serious nonetheless, as thousands of Boers galloped round the flanks of the 4th Brigade. There were such numbers of them that the 3rd Brigade was unable to get through to support the 4th, although the horse artillery batteries of both brigades were in action and pumping off shells as quickly as they could be rammed into the breeches. The 4th Brigade had therefore to go about and retire at a trot, covered by the 14th Hussars. This was a tough assignment for the 14th, who had to dismount and hold a succession of rearguard positions, with two squadrons up and one in support. As soon as they saw that the brigade was withdrawing, the exultant Boers came on in masses, but they did not dismount and so were at a disadvantage in the exchange of rifle-fire. The squadrons of the 14th, however, had to get mounted as they retired from their positions and, with the Boers pressing so closely, had to do so under fire. Several horses were hit but no men, and the dismounted men all brought out of action riding double, with one exception who was captured but managed to escape later – or was set at liberty, for the Boers had no means of looking after prisoners at that time. A fair number of transport wagons were lost by the 4th Brigade in this action, after which the Boers continued to hang about in the area, shelling the cavalry bivouacs and causing a fair amount of tension.

While the 14th were on outpost duty on the 2nd May, mostly dismounted but with one or two cossack posts, Major Brown of 'C' Squadron saw some Boers riding to cut off a wagon escorted by a party of infantry to the north-west of Thabanchu. He sent off a patrol led by Capt. Miller to warn the party that the Boers were coming, but while the patrol was trying to carry out this mission it was ambushed by the Boers and had to gallop off, Miller being hit in the back and his charger, Buster, shot dead and coming down on top of him. Some days later the Boers handed him over to the Band Sergeant of the South Staffords, and he recovered from his wound in due course; but it was a pity about Buster, who was a good horse, a bay gelding, twice winner of the regimental steeplechase, and also the Irish Military Steeplechase plate and Ward Union Hunt Point-to-Point.

Bandsmen, who were employed as stretcher-bearers and on other medical duties, wore medical brassards and were supposed to have immunity although they could not always count on it. The Boers, however, were always most scrupulous about the chivalrous conventions of war, and anyone displaying the Red Cross could come and go as he pleased.

Although the cavalry had been halted in this manner, the arrival of the infantry forced the Boers to retire north on Houtnek and Ladybrand. Roberts, with his right flank now secure, commenced to march on Pretoria after ordering French to follow as soon as the horses were fit. The Cavalry Division then returned to its old camp near Bloemfontein to rest and refit. After operations lasting fourteen days without a break, and on very inadequate rations, its losses in horseflesh had been very great, but a remount depot had now been opened in Bloemfontein, so that it was possible for them to be immediately replaced. The 14th had lost 180 horses, and as this was about the average for the Division, the extent of the constant demands for horses during the Boer War may be appreciated. In no previous campaign had such devastating losses been so constant a feature of the operations, and it seems to have been largely due to the difficulty of finding water on the high veldt when needed. The experience tended to make the British cavalry somewhat excessively water-conscious, so that in subsequent wars it was sometimes apt to think more in terms of water than of the purely tactical situation.

The 4th Cavalry Brigade marched from Bloemfontein on the 7th May, in rear of the Division and therefore responsible for the baggage-train which, consisted of a vast number of wagons

1900

drawn by oxen, mules and horses, was continually straggling out and getting bogged-down. The 14th, acting as rearguard to the Brigade, were constantly having to send squadrons back to protect and bring on the wagons, and this placed an additional strain on the horses which were still out of condition, for the halt at Bloemfontein had been too short for them to pick up. Nevertheless the regiment took part in an action on the Zand River during the 10th May, which consisted almost entirely of galloping about on the enemy right flank until the Boers gave way before an onslaught delivered by Roberts against their centre. When the march continued on the following day neither men nor horses had been fed, for the baggage had not arrived, so that they had to ransack the various farms on the line of march, but with little result. The order to trot was passed back as the Cavalry Division approached the Valsch River, and the pace was soon increased until the whole Division was at the gallop, which was kept up for nearly half-an-hour. The haste was necessary in order to forestall the Boers at the Valsch River Drift, through which the leading squadrons galloped under shell-fire, just as the enemy arrived to defend the crossing. The Boers retired when they found that they were too late.

The cavalry reached Kroonstadt on the 12th May, after a march of at least 150 miles, punctuated by a great deal of skirmishing and on a starvation diet. The road behind them was littered with the dead bodies of horses, mules and oxen, and an epidemic of enteric broke out among the troops. But the Boers were on the run, and Roberts had every intention of keeping them moving. Winston Churchill asked a Boer chaplain if he thought his countrymen would continue to resist. 'I told my flock often that it would not be child's play,' he answered, 'and we must go down fighting.'

'You preach a strange gospel of peace, Sir.'

'And you English have strange ideas of liberty.'

This retort, indicating a condition of mind apparently quite incapable of understanding the real cause of the war – the Boer maltreatment of the Uitlanders, to whom they had denied human rights and liberty – is not a bad example of the cause of war generally: the uselessness of argument unless backed by the sword.

Roberts halted at Kroonstadt for ten days, being forced to do so in order to get up supplies, which was a difficult and lengthy business, as the single line of narrow-gauge railway on which he was dependent had been blown up by the Boers in several places. There was little rest for the cavalry, however, for they were constantly out on patrol, from which they seldom returned without having had a skirmish. On the 18th, the 14th rode out to burn down a farm from which it had been reported that fire had been opened on British troops after the white flag had been hoisted. The Boers made an effort to surround the 14th and stop them burning the farm, but they were held off, and the regiment returned to Kroonstadt after burning two farms for good measure and bringing with them both farmers and 134 head of cattle.

Making a wide detour to the north-west, French with the Cavalry Division crossed the Vaal River unopposed at Parys, and so entered the Transvaal on the 24th May – Queen Victoria's birthday. Pushing on, he discovered Louis Botha and his men ensconced among the hills along the north bank of the Klip River – a winding stream with wide, marshy banks. A series of cavalry skirmishes followed, accompanied by the usual hardships suffered by the non-arrival of the transport. Not only was there no food or forage, but the nights had become bitterly cold, and no-one had any blankets. The cavalry bivouacs along the slopes of the kopjes were therefore far from being havens of rest, but as the troops were continually being called out to fight the grass fires which had been started by the shell-fire, there was no danger of them actually freezing to death.

On the 27th, the Division advanced to Vlakfontein, where French made a reconnaissance with the 4th Cavalry Brigade. The Boers were around in considerable numbers, and as the Brigade advanced in squadron columns at the trot their shells crashed right among the ranks, but for some reason they did little damage. It was thought that the Boer ammunition must have been of very poor quality, but this could not altogether have accounted for its lack of effect against the cavalry, for the horse artillery batteries nearly always suffered heavy casualties in action.

From the summit of the hills, the long line of factory chimneys along the Rand Ridge before Johannesburg now came into view. 'I might have been looking from a distance at Oldham,' said Winston Churchill. The 14th were continually galloping forward, dismounting, and attacking up the kopjes, always finding, when they got to the top, that the Boers had decamped. They had a few men and horses wounded, some of the latter being officers' chargers which could ill be spared. When Major Brown's charger was brought down during an action at Klipriveirsberg on the 28th May, Cpl. Dove galloped up and offered his own horse, but Brown was content to get under cover hanging on to

1900

Dove's stirrup, for which service he had Dove promoted to sergeant.

The battle for Johannesburg commenced on the 29th May, when Roberts advanced along both sides of the railway. Ian Hamilton made a frontal attack against the western side of the Boer positions, and French endeavoured to turn the western flank. He manoeuvred the Division with great skill, making full use of his mobility, and succeeded in hiding his intentions from the enemy for some time. When they awoke to their danger, they commenced to prolong their flank to the right, but as they had no time to organise an effective defence the cavalry were usually able to get them on the run by galloping at them, although the 14th had to dismount and attack on foot several times. 'C' Squadron, led by Major Brown, was specially complimented by Sir John French for the gallantry and efficiency with which 'under very heavy shell and musketry fire', it captured and held a kopje on one of these occasions, in collaboration with the 7th Dragoon Guards.

During what was known as the Battle of Orange Grove, on the 30th May, the Boer defences gradually crumbled, and the city of Johannesburg surrendered on the following day. When the cavalry advanced they found the enemy demoralised and in full retreat. Reports reaching Lord Roberts indicated that French's guns had been heard at Pretoria, twenty-five miles off, causing a panic among the burghers and the flight of President Kruger. Roberts accordingly made but a brief halt at Johannesburg and marched for Pretoria on the 3rd June, although he was still worried about the security of his communications, for the Boer raiders were again active on his right flank and had captured Heilbron.

During his advance on Pretoria, Roberts kept the Cavalry Division well out to his left, with orders to continue with their attempts to get round the enemy flank. The opposition met with was chiefly from long-range shell and rifle fire, but 'C' Squadron fought a dismounted action on the 3rd June, when it was sent up to support the 1st Cavalry Brigade which was held up near Kalkheuval. The horses continued to founder from the shortage of water and forage, and the heavy demands made upon them. During the advance to Pretoria the regiment became reduced to 135 mounted men, but Roberts was relentless in his determination to push on and finish off the war which, with the Boers defeated, he could see no sense in continuing. The advance was so rapid in consequence, that men whose horses had foundered had no hope of catching the regiment up at the next halt, and they were therefore ordered to lead their horses within reach of water, off-saddle and turn them loose, then to report to any unit they could find – with their saddles. It was the only possible solution, but it meant that when the regiment did receive a draft of remounts the men could not be found to mount them.

After retreating from Pretoria, Louis Botha had taken up a position along a ridge about fifteen miles to the north and extending on either side of the railway. Roberts sent several messages to him in attempts to persuade him to come to terms, but he had been encouraged by the success of De Wet's raids, and his evasion of the many attempts made by Lords Kitchener and Methuen to catch him in the country between Winburg and Heilbron. Having had to reinforce the troops guarding the railway and chase De Wet and other commando leaders, Roberts' army at Pretoria had become reduced to 30,000 men, and the Cavalry Division, once 6,000 strong, could parade only 2,000. It was estimated that 5,000 remount horses were required, for those still in the ranks were footsore and debilitated, so that they had to be led on the line of march and mounted only when action was imminent.

The soldiers, officers and men, were dirty, ragged, tired, cold and hungry; so much so that Roberts at last noticed their condition and temporarily switched the target of his powerful personality from the Boers to his own supply services. Food, forage and clothing arrived accordingly. In the 14th, all their old clothes were in such a state that they had to be burnt, for the lousiest tramp would not have touched them. For a short time their ration-scale went up to $1\frac{1}{2}$ lb. of meat a day with the usual additional items to match, but the horses were not so lucky, and were still kept short at 4 lb. a day below the normal scale.

There was no rest, however, for while at Pretoria the cavalry were constantly out on patrol or on outpost, and the march against Louis Botha commenced on the 8th June. The Battle of Diamond Hill followed, lasting two days, with the cavalry far out to the west, engaging Delarey's commando while trying to get round the Boer flank. This proved impossible, for Delarey kept prolonging the flank, and the cavalry horses could not outpace the Boers in the condition they were in; but the threat to the flank forced the Boers to weaken their centre, so that the infantry were able to beat them without any great difficulty or casualties. The 14th were in close action during the whole of this battle, mostly fighting dismounted. The regiment could only get about seventy men into the firing line, for more horses had foundered during the march from Pretoria, but they gave a good account of

1900

themselves and, for the first time during the campaign, ran out of ammunition, which caused some anxious moments. It seems, however, that their opponents were also running short for the firing died down on both sides and eventually ceased completely, leading to a strange interlude during which British and Boers got up to stretch their legs within short range of one another. At Diamond Hill the Royal Horse Artillery, upon which the cavalry were always greatly dependent for close support, was not so effective as usual for it was also very short of horses. Many of the teams were down to three or four horses, and there were often none for the gunners who had to ride on the limbers. The batteries had therefore great difficulty in getting into action, which placed the cavalry at a serious disadvantage. Nevertheless, for some inexplicable reason, the casualties were light, and the 14th were surprised to find that theirs amounted to only two men wounded.

The Boers withdrew before dawn on the 13th June. The cavalry mounted at once and set off after them, but halted after a few miles, for French realised that the enemy were well away, and that it would be hopeless to try and catch them up on worn-out horses. The 14th rode back to Kameeldrift, where they rested for three weeks and received a fresh supply of remounts.

Finding that he was not being pursued, Louis Botha halted at Middelburg, about a hundred miles from Pretoria, while the British cavalry rode back to the Diamond Hill area and established a line of outposts. The line extended along the Magakiesburg Ridge, facing Grobler's commando which had formed a laager at Wonderboom Farm, only a few miles from Pretoria, from which parties of Boers were continually riding out and exchanging shots with the outposts. Roberts did not bother with them, being engaged in consolidating his position in collaboration with Generals Buller and Hunter, and attempting to check the Boer raids against his flank and rear. At the end of June Louis Botha rode out in force to see what was going on, and some sharp skirmishing took place on either side of the railway near Van der Merwe, but the Boers retired when reinforcements came out from Pretoria. Delarey's commando, however, rode round the rear of Grobler's laager and joined De Wet and Prinsloo in raiding the railway south of Pretoria, halting a supply train and carrying off its cargo which included mail for the 14th, which the regiment had been looking forward to for weeks. The 'Queen's Chocolate' got through, however, and each officer and man was issued with a gilt tin of it, embossed with Her Majesty's profile. A few of the recipients posted their issue home to their relatives as a souvenir, but the great majority thankfully devoured it at once.

1900

On the 7th July, De Wet was run down at Bethlehem by Generals Clements and Paget, and very roughly handled although he got away as usual. Four days later his defeat was avenged by Grobler and Delarey, who combined to make savage attacks against the British outpost line north of Pretoria.

The use of cavalry for outpost duty was normally avoided as much as possible for it imposed a heavy strain on the horses which, even when they were not on duty in the vedettes or cossack posts carrying their riders, could seldom be unsaddled. The force at Roberts' disposal, however, though large was still insufficient to protect his communications, chase after the raiders, and yet allow him to keep enough in hand for a further advance. Even with the help of the cavalry, the line could only be very thinly held and a difficulty arose in the cavalry outposts by the fact that the raw and untrained horses which they were forced to use were very liable to stampede, and therefore required one holder for every two horses instead of the normal one for four.

This, of course, further weakened the firing line, in which a thousand yards of front had in many cases to be held by a hundred men – and these armed with carbines against the Boer rifles. As not infrequently happens in war, the regiments were getting very mixed-up, with all sorts of strangers in their ranks; the 14th getting enough Lancers to be able to form them into a separate troop. This was a good thing in one way, in that it confused the Boers, who often thought that they were up against more than one regiment and were accordingly led into the exercise of an exaggerated and unnecessary caution.

The 14th were in the line at Derdepoort, but were resting when patrols sent out by the outposts of the 7th Dragoon Guards on the 10th July found the enemy in force north of Waterval. On the following day, 'C' Squadron was sent to co-operate with the 7th D.G. in an attack on the line of kopjes held by the enemy, but nothing came of it other than fairly heavy casualties to the 7th. The Boers had been about to advance themselves and fierce, though sporadic, fighting continued for the next four days. Neither side made any headway and on the 17th the cavalry were relieved by infantry, and the Cavalry Division marched eastwards.

14th King's Hussars, 1900. Trooper *(left)* and officer. In November 1900 at Pretoria the 14th were issued with the long Lee-Enfield rifle shown carried in the Trooper's bucket. This replaced the short-range carbine.
The weight of rider and equipment was about 300 lbs.

July 1900 The advance on Middelburg
31st August 1900 Capture of Machadadorp
13th September 1900 Capture of Barberton
13th October 1900 Mahon's Cavalry Brigade at Dalmanutha
Major E. D. Brown awarded the Victoria Cross

1900

Operations in the Transvaal

21

LOUIS BOTHA, who had been watching events from his headquarters at Middelburg, had reinforced both Delarey and Grobler during their attacks on the outpost line at Pretoria. A week later he arrived himself at the head of the rest of his men and attacked the British positions east of the city. Roberts then decided that Middelburg would have to be taken, and he advanced upon it on the 23rd July, marching along the railway line, with French as usual trying to get round the enemy flanks with the cavalry and mounted infantry.

Louis Botha, who had barely 4,000 men under his immediate command, could not seriously oppose the formidable host deployed by his opponent, and the Boers accordingly fell back as the cavalry advanced, sometimes firing ragged volleys from the saddle, to which the cavalry replied in like manner with no damage done to either side. Conditions for the British troops were miserable in the extreme. A freezing wind drove blinding clouds of sand and dust into the faces of the marching troops, and was followed by a steady downpour of rain, turning the march route into a quagmire in which horses, oxen and mules foundered and died in great numbers. Owing to the Boer raids on his communications, Roberts had not been able to accumulate enough supplies and transport before starting, and what he did manage to

1900

collect was now bogged-down and unable to keep up with the army, so that the troops had often to shiver away the nights bivouacked on the bare hillsides, without either food or shelter. Many men died of exposure under these conditions, which were as bad as those experienced during the Peninsular and Crimean Wars. On the night of the 25th July, after the 14th had been in action most of the day, during which they had been transferred from the 4th to the 1st Cavalry Brigade, 'no wheels reached the regiment who were lying out in complete exposure on Naauwpoort Hill. The Brigadier and staff crept under a Cape-cart in a mealie field and spent the night leaning against each other in a little group.' The only comfort lay in the fact that the Boers were no better off – 'The Boer picquets were quite close to ours, but all were so miserable that no firing occurred at all.'

As far as Roberts was concerned, however, the operations against Louis Botha were proceeding as planned and did not require his personal direction. Rather to the annoyance of his long-suffering soldiers, he therefore returned to Pretoria by special train, taking his staff with him. He was concerned with the increasing activities of the Boers in the Free State, especially De Wet, who had escaped as usual from the cordon which was being drawn around him on the border, and was now on the Vaal River, watched by Lord Methuen and Birdwood's Cavalry Brigade. Prinsloo, however, had not been so fortunate – or clever – as De Wet, and surrendered on the 30th July with his whole commando, which exceeded in numbers that of Cronje at Paarde Berg.

Dawn broke on the 26th July upon conditions of such misery that 'no one offered to fight', although there was every opportunity to do so. The opposing lines of picquets were nowhere farther than two hundreds yards apart, and one of the Boer picquets was found to have been posted in between two of the 14th Hussars' picquets. When the Boers discovered their awkward situation, they gathered up their few possessions and sloped off to the rear, unhindered by the 14th. The regiment was in position across a drift over the Klein Olifant River, which was blocked by overturned transport and dead animals, while the road and adjoining fields on the south bank were jammed solid with carts and wagons of every description, with their teams still in harness un-fed and un-watered, for although they were on the banks of a river only those which happened to be in front could get to it for a drink.

The Boers were fortunately in no condition to take advantage of this state of affairs, but withdrew towards Middelburg pursued by the 1st Cavalry Brigade. The 14th, whose start was delayed from having to call in their picquets, caught up the Brigade while it was in action at Sterkwater, and rode up on the right flank. As the Boers withdrew before it, the regiment moved on, led by 'C' Squadron, with one troop in front in line of sections, one in support, and one in echelon on the left rear. The squadron was shelled as it advanced, but suffered no damage, and the Brigade reached Middelburg without serious opposition to find that Louis Botha had decamped.

The Cavalry Division then rode on towards Machadodorp, which the Boers declared their intention of holding to the last man. It was only in the last eight miles that their resistance really stiffened, however, when the cavalry took up a defensive position east of Belfast and entrenched themselves. The 14th, whose strength at this time was 340 men and 250 horses, were stationed about fourteen miles south of Belfast, with a very considerable frontage to watch and defend. Lack of supplies had obliged them to send out foraging parties. 'Living at free quarters', to use the ancient military term, was at first engaged upon with a kind of sheepish reluctance and profuse apologies; but when it was found that, by doing so, the soldiers and their horses for the first time in the campaign enjoyed ample and more-or-less regular meals, their feelings of diffidence were dismissed as irrelevant and morale was soon restored to normal.

There was at first no sign of the Boers, but mounted patrols discovered their line about five miles off. Such a situation was more dangerous than when the opposing forces were in close contact, for it was impossible to know what the enemy were up to. The outpost work was consequently very arduous, for patrols had to be kept out continuously, and the utmost vigilance maintained. The 14th kept two picquets in the line by day and three by night, each picquet being the equivalent of a troop. Two or three sentry-posts were put out in front of the picquet in entrenched positions, while the remainder formed a mounted reserve in rear with their horses saddled. The patrols, which had long-distance missions, were sent out by regimental headquarters and not, as is the usual custom, by the outpost commanders. It was not, in fact, a sound tactical arrangement, but was forced upon the regiment by the heavy nature of its task and the lack of strength and resources with which to carry it out properly.

After his return to Pretoria and a re-consideration of the general situation, Roberts had become not a little perplexed regarding the best move to take for finishing the war quickly and decisively. The activities of the Boer raiders on his flank and rear

1900

had obliged him to disperse his forces over a vast area, often in small garrisons which were liable to become cut-off and so necessitate further dispersal in the shape of relieving columns. It was impossible to find any immediate answer to this problem and he decided, therefore, that he must again march against Louis Botha who lay before Machadodorp with 6,000 men, representing the only formed Boer army left in the field. Its defeat would cut the Boers off from the supplies of arms and munitions which they had been receiving from abroad through Lorenco Marques and Komatipoort, dealing them a blow from which they could scarcely recover.

For the attack against Machadodorp, Buller was ordered to move up from the Natal railway through Ermlo against the enemy flank, while Roberts himself led the direct advance from Middelburg against their centre. At the same time, various independent forces were deployed for the protection of Pretoria and the flanks of the advance.

Buller advanced on the 8th August, drove back Christian Botha who was guarding the enemy flank, and occupied first Ermlo and then Carolina, about twenty-five miles south of the main enemy positions. The Cavalry Division had meanwhile moved forward ahead of the main army. The 14th, with the 1st Cavalry Brigade on the right flank, came within sound of Buller's guns on the 23rd August. The regiment, like the others, was moving across the difficult country with squadrons in single rank extended to four paces, a novel departure from the normal formation of two ranks closed up and ready to charge. By taking away the rear ranks, the number of squadrons in a regiment was of course increased from three to six, enabling a much wider front to be covered, while the target presented was a very difficult one, especially when moving at a trot or faster. The Boers in fact could make nothing of it, and casualties were very few in spite of constant rifle and shell fire. Buller appears to have got the measure of the Boers at last and, while operating under the direct orders of Roberts at any rate, displayed a creditable skill on the battlefield. The general plan therefore worked without a hitch and Louis Botha, with his flank crumbling, evacuated Belfast and Machadodorp in turn.

As soon as Buller's attack developed, Roberts had sent French with all the cavalry and supported by the Guards Brigade into the hills north of Belfast in order to threaten the Boers' right flank. The Boers offered no serious opposition at first, but when Louis Botha realised that his situation was becoming precarious, they began to show more resolution and even launched one or two counter-attacks. On the 27th August the 14th, who were holding a line of kopjes far out on the left of their Brigade, had several men and horses wounded while defending their position. Sergeant Dove, who led a troop in a mounted attack along a spur, was specially mentioned for his conduct in this affair.

On the arrival of the 11th Infantry Division, French brought the cavalry out of action and led them to the north in an attempt to get across the Boer line of retreat. Although the country was difficult for movement because of marshy ground between the ridges running across the line of advance, the cavalry kept up a hot pace and seldom dismounted. When the advanced guards were fired upon, the horse artillery batteries came up at full gallop and, on the shout of 'Action front!' presented an exhilarating spectacle, the sight of which in a great measure compensated for the hardships of the campaign. Wellington had always expressed his grave displeasure, if he saw one of his horse troops going into action at a pace shorter than a gallop, and after nearly a century of practice and experience the Royal Horse Artillery had become unsurpassed for gallantry and efficiency, dismounting in the act of pulling up, unlimbering and swinging round the trails, unhooking the teams as they brought the limbers round to the exact spot required, and the first ranging shots were usually away before the teams were clear. Against what now amounted to a demoralised enemy galloping about in futile attempts to prolong their flank, the dash and verve shown by the cavalry and horse artillery was irresistible and the Boer front steadily crumbled. Unfortunately the country became increasingly difficult and when the 14th rode against Watervalboven on the 30th August the leading squadron was forced into single file, moving along a narrow track through the hills. Even the pack animals had to be left behind, and artillery support became out of the question. The Boers consequently became more actively aggressive, so that the cavalry operations developed into a series of probing attacks with frequent withdrawals, in many of which the 14th were lucky to escape without serious loss.

On the 31st August, Buller entered Machadodorp, and Louis Botha fell back to Lydenburg. He then divided his force, sending half to the north and leading the remainder to the east. Roberts ordered Buller to concentrate on the defeat of this second half, with Louis Botha at its head, and Buller therefore continued his advance through Lydenburg, while French with the cavalry moved south of the railway through the Barberton country.

The Cavalry Division reached Carolina on the 7th September and headed at once towards Barberton, a distance of about

1900

1900

seventy miles. With the Division was a company of mounted infantry, the Suffolk Regiment and the King's Shropshire Light Infantry. As the country was even worse than that in the north, mounted engagements were not expected and, indeed, it often proved impossible to ride and the cavalry had to dismount and lead their horses in single file along rocky mountain tracks. The Boers, had they chosen, could have imposed serious delays on the Cavalry Division in such country, but they showed no willingness to stand and fight. Most of them, in fact, had lost interest in the war and were more than anxious to concede defeat and get back to their farms; but they were too scared of their leaders to desert.

The 14th, who for some undisclosed reason were in the irritating position of riding with the 1st Cavalry Brigade while their baggage accompanied the 4th Cavalry Brigade, had plenty of hard work and excitement, for although the Boers made no serious stand, there were lots of them about on the lookout for opportunities to kill a few soldiers without danger to themselves. On one occasion about thirty of them, dressed in British uniforms, made a mounted attack on a cossack post held by the regiment, but the post was not taken-in by their fancy dress and sent them away in a hurry. On the 12th September the regiment, which was leading the brigade, was fired on from the flank by some mounted Boers who were chased off by Lieut. Hill-Whitson's squadron, while the rest of the regiment dismounted in order to lead their horses up a very steep and rocky hill. There was no opposition on the way up, but on the summit Lieut. the Hon. H. Grosvenor's squadron was attacked while on a ridge to the right, but mounted and dispersed the Boers at the cost of one horse killed. The regiment had been ordered to take a kopje known as Nel's Hoek, against which it now advanced mounted with squadrons in file, and moving at a brisk canter in spite of the rough ground, for the Boers were shooting at them from both flanks. They reached their objective without loss, and the Boers promptly decamped.

On the following morning the 1st Cavalry Brigade – Greys, Carabiniers, Inniskillings and 14th Hussars – was joined at Nel's Hoek by General French who rode with it towards Barberton, sending the Greys to cut the railway line behind it to prevent the removal of artillery and supplies. Captain Tottenham's squadron, which was leading the Brigade, met the Landrost coming out of the town in a Cape-cart to surrender, and when the squadron rode in it was greeted with hearty cheers by the citizens, who were mostly British. There were also many Boers, waiting to surrender their arms, who had not bothered to attempt an escape. A great number of wagons loaded with supplies, 40 locomotives and £10,000 in gold were captured – a surprising haul which was due apparently to Louis Botha having been taken ill and so unable to maintain control and morale among his tough followers.

1900

Lord Roberts was now sick of the war, which he could see no point in continuing. For some time, he had been carrying governmental authority for the annexation of the Transvaal, to be put into effect at his discretion. He made the proclamation on the 1st August, and at the same time asked to be relieved of his command in favour of Lord Kitchener, with whom he had already discussed the measures necessary for destroying the burghers' will to fight, if their leaders still continued recalcitrant. He hinted at these measures in a lengthy proclamation, which ended:

'the war is degenerating and has degenerated into operations carried on in an irregular and irresponsible manner, and in many cases by insignificant bodies of men. I should be failing in my duty to Her Majesty's Government and Her Majesty's Army in South Africa if I neglected to use every means in my power to bring such irregular warfare to an early conclusion. The means which I am compelled to adopt are those which the customs of war prescribe as being applicable to such cases; they are ruinous to the country, entail endless suffering to the burghers and their families, and the longer this guerrilla warfare continues the more vigorously must they be enforced.'

Up to this time the Boer War had undoubtedly merited its description as a 'Gentlemen's War', with each side going out of its way to show its consideration and regard for the other. There is even something faintly amusing in the sportsmanlike manner with which Boer and Briton refused to hit the other fellow when he was down, and in the flags of truce conveying requests for medical aid and other favours, or offering or suggesting surrender to avoid unnecessary suffering. Following Roberts' proclamation, the war became not quite so gentlemanly, but it never degenerated into a cad's affair with nothing barred and no standards of decency, like the wars of more recent times. As the war dragged on, with large numbers of Boer prisoners breaking their parole and rejoining the commandos, the warning issued by Roberts had to be followed by action. Prisoners of war were no longer put on parole but were deported, farms and crops were destroyed and livestock driven off, while the farmers and their families were placed in camps surrounded by barbed-wire and strongly guarded. They were known as 'Concentration Camps', a term which had no particular significance at the time, but which was later adopted by Hitler for the German political camps with

1900

their sinister reputation for mass-murder, torture and unorthodox medical experiments. Although there was, of course, no shadow of resemblance between the two, the unfortunate similarity of name has since given rise to the scandalous fable that Great Britain first started the idea. In fact, it is doubtful whether the Boer guerrillas could ever have been suppressed had not their sources of supply and intelligence been closed to them in this manner.

On the 8th October the Cavalry Division was reorganised at Machadodorp. French had returned to Pretoria, taking with him several of the regular cavalry regiments, and the remainder were formed into three brigades of which only the 1st Brigade with the Greys, Carabiniers and Inniskillings remained unchanged. General Dickson's Brigade became a composite force of all arms, based on the 7th Dragoon Guards and the Suffolk Regiment, while the 8th and 14th Hussars, with Mahon's Horse and 'M' Battery, R.H.A., made up a new brigade commanded by Colonel B. T. Mahon of the 12th Lancers, formerly commander of Mahon's Horse, one of the many regiments of irregular cavalry raised during the war to counter the mobility of the Boers.

On the 12th October the Cavalry Division, led by Mahon's Brigade, marched to Heidelberg on the orders of Lord Roberts 'to clear a part of the country which has not hitherto been visited by our troops.' In fact, the area had already been traversed by Buller on his way up from Ermelo to the fighting round Machadodorp, and Mahon's Brigade used one of his camping grounds at Geluk near Dalmanutha, at the end of their first day's march. It turned out to be a bad choice of ground for a bivouac, when the Boers had been hovering about all day. During the night they crept up around it, and shelled it at daybreak preparatory to attacking. The Brigade, which was only about 600 strong, was heavily outnumbered and Mahon had to retire on Dalmanutha. A serious situation then developed, for the Brigade had a large transport column with it which the Boers were particularly anxious to capture, for they were very short of supplies. As soon as they saw the transport on the move to the rear, escorted by two squadrons of the 14th, they attacked with great determination and got round the flanks of the 8th Hussars, whose last picquet was nearly surrounded and lost two officers and several men killed and wounded.

'A' Squadron of the 14th, commanded by Capt. Tottenham, was in a covering position with a series of entrenched picquets dug in along the forward slope of a ridge, behind which were the reserve troop and the horses. When the 8th Hussars had withdrawn, and the transport column was out of range, Major E. D.

Brown, who was acting second-in-command of the 14th, rode back with orders for 'A' Squadron to retire, which was carried out by sections leaving their trenches one at a time and running for their horses, which meant crossing 150 yards of open ground under a hot fire at close range. Fortunately the Boers were excited, and blazing away in all directions without taking aim, but it was all very unpleasant and, as they got round the flanks, the guns of 'M' Battery, R.H.A., the horses of 'A' Squadron, a troop of 'C' Squadron and a troop of the 8th Hussars, all of which were being held in the same place, gave them targets which they could hardly miss.

As had happened at Colenso, and on many other battlefields of the Boer War, 'M' Battery was in an exposed position far too close to the firing line, so that many of its officers and men were shot down, and so many of its horses killed or wounded that the guns had to be man-handled out of action and could only retire at a walk under a hail of bullets. In fact, they were only saved from capture by the extraordinary gallantry of the gunners and drivers, although a great deal of credit could also be claimed by 'A' Squadron which kept the Boers off until the guns were clear.

Colonel Hamilton of the 14th had meanwhile placed 'C' Squadron into position to cover the retirement of 'A', which was being superintended by Major Brown who was with the horses under close-range fire from both flanks. Fortunately, the Boer fire was still very wild, partly owing to the activities of the reserve troop, which was replying to it with a great deal more accuracy. The horses, however, were getting very restive as numbers of them were hit and upsetting the others by their screams and plunges. They included those of a troop of the 8th Hussars, which had gone back without them, and this added to the confusion. As 'A' Squadron came in and began to get mounted, Major Armitage of 'M' Battery rode up and asked for help for his wounded. Captain Chalmers, the Medical Officer of the 14th, went back with him accompanied by a trumpeter, to be greeted by a heavy burst of fire as soon as the Boers saw them. Chalmers rode on shouting 'Doctor!' and they let him advance with the trumpeter but shot Armitage's horse, so that he had to go back. Chalmers found the wounded by an overturned ammunition wagon, but had to attend to them lying down owing to the heavy fire, while the trumpeter, Stride, waved bandages. When the firing died down the Boers came up for a chat, and told Chalmers that they had intended to make a night attack, but had had to call it off as the British lit no fires that night to give them the direction.

1900

1900

They were pleasant and polite as usual, but stole Chalmers' horse and raincoat.

Two troops of 'A' Squadron had meanwhile got mounted and away, but the last troop and one of 'C' had more difficulty, being under both shell and rifle fire. Three men had to be helped on to their plunging horses by Major Brown, who then rode over to Sergeant Hersey, whose horse had been killed, and took him up behind until another horse was caught for him. Brown, accompanied by his trumpeter, Leigh, then rode back to make sure that no one had been left, and found one man retiring on foot. As this man was too heavy to ride double, the trumpeter gave him his horse and mounted behind Brown – all this under heavy fire. Sergeant Hersey had also come back and took up another dismounted man.

As the Boers had closed in along the line of retreat, Tottenham became obliged to halt 'A' Squadron and take up another defensive position until 'C' Squadron was ready to cover a further withdrawal. Although in this position the horses were under cover, so that it was easier to get away when the moment came, they were still restive from the bullets flying low over their heads and would not stand still to be mounted. All got clear, however, except Lieut. Browne, whose horse was pulling him about at the end of its reins and trying to break away. His predicament was seen by Major Brown who was again on the look-out for such incidents and who galloped back to his assistance, held his horse, and brought him out safely.

Having disengaged in this manner, the 14th rallied a mile or two away and sent back patrols, who found the Boers gone and the stretcher-bearers attending to the wounded, surrounded by vultures which did not, however, approach any human casualties but gorged themselves on the horses. The casualties in the Brigade amounted to about seventy in killed and wounded, of which number ten belonged to the 14th who also lost about twenty horses. There were several narrow escapes, such as that of S.S.M. Russell, whose reins were cut in front of his hands, a button cut off and a bullet lodged in his pocket-book. Major E. D. Brown was afterwards awarded the Victoria Cross for his conduct in the action which was certainly most gallant. Apart from the fact that he saved several officers and men from death or capture, his example of cool courage in the face of great danger was an inspiration to all ranks, and prevented the disorder which might well have occurred under such circumstances. Others also risked their lives to bring unhorsed comrades out of action, Sergt. Hersey, who was wounded, in particular, Trumpeter

Leigh and Pte. Sexton who brought out his own officer, Lieut. Harvey. Not all horses, of course, were able to carry two men. Those which could were the officers' chargers and the English or Irish troop horses; very few of the 'Colonial' horses could do so, especially in the condition to which they had been reduced by the hardships of the campaign. Chargers, which were heavyweight hunters, were becoming distressingly few in numbers at this time although each officer had brought two or three into the field at the beginning of the war. Many of them, like Buster, were without blemish as examples of a good horse, and they were impossible to replace outside England or Ireland.

During the onward march of the Brigade several skirmishes took place against parties of Boers hanging about on the flanks and rear, who were found to belong to a force of about fifteen hundred led by General Smuts. The Boers had become incensed over the burning of their farms in accordance with Roberts' new tough policy for bringing the war to an end. Smuts issued a warning that if it continued he would shoot his prisoners of war and fire on ambulances. He did not in fact proceed to such extremes, but the war did begin to degenerate into a rather squalid affair with the Boers playing various dirty tricks which inevitably led to reprisals. One of these, which much annoyed the British, was 'the abuse of the white flag'. In an attempt to stop the burning of farms, they garrisoned those within reach of the British forces and, after firing on the foraging parties, hoisted the white flag of surrender as soon as an attack was started. Then, when the British troops ceased firing and exposed themselves, the white flag was hauled down suddenly and they would find themselves in the middle of a hot fire at close range, suffering many casualties. The Boers then got to horse and made off, so that they could not be caught and made to account for such behaviour. Some of them also rode up to British picquets dressed in British uniforms, and opened fire on the soldiers while they were off their guard. Furthermore, some of the bodies of British soldiers had wounds which indicated that they had been shot in cold blood while wounded and incapacitated. However, such deplorable incidents never became widespread, and may have been partially attributable to the foreign mercenaries serving in the commandos, who were generally low types with few scruples. Some of them, Portuguese, were captured by the 14th, and S.S.M. Collard was photographed holding one of them above his head with one hand. Collard had been a pupil of the great weight-lifter Sandow, who could lift a horse at his gymnasium in St James's Street, and it is curious to find such a man in the ranks

1900

of a light cavalry regiment; but he was not the only large man in the 14th, and the records of both the 14th and 20th Hussars show that even in Napoleon's day they had many such men, so that the popular conception of a light cavalryman as being necessarily light in weight cannot be altogether accurate. They could not, however, have reached the weight standards of some of the heavy regiments particularly the Household Cavalry who had to be sent home at this stage of the Boer War because there were no horses left in South Africa big enough to mount them.

Roberts was still firmly of the opinion that the Boers could not hold out much longer, and he had apparently converted his Generals to this view. It was expressed by French on the 21st October, when he made a complimentary address to the 14th at Bethel. After congratulating the regiment for its 'splendid and gallant behaviour' at Geluk on the 13th October, and at Diamond Hill and elsewhere, he concluded: 'Throughout this long and trying campaign you have borne, without a murmur, short rations and exposure, hard work and harassing outpost duty; but the war is nearly over, and can last but a few weeks longer – perhaps for you only a few days, as we are going to Pretoria.'

In fact, the Boer resistance was steadily increasing all over the Free State and the Transvaal, while raids were still being carried out into Cape Colony and Natal. The commandos had mostly split up into small bands of guerrillas, which were most difficult to catch and were yet capable of causing serious damage and disturbance. Nevertheless, the Canadian contingent and many of the volunteer and yeomanry regiments were sent home, in the belief that there was no further use for their services. Roberts and Buller also left the field although the Boer raiders were so active along the railway that special precautions had to be taken for the protection of Roberts' train – for it would have been embarrassing, to say the least, had the Boers caught him. The 14th had to take out 'three half-squadrons' to picquet the line between Heidelberg and Roodekop, until the train was safely past and similar security had to be provided all along the line as far as Cape Colony.

The 14th, who had arrived at Pretoria on the 3rd November and gone under canvas for the first time in six months, were entirely re-equipped and had their carbines replaced by rifles which, they noted with satisfaction, were sighted up to 2,800 yards, as opposed to the mere 1,200 yards of the carbines. Such excessive ranges were, of course, only effective for volley-firing, which had not hitherto formed part of the cavalry training. The British infantry were adept at it and at Omdurman, for example, when they opened fire by company volleys at 1,800 yards, knocked over 30,000 dervishes out of a total of 50,000. It was an art in which it was not so easy to become proficient as might be supposed, but the 14th put the Boers to flight on several occasions later on, with volleys by half-squadrons at ranges up to 1,000 yards. Like the dervishes, the Boers had no reply to it, for it could only be used by disciplined regular troops. The Boers, however, often opened fire at very long ranges, and although they seldom caused any damage by doing so, it had always irritated the cavalry that their carbines were ineffective on such occasions.

While at Pretoria the 14th also received 300 remounts, which enabled the 212 men without horses to be mounted and brought the effective strength of the regiment up to over 400 all-ranks. The 4th Cavalry Brigade was re-formed under the command of Lieut.-Colonel G. H. C. Hamilton of the 14th, with the temporary rank of Brigadier-General. As the 8th Hussars were sent elsewhere, it consisted of two regiments only, the 7th Dragoon Guards and 14th Hussars, with 'O' Battery, R.H.A. On the 22nd November it marched to Heidelberg with orders to clear the area of Boers – a tall order to say the least, for it was overrun by gangs from Hans Botha's, Delarey's and De Wet's commandos, carrying out their new 'hit and run' tactics. Skirmishes with them took place almost daily at long range, while the country was cleared of livestock. Large herds of cattle, sheep and horses were rounded up and driven into corrals at Heidelberg, while many farms were burnt. As the Boer families were often still living in the farms ordered to be burnt, they had to be evacuated and brought away, eventually to be incarcerated in concentration camps. On the 3rd December, when the 14th rode out on a stock-raiding expedition with the 7th Dragoon Guards, they reported their total 'bag' as 3 wagon-loads of women and children with household effects, 3 wagon-loads of forage, and 500 head of cattle.

This business of cattle-rustling and kidnapping of women and children was strange employment for British soldiers, but not as distasteful as it may sound, for all he knew it to be unavoidable and, as the Boer women were as phlegmatic as their men, there were seldom any distressing scenes, and life in the field was not too bad during this period. The soldiers and their horses were well fed for a change, and there was little hardship. But there was still danger, and soldiers were still getting killed. It therefore greatly annoyed the troops to find that the British public, after giving a resounding welcome to Roberts and the returning volunteers, had thereafter lost all interest in the war and refused to take the necessary mopping-up operations seriously. It was certainly dis-

1900

heartening for troops in the field to read in the newspapers that the public at home in whose service they were risking their lives was 'tired of the war'.

Colonel E. D. Browne-Synge-Hutchinson, V.C., C.B. He was awarded the Victoria Cross for conspicuous bravery at the Battle of Geluk, 13 October 1900, during the South African War, and was thrice mentioned in dispatches. Commanded the 14th from 1907 to 1911.

1901 Dealing with the guerrillas
September 1901 Drives against the Boers, the Blockhouse Line, the affair at Acton Homes
December 1901 The 20th arrive in South Africa
February 1902 The 14th as stops and the 20th as beaters
31st May 1902 Treaty of Peace
March 1903 The 14th and 20th shipmates on the *Dunera*

End of the South African War

22

Lord Kitchener's first action on taking over from Lord Roberts was to open peace negotiations with the Boers, using some of those who had submitted as intermediaries. The Boers, however, regarded this attempt at negotiation as a sign of weakness. Some of the intermediaries were shot and the Boer raids were intensified, with De Wet going so far as to invade Cape Colony and cause alarm as far south as Cape Town itself, although he was fairly speedily thrown out again. Kitchener then went ahead with his plans for the blockhouse line, and as a preliminary made an attempt on a large scale to clear the eastern Transvaal. The operation was carried out chiefly by mounted troops under the direction of French, who was ordered to move eastward on a broad front, driving back the Boers against the Portuguese frontier and thereby forcing them to stand and fight. French accordingly advanced in seven parallel columns on a front of over sixty miles, in one of the first great 'drives' which were thereafter to be the principal feature of the British operations.

Roberts and Kitchener, although commanders of very great ability, both suffered from the same defect of having but scant knowledge of the British soldier and of the British Army generally. They were both 'sepoy generals' who had spent most of their

1901

careers leading armies chiefly composed of orientals against other orientals, and this proved to be something of a drawback when leading British armies against Boers. It accounted for example, for the constant breakdowns in the supply services and for the terrible wastage in horses which could have been largely avoided had the scope and requirements of British cavalry and artillery been better understood. Although the Army Service Corps had been formed in 1870, it was still an innovation which was unknown in India, and the bad old system of relying on civilian transport with rations and forage provided by commissaries and contractors still prevailed in most parts of the British Empire. The strong *esprit de corps* which prevailed in all units of the British Army, and which in no small measure contributed to their fortitude and resolution in adversity, was barely appreciated and often ignored, so that units were often split up and divided between different formations for no sufficient reason.

This fate descended on the 14th at the end of 1901, and the regiment never again fought as a single unit until nearly the end of the war. The former cavalry brigades had been disintegrating for some time, and giving place to various mobile columns – Hamilton's Force, Pulteney's Column, and so on – with the idea, presumably, of defeating the Boers with their own methods, by becoming more guerrilla than they were. But in the event, the irregular columns were no more successful than the conventional formations – rather less so, if anything.

The 4th Cavalry Brigade disappeared when only the Brigade Headquarters and the 14th Hussars – less one squadron – were all that were left in it, after which Regimental Headquarters and three squadrons joined Gordon's Column while the fourth squadron went to Pulteney's Column. The Brigadier, Gilbert Hamilton of the 14th, then took command of the former 1st Cavalry Brigade and Gordon's Column, the two formations then becoming Hamilton's Force. General Gordon then took over command both of Hamilton's Force and Pulteney's Column, calling it Gordon's Column. It would almost appear in fact, that the cavalry and mounted infantry disintegrated as such and were turned into guerrilla bands by the senior officers, each of whom used his seniority to grab the bands led by officers junior to him and so, like some mediaeval baron, increase the size of his own following.

It would be tedious to describe the subsequent operations in detail, for they consisted mainly of rounding up stock, burning farms, and ineffectually galloping after the Boers as they ran for it after opening fire from over a mile away – one man of the 14th had his collar-bone smashed by a bullet which had travelled 1,800 yards. Information of the whereabouts of Boer laagers was often brought in by the Kaffirs, some of whom were employed as scouts, while others worked against the Boers on their own account; but they were far from trustworthy allies and were sometimes suspected of murdering the wounded of both sides and stealing their arms and valuables. Their information was usually checked by patrols, which often ran into trouble. A patrol of twenty-five men led by Lieut. the Hon. H. Grosvenor, which was investigating Kaffir reports of a large number of Boers at Varkenskraal, suffered fourteen casualties and narrowly escaped complete extermination. This mishap, however, seems to have been largely due to attempts by the patrol to bring away the wounded and those who had been unhorsed. Grosvenor himself and Pte. Shenton were both recommended for awards for carrying wounded men away under heavy fire at close range, although it would probably have saved further casualties had the wounded been left, and a medical party sent back for them. As for those whose horses had been killed under them; there were of course, sound reasons for carrying them away if it could be done without unduly endangering the patrol; but the only danger to the men themselves was the loss of their arms and boots. The Boers were not at that time in a position to deal with prisoners, and so usually let them go after depriving them of everything they possessed which was worth taking, including their boots. Some unfortunate men were even sent back to their units without their trousers, but it is not clear whether the Boers had taken those garments because they had need of them, or had just done it for a joke. In any case, it would scarcely seem worthwhile for a man to risk his life in order to save a comrade from losing his trousers, although gallantry, however misguided, must always be respected.

The drives by parallel columns did not have the success which had been hoped for. As the columns were continually being diverted from their true line of advance by following parties of Boers, the intervals between them either became too wide, so that the Boers slipped away between them, or else the columns converged, as happened when the flank guards of Gordon's and Babington's columns exchanged shots under the impression that they had found some Boers. 'A' and 'B' Squadrons of the 14th were riding with Babington's Column at the time, and judging from their experiences this mix-up may have been partly due to the happy-go-lucky attitude of the Imperial Light Horse, a corps of volunteers distinguished for their gallantry and horsemanship but sadly lacking in the basic military skills. After Gordon's and

1901

Babington's flank guards had been disentangled by the efforts of several trumpeters, who galloped about sounding the cease-fire, the 14th sent out a patrol under Sergt. Ridgwell to investigate more horsemen who were seen coming down the hills above Naauwpoort. When the patrol left, the Imperial Light Horse were sent forward to occupy a ridge in front, and rode off in close column of sections without taking any precautions for security, which they thought to be unnecessary when Ridgwell was somewhere ahead of them. The ridge turned out to be occupied by several hundred Boers, who held their fire until the Light Horse dismounted in order to lead their horses up, when they opened a murderous fire at under 100 yards range. The Light Horse lost 23 killed and 41 wounded in this deplorable affair, for which the 14th were afterwards blamed for not making sure that there were no enemy about before letting the Light Horse advance. It was not unusual for regular soldiers to be made the scapegoats when the amateurs had mishaps such as this, but it was nevertheless extremely irritating, especially as Sergt. Ridgwell had not gone over the same ground, but had got into trouble on his own account further ahead, when he ran into great numbers of Boers and lost two men killed, while he and two others were captured. The two squadrons of the 14th went forward immediately these disasters occurred and drove off the Boers, afterwards sending officers' patrols out to keep an eye on them. 'B' Squadron was complimented by General Babington for the manner in which it attacked and captured one of the Boer positions. Evidently, therefore, he was an eye-witness of these events, so that it seems strange that he did not exercise more personal control over the Imperial Light Horse, instead of expecting the 14th to look after them. While the column was on the way back from this drive, the two squadrons became heavily engaged with large numbers of Boers near Ventersdorp, and had to retire by troops in succession. The Boers, who seemed to be trying to get round the flanks, did not dismount but galloped about firing with their rifles across their knees. In spite of a vast expenditure of ammunition, they only succeeded in wounding a few of the 14th horses and hitting the shoeing smith in the leg.

In general, the operations failed in that it proved impossible to force the Boers to stand and fight in any worthwhile numbers. Nevertheless, after two months, 745 of them had been killed, wounded, captured or had surrendered, and an enormous quantity of livestock had been rounded up. Transport, arms and supplies had been captured and many farms burnt. One of the latter belonged to General Smuts, near Kliffontein. Mrs Smuts was at home at the time, and had to be forcibly evicted, after which Cpl. Gregory of the 14th attempted to soothe her ruffled feelings with a cup of tea, upon which she remarked, 'Mr Gregory, you are the only gentleman in the whole British Army'. Great numbers of other Boer families were likewise evicted and brought into the concentration camps, but it was all done in as friendly a manner as possible, and although the Boers professed to be horrified at such inhumanity and promised the direst retributions they were unable to work up any hatred against the British soldiers. Sergt. Taylor and another man of the 14th, who were captured on patrol reported that the Boers told them, 'Now we are going to shoot you because of our women and children you are starving at Potchefstroom (concentration camp),' but actually they merely took their boots off and told them to get out.

As French's columns had been unable to corner Louis Botha, Kitchener arranged to meet him in Middelburg and the two endeavoured to come to terms with a view to ending the war. They would probably have succeeded had Kitchener not been hampered by the British Government, which insisted on 'unconditional surrender', while Louis Botha was equally hampered by Paul Kruger, who was still nominally the Boer President, although he was at the time in France trying to obtain armed support for his cause. The talks therefore came to nothing, and the two parted as personal friends who had been forced into combat from circumstances beyond their control. Kitchener then patiently continued with the construction of his blockhouse lines, and in improving the conditions in the concentration camps, which now housed over 100,000 Boers, mostly women and children, who had been dying at the rate of a hundred a month and causing an international scandal thereby.

The blockhouse lines swallowed up so many of Kitchener's troops that he had to ask for reinforcements, pending the arrival of which the areas covered by the cavalry and mounted infantry operations became wider and wider so that individual units had to be further split up and dispersed. The 14th were together for a week or two in Newcastle at the end of April, when they were supposed to have a rest, but they were soon riding out again, patrolling along the Buffalo River. Lieut. Lace with 15 men caught a party of about fifty Boers at a moment when they were all drunk after looting a store, but although his patrol shot down about fifteen of them the others were not too drunk to be unable to ride, and Lace was unable, with his small party, to round them up. This was the sort of life now led by the cavalry, one of high adventure and constant excitement, with little risk attached.

1901

There was a lot to be said for it, except that now that the country had been cleared of livestock and forage, and most of the farms destroyed, horses and men were again on very short commons with a horse lucky to get a couple of handfuls of grain in twenty-four hours, and his rider a couple of army biscuits. By the end of July, the regiment was split up into nine separate detachments, widely dispersed over a large area. The detachments were posted along the blockhouse line, ready to ride to the assistance of any of the adjacent blockhouses which were being attacked, or which reported Boer movement along the wire. A typically exciting adventure was experienced by Lieut. Foster of 'A' Squadron, who rode out with a patrol from Acton Homes on the Upper Tugela in September, when a report came in that the Boers were raiding a hotel and post-office kept by an Englishman, Orwin. When Foster arrived, he was fired on from the windows of Orwin's billiard-room and withdrew to the neighbouring Pig-Sty Hill. Orwin had meanwhile locked himself in his telegraph-office and, with the Boers banging on the door and shouting all manner of threats, signalled the situation to Acton Homes.

Major Brown of 'A' Squadron, who was in command at Acton Homes, had just been about to ride out and head the Boers off as they fled from Lieut. Foster, when Orwin's telegram was handed to him. Realising that the Boers were out in strength, he sent the rest of Foster's troop to Upper Tugela and galloped round to the far side with some mounted irregulars and a field-gun. With his whole troop behind him, Foster rode after the Boers, who were driving off a number of loose horses and cattle, but he was charged by a hundred of them and had to fall back. Brown's field-gun then opened fire, scattered the Boers and stampeded the captured stock which ran back to its home pasture. A running fight developed during which some Boers were killed or captured. One of the latter escaped on the horse of the soldier of the 14th who was supposed to be guarding him, but was stopped by the Squadron-Sergeant-Major, Sutherland. The Boer, who, like many of his friends, had over-indulged in the liquor found in Orwin's hotel, drew the sword carried on the troop horse and tried to cut the Sergeant-Major down. Having a rifle in his hands, and with his horse to manage, Sutherland was unable to draw his own sword and make a fight of it, but was obliged to shoot him – a tame ending to a promising encounter. The Boers were chased for several miles, but got away into the mountains. However, Brown's brisk action had saved the livestock, and the Boers got nothing out of their raid except a drink at Orwin's expense. A signal from Army H.Q. at Natal congratulated Brown.

1902

Similar kind of fighting went on for the whole of 1901, with the Boers gradually being worn down and becoming more and more dependent on captured arms, clothing and ammunition, and on raided supplies. Still, they kept going, and showed no signs of surrender, encouraged by many small successes. Kitchener then abandoned the practice of making drives in parallel columns, which the Boers avoided by slipping out between them. A better-organised system was introduced, in which sweeps were made by thousands of mounted men, unencumbered by transport, riding on a wide front and keeping touch throughout. This required a considerable increase in the mounted men available, which he achieved by various expedients, not only mounting more infantry but gunners as well, who were ordered to put their guns into grease, take up rifles and get to horse, which was a novel experience for them. Every hole and corner of the Empire was searched for cavalry regiments which might have been overlooked. As was always the case in India, the native followers of a British regiment found out about its future movements long before the Colonel had heard of them, and those belonging to the 20th Hussars in Mhow in November, 1901, were seen to be wearing the dismal expressions usual to men whose source of livelihood was about to escape them. The 20th had long since given up all hope of taking part in the Boer War, and one or two of their officers had managed to get to South Africa on their own account; Lieut. H. R. Lee being wounded while serving with the 16th Lancers, and Major N. Legge killed while commanding a mounted infantry battalion. Rumours, however, which were frankly disbelieved, were confirmed by orders on the 22nd November and the regiment spent Christmas at sea in two ships, the *Saint Andrew* and *Custodian*, being at a total strength of 20 officers, 666 rank and file, 71 chargers and 668 troop horses. After disembarking at Durban, the regiment went by train to Newcastle, and then, as soon as the horses were fit, marched, or 'trekked' as they now called it, to Perdekop by a roundabout route which took them ten days.

A blockhouse line had been constructed running from Harrismith along the central railway line to Kroonstadt, and another line to the north, between Frankfort and Heilbron. De Wet and his commando were known to be operating inside the enclosed area and, at the beginning of February, just before the 20th arrived, a 'drive' was organised against him which brought in 300 prisoners, although De Wet himself escaped through the fence in the south. Another drive was then arranged from north to south, starting on the 21st February. This time the 20th Hussars took part, advancing south from Perdekop with two squadrons for-

1902

ward in extended line, ten paces between each man, and the third squadron concentrated in support. At Harrismith, the other end of the 'drive' were the 14th Hussars, dismounted and entrenched at intervals along the wire between the blockhouses. This arrangement made it impossible for the Boers to escape through the wire as De Wet had done, so that it was a pity it had not been considered necessary before. It was thought at the time that De Wet had escaped by driving a large herd of cattle against the wire, but he himself said that he had merely cut his way through with a pair of wire-cutters.

Both regiments had quite an exciting time. The Boers made several attempts to break through the line of 'beaters' provided by the 20th, but were frustrated each time and the regiment eventually collected 400 prisoners, who had surrendered, although the 14th shared the credit for this bag by keeping the Boers in the trap. As the 20th had only just arrived on the veldt, their performance was especially creditable. It was because they were all fully-trained regular soldiers, who had been some years in India and were accustomed to heat. India also offered exceptional facilities for training units and formations, especially cavalry. The horse-management of regiments on the Indian service was in general far superior to that of the cavalry at home, and the losses in horseflesh experienced by the 20th were consequently far below the average, although it is true that they had arrived too late to take part in any of the endurance tests under Roberts.

The business of acting as stops during the drive involved the 14th in an immense amount of digging, an activity very unpopular with the British soldier. Posts of ten men each were dug in between each blockhouse, so that no part of the wire was more than two hundred yards away from either a post or a blockhouse. A considerable length of dummy trench also had to be dug, in order that the occupied trenches should not be too obvious. After all this, the first attack came from the rear, being delivered by some of De Wet's men outside the wire, who crept up in an attempt to make a gap for their comrades to escape by. The 14th were not expecting it, for they had apparently not been told that De Wet was at large and thought that he was still safely inside. The Boers were driven off without difficulty, but their appearance made it evident that a form of all-round defence was necessary, which meant considerably more digging, ending with two lines of trenches which could be occupied as expedient – for the 14th had a long frontage to hold and very few men to do it with, so that they had to keep mobile.

1902

During most of the ensuing period, shooting was heard in front as the trapped Boers tried to get through the line of beaters, but bullets arrived from the rear, where De Wet had posted a line of snipers. Not unnaturally, this kept everyone in a state of jumps, and when Captain Tottenham was riding round his posts his horse was shot in the head by one of the sentries, who had been ordered to shoot first and challenge afterwards. Tottenham was fortunately riding a troop horse at the time, and not one of his valuable chargers, so that he was able to treat the incident lightly, congratulating the sentry on his good shooting. Another sentry, not such a good shot, missed an antelope at close range in the dark. The animal took fright and blundered into a blockhouse, setting off the burglar alarm and causing the whole squadron to stand-to.

The drive, however, was very successful; 735 Boers were captured and 28,000 head of cattle, while another 65 Boers were killed trying to break out. It was evident that the Boers would not be able to hold out against this sort of treatment for very long.

The Boer leaders were, in fact, reluctantly arriving at the conclusion that it was senseless to go on with the war. Although guerrilla operations were still possible, the morale of the burghers had completely collapsed, and they no longer made any pretence of being prepared to risk their skins nor, to their credit, did they make any serious attempts to kill British soldiers except in self-defence. De Wet and other commando leaders were known to be riding round the laagers in order to find out the general reaction of the Boers towards surrender, often doing so under flags of truce to enable them to pass freely through the British lines on this mission.

The 'drives' were meanwhile continued, and both the 14th and 20th were constantly out, riding on a front of about a mile and sometimes covering distances of sixty miles a day. Skirmishes were fairly frequent, occasionally resulting in a few casualties, but the Boers usually galloped off without ado. Direction was often difficult to keep, especially at night, when moving on such wide fronts, so that many men often went missing. They invariably turned up again, however, for the Boers no longer tried to kill or capture lost soldiers. Cpl. Morrison of the 14th, who was captured after his horse had foundered while he was trying to find his way back to the regiment, was set free at once, after being told by the Boers that the war was over and they wanted no more prisoners. An incident occurred at the end of one of the last 'drives' which showed that the sword, though seldom drawn in this war, was still a useful weapon on occasion. The Boers had

1902

been driven against the blockhouse line near Geelplatz and, when they found themselves trapped, turned and galloped through the volunteer regiment on the left of the 14th. As this regiment had no swords it had to make an attempt to meet the Boers with fixed bayonets, but this proved to be hopeless on horseback and so they all escaped.

A peace conference between British and Boer delegates had assembled at Vereeniging on the 15th May and lasted a fortnight, during which operations continued more or less as usual, for Kitchener would not agree to an armistice. Peace was decided upon on the 31st May, and the Treaty signed at Pretoria at 10.30 p.m. on that date, when orders for the cease fire were sent by telegraph to all formations in the field. The 14th received the news while on outpost duty at Lindley, while the 20th were in camp at Heilbron having just returned there after taking part in a lengthy 'drive'. Shortly afterwards a detachment of the 14th was sent home to attend the coronation of King Edward VII, but the 20th were not represented at this ceremony, presumably because the regiment was based in India at the time.

The peace negotiations, being handled by British officers on Kitchener's staff, who had personally fought in the war and respected their opponents in the manner usual with soldiers, were conducted in the same sportsmanlike spirit which had characterised the whole war. There was a great deal of hand-shaking and exchange of compliments, which went far in preventing the seeds of bitterness and resentment from growing and festering in the hearts of the vanquished. Kitchener himself went out of his way to be friendly with his recent opponents, whom he met at Vereeniging and congratulated on the decision which they had made, which he declared to be in the best interests of their country. He then won their hearts by saying that if he himself had been a Boer he would have been proud to have fought so well in the field. The Boer delegates greeted this chivalrous speech with cheers, and their chairman replied by saying how pleased they all were to meet as a friend one whose worth as a soldier they had tested in battle.

In this agreeable atmosphere ended the last gentlemen's war. A great number of men had died in it and there had been vast destruction, with families left bereaved and homeless. But suffering was soon alleviated with the return of peace and prosperity, and although the dead could not be brought to life the fact that neither the Boer nor Briton had given his life to no purpose was a consoling thought. Among the British soldiers who gave their lives were 5 officers and 84 rank and file of the 14th King's

1903

Hussars, and 8 rank and file of the 20th Hussars.

After the conclusion of peace, the 14th went into camp near Kroonstadt and the 20th at Pretoria. Neither regiment was given any indication as to when it was likely to leave South Africa, and both settled down to a fairly leisurely routine during which all ranks went home in batches on four months' leave. The 14th gave a dance on the 22nd November, the anniversary of Ramnuggur, which was the only event of interest until March, 1903, when orders were received for the horses to be sold preparatory to the regiment's return to England. The Boers arrived in camp in large numbers to bid for the horses and exchange wartime reminiscences with the soldiers. Although not a nation of horse-lovers like the British, they at least understood and treated them reasonably, so that handing them over was not the painful affair experienced after campaigns in other countries, when the inflexible determination of the British Treasury to get hold of every penny it could lay hands on, often led to home-bred troop horses accustomed to friendly treatment, being sold into conditions of savage ill-treatment. Even so, the horses of the 14th accompanied their new masters with some reluctance, and one of them soon returned, dragging a cart behind him, and making straight for his old place in the lines.

The 14th sailed from Cape Town on the 28th March, 1903, in the *Dunera*, which then went on to Durban to pick up the 20th. The two regiments, with no presentment of their future close association, separated again at Suez where the 20th disembarked. They were not, however, sent back to India to resume their interrupted tour, but went into Abbassia Barracks, near Cairo. The 14th, on return home, went back to Aldershot, where their march from the station to the West Cavalry Barracks attracted much attention, not because they were soldiers returning from active service, but because a South African baboon was marching behind the band. Regiments returning from overseas not infrequently brought back a regimental pet, but Kruger the baboon was certainly an unusual one, who obviously enjoyed his position as mascot to the 14th.

315

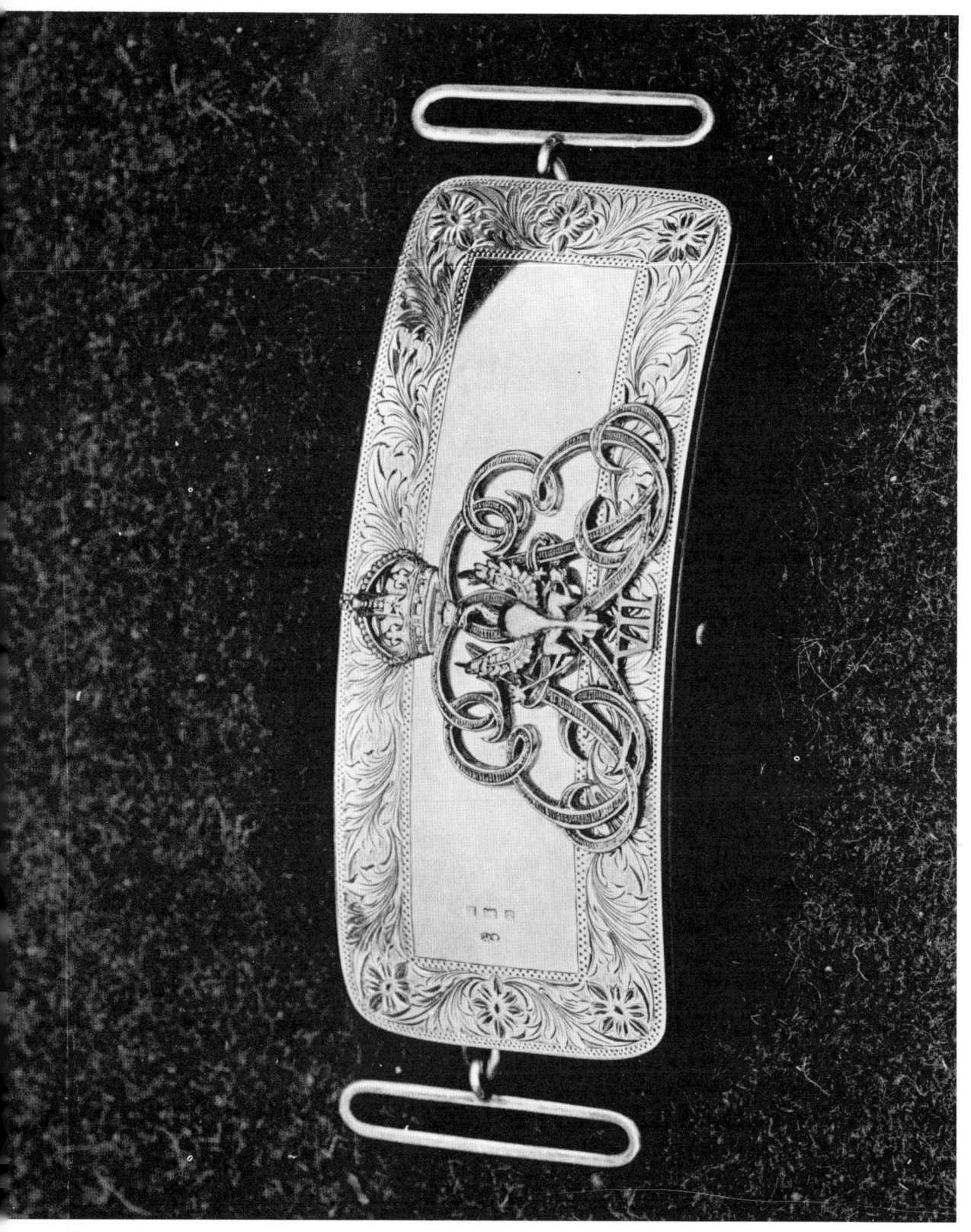

14th King's Hussars officer's silver cross-belt pouch (1902) with King's Crown, Royal Cypher (King Edward VII) and Prussian Eagle badge.

1903

1908 Army re-organisation
1904 20th return from Egypt
1906 14th sail for India
1911 20th join the 5th Cavalry Brigade
4th August 1914 Declaration of war on Germany
17th August 1914 The 20th cross to France
22nd August 1914 The 20th fire their first shots

Outbreak of the First World War

23

THE Boer War proved an invaluable experience for the British Army, revealing many weaknesses in its organisation and administration which there was still time to put right before it had to face the greatest test in its history. At the beginning of the war it had not changed much since the Crimea, being merely a collection of regiments without any brigade or divisional organisation, having no General Staff and only rudimentary administrative services. For keeping the peace throughout the British Empire it was adequate, but it could take the field in any major war only at such a disadvantage as to make its subsequent achievements seem almost miraculous.

In the Boer War, unlike the Crimean War, great numbers of civilians had enlisted 'for the duration', and their experiences had awakened public interest at a time filled with menace when Great Britain, outside her Empire, had no friend or ally in the world. Recognising the dangers of isolation, a succession of British governments searched for allies, finding the first in Japan and the second in a formerly hostile France, won over by the charm of King Edward VII. These alliances, however, were soon proved to be as dangerous as isolationism. In 1904 the Russo-Japanese War broke out, in which French sympathies lay with Russia, while Great Britain sided with Japan, not only on account of her

317

1907

new alliance but because the Russian Fleet mistook a collection of British fishing vessels for Japanese destroyers and opened fire on them. Empire-building activities in North Africa by France then brought her into conflict with Germany, which also had ambitions in Morocco. The Kaiser landed from his yacht at Tangier and made one of his bombastic speeches to the assembled German colony, following it up by official governmental threats against France. As France had agreed to allow Great Britain a free hand in Egypt in return for British support in Morocco, the British Government felt obliged to come to her aid with diplomatic overtures which, while averting the current crisis, had the effect of aligning Great Britain on the side of France against Germany. This encouraged France to wheedle Great Britain into allowing conferences to be held between the naval and military experts of both countries, which further worsened relations between Great Britain and Germany.

In 1907, Great Britain found a new friend in Russia, and an Anglo-Russian Convention at last removed the long-standing Russian threat to India. Germany retaliated by making overtures to Turkey whose Sultan, 'Abdul the Damned', had alienated every other civilised nation by his wholesale massacres of Christians. Abdul was shortly afterwards deposed by the 'Young Turk' revolution, but the new rulers of Turkey proved to be even more unpleasant characters than Abdul. Only Germany would associate with them, but the revolution gave Austria-Hungary an excuse for annexing the former Serbian provinces of Bosnia-Herzegovina. Russia protested and was backed by Great Britain which was not, however, prepared to go to war over the question. When, therefore, Germany came to the support of Austria-Hungary in repayment of her support of Germany over Tangier, Russia and Great Britain backed down. The 'mailed fist' had thus triumphed at last, and the shadows darkened accordingly.

Great Britain, being an island protected by the largest navy in the world and at the head of a vast empire, was not particularly alarmed by the sinister happenings in Europe but, as the continued maintenance of peace had become problematical, to say the least, it was at last decided to do something about the Army and rectify the shortcomings disclosed by the Boer War. In 1908, the Territorial Army was formed out of the old Yeomanry and Volunteers; the Militia was redesignated the Special Reserve, with the duty of reinforcing and finding drafts for the Regular Army, and the latter was organised into one cavalry and six infantry divisions with adequate supporting arms and adminis-

1908

trative services. The credit for this achievement is usually given to Richard Haldane, the Liberal Secretary of State for War, but in fact, as he was a lawyer with no knowledge of military matters, he had to rely upon the advice of General Sir Douglas Haig, to whom posterity has shown singularly little appreciation for this and later services to his country.

The Army reorganisation occupied the greater part of the decade following the Boer War, and during this period regiments carried on much as they had always done both at home and overseas. Aldershot, the main centre of all British military training and experiment, had become a place of considerable importance and interest, and was invariably visited by foreign potentates while guests of the King. Among the first of these was the President of France who arrived in 1903 accompanied by the King. The 14th provided the escort for the royal carriage and afterwards took part in the usual review. The following year brought a visitor whose political importance may have been appreciated by the Prime Minister and Foreign Secretary but scarcely at that time by anyone else. The Archduke Franz Ferdinand was the nephew and heir of the Emperor of Austria-Hungary, with whom he had fallen out by marrying outside the royal circle. He was suspected of political intrigue under the influence, so it was believed, of his wife, and was therefore much distrusted in his own country. In this unhappy position, he was taken under the wing of the Emperor of Germany who saw in him a useful tool for increasing German influence in Austria, and who won him over by the simple expedient of being polite to his wife – which no one else was. As German machinations on the Continent were naturally being closely watched by the British Government, the Archduke was then invited to England as one of the diplomatic moves by which foreign affairs were then generally conducted, and while in England he had, of course, to be shown Aldershot. A man of distinguished appearance and great charm, he made a favourable impression on the officers presented to him, among them those of the 14th, whom he specially complimented.

In 1904, the 20th Hussars returned from Egypt and were stationed at Brighton, with a detachment at Canterbury. In the same year, the 14th moved to Shorncliffe and, on the formation of the 2nd Cavalry Brigade, were brigaded with the 7th Dragoon Guards and 20th Hussars. In 1906, the 14th sailed for India, and were stationed at Bangalore, and two years later the 20th left Shorncliffe, where they had relieved the 14th, and went to the Curragh, after sending a draft of 72 rank and file to join the 14th in India.

1908

Various changes in the arms and equipment of the cavalry were being introduced during these years, as the result of experience gained in the Boer War. The short Lee-Enfield rifle, as issued to the infantry, was carried in a leather bucket attached to the off-side of the saddle. This weapon, although an excellent one in the hands of a trained soldier, was balanced and designed for infantry, and the long sword-bayonet was really part of it. The bayonet was not at first issued to the cavalry but later on, when the cavalry were required to become expert in all infantry weapons, it was carried attached to the bandolier for use dismounted. The main cavalry weapon was still the sword, but the pattern of this was changed to a rapier, 43 inches long. When brought down to the 'in line' position during a charge, the point of this sword projected well beyond the horse's nose, so that it was almost as good a thrusting weapon as the lance. Another innovation was the picketting peg attached to a short length of rope with a leather collar at the end. It was carried on the saddle, and horses were picketed by the foreleg when in bivouac. Previously, the usual custom had been to run out a long rope and tie them to it by the headcollar on either side. The new picketing peg was a rather doubtful improvement. When the 14th were on manoeuvres near Southampton in 1904, an alarm among the 8th Hussar horses near-by caused some of them to pull up their pegs and charge the horses of the 14th, which also pulled up their pegs and stampeded. Matters were made worse by the pegs being fastened to the horses' forelegs by lengths of rope, consequently striking and tripping up other horses. The 14th had nearly a hundred horses injured in this incident and six were killed.

In addition to the reorganisation of the Army, plans were also made for its smooth and speedy mobilisation. Except for the air battalion it was entirely dependent on the horse, but arrangements for assembling the vast number of horses required on mobilisation, and for subsequent reinforcements, were seriously lacking. In 1909, the 20th Hussars in Ireland were ordered to try out a scheme whereby fifty trained troop horses at a time were let out to farmers and other civilians free of charge, on the understanding that they would be subject to periodical inspections and called in for a month's training in the ranks annually. The regiment was meanwhile issued with fifty additional remounts above establishment for training. The scheme apparently proved successful, for the number of horses let out to civilians was later increased to seventy-five.

In 1911, the 20th Hussars returned to England and were stationed at Colchester, sending a detachment of 100 all-ranks to

Colonel E. D. Browne-Synge-Hutchinson, V.C., C.B. Awarded the Victoria Cross during the South African War. Commanded the 14th King's Hussars 1907–1911. He is wearing the uniform of the Order of St John of Jerusalem.

1913

the coronation ceremonies of King George V. The regiment now belonged to the 5th Cavalry Brigade, commanded by Brigadier-General Sir Philip Chetwode, with the Greys and 12th Lancers. It continued to send annual drafts of trained men to the 14th Hussars in India, cavalry regiments overseas being linked to those at home for this purpose. The practice of 'boarding out' horses to civilians in order to build up a reserve also continued, but steps had now to be taken to prevent these horses from being docked while boarded-out. This horrid practice was not tolerated in Ireland, but it was still carried out in England, where the carriage horses in smart circles were also fitted with bearing reins which forced them to keep their necks arched and move with a prancing motion, in order to give an impressive appearance to the turn-out.

In 1911, the friction which had been steadily increasing between France and Germany over Morocco came to a head when the German gunboat *Panther* arrived at Agadir, with orders to look after the interests of German nationals. Germany then demanded the cession of the greater part of French possessions in the Congo, as the price of recalling the *Panther*. The episode was a bluff, apparently designed to test the strength of the *entente* between France and Great Britain and it did in fact achieve that result, for Great Britain re-acted sharply. Her attitude was emphasised by Lloyd George in a speech at the Mansion House in July: 'If a situation were to be forced on us in which peace could only be preserved by the surrender of the great and beneficent position Britain has won by centuries of heroism and achievements, by allowing Britain to be treated, where her interests were vitally affected, as if she were of no account in the Cabinet of Nations, then I say emphatically that peace at that price would be a humiliation intolerable for a great country like ours to endure.' This forthright speaking concluded the incident after a period of tension, for Germany was not yet ready to back her policies with armed force, but only a respite had been achieved and Europe began feverishly preparing for the worst.

A few months later Italy declared war on Turkey with the idea of gaining possession of the province of Tripoli, but made peace again on the outbreak of the Balkan wars of 1912, when Turkey was driven back within the defences of Constantinople. Her defeat was a severe blow to the Central Powers, for Turkey was the protegé of Germany, while Austria was discomfited by the success of Serbia, to whom her southern Slav subjects had long been looking for liberation from Austrian oppression. In 1913, however, the Balkan States fell out among themselves, and

1914

Bulgaria was beaten by Serbia and Greece. Taking advantage of the turmoil, Turkey advanced again and reoccupied Adrianople. This pleased Germany, but the second victory of Serbia displeased Austria, by giving renewed hope to the Slavs and disturbing the situation along her southern frontiers. Bulgaria, under King 'Foxy' Ferdinand, was also now more than ready to join any alliance which would enable her to get her own back on the Serbs and Greeks.

On the 28th June, 1914, the Archduke Franz Ferdinand, Inspector of the Austrian Army, visited Sarajevo, capital of the annexed province of Bosnia, in connection with some army manoeuvres. While driving through the streets he and his wife were assassinated by a Bosnian Serb. The circumstances were so peculiar as to suggest that the unpopular Archduke had been deliberately sacrificed, or 'put on the spot' by his government in order to provide an excuse for the liquidation of Serbia where the assassination plot was said to have been conceived. After conferring with Germany and being assured of her support, Austria delivered an ultimatum to Serbia in terms which were impossible for a free country to accept, and war was declared on the 25th July.

As the Central Powers had anticipated, Serbia then appealed to Russia for aid and the Tzar reluctantly ordered general mobilisation. This was immediately followed by Austrian mobilisation and a German ultimatum to Russia to cease mobilising or take the consequences. On the 1st August, Germany and Russia were at war.

The desperate efforts made during this period by Sir Edward Grey, the Foreign Secretary, to preserve peace, caused the Germans to believe that Great Britain would not fight, and so had the reverse effect to that intended. On the 31st July, Germany delivered an ultimatum to France to surrender her frontier fortresses, and another to Belgium on the 2nd August demanding a free passage for German troops in violation of the Belgian neutrality Treaty of 1832, signed by Prussia, Great Britain, France, Austria and Russia. For Great Britain, this represented the last straw and an ultimatum was presented to Germany which came into force at midnight on the 4th/5th August, after which the two nations were at war. Standing at a window of the Foreign Office as dusk was falling, Sir Edward Grey sadly observed, 'The lights are going out all over Europe; we shall not see them lit again in our lifetime.'

In England, the people enjoyed the hottest Bank Holiday in years on the 3rd August, with no comprehension of the magnitude

1914

of the sickening disaster about to fall upon them. Everything in fact, was going on as usual, with the Territorials on their way to camp. On the Sunday the 20th Hussars had marched to church in full-dress as usual, presenting a fine sight in their frogged hussar jackets, with crimson plumes and busby-bags, having no idea that it was the last time the regiment would ever appear so dressed. The regimental quarter-guard was still wearing it when a telegraph boy on a red bicycle arrived at the barrack gate and handed a telegram into the guard-room at 5.30 in the afternoon of the 4th August. It was from the 5th Cavalry Brigade at York, and contained a single word, 'Mobilise!'

The procrastinations of Sir Edward Grey, though understandable, had got the mobilisation of the British Army off to a bad start by causing the first day to be that immediately following the August Bank Holiday. Nevertheless, thanks to the admirable arrangements worked out by Haldane – or Sir Douglas Haig, rather – it was carried out with astonishing smoothness and efficiency. Within five days the Cavalry Division and four infantry divisions were ready to embark, and the fantastic task of collecting 120,000 horses and having them clipped and re-shod, given veterinary inspections, weeding them out and despatching them all over the kingdom, was accomplished in twelve days. The British Expeditionary Force, complete in every detail and, though very small by continental standards, what may, without exaggeration, be described as the finest army for its size that the world has ever seen, crossed the Channel between the 12th and 17th August. The 20th Hussars, at a strength of 24 officers and 519 rank and file, commanded by Lieut.-Colonel G. T. G. Edwards, crossed on the 17th August with the rest of the 5th Cavalry Brigade, commanded by Brigadier-General Sir Philip Chetwode, Bt. It was independent, being directly under General Headquarters, and did not belong to the Cavalry Division which was composed of the first four cavalry brigades and was commanded by Major-General Allenby.

The concentration area of the B.E.F. was on the left bank of the Sambre, between Maubeuge and Le Cateau, with the five cavalry brigades to the east of Maubeuge ready to link up with the French Fifth Army. The concentration was complete by the 20th August – just over a fortnight after mobilisation, a remarkable achievement. While his army was concentrating, the Commander-in-Chief, General Sir John French, visited the French General Headquarters and those of General Lanrezac, commander of the French Fifth Army. A plan was concerted whereby the B.E.F. would march north-east, on the left of the

1914

Fifth Army, through Soignies towards Nivelles. It was anticipated that the German right flank would be in the area of Mons, in which case the B.E.F. would wheel eastwards and envelop it.

Sir John French was not impressed, either by the plan or by the French Generals, Joffre, the Commander-in-Chief, and Lanrezac, but his orders were to co-operate with them, while retaining an independent position and full responsibility for the safety of the B.E.F. He set his army in motion accordingly, but with much inward misgiving and definitely prepared for the worst.

Unlike those of their allies and enemy, the General officers in the B.E.F. all had actual war experience, as had most of the field officers and a good proportion of the rank and file. Among the General officers this experience had, for some years before the war, led them into a somewhat pessimistic estimate of the chances of the French Army getting the better of the German on the battlefield, so that Sir John French was by no means alone in viewing the outcome of the conflict with some apprehension. However, the experience of the commanders, combined with the fact that the B.E.F. was undoubtedly the best trained and equipped army which Great Britain had ever put into the field, enabled it to exert an influence on events out of all proportion to its numbers. Its weaknesses were that the commanders had not had sufficient practice in the handling of large modern formations owing to the lack of suitable training areas in the United Kingdom, and that there were insufficient trained staff-officers, for the General Staff had only been formed in 1904, and potential staff-officers were still slow in coming forward ten years later. Largely for this reason, the organisation of the B.E.F. into Army Corps was left until the last possible moment, when the six infantry divisions were formed into three Army Corps of which the first two, with staffs hastily assembled, and commanded respectively by Sir Douglas Haig and Sir Horace Smith-Dorrien, were now in France, supported by the Cavalry Division, the 5th Cavalry Brigade, and four squadrons of the Royal Flying Corps, with a total of 48 aircraft.

On the evening of the 20th August, orders were issued by G.H.Q. for the advance of the B.E.F. in accordance with General Joffre's plan for the envelopment of the enemy's right flank. The advance was to be covered by the 5th Cavalry Brigade, which was ordered to march on Binche and there remain, in advance of the British right, while the Cavalry Division, after marching on the left of the 5th Cavalry Brigade on the 21st August, was then to move across the front to Lens. As a preliminary to the envelopment movement, the 1st Corps marched north-easterly while the 2nd Corps, after passing Mons on the 23rd August, was to wheel easterly so that the whole army would be inclined ready to fall on the enemy flank. Its own left flank was to be watched by the Cavalry Division and a French Cavalry Corps under General Sordet.

Little was known at this stage of the strength, dispositions and plans of the German armies, and bad visibility made it impossible for the Royal Flying Corps to discover anything. It was, therefore, left to the cavalry to get information by the old-fashioned method of riding forward on a wide front and looking for Germans.

On the night of the 21st August the 20th Hussars bivouacked near Binche, a village at the junction of several roads leading northerly. Orders for the following day were given verbally during the night, and consisted chiefly of instructions for officers' patrols to ride out at 4 a.m. The 20th provided two such patrols, led by Lieutenants Thomson and Goodhart, who rode towards Godarville and Seneffe respectively. In the British cavalry, patrols consisted of about a dozen men, who rode in file along each side of the road preceded by advanced and rear points provided by two trained scouts. Each patrol in this case was accompanied by a French N.C.O., of whom twelve had joined the regiment as interpreters and had been allotted one to each troop.

Although, during the march to Binche, the French guns could be heard in action far away to the north-east, nothing could have looked more peaceful than the fair countryside through which Thomson and Goodhart led their patrols. Although, therefore, everyone felt a certain nervous tension or excitement, it was not easy to realise that this was in fact the real thing and not a training manoeuvre on Laffan's Plain. It had not occurred to Goodhart for example, to load his revolver in case he might have to shoot someone.

Thomson got to within 25 miles of Brussels before discovering that he was surrounded by vast masses of Germans of all arms. He had to ride for his life, leaving behind one of his men, O'Shaughnessy, whose horse was shot as the patrol was moving at the gallop. O'Shaughnessy rejoined the regiment some days later in civilian clothes, having got through the German lines by pretending to be deaf and dumb – not an easy subterfuge for an Irishman, and showing a high degree of courage and initiative.

Goodhart had ridden about ten miles north of Binche, when he got his first sight of the enemy patrolling far away on his flanks.

1914

Then, from the top of a hill overlooking Seneffe, he saw a troop of cavalry dismounted and a mounted patrol thirty strong starting up the hill. He dismounted his patrol and lined a ditch, ordering his men not to fire until he gave the word. One of them was unfortunately too excited to obey and opened fire on the enemy points at 300 yards, thus alerting the whole squadron and making it advisable for Goodhart and his patrol to get away fast. He noted later that these shots were fired well before 8 a.m., which was the hour at which a patrol of the 4th Dragoon Guards opened fire near Soignies with what was claimed to have been the first shots fired by the British Army in the war.

Having an enemy squadron on his tail and knowing others to be on his flanks, Goodhart was not, of course, interested at the time in any speculation as to who fired the first shot. Pulling up to question a peasant on a bicycle, he learned that an 'English milord', the Earl of Leven, was retiring along a parallel road with a troop of the Greys, after spending the night at his farm. Shortly afterwards he sighted a troop, mounted on 'dirty-coloured' horses, which he took to be Lord Leven and his men – for the Greys had camouflaged their horses with Condy's Fluid. Riding over to speak to them with every confidence, he discovered rather late that they were Uhlans and so had to pull his horse round and rejoin his patrol at a gallop. While doing so, he looked over his shoulder and 'saw an ugly Hun with a lance not more than two horses' lengths behind me.' He got out his revolver and tried a shot only to find, as already mentioned, that it was unloaded, but his horse – a polo-pony in happier days – easily outdistanced the Hun and took him safely back to his patrol. In the skirmish which followed, three 'Huns' were unhorsed and their horses captured and brought in, representing the first booty captured from the enemy, whoever may have fired the first shot.

The firing in front was heard in Binche, where Lieut. Hall's troop was holding the railway bridge. Lieut. Sparrow's troop was sent out to support the two patrols and cover their withdrawal, joining a troop of French cavalry just north of Binche. On the appearance of some German cavalry, Sparrow dismounted his troop and opened fire in order to cover a charge by the Frenchmen. The Germans galloped off, pursued by the French, who came back shortly afterwards, after sighting the enemy main body. After Thomson's and Goodhart's patrols had come in, Sparrow rejoined the regiment, which was withdrawn that night to Faroeulx, five miles to the south-west.

23rd August 1914 Mons
24th August–5th September 1914 Retreat from Mons
8th September 1914 Crossing of the Petit Morin and
9th September 1914 Marne
10th and 12th September 1914 Cavalry Pursuit
to the Aisne
1st October 1914 B.E.F. moved to Flanders
11th October to 22nd November 1914 The First Battle
of Ypres

1914

Mons, the Marne, and first Ypres

24

THE information brought in by the British cavalry patrols during the morning of the 22nd August indicated that dense masses of Germans were moving in the direction of Mons. This was confirmed by air reconnaissance during the afternoon, by which time the 5th Cavalry Brigade had learned that the French Fifth Army on its right was being driven back across the Sambre. During the day elements of the German 13th Division arrived before Binche, but were stopped by the Greys who were holding the bridges over the Sambre. The 20th were on the right of the Greys at this time, but were not attacked. The Third Division of the French Cavalry Corps made an unexpected appearance at Binche owing to the Corps being heavily attacked during its march west, which had obliged General Sordet to retire across the Sambre Canal. The French cavalry had not changed much in appearance since Napoleon's time, and its armoured Cuirassiers, and Dragoons with horsehair tails hanging down the backs of their cumbrous helmets, seemed a little out-of-place on the battlefield of 1914, with its machine-guns and magazine rifles. The only firearm it carried was the *mousqueton*, a light carbine of short range and quite useless against modern infantry. The French infantry, sweating in its ill-fitting *capotes* under mountains of kit and equipment, was equally unimpressive

1914

but, by British standards, the German cavalry and infantry were not much better.

The superiority of the British over the German cavalry was proved in the early encounters which took place all along the front during the 22nd August, but four Cavalry Brigades could not do much against 325,000 men massed along an 18-mile front. As it became clear that these sort of numbers of Germans were marching against him, Sir John French hastened the advance of the 72,000 men of his four Infantry Divisions to enable the Cavalry Division to be drawn off on to the left flank. The 5th Cavalry Brigade was to remain on the right flank keeping touch with the left of the French 18th Corps on the Sambre. The British 2nd Corps, of the 3rd and 5th Infantry Divisions, had arrived along the Mons Canal in the evening of the 22nd, but the 1st Corps, of the 1st and 2nd Infantry Divisions, was still some distance in rear. Until it came up, there was a huge gap in the allied line, between the right of the 2nd Corps at Mons, and the French left on the Sambre which, once the Cavalry Division had moved across to Lens, was watched only by the 5th Cavalry Brigade.

This situation being extremely grave, the 1st Corps had to continue its advance by forced march, all through the night without a halt, although large numbers of the infantry were reservists fresh from sedentary work in offices and factories. However, the whole Corps was more or less in position by the evening of the 23rd. The Cavalry Division moved off to the left and the British Expeditionary Force was aligned along the canal from Conde to Mons, with the front of the 1st Corps inclining south-easterly from Mons to the Sambre. This position, it will be remembered, had been designed by General Joffre to enable it to swing round against the flank of the enemy advancing to the Sambre, but it was now evident that the B.E.F. was itself in great danger of being enveloped by the vast masses of the German First Army, which considerably outflanked it; and on the left flank, between Conde and the sea, there were only some French Territorials of very doubtful quality.

A minute drop in the Continental bucket filled to the brim with French and German soldiers about to fall upon one another with the utmost savagery, the British Expeditionary Force might well have been swallowed up and have disappeared in the holocaust with scarcely a trace remaining. This in fact, had been the fate envisaged for 'the contemptible little army' by the Kaiser. The German field commanders, however, were already beginning to take it more seriously, and were becoming worried about its intentions and precise whereabouts. Furthermore, both Germans and French had been surprised and impressed by the appearance, behaviour and tactical efficiency of the British cavalry and other advanced troops. The Francophile General Spears, then a liaison officer with the French Fifth Army, has described the glow of pride felt as he silently compared the troops of the British 1st Corps with the French, and the astonished respect with which the French officer he was escorting observed them, 'really splendid, perfectly turned out, shining leather, flashing metal, beautiful horses, and the men absolutely unconcerned, disdaining to show the least surprise at or even interest in their strange surroundings.'

While the 1st Corps was moving into position, the grave news reached Sir John French that the French Fifth Army on his right was being driven back from the Sambre. A request then came from General Lanrezac, late at night on the 22nd August, that the British should attack the flank of the Germans who were driving him back. As French knew that the German First Army was coming straight for him, he was unable to agree to making any attack, but he did agree to stand fast at Mons for twenty-four hours in order to protect the French flank. This, in view of the terrible disparity in numbers between the B.E.F. and the German First Army, was not an easy undertaking to give.

The historic Battle of Mons began in the morning of the 23rd August, when the German First Army arrived before the positions of the British 2nd Corps along the Mons-Condé Canal. The positions of the British 1st Corps were roughly from Mons southeasterly to Peissant. On the right, the French Fifth Army was in retreat before the German Second Army, whose right wing was bearing down upon the British 1st Corps. The 5th Cavalry Brigade was still south of Binche, but the Cavalry Division had moved west. Most of the French Cavalry Corps, however, was still in the east, having been halted before Beaumont in the rear of the French left flank. When the opening shots were fired, the 2nd Infantry Division was still moving forward into position south-east of Mons. Until it arrived there was a large gap in the British line, which was being temporarily watched by the 5th Cavalry Brigade.

During the day, the whole weight of the German attack fell upon the 2nd Corps, which maintained its positions with ease against fantastic odds. There was little fighting along the front of the 1st Corps where the 20th Hussars, in Brigade reserve, were able to off-saddle during the morning. In the afternoon, however, the cavalry of the 1st Division, a squadron of the 15th Hussars, sent news of enemy movements on the right flank, and 'B'

1914

Squadron of the 20th was ordered to Peissant on the Sambre. On arrival, a patrol under Lieut. Soames was sent out and ran into large numbers of Germans of all arms. The patrol had to fight its way back and Soames – a very popular officer – was killed. One man was wounded, with two others unhorsed and missing.

By the evening of the 23rd, Sir John French, though well-satisfied with the result of the day's fighting, was becoming very anxious about the position on his right flank, where the information gained by the cavalry patrols and air reconnaissance indicated that the French were being heavily attacked, and that large enemy columns were continuing to move up, so that the attack was likely to continue. Towards midnight, it became apparent that the French were still retiring, leaving the B.E.F. exposed in advance of the line so that an immediate retreat was necessary. Naturally, this took time to arrange, especially as the methods of communication were still primitive. Sir Douglas Haig, the 1st Corps Commander, was on the telephone, but Sir Horace Smith-Dorrien, the 2nd Corps Commander, was not. It was, therefore, not until the early morning of the 25th August that the retreat from Mons actually began. The enemy, fortunately, had been so badly mauled during the 23rd August that he held back during the 24th, which passed fairly peacefully and the 1st Corps was able to commence its retirement on the following morning without serious opposition.

The troops of both the Divisions in the 1st Corps were exhausted after being eighteen hours under arms following long marches into position. To cover their retirement a special rearguard was formed, consisting of the 5th Cavalry Brigade, 'J' Battery R.H.A., the Guards' Brigade, and the 36th and 41st Brigades R.F.A. It concentrated at Bonnet with orders to make a demonstration at daybreak in order to delay the enemy's leading troops. The 20th Hussars saddled up at 4 a.m. and took up a dismounted position along the Mons-Maubeuge Road to cover the retirement of the 2nd Division whose rearguard passed through shortly after the arrival of the regiment. Patrols were sent out which met German cavalry patrols, but the Germans were riding with extreme caution, and would not come to close quarters. The regiment was under long-range shrapnel-fire for the whole morning, but saw no enemy until it was about to withdraw, when some infantry came out of a wood in close order and were halted by the long-range fire of 'B' Squadron. The regiment then fell back to a position which had been reconnoitred four miles in rear, from which it withdrew in the evening and retired to Hargnies, overtaking the infantry rearguard and riding slowly, with many hold-ups, along roads jammed with marching troops and vehicles of every description. There was a long column of French transport: 'I am not wishing in any way to cast aspersions on our gallant Allies,' wrote Captain Darling, the Signals Officer of the 20th, 'when I say that the appearance of this column was rather a shock to us.' To the British troops, it gave the impression of belonging to an army whose morale had given way after a heavy defeat, for they had not seen enough of the French Army at that time to know that the normal appearance of its units was far from impressive. In contrast to a British transport column, with its soundly constructed wagons drawn by well-matched teams of light draught horses or mules, with their harness in good condition and their drivers well turned-out, a French column usually consisted of requisitioned farm or tradesmen's carts drawn by broken-down horses indifferently harnessed to mules, and driven by dirty and ill-clad soldiers who sat crouched over reins made of rope, sucking at their pipes and seemingly only half awake. The French, however, had their own methods and their own ideas – neither of which have changed very much from Napoleon's time to the present day – and it would be a mistake ever to judge them solely by their appearance. Nevertheless, on this particular occasion they had undoubtedly been soundly beaten, and the general situation was very serious.

From the beginning, Sir John French had been unable to get on good terms with General Lanrezac, with the result that there was no cooperation or consultation between the two. The sudden retreat of the French Fifth Army, which might well have led to the complete destruction of the B.E.F., had now degenerated into something resembling a rout, with disorganised French Divisions making for the Sambre along routes which Haig had intended using for the 1st Corps. Fortunately, the retirement of the 1st Corps was not seriously pressed; unlike the 2nd Corps which, on the 25th August, was brought to bay at Le Cateau and forced to stand and fight against the orders of Sir John French, who thereafter lost confidence in Smith-Dorrien, the Corps commander. The 2nd Corps beat back the German pursuit and was successfully extricated from a highly dangerous position, but French had by this time somewhat lost his nerve – for although very capable he was no Wellington – and could think of nothing other than getting his army safely off the field in order to reorganise and make fresh plans.

The 20th Hussars were meanwhile making their way south through the confused jumble on the roads, often sound asleep in their saddles for they seldom halted for more than an hour or two.

1914

Unlike almost every other major retreat in military history, there was no starvation on the Retreat from Mons, for the supply services functioned more or less as usual – an astonishing achievement under the circumstances. Men and horses were therefore well-fed, and their only trouble was sheer exhaustion from which, of course, the infantry suffered more than the cavalry. The flank being exposed, there were constant brushes with the enemy who, however, fortunately showed little enterprise. The 20th did occasionally spend a night in billets, and always had patrols out on the flank from dawn onwards. On the 27th, when the regiment was in a covering position near Andigny, some skirmishing developed with enemy patrols which were driven off with casualties on both sides.

On the 28th August, the 5th Cavalry Brigade went into action to stop an enemy attack from St Quentin, from which the French had been evicted the day before. This was quite a lively affair, which opened with German cavalry galloping forward, dismounting in full view within 500 yards of the Brigade and opening fire while standing in front of their horses. It was not the sort of manoeuvre which one would have expected of regular cavalry in the Peninsular War, and was certainly unsuitable in 1914. Their horses were stampeded by 'J' Battery, and the men charged by the 12th Lancers and Greys. This finished them, but the 20th, who were riding on the left flank, found a German battery going into action in front. Colonel Edwards decided to attack in order to divert its fire from the rest of the Brigade, and led the regiment forward at a gallop, with a troop out on either flank. He did not, fortunately, attempt a charge, but sent in 'C' Squadron dismounted, while 'B' manoeuvred to the flank finding that the ground made a mounted attack impracticable. The led horses of 'C' Squadron then began to suffer casualties from shrapnel and had to be taken back a considerable distance. The squadron then retired covered by Lieut. Sparrow's troop, which charged some dismounted Germans and got in with their swords, which caused great satisfaction. The enemy attack having been halted and disorganised by that time, the Brigade withdrew, covered by the 20th who put out rear parties but were not interfered with.

The regiment crossed the Aisne below Soissons on the 31st August, having seen no more enemy after the 28th. Patrols under Lieutenants Hall and Sparrow were sent out on the following morning to see if any enemy were approaching the river crossings, and both had similar adventures, from which they were lucky to escape unscathed. They had found the enemy in strength north of the river, and in possession of at least one bridge which had not been blown. Both of them had several brushes with the enemy and found, as they returned, that their retreat was cut off. Hall's patrol in fact, rode into a car-load of German officers travelling north, an encounter which so surprised both parties that they had no time to do more than swear at each other before separating. His patrol was also charged from the rear by a party of Uhlans with lances, but they were put to flight by the rear point, Pte. Hayhurst, who drew his sword and rode at them single-handed. This may sound improbable, but in fact the dash and gallantry displayed by Hayhurst disconcerted the Germans, who imagined it to be part of a trap, such as they were always on the look-out for.

Shortly after the patrols returned, the regiment, which was covering the retirement of the 1st Guards Brigade under the orders of its commander, Brigadier-General Maxse, was attacked while holding a covering position in the middle of a forest about four miles north-east of Villers Cotterets. As the Guards Brigade had by that time rejoined the 1st Division at Villers Cotterets the covering role of the regiment had ended and it was ordered to withdraw. The enemy being round the flanks, this was easier said than done, but in the end the enemy were halted and the regiment retired by squadrons with a few casualties. Among them was Sergeant Cook, who managed to stay in his saddle, although suffering much pain. When he was at last placed in an ambulance he enquired about his mare, a good horse of which he was particularly fond. He was told that it had been allotted to an officer of another regiment, whereupon he sprang from the ambulance, found his mare and rejoined his squadron. Like Pte. Hayhurst's single-handed charge, this was a good example of the fearless and indomitable spirit possessed to an extraordinary degree by all ranks of the old regular army in 1914. Reflecting the pride and self-confidence of the British people, whose country was at the head of a mighty empire, it was shared by the soldiers of the national armies which followed the regulars into the field, but they of course had not had the time to acquire the same standards of training, discipline and sense of tradition which had characterised the old regulars, whose exploits have never been equalled.

Sir John French, finding the enemy pressure somewhat relaxed, had urged that a defensive position should be established along the Marne. This was not agreed to by the French, whose Fifth Army was nearing the Marne with the Germans close behind. It was therefore decided that the B.E.F. should retire on Paris, and it crossed the Marne accordingly on the 3rd

1914

September. Thereafter its retirement was to continue in a south-westerly direction, and as this would present its flank to the advancing German First Army, it was necessary to hold the high ground north of the Marne while it was being carried out.

The 3rd and 5th Cavalry Brigades were therefore ordered into covering positions beyond Meaux, the 20th Hussars being allotted a sector on some high ground west of Avernes, with Lieut. Sparrow's troop holding a crossing over the Ourc, supported by the rest of 'C' Squadron. The German cavalry appeared in the afternoon in considerable numbers, covered by Horse Artillery which shelled the squadron and caused some casualties, while Sparrow's troop nearly got cut off. The squadron withdrew to Jaignes, dismounted and took up a position in front of the village, where it was again attacked but held the enemy off with rifle fire at 600 yards. Becoming outflanked, the squadron made another short withdrawal under shrapnel fire, after which the Brigade was ordered back across the Marne, having by that time delayed the enemy advance long enough for the infantry to get clear. The final retirement of the 20th was covered by 'B' Squadron, which had several casualties, including Captain Cristy, who was killed. The last man across the Marne was the C.O., Colonel Edwards, who stayed to the end to ensure that all patrols had come in. During the next few days the regiment suffered further casualties in brushes with the enemy, and on the 5th September bivouacked at Segres. This proved to be the end of the march south, for the Retreat from Mons was over.

After the British withdrawal from the Marne, the German First Army began to wheel eastward. This was in accordance with the original plan of operations which had previously been upset by the presence of the B.E.F. on the French left flank and its unexpectedly strong resistance. Now being convinced that the B.E.F. was defeated and need no longer be reckoned with, von Kluck, the First Army Commander, decided that it would be safe to carry out what would otherwise have been a highly dangerous flank march across the British front. He was very nearly right, for Sir John French, after temporarily recovering his nerve, had lost it again when his proposal to accept battle on the Marne was turned down by Generals Joffre and Lanrezac. He could no longer bring himself to put any trust in Lanrezac, and was at odds with both his corps commanders whose desires to halt and face the enemy during the retreat he had constantly frustrated – except at Le Cateau. He had been gravely distressed by the losses suffered by the 2nd Corps at Le Cateau, and by the exhaustion of the troops which was apparent on the line of march, which gave him the mistaken impression that unless he could get the B.E.F. out of the field to rest and refit, it was done for. When, therefore, Joffre proposed that the French Fifth Army and the B.E.F. should turn about and fall upon the flank of the German First Army he at first refused to co-operate, but at length succumbed to the combined blandishments of Joffre and Kitchener – who had hastened over to Paris to exert his personal influence. Both he and von Kluck then soon found out the B.E.F. had not been beaten after all.

Whereas the German First Army had been gravely weakened by casualties and the diversion of troops for the defence of East Prussia against the Russians, for the sieges of Antwerp and Maubeuge, and to hold off the newly-formed French Sixth Army under General Maunoury which was concentrating north-east of Paris, the French Fifth Army had been heavily reinforced from the eastern flank, on which fighting had died down. Von Kluck was also unable to co-ordinate the movements of the First Army with those of the Second Army under von Bulow on his left. A gap of some thirty miles opened between the two armies and when, on the 6th September, the B.E.F. counter-marched, the fortune of war led it straight into this gap, which was held only by cavalry and light infantry (Jagers). Receiving further favourable news to the effect that his *bête noire*, Lanrezac, had been replaced by General Franchet d'Esperey, Sir John French quite recovered his spirits.

The 20th Hussars were in equally high spirits, when they saddled up at 4 a.m. on the 6th September, preparatory to leading the Brigade back north. So far, the regiment had suffered few casualties and no shocks or surprises. The operations had been such as they had been trained to carry out and, like the rest of the B.E.F., they had proved themselves to be far better at the business than the enemy, whose sole advantage had been weight of numbers. Nor had the lengthy retirement any depressing effect on their morale, for professional soldiers, such as they were, were accustomed to think of war in terms of manoeuvring. By some quirk or stubbornness of character, however, British soldiers are generally at their best when things are going against them, and are liable to over-reach themselves when they feel that the tide has turned and they have the upper hand.

Riding out as advanced guard to the 5th Cavalry Brigade, with 'A' Squadron in the lead, the regiment came under shell-fire, when the Brigade deployed and 'B' Squadron was sent to support the 12th Lancers who went into action near Ormeaux. But such

1914

enemy as there were retired immediately, and by the following morning all ranks were under the impression that they were engaged in a pursuit. There was, in fact, every evidence that the enemy were on the run, for the roads were littered with the debris usually to be found in the wake of a retreating army. The 5th Cavalry Brigade began to get up speed and the Quartermaster of the 20th, Bill Adams, was so anxious not to be left behind that he lightened the transport wagons by throwing out such stores as he could not envisage any future use for, such as picks and shovels. The heavy baggage of a cavalry regiment was carried in General Service Wagons, each drawn by a pair of draught horses driven on the long rein. They were not devised to keep pace with the regiment, but were supposed to move along the roads in convoy at a walk. If the road was clear and there was any special hurry, they could move at a trot, but the drivers were not expected to 'spring 'em' at a canter or gallop, as Bill Adams apparently insisted upon on this occasion. His departure from the regulations was tolerantly disregarded, as evidence of a good spirit, but the loss of its picks and shovels was embarrassing to the regiment later on, as things turned out.

A fair number of enemy rear units, mostly cavalry and cyclists, were met with as the regiment advanced to Rebais and many were killed, Lieut. Sparrow getting a cyclist with his revolver and Cpl. Goring two Uhlans with his sword. He took their lances as trophies and is believed somehow to have got them back to his family at home, as souvenirs of the Great War.

With the arrival of the 4th and 6th Infantry Divisions the 3rd Corps had been formed in France at the end of August under the command of Major-General Pulteney. Sir John French therefore now had three Army Corps under his command, and his left was secured by the French Sixth Army instead of a handful of French Territorials. His mission was to advance across the Marne, after securing the Grand Morin and Petit Morin in turn, keeping in touch with the French Fifth Army on his right and the French Sixth Army on his left. The three corps advanced on a front of about ten miles behind the Cavalry Division on the left and the 3rd and 5th Cavalry Brigades, commanded by Brigadier-General Gough, on the right. These two Brigades were later formed into the 2nd Cavalry Division under the same commander.

The 20th Hussars reached the Petit Morin early on the 8th September, coming under artillery fire and finding all crossings strongly held. The Brigade was halted until the 1st Guards' Brigade arrived, led by the Black Watch and the 117th Battery, R.F.A. All the cavalry had been held up in a similar manner, and

The capture of Medicina (Northern Italy) 16th April, 1945. Major P. F. W. Browne leading his Squadron into the town.

the forcing of the Petit Morin by the infantry was in fact a major engagement skilfully and resolutely carried to a successful conclusion; but the 20th Hussars did not appreciate this fact and became very impatient at being held up and unable to take part in a battle which, it appeared to them, the infantry were taking an uncommonly long time about winning.

After being driven from the Petit Morin, the enemy facing the B.E.F. made no further resistance and retired across the Grand Morin and the Marne without even blowing the bridges. The 5th Cavalry Brigade crossed the Marne on the 9th September and continued the advance, with the 20th Hussars ending the day in billets at Domptin. Here they were visited by Sir John French, who was riding round the Brigade on horseback and complimenting each regiment on its good work. The Battle of the Marne was over, and the 20th were greatly surprised when they learned later that there had been such a battle and that they had taken part in it. They had been fortunate in fact, to have been riding on the right wing, while the heavy fighting was going on in the centre and left, but their role was an important one and they deserved the Battle Honour. The Battle of the Marne, which ended all German hopes of a quick victory in the war was, although not fought to a finish, one of the decisive battles of history, and the allied success was predominantly attributable to the advance of the B.E.F., which carried all before it while the French armies on its flanks, particularly the Sixth Army, were in trouble. Although there were well over a million men on either side, along the hundred mile battle line between Verdun and the Ourcq, there is still no doubt that it was the forcing of the Petit Morin by the B.E.F. which led to the German decision to retire the whole of their right wing. It was, however, an orderly withdrawal covered by rearguard actions, and not the rout which more vigorous pressure by the French Fifth and Sixth Armies should have brought about.

On the 10th September, Sir John French ordered an immediate pursuit without waiting for French co-operation. The 20th Hussars saddled up at 3 a.m. and rode out as advanced guard to the 5th Cavalry Brigade, marching with two squadrons up and covering a front of about five miles. The 3rd Cavalry Brigade was on the left, and the 2nd and 3rd Infantry Divisions in rear. After riding through Marigny, 'B' Squadron hunted some enemy stragglers through a wood, and at about 6.30 a.m. the regiment reached Veuilly, which was found to be held by an enemy rearguard. At this moment the Brigade was wheeled westwards towards Premont in order to join the 3rd Cavalry Brigade in an

1914

attack on a German column moving towards Chezy. Veuilly was left for the infantry to deal with, to the annoyance of the 20th, who felt that they could have captured it much quicker. Furthermore, the sudden change of direction brought the Greys and 12th Lancers into the lead when the Brigade, under cover of long-range fire from 'J' Battery, rode down 300 Germans and captured 30 wagons and four machine-guns. Similar cavalry actions took place elsewhere along the front, and after the infantry had gone into action the German retreat began to show signs of falling into disorder, and great numbers of stragglers were made prisoner.

Meeting with but slight opposition, the cavalry arrived on the heights overlooking the Aisne on the 12th September. It had not been expected that the enemy would defend the river, but it turned out to be an ideal defensive position which was being held in strength. The crossing was forced by the infantry, and heavy fighting developed with no opportunity for the cavalry to engage. The 5th Cavalry Brigade was ordered to cross the river by a pontoon bridge at Vailly on the 14th September, but when the 20th Hussars arrived it was found that the infantry were still in action just beyond Vailly, and that the whole valley was under heavy artillery fire. The regiment dismounted and led the horses over, but had no sooner done so than the Brigade was ordered back again, so that the 20th twice had the unpleasant experience of walking their horses over a swaying pontoon bridge under heavy shell-fire, losing Lieut. Greenslade and ten others in killed and wounded.

By the 18th September the most desperate efforts by the Allies had failed to drive the enemy from their selected positions along the Aisne, but at this stage of the war there was still a way round the German right flank, and during the night of the 1st October the B.E.F. started to withdraw from the Aisne preparatory to moving across to Flanders and the left flank of the Allied line. The Battle of the Aisne having been an infantry affair of attacks against entrenched positions, the cavalry could play little part, and the 20th Hussars only once went into action, when they lost a man and some horses killed while holding the crossing over the Vesle River at Condé.

The disengagement of the B.E.F. from the Aisne, after its relief by the French, was a tremendous and dangerous operation which had to be carried out in great secrecy. The 2nd Cavalry Division – made up of the 3rd and 5th Cavalry Brigades – was the first to leave, marching by road on the night of the 2nd October. It was followed the next night by the 1st Cavalry Division. The infantry were moved by rail; the 2nd Corps leaving first, followed by the 3rd and 1st Corps in that order. The two Cavalry Divisions, commanded by Major-Generals de Lisle and Gough respectively, now formed the Cavalry Corps, under Allenby, who had orders to cover the concentration of the 2nd Corps in an area north-east of Abbeville.

Although the Allies had succeeded in halting the German offensive, the situation was still very grave. On the eastern flank, the Russians had been defeated at Tannenburg, while in the west the port of Antwerp had fallen, in spite of the gallant efforts of the Belgian Army and the British Royal Naval Division. Nevertheless, it was still intended that the role of the B.E.F. in Flanders was to be an offensive one and not merely defensive. If it moved fast there was a possibility of turning the enemy's flank, and its initial deployment was made with this end in view. The Cavalry Corps and the 2nd and 3rd Army Corps marched north of Ypres, and by the 11th October the Cavalry Corps arrived between Merville and Hazebrook, with the 2nd Corps on its right around Bethune, and the 3rd Corps moving up on its left. The completion of the Allied dispositions on the western flank then resulted in an attenuated line reaching from Bethune past Ypres and along the Yser to the sea, with the Cavalry Corps in occupation of the Messines and Wytschaete ridges.

A general engagement commenced along the front of the 2nd Corps on the 11th October, and sufficient progress was made to cause Sir John French to issue orders for an advance eastwards, with the Cavalry Corps forcing the passage of the Lys.

The 5th Cavalry Brigade arrived at Wytschaete on the 15th October, after 'some scrapping with German patrols', and an attack on the Mont des Cats, in which the Greys and 'C' Squadron of the 20th were dismounted. The country was intersected by dykes and boggy streams, and becoming difficult for cavalry, but patrols under Lieutenants Thomson and Sparrow rode forward to reconnoitre the crossing over the Lys at Comines and Wervicq. They found that the former bridge had been blown but that the latter was still intact. Sparrow, who was rather prone to hair-raising adventures, got cut off by the enemy but escaped by leading his patrol over a wire fence, which every horse jumped without mishap. As the Brigade advanced, the regiment was directed to Comines, and on the way Lieutenants Thomson's and Goodhart's troops of 'C' Squadron, which was left flank guard, galloped enemy positions at Hollebeke and Houtham. Thomson's troop, supported by a squadron of the 10th Hussars, killed seven Germans without loss to themselves. The regiment had then to continue the advance dismounted.

1914

A successful mounted attack was made by the 20th Hussars on the 18th, when Tenbrielen was captured with the loss of one man, Cpl. Charlotte, who was buried in the churchyard; but mounted action was becoming increasingly difficult, and the cavalry began to entrench themselves, using their horses only for getting about. The enemy had begun to make heavy counter-attacks, in meeting which the 20th were at first able to use other people's trenches, and did not have to do any digging themselves. On the 19th, however, they were ordered to dig themselves in near Warneton, and remembered that their entrenching tools had been jettisoned on the battlefield of the Marne. It was a very awkward situation: 'spent most of the night digging a trench with the aid of broken plates, mess tins, knives and forks', wrote Lieut. Hall. Some spades were borrowed from Oostaverne, the nearest village in the rear, but the peasants parted with them reluctantly, and only after promises of their prompt return when done with. The sight of the enemy 'digging like beavers', along a ridge 800 yards in front, was a great encouragement to the 20th to do likewise and although, with their make-shift tools, properly finished trenches could hardly be expected, they did manage to make themselves fairly reasonable cover against the ever-increasing shell-fire.

By this time the British attempt against the enemy flank had been halted and the Germans, heavily reinforced by Divisions brought over from the eastern flank and Antwerp, took the offensive in their turn. The B.E.F. had been reinforced by the 7th Division and an Indian Division, and now consisted of four Army Corps and the Cavalry Corps, but its casualties had been very heavy and its line formed a vulnerable salient of which the apex was the town of Ypres, whose military value was not so much tactical as prestigious – the Germans were determined to have it, and the B.E.F. equally determined to hold on to it. The resultant operations were subsequently known as the First Battle of Ypres, during which the old British Regular Army perished as such. Faced by much the same gigantic odds as it had experienced at Mons, it received no orders to retire and so stood fast, once again preventing an enemy breakthrough and this time saving the Channel ports, whose capture would have had the gravest consequences.

In the Boer War, as previously described, the infantry had often to get mounted and try to emulate the cavalry. In this war, starting at Ypres, things were to go rather the other way round, with the cavalry dismounting and trying their hand as infantry. Although possibly not up to the standard of the regular infantrymen, they were very fair shots – good enough to halt most German attacks – but better with the sword than the bayonet, a weapon which, if clumsily handled and driven in too far, is not easy to get out again. Later training corrected this fault, but at Ypres there was nothing that could be done about it, and the heaviest German attacks were fortunately directed against those parts of the line held by the infantry.

The 20th Hussars, in their position between Warneton and Oostaverne, had a fairly quiet time until the end of the month when, under cover of a heavy bombardment, the enemy attacked along the front of the 5th Cavalry Brigade and the 4th Cavalry Brigade on its left. The first regimental casualty was Lieut. Carew, who was killed by a sniper. The 12th Lancers on the right then fell back under orders, which brought the enemy on to the flank of the 20th, who had also to retire to avoid encirclement. The retirement was covered by Carew's troop, now commanded by his sergeant, Bassinthwaite. This troop fought to the end to enable the regiment to disengage, and only one man escaped, the others being all killed or captured. A new, previously prepared position was taken up near Oostaverne. A further enemy attack drove in the left of the 4th Cavalry Brigade which obliged 'B' Squadron, which was also in action firing rapid, to change position facing the exposed flank. The line held by the regiment then became very extended, and part was held for a time by R.H.Q. Some French troops then came in and the 12th Lancers, with 'B' Squadron in support, made a successful counter-attack during which 'B' Squadron went to close quarters and avenged the loss of Carew and his troop.

The 2nd Cavalry Division was relieved by the French on the 1st November. An enemy bombardment commenced just as the 20th were withdrawing, and Lieut. McConnel had to cover the retirement with two machine guns. It was the second time he had done this, and he was awarded the D.S.O., as was 'B' Squadron Commander, Capt. Little, for his handling of the squadron at Wytschaete on the previous day.

Under the heavy and relentless enemy pressure, the British line at Ypres was getting very mixed-up. Many British infantry battalions had practically disappeared, and their trenches were being held by an extraordinary conglomeration of men from other regiments, cavalry, infantry, Army Service Corps, French, Belgians and Indians. The cavalry were as far as possible sent back to their horses, which they then used to dash about from one part of the line to another, 'plugging gaps'. The 20th rode about plugging gaps during most of November, on one occasion

1914

relieving some Frenchmen, who were commanded by an N.C.O. They seemed to be worried by the presence of the officers of the 20th, saying that their trenches were not sufficiently *chic* for officers. In fact, they were the best trenches that the 20th had been in, with overhead cover and loopholes, through which one could put in some rifle practice at the 'Huns' seventy-five yards away. The regiment was remarkably lucky in that it was never heavily attacked, so that its casualties were exceptionally light for such operations, during which many infantry battalions could barely muster a hundred men.

The regiment came out of action on the 22nd November, and went into billets at Steenwerk until the 15th January, 1915. Short leave was started, and leave parties went off in turn for seventy-two hours in England. During December, the regiment was inspected by the King and Sir John French.

A Tigris river-steamer with a 'Mahalla' on the left and a barge full of animals on the right. They are passing Ezra's Tomb. The river's bends were too sharp to allow for towing. Sketch by Pte. M. Baggott of the 14th.

8th November 1915 The 14th leave India for the Gulf
29th October 1915 The first action on the Tigris
1st December 1915 The engagement at Umm-al-Tubal
6th January 1916 Kut beseiged, Ali-al-Gharbi,
Battle of Sheik Saad
13th January 1916 Battle of Hannah
29th April 1916 Surrender of Kut

1914

Start of the Mesopotamian Campaign

25

At the outbreak of war, the 14th (King's) Hussars were stationed at Mhow, where they had moved from Bangalore in 1911. Eight pleasant years had passed since the regiment had landed at Bombay off the transport *Assaye*, during which it had acquired a very high reputation for sportsmanship, efficiency, riding and horse-management. It was commanded by Lieut.-Colonel R. C. Stephen, who had taken over from Colonel Browne-Synge-Hutchinson, V.C., in 1910. His predecessor, whose winning of the V.C. in the Boer War as Major E. D. Brown, has already been described, was responsible for the institution of the Regimental Medal in 1909, for award to a King's Hussar of any rank who has contributed in some conspicuous manner to the military efficiency or military honour of the regiment.

In 1914, to an Englishman in India, 'home' was a long way away. It took a month to get there, and although a traveller could cut this down a bit by landing at Marseilles and finishing the journey by train, this did not apply to the mails, which went all the way by sea. The distance in time and space was further emphasised by the self-contained life of the average Indian station, such as Bangalore, Mhow or Meerut, with its polo, cricket and club life, where everyone knew everyone else and the annual separation caused by some of the community departing

1914

to the hills at the beginning of the hot weather was quite a wrench. Under such conditions, the outbreak of war in Europe caused no disturbance whatever in India, either among the British or among the native population, and everything went on as usual. The soldiers, of course, both in the British and Indian Armies, knew that their services would be required in the field sooner or later, for the implications of a war with Germany had long been the subject of military study. They were naturally excited and impatient to be off, and it was particularly frustrating and unpleasant for a regiment like the 14th to be kept inactive when such stirring events were happening in Europe. In January it had been reported on by the Inspector-General of Cavalry as 'A very fine regiment – fit to take the field', and consequently expected to be among the first troops to leave India. Nothing more happened, however, than a move to Meerut in November to relieve the 13th Hussars, and on the 1st January, 1915, the regiment took part in the annual 'Proclamation Parade', as usual in full dress – this being the last occasion on which it was worn. The regiment was particularly well-mounted at this time on big Australian horses, known as walers, which for some years had been replacing country-bred horses in British regiments. Its last appearance in full dress was therefore a most impressive one, such as has never been seen since.

From the outbreak of war every possible expedient had been employed by the very efficient British propaganda machine to whip up hatred and scorn for the Germans throughout the British Empire. Generally described as 'Huns', the feeling against them gradually rose to rather ridiculous heights. Anyone with a German name made haste to change or Anglicise it, even the King himself, whose ancient family name of Guelph was changed to Windsor. In England, it did not even do to own a dachshund, as almost anything even remotely hinting of German origins or connections was suspect. It was not long, therefore, before the attention of the King was directed to the Prussian Eagle worn by the 14th Hussars and, on his desire for it to be changed 'for the present' having been conveyed to the regiment through the Army Council, it was replaced in May, 1915, by the second crest – the Royal Crest within the Garter.

The order to mobilise reached the regiment at last on the 27th October, 1915, and it embarked at Karachi on the 8th November in three transports, at a strength of 18 officers and 443 rank and file, with 490 horses. One in every three horses had by this time been replaced by country-breds, but they were carefully selected, good horses. It is safe to say that never before had the regiment taken the field so well-mounted. The quantity of kit carried on the horse was still considerable: on the off-side, a rifle in a leather bucket, and on the near-side a sword. Grooming kit was in two wallets on the front of the saddle with a rolled blanket on top, and the rolled great-coat was strapped to the back of the saddle. Hanging on either side were a nose-bag with 5 lb. of grain, a corn-sack with 9 lb. of corn, a case with two spare horse-shoes, a canvas water-bucket, ropes and picketing gear. A bandolier with 90 rounds was carried round the horse's neck. On the rider was another bandolier with 90 rounds, haversack, water-bottle, knife and bayonet, and mess-tin. The weight carried by the horse was about eighteen or twenty stone.

A farewell party was given to the officers of the regiment at the Meerut Club by the Earl of Suffolk. About a hundred guests sat down to dinner in the last civilised surroundings which the officers were to experience for some time. Soft lights, champagne and music, a fine dinner served by efficient Indian waiters, dancing afterwards and flirtations on the verandah or in a garden lit by fairy lights; it was all far removed from war and remarkably similar, in its general atmosphere, to the famous Ball on the eve of Waterloo.

The 14th were not bound for Europe and the Western Front, as they had been expecting for over a year, but for a theatre of operations within a week's sailing from Karachi. Shortly after the outbreak of war, the pro-German attitude of Turkey had caused anxiety to both the home and Indian governments with regard to the safety of the oil refineries at Abadan in the Persian Gulf, which could easily be reached by Turkish troops from Basra. When, therefore, an Indian Corps was dispatched to the Western Front in 1914, an independent Brigade sailed with it under sealed orders, in accordance with which it was landed at Bahrein. When war broke out with Turkey in November, this Brigade was moved to the Shatt-al-Arab, and after landing, was reinforced by the rest of the 6th Indian Division under General Barrett, who was ordered to march on Basra. After defeating a covering force of Turks and Arabs, Barrett arrived before Basra to find that the Turks had fled. All the Sheiks in the area were pro-British as, therefore, were their tribesmen, so that Barrett and his men received a rousing welcome when they marched into Basra. Advancing again, he captured the village of Qurna against stiff opposition and, by extending his left to Shaiba, covered Basra from attacks across the desert from the Euphrates, as well as down the Tigris.

The area of the oilfields was thus made secure until April,

1915

1915, when the Turks launched a heavy counter-attack on the British positions. The skill of General Barrett and the heroism of his men, who fought against great odds under terrible conditions, again defeated the Turks who fled in disorder. It had previously been decided, however, by both the home and Indian governments, that for political reasons it was now necessary to advance and take Baghdad. German emissaries were stirring up trouble in Persia and Afghanistan, and it was feared that unless the Turks were driven out of Mesopotamia and British prestige thus heightened throughout the East, a spirit of unrest might well arise in India. The 12th Indian Division was therefore sent to reinforce the 6th. The two Divisions with the 6th Indian Cavalry Brigade (7th Lancers, 16th and 33rd Cavalry and 'S' Battery R.H.A.) became the Mesopotamian Expeditionary Force. It was commanded by General Sir John Nixon, an Indian cavalryman. There was a distinct tendency at this time to appoint cavalrymen to high command in preference to infantrymen, and it would appear that the principal reason for this was their more dashing personalities, although in some cases influence in the right circles may have had something to do with it. Nixon, at any rate, was undoubtedly a dashing personality, to whom the old precept that the best form of defence is attack was second nature.

With Nixon's arrival in the Gulf, the Mesopotamian Campaign got under way. Having commenced as a minor security operation, it had now become a 'side-show', and the successes, reverses, blood-letting and fearful hardship which paved the road to victory were all part of the Great War. Whether or not it was right to embark on it can never be determined. The fact remains that it forced the Turks to commit large forces which they might well have used more effectively in Europe, the Dardanelles or Palestine and Egypt.

Undeterred by arrival of the hot weather, and the fact that he was short of transport, tents, medical equipment and supplies, Nixon prepared, as well as he could, for an advance to Amarah, nearly a hundred miles up the Tigris beyond his advanced post at Qurna. Meanwhile he sent a Brigade Group to clear the Turks out of Persian Arabistan, where they were interrupting the flow of oil from the oil-fields to Abadan. This expedition was completely successful, and returned to Basra in June. The 6th Indian Division, under General Townsend, then commenced the advance on Amarah. Townsend's first task was to drive the Turks from their forward positions before Qurna. This necessitated an attack across seven thousand yards of open desert without cover of any kind, with the added embarrassment that the whole area was flooded by overflow from the Tigris, in places to a depth of three or four feet. Townsend, a General who deserved a better fate than the one which he in fact encountered, collected a large number of small native boats in which he embarked his infantry and delivered an amphibious attack supported by a flotilla of gun-boats on the Tigris and some field-guns on rafts. It was too much for the Turks, who fled in disorder and did not stop running until they were well beyond Amarah, which was captured on the 3rd June by Townsend himself, and some thirty soldiers and sailors.

With a view to protecting his communications with Amarah, Nixon then extended his front to Nasiriyeh on the Euphrates, which was captured on the 25th July, after six weeks' fighting under the most frightful conditions. Nixon then turned his thoughts back to the Tigris, in contemplation of an advance to Kut-el-Amarah, another hundred miles up-river from Amarah, although his army was now not only too widely-dispersed for its strength, but exhausted as well.

The capture of Kut was entrusted to General Townsend who, on the 23rd August, received orders to effect 'the destruction and dispersion of the enemy . . . and the occupation of Kut'. Manoeuvering the 6th Indian Division and the 6th Indian Cavalry Brigade with great skill, he outwitted the Turks who retired – but not in disorder this time – to a strong position which they had previously prepared at Ctesiphon, eighty miles beyond Kut, which Townsend reached on the 30th September.

The exhaustion of the troops made an immediate pursuit of the enemy out of the question, but his unbroken series of victories over the Turks – whose readiness to do a bolt also pointed to poor morale – led Townsend to concur in Nixon's plans for an early advance on Baghdad. The Indian Government also concurred, for the Viceroy was again getting worried over the possibility of unrest in India, consequent on the lowering of British prestige after the failure of the Dardanelles expedition and set-backs on the Western Front. There was a good deal of misgiving on the part of Kitchener and the Imperial General Staff who, studying the position in Mesopotamia from a purely military angle, were unable to share Nixon's confidence in a successful outcome. However, Nixon was the man on the spot and his opinions, especially when backed by the Viceroy, were not lightly to be disregarded. It was agreed that the attempt should be made, and that two Indian Divisions should be transferred to Mesopotamia from the Western Front. To meet General Nixon's urgent request for another British cavalry regiment, the General Staff in India also

1915

agreed, though with some reluctance in view of the worsening internal situation, to send the 14th Hussars.

When the 14th sailed from Karachi, the officers, men and horses were all suffering from the debilitating effects of the hot weather – for in Meerut, it was very hot indeed. They soon picked up, however, once they were at sea, for conditions in transports had greatly improved since the turn of the century, and the soldiers in particular benefited considerably from a sea-going ration-scale which seemed to them positively luxurious after the sparse and unvarying diet to which they were accustomed in India, and which was little better than that issued in jail. After a week's voyage, the regiment arrived off Basra on the 14th November and transferred to four river steamers, which set off up the Tigris for Kut without delay. The horses were carried on flat lighters or barges, on to which they were unloaded from the transports on slings. After a week's idleness on excellent rations, the horses were in a very lively mood, and transferring them to the lighters was a hard and dangerous business. Ninety were carried on each lighter, with their heads facing outwards, secured to a single rope running round the side of the vessel. A wooden partition separated port from starboard, which the horses relieved their feelings by kicking to pieces, making conditions very unpleasant for their minders, who had to fill nose-bags and water-buckets in rear of the horses and then take them round the front. One lighter was secured on each side of a steamer for the journey up-river, which was miraculously completed without serious mishap, although the steamers were constantly having to heave-to while horses which had fallen overboard were recovered.

The regiment disembarked at Kut between the evening of the 20th and the 23rd October. On the 24th a message was received from Townsend that the 14th were urgently required, and they marched early on the following morning with two companies of the Royal West Kents and some transport and medical details, all under command of Major R. W. Hewitt of the 14th. No one was aware that three days previously Townsend had met with his first set-back.

During the afternoon of the 21st October, Townsend had launched a flank attack against the prepared enemy positions at Ctesiphon, being unaware that they had been heavily reinforced and outnumbered him by at least 8,000 men. Furthermore, they were regular troops of a quite different quality to those previously encountered, while Townsend's men were tired, he had no reserves immediately available, and his administrative services had come close to breaking down. Nevertheless, he very nearly succeeded in getting the Turks on the run once again, after getting through to the enemy's second line and taking large numbers of prisoners and guns. In this wonderful achievement, however, his men fought themselves to a standstill and suffered so many casualties that Townsend, having no reserves to exploit his success, was obliged to disengage and re-form. While he was doing so, the Turks launched a heavy counter-attack, which he beat off after a night's heavy fighting. Both sides then retired, each believing that the other had been reinforced and was advancing. Townsend was thus able to get clear, but he was in desperate straits and quite unable to cope with his large number of wounded, whose sufferings were indescribable. Discovering the true situation, the Turks turned about and followed Townsend down the Tigris, being kept at long range by the 6th Indian Cavalry Brigade. On the 28th he reached Aziziyeh, where he wrote, 'I was glad to find the 14th Hussars and half a battalion of West Kents, sent up to reinforce me.'

On arrival at Aziziyeh, the 14th joined the 6th Cavalry Brigade under Brigadier-General H. L. Roberts, while the half-battalion of the West Kents joined the 30th Infantry Brigade. Although the total strength of the reinforcement was under 800 men they were all British regulars – no soldier in the 14th had less than five years' service – and no one, friend or enemy, had any doubts as to the quality of such men, or that they were the equal of many times their own number of all other kinds of soldiers. They were therefore given a rousing welcome by the Indian troops, who formed the greater part of Townsend's force. The regular Indian Army, which had British officers, recruited only from the warrior castes of India, which form a very small part of the total population, so that the source soon dries up in a major war. This had not happened at this time, and the Indian battalions in the field were performing, under the most adverse conditions, feats of arms which were beyond both praise and criticism. They required, however, both good leadership and the force of example. The first was given them by their officers, to whom they were devotedly loyal, and the second by the British troops whom they so greatly admired and on whom they modelled themselves. It was customary for each Indian Brigade to consist of one British and three Indian battalions, an admirable arrangement which not only made for good comradeship, but inspired the British soldiers with the feeling that they were responsible for setting an example, and the Indian soldiers with the desire to emulate and impress the British. So many British units had by this time left India for the Western Front, that there was a scarcity of them in Mesopotamia and the British element in the 30th Brigade for example consisted only of a company of Hampshires until the West Kents arrived. The Cavalry Brigade had no British regiment until the 14th joined it, which explains Nixon's urgent requirement for a British cavalry regiment, in a theatre of operations where reconnaissance and security were of very considerable importance. Only one aircraft out of a total strength of four was in working order at this time, so that the cavalry were the only means of obtaining information of enemy movements.

Townsend was dependent for supplies on the Tigris, on which a number of barges and other supply vessels were protected by a flotilla of gun-boats. They were continually going aground and being attacked by Turks and Arabs. One of the gun-boats, the *Shaitan*, went aground eight miles above Aziziyeh on the evening of the 28th, and had to be lightened of her guns and ammunition while three of her sister ships stood by. She was then attacked by the 2nd Tribal Brigade and some Arabs of the Turkish advanced guard, and the Senior Naval Officer wirelessed Townsend for help. He sent out the Cavalry Brigade, led by the 14th, who advanced in line-of-squadron columns at the trot towards the village of El Kutunie, where the *Shaitan* was aground, while the 7th Lancers swung south along the river bank. Large numbers of Arabs were soon sighted among the trees and long grass north of the village, and Major Hewitt sent in 'A' Squadron, led by Lieut. J. A. T. Miller. The squadron drew swords and galloped through a blinding dust storm, which had suddenly blown up. This covered its approach from the enemy, whom Miller caught in the act of forming up and charged right through them, scattering them in all directions. Most of them fled towards the river, some on horseback, some on camels and others on foot. About forty were cut down by Lieut. Woodhouse's troop, and another hundred by the 7th Lancers, while many more were shot swimming the river. The main columns of the enemy advanced guard were then seen approaching and the Brigade was concentrated to receive them, while 'S' Battery went into action. The shelling halted the enemy, whose nerve had evidently been shaken by the brisk manner in which the Arabs had been dealt with. He made no further advance and the Cavalry Brigade withdrew. This spirited action enabled Townsend to dismantle his pontoon bridge at Aziziyeh, embark his heavy guns and continue his retirement on Kut. 'The advent of the 14th Hussars (British) had,' he wrote, 'put new spirit and dash into the Indian

Cavalry.' In its first action in the campaign, the regiment had suffered no casualties, either in men or horses, but two men and several horses were wounded by shell-fire while in bivouac the following night.

Delays caused by mishaps to the river craft obliged Townsend to give battle at Umm-al-Tubal on the 1st December. Aware that the Turks were close upon him, he issued orders for an attack at dawn, but as soon as it became light enough to see, he found that the Turks were deployed, and advancing to the attack themselves. They were in considerable numbers and far outflanked his right, so that he sent out the Cavalry Brigade to that flank with the traditional order, 'Forward and Charge'. On arriving on the flank, however, the Brigadier could see no opportunity for a charge, and ordered an attack dismounted. 'S' Battery and the Machine-Gun Section of the 14th, under Lieut. Pope, were halted to give covering fire, while the regiment deployed and advanced; opening fire at 1,200 yards. The 14th described themselves as 'a regiment of marksmen', and they were in fact unusually skilled shots for cavalrymen. Even at this long range, they were able to halt and break up the advance of the enemy left wing – the Turkish 51st Division – enabling Townsend to break off the action and withdraw. He wrote afterwards that he was strongly tempted to advance and fight it out. If he had, it is quite possible that the Turks would have been routed, but as he was outnumbered two to one, and his men were hungry and exhausted, he dared not take the risk. The Machine-Gun Section of the 14th had seven casualties in this affair, not counting a bullet through Pope's helmet, but it did considerable execution among the Turks and saved 'S' Battery from having to withdraw to avoid encirclement.

As the British forces retired down-river, enemy cavalry and infantry were seen on the exposed flank. The 14th were sent out against them, and the sight of the steady advance of the regiment at a trot brought them to a halt. As it was evident that they were on the point of doing a bolt, Hewitt formed the regiment into line, drew swords and moved on at a gallop when the enemy were still 800 yards distant, which was too far for horses to gallop and still retain sufficient reserve of speed for a charge. However, no charge was necessary for the Turks fled without ceremony and disappeared into an area of broken ground, where Hewitt did not feel that duty required him to follow. On this day the regiment lost five men and nine horses killed or died of wounds, with fifteen men and twenty-five horses wounded.

Kut-al-Amara was reached on the 2nd December, with the

1915

infantry in such a state of exhaustion that large numbers dropped by the wayside, although they well knew that if the Arabs got hold of them they would be tortured to death. The majority of stragglers were picked up by transport carts, which had been emptied for the purpose, although the supplies thus jettisoned were vital, for Townsend could retreat no further and had to face a siege. The town was put into a state of defence without delay, and there was some doubt whether or not to keep the cavalry, not on account of their fighting strength but for horsemeat. Fortunately, Nixon decided that they were essential in the field, and the Cavalry Brigade was ordered to march to Ali-al-Gharbi, a small town on the south bank of the Tigris about seventy miles from Kut. Leaving a guard of sixteen men with the regimental baggage and 25 sick and wounded horses in Kut, the 14th marched to Ali-al-Gharbi accordingly, reaching it – after a brush with about twelve hundred Arab horsemen – on the 8th December. It was the end of eleven days' marching and fighting, during which the regiment had covered over 200 miles. It was now bitterly cold, and no one had any kit other than what could be carried on his horse – which was not much for, as had been the custom of cavalry for centuries, the burden carried by the horse in marching order was lightened before going into action by jettisoning such non-essentials as blankets and greatcoats. When all went well, they were picked up again later, but seldom indeed, does all go well in war. Certainly not in 1915, either in the east or the west. No replacements for lost kit were available even in Basra, and the 14th – not for the first time in their history – had patiently to endure the lack of all normal essentials for a prolonged period. However, for the time being the 14th and the rest of the Cavalry Brigade at Ali-al-Gharbi were in very comfortable circumstances compared with the unfortunate 6th Indian Division, which, since the 7th December, had been closely invested within the extremely insalubrious town of Kut. Forage and rations were fairly plentiful, and the latter were supplemented by parcels of clothing and luxuries forwarded by women's voluntary organisations at home and in India. The 14th accordingly had quite a pleasant Christmas, unaware that the garrison of Kut had to spend it in repelling a heavy enemy attack. This it did to such purpose that the Turks made no further attempts to carry the town by storm, and settled down to a blockade. Their peace was disturbed on several occasions by determined sorties, which showed that the 6th Division in its reduced circumstances had lost none of its fighting spirit.

Townsend had not, naturally, relished the prospect of be-

1916

coming besieged. He had halted at Kut in the first place to rest and reorganise; expecting, if the worst came to the worst, to be relieved within a month. When Nixon told him that he would have to hold out for two months, he had wanted to retire on Ali-al-Gharbi while there was still time but Nixon, who was still determined to renew the offensive and get to Baghdad by the spring, made him stay where he was, promising to get a relief expedition organised immediately. This began concentrating at Ali-al-Gharbi in December, with the arrival of the 7th Indian Division from France under Major-General Sir George Younghusband. The 3rd Indian Division, also from France, was to follow, and the two Divisions, with the 6th Cavalry Brigade, guns and services, were then to be organised into the Tigris Corps, commanded by Lieut.-General Sir F. J. Aylmer, V.C.

Not realising that he had given the Turks such a hiding over Christmas that they had decided to starve him out rather than risk another attack, Townsend became worried about his ammunition supplies, and wirelessed that he must be relieved by the middle of January. Aylmer could not get his Corps ready in time, for shortage of shipping had caused confusion and delay, with formations getting mixed-up and disorganised. He therefore ordered Younghusband to advance on the 3rd January to Sheikh Saad and pin the enemy down in that area until the rest of the Corps arrived.

The British military cliché – *to do nothing is to do something definitely wrong* – which someone thought up about this time, has been responsible for many departures from principle with sad results. Whether it was responsible for Aylmer's decision to advance against superior numbers, with inadequate preparations and without first concentrating his force, is perhaps doubtful, but he certainly felt that he had to do something, even though he knew that Townsend's position was in no immediate danger.

The Turks were known to be entrenched on either side of the river about three miles below the village of Sheikh Saad, and Aylmer accordingly divided his force, and advanced up both banks of the Tigris, taking with him a bridging train to make a pontoon bridge at the Musandaq Reach, where the force bivouacked on the night of the 6th January. The troops on the right bank, commanded by Major-General Kemball, marched in two columns with the 6th Cavalry Brigade about two miles out on the left flank, led by the 14th Hussars less Lieut. Brooke's troop which was leading the infantry advanced guard. The Cavalry Brigade, which had been ordered to work round the enemy flank, was slowed down by the maze of irrigation ditches running into

1916

the Tigris, and a fairly thick mist made it difficult for 'A' and 'C' Squadrons under Major Hewitt, to keep direction. At about the same time that Lieut. Brooke's troop came under fire along the river, the two leading squadrons of the regiment were also fired on at long range from enemy trenches in front. 'C' Squadron dismounted and replied from cover, but at this moment masses of Arabs on horses, camels and on foot appeared on the left flank of the Brigade. They disappeared again when 'S' Battery went into action, and a general engagement followed, which lasted three days. While the infantry were attacking along both banks of the Tigris, the cavalry continued to manoeuvre against the flank, not only with a view to turning it, but to find out the enemy dispositions. This was done by hard riding and considerable dash; 'B' Squadron under Captain T. R. Bruce getting within a hundred yards of the Turkish trenches, before retiring under a heavy fire without leaving any of its wounded or dismounted men behind, although collecting them under such circumstances required exceptional courage and coolness. Some very well-deserved decorations were won in this affair, which included the D.C.M. for Squadron-Sergeant-Major Wright, who galloped right up to the Turkish trench and fired his revolver in order to create a diversion.

On the morning of the 9th January, reconnaissances by the 14th Hussars found the Turkish trenches empty. The enemy had, it turned out, retired during the night to a position along a tributary river known as the Wadi, on the left bank of the Tigris, about ten miles up-river from Sheikh Saad. General Aylmer, however, was unable to do more than occupy Sheikh Saad, for his administrative difficulties were considerable, and he had had nearly four thousand casualties among which the sufferings of the wounded, under medical arrangements which were grossly inadequate, were most grievous. Realising, however, that the enemy left flank on the Wadi was vulnerable, he ordered the Cavalry Brigade across the Tigris and marched as soon as he could, attacking on the morning of the 13th January. Owing to administrative chaos, the operation was something of a shambles, in which formations lost direction and advanced without any clear ideas as to their objectives. The Cavalry Brigade, when trying to find the enemy left flank, came under such heavy artillery fire when riding over flat ground without any cover, that it was dismounted and advanced on foot. The 14th Hussars, who were in the lead, marched 'at a rapid pace', but could not close the enemy until it was nearly dark. After shots had been exchanged for a while at a range of about 600 yards, the Turks with-

1916

drew under cover of darkness to a previously prepared position at Hannah, where their left was secured by the Suwaikiya Marsh. Having, for one reason or another, missed this opportunity for turning the enemy flank on the Wadi, the cavalry had to take a back seat for a time, being of little use in the situation now developing.

Generals of the twentieth century suffer to a degree unknown to their predecessors, from being tied to the apron-strings of their respective governments. 'War,' said M. Clemenceau, the Prime Minister of France, 'is too serious a matter to be left to Generals.' The unfortunate Sir John Nixon in Mesopotamia, who had taken the field with such dash and enthusiasm, had two governments to deal with – British and Indian – which were not infrequently at variance in their opinions. This, in combination with the strain of responsibility and excessive exertions in a climate more suitable to condemned souls than living mortals, had broken down his health and forced him to apply for a relief. He was duly relieved by Lieut.-General Sir Percy Lake, and was made in due course to accept the blame for the failures of the campaign, in which his initial brilliant successes seem to be entirely forgotten. Although it could not be avoided, his relief at this stage was unfortunate, for one can learn more from failure than from success, and he was not the man to make the same mistake twice.

A change of command more welcome to the 14th Hussars occurred when their former commanding-officer, now Brigadier-General R. C. Stephen, arrived to take over the 6th Cavalry Brigade from Brigadier-General Roberts who had returned to India on sick leave. He was not the only one sick in the 6th Cavalry Brigade, which Stephen found in poor shape after the first battle of Hannah. This had taken place during the third week of January, 1916, under the most appalling conditions in a sea of mud and stinking slime, provoked by an icy rain which poured down continuously. The cavalry were thrown out to protect the flanks of the attacking infantry and did not go into action, but they had their share of hardship and misery, being reduced on occasion to bivouacking in areas knee-deep in mud where it was impossible to find anywhere to sit, let alone lie down and sleep, so that the troops had to spend the night walking about to keep warm, with their soaking blankets over their heads. In the 7th Indian Division, there were nearly three thousand casualties, suffered during abortive attacks against strong entrenchments without adequate artillery support, and the wounded were left lying about on this sort of ground, until they either died or were picked up in springless carts, in which their sufferings were far

1916

worse – so much so that many able to make a last effort rolled out of the carts to die on the ground, rather than endure them a moment longer. Long ago in the Crimea, Florence Nightingale had commented on the neglect of the sick and wounded in terms which ensured that their sufferings would never be forgotten, but there was no one to do the same for those who perished in the Mesopotamia Campaign, although their lot was certainly as bad.

Immediately on his arrival, Sir Percy Lake set about trying to establish some sort of order in Basra, where reinforcements of all arms were disembarking without any arrangements for their reception. At the same time he was under most urgent pressure to rescue Townsend at Kut. It was a desperate position to be in, especially as neither he nor any formation commander had any trained staff officers. When the 13th Division arrived, he was unable to send it forward for lack of transport, and as Townsend's position was getting desperate, the 7th Division made another gallant attack at Hannah which, with a little more luck might well have been successful, but it had no luck at all, and although the Cavalry Brigade on the left flank came within sight of Kut the attack was halted after the Turks had thrown in their reserves. When the 14th Hussars got back to Ora on the Tigris, neither men nor horses had eaten or drunk for two and a half days.

The final attempt to relieve Kut began on the 5th April, when the 13th Division – which consisted entirely of British Territorial and Special Service units – attacked Hannah and found that the Turks had withdrawn to Fallahiya. This the Division captured the same evening at a cost of nearly two thousand casualties. The 7th Division then went through and lost sixty per cent of its remaining strength before the main enemy positions at Sannaiyat – the 43rd Oxfordshire and Buckinghamshire Light Infantry lost every officer left in the battalion, and of the rank and file only forty-six were left on their feet. Attacking on the right bank of the Tigris, the 3rd Division captured and held Bait Issa, and finally the 7th Division tried once again and was wiped out. The Black Watch, whose gallantry had attracted the attention of the 14th Hussars on several previous occasions, came out of action with forty-eight left out of their original strength of 840. All this while the Cavalry Brigade had been protecting the left flank on the right bank of the Tigris, meeting only with Turkish cavalry who were of no account and turned tail on each occasion without risking coming to blows.

On the 29th April, 1916, Townsend surrendered with 2,750 British troops and 6,500 Indians. The decision to hold Kut had cost over forty thousand casualties and, in retrospect, appears to

1916

have had little justification, with the relief operations shockingly mismanaged. It is a tale, however, of gallant endeavour in the face of heavy odds under every conceivable disadvantage, including that of abnormal rainfall, and it must not be forgotten that the Turks were made to pay for their success in full measure.

At the end of these operations the 14th encamped at Gomorrah, on the right bank of the Tigris, where the conditions were such that upwards of forty men reported sick daily. Soon, everyone in the regiment was suffering from fever, jaundice, dysentry, and so on. One man died of cholera and the commanding-officer, Colonel Hill-Whitson, and seventeen men were invalided. Major Hewitt, therefore, again took over command.

Lieut.-Colonel R. W. Hewitt, D.S.O. Served successively with the Royal Norfolk Regiment, the mounted infantry, and the 14th King's Hussars. He commanded the last-named in Mesopotamia. Mortally wounded at the Battle of Ramadi, 29 September 1917.

Men of the 20th Hussars with a chicken which they had purchased for their Christmas dinner at Bailleul, December 1916.

February 1915 The 20th in the trenches at Zillebeke
March 1915 Battle of Aubers Ridge
April 1915 Second Battle of Ypres
May 1915 The 20th in the trenches at Vlamertinghe
July 1916 The Battle of Loos, the Battle of the Somme, the Dismounted Cavalry Division

1915

The Western Front 1915–1916

26

On the Western Front, 1915 opened with the British Army holding a line along the low ground of the Lys Valley, overlooked on the 1st Army front by Aubers Ridge and in the 2nd Army by the Messines Ridge. An offensive was therefore planned to start on the 10th March, with the capture of Neuve Chapelle by Sir Douglas Haig's 1st Army as a preliminary to securing the whole of the Aubers Ridge.

Haig, like Sir John Nixon and most other cavalry generals, was a thruster who disliked awaiting an attack and preferred always to take the offensive when at all possible. The position of stalemate which had now developed on the Western Front, with both sides well dug in and their flanks secure, did nothing to modify his opinion that the war could only be won by offensive tactics – and indeed, he continued to hold it up to the day of final victory. Nor did his methods change, for, if one was bent on the offensive, they were the only sound tactics to adopt under such circumstances. He always hoped, that by establishing a preponderance of force, he would be able to break through the enemy line on a wide front, and, having done so, exploit the break-through before the enemy had time to react by sending the cavalry through the gap. The trouble was – to put it simply – that when making the gap, the infantry and artillery made such a mess of the battlefield

1915

that it was impossible for the cavalry to ride over it. Haig has accordingly been subjected to a vast amount of often ill-considered criticism for sticking to his guns over this matter. 'The Gap', in fact, soon became something of a standing joke among the cavalry at the time. The cavalry indeed had become bewildered for, once trench warfare had started, they were unable to envisage any useful employment for themselves in the future and, although they were only too happy to take their turn in the trenches with the infantry, it was not what they had been trained for.

A commander in the field, however, is not in the same position as the captain of a football team, whose only concern is to get the better of an opposition whose numbers and equipment are exactly the same as his own – and, if he fails there is no great harm done. The commanders on the Western Front, French, Haig, and Smith-Dorrien, were in no position to play a waiting game, in spite of the fact that with grossly inadequate resources they were having to face a military machine of a size and efficiency which had never been seen before, and by the side of French and Russian allies whose reliability had been seriously over-estimated. They had really no other alternative but to keep pounding away; a job for infantry and guns, and not for cavalry. But the cavalry still represented the only available mobility, and so could not be dispensed with altogether, especially as, in the business of plugging gaps as opposed to exploiting them, they had proved themselves exceedingly useful, if not indispensable. The regular cavalry regiments, however, were by no means lacking in officers with brains and ambition, such as Captain G. K. Mason of the 14th, who was attached to the 20th in 1914 and 1915 until wounded by shrapnel. Like many others, he was disconcerted by the way things had turned out, finding that all his training and study were apparently proving useless under such unforseen conditions as existed on the Western Front. Such conditions, he asserted, required nothing from an officer other than the quality of leadership, so that a clerk or shop assistant, provided he had this quality, could go straight from his desk or counter into a trench and be just as valuable there as a regular officer who had spent his life in the study of war. Views such as this were fairly widely held and expressed, tending to give a wrong impression to the whole conduct of operations. The grievous casualties among regular officers in the first months of war had forced the commissioning of vast numbers of 'temporary gentlemen', whose only qualities as officers were courage and leadership. They were in no way comparable to regular officers and when, knowing nothing of the business, they led forward to the attack soldiers whose training had been limited by the time factor to loading and firing their rifles, it is not surprising that sickening casualties resulted. What is surprising is the fact that their morale never weakened from first to last. Defeat never entered their heads; they were always ready for another 'go at Fritz' under conditions so frightful as to strain the imagination, and they won through in the end, after both the Russian and French armies had crumbled into mutiny.

At the end of 1914, the British Expeditionary Force on the Western Front had grown to eleven infantry and five cavalry divisions, and it was reorganised into the 1st Army, under Sir Douglas Haig, the 2nd Army, under Sir Horace Smith-Dorrien, the Cavalry Corps, under Sir Edmund Allenby, and the Indian Cavalry Corps, under Major-General Rimington. It was thus no longer 'contemptible' in numbers – or in quality – but the majority of officers and men had had very little training and much of their equipment was makeshift and not up to previous standards.

The increasing strength of the B.E.F. should have enabled Sir John French to deepen his front and form a reserve adequate to exploit an attack, but he was obliged to agree to take over more of the front line from the French, and so had to commit the newly-arrived 27th and 28th Divisions which took over from two French divisions on the British left, extending the front to the Ypres-Zandvoorde road. Even this was not enough, and the 2nd Cavalry Division was dismounted in order to relieve the French on 1,400 yards of the front on the left of the 28th Division, although behind this sector were two French Territorial Divisions and five Cavalry Divisions. It was a dangerous part of the front, being within the salient held by the French 8th Army before Ypres.

Before going up to the line, the dismounted 2nd Cavalry Division carried out a week of intensive infantry training which ended on the 13th February, when the 20th Hussars were conveyed to the square in Ypres by 'motor-bus', for the cavalry were still not being expected to use their feet like the infantry – whose 27th Division marched seventeen miles to the trenches, wearing 'indifferent foreign service boots', which were in fact second-hand and probably salvaged from casualties. The 20th did a week's duty in the front line east of Zillebeke during February, occupying a line of French-constructed breastworks in a wood. Although the enemy front line was only forty yards away, they had a quiet time, for the trees prevented shelling, and those

1915

between the opposing lines had been felled, which made an attack difficult. Apparently getting bored, Sergeants Gray and Curran went out on their own in broad daylight and bagged a Hun behind the enemy lines, coming back safely although Curran, an Irishman, had wanted to go on and shoot some more Huns.

The only casualty at this time in the regimental sector was Lieut. Barr, who was killed by a sniper, but 'C' Squadron lost seven men killed and three officers and three men wounded while counter-attacking a trench of the 16th Lancers, which had been blown up and occupied by the enemy with a loss to the 16th of no fewer than ten officers. A similar attempt by the enemy to blow up 'A' Squadron's trench was apparently frustrated by Lieut. McConnel, who blew up the enemy sap which they were digging towards the position.

Although a good deal better off than was the case in Mesopotamia, the wounded on the Western Front had a hard time of it. Getting them under cover was a risky business, for stretcher-bearers could not count on the immunity experienced in the Boer War. There were no pain-killing drugs, such as morphia, in the front line, and a wounded man had to endure some very rough handling on his way to the regimental aid post. Here his 'First Field-dressing' was changed for bandages by the Medical Officer, and he was sent back to the Field Hospital either in a stretcher or a horse-drawn cart, but he would have to wait until nightfall before starting this journey. The Field Hospital was usually a theatre or public building flying the Red Cross. There were no beds in it and seldom any mattresses. The wounded lay huddled together on the floor which had sometimes been strewn with a thin layer of straw, which soon became soaked in blood. However, if a man managed to survive the Field Hospital, things progressively improved until he eventually arrived in some country house in England, whose owner had turned it into a convalescent home, and where a wounded man completed his cure under very comfortable circumstances indeed. 'A Blighty one', which was the expression used for a bullet in a non-vital and not too painful part of the body, accordingly became something which most soldiers looked forward to, as the war went on.

When the Aubers Ridge battle started on the 10th March, the 20th Hussars, with the rest of the cavalry, hastened back to their horses and saddled up, ready to ride through the gap. As this was the first time that they had heard this expression, they followed up the infantry with lively anticipation, and when the 5th Cavalry Brigade at Rouge Croix was eventually ordered forward

1915

at the trot, swords were eased in their scabbards to make sure they would draw easily. But although the infantry captured Neuve Chapelle, they were unable to get the enemy on the run, and the offensive gradually came to a halt. The 2nd Cavalry Division therefore had to retire disappointed, and the 20th went into billets at Verte Rue until the 23rd April, during which time a welcome relaxation was staged, in the form of a Divisional Horse Show.

At the beginning of April, while Haig was getting ready for another attack on Aubers Ridge, the enemy launched an offensive against the Ypres salient, now held by the 2nd Army. In the Second Battle of Ypres, the Germans gained some initial success by means of the surprise use of poison gas, against which the allies had no defence. Squirted out of cylinders laid along the trench parapets, it was dependent on a following wind and its effects, far from being decisive, were chiefly to enrage the British and Canadian troops, whose comrades got a dose of it, against this further example of Hunnishness. A ferocious battle developed which lasted until the 3rd May, when the enemy attack was finally halted. During the battle, the cavalry were not at first called upon, so that the 2nd Cavalry Division was able to hold its Horse Show undisturbed, but the cavalry brigades were soon once again functioning as a mobile reserve and plugging gaps in the line. The 5th Cavalry Brigade was summoned to horse on the 23rd April. For a few days the 20th Hussars remained mounted and sending out officers' patrols, but on the evening of the 26th the regiment dismounted and occupied various reserve trench-lines in the neighbourhood of Hooge, suffering several casualties from shelling. While leaving the trenches on the 2nd May, 'C' Squadron had a whiff of gas, and had to stuff handkerchiefs into mouths, which was the only protection available at that time. The first 'respirators' were issued shortly afterwards. They consisted of locally made pads soaked in chemicals, which had to be stuffed into mouths and breathed through.

On the 8th May the Germans launched another heavy offensive and broke through at Frezenberg. The 3rd Cavalry Division dismounted and went into the line, where it had to withstand a full-scale attack and suffered heavy casualties while doing so. On the night of the 14th it was relieved by the 2nd Cavalry Division, and the 20th Hussars took over some front-line trenches before Vlamertinghe from the 3rd Dragoon Guards, who had had eighty casualties including their commanding-officer. The 20th were more fortunate, for the 3rd Cavalry Division had given the enemy a 'bloody nose', and he had retired into his dug-outs 1,000

1915

yards away, where he showed no disposition to emerge. The 20th had some casualties from shelling, but were otherwise able to spend this period in the front line repairing the trenches, which had been so knocked about that it was astonishing that the 3rd Dragoon Guards had any survivors.

At the end of May, the 2nd Cavalry Division relieved the 1st Cavalry Division in the Ypres salient, just after a heavy gas attack which left the atmosphere strongly polluted for a time. Thereafter the front remained fairly quiet for some months, during which the cavalry furnished working parties and patrols, but in the 20th time was found to sort out the horses into matched squadrons. It had long been the practice in the smarter cavalry regiments to have all horses in a squadron of the same colour; in the 20th, 'A' always had bay horses, 'B' brown and black, and 'C' chestnut, with the band on greys and the drum horse skewbald. Such a refinement was difficult to maintain in war time, and the horses had become mixed-up. Sorting them out was not as easy a matter as might be supposed, for it was disagreeable for a squadron leader to lose a good horse in exchange for an indifferent one merely on account of colour, especially as the colour of a horse – or, strictly speaking, of his nose – is not always easy to determine. The resultant 'horse-coping', however, served to while away a dreary period behind the lines.

Sir John French had been hoping to avoid launching another offensive until the following spring, for he was short of both men and munitions, but General Joffre was planning to attack in Champagne against the right of the salient formed by the German advances, and pressed French to co-operate with the 10th French Army in an attack against the left of the salient in Artois. As the Russians were repeatedly calling for a major effort to be made in the west to take the pressure off themselves, after the failure of the attempt to force the Dardanelles, Joffre was supported by the British government and French was forced to agree to an attack by the 1st Army in the area between Lens and the La Bassee Canal, although this part of the front was open except for coal mines and villages and very unfavourable for an offensive.

In the resultant Battle of Loos, the cavalry were again earmarked for exploiting breakthroughs, and the 20th were in the saddle almost continuously but their services were not called upon except to help in the dismal task of burying the dead, for there were no gaps in the line in the 2nd Cavalry Division area, either to plug or to exploit, although the other cavalry divisions were very actively employed. The second year of the war ended with the 20th Hussars in billets at Fauquemberges and Renty.

1915

The Battle of Loos having achieved no worthwhile result, although the casualties suffered in it were appalling, Sir John French – who had engaged in it only under duress, and against his better judgement – was relieved as Commander-in-Chief by Sir Douglas Haig. There were now thirty-six British Divisions in the field, but the state of training of the great majority was so indifferent that even Haig became reluctant to fight before he had to. A combined allied offensive was planned for the summer of 1916, by which time he felt that his armies would be better prepared, but in February that year the Germans, with considerable cunning, launched an attack on Verdun, an obsolete fortress on the Meuse. The garrison stood fast, and the defence of the fortress became a matter of acute national pride for the French, who poured troops into its inadequate trench system and reinforced it from all other parts of their front. More and more of the front line had in consequence to be taken over by the British, whose line, after relieving the French 10th Army at Arras, ran from Maricourt on the Somme, through Ypres to the sea. This was far too extensive a front for the strength of the British armies, but Joffre nevertheless insisted on launching a combined offensive along the Somme where the two allied armies joined. It was a particularly bad choice of battleground for the British, whose waterlogged trenches were overlooked by those of the enemy on higher ground. Being also the junction between French and British, it was in that area that the Germans were in special strength and alertness, either to repel a combined assault or to exploit any opportunity for driving the Allies apart. As in the case of his predecessor, political pressure left Haig with no choice but to co-operate. In such a position, there was no way in which he could out-manoeuvre the enemy by exercising his military skill, and he could only attempt to hammer his way through. Collecting all the artillery he could lay hands on, he lined it up wheel to wheel and, after a concentrated bombardment lasting a week, sent the infantry forward on the 1st July.

At the beginning of the year, an arrangement had been worked out under which the three divisions of the Cavalry Corps between them contributed to the formation of a dismounted division for the close support of the infantry, and to relieve them in the front-line trenches or plug gaps as required. Each Cavalry Division contributed one dismounted brigade of three battalions, one of which was provided by each cavalry brigade and made up of three companies representing the three regiments in the brigade. The officers, from the commander of the dismounted division downwards, were detailed in rotation for a period with the

1916

division. The idea behind this was presumably to impress upon the infantry that the cavalry were quite prepared to 'go slumming' in the trenches, and did not spend all its time riding about in the rear. There was otherwise no particular point in the formation of a dismounted division, for the cavalry, as already described, had been taking its turn in the trenches from the beginning. During the Battle of the Somme, however, the cavalry were again cast for the optimistic role of exploiting a gap or gaps by the use of their mobility and spent much of the summer practising for this role.

The dismounted company provided by the 20th Hussars for the 5th dismounted battalion consisted of two platoons from each squadron, and was commanded by Captain Micholls, but he and the other officers were relieved from time to time, as was the commanding-officer of the battalion, in which duty Colonel Cook of the 20th took his turn in due course. While the company was in the trenches, in the neighbourhood of Vermelles, action was limited to local raids and attacks by both sides, but there was constant shelling, sniping, mortaring, bombing and attempts to blow up one another's trenches by mines. This kind of activity was invariably provoked by the British, whose insatiable desire for putting Huns underground was a peculiar feature of trench-warfare on the Western Front. It was not the result of hatred or even dislike for the Germans who were generally regarded with tolerant respect. It seems that in the British Army, the high command was always anxious in case the soldiers should become bored, and lose their fighting spirit by remaining inactive under the harsh conditions of the front-line trenches, and officers were therefore encouraged to devise local adventures. As a consequence, there was a considerable difference in atmosphere between the French and British trenches when there was no major engagement taking place. The former were so quiet and peaceful that it was even reported that newsboys from the neighbouring towns were seen selling papers in them; and it is a fact that the French always disliked taking over British trenches, for the enemy was always sure to have been thoroughly stirred up and extremely lively.

The 20th Hussars were as ready as any other British unit to bag Huns whenever opportunity offered. A favourite method was the bombing raid which, although sometimes useful for clearing the enemy off an enfilade position, usually had no other object but to exercise the soldiers and kill a few Huns. Such attacks were led by specially-trained subalterns, with grenadiers, riflemen, and a Hochkiss gun. Lieut. Jeffrey, one of the bombing-officers of the

20th who was known, for some reason, as the 'Iron Man', had more than the usual devotion of the specialist towards the hand-grenade, and had invented a sling for projecting the missile further. He was killed in February, 1916, while leading an attack against some enemy craters. Seven men died with him and two were wounded but the attack, made in conjunction with another led by Lieut. Hatton, was completely successful and many Huns were sent to their last account.

While the dismounted division was in the trenches, the three mounted divisions, in addition to practising 'gap tactics', were busy constructing 'cavalry tracks', to enable them to ride across the dismal wastes into which the devastated countryside within range of the guns had now degenerated. A larger version of the infantry's duck-board tracks, they passed over waterlogged ground, shell-craters and trenches. The Cavalry Corps had been broken up, and a Cavalry Division placed under command of each Army; the 2nd Cavalry Division going to the 2nd Army near Boulogne. The 20th Hussars were billeted at Licques, but before the Somme offensive started the 2nd Cavalry Division was moved to the Hazebrouck area, as mobile reserve to the 2nd Army.

The first assault on the Somme on the 1st July was delivered by 19 British and 5 French Divisions. The British troops, young and half-trained, advanced in waves which the German machine-gunners, coming up from their deep dug-outs as soon as the artillery barrage lifted, mowed down in enfilade. When the sun set on that day there were 57,000 British casualties lying dead or wounded on the field. It is doubtful whether any other troops in the history of the world have, or would have, stood up to such conditions without breaking, but the British soldiers pressed on and made some small gains, capturing Mametz and Montauban.

Haig would not accept defeat and renewed battle on the following day, upon which the Fricourt salient was taken. This was an important achievement which was worth exploiting, and day after day the British infantry attacked, striving to enlarge the bulge driven into the enemy line. By the 17th July, Longueval, Bazentin le Petit and Orvillers were in British hands, as well as 10,000 prisoners. A German counter-attack on the 18th July won back the ridge which had been Haig's main objective, and he had lost another 80,000 men but, none-the-less, a foothold had been established in the enemy's defensive system, and so he continued to call for fresh efforts by his troops, and the battle went on. Each desperate attack was followed by an equally desperate enemy counter-attack, and the fighting raged to-and-fro week

1916

after week, until the British gradually began to get the better of the Germans, who were suffering very heavy casualties by being forced to counter-attack across open ground. In a final effort in the middle of September, which cost them 100,000 casualties, the British captured High Wood and Martinpuich, firmly establishing themselves along the ridge which had been their original objective.

During this series of battles on the Somme, the cavalry were mostly kept mounted as mobile reserves, but with few chances of intervening although some regiments went into action dismounted and one at least – the 7th Dragoon Guards – went in mounted and, armed with lances, killed a large number of Germans at High Wood without, apparently, suffering many casualties themselves. The 20th Hussars, who had been furnishing patrols and working parties during July and August, went up to the front at the beginning of September and bivouacked near Bray. They were still intended to go through the infantry when an opportunity offered, and a dismounted party went forward to work on the cavalry track. This scheme had, however, to be abandoned, in spite of the infantry success, for the area had taken such a pounding during the battles that the heavy rain which followed turned it into a morass, which was impossible to ride over, even along the cavalry tracks, which became covered in liquid mud. The pack horses and mules, used for getting ammunition forward to the infantry and guns, could move across this dreary waste only with the greatest difficulty, and some of the horses of the 20th had to be sent forward to help. Officers' patrols also went up to keep in touch with the infantry, and 'B' Squadron rode forward as far as Carnoy in the hope of finding an opportunity for action; but the rain continued all through October until even the infantry operations became restricted and the fighting gradually died down.

By this time, the British casualties were greatly decreasing, as the troops and their leaders gained experience. The first tanks made their appearance on the battlefield. Few in number and of rudimentary design, they gave the Germans an unpleasant surprise, but had little influence on the operations and it was only the few mechanically-minded enthusiasts who were able to foresee that they would one day entirely replace cavalry on the battlefield.

As the British losses decreased, so those of the enemy steadily increased. When the weather finally put a stop to the allied offensives in mid-November, just after the British capture of Beaucourt with many prisoners, the German casualties on the

Somme totalled well over 650,000 men. A shattering blow had also been delivered to their morale and confidence in victory, and it was only the weather which saved them from complete defeat on the Somme front. The offensives had also given the French a chance to rally after their devastating experiences in the defence of Verdun, and they began to strike back. The year 1916 ended, therefore, with the allies in possession of the initiative on the Western Front.

Top Clearing out snipers at Khazimain. *Bottom* On the track of the Turk, February 1917 (this picture was used as the Regimental Christmas card that year). Sketches by Pte. M. Baggott of the 14th.

May to November 1916 Operations at Es Sinn and on the Hai
December 1916 Offensive at Sannaiyat
January and February 1917 Attack on the Hai Salient
March 1917 Capture of Aziziyah
11th March 1917 Entry into Baghdad and surrender of Khazimain
April 1917 Pursuit to Tikrit
May 1917 The 14th on the Euphrates
9th April 1917 The Battle of Arras
10th April 1917 The Gallop at Monchy
20th November 1917 The Battle of Cambrai
25th November 1917 Bourlon Wood

1916

Mesopotamia and the Western Front 1916–1917

27

AFTER the fall of Kut, British military policy in Mesopotamia changed to the defensive, for it was impossible to spare further reinforcements for General Lake at the expense of the Western Front and Egypt. Fortunately, the advance of Russian columns through north-west Persia, with the dual role of co-operating with the Tigris Corps and protecting the flank of the Russian advance in the Caucasus, had the effect in the Middle East of distracting attention from the British reverse and no serious consequences resulted in India and Persia, as had been feared. Lake was accordingly directed to maintain a bold front on the Tigris, and assist the Russians by keeping the Turkish Army Corps busy around Kut and Sannaiyat. This was not in fact easy, for the Tigris Corps, lying astride the Tigris before the Turkish defences at Sannaiyat and Es Sinn, was in such poor shape that Lake was strongly tempted to withdraw in order to shorten his strained lines of communication and undertake some measure of rehabilitation. From a purely military angle, this was probably the correct action to take, but political considerations of prestige and support for the Russians eventually forbade it – and there was also the fact that the climate, bad enough at Sannaiyat, became progressively worse down-river to the Persian Gulf, so that it was really advisable to keep the unfortunate troops where they were,

1916

for their health's sake. The 14th Hussars, at Gomorrah camp, were fortunate in having to keep two squadrons in the saddle 'on observation duties', which entailed long rides every morning and evening, and to a certain degree took their minds off the hell into which their lives had degenerated on the Tigris, once the hot weather started. Apart from the intense heat and lack of air, against which there was no defence, they lived within a dense cloud of flies, which crawled all over the bodies of men and horses, so that from a little distance a squadron of cavalry looked as if they were wearing chain mail. Many of these flies inflicted painful bites, and it was impossible to eat without swallowing them, for they swarmed over every plateful of food and each morsel on the end of a fork. Flies, of course, are a curse which every army has to put up with in the field, even in Europe, and before the invention of detergents they were responsible for much of the disease to which soldiers are subject while on active service. They plagued the soldiers in the Dardanelles, Egypt and Palestine, but the flies in Mesopotamia were in a class by themselves and, without any doubt, had no equals anywhere in the world, either as to numbers or voracity. Besides the flies, there was the sand, hot enough to blister the flesh, and every so often whipped up into sandstorms which lasted for days, up-rooting tents and covering everything. It was impossible for anyone to put into his mouth a piece of break or meat which was not smothered in sand and black with flies.

Even under such conditions, there is always something that can be done to make life more tolerable, given time. The 14th, under the impression that they would remain at Gomorrah for the rest of the hot season, were just beginning to make certain improvements to their camp in the light of experience when, on the 19th May, 1916, the order came to mount and ride. As already mentioned, General Lake's instructions were to 'contain' the Turks before Kut, and prevent them from withdrawing troops to face the Russian advance through Persia. Kalil Pasha, the Turkish commander, had been observing the Russians' advance with much anxiety and now, being convinced from what he knew of the condition of the Tigris Corps that it would be unable to advance for the time being, he withdrew his cavalry and 2nd Division from the right bank of the Tigris and sent them to the Persian front, leaving three Divisions holding the Sannaiyat positions on the left bank and the line of the Hai River on the right bank. This was a much smaller force than the Tigris Corps, which in theory should therefore have been able to overwhelm the Sannaiyat positions. The health of the troops, however, and the lack of essential equipment, especially bridging material, made any large-scale operation out of the question and the commander, General Gorringe, was obliged to limit his activities to moving the cavalry and 3rd Division up the right bank to occupy the abandoned Turkish positions.

The first objective for the 3rd Division was the enemy position at Es Sinn which lay across the Tigris, and was linked by a pontoon bridge at Maqasis. The cavalry were ordered to seize and hold this bridge until the infantry arrived, although the infantry were seventeen miles nearer to it than the cavalry and, as the approach march had to be made by night, should, in the ordinary way, have been able to get there first. The heat was so terrible, however, even by night, and the infantry were in such poor shape, that the cavalry were able to get ahead by hard riding. The 14th had struck camp, saddled-up and were ready to march at sundown, but there was no transport for their camp equipment and stores which they were not allowed to leave. Some carts arrived after a while, and over two hours were spent in loading them, which was very hard work as the loads had to be rearranged to go into a smaller number of carts. The regiment finally left at 10 p.m. – two-and-a-half hours late, which was made up by cutting the night's halt down to two hours. As the business of off-saddling, pegging-down, and posting vedettes took, including the reverse procedure, nearly half this time, there was not much rest for anyone. No food had been issued since mid-day, when it had been too hot and the flies too bad for it to be possible to eat much of it. Each man, however, carried a tin of bully beef and a couple of biscuits. One man in six had a tin of plum and apple jam, and water-bottles were filled with brackish, evil-tasting water which was almost hot enough to shave with. There was thus no excuse for anyone fainting from lack of nourishment, but such a diet, in such a climate and under such conditions did nothing to raise the soldier's spirits, especially as he was perpetually tormented by a raging thirst which the contents of his water-bottle increased rather than diminished. But the cavalry were still better-off than the infantry, whose sufferings were unspeakable.

The march continued in daylight, when an aeroplane dropped a message saying that the Turks were evacuating Maqasis and towing their bridge away with a steamer, whose smoke could in fact be seen up-river from Maqasis near Abdul Hassan. The cavalry had now come up with the 3rd Indian Division, which was marching across the desert on a wide front and looking like a dense crowd of refugees, rather than a disciplined force going

1916

into action. By 1.30 p.m. both British and Indian soldiers had reached the end of their tether and the commander, General Keary, was obliged to halt, while the cavalry went on to Maqasis and watered. While they were doing so, shells came over from Kut and the left bank of the Tigris, but the watering was completed before the Brigade withdrew. The whole force bivouacked at Imam al Mansur, along the dry watercourse known as the Dujaila Depression, and during the night orders came for the cavalry to march at 3.30 a.m. and secure the Turkish pontoon bridge across the Shatt al Hai, below Kut.

Leading the Brigade, the 14th moved off at a trot, with 'B' Squadron in advance, followed by 'C', 'A' and 'D' at intervals of 300 yards. At first light, 'B' came under fire at 600 yards range, swung to the left and dismounted under cover of a low bank. The other squadrons aligned themselves to right and left as they came up, and fire was opened. Colonel Hewitt then sent 2nd-Lieut. C. G. Deakin's troop of 'D' Squadron up the right bank of the Tigris in an attempt to find the Turkish bridge over the Hai, and whether an advance on that flank would be possible. Handling his troop with considerable dash, Deakin arrived before the Turkish entrenchments at the junction of the Tigris and Hai, just below Kut. After dismounting and opening rapid fire, he was apparently just about to mount and make an attempt to gallop the opposition when he was stopped by the arrival of the rest of his squadron which went into action on his left.

The whole regiment was then in action, and Hewitt ordered 'A' and 'D' Squadrons forward, bringing the other two in behind them. When dismounted, however, the whole regiment could not put more than 150 rifles into the firing line, and as the Turks were entrenched in strength and determined to defend the bridge, the Brigade Commander decided against supporting the 14th and ordered them back. The retirement commenced at 8 a.m. under cover of 'C' Squadron and the machine-guns. Very fortunately, the Turks made no move other than to open a heavy but inaccurate shell-fire, for the regiment was at least three miles in advance of the rest of the Brigade, and could easily have been completely wiped out. Captain Mewburn and 2nd-Lieut. Deakin were both killed during the retirement. Fifteen men were wounded, eight horses killed and twenty-two wounded.

After watering at Atab, lower down the Hai, the 6th Cavalry Brigade went into camp at Sinn Abtar, behind the Dujaila Depression. Mewburn and Deakin were buried side by side in the same grave that evening, being the first officers to fall in the Mesopotamia Campaign. They were both very popular in the regiment and their loss was sadly felt. Deakin had joined at Meerut late in 1913, and had shown great promise, both as a soldier and sportsman.

After this affair, the cavalry were withdrawn and went into various camps along the Tigris; the 14th, with Brigade H.Q., being at Arab Village, a few miles east of Fallahiya. The 3rd Indian Division remained to face the Turks along the Hai, having occupied the former enemy positions at Maqasis, Es Sinn and Dujaila. There was nothing more that could be done for the time being, for the Tigris Corps was worn out from exhaustion and disease, and the supply organisation had almost completely broken down. The 14th remained at Arab Village until the end of the year, trying to exist on an unvarying ration of bully beef for the men and barley for the horses, with the condition of both men and horses steadily deteriorating from monotony and deadly heat. The only event of interest was the arrival of a *sotnia* of 150 Cossacks, with whom the British cavalrymen appear to have been much impressed. The Russian supply services, however, were just as chaotic as those of the British, with the inevitable result that General Baratov suffered a severe set-back in Persia and had to retire on Kermanshah. The danger of a Turkish invasion of Persia followed, and so disturbed the British and Indian governments that General Lake was pressed to make another offensive. It was quite impossible for him to agree, and he replied that he could only make an 'administrative offensive', by which he meant the reorganisation of his supply services, which he was indeed carrying out with vigour. He was, however, relieved by General Sir Stanley Maude, and left the field un-lamented by the troops who not unnaturally blamed him for their excessive sufferings, although this was not quite fair. Maude on the other hand was a commander well-known in the Tigris Corps for his able leadership of the 13th Division, and his appointment gave general satisfaction. He took over command with no illusions: 'It is a campaign,' he said, 'so full of difficulties and complications as can hardly be realised at home.'

By November, 1916, the general condition of the army in Mesopotamia had improved to an extent which could not have been credited a few months previously. The morale and fighting efficiency of the troops had quite recovered, and the administration was functioning with increasing smoothness. As a final touch before resuming the offensive, the C.-in-C. reorganised the Tigris Corps into the 1st Army Corps, of the 3rd and 7th Divisions, the 3rd Army Corps of the 13th and 14th Divisions, and a Cavalry Division. This last, commanded by Brigadier-General S. F.

1916

Crocker, consisted of the 6th and the newly-arrived 7th Cavalry Brigades. The 6th Cavalry Brigade now consisted of the 14th Hussars and the 21st and 22nd Cavalry of the Indian Army, with the 6th Machine-Gun Squadron, 2nd Field Troop, Sappers and Miners, Signal Troop and Field Ambulance all from the Indian Army. The faithful 'S' Battery, R.H.A., still belonged to the Brigade, providing, with the 14th, the only British element in the formation. The Brigade was temporarily commanded by Colonel Henslow of the 22nd Cavalry. Colonel Stephen of the 14th had been invalided and the real Brigadier was General Crocker, now commanding the Division. The 7th Cavalry Brigade consisted of the 13th Hussars, with the 13th Lancers and 14th Lancers, Indian Army, 'V' Battery, R.H.A., and the usual attached troops. The regiments were now all up to strength, and the total number of cavalry amounted to 3,500, although some of these were with the infantry divisions or on detachment.

The Turks, with three divisions, were still strongly entrenched before Sannaiyat and along the Shatt al Hai, where their right flank was somewhat in the air and watched only by mounted Arab irregulars. The opportunity thus offered for an outflanking movement against the Hai was not, of course, lost on General Maude, but he had to be careful about putting it into operation. It was necessary to inflict a defeat on the enemy, and not merely to get him on the run, as might well happen if his flank was threatened by superior forces. Maude had therefore to keep the Turks pinned down at Sannaiyat, while striking against the Hai. Making arrangements accordingly, he issued orders for an advance to the Hai on the 10th December.

The offensive opened on the 13th December, with a bombardment by all available artillery against the Turkish positions at Sannaiyat on the left bank, while the 1st Corps manoeuvred to give the impression of an impending attack. During the night, the Cavalry Division was to march and secure a crossing over the Hai at Basrugiyah, afterwards riding hard along the west bank towards the bridge at the Shumran bend, while the 3rd Corps advanced to the Hai.

The cavalry marched from Arab Village at 5.30 p.m. on the 13th and crossed the Hai at Basrugiyah at daybreak without opposition, for the Turks were not expecting any such move. The Division then rode towards Shumran, with the 7th Brigade leading and the 6th in echelon on its left rear. The 14th Hussars rode on the left rear of the Brigade. A few shots were exchanged with Arab and Turkish horsemen, but no serious opposition was met with until two miles from Shumran, when the Division came under rifle-fire and shells from a Turkish gun-boat on the Tigris. General Crocker took ground to his left, but hesitated to gallop the bridge until he knew more about the enemy dispositions, and Captain T. R. Bruce with 'B' Squadron was sent forward at the gallop to find out. This was a very unpleasant assignment, which might well have resulted in heavy casualties. Bruce formed up with two troops forward and one in support, extended to four paces and moved off at a high speed behind two advanced patrols. The enemy opened up with rifles and machine-guns, but he kept on until he got within 700 yards of the bridge and could pin-point its exact position, and could see the enemy on and around it. With a neat and well-executed movement, he then got his squadron about and safely out of range with two horses wounded as his only casualties. It was an interesting performance, amd one of many examples during the war which showed that cavalry, provided it could get up speed, was able to ride through fire which would have decimated infantry.

As by this time the 3rd Corps had arrived on the Hai, General Crocker withdrew the Cavalry Division into bivouac at Atab. By the time it unsaddled it had marched forty-five miles, with only one short halt at daybreak to water and feed. An aeroplane was sent out to drop bombs on the Shumran bridge, and reported that it was being dismantled and towed away. The bombs were dropped nevertheless and caused much damage and confusion. For the next three days, the Turks were left without any communication by bridge across the Tigris.

General Maude had very sound views on the use of cavalry, which had a considerable influence in the success of his operations. By employing their mobility to the full against an enemy whose own cavalry was extremely indifferent, he was able to surprise them and distract their attention from the movements of his infantry on this and many other occasions, so that in the Mesopotamia Campaign the cavalry, though not as spectacular in action as it used to be, regained much of its former importance in the field.

The operations by the 3rd Corps and Cavalry Division continued on the 15th December, and by the 18th had reached the line Imam al Mansur through Atab to Kala Haji Fahan. During these three days the Cavalry Division covered over ninety miles at a brisk pace, riding on the left flank and up the western bank of the Hai. South of Kut and up to the Dahra Bend in the Tigris, the country was a maze of Turkish trenches, some occupied, others not, but there were great stretches of open desert, watched by the Arab irregulars whom the cavalry were

1916

always having to gallop at and drive off. Near Kala Haji Fahan on the 15th, the 14th Hussars dismounted under fire and advanced on foot against entrenched Turks, losing two men killed and a number of men and horses wounded, while covering the advance of the 13th Infantry Division. This was the only dismounted action during the operations, which were brought to an end on the 20th December by continuous and heavy rain. For a few days the 3rd Corps was able to advance slowly and consolidate its gains, while the 1st Corps extended its front to include the right bank of the Tigris and link up with the 3rd Corps. The whole battlefront then gradually dissolved into a sea of liquid mud, under a downpour which lasted until the 6th January, 1917.

The position now was that the 1st Corps had two Brigades facing the Turks at Sannaiyat on the left bank of the Tigris, and had taken over the right bank from the 3rd Corps as far as Maqasis. The 3rd Corps line ran along the right bank from Maqasis, past Kut and south along the Hai to Atab. The main Turkish positions on the right bank were at the Khudhaira Bend above Kut, and the Hai salient south of the town. Once these had been taken, Kut could be recaptured and the Turks would have no option but to withdraw from Sannaiyat.

As soon as the rain ceased, General Maude ordered the 1st Corps to take the Khudhaira Bend, assisted by a demonstration against the Hai salient by the 3rd Corps and a raid by the cavalry against Bughaila, forty miles up the Tigris. These last two operations had to be halted owing to a thick mist, so that the assault at Khudhira had to be made without the assistance of any diversions, and it was not until the night of the 18th January that the Turks gave up and withdrew across the Tigris, by which time they had caused 1,639 casualties to the 3rd Indian Division. During the offensive the Cavalry Division carried out a raid on Hai Town, partly as a diversion and partly to find out what local supplies were available. The 14th stayed three days in the town; a strange experience, for business was being carried on as usual, with the shops all open and well-stocked and the thunder of the guns before Khudhira completely ignored. The Arab horsemen came down upon the rear of the Division as it withdrew, but the 14th, who were advanced guard, saw nothing of the skirmish, in which a number of Arabs ended their days on the points of the lances ably wielded by the 14th Lancers.

On the 23rd January, the 3rd Corps commenced the battle for the Hai salient. It had been intended that the Cavalry Division should make a diversion by crossing to the left bank of the Tigris and riding round the north of the Suwaikia Marsh – a very long ride which might have had interesting results. Heavy rain unfortunately made this exploit impracticable, and the cavalry had to confine their activities to the left flank of the 3rd Corps, upon which they rode as far as Bughaila, shelling the Turkish communications en route. On the 8th February, when the Turks in the Hai salient were making a last stand in a liquorice factory on the river bank below Kut (the same factory had also been defended by Townsend's men) the Cavalry Division made a dismounted holding attack against the enemy right flank at Shumran. The 14th Hussars attacked along the Massag Canal, and engaged the Turks at about 800 yards. The Turks abandoned the factory on the following day and became bottled up in the Dahra Bend, where they were mopped up on the 15th February by the 13th and 14th Divisions, which took over 2,000 prisoners and vast quantities of arms and supplies.

General Maude's next step was the capture of the Sannaiyat positions. His plan, as usual, included a diversionary movement, which in this case commenced with a raid across the Tigris at Maqasis to distract the enemy's attention both from Sannaiyat and Shumran, where the 3rd Corps was to cross the river in force. The operations started on the 22nd February and went more-or-less according to plan, although the fighting was most desperate, with both sides displaying the greatest valour and resolution. By the 24th February, the enemy was in full retreat along the left bank of the Tigris, and the 3rd Corps had the 14th Division across the river at Shumran. The Cavalry Division was then ordered to cross at Shumran, pass through the 14th Division and take up the pursuit.

The cavalry were awaiting the order and left their bivouacs on the right bank at 4.30 a.m., but they were held up at the bridge, which had broken down under the passage of the 14th Division and its guns. It was several hours before the cavalry could get across, by which time the 14th Division had been halted before the Dahra Ridge, which the Turks were holding in strength. After some manoeuvring, the cavalry got round the enemy left flank, whereupon he retired from the Dahra Ridge and took up a strong rearguard position with his right on the river. The cavalry dismounted and made a vigorous attack, but with only two batteries of horse artillery in support were unable to get the Turks on the move before nightfall. Patrols sent out during the night found them withdrawing, and the cavalry were ordered to ride in pursuit at daybreak.

On the morning of the 25th February, the Cavalry Division

1917

advanced on a wide front with the 7th Brigade on the right, slightly ahead of the 6th Brigade, which had its flank on the river. Air reconnaissance had found the Turkish main body at Bughaila and a rearguard of about 2,000 men with 20 guns at Imam Mahdi. General Maude was anxious for the cavalry to reach Bughaila by the evening, but he apparently gave orders for Imam Mahdi to be captured, which were taken too literally by the Divisional Commander.

The 14th Hussars rode with 'B' and 'C' Squadrons forward, in line with the 21st Cavalry on the right. All went well for a time, and numerous enemy stragglers were rounded up, but when the Brigade came under fire from Imam Mahdi some confusion developed from the Division being halted and ordered to attack the town, where the enemy were occupying a dry canal. The 21st Cavalry dismounted, and attacked with 'B' and 'C' Squadrons of the 14th on their left, while 'A' Squadron, with two squadrons of the 22nd Cavalry, commenced to work round the right. The 7th Brigade meanwhile, instead of being allowed to continue the pursuit towards Bughaila, was also dismounted and sent in on the right of the 6th Brigade, so that the whole Division became committed to an attack against an entrenched enemy of about equal numbers and a far greater strength in artillery. At about 2.30 p.m. General Crocker received a wireless signal from Maude that the cavalry were to march at once to Bughaila, and he therefore ordered the Cavalry Brigades to break off the action and concentrate. As they were both in close action dismounted, this was easier said than done, and it was not until nearly sunset that the Division was concentrated. By this time the men were very tired and the horses badly in need of water, so Crocker took the Division back to its transport, about twelve miles in rear.

The officers of the 14th Hussars were irritated and perplexed over this mishandling of the cavalry, which lost a great opportunity for cutting out the enemy rearguard and turning his retirement into a rout, in the manner in which they had been trained and practised. They were inclined to blame their Brigadier, and were delighted when Brigadier-General Holland-Pryor arrived to take over the 6th Cavalry Brigade that evening. It appears, however, that a misunderstanding between Generals Maude and Crocker was responsible for the error in tactics.

Maude's orders for the 26th were for the 3rd Corps to push on with all speed, while the Naval Flotilla of three gunboats steamed up-river and shelled the retreating Turks. The Cavalry Division was to do what it should have done on the 25th – move wide of the enemy's left flank and strike at Bughaila. The fire from the gun-boats broke up the Turkish columns, Bughaila was evacuated, and the Cavalry Division pressed on, overtaking the enemy's rearguard about eleven miles further north. The 6th Cavalry Brigade was sent against it, and found that it was already under fire from the Flotilla. 'S' Battery unlimbered and joined in, but when the Brigade advanced it was heavily shelled by the Flotilla, whose gunners had a very limited field of view and no clear understanding of the situation. Attempts to get in touch with the gunboats by heliograph failed, and the Brigade was obliged to halt and watch the demoralised Turks streaming away towards Aziziyah, with the gunboats chasing after them. Some Turkish cavalry which came up to cover the retreat were quickly put to flight by the Brigade which then closed in on the river, opened fire and collected several hundred prisoners.

After a cold, wet night in the desert without either food or covering, the Cavalry Division saddled-up at dawn to continue the pursuit, but was ordered to stand fast and did not get away until 10 a.m. A very odd feature of this phase of the Mesopotamia Campaign was that Maude would allow his formation commanders no freedom to act on their own initiative. They were only allowed to carry out the exact letter of his orders, and had to ask his permission before deviating from them an inch. This was because he himself was tied to the apron-strings of the War Cabinet, which had placed him under severe restrictions under which he was, strictly speaking, forbidden to advance beyond Kut, in order to save casualties, supplies, and the chance of a set-back such as had befallen Nixon. The chief sufferers from this hesitant policy were, of course, the cavalry for whom it was especially galling to be constantly checked from the rear when, after a long period of frustration, they had the opportunity at last to gallop forward.

During the advance on the 27th February, the 7th Cavalry Brigade turned off to take a Turkish hospital, while the 6th Brigade continued the pursuit, collecting hundreds of stragglers but meeting no opposition until it came under shell-fire three miles from Aziziyah, when the 22nd Cavalry dismounted and the 14th Hussars rode round to find the enemy flank. At this moment the Brigade Commander received orders to rejoin the Division, in accordance with further orders from Maude that the cavalry were to stand fast. Holland-Pryor did not pull out, however, but asked permission to stay where he was, and for his transport to be sent up to him. Rather surprisingly, both requests were eventually agreed to, and meanwhile he ordered the 14th, who had dismounted and gone into action with rifles and Hotchkiss guns, to

1917

concentrate along a low ridge and send out patrols. Although it was quite dark by this time, two mounted patrols were sent out under Captain Bridges and Lieut. Whadcoat, and rode fast towards the enemy watch-fires, the lighting of which, under the circumstances, pointed to a breakdown in the Turkish discipline. The patrols were able to locate the position of the two field-guns which had been shelling the 6th Brigade, and were also able to report that there were a considerable number of Turks defending Aziziyah, although Bridges declared that their discipline was so poor that he could have reconnoitred the whole Turkish camp without interference, had he felt it to be worthwhile. The two guns, and six others dug in by the river, were afterwards taken by Lieut. Macintyre's troop and brought into Divisional H.Q., when General Crocker presented two of the gun-plates to the regiment, which still has them in its possession.

On the 1st March, the Cavalry Division marched to Aziziyah, 51 miles from Baghdad, to find that the Turks had gone. On the following day, Maude received a telegram from the C.I.G.S. giving rather hesitant approval to an advance on Baghdad. Before moving on, Maude concentrated the 3rd Corps and the Naval Flotilla at Aziziyah, and brought up supplies. It was not, therefore, until the 5th March that the cavalry were ordered to advance, and by that time the Turks had reorganised themselves and put a strong force of all arms into position at Lajj, twenty miles up-river from Aziziyah, as a last attempt to bar the road to Baghdad.

The 5th March was a hot and blustery day, with clouds of dust blowing which greatly limited visibility both from the ground and the air. The reconnaissance aircraft were able to locate what they described as 'a small force' of Turks digging in at Lajj, so that the 7th Cavalry Brigade, which was leading the advance, was expecting opposition but went into action thinking that there was only about a battalion to deal with, whereas in fact the whole of the Turkish 51st Division was awaiting them, well dug-in. The Brigade made a spirited attack, during which the 13th Hussars carried out a gallant charge and cut down the enemy in fair numbers, but they lost 9 officers and 77 rank and file in the action. The 14th Hussars, who were leading the 6th Brigade, went into action dismounted and fought until dark, when the Brigadier recalled them and concentrated the Brigade. The 14th had six casualties in this affair, including Captain A. G. L. Astley, who was killed. The Turks, who thought that they had been attacked by an infantry division and two cavalry regiments, and were frightened of being out-flanked, retired during the night.

The cavalry attack may therefore be said to have been very successful, and it certainly saved the British and Indian infantry a great deal of hard fighting.

The Cavalry Division marched through Lajj on the following day, with officers' patrols out in front, one of which, led by Lieut. Moule, came within sight of the Diyala River and returned with forty-three prisoners and information that the Turks were crossing the Diyala. The 6th Cavalry Brigade reached and reconnoitred the Diyala River on the following day, coming within sight of the mosques and minarets of Baghdad, which raised their spirits considerably.

When the 13th Infantry Division arrived on the Diyala it met strong enemy resistance and heavy fighting developed. While it was going on, a pontoon bridge was constructed over the Tigris at Bawi and on the night of the 8th March General Maude sent the Cavalry Division across it with orders to ride for Baghdad, followed by the 1st Corps. Progress was slow as the country was very difficult, being intersected by deep nullahs and dry canals, while a heavy dust-storm caused the cavalry to lose direction for a while. However, shortly after dawn on the 9th, the 6th Cavalry Brigade found the enemy occupying a line of sandhills to the front, while officers' patrols reported lines of trenches behind them. The Turks were apparently too busy to notice the approach of the cavalry, and Holland-Pryor decided to gallop them, which would almost certainly have stampeded the lot. Unfortunately he was prevented by the Divisional Commander, who preferred to move the Division west, to locate the enemy's right flank. Another fine opportunity was thus lost by the cavalry, which, had it been correctly handled, could have saved the infantry over 700 casualties. The 7th Division was coming up just as the cavalry were moving west, and was informed of the situation and the cavalry's intention by heliograph. In the resultant engagement the infantry attack was halted after hard fighting while the cavalry, after finding the enemy flank at Shawa Khan and firing a few shots at it from the horse artillery batteries, were withdrawn back to the Tigris to water. The horses had been without water for twenty-four hours and were feeling it badly; but a horse does not seize up when he runs dry, like a motor engine, but can go on as long as a man can without water. It is not clear why General Crocker should have pulled out in this manner at a critical moment, for if the horses really were too done-up to go on, he could have engaged dismounted, rather than leave the infantry in the lurch.

The appearance of the cavalry on their flank did, however,

1917

cause the Turks to withdraw during the night to their main position at Um al Tubal, where the 7th Division, suffering very much from the extreme heat, scorching wind and dust, attacked again on the morning of the 10th, at the same time as the 13th Division was forcing the passage of the Diyala on the left bank. After putting up a stiff resistance during the day, the Turks again withdrew by night and retired up-river. The Union Jack was hoisted over the citadel in Baghdad by the Buffs on the morning of the 11th March, and General Maude entered the city that afternoon, after ordering the Cavalry Division to march on Khazimain, eight miles to the north. Leading the 6th Cavalry Brigade, the 14th Hussars halted before Khazimain at 3.30 p.m., while Colonel Hewitt rode into the town with a party from the regiment to receive its surrender. He returned with the sheik and leading townsmen, several released British prisoners and a hundred Turkish prisoners. The Brigade then went into bivouac on the outskirts of the town.

Baghdad was at the centre of several converging routes from the north, covering which there were no natural defensive positions. As there seemed every likelihood that the Turks would attempt to recover the city, General Maude had therefore to push out beyond it, and by the end of March, after hard fighting in intense heat, he had secured the line Sharaban – Mushaidi – Faluja, and was able to cover the approaches along the rivers Diyala, Tigris and Euphrates. The 6th Cavalry Brigade and the 3rd Infantry Division were left to hold Baghdad at the start of these operations, but the 7th Cavalry Brigade went out after resting its horses, and while reconnoitring along the Khalis Canal on the 26th March, found the Turks in strength around Delli Abbas and after a lively engagement withdrew along the road to Baqubah, where it was joined by the 6th Cavalry Brigade. The whole Division, now commanded by Major-General L. C. Jones, then bivouacked about six miles from the enemy positions.

General Maude had received intelligence that the enemy was about to make an attack through Delli Abbas against his advanced positions on the Tigris left bank and concentrated the 13th Division to meet it, at the same time ordering the cavalry to 'retard, and operate vigorously against, any advance along Lambarak-Muhurar road'. On the 27th March, the 6th Cavalry Brigade was sent to reconnoitre between the Diyala and the Khalis Canal, and was attacked soon after mid-day by 2,000 Turks with five guns. The Brigade was halted at the time, with the 21st and 22nd Cavalry reconnoitring forward, while 'B' and

'C' Squadrons of the 14th were dismounted and holding positions on either side of the Delli Abbas road, with mounted patrols forward. By working towards the Dialah River on the right and the Khalis Canal on the left, the two Indian Cavalry Regiments had left the front open, so that when the Turks appeared and advanced with great determination, 'B' and 'C' Squadrons became heavily engaged. 'S' Battery R.H.A. came into action on the right and was soon knocking over large numbers of Turks with well-aimed salvoes of shrapnel. Nevertheless the Turks still came on fast, in the face of the rifles and Hotchkiss guns of the 14th, while the 21st and 22nd withdrew along the flanks. Once they were clear, 'B' and 'C' Squadrons began to be enfiladed and had to get their horses and gallop to a position in rear. This was then held by 'B' and 'C' Squadrons, with two squadrons of the 21st, supported by 'A' and 'D' Squadrons, one squadron of the 22nd, and two machine-gun troops. The Turks could make no further headway against this arrangement, and their attack came to a halt. During the night the 6th Brigade was withdrawn to a position prepared by the 7th Brigade, but as the enemy did not appear next morning, the 7th Brigade rode out to find him and pushed him back all day. Thus ended a very satisfactory engagement for the cavalry, especially as their casualties did not amount to more than ten in killed and wounded, including the Brigade-Major of the 6th Brigade – the second officer holding this appointment to be killed in action during the campaign. The action, in which the 14th played so conspicuous a part, was a highly important one and had a considerable influence on the course of the operations dealing with the Turkish counter-offensive.

During the following days, and up to the middle of April, the Turks continued their attempts to drive the British forces from the left bank of the Tigris. The Cavalry Division, with the 13th Infantry Division coming up on its left flank, remained between the Diyala and the Khalis Canal, fighting numerous delaying actions over difficult ground much of which was intersected by dry irrigation ditches. The 21st and 22nd Cavalry temporarily left the 6th Brigade on reconnaissance duties, so that the Brigade consisted only of the 14th Hussars, 'S' Battery and a machine-gun troop. Riding up the Khalis Canal on a two-squadron front, with patrols well out in front and 'S' Battery in close attendance, the Brigade – or regiment, rather – watched for opportunities of falling on any Turks marching south through Delli Abbas. Such Turks, however, knew that the Cavalry Division was in the area and consequently advanced with some caution and without

1917

exposing themselves to a mounted attack. The cavalry had therefore to revert to the dragoon method of combat, although in this case it entailed some very hard riding and bore little resemblance to the practices of mounted infantry. The usual pace was the trot, with the squadron leaders riding well ahead and doing their own scouting. When the enemy were sighted the squadron leader picked out some suitable position from which to engage them and signalled the gallop – swinging the right arm round in a circle. 'S' Battery of course, also had an officer forward, and it too went into action at a gallop when a target appeared. The enemy was usually engaged by rifles, machine guns and horse artillery at a range of 800 yards, and there is no doubt that the Turks received a severe drubbing at the hands of the 14th on several occasions at this time.

When the infantry began to go into action about the 12th April the Turks, after a brief attempt to stand west of Delli Abbas, commenced a withdrawal in which they soon outdistanced the British infantry, while the cavalry, attempting to get across their line of retreat, was obliged to pull out and ride for the Tigris owing to lack of water. On the 23rd April, Samarra was captured, and the Turks withdrew to Tikrit. On the 29th, the 14th Hussars were ordered back to Baghdad and, when taking leave of General Holland-Pryor, were informed that they were 'the best regiment he had ever seen'.

It transpired that the regiment had been recalled in order to join a small punitive expedition on the Euphrates. It consisted of a battalion of the Dorsets, two Gurkha battalions and a field battery; and its object was to exact retribution from the Arabs for the murder of a British officer. The 14th had one man killed on this expedition, during which the two squadrons carried out a reconnaissance as far as Musaiyib. The regiment returned to Baghdad on the 10th May and rejoined the Cavalry Division which had gone into summer camp at Chaldari, seven miles up the left bank of the Tigris.

The advance to Baghdad, now successfully accomplished, had been undertaken largely in order to assist the Russian advance on Mosul. This had now to be dismissed from Maude's calculations, for the Bolshevik revolution had broken out and the Russian armies in the field were left without either money or supplies. It soon became apparent that they could no longer be relied upon as allies, and they gradually disintegrated, leaving the British to play a lone hand on the Tigris. The situation might well have become very serious, but for Allenby's victories in Egypt and Palestine, which attracted to the Middle East Turkish reinforcements originally destined for Mesopotamia. Allenby's and Maude's successes in conjunction also kept up morale in India, by renewing confidence in an eventual British victory in the war.

The Palestine and Mesopotamia Campaigns still, however, remained 'side-shows' whose principal value lay in the maintenance of the unity and sense of purpose of the British Empire. Only in Europe could Germany be decisively defeated, and on the Western Front the situation was still grim. At the end of 1916, General Joffre was succeeded in command of the French armies by General Nivelle, a good-looking extrovert whose self-confident powers of expression won the heart of Lloyd George, who was constantly at variance with the British Generals. Nivelle produced a plan in which a French attack in Champagne would coincide with a British offensive on either side of Arras with the object of eliminating the German salient on the Somme. Haig, who had not been consulted in the matter, was ordered to co-operate, even to the extent of acting under Nivelle's general direction.

The British attack at Arras was preceded by the German withdrawal to the Hindenburg Line, a practically impregnable series of fortifications which the enemy, like Wellington and his Lines of Torres Vedras and Marshal Villars' *non plus ultra* Lines of 1711, had constructed as a last defence. The British Army, which now had a million men in the field, followed up across the dreary wastes which thousands had died in defending, but there was no immediate enemy withdrawal at Arras, where, after a week's bombardment by nearly three thousand guns, the 1st and 3rd Armies advanced on the 9th April, 1917. The attack went well, and by the 14th April, Vimy Ridge and the Scarpe Valley had been taken, with 13,000 prisoners and 200 guns.

During the preliminary bombardment, the Cavalry Corps assembled south of Arras, ready to move eastwards along the Scarpe and exploit a breakthrough in the neighbourhood of Monchy-le-Preux. It was very cold, with pouring rain turning occasionally to sleet, and the cavalry had no cover, except for a few open cattle-sheds in which some of the luckier horses found shelter. The spirits of both men and horses were far from lively, for after so many previous disappointments no one expected to get his sword through a 'Hun'. When, however, the cavalry were called forward and rode through Ronville to Telegraph Hill west of Tilloy, which the infantry had taken that morning *en passant*, it began to look as if a chance was coming at last, and the cavalrymen started to prick forward with great eagerness. This feeling of exultation did not last long, for the sleet turned to snow and the 'cavalry tracks' disappeared. Horses fell into shell-holes and often could

1917

not get out again while the enemy, becoming aware of the cavalry advance, started shelling, which caused a number of casualties. The cavalry were then withdrawn, and spent another night in the snow, losing many horses from exposure, but they saddled-up again at noon on the 10th April and the 2nd and 3rd Cavalry Divisions went forward to Monchy, following a premature report that it had been taken. The infantry, in fact, were held up on its outskirts, but the town was galloped by the 8th Cavalry Brigade. The 20th Hussars, who had just come through Tilloy les Mouflains at the trot with the rest of the 5th Brigade, formed line of troop columns with 'B' and 'C' Squadrons forward and 'A' in support. The Greys came up on the right, and with the 12th Lancers in support the Brigade advanced at a gallop on the left of the 3rd Brigade. The snow fell so heavily that no one could see anything ('we merely followed the Colonel') and the enemy stopped shelling, for he could not see anything either. As the ground was covered in trenches, shell-holes, and broken-down barbed-wire fences, its negotiation at high speed in a thick snow-storm in this manner was very surprising, although it has been proved on many campaigns that horses galloping in line will take obstacles without flinching which they would never dream of facing in cold blood. The 20th Hussars were brought to a halt at last when they rode into a maze of barbed-wire and had to cut themselves out with wire-cutters. The snow ceasing at that moment, they were able to see that they had in fact reached the ridge which was their objective. The gallop had caused the enemy to abandon his forward positions and retire to his main line of defences. It had also greatly assisted the exhausted infantry and was instrumental in the capture of the key position of Monchy-le-Preux. There was, however, no gap to exploit, although the gallant infantry had broken into the Hindenburg Line at some points.

The enemy had already begun to launch heavy counter-attacks, and as one was expected at any moment, the cavalry stayed where they were. The 20th Hussars spent the night without rations or forage, standing in snow and mud a foot deep, with one man holding two horses while the other man rested in a shell-hole. Shelling went on intermittently the whole night. Patrols were sent out to gain touch with the infantry, and in case of a counter-attack the line was strengthened by Hotchkiss and machine-guns sent forward from Brigade. The shelling continued in the morning, and the Brigade was eventually withdrawn some distance. Finally, as it was evident that no breakthrough could be expected, the Cavalry Corps was taken out of action about the 20th April.

1917

The casualties suffered by the 20th Hussars at Arras amounted to 2 officers and 5 men wounded; one man died and 37 horses were killed or died of exposure.

Nivelle's offensive on the Aisne was launched on the 16th April. Like the British effort at Arras it had considerable initial success, but was soon brought to a standstill after the French had suffered such heavy casualties that the discipline broke down in many divisions, which lapsed into a state of mutiny. Nivelle was replaced by General Pétain and, while with great difficulty he was restoring discipline, the British Army had to take over the whole brunt on the Western Front, and continue the offensive at great cost. A very difficult and dangerous situation was saved by a successful attack on the Messines Ridge during June by General Plumer's 2nd Army, which ended in the elimination of the German salient south of Ypres. The enemy was badly shattered by these massive blows, which were succeeded by the Third Battle of Ypres, or Passchendaele as it is usually called, which raged from August until November. By that time the British Army had succeeded in pinning down the Germans and given the French time to recover their morale; but the cost was nearly 400,000 casualties.

Messines and Passchendaele were defensive battles fought for limited objectives, and with no 'break-through' envisaged. The cavalry were not therefore called forward to wait for 'the gap', and spent most of the summer relieving infantry units in the trenches. The Cavalry Corps was, however, called forward mounted when Sir Julian Byng's 3rd Army launched an attack before Cambrai on the 20th November, hoping to break the Hindenburg Line with the help of tanks. About 400 tanks advanced on that day, without any preliminary bombardment, followed by six infantry divisions with two in reserve, on a six-mile front. All went well, and the first and second offensive systems of the Hindenburg Line were over-run, but the key positions round Bourlon Wood and village were taken only after many days of desperate fighting. By the 29th November, 10,500 prisoners and 142 guns had been captured and a large gap had been made in the Hindenburg Line to a depth of five miles. The cavalry rode up to the Scheldt Canal, intending to cross by the bridge at Masnieres, but this was too badly damaged for cavalry to use, and the whole countryside was in such a mad shambles of broken wire, blown-in trenches, shell-holes, overturned guns and wagons, rubble from emplacements, felled trees and corpses, that it was scarcely possible to ride over it. The Canadian Cavalry Brigade and one or two British regiments had some gallops, but at heavy cost. The 20th

1917

Hussars and most of the others turned back from Masnieres, dismounted and lent a hand on foot.

On the 25th November, the 20th Hussars provided a company of five officers and 218 rank and file for a battalion found by the 5th Cavalry Brigade, which went into trenches along the north side of Bourlon Wood, where there was heavy fighting in which Captain Silvertop, who commanded the 20th Hussar Company, Lieutenant C. N. S. Woolf and five men were killed, and an officer and 24 rank and file wounded. Then, on the 30th November, the Germans launched a heavy counter-attack and broke through between Masnieres and Epéhy. The 5th Cavalry Brigade, which was having baths at Fins, was turned out and the 20th Hussars, who were the first into the saddle, rode off to the sound of the guns without waiting for the others. Near Gouzeaucourt the regiment dismounted and went into action in company with the 470th Company of the Royal Engineers attacking over a distance of 1,000 yards and 'killing the Germans encountered en route'. The Coldstream Guards joined in on the left, and Hodson's Horse of the Indian Army on the right. Major Little, second-in-command of the 20th, later collected the remnants of three infantry companies, all of whose officers had become casualties, and led them forward to fill the gap between the regiment and the Coldstreams. Some very brisk fighting ended in the capture of Gouzeaucourt, when the regiment came out of action. Major Little got a bar to his D.S.O. for his services in this affair.

The Battle of Cambrai ended on the 7th December with the evacuation of the Bourlon ridge for possession of which a vast quantity of blood had been shed. On balance, however, the general result went in favour of the British, although it was far short of what had been hoped for. On the 18th December the dismounted company of the 20th, now led by Captain Sanford, went into the trenches at Cote Wood, and remained there until the end of January. The rest of the regiment were billeted near Amiens.

British cavalry awaiting orders to move forward during operations in the Arras area, 26 May 1917. Opportunities for cavalry to operate in the mounted role were few and far between on the Western front. The 20th Hussars were frequently employed as infantry.

Top The 14th Hussars in action against the Turks at Ramadi. *Bottom* Farrier-Sergeant Hayward rescuing Lieutenant Hamer in a Turkish counter-attack. Sketches by Pte. M. Baggott of the 14th.

September 1917 The action at Ramadi
November 1917 Tikrit
December 1917 The Jabal Hamrin
21st March to 15th July 1918 The last German offensive
8th August to 11th November 1918 The last Allied offensive

1917

The Last Twelve Months

28

In contrast to the never-ending turmoil on the Western Front, Mesopotamia during the last months of 1917 had become almost a haven of peace – though certainly not of comfort. Although, owing to the disintegration of the Russian Armies, General Maude had been baulked of a decisive victory, he had hit the Turks so hard that they were incapable of mounting any offensive, while he himself was unable to make any further advance for a variety of reasons, principally because he lacked the resources for lengthening his lines of communications.

The remnants of the Turkish army on the Tigris lay between the Jabal Hamrin mountains north of the Diyala River and Samarra, where an advanced detachment covered the main body of their 18th Corps at Tikrit. On the Euphrates, the Turks had a detachment of about 1,000 all-arms at Ramadi, some sixty miles west of Baghdad. Very inadvisedly, Maude sent the 7th Infantry Brigade to drive away this detachment in the middle of July, when the heat was so intense that any metal object – or even a tumbler – burnt the hand if picked up inside a tent, and the desert sand would scorch the soldier's feet inside his thick ammunition boots. The 7th Infantry Brigade was defeated by this heat and obliged to retire, giving the Turks an opportunity for reinforcing Ramadi, through which they had been obtaining supplies sent up

1917

by the Arab tribes along the lower Euphrates, and which served them as an advanced base for projected operations against the British left flank.

As soon as the weather cooled in September, Maude sent another force against Ramadi, consisting of the 50th Brigade Group at Faluja, with the 6th Cavalry Brigade and most of the 15th Division from Baghdad. The strength of the Turkish garrison was correctly estimated at 100 cavalry, 3,500 infantry and 10 guns, with a few hundred Arab irregulars. The main enemy positions ran along the Euphrates Valley Canal east of Ramadi, and across the southern front of the town to the Aziziyah Canal. General Sir H. Brooking, who commanded the British force, planned to mislead the enemy into believing that his attack would be made along the Euphrates, while in fact he intended to put it in from the south, between the two canals, and sent the 6th Cavalry Brigade to the high ground west of Ramadi and across the Turkish lines of retreat.

In the 6th Cavalry Brigade, 'S' Battery had been replaced by 'V' Battery, R.H.A., but otherwise it still consisted of the 14th Hussars, 21st and 22nd Cavalry. The Brigade arrived at Madhij, on the right bank of the Euphrates, on the 28th September. A pontoon bridge had been laid across the river at this point with the object of making the enemy think that the cavalry were going to cross and come up the left bank but instead, after watering, the Brigade moved south-westerly at a brisk pace. The infantry had meanwhile commenced their attack, and by the time the cavalry reached the Euphrates Valley Canal the dam, which was the only crossing-place, was in their hands, so that the cavalry were able to cross immediately and continue towards the Aziziyah Canal. This was dry except for a few pools of brackish water, which the horses had to make the best of, while ramps were being cut in the banks to take the guns and transport. After crossing, the Brigade trotted on south of the high ground beyond Ramadi, and eventually struck the Hit-Ramadi road without the approach march having been observed by the enemy.

After chasing fifty enemy horse back into Ramadi, the 14th Hussars dismounted and took up a position across the Hit road, with two squadrons of the 21st Cavalry, the Machine-Gun Squadron and the 22nd Cavalry on their right, and two squadrons of the 21st watching the rear in case of the arrival of enemy reinforcements. Every possible security precaution was taken, with vedettes posted on all sides, and mounted patrols out continuously.

In the evening, General Holland-Pryor received a message

from General Brooking to the effect that the infantry had driven the Turks back on to the river, and that it was essential the cavalry should prevent them from doing a bolt along the Hit road. A patrol under Lieut. Moule (known in the regiment as 'Old man Moule') reported in the middle of the night that the Turks were coming. Shortly after, he rode in himself and said that he had been shot at, but the Colonel sent him out again with instructions to keep in touch with the enemy. This he did, and finally brought his patrol in a bare 150 yards ahead of the Turks, who could be clearly seen advancing over the desert in the bright moonlight.

The fire opened by the 14th Hussars spread along the whole front of the Brigade, with 'V' Battery and the machine-guns joining in. The Turks were easy targets, and their advance was quickly halted with heavy losses, but as the moon dropped down to the west behind the 14th, they in their turn became easy marks and suffered an increasing number of casualties. The line held by the Brigade was so long for its strength that every man was in the front and there were no reserves, so that the 14th were obliged to pull out a troop which was guarding the left flank on the river, in order to strengthen the centre. This let the Turks through on the flank, so that not only was the regiment enfiladed, but a hundred or two of the enemy got away up the river bank. At this time Colonel Hewitt was shot in the lower part of the back, with the bullet coming out of his chest. Many a soldier has survived worse wounds, but there was small hope of doing so in the Mesopotamia Campaign, where the country was squalid and full of disease, and the medical arrangements were scandalously inadequate. The wounded had to be taken fifty miles across the desert to Faluja, where an apology for a hospital had been arranged, travelling in springless carts which had to cross extremely rough country, including the two canals, and there were no pain-killing drugs available. After great suffering, which he bore with patience and courage, Hewitt died in the hospital shortly after arriving on the 31st September. A very popular and respected commanding-officer, he was given a military funeral attended by the whole regiment and representatives from the formations and units of the force. His loss was sadly felt by all ranks, and when the regiment paraded after return to camp, to receive a congratulatory address by the Divisional Commander, Major-General Jones, the late Colonel's charger, with empty saddle, was paraded in his usual place in front of the line.

When Colonel Hewitt fell at Ramadi, command of the regiment was taken over by Captain J. D. F. Woodhouse. Shortly afterwards the Turks gave up their attempt to break out and

1917

returned to the town. At daybreak there was no enemy in sight and Captain Bridges, who arrived with 'C' Squadron from the right of the line, took over from Woodhouse. The 21st Cavalry were then ordered up-river in pursuit of those Turks believed to have escaped. The 14th Hussars followed after burying the dead, and the two regiments rode hard for several miles, but turned back without having seen any enemy. At 11 a.m. on that morning, the 30th September, the Turkish garrison of Ramadi surrendered, and 3,545 prisoners fell into British hands, with 13 guns and a great quantity of arms, ammunition and supplies.

The casualties suffered by the 14th Hussars at Ramadi amounted to 2 officers and 9 rank and file killed; 1 officer and 15 rank and file wounded, out of a strength of 170 all-ranks engaged. The regiment was specially mentioned in General Brooking's report for its fine work in the action, and 'Old man Moule' was awarded the Military Cross for his patrol-work, on which his reports of the strength and dispositions of the enemy were so accurate as to contribute a great deal to the success of the operations, besides saving the 6th Cavalry Brigade many casualties.

Following the Battle of Ramadi, the Turks were driven from the Jabal Hamrin north of the Diyala, but the 6th Cavalry Brigade was not employed in this operation. During it, the Turkish 18th Corps advanced down the Tigris towards Samarra, in the hope of easing the situation of their friends in the Jabal Hamrin but, as soon as that position was in his hands, General Maude attacked the 18th Corps with his own 1st Corps and the Cavalry Division. The cavalry had a very hard approach march, moving always by night in the hope of taking the Turks by surprise, as they had done at Ramadi. For the same reason, they kept well clear of the Tigris; but as that river provided the only water-supply in the country at that time of year, they were obliged to take the horses to it each day. This meant that they were almost certainly spotted by enemy aircraft, and also that the cavalrymen got very little rest for days on end, being on the line of march all night and having to look after their horses for most of each day. Battle was eventually joined before Tikrit on the 5th November, when the Cavalry Division attempted to get across the enemy's line of retreat and repeat the Ramadi tactics on a larger scale. There was some idea at first that the whole division should charge the Turkish flank *en masse*, while the infantry attacked in front, but it was abandoned when mounted patrols discovered that the enemy's flank was well-protected by guns and machine-guns. Cavalry leaders were understandably hesitant about charging machine-guns, although experience seemed to show that these weapons were not nearly as effective against cavalry as they were against the slow-moving infantry. On the Western Front, it was the barbed-wire, deep entrenchments and messed-up ground which foiled the cavalry – not machine-guns. The idea of a massed charge at Tikrit was probably not as lunatic as it seemed, and might well have been successful. More sober counsels prevailed, however, and the 14th Hussars fought at Tikrit as dragoons. The mounted patrols of the regiment were again in evidence, and it is interesting that Lieut. Whidborne was able to lead his patrol close enough to be able to report the exact locations of the enemy machine-gun emplacements, although he was under heavy fire and had his charger wounded.

After the capture of Tikrit, which the Turks evacuated, it was garrisoned as a forward position, and the bulk of the 1st Corps withdrew to Samarra. The Turks, beaten and demoralised, had now been driven far from Baghdad, and the British forces, full of spirit and confidence, were ready to push on to Mosul whenever ordered. Unfortunately, General Maude was not fated to crown his immense achievements by directing the operations which led to final victory. He died of cholera on the 15th November leaving to his successor, Lieut.-General Sir W. R. Marshall, an army which was unrecognisable as the one which he had originally taken over, and a military situation which was difficult to improve upon.

On taking over command, Marshall received a directive from the C.I.G.S. which in effect limited his activities to the maintenance of an active defence, for in view of the general situation, the War Cabinet could not contemplate any large-scale operations in Mesopotamia, resulting in further calls upon its already overstrained resources of men, money and material. The only enemy still within reach of a limited offensive by Marshall were on the Diyala above Mansuriya, and holding the passes over the Jabal Hamrin. He decided to send the 3rd Corps to drive in the enemy's covering positions, which extended from Suhaniya along the Diyala above Abu Zenabil, and advance up the Narin River to attack their main positions about Qara Tepe, in concert with a flanking movement by the Cavalry Division up the Shatt al Adhaim and across the enemy's rear towards Kifri.

The infantry attack, skilfully conducted with superior numbers, was highly successful and Qara Tepe was captured at slight cost. The advance of the Cavalry Division was unfortunately spotted by Turkish aircraft, and its patrols reconnoitring the passes over the Jabal Hamrin towards Kifri found that they were too strongly defended for cavalry to be able to force, other than by

1918

a laborious dismounted assault. This was not in accordance with Marshall's plan, and he therefore withdrew the Cavalry Division, whose threat to the enemy flank had at least greatly assisted the main operations. The patrols sent out by the 14th Hussars, particularly those led by Lieutenants R. A. G. Woodhouse and P. Cropper, were, as usual, efficient and adventurous, securing useful and accurate information at considerable risk. The regiment, which had a sergeant killed and two men wounded before the Jabal Hamrin, spent quite an enjoyable Christmas at Sadiyeh, where many of the officers went pigsticking. The largest boar killed stood 38 inches – a very sizeable pig and well up to Indian standards. So 1917 came to an end and 1918 began, the last year of the war.

The beginning of 1918 was a time of hope and cheer in the East, where the successes on the Tigris had been more than matched by those in Palestine, for Allenby had entered Jerusalem on the 11th December. But in the West the outlook was still grim, for the collapse of Russia had enabled Germany to transfer vast numbers of seasoned soldiers to the Western Front, where she made no secret of the fact that she was preparing for a devastating and decisive blow.

There was no pigsticking for the 20th Hussars at Cartigny. Even had there been pig available the horses would not have thought much of the idea, for they were having to spend the winter in the open on far from generous rations and their condition was steadily worsening. This did not worry the High Command for whom men, not horses, were the chief anxiety. In the testing time which was fast approaching there was no longer any thought of employing cavalry as such. Every man who could fire a rifle – and even those who had not previously done so, of whom there were quite a number employed on various jobs on the Western Front – was going to be required in the front line on his own feet.

Early in February the mounted part of the Cavalry Corps was moved up to the area between Peronne and the Oise. Here it was behind the 5th Army, which had relieved the French west of the Oise, and which was holding a length of front too long for its strength and in inferior positions. As the Oise was the boundary between the British and French armies, the 5th Army was obviously in a very vulnerable position, and the Cavalry Corps was intended as a mobile reserve ready to plug such gaps as must inevitably occur. Preparations for meeting a large-scale offensive were intense, and when not reconnoitring routes to the front and planning counter-attacks, the cavalry put in a great deal of very

1918

hard work on the defences – especially a dismounted company of the 20th under Captain Hall, 224 strong, which spent a week constructing trenches and wire entanglements north-west of St Quentin.

Strong representations were being made by Sir Douglas Haig for all available reinforcements in the United Kingdom to be sent to him immediately, for the French Army had still not recovered its morale and it was likely to be the British who were going to have to play the major part in stemming the forthcoming onslaught. But although Haig made a personal visit to London he could not get the Prime Minister, Lloyd George, to authorise the dispatch of the 400,000 soldiers still at home. Lloyd George did not want a repetition of the casualties of the Somme, which he attributed to Haig's prodigality with soldiers' lives whenever he had plenty at his disposal, and refused to recognise the fact that the sacrifice had had to be made in order to prevent the collapse of the French Army. After the enemy offensive had been launched and Haig's lack of reserves really began to be felt, the Prime Minister managed to some extent to evade the consequences to himself arising out of his refusal to support the Commander-in-Chief by getting him placed under the 'direction' of General Foch, an arrangement by which the Frenchman would enjoy the credit for any future successes, while Haig would continue to accept the responsibility for the casualties and set-backs.

On the 14th March, the 5th Cavalry Brigade dismounted practically everyone except the horse-holders and formed itself into a 'Dismounted Brigade Group', which was more-or-less the same strength as an infantry battalion. The 5th Dismounted Brigade, as it was now called, joined the 43rd Infantry Brigade in the line before Montescourt. The general warning 'Prepare for attack', was issued on the 20th March, and in the early morning of the 21st the roar of 6,000 German guns opened the long-awaited offensive. The blow was delivered along the front of the 3rd and 5th Armies, and after several break-throughs had been made around St Quentin, the 5th Army Commander, Sir Hubert Gough, ordered a general retirement to the line of the Somme. Thereafter the situation of the 5th Army became more and more chaotic, so that to follow the fortunes of any particular unit is practically impossible – they were all mixed-up but never demoralised, each man fighting for himself under the orders of any officer who was there to take the lead.

At the beginning of the offensive the 5th Dismounted Brigade covered the withdrawal of the 43rd and 54th Infantry Brigades across the Crozat Canal, and thereafter joined the 3rd Dis-

399

mounted Brigade under the command of its G.O.C., Bell Smythe. The combined force was under the orders of the 14th Infantry Division, to which it gave support during the desperate fighting which followed. On the 23rd March the 20th Hussars and half the Greys found themselves holding a railway embankment south of Jussy under the orders of the 9th Scottish Rifles, and when the battle was at its height with the enemy breaking through on the flanks, Major Little was sent off to collect stragglers and raise his own unit, afterwards taking up a position along the Faillouel-Flavy Le Martel road. He collected quite a large number of leaderless but great-hearted men and, after being joined by squadrons of the Greys and 12th Lancers, put in a gallant counter-attack which he had to halt when vast numbers of Germans got round his left, but he stood his ground for over two hours after refusing his left flank in the old Wellingtonian tradition.

Major Little's was but one among dozens of similar efforts made to stem the advance of hundreds of thousands of well-trained and determined Germans. The British soldier, officer and man, is at his best under such conditions, which seem to bring out his finest qualities. Troops of the French 3rd Army began to arrive on the battlefield, and often became mixed-up with British units and formations but there is no doubt that they were not half as good as the British at this sort of improvised fighting. Outnumbered by more than three to one, the 5th Army was steadily forced back, fighting for every yard of ground and on the lookout for every opportunity for staging local counter-attacks. When the cavalry fell back they at length reached their horses and began to get mounted again, with the object of forming mobile reserves. Regiments were still very mixed-up, and there was no question of finding one's own horse and riding under one's own commanding officer. On the 24th March for example, two temporary cavalry regiments were formed at Beaurains, one out of the 4th Cavalry Brigade and the other, commanded by Major Little, from the 5th Cavalry Brigade. Both regiments were under the command of Lieut.-Colonel Cook of the 20th, and were known as 'Cook's Detachment'. Innumerable other temporary formations of both cavalry and infantry were being raised in a similar manner out of leaderless sub-units, stragglers and administrative staffs, and known by the names of their commanders. Their morale and discipline was as high as ever and in fighting back the hordes of advancing 'Huns' they showed as little concern for death, wounds and exhaustion as the Old Contemptibles, whose spirit and resolution they fully matched at this time of grave peril.

One cannot say the same for the French, who seemed to have

1918

lost all heart, and who could not be trusted to hold a position long enough to enable some British formation to get a brief rest. The cavalry were consequently in constant demand and Cook's Detachment, after dismounting and going into action at Lagny in support of British troops, was immediately pulled out again and ordered to mount and ride to the assistance of the French, who were hard-pressed at Cattigny. The French, as they usually did at this time, retired as soon as Cook's Detachment came to the front, and although the G.O.C. 10th French Division sent up reinforcements, they also failed to stand, and the whole line was driven back, with the enemy round the flanks and the British cavalrymen mixed-up with the French. Colonel Cook was killed, and many another 20th Hussar also lost his life in this action, which ended with a retirement to Thiescourt. Here the Detachment remounted and rode back to Compiègne, where the 5th Cavalry Brigade was re-formed and sorted out, with the remnants of the 20th Hussars, parading as a Regiment once more, under the command of Major Little.

Among those who rejoined the regiment at this time were about a hundred men led by Captain W. D. Hall and Lieut. J. C. Bland, who had been riding with 'Fane's Regiment', which had been assembled out of the horse-holders of the 5th Cavalry Brigade and various oddments, and placed under the command of Colonel Fane of the 12th Lancers. Fane's went into action both mounted and dismounted at several points in the neighbourhood of Chiry, mostly in support of the French, who seem to have put up a rather better performance in this area than elsewhere.

On the 28th March, the whole of the 2nd Cavalry Division rode off to plug gaps south of Montdidier but until the 30th, when the Greys and 12th Lancers dismounted to support the infantry, the situation was restored without the help of the cavalry. On the 31st, the 20th Hussars, who were in the Bois de Hangard near Amiens, organised a dismounted company of 138 all-ranks, officered by Captain Hall and Lieutenants Taylor, Austin and Fairbrother. On the following morning this company supported the 4th Dismounted Battalion in a counter-attack against Rifle Wood, near Domart-Sur-Luce, and suffered heavy casualties, including all three subalterns, from the enfilade fire protecting the forward edge of the wood. Led by Hall, the company nevertheless rushed the wood and cleared it of enemy after some fierce hand-to-hand fighting, thereafter holding it until relieved by infantry. The total casualties of the 20th Hussars in this action were 3 rank and file killed, 3 officers and 39 rank and file wounded, with one missing.

1918

The other dismounted units of the 2nd Cavalry Division were all equally successful, and the Division was warmly thanked by the commander of the 4th Army for its 'brilliant achievement'. He ended his message, 'I fear they have suffered heavily, but their victory had been invaluable at this critical juncture.'

At the beginning of April the 5th Cavalry Brigade was withdrawn to Bois l'Abbé, with the 20th Hussars reduced to a strength of 13 officers, 150 rank and file and 245 horses. In stemming the great offensive, the British Army had suffered 300,000 casualties and had been forced right back across the Somme to the gates of Amiens. The heroic 5th Army had ceased to exist and Sir Hubert Gough, whose dispositions and conduct of his Army's retirement had been faultless, was dismissed by order of the Cabinet and replaced by Sir Henry Rawlinson at the head of a new '4th Army'. The German offensive, however, had begun to peter out without having achieved its object – a break-through between the British and French Armies – and General Ludendorff, its instigator and planner, was becoming anxious, for he well knew that time was not on his side and that no victory would be possible for Germany once the resources of the United States, which had entered the war in 1917, were fully deployed. He therefore continued to hammer away with fresh reserves at what he knew to be the weakest points in the allied line, and on the 11th April Haig issued his order: 'With our backs to the wall and believing in the justice of our cause, each one of us must fight on to the end.'

His own lack of reserves had forced Haig to transfer troops from his left to bolster up his right, which had gravely weakened his line between Ypres and Bethune. For some time, Ludendorff had been preparing a subsidiary offensive in this area, well-knowing it to be thinly held. On the 9th April the enemy attacked at Neuve Chapelle, at a point held by a raw Portuguese Division, which was quickly got on the run. Pouring through the gap the Germans were able to outflank the British divisions on either side, and crossing the Lys, reached Armentières. The 2nd Cavalry Division, which was being held as G.H.Q. reserve, was ordered across to the 1st Army front on the 11th April. It was not an easy move, for all available rolling stock was being used for the transport of infantry and supplies, so that the cavalry had to ride – and fast at that. The difficulty of this was that all roads were crammed with transport, guns, tanks, refugees and occasional columns of marching infantry, all of which the cavalry had to push their way through, leaving the roads when possible and getting up speed at night.

The Division arrived in the 1st Army area on the 13th April, by which time the German thrust had been halted, and the Division was moved to the left flank around the Foret de Nieppe. The 20th Hussars, who had received drafts of reinforcements, mainly from the Yeomanry, were now at a strength of 19 officers and 442 rank and file. Fighting gradually died down all along the front as the enemy effort spent itself, and, after some weeks of patrolling, the 20th Hussars went into billets at Aiz-en-Issart, there to prepare for the last battles of the war.

Ludendorff's last effort came on the 15th July, when he attacked on both sides of Rheims. He was again held, and this time the French counter-attacked on the flank of the German salient and came close to routing its defenders. Haig was now getting ready to drive forward to final victory, which he was confident of achieving within the year, although he seems to have been the only man in the world at the time to believe such a thing to be possible. The attack was launched on the 8th August, at the traditional 'one hour before dawn'. It was conducted by Rawlinson with the 4th Army, which included the Australian and Canadian Corps, and the Cavalry Corps, with a great quantity of the latest tanks and a vast deployment of artillery. The 1st French Army, on the right, had been placed under Haig's command. The date, wrote Ludendorff, was 'the black day of the German Army in the history of the war'.

The cavalry advanced in support of the Australians and Canadians east of Amiens, which they rode through during the night. It was within range of the German guns, and had been evacuated by its inhabitants, but the streets were heavily congested by marching troops, mostly tanks and transport. The cavalry had difficulty in getting through, and the 20th Hussars were held up in a traffic jam for over an hour, expecting an enemy bombardment to start any minute. As a result of the most thorough security precautions however – which included the flying of R.A.F. aircraft along the line to drown the noise of the tanks – the Germans were quite unaware that they were in immediate danger of a major assault.

By the afternoon of the 8th August the German 2nd Army had been shattered and driven back nine miles, suffering losses of 30,000 men and over 400 guns. The cavalry had done a good deal to keep the enemy on the run, and the 1st Cavalry Division, in the lead, was able to gallop about and do considerable damage at slight cost, the 5th Dragoon Guards capturing a train full of 600 reinforcements and three batteries of guns nine miles behind the original enemy front line. The 3rd Cavalry Division was not so

1918

fortunate, having to dismount and attack on foot through the wooded country beyond the Luce, and the 2nd Cavalry Division, which was in reserve and hoping to be sent in behind the 1st Cavalry Division, was instead sent across the Luce to support the 3rd Cavalry Division. Both Divisions were then withdrawn as the infantry came up, and the 2nd Cavalry Division was then sent to support the Canadians, the 20th Hussars going into action near Beaucourt on the following day. Here the whole of the 5th Cavalry Brigade attacked with the Greys on the right and the 20th on the left, moving at a trot behind a screen of patrols. The object was to pass through the Canadians and stop the retiring Germans from taking up intermediate positions, but although this was done to a certain extent it was generally frustrated by the skilful placing of the enemy machine-guns whose crews – as they nearly always did – fought to the last man. As already mentioned, so long as it was possible to gallop, cavalry could often cross ground under machine-gun fire without undue losses, but in this area there was a good deal of old wire about which, as the ground was very open, made things very awkward indeed. The leading troop of 'C' Squadron, for example, led by Lieut. Mann, came under heavy machine-gun fire while galloping across the open for the cover of a gully. Owing to wire in front, the troop had to wheel in towards the machine-guns in order to get round. It got within 500 yards of the guns before it was possible to wheel to the front again and reach the shelter of a gully. The sight of this troop, mounted on light chestnuts, galloping through a hail of bullets which were kicking up the dust around it, was very harrowing for the rest of the squadron. Several of the fine horses were brought down, but not a man was hit, and the squadron was able to take advantage of the distraction by galloping across to the gully from a different direction, reaching it unscathed before the enemy had time to find the range.

At the beginning of the offensive, the enemy machine-gun nests had been successfully dealt with by the tanks, but at the cost of such heavy casualties that there were now no longer enough to go round. The 'Whippet Tanks', which were supposed to support the cavalry, never appeared, and when the advance reached the old battlefields of the Somme – still a mess of broken-down trenches, shell-craters and wire-entanglements – over which it was impossible to engage mounted, the Cavalry Corps was withdrawn temporarily. At this period most regiments, including the 20th Hussars, were employed as Divisional Cavalry on a basis of one squadron to each infantry division. The duties were chiefly patrolling along the flanks of the advance in order to keep touch with neighbouring formations and also with the enemy when, as sometimes happened, he disappeared during the night. It was very essential work, which made a considerable contribution to the success of the operations, but being unspectacular it has received scanty recognition, in spite of the casualties suffered while carrying it out. A very unpleasant feature of the advance was the saturation of the ground by liquid mustard gas, which the enemy sent over in shells, some of which were nearly always included among the shrapnel and high-explosive of their defensive fire. The cavalry suffered more from this than the infantry, for the horses had no protection and often could not graze, while both men and horses were often poisoned by gas-impregnated water.

During the second and third weeks of September the 20th Hussars were at Behencourt, training for the open warfare which must inevitably follow the enemy's defeat on the Hindenburg Line. On the 29th September, the regiment marched to Roisel, in support of the 5th Australian Division. By this time the British Army, advancing on a forty-mile front, had driven the enemy back twenty-five miles and the final push across the Hindenburg Line was about to start. By the 1st October, most of the Line was in British hands, and a situation began to develop in which the cavalry would be able to do some riding. 'C' Squadron was the first to do so in the 20th, riding through the 32nd Division after a successful attack before Joncourt. The squadron, which was at a very low strength from casualties – chiefly gas – split up into three patrols led by Lieut. Mann, the only subaltern left, S.S.M. Adams and Sergeant Brook. They found the enemy in position and not retiring as had been expected. S.S.M. Adams, who was a very dashing type of cavalryman, was unable to resist making a fight of it and galloped the trenches. It was a gallant effort, but he and each one of his men were hit, and came back just as the squadron leader was restraining Lieut. Mann from following his example. Mann was unfortunately killed on the following day, during an enemy counter-attack near Montbrehain. After this counter-attack had been beaten off, the whole regiment concentrated ready to take part in a combined effort by the Cavalry Corps at Le Cateau, meanwhile continuing to send out reconnaissance and liaison patrols which suffered several casualties, including Lieut. Jackson, who was killed near Molain. The cavalry then again split up, and the 20th Hussars were sent as Corps and Divisional Cavalry to various formations in turn, commencing with the 2nd American Corps and ending, on the 1st November, with the 32nd Division.

1918

When, on the 4th November, the 32nd Division attacked across the Sambre and Oise Canal, the regiment was under the orders of the 97th Infantry Brigade in reserve. The 97th passed through the leading brigades on the 5th November with 'C' Squadron on the left flank and the remainder of the regiment following. The Germans were still putting up a determined resistance at some points, and 'C' Squadron lost two men killed and an officer and two men wounded; but the scent of victory was in the air, for not only were the Germans being steadily driven back, but the inhabitants of the villages were wild with delight at the arrival of the British. Lieutenant Bland, with two troops, reached Favril and captured two heavy guns and 49 prisoners. The two troop leaders had some difficulty here in extricating themselves – reluctantly but with a stern sense of duty – from the arms of the village girls welcoming them as deliverers.

On the 6th November, the 20th Hussars passed through the 97th Brigade and took the lead until held up near Maroilles, but the advance was continued at the next dawn, when the regiment reached Avesnes. Here it was held up by a line of machine-gun posts and dismounted under cover, leaving patrols out in touch with the enemy. The leader of one of these patrols was the irrepressible S.S.M. Adams, still in the saddle in spite of an unhealed wound in the thigh and gas-poisoning from drinking a cup of 'gun-fire' tea made from water impregnated with mustard. Ignoring both these disabilities with a stoicism worthy of Captain Brotherton in the Peninsula, he led a charge against the enemy in which he was wounded and unhorsed, so that the regiment did not see him again until after the armistice. Captain Clark, the Medical Officer, and one man were killed, and seven wounded, while the regiment was keeping the enemy occupied pending the arrival of the infantry.

Before noon on the 9th November, the 20th Hussars were riding five miles ahead of the infantry, eventually getting in touch with the enemy near Touvent. They bivouacked that night at Pont de la Ville, completely out of touch with any British formation. At this time Colonel Little was commanding the Brigade, and Major Sanford had taken over the regiment. He pushed on at dawn and outflanked a line of machine-guns, forcing the crews to withdraw. Another line had just been discovered along a spur beyond Eppe Sauvage, when a galloper arrived with orders to change direction north-east, and join 'Bethell's Force' of the 5th Cavalry Brigade and two infantry brigades, which were marching on Renlies. The regiment bivouacked that night near Clair Fayts on the Belgian Frontier, in close touch with the enemy who

1918

were holding a line less than a mile away. It had been without rations for two days, except for the emergency 'iron ration', and on the morning of the 11th November the advance was held up until the arrival of the wagons. Before this happened, orders were received from the 66th Division to send patrols forward as far as possible without coming to blows, in order to secure as much ground as was practicable before the impending Cease Fire. Patrols under Lieutenants Dawnay and Burt were sent forward accordingly, and when a staff officer followed them at 11 a.m. with news of the armistice, Burt was busy stalking a German machine-gun near Sivry Station. 'A' Squadron, under Captain Hall,* which had been detached from the regiment for duty with the 137th and 138th Infantry Brigades, also arrived at Sivry at this juncture, having just had orders to join the 199th Brigade and get in touch with the enemy at Sivry. He was halted by the Brigade Major with the information that the war was due to end in ten minutes.

At 11 a.m. all trumpeters of the 20th Hussars assembled outside the regimental headquarters at Clair Fayts and sounded the *Cease Fire*. Victory at last, and the war was over.

---

*Captain (later Lt.-Col.) W. (D'Arcy) Hall was awarded the M.C. and Bar and the Croix de Guerre for his wartime services.

Top Men and horses of the 14th/20th crossing the Indus river in 1936.
Bottom Annual dismounted inspection by General Sir George Barrow at Abbassia, 1932. The 14th/20th had arrived in Egypt the previous year.

28th October 1918 The 14th with Bridges' Column and Dunsterforce, Operations in North Persia, Turkey defeated
February 1919 The 14th come home
March 1919 The 20th come home
July 1919 And sail for Egypt
28th June 1920 The 20th join the Army of the Black Sea
13th July 1920 Their charge at Gebze
October 1920 The 20th ordered to disband
January 1922 But amalgamate with the 14th
October 1923 The 14th/20th return home
October 1930 They sail for Egypt
December 1933 And India
31st March 1939 Mechanisation
3rd September 1939 Outbreak of the Second World War

Aftermath

29

In the east, Turkey had surrendered on the 31st October, 1918, after Allenby had destroyed her army in Palestine, and Marshall had advanced to the gates of Mosul. Marshall, who had had to part with two of his divisions as reinforcements for the Western Front, had not been in the position to make any advance in Mesopotamia until the end of the summer; a fact which greatly disturbed the over-nervous Government of India. The collapse of Russia had left open the ancient invasion routes through Persia, and although Turkey was too heavily committed elsewhere to be able to contemplate an invasion she could, and did, send propaganda missions through Persia and towards India. Such missions could well stir up trouble and chaos in the highly sensitive Middle East, and even in India. Marshall was accordingly instructed to organise a British Mission, not only for propaganda purposes, but to endeavour to close Persia to the Turks by reorganising the scattered remains of the Russian, Caucasian and Armenian forces which the Russian Revolutionary Government had abandoned and left to fend for themselves.

The British Military Mission was led by Major-General L. C. Dunsterville, and consisted of twelve officers, two clerks and an armoured car, being known as 'Dunsterforce'. Its instructions were to 'frustrate enemy penetration in North West Persia', with

1918

the help of the Russian General Bicharakoff, who was on his way to Kermanshah with 500 Cossacks. Pending the arrival of Dunsterforce it was decided to send a mounted column to Kermanshah to meet Bicharakoff, and Lieut.-Colonel E. J. Bridges, of the 14th (King's) Hussars, was appointed to lead it. The column, known as 'Bridges' Column', consisted of the 14th, with sections of 'S' Battery, R.H.A., 15th Machine-Gun Squadron, 131st Field Ambulance, and wireless and transport detachments. It left Sadiyeh Camp on the 13th January, 1918, and arrived at Qasr-i-Shirin, just inside the Persian border, on the 18th after an uneventful march of 102 miles. Here it found a battalion of the Hampshires with two troops of the 12th Lancers and some administrative services. They had marched into Persia to collect certain wireless and survey detachments which had been attached to the Russians at Kermanshah. The commander, Colonel Matthews, reported that the roads onwards were almost impassable at that time of year, and as no news had been received from Bicharakoff at Army Headquarters, Bridges was told to stay where he was until further orders.

The situation at Qasr-i-Shirin was far from pleasant. The whole country was devastated and famine-stricken, the home of savage Kurdish tribes who were well-armed with modern rifles and under the influence of German and Turkish agents. The Jangali tribes, who lived along the south-western shores of the Caspian, were under the influence of the Bolsheviks, who were encouraging them to move southwards on Teheran. Although there were none as far south as Hamadan and Qasr-i-Shirin, their activities helped in stirring up unrest throughout the country, over which the Persian Government scarcely pretended to keep any control.

Under such circumstances, the troops at Qasr-i-Shirin had to exercise the utmost vigilance, and the 14th were constantly out on patrol, reconnaissance and protective duties along the roads. General Dunsterville arrived on the 27th January armed with a letter of authority appointing him 'Chief of the British Mission to the Caucasus and British Representative at Tiflis'. He set off at once to Enzeli on the Caspian where he hoped to find a ship to take his party to Baku, but when after the greatest difficulty he reached Enzeli in late February, he found it under the control of the Bolsheviks and had to return to Hamadan. On the 18th February, Bicharakoff arrived with his Cossacks from Baghdad where he had been conferring with Marshall. He was now on his way back to Hamadan, having advised Marshall that he had little hope of being able to collect a Russian force, for the Russians were all gradually filtering back into the arms of the Bolsheviks. The 14th Hussars, however, were again favourably impressed by the Cossacks, who were fine-looking fellows and well-disciplined. So far absolutely nothing in connection with Dunsterforce had gone according to plan or anywhere near it.

During March and April, the 14th were employed in trying to restore some kind of law and order in the country under the guidance of Political Officers. A Political Officer accompanied Captain Ambler and 'B' Squadron on a punitive expedition against the Kalhurs, who were surprised in their camp some twenty miles off. After dispersing them, the Squadron brought back 600 head of sheep and cattle which the Kalhurs had stolen from other tribes. On the 11th April, Captain Pope with 'C' Squadron was ordered to Hamadan to support Dunsterville who was now endeavouring to raise a force of levies from the local tribes. A few days later Major J. D. F. Woodhouse with 'A' Squadron rode out against the Sinjabis. The squadron was accompanied by the Kalhurs (previously disciplined by 'B' Squadron), who were of considerable assistance and saved 'A' Squadron the trouble of chasing the Sinjabis after getting them on the run.

Apart from its main object of restricting the enemy influence in Persia, the presence of Dunsterforce gave flank protection to the troops on the Tigris, with whom a close liaison was maintained. At the end of April, Captain Featherstonhaugh with 'D' Squadron was attached to the 37th Brigade for an attack on Kifri, while a troop of 'B' Squadron under 2nd/Lieut. Youngman joined a covering force demonstrating along the Diyala. 'D' Squadron pursued the Turks fifteen miles beyond Tifri and took seventy prisoners during the operations, marching in all nearly two hundred miles. The affair ended with the capture of Tuz Khurmatli, after a charge by the 6th Cavalry Brigade which killed 200 Turks with the sword and captured another 500.

On the 1st June, Dunsterville arrived at Kasvin fifty miles from the Caspian, accompanied by 'C' Squadron. The regiment was now scattered over an area of four hundred miles between Kasvin and Ruz. Also at Kasvin was Bicharakoff, still with his escort of Cossacks who were acting as rearguard to the remnants of the Russian army leaving Persia. On the 8th June, Bicharakoff and the Cossacks left Kasvin for Enzeli to take ship for Baku. 'C' Squadron marched with them under the orders of Bicharakoff who sent it on ahead. On arriving at Manjil the bridge was found to be blocked by a force of Jangali tribesmen under German officers which Bicharakoff's Cossacks attacked and routed. He

1918

then pushed on to Enzeli, leaving 'C' Squadron to hold the bridge until Matthew's Column arrived. The Squadron had built a blockhouse at each end of the bridge when the Hampshires arrived on the 18th June, and it remained at Manjil until the middle of August, bivouacking in the open in this remote spot, high and windy, and surrounded by desolate, rocky hills. On the 18th August it was ordered to Zenjan, and while riding down a defile near Kaskal was attacked by tribesmen and had a horse wounded. But they captured four horses, four men, and a great quantity of ammunition from the tribesmen. The onward march was by goat tracks across mountains 7,000 feet high, and over thirty miles were covered in the one day before the Squadron bivouacked in the Zenjan Valley.

Whilst at Zenjan a picket held up a bullock cart carrying two small barrels. Captain Pope ordered them to be opened and found they were caviare. The officers and sergeants shared one and men the other. When asked if there were any complaints, a trooper said, 'Yes, Sir, we don't like this 'ere fish jam.'

Seventy miles north-west of Zenjan, across the Kuflan Kuh mountains, Major Wagstaff, one of Dunsterville's officers, was watching the movements of the Turks at Tabriz. He had with him a platoon of Hampshires and about 600 levies while a couple of platoons of Gurkhas were at Zenjan. 'C' Squadron with men and horses very tired, had only just off-saddled at Zenjan when an urgent message arrived from Wagstaff to come to his assistance, as the Turks were coming out of Tabriz. The officers and men of the squadron had, incidentally, worn out their boots, an unusual experience for cavalrymen, and their clothing was in rags. The Gurkhas were sent on ahead, and the squadron caught them up two days later, while riding on through Mianeh to Turkmanchai, patrolling towards Tabriz.

As it appeared that the Turkish 11th Division was concentrating at Tabriz preparatory to cutting off Dunsterville's communications with the Caucasus, reinforcements were sent to Wagstaff consisting of a field and a mountain battery, a company of Hampshires and two armoured cars. They arrived just before the Turks attacked on the 6th September, when a fighting withdrawal commenced, with 'C' Squadron operating on both flanks and the Hampshires and Gurkhas in the centre. From time to time the squadron had to close and hold a rearguard position to enable the infantry to disengage. On one occasion they fought for seven hours on end against an enemy force of about 500 all arms, during which the ground yielded to the enemy did not exceed $2\frac{1}{2}$ miles. The retirement continued over the Kuflan Kuh, with the squadron holding the pass until the infantry got clear when it had to retire through a ravine with great difficulty. Subsequently, when the Turkish advance slackened, the squadron made an 'offensive reconnaissance' back to the foot of the Kuflan Kuh, and by working round their flank forced the Turks back into the mountains. After this it was ordered back to Kasvin, where it was joined by Captain Ambler with 'B' Squadron at the end of October.

While 'C' Squadron was thus engaged, 'D' Squadron and some armoured cars were fighting another 500 Turks at Sain Kala, a hundred miles to the westward. The situation was exceedingly complicated, for thousands of refugees were fleeing before the Turks and the Jelu levies were mixed up among them and doing little in the way of fighting. Spread out over a considerable area and acting independently, the three troops of the squadron, led by Lieutenants Whidborne, Shard and Burton, galloped about, shepherding the refugees, fighting the Turks and trying to reorganise the levies. Sergeant Hallard with twelve men rode to the rescue of a Dunsterforce party whose officer had been killed and who were surrounded by Turkish cavalry and mounted irregulars. Hallard was awarded the D.C.M. for successfully extricating this party and covering its retirement. It was indeed a remarkable performance, carried out at the small cost of two men wounded.

Dunsterville was at this time in Baku, trying to keep it out of the hands of the Turks. The British Government had previously expressed its dissatisfaction with his efforts, alleging that he was wasting too much time making friends with the Bolsheviks instead of organising resistance against the Turks. In fact he had no choice but to attempt to come to terms with the Bolsheviks. It is doubtful if he could ever have got to Baku at all had not his associate Bicharakoff actually turned Bolshevik in order to get himself appointed Commander-in-Chief in Trans-Caucasia. He and Bicharakoff, however, were now having great difficulty in organising the defence of Baku, and it seemed that they would soon be obliged to evacuate the port, although the Bolsheviks threatened to sink their ships if they did so. Meanwhile, the British troops in North Persia, which had originally consisted only of Bridges' and Matthews' Columns, sent in to support Dunsterforce, but which had been slowly and reluctantly increased, were placed under the command of Major-General W. M. Thomson. This appointment gave satisfaction to the 14th Hussars who hoped that future operations would be conducted in accordance with some recognisable plan.

In September, the 14th Hussars less 'B' and 'C' Squadrons, were at Bijar with the rest of Bridges' Column, which now in-

1919

cluded a battalion of the Gloucestershire Regiment, a Field Company, R.E., a section of a Mountain Battery and a machine-gun section. News of Dunsterville's evacuation of Baku caused some anxiety over the situation in North Persia, especially as Turkish cavalry were reported to be within seven miles of Bijar. The Turks, however, then began to pull out following their collapse in Palestine and the start of Marshall's final advance in Mesopotamia. The news of their defeat at Sharqat on the 28th October was quickly followed by that of an armistice, which was celebrated by a salute of 21 guns by the Mountain Section. The 14th Hussars returned across the Jabal Hamrin into Mesopotamia on the 17th December.

In February, 1919, a squadron was formed to remain in Mesopotamia as part of a composite regiment with similar squadrons of the 7th and 13th Hussars. The remainder of the regiment returned home, part for demobilisation and the rest to form a cadre which, on arrival at Tidworth by train, was met by the regimental band which had been attached to the 5th Reserve Cavalry Regiment.

In Europe meanwhile, after a stand-fast on the Armistice Line to allow the vanquished enemy to get clear, the British advanced guards crossed the German frontier on the 1st December, 1918. The 20th Hussars were quartered at Berg Reuland and, after demobilisation and drafts to other units had reduced the regiment to a cadre of 135 all-ranks, it returned home in March, 1919, and was posted to Colchester. In July of the same year, after being brought up to a strength of 16 officers and 433 rank and file, it embarked for Egypt and went into camp at Tel-el-Kebir, where it was inspected by General Sir Edmund Allenby who presented the 'Mons Star' to the 24 'Old Contemptibles' still serving.

Since the Armistice, which had been celebrated in London with unparalleled scenes of enthusiasm, Great Britain had disbanded her vast wartime armies with positively indecent haste and little regard for the realities of the international situation, which was very far from stable. In fact, although 'the War' was certainly over, the military commitments of Great Britain were still considerable. Besides contributing to the armies of occupation, she had to provide expeditionary forces for the North Russian Expedition, the 3rd Afghan War, and the Waziristan Campaign in 1919, and for the Arab Insurrection in Iraq in 1920 – a year in which the Turks, thought to have been beaten to their knees, suddenly showed fight again. The Peace Conference, which lasted a whole year in Paris and resulted in the map of Europe being entirely re-drawn, produced as one of its many

1919

sidelines the Treaty of Sevres, which partitioned Turkey. Except for Constantinople, the whole of Eastern Thrace was handed over to Greece, as well as a large area inland from Smyrna, while France and Italy were allotted 'spheres of influence' in Anatolia, and Armenia was declared mandated territory. The Treaty was signed by the Sultan's Government in August, 1920, although Mustapha Kemal and the Nationalists had repudiated its terms months previously. It was the Nationalists who held the real power in Turkey and in June they had broken out into open revolt and concentrated in the Ismid area, taking possession of the whole south coast of the Sea of Marmora. Pending the arrival of Greek forces, the allies sent troops to Constantinople to enforce the Peace Treaty. The British contribution was a British/Indian contingent commanded by General Sir Edmund Ironside who had just returned from North Russia. He was considered good at this sort of adventure, which required tact and diplomacy as well as military skill. As the French and Italians refused to do anything but sit in Constantinople, and the Sultan was merely a puppet, it was necessary for Ironside to stop Turkish infiltration into the Ismid peninsula and up to the shores of the Aegean.

The 20th Hussars left Egypt to join the 'Army of the Black Sea' on the 28th June, at a strength of 13 officers and 523 rank and file, commanded by Lieut.-Colonel M. C. Richardson, and joined Ironside at Deringe on the 20th July. The Turks had meanwhile advanced along the coast of the peninsula and occupied the village of Gebze where they blew the bridge. It being urgently necessary to throw them out and repair the bridge, Ironside sent a detachment consisting of the 20th Hussars, 2/39th Royal Garhwal Rifles, a Field Battery and some Royal Engineers to take the necessary action.

This resulted on the 13th July, 1920, in the 20th Hussars being drawn up in mass on the Turkish right flank watching the Garhwalis make a frontal attack. As this developed the Turks moved forward and occupied prepared positions in front of Gebze. The distance from the 20th Hussars was about 1,000 yards, across very reasonable and open ground. The enemy were in full view and the glorious opportunity was not lost on Colonel Richardson.

An officer of the Garhwalis who witnessed the operation wrote: 'Our artillery opened fire and I could see the shells falling on the enemy position. Suddenly, as I watched, I saw movement on the ridge to the north. Over the crest of the ridge came the whole of the 20th Hussars, two squadrons abreast in columns of troops with the third squadron in depth, nearly three hundred men in all. Their sabres were drawn and glistened in the early morning

1920

sunlight, their trumpets sounded as they moved, slowly at first, but gathering speed as they approached the enemy's flank. Our artillery stopped firing. The Turks huddled together as best they could in small groups facing the oncoming horsemen. Some lay down and fired, some knelt, a few fired standing. All stood their ground, though lamentably positioned and with little hope of checking the cavalry. The Turk was always a dour fighter.

'Now the Hussars reached the Turkish flank. We could see their sabres flashing in the sun as they struck, withdrew, and struck again. All the time the trumpets echoed, fierce and thrilling, lifting one's spirits in some form of savage exultation. The charge swept clean through the Nationalists' line. Beyond it the Squadrons rallied, regrouped, turned and charged back through the bewildered Turks, now making off for the cover of the vineyards round the village itself. Not more than thirty minutes after appearing over the ridge the Hussars had vanished whence they came, leaving huddled bodies on the plain to bear testimony to their passage.

'The last of the Nationalists disappeared into the thick country behind Gebze and it was time for me to advance with my company to take possession and to complete the job begun so competently by the cavalry. There was no more resistance.'

The last cavalry charge in British military history was over and with it disappeared finally the colour and panoply that, in earlier days, lent romance to war. From this date onwards the graceful, champing charger was finally to give way to the squat, sinister and unlovely steel tank. The thrilling music of the trumpets was to be replaced by the nattering twitter of the radio set, the glistening sabre by the snub-nosed automatic.

Sic transit gloria mundi.

The only casualty to the 20th Hussars was Lieutenant Groves who was badly wounded in the knee and several horses were wounded.

With the arrival of Greek forces, the activities of the Turkish Nationalists temporarily died down, and the 20th Hussars, after one or two skirmishes in which an officer and two men were wounded, were quartered in the Turkish barracks at Soglani. The allies had become divided over the question of Turkey, and France and Italy began secretly to support the Nationalists, leaving Great Britain as the sole friend of the Greeks. Mustapha Kemal, being well-aware of the run-down of British military strength, had ceased to regard Great Britain's friendship for his enemy as being worth very much, and proceeded to take over Armenia and part of Trans-Caucasia, involving much bloodshed.

1920

In spite of the serious threats to peace in this and other parts of the world where Great Britain was responsible for its maintenance, the government continued its planned reductions in the Army even after demobilisation had been completed. Twenty-six battalions of infantry of the line were earmarked for disbandment, and the cavalry were to be reduced by one regiment of Household Cavalry and eight of the line. As one of the junior cavalry regiments, the 20th Hussars were informed that 'His Majesty the King was graciously pleased to approve' the disbandment of the regiment 'as soon as the exigencies of the service permit'. The exigencies of the service did so permit, after the regiment was relieved by the 3rd Hussars in October, 1920.

After transferring 225 men to the 3rd Hussars and another 118 to the 11th Hussars in Meerut, the remains of the 20th Hussars, now commanded by Lieut.-Colonel A. C. Little, who had taken over in June, returned home for the melancholy purpose of disbandment. At this same time the Turkish Nationalists beat off the second of two Greek offensives. In the following year they defeated the Greeks altogether, and Mustapha Kemal announced his intention of marching on Constantinople, which resulted in the launching of the British 'Chanak Expedition' of 1922 and 1923, and the downfall of the soldier's plague, Lloyd George, who had once told Sir Douglas Haig that he knew nothing of military matters, and who never, seemingly, considered it worth his while to learn.

Turkey was not the only thorn in the side of the British Empire in those days of post-war disarmament. British soldiers were under arms in India, Ireland, Palestine, Egypt and the Sudan, carrying out various tiresome and dangerous but necessary duties in aid of the local authorities. The British Army was therefore fully extended and certainly earning its keep. Although this fact did not lead the Government to have second thoughts over its drastic measures or its reduction, a compromise was reached by which certain cavalry regiments were paired and amalgamated.

This new idea was conceived just in time to preserve the title of the 20th Hussars who, in January, 1922, consisted only of the C.O., 2 i/c., Adjutant, Quartermaster, R.Q.M.S., one S.Q.M.S., and the Officers' Mess Sergeant. They were attached to the 2nd Life Guards while completing the winding up of the regimental affairs. On the 29th March, the C.O. with somewhat mixed feelings, received the order to resuscitate one squadron for amalgamation with the 14th King's Hussars, to be known as the 20th Hussar Squadron and retaining its own regimental badges. Similar amalgamations took place in regiments including and

1922

junior to the 13th Hussars, and in the Dragoon Guards regiments including and junior to the 3rd Dragoon Guards. (Also, the 16th Lancers were amalgamated with the 5th Lancers.) Everything possible was done to preserve the separate identity of the amalgamated regiment although such extreme measures did not, as might have been foreseen, stand up to the test of time. The 14th and 20th Hussars had long been exchanging drafts both of officers and rank and file, so that their eventual amalgamation was an inevitable result of changing times. They did not, however, take kindly to the idea. The regimental spirit, based as it is on long comradeship and dangers shared, cannot be destroyed in a hurry, but with the passage of time and the experience of fresh campaigns a new one takes its place.

The amalgamation was carried out smoothly in the 14th/20th and the situation was helped by the fact that a number of officers of the 20th had already been transferred to the 14th, when the 20th Hussars were 'disbanded'. In the amalgamated regiment, 'A' Squadron was designated the 20th Hussars Squadron and wore the yellow plumes and badges of the 20th, while the remaining squadrons wore the white plumes and badges of the 14th. The wearing of the Prussian Eagle badge – discontinued in 1914 – was not officially authorised until 1931. But it was, in fact, in use as early as 1926.

The 14th Hussars left Tidworth for Cologne in November, 1920, after celebrating the anniversary of Ramnuggur on the 10th September. Present at the celebrations was Troop-Sergeant-Major J. Stratford, aged 91, who had actually taken part in the charge and had ridden with the regiment throughout the Sikh War, Persian Campaign and Indian Mutiny. He still had another twelve years to live. Also present was Mrs Summerill, born in the regiment in 1834, who had been with it as a girl during the Sikh War and Indian Mutiny.

At Cologne the regiment was quartered in a German cavalry barracks at Deutz. Because of the fantastic inflation of the German currency the pound sterling was worth something like 350 billion marks. The troops were paid in sterling and officers and men were exceedingly well-off and able to enjoy life to the full. Occupied Germany had much to offer to those able to pay for it. The inflation was partly due to economic conditions, and partly to the French insistence that Germany should be made to repay the cost of the war to the allies. This was in fact impossible, but when Germany endeavoured to make this clear the French advanced up the Rhine as a threat to the whole country. Somewhat reluctantly the British collaborated in this move and on the

7th March the 14th Hussars, less 'C' Squadron, moved to Dusseldorf as part of an allied column. For some weeks the regiment rode about through the Ruhr by troops, and at the end of May 'B' Squadron advanced to Herne and put out an outpost line to cover the movement of a French column. The Germans then agreed to pay 'reparations', but as their treasury was completely empty this gesture did not amount to much.

The 14th Hussars returned to Cologne except for 'A' Squadron which was sent by train to Silesia. Fighting had broken out between Germans and Poles in consequence of the establishment of the 'Polish Corridor' between Germany and East Prussia. The squadron spent a whole year in Silesia – based on Lublinitz – and constantly patrolled along the Polish frontier under severe conditions, with the winter temperature at times as low as 8 degrees below zero. 'A' Squadron became the 20th Hussars squadron on the 1st October, 1922, which was the official date of amalgamation. The title of the regiment became the 14th/20th Hussars. Only a year previously the title of the 14th (King's) Hussars had been changed to the 14th King's Hussars; the bracket being removed which was a welcome innovation. Now, however, the title of King's was dropped altogether by the amalgamated regiment, although the officers' mess dress retained the dark blue facings of a 'Royal' regiment. The distinctions between Royal regiments and the others was always jealously preserved in the infantry, although generally quite fortuitous in origin and in no way indicating that one was a better performer on the battlefield than the other. The cavalry appear generally to have been less interested in the matter, and the main concern of the officers of the 14th was the preservation of their sable eagle, Prussian or not. The eagle re-appeared at this time on the officers' mess dress without, one may assume, the formality of Royal consent.

The 14th/20th Hussars, under the command of Lieut.-Colonel J. G. Browne, returned home from Germany in October, 1923. Their ship ran into a gale off Dover and was obliged to stand out to sea again, sailing round in circles for over five hours. The regimental baggage, which had been stowed on deck, broke loose and much was lost. When the regiment was at last able to disembark it was found that the N.A.A.F.I. hut on shore had been washed into the sea, and with it the meal prepared for the officers and men, few of whom, however, were in any condition to eat. On its arrival home the regiment returned to Tidworth and joined the 2nd Cavalry Brigade with the 12th and 17th/21st Lancers.

The arrival of aircraft, armoured fighting vehicles, machine-guns and poison gas in ever-increasing quantity and efficiency

1924

had led to a constant re-appraisal of the conduct of war. Conclusions were not easy to draw in the light of experience, for the operations of the First World War had all been conducted differently in accordance with the situations prevailing in the various theatres of war, although all had ended in victory. A study of the operations on the Western Front might well have led to the conclusion that cavalry would have no further place on future battlefields, yet Allenby had been greatly dependent on cavalry for the success of his brilliant campaigns in Egypt and Palestine, and the British Army had still to be prepared to fight anywhere. Nevertheless, the First World War had given the cavalry a shock, and considerable doubt had been sown in the minds of its officers with regard to its future role. The ideas of the officers varied between those held by the keen progressive soldiers who considered that the days of the horse were numbered, and the more conservative types who refused to admit any such thing. The following fifteen years therefore saw the introduction of a series of experimental compromises between the two extreme schools of thought, which ended with a victory for the progressives and the disappearance of the horse.

The anxiety of the cavalry to move with the times was demonstrated in an unusual fashion when the C.I.G.S. visited the Cavalry Brigade at Tidworth in 1924. On such occasions in the past, a cavalry regiment or formation would have received the inspecting officer drawn up in mass, and after showing off its horsemanship in a ceremonial ending with a gallop past, and possibly a charge, would have carried out various field movements and sword exercises. When the C.I.G.S. arrived this time there were no cavalry to be seen at all, for the whole Brigade had deployed and taken cover. The C.I.G.S. was much impressed by this example of progressive thought, but presumably still had to insist on actually seeing the Brigade in order to make his report.

The horse continued as the object of principal interest in a cavalry regiment, although as an instrument for sport rather than war. While the 14th/20th were in Germany they achieved many outstanding successes in show-jumping and steeplechasing, but they had not brought their horses home with them and so, on arrival at Tidworth, had to start again with a new lot, obtained from the Remount Depot and drafts from other regiments. Captain A. R. Sturt, whose exceptional ability in judging and training horses had been largely responsible for the successes on the Rhine, where his 'Sea Count' and 'Flighty' had become well-known competitors in every Inter-Allied Horse Show, soon produced another outstanding pair in 'Charles O'Malley' and 'Aunt

1926

Sally'. They won many events at Bath, Andover and Olympia, where Sturt and Lieutenant Pemberton both reached the final round of the Prince of Wales Cup. All officers hunted and played polo, and a commission in a cavalry regiment was still an expensive privilege, although much less so than had been the case before the war. At this time the average annual expenditure of a subaltern was well over his pay which was about £250 a year.

In 1924 the private soldier in the cavalry was redesignated Trooper. The rank of Private Gentleman, Private man or plain Private, had been in use for three centuries. It is not clear why it should have been considered necessary to change it, except that Privates in the cavalry had been known unofficially as Troopers for many years. This reason had not applied to the previous changing of the time-honoured rank of Cornet to the continental Second-Lieutenant for which there does not appear to have been any justification whatsoever.

The 14th Hussars had always prided themselves on their good marksmanship and this tradition was still maintained. The achievements of the 14th/20th in the Army Rifle Association competitions of 1925 are unique. In that year they won the following in the ARA Competition: The Queen Victoria Trophy, King George Cup, Royal Irish Cup, Young Soldiers' Cup, Squadron Shield (1st and 3rd), The Duke of Connaught Cup (1st and 3rd), and the Revolver Cup (1st and 2nd), receiving 7 cups, 6 large silver medals, 1 large bronze medal, 1 medium silver medal, 64 small silver medals, 17 small bronze medals and £36 in prize money.

Whilst commanding the regiment, Lieut.-Colonel Hurndall captained the English Polo Team which went to America for the international matches for the Westchester Cup.

The cavalry training during this period was largely devoted to inconclusive encounters or co-operation with tanks, but the old skills were still practised regimentally and every cavalryman had to be an expert swordsman, capable of galloping over a series of obstacles while making the correct thrusts at dummies on either side. At the Brigade Horse Show and Assault at Arms, the 14th/20th were often first in practically every event – Inter-Troop and Inter-Section competitions, Hotchkiss and Machine-Gun, Dummy Thrusting, Tent-Pegging, Lance, Sword and Revolver. The competitors from the 14th/20th in fact proved themselves better with the lance than the Lancer Regiments in the Brigade, especially S.Q.M.S. Wash and S.S.M. Trueman. Trueman was a gallant soldier who wore the Military Medal, won with the 20th Hussars on the Hindenburg Line. A Riding Instructor, he was a

1929

fine example of the old school of cavalryman and a magnificent horseman, winning the Skill at Arms competition at Olympia in 1927. He later became R.S.M. and during the second World War was a Lieut.-Colonel in the 20th Lancers (India Cavalry). In 1927 he had seven wins to his credit, an achievement equalled by Lieut. J. B. Pemberton with his good horses 'Lapwing' and 'Phoebe', who gained two firsts at the International Horse Show at Nice and five more at other important meetings.

In 1926 the Regiment moved to York where it was quartered in the Cavalry Barracks un-brigaded. On leaving Southern Command, it was reported on by the G.O.C.-in-C. as being 'An excellent regiment in every way, above the average. I should be glad to take it with me on service'. Commanded by Lieut.-Colonel F. B. Hurndall, M.C., it was at a strength of 27 officers and 539 rank and file, but the horses, including chargers, pack and light draft, numbered only 393. This was due to the event of mechanisation, still only experimental. 'C' Squadron was dismounted and turned into a Machine-Gun Squadron of 4 troops with 2 guns each and was 'to be mechanised in due course', while some of the horsed transport was replaced by lorries.

The 'harmonisation' of horses with motor vehicles did not prove practical and machine-gun squadrons were later re-mounted with the guns on pack, but the cavalry generally were in a state of much confusion during these years. The whole Army was in fact confused, being plagued on one hand by the writings of large numbers of military theorists with little or no practical experience, and on the other hand by a pacifist press for ever insisting that there could not possibly be another war. At the same time, the bottom dropped out of the nation's economy, leaving less money than usual available for the fighting services. Some experiments continued, however, such as the issue of 'Baby Austins' to the cavalry for scouting purposes, and light tracked vehicles for carrying the machine-guns.

After spending a few months at Catterick Camp, the regiment left York for Aldershot in October, 1929. In this year the 14th Canadian Light Horse were allied or affiliated to the 14th/20th Hussars, in accordance with the general policy of linking regiments of Canadian Militia to British Regiments. The regiment, now under the command of Lieut.-Colonel C. G. Darley, was 25 men over establishment in this year, although recruiting in the Army generally was at a low ebb. In one way or another, the regiment had succeeded in establishing itself in the public esteem, probably chiefly on account of the fine appearance of its men and horses, the excellence of its musical rides and other public displays, and the continued success of its competitors at Horse Shows. Lieut. Pemberton on 'Devilled Kidney' won the Canadian Gold Cup twice running at Olympia, and S.S.M. Trueman's wins in every conceivable mounted event are too numerous to mention. In 1929 he got eleven first prizes on 'Lapwing'. In 1928 the Foxhunter Steeplechase over the Grand National Course had been won by Captain G. S. Poole on 'Pippins II', the only officer of the Regiment ever to ride a winner at Liverpool. All ranks were hard riders with no concern for the risk of broken bones, but it was a sad day for everyone when 2nd/Lieut. Joicey, a newly-joined subaltern, was killed in a steeplechase at Folkestone.

Although over establishment, the regiment opened for recruiting in January, 1929, and got 97 recruits in one week. At this time, cavalry regiments opened for recruiting in turn, for a week at a time, with the 14th/20th seldom getting less than 40. The regiment, however, was not allowed to profit by this popularity, for it was ordered to dispose of its surplus above establishment to other regiments who were under establishment, so carrying out the function of a cavalry recruiting depot. In 1929, Queen Alexandra's (Wellington West Coast) Mounted Rifles, of the military forces of New Zealand, were allied to the regiment.

In October, 1930, the 14th/20th Hussars marched from Aldershot to Hounslow where they were quartered in the cavalry barracks. While there they provided a detachment for the Lord Mayor's Show and two events, an Activity and a Trick Ride at the Royal Tournament, Olympia. In September, 1931, the regiment sailed for Egypt in the H.T. *Somersetshire*, and went into Abbassia Barracks near Cairo. It was therefore unfortunately unable to send a party to the funeral of the last of the 14th Light Dragoons, Troop-Sergeant-Major John Stratford, who died at Wolverhampton on the 16th January, 1932, aged 103 years. The oldest pensioner of the British Army, he was buried with full military honours by the 1st Battalion The South Staffordshire Regiment, with a bearer party from the Staffordshire Yeomanry, with whom he had served as Troop Sergeant Instructor for 16 years after leaving the 14th in 1871. The regiment was represented at his funeral by Lieut.-Colonel V. E. Mocatta and a number of old comrades. Born in 1829, in the reign of George IV, he had fought at Ramnuggur, Chillianwalla, and in the Persian and Central India Campaigns, thus providing a unique link with the past, especially as he retained his faculties to the end. A Bronze Tablet to his memory was erected by the regiment in St Peter's Church, Wolverhampton, and his medals are kept in the Sergeants' Mess.

The medals of Troop-Sergeant-Major John Stratford of the 14th who died aged 103 in 1932. *From left to right:* Punjab 1848–9 with bars; India General Service with Persia bar; Indian Mutiny with bar; Long Service and Good Conduct Medal; Meritorious Service Medal.

On arrival in Egypt the regiment were brigaded with the 12th and the 17th/21st Lancers, and the Vickers machine-guns transferred from lorries to pack saddles. Lieut.-Colonel J. A. T. Miller assumed command of the Regiment. On 31st October, H.M. The King approved the alliance with the 20th Light Horse, Australian Military Forces. In 1933, the 17th/21st Lancers moved to India being relieved by the King's Dragoon Guards. L./Cpl. Blackwell won the Command Lightweight Boxing, and the regiment won the Inter-Regimental Polo Tournament.

On the 31st December, 1933, the regiment sailed from Port Suez in H.T. *Nevasa*, for India. The regiment arrived at Risalpur on the 12th January, 1934, and was brought up to the Indian Establishment by a draft of 90 rank and file from the 15th/19th, The King's Royal Hussars who were leaving for home. This brought the strength up to 572 rank and file, with 559 troop horses, so that the regiment was once again fully mounted. The Risalpur Hounds, amounting to 19 couple, were also handed over by the 15th/19th. Major A. V. Pope took over as Master, and was soon showing excellent sport although at first the strange country and strange quarry in the shape of the jackal were confusing.

In 1933, the aged President of Germany, Field-Marshal von Hindenburg, invited Adolf Hitler, leader of the National Socialist or Nazi Party, to take office as German Chancellor. During his rise to power, Hitler had made no secret of his ultimate aim, which was to lead Germany in a war of revenge and wipe out the stigma of defeat in 1918. The danger was obvious, but

1936

Great Britain was in no position to take any defensive measures, for not only was the country still suffering from an economic slump but had become strongly pacifist and opposed to war as an instrument of policy. Aspirants to political power therefore felt themselves obliged to keep off the subject, and pin their faith to the League of Nations to which Germany belonged and which had 'outlawed' war, to the great satisfaction and comfort of the British people. The fighting services continued to be almost completely neglected, especially the Army, which at home had sunk to a collection of units at cadre strength, still armed with the weapons of 1918. In India things were not quite so bad. The Indian Government was not, of course, worried about people like Hitler, but was merely concerned with internal security and the defence of the North-West Frontier, for both of which, men were more important than up-to-date weapons. Even so, a new light machine-gun was urgently needed to replace the indifferent Hotchkiss and the cumbersome Lewis, and the Indian Government got tired of waiting for the War Office to decide on the rival merits of the Vickers-Berthier and Bren. The Vickers-Berthier was therefore purchased and issued to the army in India. In the cavalry the V.B. replaced both the Vickers machine-gun and Hotchkiss light machine-gun. The machine-gun troop was re-armed with four V.B.s and a fourth troop with one V.B. was added to each squadron.

In October, 1936, the regiment changed station to Lucknow, where Captain J. D. G. Chaytor took over the Lucknow Hounds. After hunting them for a full season and giving fine sport, he was unfortunately killed in March, 1937, when playing polo in the Inter-Regimental. He was the second officer of the 14th/20th to lose his life at polo during this tour in India; the other being Captain R. H. Hannay, who was killed in December, 1935. Fatal accidents at polo were not uncommon in India, where the game was faster than at home. The regiment had many good players and could turn out four teams of good standard.

A high standard of marksmanship was maintained and by the time the Second World War broke out the regiment had won the Duke of Connaught's Cup fourteen times, often as in 1936, taking second and third places as well. At the Imperial Delhi Horse Show, Lieut. E. B. Studd on 'Warrant' won the Open Jumping, and S.S.M. (R.I.) Brown and Sgt. Blake were 1st and 2nd in the British Other Ranks Jumping. The following year the Open Jumping at Delhi was won by Lieut. C. F. Johnston on 'Bing Boy', and Lieut. G. N. Loraine-Smith won the Patiala Gold Cup at Lahore on 'Lord Bow'.

Mounted officer and dismounted trooper. Lucknow, India, 1936. It was in this year that the Regiment was re-designated the 14th/20th King's Hussars, thus reviving its old distinction.

In 1936, while the 14th/20th were enjoying the social and sporting life of an Indian 'station', which had continued unchanged in its scope and form for seventy years, German forces re-entered the Rhineland which had been demilitarised under the Treaty of Versailles, and Italian forces invaded Abyssinia for no other reason than conquest. Neither the German nor Italian armies amounted to much at this time, and the British Army – if it had called up its reserves – could certainly have disposed of either of them without much difficulty, ill-armed and attenuated as it was. In the previous year, however, Hitler had been successful in negotiating a naval treaty with Great Britain. In effect, this brought the Treaty of Versailles to an end so that Great Britain did not now feel justified in opposing his reoccupation of the Rhineland and restrained France from taking any action. The savage aggression by Italy against a peaceful country like Abyssinia was another matter, but even here, Great Britain declined to give Abyssinia any help in her extremity. An attempt to make Italy see reason by peaceful persuasion in the form of economic sanctions was made, but it was contemptuously ignored and its only effect was to give Hitler the opportunity for concluding a defensive pact with Italy. The establishment of the 'Rome-Berlin Axis' was thus achieved in accordance with Hitler's foreign policy the aims of which he had never bothered to keep secret. Abyssinia was brought down and enslaved under an onslaught from tanks and aircraft combined with the lavish use of poison gas. A dignified appeal was made by the Emperor, but was fobbed off by the League of Nations, which told him to make the best of things.

Public opinion in Great Britain and the British Empire was unfortunately distracted at this time by the crisis over the Throne, following the death of George V. This was resolved within a few months by the abdication of his successor, Edward VIII, and the succession of the Duke of York as George VI. But, by that time, the two confederates, Hitler and Mussolini, had reached the point of no return. There was no longer any hope of stopping them other than by force of arms, and Great Britain was still neither ready nor prepared to make war.

The accession of George VI as King Emperor was proclaimed from the steps of the Council Chamber in Lucknow on the 14th December, 1936. Two days later the regiment was notified that as a result of representations made to His Majesty by the Colonel of the Regiment, General Sir George Barrow, the King was pleased to approve the regiment being re-designated the 14th/20th King's Hussars, thus reviving its old distinction.

While on the frontier and at Lucknow, the regiment, now under the command of Lieut.-Colonel A. V. Pope, carried out a great deal of experimental training in co-operation with light tanks, lorried infantry and motor transport. The conclusion reached was that horsed cavalry were still useful, being able to move across country both by day and night with speed and secrecy. Everyone was well-aware, however, that the regiment was bound to be mechanised sooner or later, but until it happened the standard of horsemanship remained as high as it had always been in the regiment.

In February, 1938, the German Army marched into Austria without meeting any resistance, and Hitler entered Vienna in triumph and announced the annexation of the country. He then announced his plans for the 'liberation' of the Germans settled in the Sudentenland of Czechoslovakia, with the obvious intention of annexing that country also. This behaviour was becoming too

1938

much for even the British Government to swallow, but it still managed to avoid war by various diplomatic manoeuvres. The Czechs were persuaded to agree to cede the Sudentenland to Germany and the British Government recognised the Italian conquest of Abyssinia in the hope of obtaining the support of Mussolini in its dealing with Hitler, being unaware that the two were in secret alliance. However, when Neville Chamberlain, the Prime Minister, met Hitler in Munich to try to persuade him that enough was enough, Mussolini did throw his weight into the scales in support of Chamberlain, thus acknowledging his obligation. This enabled Chamberlain to return to London with Hitler's signature on a pact, which he waved over his head with happy cries of 'peace in our time'.

Nevertheless, Chamberlain although publicly optimistic, had not gone completely off his head. Recognising that the International Situation was still extremely grave, he introduced various measures of re-armament, including conscription, or 'National Service' as he preferred to call it. The British Army was completely mechanised, on paper at least, and the cavalry of the line joined the tank regiments in forming the Royal Armoured Corps. At long last also, the Lewis and Hotchkiss guns were replaced by the Bren – in spite of the fact that the army in India was already armed with the Vickers-Berthier.

In January, 1938, the 14th/20th King's Hussars rode out on manoeuvres on horseback for the last time. In his report on the manoeuvres, the District Commander wrote: '14/20 advance very good. 24 miles in 4 hours 10 minutes. Patrols sent out at 1010 hrs reported very good information all day and exact enemy positions. Some must have covered 50 miles in the day.'

In 1938, in the Inter-Regimental Polo Tournament, the regiment lost in the semi-finals to the 17th/21st Lancers who finally won the tournament. The next year the regiment did not enter for the Inter-Regimental but sent six officers to Jaipur where they received intensive coaching.

In August, 1938, the regiment said goodbye to its horses, sadly but without ceremony. Each officer was allowed to retain one charger and had half use of another from a pool based on 50 per cent of the authorised officer establishment. In November the first three tanks arrived with a detachment from the Royal Tank Corps under Captain L. C. Rumsey to show the regiment how to work them. Tanks continued to arrive in twos and threes, and the 31st March, 1939, is recorded as the official date upon which the 14th/20th King's Hussars converted from a mounted unit into a mechanised one. All ranks of the regiment were transferred from

1939

the Cavalry of the Line to the Royal Armoured Corps on the 11th April, 1939. At this time the regiment was in Secunderabad where it had arrived from Lucknow in the previous September.

In March, 1939, Hitler proclaimed the dissolution of the State of Czechoslovakia. Great Britain had sent a diplomatic mission to Russia in an attempt to enlist the aid of that country against Germany, but Hitler was again ahead and signed a pact with Russia in August. He had already strengthened his alliance with Italy by the 'Pact of Steel' in May. He was now determined on the invasion of Poland and the elimination of the Polish Corridor between Germany and East Prussia which had been created by the Treaty of Versailles. Great Britain and France could stand aside no longer. Ignoring their ultimatum, Hitler invaded Poland on 1st September, 1939, and Great Britain and France declared war two days later.

Secunderabad, 1939: one of the first parades held after mechanisation. The tanks are Vickers Mk II and VI B.

Top A tank of the 14th/20th helping to round up Persian prisoners.
Bottom A gendarme reporting to a tank crew that a Persian horsed cavalry brigade is about to attack. (Imperial War Museum photographs)

Events in 1939 and 1940
3rd July 1941 The 14th/20th land at Basra
August 1941 to October 1943 Operations with Iraq Force and Paiforce
October 1943 The 14th/20th move to Egypt
April 1944 And Syria
May 1944 The Greek Mutiny
21st January 1945 The 14th/20th land in Italy
9th April 1945 Crossing the Senio
16th April 1945 Medicina

1940

The Second World War

30

Although Great Britain and France had declared war on behalf of Poland, they were unable to give her any assistance, and she was soon overwhelmed and partitioned between Germany and Russia. The period of the 'phoney war' ensued, during which the British and French armies lay impotently along the German and Belgian frontiers, while Hitler occupied Denmark and Norway, and Russia attacked Finland. The German conquests of Holland and Belgium followed, during which the 'phoney war' ended and the real one commenced, to end with the British Army being driven into the sea, and the capitulation of France. Mussolini held his hand until it was obvious that France was at the end of her tether, when Italy entered into the war on Germany's side. Great Britain then stood alone against Germany and Italy and, while defending her shores against an anticipated German invasion, took active steps to halt Mussolini's activities in the Middle East. British Somaliland, which was defended by only five battalions, was overrun by August, 1940, but British and Imperial reinforcements then arrived and, led by General Sir Archibald Wavell, threw the Italians out of Somaliland, Eritrea and Abyssinia. Wavell also counter-attacked the Italian 10th Army, which was massed for an advance into Egypt, and having completely destroyed it, occupied the whole of Cyrenaica.

1941

The outbreak of war came at an awkward moment for the British cavalry in India, for they were in the middle of mechanisation. Some regiments were more advanced than others, but this was of little relevance, for under the powerful stimulus of war they could all have speedily reached the same standard had the necessary arms been available. Tanks, however, were hard to come by at this time, and any in India that were in good condition were liable to be called in and shipped off to the Middle East, making it very difficult for the mechanised cavalry to prepare itself for war.

In the struggle for tanks, the 14th/20th King's Hussars were more successful than many other regiments in India which were in the same predicament, and the regiment was fully mechanised and ready for the field in May, 1941, when it was ordered to mobilise at Meerut as a unit of the 2nd Indian Armoured Brigade. It was equipped with Mark VI B Light Tanks and Bren Gun Carriers. These light tanks had been designed to mount two guns co-axially. The main armament was a ·5 in. Vickers heavy machine gun and the secondary armament was a ·303 in. of the same make. However, as no ·5 in. guns had reached India, the tank had only the ·303 in. in it and the hole in the mantlet of the turret for the ·5 in. was filled with a wooden plug.

Prior to mobilisation it had, like most of the other British cavalry regiments in India, provided the nucleus – 9 officers and 102 N.C.O.s and tradesmen – for the formation of a new regiment, in this case the 26th Hussars. Lieut.-Colonel J. B. Norton was appointed to command this regiment. Captain A. J. C. Stanton who had won the Sword of Honour at Sandhurst and who was later killed by the Japanese in New Guinea was appointed Adjutant. The bulk of the rank and file for these new regiments was found from volunteers from the infantry who were a mixed lot, ranging from 'Sergeant-Major's Volunteers', or in other words those men whom their commanding officers were anxious to get rid of, to genuine volunteers who were interested in machinery. Those posted to the 26th Hussars appear to have been a reasonable lot, and only a few had to be returned with thanks to their former units.

In June, 1941, the 14th/20th King's Hussars embarked at Bombay and sailed for Basra with the 2nd Indian Armoured Brigade. The Regiment, commanded by Lieut.-Colonel L. H. S. Groves, who had taken over from Lieut.-Colonel A. V. Pope in January, travelled in a couple of tramp steamers converted into troopships; the men in the S.S. *Rhona* and the unattended tanks in the S.S. *Regula*. The separation of the men from their vehicles, which was not the fault of the regiment, was not a good arrangement, for everything on the tanks that was attractive and removable was purloined by the Lascars in the *Regula*. Owing to rough seas during the voyage and bad securing of the vehicles in the ship's hold, some of the bren carriers had broken loose and had been slammed around by the ship's movement thus badly damaging many of the tanks. Repairing the damage kept the fitters and crews very busy for many days after disembarkation. The regiment landed at Basra on the 3rd July, a time of year at which the temperature in the Persian Gulf is well over 120 degrees in the shade. Camp was made at Shaiba, in a dreary stretch of desert completely empty save for a few tamarisk trees and a large canvas container full of water, in which 'C' Squadron were already disporting themselves. It was then discovered that it was not in fact a swimming pool, but the only available supply of water for drinking and cooking. The camp site, as was usual in those parts, was infested by scorpions and black with flies. This period spent in the Shaiba desert was particularly trying for all ranks. There was almost no tentage and the bulk of the men worked and slept in the open. A certain number of heat exhaustion cases occurred and in order to minimise this hazard every soldier was made to take salt at muster parade each day under the eye of his troop Leader.

The frustrations and difficulties of working under these conditions were aggravated when the regiment was told to paint out all their carefully executed Brigade numbers on the vehicles and to substitute some new numbers. This was yet another task to be done by the sweating and thirsty crewmen.

The 14th Hussars had, as already related, made the acquaintance of this plague-spot in 1915. On the outbreak of war, the Italian Legation at Basra became the centre of Axis propaganda. This had the effect of inducing Rashid Ali, the Iraqi Prime Minister, to throw in his lot with the Axis. Backed by four Iraqi generals, known as 'The Golden Square', he overthrew the Regent, who in March, 1941, took refuge in a British warship. In the old Imperial days, the traditional British method of dealing with any such local trouble East of Suez was to send an Indian Brigade (1 British and 3 Indian battalions), and this duly arrived in April. The Iraqi army had meanwhile attacked the important British air base at Habbaniya, 40 miles west of Baghdad, but it was driven off after 300 British troops had been flown in from Basra. The advance of the Indian Brigade from Basra being held up by floods and demolitions, a mechanised column and the Trans-Jordan Frontier Force of the Emir of

1941

Trans-Jordan were sent across the desert from Amman. This defeated the Iraqi Army at Falluja and they arrived before Baghdad at the end of May, whereupon Rashid Ali and the 'Golden Square' fled the country.

Although the situation in Iraq (Mesopotamia) had thus been got under control before the arrival of the 2nd Indian Armoured Brigade, more trouble started in Iran, where German infiltration reached such proportions as to affect the neutrality of the Iranian Government. Fortunately, on the 22nd June, Hitler invaded Russia, so that in dealing with Iran, Great Britain could count upon Russian support instead of enmity, which could have made the position very serious. In August an Anglo-Soviet ultimatum was presented to the Iranian Government, demanding the ejection of all German nationals. The Iranian Government declared its strict neutrality, and denied giving hospitality to any German nationals. British and Soviet troops accordingly invaded Iran on the 26th August.

By this time 'Iraq Force' had been concentrated, consisting of the 2nd Indian Armoured Brigade and the 8th and 10th Indian Divisions. It was commanded by Lieut.-General E. P. Quinan, who was instructed to move into the oilfields round Abadan, and at the same time force the Pai Tak Pass and take over the oilfields near Khanaquin on the western frontier. Quinan had therefore to divide his force into two. The 8th Indian Division, with a squadron of the Guides' Cavalry and the 13th Lancers attached, marched against Abadan, while the 10th Indian Division, commanded by Major-General W. J. Slim, with the 2nd Indian Armoured Brigade attached, moved up to Baghdad preparatory to forcing the Pai Tak Pass. The 2nd Indian Armoured Brigade, commanded by Brigadier J. A. Aizlewood, now consisted only of the 14th/20th Hussars – as far as armoured troops were concerned – but the Warwickshire Yeomanry were attached from the 9th Armoured Brigade, and Aizlewood was also given two battalions of lorried infantry, the 1/5th and 2/7th Gurkha Rifles. He also had the 15th Field Regiment R.A., a medium battery, and the 32nd Field Squadron, Q.V.O. Madras Sappers and Miners.

The 14th/20th King's Hussars left Basra for Baghdad on the 11th July, with the tanks travelling by rail and the wheeled vehicles by road. The heat was so intense that even the rail party suffered severely. For the road party, conditions were quite intolerable. There was no actual road, and the column had to move across the open desert where the sand and dust were whipped up into sandstorms by a strong, burning wind which blew incessantly. This westerly wind blew so strongly and was so filled with stinging sand that the left sides of the men's faces were stripped raw and the edges of vehicle mudguards and bonnets were sandblasted into a gleaming silver polish. Colonel Groves and the Adjutant, Captain McAllen, both collapsed at Ur of the Chaldees and had to be sent by train to Baghdad where McAllen died. Command of the road party was taken over by Major Studd, with Captain Parry-Crooke as Adjutant, but after the regiment had concentrated at Baghdad, command was taken over by Major R. J. Stephen who had led the rail party.

The 14th/20th King's Hussars had reached Baghdad on the 13th July, and spent nearly six weeks under most unpleasant conditions while awaiting orders. It was impossible to carry out any training, for the tanks were too hot to enter and, in fact, once the sun had got up it was possible to fry eggs on the hulls. During the period in Baghdad first parade each day at dawn was followed by a smart double down to the Tigris River about a quarter of a mile from the camp in the date palms, followed by a swim in the murky fast flowing waters. Diving into the river produced many surprises as dead animals and even a female corpse were grappled with in the muddy water.

The local Baghdad citizens seemed to regard the regiment as a

1941

The quaint scout cars of the Reconnaissance Troop carried a crew of three, a Bren LMG, and wireless. They were issued after the Persian operations and never actually came under enemy fire.

1941

thieves' paradise, and nightly they eluded the sentries and stole from both tents and vehicles. However, some officers laid an ambush and by dexterous use of pick helves and tent mallets succeeded in dissuading the local gentry from further light-fingeredness.

The 9th Armoured Brigade arrived, composed of the Household Cavalry, Warwickshire and Wiltshire Yeomanry, all riding in lorries for they did not have any tanks, being armoured only in name. They would have been of far more use on horseback, and it was a strange proceeding to dismount cavalry regiments before there were any vehicles available to give them. The 14th/20th were fortunate in this respect, although their tanks were already obsolete and would not have been capable of engaging a German Panzer formation. Colonel Groves returned from hospital on the 4th August, and on the following day the regiment began moving to Khanaquin on the Persian frontier.

The road leading from Baghdad into Persia crosses the frontier near Khaniquin, and then ascends in a series of twists and curves to the Pai Tak Pass, 6,000 feet above sea level and about twenty miles beyond the frontier. It was thought that the Pass might well be held in strength, and General Slim therefore divided his force into two columns, one to force the Pass and the other to outflank it by marching through Gilan to Shahabad, where the two columns would meet before continuing the advance. A special detachment would be sent at the same time to capture the oilfield at Naft-i-Shah, about 25 miles south-east of Khaniquin.

After the Intelligence Officer, Lieut. Tayleur, had carried out a reconnaissance towards Qasr-i-Shirin, the 1/5th Gurkha Rifles in lorries, accompanied by Lieut. Durnford's troop from 'B' Squadron, advanced from Khaniquin at midnight on the 24th/25th August and seized the frontier post at Khusrawi. The noise they made was considerable, but it failed to wake the Persian gendarmerie and customs officials in charge of the post, who were all dragged out of their beds by Gurkhas and placed under restraint. The rest of the regiment, less 'C' Squadron, then crossed the frontier and headed for Qasr-i-Shirin, led by the Reconnaissance Troop under Lieut. Tayleur. The night was pitch dark and the route was by mule track over mountainous country. The track was so rough and narrow and the night so dark that the last five miles from the frontier had to be conducted at walking pace. At one moment shortly before dawn the leading vehicle, the I.O.'s bren gun carrier, was ditched in a wadi and blocking the track and it was doubtful that the regiment would reach Qasr-i-Shirin by daylight. In the event the town was reached in good time and

'A' Squadron led by Major Studd took up a position before the town to prevent the garrison escaping towards the Pai Tak Pass. Much to the disappointment of the regiment, there were few troops in the town, and the only shot fired was aimed at Colonel Groves, who immediately replied with the first shot fired in anger by the regiment in the Second World War.

As soon as the Gurkhas and Durnford's troop arrived, the column marched for the Pai Tak Pass, forty miles ahead, with 'B' Squadron, under Major Johnston, and the Reconnaissance Troop under Captain Dennistoun in the lead. A number of road blocks were found, but none of them were defended and Sar-i-Pul Zuhab, at the foot of the Pai Tak, was reached unopposed during the afternoon. Here the column harboured for the night, with the exception of the Reconnaissance Troop which probed up the Pass, supported by 'B' Squadron. As had been anticipated, the Pass was found to be strongly held, and the Reconnaissance Troop soon came under heavy fire. The troop and squadron were then withdrawn, and came back into harbour, while the Brigadier thought things out, and eventually reported to General Slim that a direct assault against the Pass would be inadvisable.

On the following day, Slim ordered the column to join the outflanking column at Gilan. This entailed a difficult five-hour march through a rocky gorge, with the regiment dispersed along the column for its protection. Gilan was reached unopposed at 4 p.m., except for the Warwickshire Yeomanry mistaking the regiment for the Persian Army and shooting Lieut. Brunton's microphone out of his hand. Meanwhile 'C' Squadron had been in action beyond the town for some hours.

'C' Squadron, under Captain Browne, with two sections of the Reconnaissance Troop under Lieut. Talbot, and a squadron of Warwickshire Yeomanry, had reached Gilan at noon on the 25th August, as advanced guard to 'Pocol', the flanking column commanded by Colonel Pocock. Hearing from a local Arab that Persian troops were around Gilan, Pocock had sent Talbot forward to reconnoitre. He found the village unoccupied and moved on, soon coming under heavy fire from almost every conceivable type of weapon in positions along a ridge lying to the south-east. Talbot and his party went to ground on the right of the road about 600 yards from the enemy and, after reporting the situation, remained in observation. Browne and Pocock then went forward, but could not see any enemy so Browne went off in his tank to look for them. About two miles up the road he came under the same sort of fire that Talbot had experienced, but as he still could not see any Persians he returned to report. Pocock told him

1941

to 'take two troops and trail his coat up the road', whereupon Browne moved off with Lieutenants Donovan and Campbell's troops, in line ahead. Browne had intended to pass along the front of the enemy's positions, wheel and return in double line ahead on either side of the road, but after the wheel had been made, the ground was found to be so bad that the pace was reduced to a crawl. Although fortunately inaccurate, the enemy shell-fire was very heavy indeed, and to drive tanks through it at walking pace was dangerous and unpleasant. Browne ordered the squadron to withdraw, and as it did so, one enemy gun was at last located about 150 yards away and was quickly knocked out. Browne stayed behind in an attempt to find more guns, and as his tank moved slowly along the lower slopes of the ridge he did locate two, which he engaged in succession with his machine-gun at close range, seeing their crews scattering in all directions. Feeling that he had then 'trailed his coat' sufficiently, he returned to report. Under the circumstances his casualties were light, only one tank being hit. Sergeant Doran and Cpl. Haddon were killed in the turret, but the driver brought the tank in safely. Another man, Tpr. Armitage, was unfortunately killed in one of the lorries, which had followed the tanks by mistake and came under heavy fire before it could turn back.

Pocock now brought his guns into action and sent Browne back up the road, with instructions not to risk casualties but to be ready to chase the Persians should they run for it under the shell-fire. As it was impossible for the tanks to deploy off the road, owing to the nature of the ground, this was easier said than done, especially as 'shorts' and 'overs' from the British batteries were bursting along the road. The Persian small-arms fire was far more accurate than their gun-fire, and the tank-drivers and others at the apertures had a nerve-racking experience. The tank hulls were later found to be thickly pock-marked from bullets, especially round the apertures. Lieut. Donovan located an enemy anti-tank gun and ordered Jones, his driver, to turn right off the road into a position from which he would be able to get a good shot at it. The tank immediately got stuck in a wadi and all efforts failed to move it. The enemy anti-tank gun was luckily out of action, but after about ten minutes the enemy noticed Donovan's plight and turned several guns on to him. He reported to Browne on the wireless, and was told to sit tight until Browne brought up a carrier to tow him out. Donovan pointed out that the small-arms fire along the road would make things risky for a carrier, but nevertheless Browne arrived shortly afterwards in a carrier driven by S.S.M. Senior, for Browne had ordered the crew to dismount. The carrier was covered by Lieut. Campbell's tank, which preceded it and kept up a covering fire, but on reaching Donovan's tank Campbell had to move out of the way while Browne brought up the carrier, got out and fixed the tow-rope, under a hot fire from enemy light machine-guns. Browne then took cover in a ditch, while the carrier towed the tank out of the wadi, a tricky operation which required two attempts. He then took off the tows and jumped back into the carrier, which then ran out of petrol. So, once again he had to dismount and fix the ropes, after which Donovan towed the carrier out of action, followed by Campbell.

After this, Browne withdrew the squadron into harbour behind Gilan for repairs and maintenance. At daybreak, Donovan was sent back up the main road on patrol. The enemy was still in position, but after he had fired on them for a while they gave up and abandoned the whole valley. Another patrol led by Campbell along a track south of the ridge found no enemy. Donovan's tank cast a track while in action near the same spot that it had stuck the day before and, once again, Browne and Senior came to his assistance and towed him clear.

Chiefly owing to the efforts of 'C' Squadron the way was now clear for an advance on Shahabad. Browne received an immediate award of the Military Cross, which he had certainly earned. His performance, in fact, compared very favourably with that of Major E. D. Brown at Geluk in 1900, when he won the Victoria Cross. A feature of both actions was the fine leadership displayed, of which the seeming indifference to danger shown by these two officers was but an incidental part.

In a final reconnaissance along the valley, 'C' Squadron picked up '4 dead Persians, 1 prisoner and a dirty picture'. Most of the remaining enemy guns were found later where the Persians had buried them before abandoning their positions.

The advance was resumed on the 26th August, with the 9th Armoured Brigade leading in their lorries, preceded by Lieut. Talbot and two sections of the Reconnaissance Troop of the 14th/20th King's Hussars. At the same time an air strike was made on the enemy positions in the Pai Tak Pass, while the 21st Indian Brigade deployed before them. The Persians gave up without a fight, and the Brigade marched through the Pass to Karind, which it reached just in time to meet some of the leading troops of the 9th Armoured Brigade. Advancing against occasional slight resistance, which caused them a few casualties, the 9th Armoured Brigade came up against the main enemy position along a steep ridge at right angles across the road near Zibiri. The Brigade

1941

halted along a parallel ridge, while the 14th/20th were called forward to lead an attack across the flat, stony valley which lay between. At dawn on the 28th August, Major Johnston took 'B' Squadron and Talbot's reconnaissance sections up to the line held by the 9th Armoured Brigade, while the rest of the regiment formed up in the rear. Before the attack started, Talbot was sent down to Zibiri to draw fire, so that the enemy gun positions could be located and engaged. It was an unpleasant assignment, but had the desired effect of causing all the Persian guns to open up against Talbot, thus disclosing their positions and fortunately without doing Talbot's troops any damage. The regiment was just about to advance at 11 a.m., when the white flag went up and the Persian emissary arrived *en parliamentaire*. He was in a hurry to complete negotiations in time to stop a Persian brigade (horsed) from making a charge on the left flank against Pocock's rear echelons, which were spread out along the road. As Pocock was unaware of the presence of this cavalry brigade, it was just as well that it was halted in time although, from a purely military angle, it would have been interesting to observe its effect against Pocock's lorries.

The Shah having ordered his troops to cease fire on all fronts, General Slim, who had arrived in Zibiri, demanded the surrender of Kermanshah by 6 a.m. on the 30th August, and the withdrawal of the Persian forces along his front. After some demur, the Persian commanders agreed, and Slim made a ceremonial entry into Kermanshah on that date. The regiment took part in the ceremonial march through the town, having halted for a day short of the town to clean up both men and vehicles. The dignity of the march was somewhat marred by Sergeant Ireland of 'C' Squadron whose tank had broken down on the outskirts of the town but determined not to miss the fun he commandeered a bicycle and rode through the streets with his squadron.

While these operations were in progress, Russian forces had been driving down from the north without meeting any resistance and Slim was instructed to press on immediately to Hamadan, so that it would be in British hands before the Russians arrived. The 14th/20th were sent off from Kermanshah at 4 p.m. on a march of 100 miles and the negotiation of the Shah Pass, 8,000 feet up and reached by a narrow track with innumerable hair-pin bends. It must be admitted that this feat could hardly have been performed on horses. It was a bit out-of-the-way for tanks, especially tanks of the vintage of those of the 14th/20th, few of which were under two years old.

The regiment received a hearty welcome from the inhabitants,

The entry into Kermanshah on 30 August 1941 by General Slim and the tanks of the 14th/20th.

as it drove into Hamadan, for they were very frightened of the Russians, whose bombers were just completing a raid over the town. Major Stephen who had gone on ahead, was already there, with a Persian battery of 150 mm guns, which had surrendered to him on the way. The Brigadier also turned up at this time and took Stephen with him to get in touch with the Russians, who were known to have reached Kazvin. Captain Swallow had already been sent up the Kazvin road in a 3-ton lorry to report on the road, but warned not to go too close to Kazvin itself. While he was trying to turn the lorry on the narrow road, after deciding that he had gone far enough, he was stopped by a Russian patrol and, after some ineffectual parleying, taken off to Kazvin for interrogation. Having at length managed to convince the Russians he was on their side, he was allowed to return to his lorry, where he found his crew surrounded by Russian soldiers and apparently enjoying themselves – for it was a curious fact, that the few words

1941

of bazaar Hindustani possessed by most British regular soldiers in those days enabled them to surmount all language difficulties in any part of the globe. One of them, L./Cpl. Boreham, was presented with an English copy of the works of Lord Byron, as a parting gift.

When the Brigadier and Major Stephen went off to meet the Russians, they took a company of Gurkhas with them. Having met a Russian armoured car about 100 miles up the Kazvin road, they left the Gurkhas to dig in a position across the road and went into Kazvin, where they had lunch with a dozen Russian officers, but were unable to surmount the language problem so well as Boreham and his comrades. The ice was at last broken when an interpreter was produced, and when more British officers arrived the usual Russian orgy commenced and lasted until breakfast on the following day, a meal at which 'methylated vodka' was served to the guests. This was the first official contact between British and Russian soldiers in the war, and it was certainly a very friendly occasion.

The friendly feelings generated on such alcoholic gatherings were not unfortunately subscribed to by the Russian High Command, which, coldly sober and subject to the terrifying scrutiny of Stalin, was suspicious of every British move. The Shah, who for one reason or another preferred the Germans to the British and detested the Russians, endeavoured with oriental guile to organise an open break between the two allies. A visit by Sir Archibald Wavell to the Russian Commander-in-Chief frustrated his efforts, but he did succeed for a time in postponing the eviction of German nationals from Persia in accordance with allied demands. The threat of an armed allied descent upon Teheran then forced his abdication in September, and the Germans were expelled, although not until the allies had in fact occupied the city.

Until the abdication of the Shah, the situation in Iran remained tense, as may be imagined in a country still under arms and smarting from defeat, and occupied by British, Russians and Germans also under arms and trying to get the advantage over one another. The British forces had therefore to keep on the alert during this period, and yet avoid any unnecessary contact with the others. While deliberations were going on at a high level the soldiers, as usual, were kept somewhat in the dark. Lieut. Woodley of the 14th/20th for example, was sent to do a road reconnaissance to Sultanabad, 200 miles away, using his own initiative and without any clear directions. Driving into the town he went to the only hotel for refreshment, and was indignant to find it full of German and Italian 'agents'. He immediately sent for the Chief-of-Police and forced him to lock them all up. On his return journey, he was halted a mile out of town by General Slim, who was doing a quiet personal reconnaissance dressed in inconspicuous clothing and equipped with a pair of powerful field-glasses. It appeared that he had been under the impression that Sultanabad was occupied by German forces, and he was not best pleased to find that Woodley had driven in without ceremony and had them all locked up.

The successful conclusion of the Iraq and Persian campaigns, and the consequent elimination of all Axis influence in this part of the Middle East, was a matter of the highest importance. Apart from establishing contact with the Russians and securing the vital oil-fields, it protected India from the dangers of enemy infiltration and denied to the enemy a potential jumping-off ground for an advance to the eastern shores of the Mediterranean. Once secured, however, it had to be defended, and thus swallowed up troops which Wavell and his successor, Sir Claude Auchinleck, could certainly have put to good use in the Western Desert.

In this campaign the 14th/20th King's Hussars, making their third visit to Iran in the history of the regiment, had driven their tanks over almost exactly the same areas as the 14th Hussars had ridden their horses across during the First World War. But whereas the 14th had been engaged in major operations involving a great deal of hard fighting, the adventures of the 14th/20th, however important the outcome, were little more than an expedition or side-show. At a time when the Eighth Army was hard-pressed, and having its work cut out to defend Egypt, it became increasingly frustrating for a regiment such as the 14th/20th, to be kept inactive 6,000 feet above sea-level in a remote Persian township like Hamadan. But there was no help for it, and it was doubtless just as well for the regiment that the fortune of war should have spared it the unpleasant experiences of the Armoured Corps in the Western Desert during 1941 and 1942.

In September, 1941, the British occupying forces in Iraq and Iran were organised into a single command and renamed 'Persia and Iraq Force' (Paiforce). Its duties were not only those of defence and internal security. To quote Winston Churchill: 'The creation of a major supply route to Russia through the Persian Gulf became our prime objective . . . ports were enlarged, river communications developed, roads built, and railways reconstructed. Starting in September, 1941, this enterprise, begun and developed by the British Army, and presently to be adopted and completed by the United States, enabled us to send to Russia,

1942

over a period of four and a half years, five million tons of supplies.'

Works services such as these were the concern of the infantry and engineers, and did not come within the province of an armoured regiment. For a time, the 14th/20th had therefore little to do except look after its vehicles and make the most of such pleasures as Hamadan and the surrounding country had to offer. These included football and rough shooting; also pigsticking on Arab horses, which always take very readily to the sport. One heat ridden by Majors Studd and Mann and Captain Parry-Crooke, led to a run of fifteen miles and the death of a boar of 40 inches – far bigger than most of those hunted in India. During the regiment's stay in Hamadan it was on the extreme end of a long L. of C. which started in India. Railhead was in Khaniquin some 200 miles away and all the rations and needs of the regiment were hauled by its own trucks from railhead. Naafi supplies never seemed to get through and the soldiers sadly missed their cigarettes and weekly bottle of beer; not to mention the officers whose spirit ration was half a bottle each month. It did not take long for the regiment to appreciate that Persia produces excellent mild and cheap cigarettes and also good wines, cherry brandy and vodka. When Naafi supplies did finally catch up, their arrival was hardly noticed.

In October, the regiment marched from Hamadan to Quayara on the Tigris, 40 miles south of Mosul. The march, with the tracked vehicles carried on civilian lorries, took a week. The 14th/20th were an odd looking crew at this time. Standard British uniforms were seldom seen. Most of the officers wore a variety of sheepskin yellow poshteen coats of local Persian purchase. Nearly all the men wore leather or sheepskin jackets and headgear which varied from flying helmets to Cossack type fur hats.

During the winter, in appalling conditions of mud and snow, the regiment trained hard at desert warfare, expecting to be sent off to the Western Desert at any moment. Colonel Groves and Major Studd did in fact go there, but on a visit only. In the spring the regiment was re-equipped with Stuart Light Tanks, which arrived in batches over a lengthy period. While they were still in process of delivery, the regiment was issued with a balance of 15 cwt. trucks, and so, as an armoured regiment, was not for a while fit for action. This, however, was not the only factor which kept it on the Tigris at a time when the Eighth Army was falling back on Alamein. The Germans had advanced along the Black Sea, capturing the Crimea and moved into the Caucasus. Their objective was the Caucasian oilfields, but it was feared that they might well force Turkey into the war, or at any rate violate her territory and come down upon Iraq. Paiforce was alerted accordingly, and defensive measures were taken round Mosul and Quayara. An extended sapper reconnaissance was carried out into Kurdistan, passing Lake Urmia and returning by way of Kermanshah. It was escorted by Captain B. C. L. Tayleur with the Reconnaissance Troop, travelling in so-called scout cars, which were in fact large four-wheeled vehicles protected by armour plating and carrying crews of three, with a Bren gun in each. These scout cars were built in India and armoured with plate made by the Tata Indian Steel Works. The crews always doubted the bullet resisting qualities of the steel and one or two odd bulges in the plates of some cars showed that private tests had been carried out. Besides the sapper party – of the Madras Sappers and Miners – and the Reconnaissance Troop of the 14th/20th, there was a platoon of the Bombay Grenadiers and a mortar section. After the administrative vehicles had been added, Tayleur had a small army under his command. It was an adventurous trip, during which the party ran into Russian cavalry among the wild heights of Kurdistan, and had the usual difficulty in extricating themselves from the predatory grip of the Russians who, then as always, had a pathological dislike of letting anyone go, once they had got hold of him.

In November, 1942, the 14th/20th King's Hussars were moved to Shaiba, where they were re-equipped with Grant tanks. In the following February, Lieut.-Colonel Groves relinquished command and returned to the United Kingdom. He was succeeded by Lieut.-Colonel H. A. R. Tilney, who had rejoined the regiment shortly before, after an absence of ten years. The 'Python' scheme was introduced at this time, entitling those with long service overseas to repatriation. This resulted in the loss to the regiment of most of its old and experienced soldiers. The replacements, however, who came from the 7th Queen's Own Hussars and the Lancashire Fusiliers (who had been converted to an armoured regiment) proved to be excellent, and many of them eventually changed their coat and became 14th/20th King's Hussars.

In May, 1943, the whole of the 31st Indian Armoured Division, which had for several months been expecting a summons to the Western Desert, was moved instead to Quayara, near Mosul, a location which was only too familiar to the 14th/20th King's Hussars. The Division, commanded by Major-General R. E. Wordsworth, was composed of the 252nd Indian Armoured Brigade, the 43rd Gurkha Lorried Infantry Brigade, and Divisional Troops, consisting of the 15th and 144th Field Regi-

1944

ments R.A., the 79th Anti-Tank Regiment R.A., the 13th Lancers and the Madras Sappers and Miners. With the 14th/20th King's Hussars in the 252nd Brigade, were Hodson's Horse, the Scinde Horse, and the 1st/4th Bombay Grenadiers. Every one of these units was efficient and battleworthy, and to be kept out of the field at a time when victory was at last in sight was extremely galling for them. In October, the Division finally left the Tigris, to everyone's great relief, and moved to Burg-el-Arab, 30 miles west of Alexandria. A month previously, the Allies had landed on the toe of Italy after the Italians had unconditionally surrendered. Naples was occupied on the 1st October, and on the 13th Italy declared war on Germany. At this time, the regiment was re-equipped with diesel-engined Mark III Sherman Tanks; quite the latest thing in battlefield machinery. They were so different from any of the various types of ironmongery which the regiment had been driving before, that some intensive 'conversion training' was necessary in order to get used to them. Everyone put his back into this, being convinced that the 14th/20th King's Hussars would soon be chasing the Germans out of Italy.

This moment, however, had still not arrived, for in April, 1944, the Division was sent off to Syria to practise the movement of armoured formations in mountainous country. It was envisaged at this time that the Germans would make a stand in the Austrian Alps, and they were already taking full advantage of the mountains in Northern Italy. Some infantry units had already been trained as 'mountaineers' in order to deal with this situation, so that it was nothing out of the way for the 31st Indian Armoured Division to be sent off for special training. It was nevertheless extremely irritating for regiments such as the 14th/20th, already well-acquainted with mountain country and in every way fit for action, to be thus again informed by implication that they were not yet up to the standard necessary for engaging the Germans. Ever since the end of the 'Phoney War', the British tendency had been to produce more and more specialists and specially-trained 'Private Armies' of every description: Commandos, Special Air Service, 'Phantoms', and Mountaineers. There was simply no end to them, and orthodox units were made to feel their inferiority in a manner scarcely calculated to maintain morale although, thanks to their inward knowledge of a martial inheritance second to none in the world, they did maintain it. Regiments of the British Regular Army had been fighting for centuries over every conceivable type of terrain against every conceivable type of enemy, with an adaptability which made light of forests, deserts, mountains and even salt water. Why their potentialities should

1944

have been so widely disregarded in this war is a mystery, except that Winston Churchill had a passion for the romance of the unorthodox – though none should have remembered better than he, that there were no 'Commandos' at Badajoz.

A sudden alarm in April, 1944, when the regiment was stood-to for an urgent move at short notice, brought hope to every heart. Colonel Tilney flew off in an aeroplane, leaving Major Stephen to bring the regiment – less its tanks – to Alexandria. But the situation proved to be nothing more alarming than the mutiny of a Greek Brigade beyond Burg-el-Arab. Within 72 hours of leaving Hermon, the regiment had driven 800 miles and drawn 52 Sherman tanks and 11 Stuarts out of 'care and maintenance', cleaned the jelly off them, stripped down, reassembled and calibrated the guns, checked all wireless sets, drawn ammunition and confronted the Greeks in line of battle. The wretched Greeks gave in without further demur, as did others in the Greek Naval Barracks after a demonstration by 'B' Squadron. They were all packed into trucks and escorted by the regiment 'many miles into the back of beyond', after which, in spite of energetic protests by Colonel Tilney, the regiment was sent back into Syria to rejoin the Division.

In June the regiment moved up to Aleppo with the Division which, for a couple of months, made 'a show of force' along the Turkish frontier. This was in fact part of the D-Day deception plan and was instrumental in keeping at least six German Divisions in Greece looking East instead of West. Thereafter it ranged far and wide throughout Syria and Palestine, engaged in Tank and Infantry co-operation training with the 5th Infantry Division. In July, Commanding-Officers were told by the Divisional Commander that there was no longer any chance of the Division becoming operational. There was nothing to be done but to make the best of it, and the regiment turned its thoughts to the coming post-war period, and commenced a series of lectures and courses to prepare the rank and file for their return to civilian life. One of the lecturers was W.O.I. Michael Stewart of the Army Educational Corps, whose efforts were so appreciated by the regiment that it presented him on leaving with an engraved silver cigarette case. W.O.I. Stewart became the Secretary of State for Foreign Affairs in 1966, which shows that, when lecturing the regiment on civilian life and opportunities he must certainly have known what he was talking about.

Fortune, that 'fickle jade', then, as usual, demonstrated her fickleness by arranging that, the moment the regiment abandoned hope of ever getting to the front, it was immediately sent

1945

there. The orders, which came in December, that the 14th/20th King's Hussars were to relieve the 3rd Hussars in Italy in January, 1945, coincided with orders to convert to an armoured car regiment for internal security duties in Palestine. South African Marmon Harrington cars were issued but, when found to be unreliable, replaced by Humbers. All this was not done in a day, and at one time the regiment was driving four different sorts of vehicle – Shermans, South Africans, Humbers and AECs – and not sure whether it was really going to fight the Germans or merely keep order in Palestine. In spite of all its set-backs and disappointments, however, its morale had never weakened and was now, with renewed hope, higher than ever. After carrying out a major exercise in the mountains in villainous weather without a single mishap, 'the best Christmas of the War' was celebrated, with the advance party of the 3rd Hussars as guests. The 3rd Hussars had been decimated in Italy, but the prospect of this happening to the 14th/20th in no way affected anyone's spirits. For the soldier, faced with the distinct possibility of death or suffering in the near future, going to war is a fearsome experience; but an even worse experience is to be left out of it when others are fighting and suffering. The ability to enjoy a celebration before leaving safety for the field is thus no paradox.

At the final visit of the Mechanical Inspectorate before the regiment left for Italy, it was given the classification 'Excellent', in respect of its vehicle maintenance. It was a classification which had never before been gained by a field unit. A special visit was also made by the Commander-in-Chief who paid high tribute to the regiment's 'spirit, efficiency and boundless patience'. The main body of the 3rd Hussars arrived on the 15th January, and the 14th/20th entrained that night for Haifa, sailing two days later for Taranto.

The regiment arrived in Italy on the 21st January, 1945, to find the country in the grip of a bitter winter which was a severe contrast to the Middle Eastern climate. By this time the Allies had advanced to the line of the Senio River, with the Eighth Army on the right beyond Ravenna, and the American Fifth Army on the left astride the Apennines. The Germans were still resisting stoutly with their morale unimpaired, in spite of the decline in their fortunes which made it obvious to them that they had nothing to look forward to but final and devastating defeat. The object of the Allies was to keep them on the move and prevent them from sending reinforcements to the west. Hard weather and a shortage of ammunition and supplies had halted operations for the moment, but a combined offensive was planned for the spring.

1945

At the end of January, the regiment, less 'B' Squadron, was informed that it would operate under XIII Corps as an independent armoured regiment on the left of the Eighth Army, and on the 1st February it was moved up to San Donato near Florence, where the XIII Corps was in reserve. 'B' Squadron, under Major Mann, was sent to relieve a squadron of the 12th Canadian Armoured Regiment at San Clemente, and by the 7th February was in the front line with three troops and two troops back (one troop of 'C' Squadron was under command).

By the 15th February, the regiment was deployed as follows:

R.H.Q. and 'A' Squadron at San Donato, with a Tactical H.Q. at Castel Del Rio.

'B' Squadron and one Troop 'C' Squadron at San Clemente.

'C' Squadron less one Troop at Fontanelice.

'C' Squadron was in support of the 6th Armoured Division in a counter-attack role. The Germans were in a strong position on a ridge 1,200 yards in front, but the squadron was not allowed to shoot at them for fear of reprisals against the infantry, who were trying to get a rest and wanted as much peace and quiet as possible. This was annoying, as the enemy kept their guns warmed-up and shelled 'C' Squadron from time to time as a matter of routine, but without causing any damage or casualties.

'B' Squadron, on the left of the 10th Indian Division, were encouraged to shoot. The squadron had always prided itself on its gunnery, in which Captains Sturt and Heath had a special interest. It was frequently called upon by the neighbouring Field Regiment to take on targets at the closer ranges up to 8,000 yards, with excellent results, and requiring at the most three shots to register indirect targets at this range. However, after 'A' Squadron had relieved 'C', which later relieved 'B' and so at last was able to do some shooting, it proved so good at it as to receive several complimentary mentions in the daily Intelligence Summaries.

On the 12th March, a warning order was received from H.Q. Eighth Army for a move to a new concentration area near Cesena, to be completed by the 18th. 'C' Squadron was to be left behind until relieved, and 'A' Squadron (Major Studd), was to exchange its Sherman tanks for Kangaroos (armoured troop carriers), which turned out to be converted Priests (self-propelled guns) from which the 105 mm guns had been removed, and additional armour-plating added. After its conversion, 'A' Squadron was to be able to mount a whole infantry battalion, and to enable it to do so, 'B' and 'C' Squadrons had to give it the personnel of one tank troop apiece. The regiment was not best pleased at being 'mucked

1945

about' in this manner, but everyone cheered up considerably on learning that the infantry which they were going to escort round the battlefield were their old friends of the 43rd Lorried Gurkha Brigade, with whom they had practised such tactics *ad nauseam*, and who were just as anxious to try them out on the Germans as the 14th/20th were themselves.

The conversion of 'A' Squadron in this manner was a highly complicated business, which the whole regiment had to put its back into in order to get it done in the short time available and carry out some training with the Gurkhas. Each Kangaroo had a crew of two: the commander/wireless operator, and the driver. Each troop in the re-organised squadron carried a complete Gurkha company, while the squadron H.Q. troop carried the battalion H.Q. and H.Q. Company. The wireless network was complex, for besides the normal squadron communications, additional communications had to be provided for the Brigadier and Battalion Commander, and for various specialist officers including R.A. and R.E. This meant that several Kangaroos had to carry as many as four wireless sets.

The main German line of resistance, the 'Genghis Khan Line', ran along the southern shore of Lake Comacchio and across the lower valley of the Po to the Senio River. Continuing westwards over the mountain tops of Monte Grande and Belmonte it crossed the Reno to Vergato. On the Allied side, Monte Grande was the junction between the Fifth and Eighth Armies, and for the coming offensive formed the pivot upon which the Eighth Army, attacking a few days before the Fifth, would swing north-westerly towards the Po valley.

On the Eighth Army front, the order of battle from right to left was the Vth Corps, the IInd Polish Corps, the Xth Corps and the XIIIth Corps. The plan was for the Vth and Polish Corps to attack across the Senio and secure crossing bridgeheads beyond the Santerno, from which the Vth Corps would advance north towards Bastia and Argenta. The Polish Corps would advance towards Medicina on the right, towards Budrio, and to Castel San Pietro on the left. The Xth and XIIIth Corps were to create as much uproar as possible in order to mislead the enemy as to the main direction of the offensive, and then to advance as opportunity offered.

The task of the 43rd Lorried Gurkha Brigade Group was to follow up the Poles and break through when the moment arrived. Unlike the 14th/20th, the Gurkhas had been fighting in Italy since the previous September – on their feet, not in lorries, which were seldom of much practical use in this theatre where the country was either mountainous or enclosed. Now they were to be carried into action in Kangaroos driven by their old friends the 14th/20th King's Hussars.

'War,' said Napoleon, 'is a great and impassioned drama.' Had he been sitting on his horse on the banks of the Senio River, watching the opening of the Vth Corps offensive during the afternoon of the 9th April, 1945, he might well have felt that he had been guilty of a gross understatement. Fleets of heavy bombers arrived, and for an hour and half their bombs rained down along the German line, raising a dense cloud of yellow dust and smoke. They were succeeded by an artillery bombardment reminiscent of those on the Somme thirty years before and when the infantry went into the attack they were accompanied by flame-throwing tanks squirting out long streams of fire, while the sky above was black with fighter-bombers diving down with their cannons roaring, and followed by medium bombers dropping sticks of bombs. It was a strange thing, however, as Napoleon might further have reflected, that this impressive holocaust did not result in nearly as many dead men as he had been accustomed to expect during his own campaigns in this same country.

The Germans at any rate were not dismayed, but put up the most determined resistance. Nevertheless the advance of the Vth Corps went well, although the skilful withdrawal by the enemy prevented the destruction of the German divisions in the salient before Bologna, which had been hoped for. The Polish Corps had more difficulty. Some days before the offensive the Poles had heard the news of the Yalta Conference, at which Churchill, Stalin and Roosevelt had discussed the policy to be followed during the closing stages of the war and after final victory. The Russian demands with regard to the restriction of Poland's frontiers were acceded to, and this caused such resentment in the Polish Corps that its commander, General Anders, had great difficulty in persuading its officers and men to go into action. They were then bombed by some of the United States' aircraft while forming up, but having at length given General Anders their undertaking to go on with the fight, they did not allow this mishap to weaken their resolution. The 43rd Lorried Gurkha Brigade, including the 14th/20th, was under General Anders' orders and Colonel Tilney had to report to his H.Q. for briefing. At lunch in the officers' mess, his neighbour remarked: 'Apart from our hatred of Germans we have nothing left to fight for. All of us have lost everything – yes, *everything*! Country, family, home, possessions; the Russians or Germans have them all.' As may be imagined, Tilney was at a loss for a reply.

1945

The 2nd/8th and 2nd/10th Gurkha Rifles went into action on foot when the Poles were held up along the Santerno River on the 12th April, and led the way to the Sillaro River. Here the 2nd/8th Gurkha Rifles, supported by the 2nd Royal Tank Regiment, had some heavy fighting along the south bank, but the 2nd/10th Gurkhas came up and forced a crossing during the night of the 15th. Meanwhile the 14th/20th, carrying the 2nd/6th Gurkha Rifles, had moved up to an assembly area 1,500 yards in the rear, with the intention of crossing at dawn and pushing on to Medicina, about five miles beyond.

The enemy had, of course, blown all the bridges over the Sillaro. In addition all likely crossing places were heavily mined, and the south bank had been accurately registered by the German artillery. The Gurkha Rifles had not had an easy time getting over, and they were infantry, trained in the use of assault craft and bridges. Getting tanks and armoured personnel carriers over was a different problem, which the vigilance of the German gunners made difficult to solve. The accuracy of the salvoes directed against every reconnaissance party which showed itself in daylight gave everyone a very lively time, and in fact made a detailed reconnaissance impossible. The regiment was fortunate to escape casualties at this time, and the only tank hit was Lieut. Kneller's, whose ·5 Browning was blown away, while he was in the act of clearing and adjusting it.

Crossing tanks over rivers was done with the help of an 'Ark', which was a specially constructed bridging tank which, when positioned in the middle of the river, allowed other tanks to drive over it. It required careful siting, which was lacking in this case owing to the difficulties of prior reconnaissance. Two tanks of the Royal Tank Regiment got over, but no others could negotiate the further bank and had to be towed up it with great difficulty and delay. The enemy defensive fire then came down on the crossing, but fortunately an armoured bulldozer arrived at the same time and, after it had scraped a passage up the far bank the whole regiment got across. It emerged into a country of thick vineyards and orchards, intersected by canals and ditches, and by scattered groups of houses along the roads to Medicina, each of which was a potential fortification from which the enemy could hold up the advance.

It was known that the 2nd New Zealand Division was advancing on the right, but touch had been lost with the Poles on the left, and a squadron of the 2nd Royal Tank Regiment, which was under command of the 14th/20th, was therefore sent out as left flank guard. 'C' Squadron, under Major Browne, then moved on as advanced guard, with a troop of 'A' Squadron carrying a company of the 2nd/6th Gurkha Rifles under command. Forward Observation Officers from 'R' Battery 15th Field Regiment, R.A., accompanied the advanced and flank guards.

'C' Squadron soon came under heavy artillery fire, and Lieut. Camburn was wounded. The road to Medicina was, however, found to be unmined and uncratered, which was a pleasant surprise and enabled a fair pace to be kept up. It had to be assumed that the road-bridge over the Scolo Sillaro had been blown and therefore, before reaching it, 'C' Squadron was directed to move off the road and take to the country, thereafter reconnoitring for an alternative crossing. 'C' Squadron and the left flank guard then both began to come under heavy fire from self-propelled guns. Communications within 'C' Squadron were disrupted, and the Royal Tank Squadron was held up, but after numbers of Germans had surrendered and were ordered back to the rear, the advance continued.

In the meantime, Lieut. Kneller with the Reconnaissance Troop of 'C' Squadron was having to take brisk avoiding action from the attentions of several S.P. guns while trying to find a crossing over the Scolo Sillaro, while the rest of 'C' Squadron ran into a hornets' nest, with each troop fighting it out on its own against every conceivable type of opposition. Two tanks were destroyed by Bazookas and two others put out of action, all of them Shermans. One Stuart tank was also destroyed, one man killed and ten wounded. The gains were worthwhile; one S.P. gun was captured intact, 50 enemy were killed or badly wounded, and 40 others surrendered when Lieut. Kneller drove his tank along a ditch in which they were sheltering. The dismounting of a Gurkha Company enabled the Scolo Sillaro to be reconnoitred and a crossing found. It was a resolute and gallant performance in which Sergeant Hall particularly distinguished himself after his troop leader's tank had been knocked out and several others badly damaged. His own tank was hit five times and his gun put out of action, but he went on fighting with his secondary armament until obliged to abandon ship after the tank had been brought to a standstill in the middle of a 'bracket'. He was given an immediate award of the D.C.M.

Some of the leading tanks of 'C' Squadron were now shooting into Medicina, whose domes and spires (with enemy O.P.'s in most of them) were visible in the fading light, about 4,000 yards distant. The squadron was still on the wrong side of the Scolo Sillaro, and no crossing had been found, but at this moment a New Zealand Armoured Bulldozer appeared on the right, dug

1945

out a crossing and disappeared again. The whole regiment was soon across, including the Kangaroos with the 2nd/6th Gurkha Rifles, but there were still two water obstacles ahead, and Colonel Tilney came to the conclusion that it was time to dismount the Gurkhas and send them against Medicina on foot. The Brigadier, 'Tochi' Barker, drove up at this moment, however, and ordered – or at any rate strongly suggested – that the tanks continued to lead the way. Tilney was momentarily nonplussed by the order and, being a man of strong faith, got out of his tank, moved out of sight and put up a prayer for guidance. Receiving a strong impression that it was indeed time for the charge to be sounded, he returned strengthened to his tank. The only way by which tanks could advance was down the main axis, which was so certain to be mined and cratered that he had not previously considered it. Now, without hesitation, he called up 'C' Squadron and ordered it to close on the main axis, then 'Get your whips out and go like hell!' 'I confess freely,' he wrote afterwards, 'that I would not have given that order to "C" Squadron of my own accord.'

The order at any rate was perfectly acceptable to a man of the temperament of Major Browne, who was soon roaring down the road at the head of his squadron, with the guns blazing away to right and left of every building or cover where Germans might be lurking with their Spandaus and Bazookas. At 7.45 p.m. he wirelessed, 'I'm in Medicina.'

Medicina was a fantastic sight. Much of it was ablaze; the streets were full of rubble, enemy guns and vehicles, and the houses full of Germans, who had been taken completely by surprise but were quickly recovering themselves and full of fight. Tilney had followed 'C' Squadron with his tactical H.Q., but as no more tanks could get into the town he halted on the edge and ordered 'B' Squadron to bring up the Kangaroos, dismount the Gurkhas and then stand-by in case of a counter-attack. Browne had meanwhile dashed on through the town and blown up an S.P. gun, which then slewed across his path. His tank just managed to get past before a nearby building collapsed and blocked the street, and he then drove on and put two 88 mm. guns out of action, killing their crews before they had time to get a shot off. Thus he reached the station square, in which every surrounding house was full of snipers and Bazookas. He had just time to wireless orders to the squadron before his tank was set on fire and he and his operator, Sgt. Evans, were badly wounded. Burt, the gunner, was killed, but Armstrong, the driver, and McGregor, the second operator, were unhurt and so jumped out of the tank and attacked the house containing the Bazooka which had set it on fire. The two of them killed most of the Germans inside and chased the others out of the door and round the corner, after which they returned to the tank and got Browne and Evans out and under cover. All this was done under heavy rifle and Spandau fire.

S.S.M. Long, who was following Browne and endeavouring to give his tank covering fire, was then killed while firing his tommy-gun from his open turret. Captain Heath, the second Captain of 'C' Squadron, was held up by the blown S.P. gun and rubble blocking the main street. He was joined by Armstrong and McGregor from Browne's tank, who had come back under heavy fire to report, ignoring the exploding ammunition in the S.P. gun. Heath took over command and sent a troop round the south-east side to the station square, followed by a Kangaroo troop led by Lieut. Brailey. Cpl. Plumley's tank was hit by a Bazooka and set on fire. The gunner, Nixon, was killed and Plumley and the rest of the crew wounded, except for Harper, the co-driver, who baled out. Then, realising that his comrades were wounded he re-entered the burning tank and got Plumley out, just before the ammunition exploded. The others managed to get out on their own.

The Kangaroos had arrived by then and the Gurkhas went into action with their kukris. The first blood was drawn by the Subedar who chased the man with the Bazooka, responsible for blowing up Plumley's tank, and chopped him up round a corner. The Gurkhas then went off in full cry, hunting Germans through the houses and killing them in cellars, lofts and on the roof-tops. Some escaped, others managed to surrender, but great numbers came to a violent end.

Night fell at last, with the town of Medicina in British hands and not a live German left in it. It had been 'C' Squadron's day; the luck of the draw having kept it in the forefront from the beginning. The other squadrons carried out their orders in an exemplary manner. Casualties to the regiment on this day amounted to 5 killed and 23 wounded. Five tanks were destroyed and 2 badly damaged. The enemy losses could not be determined accurately, but were in the region of 159 killed and wounded. Two 88 mm. guns, 5 S.P. guns, 3 Panthers and 1 Tiger tank were captured or destroyed, and 80 prisoners were taken.

The regiment received four immediate awards for gallantry in this action: Major Browne the D.S.O., Sergeant Hall the D.C.M., and L./Cpl. McGregor and Tpr. Armstrong the M.M. Captain Heath and Lieut. Brailey later received awards of the M.C.

Above: Regimental Trumpeters in front of the Brandenburg Gate, Berlin, in 1957. 'B' Squadron was stationed there from 1957 to 1960. Below: The Regiment marching past during the ceremony of Trooping the old Guidons at Catterick Camp in 1950. The Parade was taken by the Colonel of the Regiment, General Sir Richard McCreery.

2nd May 1945 The crossings of the Giano, Po and Adige The 14th/20th reach Padua
4th May 1945 The German surrender
February 1945 The 14th/20th move to the Rhine
November 1947 The 14th/20th become a Basic Training Regiment at Catterick
January 1951 The 14th/20th go to Crookham and again become an armoured regiment
October 1952 The regiment moves to Libya
October 1955 Returns home
March 1956 And back to the Rhine
10th June 1961 Presentation of a Guidon
1962 Back to Libya
January 1964 'C' Squadron in Cyprus
1966 Return home
1967 to 1969 Back to the Rhine
1970 Warned for Far East Service
1969 H.R.H. The Princess Anne appointed Colonel-in-Chief, visits Regiment in BAOR

1945

31

The End of the War and Aftermath

After the capture of Medicina, the 43rd Brigade Group was placed under command of the 2nd New Zealand Division whose commander, Sir Bernard Freyberg, greeted Brigadier 'Tochi' Barker with the words: 'Well done! You are the only formation the New Zealand Division has ever admired from behind!' In the race for Medicina the Brigade had got ahead of the New Zealanders, but they had now drawn level, and on the 17th April reached the Gaiana Canal, which was strongly held. The Brigade left Medicina in the morning of the same day, with 'A' Squadron of the 2nd Royal Tank Regiment in the lead, followed by the 14th/20th with 'A' Squadron carrying the 2nd/6th Gurkha Rifles complete, escorted by 'B' Squadron, while the 'gallant remains' of 'C' Squadron brought up the rear.

As the squadron of Royal Tanks approached the river, it came under mortar and Spandau fire from enemy positions along the flood bank. One of its leading tanks was then hit by a Bazooka, which killed the three men in the turret. The area was no place for tanks, which made easy targets for infantry hidden in the long grass, and the 2nd/6th Gurkha Rifles were therefore dismounted while the headquarters of the 14th/20th and 2nd/6th Gurkha Rifles were established in the Casa Pasi, a strongly built farmhouse 700 yards from the river. A very thorough plan was then

1945

worked out to get the Gurkhas across the river, which was a formidable undertaking, especially as the enemy defensive fire had become very heavy – it did not cease until nightfall. Throughout this hectic day, during which the German snipers never let up, a delighted Italian farmer celebrated the liberation of his property by running from tank to tank, often in a hail of bullets, with a large flask of Chianti and gave the crews a victory toast.

An objective about 500 yards in width was selected for the attack, and was softened up by forty minutes bombardment from every gun in the Brigade Group, aided by ten fighter-bomber sorties and observed fire from the Tanks. The Gurkhas attacked at about 3 p.m. with two companies up, which were carried to within 200 yards of the nearer flood bank by Lieutenants Finneron and Stratton's troops in Kangaroos. After the Gurkhas had dismounted, these Kangaroos remained in support, bringing up ammunition and evacuating wounded and prisoners. The 2nd/6th Gurkhas took the nearer flood bank and got a platoon across to the other side, but it was heavily enfiladed from both flanks and they had to withdraw. The 2nd/8th Gurkhas came up on the right of the 2nd/6th and linked up with the New Zealanders. The whole of the next day was spent in bombarding the enemy with every form of high explosive missile at General Freyberg's disposal, including those carried by the tanks, which fired many hundreds of rounds off the map at targets up to 13,000 yards. Over 100,000 shells were fired by the Brigade and Divisional Artillery. A full-scale attack was launched at 10 p.m. by the Infantry which, supported by 'Crocodile' Flame throwers, and after heavy fighting, carried all before it. Then, while the New Zealanders swept on to the Idice River, the 43rd Lorried Gurkha Brigade Group was withdrawn to Medicina to reorganise.

At the crossing of the Gaiana, the regiment lost two killed, Tpr. Banks and Tpr. Smith, and six wounded; the 2nd/6th Gurkha Rifles lost 150. The regiment was depressed at this discrepancy, feeling that it indicated some lack of enterprise on its part. Any such feelings, however natural, were quite mistaken. The regiment was well up in front, doing everything required of it, and under heavy fire for most of the time, and its light casualties, especially among the Kangaroos, were due to nothing more than luck and the realisation of the Germans that in this particular situation they had more to fear from the infantry than the tanks. Lieutenant Stratton, who had constantly exposed himself under heavy fire at close range while getting wounded men away in his Kangaroo, was recommended for the M.C., but awarded a

Mention instead, and Captain T. Cooper, R.A.M.C., the Regimental Medical Officer, was specially congratulated for his work at the Regimental Aid Post and was later awarded the M.C.

Their defeat on the Gaiano got the enemy on the run, and although they established many strong rear-guard positions they were no longer able to make any determined stand. The Poles and New Zealanders, advancing to the line of the Idice, found it evacuated. The Poles entered Bologna unopposed on the morning of the 21st April and the New Zealanders overcame a succession of rear-guards and reached the Reno. In Medicina the 43rd Lorried Gurkha Brigade Group was not long in getting organised for the pursuit. The Gurkhas got away first – in lorries, for the first time in the campaign. The 14th/20th after re-fitting, making up tank deficiencies and reorganising the crews, set off in the wake of the New Zealand Division on the 22nd April. Before the regiment left, Lieut.-Colonel Tilney's health broke down and he was sent home after handing over command to Major R. J. Stephen.

As may be imagined, the regiment pushed on with a will, but it was not easy to keep up a good pace along roads blocked with the fantastic waste and litter of war. Furthermore, all bridges had been destroyed and the pontoons and Bailey bridges used by the infantry and guns were not always strong enough to take the Shermans. After crossing the Reno, the regiment had to wait at San Carlo while a bridge was built over the Po. This was the last seen of the Gurkhas, who went streaking off in their lorries, making for the Adige. Orders came for another squadron to be converted to Kangaroos, which were wanted by the Vth Corps. 'C' Squadron under Major P. F. S. Clifford was selected for the conversion; an arduous and complicated business which was completed in thirty hours. As the conversion increased 'C' Squadron's vehicles to double the previous numbers, various lorry drivers had to be press-ganged and made to drive the Kangaroos.

A pontoon bridge capable of taking tanks across the Po was completed by the 30th April, but when the regiment drove up to it, the New Zealanders had been over it first and sunk one of the pontoons. This caused a three-hour delay, after which the regiment crossed safely in a severe hailstorm, and to the music of dozens of Bofors guns along either bank, which were keeping up a continual fire against all moving objects in the river, in case they should be mines.

There was another hold-up at the Adige, where there was no bridge, nor any hope of one, so the regiment had to cross in rafts, at the rate of six tanks an hour, and there were a hundred armoured vehicles of one kind or another on the strength at this time.

1945

Like the crossing of the Po, the Adige had to be negotiated mostly in the dark, but there were again no mishaps, and on the 2nd May the regiment reached Padua.

Here they found the Gurkhas busily rounding up prisoners. The New Zealanders were heading for Trieste, and it was fairly obvious that the German resistance had been completely broken. This was confirmed by news later in the day, that the German armies in Italy had surrendered. On the following morning the Regiment moved to San Valentino, on the Isonzo River, where it remained until the 1st August, its fighting done. In one squadron located near Ronchi, in an attempt to bring together some of the Italian factions, the Partigani (Red Scarves) and the Isoppos (Green Scarves) were asked to dine. The regiment's Italian was limited, but they all got on quite well together.

During the war, some of the regiment's officers were detached to other units. Lieut. (later Lieut.-Colonel) D. A. H. Silvertop was Brigade-Major of the 4th Armoured Brigade during the heavy fighting in the Western Desert. Awarded the Military Cross, he later commanded the 3rd Royal Tank Regiment with distinction in North Africa and also in the North West European Campaign when his regiment formed part of the 11th Armoured Division. Silvertop greatly distinguished himself in the Normandy fighting, particularly so during Operation Goodwood, the armoured attack south-east of Caen, and also at Antwerp where his regiment played a leading role in its liberation. He was awarded the Distinguished Service Order and the Belgian Croix de Guerre.

Silvertop was killed in action in Holland on 25th September, 1944. After the war, the citizens of Antwerp named the street down which his regiment entered the city 'Colonel Silvertop Straat'. In 1968, a memorial tablet on a new bridge on the street was unveiled by a representative of the King of the Belgians in the presence of a distinguished gathering, including serving members of the 14th/20th King's Hussars, the 3rd Royal Tank Regiment, and their Old Comrades. He was buried at St Anthonis in Holland.

Major G. L. Sullivan served initially with the Trans-Jordan Frontier Force, when he took part in the fighting against the French in Syria, and led one of the few cavalry charges of the war. Subsequently he joined the East Riding Yeomanry in 33rd Armoured Brigade in N.W. Europe. During the advance into Holland in October, 1944, he had several fingers blown off by enemy fire and was taken prisoner. He escaped from his captors twice and was re-captured each time. However, while at a Dressing Station, he made his third attempt and succeeded in escaping across a canal, over some town ramparts within fifty yards of two sentries, and then took refuge in a swamp. After nightfall he received help from Dutch civilians and eventually made his way, with their help, across the River Maas to a Polish Unit. He was awarded the Military Cross.

Lieutenant (later Major) G. B. Walker, having left the regiment in 1937, joined the 4th County of London Yeomanry in June, 1939. He became Adjutant and later commanded a squadron with distinction in the Western Desert. In 1942 he was severely wounded at Sidi Rezegh, the remainder of his crew being killed. He was evacuated to a New Zealand advance hospital near Tobruk which was captured for a few hours by Rommel's troops. Apart from removing the M. & B. the Germans did not worry the patients and a week later, after they had withdrawn, Walker was flown to Alexandria where he later died of his wounds. He had been recommended for the Military Cross, but through his death did not receive it.

Captain A. J. C. Stanton joined the Regiment in 1937, and during the war became Adjutant of the 26th Hussars in India. In 1943 he was attached to the Australians who were operating against the Japanese in the New Guinea jungle. He was killed there by a Jap sniper whilst bringing in a wounded soldier. He was a keen sportsman and an outstanding officer.

On the 4th May, the German armies in Europe surrendered. Of the three major Axis Powers, only Japan remained under arms, although by this time she had lost nearly all her wartime conquests and was being driven back upon her homeland. Although in a helpless position she still refused to surrender, and as an Allied invasion of the Japanese islands would have been a very costly operation it was decided to drop an atomic bomb on her. The atomic bomb had only just been completed, as the result of years of combined British, American and Canadian research, and its devastating potentialities were not yet fully appreciated. After a final ultimatum had been rejected, the first atomic bomb was dropped on Hiroshima on the 6th August, causing frightful destruction and loss of life. Russia then declared war on Japan and invaded Manchuria and Korea, but as the Japanese Government continued to hedge over capitulation, a second atomic bomb was dropped, on Nagasaki, on the 9th August. Considerably more powerful than the first, it had the result of at last making Japan see reason, and she surrendered on the 14th August unconditionally, with the sole proviso that the Emperor remained Head of State.

1945

The Second World War was thus over and Great Britain still survived, a consummation which had seemed far from likely, not so long before.

Winston Churchill who, on taking office as Prime Minister in 1940 had felt obliged to remind the British people that the successful evacuation of the British Army from Dunkirk was not in fact a victory, was still feeling far from elated, and the jubilation of the Londoners thronging round Buckingham Palace in the traditional manner, was not for him. 'Apprehension for the future and many perplexities filled my mind,' he wrote, 'as I moved among the cheering crowds.'

In July, 1945, the 14th/20th underwent another of their periodical conversions and became an Armoured Car Regiment, in which capacity they moved to Chiavari, on the coast near Genoa, in August, and remained there until the New Year on internal security duties. The 6th South African Division was stationed around Rapallo, and provided formidable Rugby opponents as well as extremely potent issue brandy. Many of the men were able to get their first leave to U.K. for many years. Two boats, one motor and one sailing, alleged to be the property of fascists, were liberated. These proved a considerable embarrassment as, on arrival at Chiavari, their owner who, it transpired, had been working for the Allied Military Government, appeared and demanded compensation. It was pointed out that the boats had been guarded by the regiment thus preventing them being taken by the Yugoslavs, and all was settled. The German searchlight engine powering the motor boat remained a mystery. Some horses were acquired and Hungarian grooms provided. Many of these wished to remain in the service, but had to their great dismay to be repatriated. The presence of British troops had a great stabilising influence. On one occasion the dockers came out on strike, but on seeing the C.O. in an armoured car passing through the area en route for a lunch party, they went happily back to work.

When winter came, ski-ing started and a number visited the resort of Madonna di Campiglio. Just as it seemed that families were going to be allowed to join their husbands, the regiment was ordered to take over from the Lothian and Border Horse at Milan en route for Germany. The Mayor of Chiavari asked whether the regiment could remain and expressed deep regret at their departure!

In February, 1946, the regiment moved to Milan, handed over its vehicles and left Italy by train to join the British Army of Occupation in Germany. The train passed through Calais,

1947

bringing the regiment closer to England than it had been for fifteen years. On arrival in Germany, the regiment was quartered first at Luneburg. Lieut.-Colonel H. A. R. Tilney returned to command the regiment before it was moved to Wuppertal in the Ruhr. Captain G. A. L. C. Talbot was called upon to defend, at a War Crimes Trial, General Kurt Student, the German Airborne Commander in Crete, which he did with considerable ability, and the General was acquitted on appeal.

Life in the Army of Occupation from 1946 onwards was very different from that experienced by the 14th King's Hussars in 1921. Germany had now been dismembered and completely crushed, and food and fuel were drastically short. Shortly after arrival in Germany, families were allowed to join their husbands, and private cars were allowed, but the rationing both of food and petrol was very stringent. Although powdered egg was available only one shell egg per person per month was the ration for a long period. There was a certain amount of shooting and fishing, and the partridges bagged in the allotments around Dusseldorf were a great help to the larder.

Although the regiment was nominally the Divisional Armoured Regiment of the 53rd (Welsh) Infantry Division, there was not a great deal for it to do and the atmosphere was generally relaxed. Horses being easy to come by, a riding school was started and the regiment began to get mounted again, and in conjunction with the Blues, produced a Musical Ride at the Dortmund Tattoo. Several events were won at various race meetings and horse shows including the race meetings at Dusseldorf, where Major Loraine-Smith was prominent as organiser and jockey. The Regimental Steeplechase was run at Dusseldorf racecourse, being won by Lieut.-Colonel Tilney on 'Old Glory'. Major Allen and Major Woodd both jumped in the Belgian Army Horse Show at Cologne and achieved some success. Before leaving Germany in November, the regiment held its own mounted sports. 1946/47 was a very cold winter and ski-ing started again, the resort most readily available being Winterburg. There was also great enthusiasm for Rugby Football. The standard was high and the regiment had an excellent ground in the Wuppertal Stadium. Up to nine officers frequently turned out on the same occasion, and the game was a great source of interest to the regiment as a whole. This state of affairs continued after the move to Catterick where the presence of potential officers under training added to the strength of the team.

On 21st May, 1947, General Sir Richard L. McCreery was appointed Colonel of the Regiment in succession to Brigadier

1947

F. B. Hurndall. General McCreery was a 12th Royal Lancer, and had been Brigadier Hurndall's Brigade-Major in Tidworth between the wars. A most distinguished officer in every way, he had been Field Marshal Alexander's Chief of Staff, and subsequently commanded the Eighth Army in Italy, when the regiment was serving in 43rd Lorried Gurkha Brigade.

British and international affairs were not, however, as happy as they appeared on the surface, and there was every reason for Churchill's anxiety for the future. In the closing stages of the war his counsels had been shrugged aside by Roosevelt, the American President, who had been anxious to allay suspicions of 'Uncle Joe' Stalin, the Russian Dictator, that the United States was in any way more friendly with Great Britain than with Russia. Although, therefore, Great Britain had gone to war in consequence of the German invasion of Austria, Czechoslovakia and Poland, she had been unable to convince the United States of the vital necessity of occupying these countries on the heels of the retreating Germans before the Russians could get into them. Russia was given a free hand to swarm all over the whole of Eastern Europe, from the Baltic to the Adriatic, and to extend the frontiers of her Empire westwards of Berlin. Owing to the presence of British and American forces along the southern Austrian frontier, it was fortunately possible to prevent Russian infiltration into Italy and, with great difficulty, the British Army managed to keep the Communists out of Greece. Berlin and Vienna, although both were in Russian-occupied territory, had international garrisons and provided the only point of intercourse between the British and Americans on the one hand, and the Russians on the other. 'An iron curtain is drawn down upon their front,' wrote Churchill to the American President. 'We do not know what is going on behind.'

In such circumstances there was no question of Great Britain carrying out the wholesale disbandment customary at the end of a war. National Service still continued, but as most of the wartime training establishments were disbanded this was to place a considerable strain on the Regular Army. In November, 1947, when the 14th/20th at last returned home and were posted to Catterick, they had to take over the task of training recruits and National Servicemen for the Royal Armoured Corps. The regiment and most of the married families found the accommodation at Menin and Cambrai Lines, Catterick Camp, somewhat primitive after the comforts of their modern German barracks at Wuppertal. The meaning of post-war financial economy was brought home to all including the young National Servicemen,

The Guidon which was presented to the Regiment by Field-Marshal Sir Gerald Templer at Hohne, Germany on 10th June, 1961.

(below) Regimental Silver. In front is 'The Emperor', the silver chamber-pot taken from King Joseph Bonaparte's coach after the Battle of Vittoria (1813).

1948

many of whom were leaving home for the first time. Squadrons were split up into Wings to cater for the various forms of R.A.C. training, and with the arrival of over one hundred recruits each fortnight, the operations of the regiment were not unlike that of a sausage machine. The recruits, who represented a cross-section of the nation, varied widely in their abilities and with the large and changing soldier population officers found it difficult to get to know their men.

Administration in all its forms including the maintenance of the large amount and variety of equipment posed certain problems until the regiment found its feet. But the training of recruits was tackled with great enthusiasm on the square, in the classrooms and on the training areas. During the three years in which the regiment had this duty it carried out the primary training of 1,732 regular recruits and 6,167 National Servicemen, including 276 'potential officers', who went on to the R.M.A. Sandhurst or the Mons Officer-Cadet School.

These new responsibilities allowed the regiment no time for horse shows and Musical Rides, but the interest in horses continued. Horses were not so readily available in the United Kingdom as they had been in Germany, but five were bought regimentally and there were seven privately-owned. The riding school continued, with Major Allen and R.Q.M.S. Roberts (afterwards Quartermaster) as instructors. There were fourteen horses in the stables before the regiment left Catterick in 1949 and most of the officers hunted with the Bedale and Zetland. Major Allen on 'Isdes' and Lieut. Palmer on 'Sonny', were first and second in the Garrison race at the Bedale Point-to-Point. The Connaught Cup for revolver shooting continued to be won with the same regularity as before the war, and there were few forms of sport in which the regiment failed to put up a creditable performance, thus maintaining a long tradition as an all-round sporting regiment.

In October, 1948, Lieut.-Colonel H. A. R. Tilney left the regiment after commanding it for over four years. He was succeeded by Lieut.-Colonel R. J. Stephen, afterwards Colonel of the Regiment, whose father, Brigadier-General R. C. Stephen, had commanded the 14th King's Hussars from 1911 to 1915. In the same year Lieut.-Colonel Studd won the John Peel Cup at Manchester on his horse 'Topped Up'. In 1950, Lieut. Groves won this race with Lieut. Palmer again coming second. Also in 1950, Lieut. Palmer won the 8th Armoured Brigade race at the Middleton meeting.

During the first year the regiment was at Catterick, the Band,

1948

after a spell of six years as the Mortar Troop, was re-formed under Bandmaster R. Hurst, A.R.C.M. There was no special establishment for Trumpeters, who had disappeared as such along with the horses. The Band Sergeant now also acted as Trumpet-Major, with the Bandsmen parading with cavalry or state trumpets as required. Being musicians they are better performers on the instrument than the former cavalry trumpeters, and on ceremonial occasions the regiment can mount an impressive display on the trumpet, although a dual role such as this always presents difficulties. Owing for instance, to the difficulty of providing a daily duty Trumpeter, the stirring old routine calls tend to be forgotten.

In 1947, the regiment adopted the arm badge of crossed Kukris at the request of the Brigade of Gurkhas, to commemorate the close wartime association between the 14th/20th King's Hussars and the 43rd Gurkha Lorried Brigade. The Gurkhas also presented the regiment with a silver kukri as a friendly memento. The wearing of the badge was approved by King George VI in 1950.

January, 1948, saw the long-awaited arrival of the first issue of the regimental magazine, *The Hawk*, an invaluable and well-produced record of the history of the regiment from year to year. Regimental magazines first began to make their appearance in the British Army towards the close of the nineteenth century, but such ventures were always difficult for cavalry regiments which, unlike the infantry, had until recently no settled 'homes'.

Russian intransigence, which expressed itself in June, 1948, by a blockade of Berlin, led to a postponement of all further projects for the reduction of the fighting force. The blockade was defeated within a year by supplying Berlin from the air, but war was only narrowly averted and in April, 1949, twelve western nations signed the Atlantic Pact, and formed a common front against aggression from the east. Thus the North Atlantic Treaty Organisation came into being, imposing defence obligations on all its members. War then broke out in Korea which, after its recovery from the Japanese in 1945, had been occupied by the Russians in the North and the Americans in the South. As soon as the Americans withdrew, the Communist North Koreans invaded South Korea, but the Russians, when planning this new thrust, had made the error of boycotting the United Nations Assembly, which enabled the United States to gain the support of that organisation in restoring the *status quo* in Korea. The North Koreans were speedily driven back, but Communist China then intervened on their side and a long struggle ensued, in which a British Commonwealth Division fought alongside the Americans,

1952

and small token formations from fifteen other nations. The first British Armoured Regiment to go to Korea was the 8th Hussars, later relieved by the 5th R.I. Dragoon Guards. The regiment provided drafts to both, and Lieut. C. E. Paul was awarded the M.C. whilst serving with the 8th Hussars.

In 1947, the last British troops had left India, as the beginning of an idealistic attempt to change the British Empire into the British Commonwealth of self-governing countries. The British evacuation of India and its subsequent partition into the two new countries of India and Pakistan was, however, attended by such heavy loss of life as to incline the British Government to go more slowly in giving independence to the other countries of the Empire. This again, was more easily said than done, and resulted in British troops becoming engaged all over the world in a series of rear-guard actions; struggling to maintain law and order in 'emergent nations' feverish for independence.

During this period of trouble and danger, when a Third World War was only prevented from breaking out by the American monopoly in atomic bombs, the British army was re-strengthening in various minor but important ways, one of which was the relief of fighting units from the dreary and exacting duty of basic training. On the 1st January, 1951, the 14th/20th King's Hussars ceased to act as an 'Army Basic Training Unit' and, having thankfully handed over to the 65th Training Regiment, R.A.C., left Catterick for Crookham.

On arrival at Crookham, the 14th/20th King's Hussars became the Divisional Armoured Regiment to the 3rd Division; Picton's 'Fighting Division' in Napoleonic times. Disbanded at the conclusion of every war, including the Second World War, it came to life again once more in 1950 as part of the modest re-armament enforced by the behaviour of the Communist Powers. Training now became almost as intensive as in wartime, but it was a refreshing change for the regiment to get on the move again, after its dull and static role at Catterick. There was still time for almost every kind of sport, and the regiment continued to keep up its usual high standard, doing well in the Pentathlon, which had started after the war and which was a severe test of all-round sportsmanship. In addition the regiment won the Cavalry Football Cup, beating the Royal Scots Greys in the final.

The regiment continued to show its skill at Small Arms and Pistol Shooting and 1952 was a particularly successful year. As most regimental interests and particular skills are traditional, it may not be too fanciful to trace pistol shooting back to Captain Horatio Ross, a godson of Admiral Lord Nelson, who was

1952

an officer of the 14th Light Dragoons during the eighteen-twenties. Ross was a well-known all-round sportsman of his day, and it is safe to say that he would never have been 'called-out' in any affair of honour, for his skill with the pistol was phenomenal, even by regimental standards. On one occasion, for example, he won a bet with Mr George Foljambe of a hundred guineas for shooting ten brace of swallows on the wing, on the same day, with a pistol loaded with single balls.

At the prize-giving after the Aldershot Command competition, representatives of the regiment formed up in front of Field Marshal Sir William Slim twelve times – seven of which were in succession. In the end he gave up shaking hands and said: 'What, you again!' Ten cups, thirty-nine medals and £40 in prize money were won. Lieut. L. P. J. S. Bromley later won the Bisley Cup and N.R.A. Silver Medal, an event open to all ranks of the army – a remarkable achievement. He later represented the Army in a match at the National Rifle Meeting.

In 1952, a team consisting of Captain Groves and Lieutenants Palmer and Bromley won the King of the Hellenes Shield awarded to the first Army team in the British Modern Pentathlon. First and second places went to the Royal Marines and the Royal Air Force.

At the end of 1951, Lieut.-Colonel Stephen handed over command to Lieut.-Colonel B. B. N. Woodd. In October, 1952, the regiment sailed from Southampton in H.M.T. *Lancashire* for Sabratha in Libya, where it became the Divisional Cavalry Regiment of the 1st Division in the Middle-East Land Forces, taking over from the 4th/7th Dragoon Guards.

The Middle East was in a state of considerable tension at this time. The surrender of their mandates over Syria and Palestine by France and Great Britain had resulted in open hostilities between Jews and Arabs, the effects of which were still being felt. In Egypt, the monarchy had been overthrown and power seized by a junta of ruthless army officers. Although British troops had withdrawn from Cairo in 1946, they were still in occupation of the Suez Canal Zone and so for the time being able to exercise a certain stabilising influence. The 1st Division, to which the 14th/20th belonged, was in fact stationed in the Canal zone. This being too limited in extent for the training and employment of an armoured regiment, the 14th/20th had to remain in Libya where it was ready to march into Egypt should an advance have to be made against Cairo, as seemed not unlikely. Meanwhile, the regiment could only take part in Divisional exercises on a cadre basis, represented by regimental and squadron headquarters,

The Regimental Shooting Team of 1952 was outstandingly successful. At the Aldershot District Rifle Meeting it won ten cups, 39 medals, and £40 in prize money. Three major competitions were won at Bisley.

which went over to the Canal Zone as required. This was perhaps just as well, since before leaving England, the regiment had lost up to 80 per cent of its trained soldiers, who were replaced by recruits and National Servicemen. The Pentathlon Team also visited the Canal Zone, where it won the Divisional Modern Pentathlon. The events were fencing, swimming, pistol-shooting, cross-country running, and a cross-country riding test which, in spite of vigorous regimental protests, was carried out on motor-cycles and not horses. The team, Major Tayleur, Captain Mylchreest, Lieutenants Hicks and Hume, were far from being expert motor-cyclists. A trial run had to be arranged for them to learn how to ride, and how to fall off without hurting themselves. The fact that the team subsequently managed not only to survive a gruelling motor-cycle test but actually win the series against very stiff opposition, is a good example of their powers of endurance and adaptability.

Polo was started, ponies being procured from the 4th/7th Dragoon Guards and the 16th/5th Lancers. A new polo ground was made on the salt flats near Sabratha which could be used in all weathers. A race meeting was also held on it which, being a triangular and rather slippery course, had some surprising

1954

results. The Police race was fixed by a bicycle being flung under the hoofs of the leader by a discontented punter, and the American Forces race produced a winner who disappeared across the desert after passing the winning post.

A polo team visited Malta on several occasions and was most hospitably entertained by Lord Louis Mountbatten and the Royal Australian Air Force. When H.M. the Queen visited Malta a mixed party of spectators travelled by a Greek sponge boat. After many adventures and some navigational errors they eventually arrived at their destination. They tied up in the dark to the Royal Mooring from which they were speedily removed in the small hours! The regimental horses also did very well at the race meetings and these were of great value in keeping friendly relations with the horse-loving Arabs. In the Open Race of the second 1953 Meeting, Captain Palmer on 'Joul Joul', closely followed by Major Tayleur on 'Madid', beat the local fancy, Abdulla ben Ali on 'Alamein', into third place, losing the Arab punters their money, which loss, being the Will of Allah, they accepted with their usual philosophy.

In 1954, Lieut.-Colonel B. B. N. Woodd handed over command to Lieut.-Colonel R. P. D. F. Allen. The regiment remained at Sabratha, comfortably situated but all by itself, with no other British regiment within fifty miles. Thrown much upon its own resources for amusement and relaxation, much talent for entertainment was brought to light, which would otherwise have remained hidden, as is usually the case in such circumstances. The Hawk Dramatic Society, which opened with a production of *While the Sun Shines*, was a notable example.

In this year the regiment won not only the Connaught Cup as usual, but seven other A.R.A. trophies: the Revolver Cup for individual shots, won by S.Q.M.S. Cundy with S.Q.M.S. Reynolds and Sergeants Tasker and Shakespeare 3rd, 4th and 6th respectively, the Royal Irish Cup, the First Army Cup, the Squadron Shield, the Queen Victoria Trophy, the King George V Cup and the Young Soldiers' Cup. It is very unusual for a cavalry regiment to win the coveted Queen Victoria Trophy, especially since mechanisation, for the rifle is not really a tank man's weapon. Yet the 14th/20th won it twice running, by repeating all these successes in 1955 including, of course, the Connaught Cup. This feat was made all the more remarkable by the fact that the aggregate did not come into it, for the regiment won each of the qualifying competitions outright. The last and only previous occasion on which the regiment won the Queen Victoria Trophy was in 1924.

1956

In 1954, the regiment carried out a period of training in rugged desert country 100 miles south of Tripoli. To reach the training area, the Garian Jebel, 2,000 feet high, had to be surmounted. Wheeled vehicles manipulated the hair-pin bends of the road route without trouble but the tanks could only use a rough track, discovered after reconnaissance, and made usable by the efforts of the Royal Engineers. The tanks could only get round the bends by wriggling backwards and forwards inches at a time with part of their hulls suspended in space over sheer drops. There were some near misses but all made the top, the leading tank carrying the United States Ambassador as a passenger. Having got to the top the regiment enjoyed its most fruitful period of field training during the Libyan tour. Infantry, Gunners, Sappers, R.A.S.C. Tank Transporters and Aircraft of the Fleet Air Arm had been invited by the regiment to take part. An exercise was carried out with the Libyan Army which was in the process of being formed and equipped by a British Military Mission. There was plenty of space for tank training and scope for the 'Q' experts to supply the Regimental Group over long distances and through difficult country.

In 1955, civilian race meetings were organised at Busetta as a business venture, by an enterprising retired Italian Colonel. The stakes being very much more generous than those normally offered at military meetings, the regiment gave the meetings full support, in the hope of building up the Horse Fund. The regimental horses were most successful, particularly Colonel Allen's 'Fileur', previously owned by Lieut. Colonel d'Avigdor Goldsmid, commanding the 4th/7th, and also by Lieut.-Colonel Woodd, ridden either by Colonel Allen or Lieut. Fenwick. His only serious rival was 'Keria', owned by Hag Mohammed, a wealthy Arab. The 'Gentlemen Riders' of the regiment, particularly Palmer, Fenwick and Tpr. Fenner, were so superior to the local Arabs – who were far too excitable – that Hag Mohammed pestered the regiment to supply a rider for 'Keria' but the regiment, with the Horse Fund in mind, very sensibly refused to oblige. Whilst ridden by Lieut.-Colonel Woodd and Colonel Allen, 'Fileur' never lost a race.

In October of this year the regiment was relieved by the Queen's Bays at Sabratha, and returned home for a brief stay at Piddlehinton Camp, near Dorchester, before returning to the Rhine early in 1946. The fact that it was only a Light Cavalry Regiment in name – there was nothing light about a Centurion tank – had saved it from becoming involved in the series of humiliating experiences which had befallen the troops in the Eastern

1956

Mediterranean, and which called to mind some of those suffered by the 20th Hussars when soldiering in the same area back in 1806. After patiently enduring the insalubrious conditions of the Suez Canal Zone for a number of years, during which they had to put up with never-ending series of raids by Egyptian gangsters to which they were not allowed to make reply, the troops had been withdrawn to Cyprus. In revenge for an Anglo-American refusal to finance his Aswan Dam project, Nasser, the Egyptian President, then 'nationalised' the Suez Canal, in defiance of his treaty obligations. This led to the 'Affair of Suez' in which British and French troops landed at Port Said and commenced to re-occupy the Canal Zone. The operations, proceeding against little or no opposition, were soon halted at the insistence of the United States, which apparently objected to the renewal of British influence in the Middle East. The political handling of the 'Affair' by the British Government, inept beyond belief, ended in a complete and final withdrawal which ended the functions of the Suez Canal as an international waterway.

On joining the Rhine Army in March, 1956, the 14th/20th joined the 20th Armoured Brigade at Munster, thus relinquishing their role of 'Divisional Cavalry' held since 1946. Colonel Allen handed over command to Lieut.-Colonel P. F. W. Browne, who had led the regiment into action at Medicina when commanding 'C' Squadron. Later in the year, the regiment joined the 11th Infantry Brigade at Hohne, as its Armoured Regiment. The move to Hohne, site of Belsen, Hitler's infamous Concentration Camp, resulted in the regiment becoming split up all over western Germany, and interrupted its sporting programme, especially polo, which was just getting started again.

In May, General Sir Richard McCreery handed over the Colonelcy of the regiment to Lieut.-Colonel R. J. Stephen who had commanded it towards the end of the war, and again from 1948 to 1951. 'A' Squadron under Major James was in Detmold, with the Royal Hampshires, 'B' Squadron under Major D. E. R. Scarr in Berlin, and 'C' under Major Talbot at Celle, with the Gordons. Early in 1959, Lieut.-Colonel Browne retired, handing over to Lieut.-Colonel E. G. W. T. Walsh.

Although the regiment had not served East of Suez since the war, several officers were seconded to units in the Far East and the Arabian Peninsula during this period. Of these, Captain R. E. D. Harris served with the Armoured Car Squadron of the Aden Protectorate Levies from 1957–60. He was awarded the Military Cross for his part in operations against the Yemenis on the frontier near Mukeiras.

1960

The regiment provided nearly all the permanent staff for the Duke of Lancaster's Own Yeomanry T.A. as from the affiliation of the two regiments in 1947. Lieut.-Colonel E. B. Studd had commanded the Yeomanry from 1949–52, and Lieut.-Colonel B. C. L. Tayleur from 1959–61. It was during Lieut.-Colonel Tayleur's tour of command, in 1961, that the Yeomanry was presented with a new Guidon by Her Majesty the Queen at a magnificent parade in Manchester.

At this time, the troops of the Rhine Army were being kept far more active than is usual in peacetime, and 'A' and 'C' Squadrons, mounted in Saracens, covered more than 5,000 miles each in company with their motorised infantry battalions during the year. 'B' Squadron in Berlin was, of course, confined to a small area in which there was little to do but ensure the Russians kept to their own part of the city. Since the death of Stalin, the Russians had become considerably less truculent and this fact, combined with the continuous withdrawal of British troops from the former spheres of British influence overseas, determined the Government to bring an end to National Service. To the British Army, the decision was welcome in that it gave the opportunity once more of becoming professional, with highly-trained soldiers of long service. On the other hand, the problem of recruiting enough regulars to replace the National Service men caused anxiety. The 14th/20th required no fewer than 540 regular recruits to fill the gap caused by the end of National Service, and they had mostly to be found in Lancashire, the only area in which the regiment was allowed actively to recruit. This well-populated county, however, has always been a good one for recruiting, and its young men soon began answering the call of 'The Cavalry Regiment of Lancashire'. The Lancastrian intake rose from two recruits a month to seventeen.

At the end of November, 1960, the regiment was once more united at Hohne, after the three squadrons had come in from Detmold, Berlin and Celle. The Saracens were replaced by tanks, and after some months of re-organisation the regiment prepared for the presentation of a Guidon by Field-Marshal Sir Gerald Templer, which was carried out at a parade at Hohne on the 10th June, 1961. In the cavalry the old Regiments of Horse, now represented by the Household Cavalry and the Dragoon Guards, carried standards, on a scale of one for each troop. Guidons, or swallow-tailed standards, were carried by the Dragoons, on the same scale. Following later re-organisations affecting the number and size of troops in a cavalry regiment, standards and guidons were reduced in number first to one a squadron and finally to one

Presentation of the Guidon to the Regiment by Field-Marshal Sir Gerald Templer at Hohne (B.A.O.R.) in 1961.

Field-Marshal Sir Gerald Templer reviewing the Regiment at the Guidon presentation parade at Hohne, 10 June 1961.

a regiment. Light Dragoons, Hussars and Lancers also carried guidons until stopped by an order of William IV dated 1834. The official reason given was the 'dispersed duties' of Light Cavalry although Light Infantry, whose duties were equally 'dispersed' were still allowed to carry colours which, however, they seldom took into action. The consecration, or more accurately, dedication, of colours at a religious ceremony was not usual before the end of the nineteenth century, after standards and colours had ceased to be carried in action. The 14th and 20th Hussars both carried guidons in action during the Napoleonic Wars. Six of the 14th and three of the 20th are still in existence, all faded and battle-scarred. The three most serviceable were trooped on a parade at Catterick, on the 20th July, 1950, held in commemoration of the assumption of the title Duchess of York's Own, by the 14th Light Dragoons in 1798, and also of the exploit of Cpl. Hanley at Blasco Sancho in 1812 when he and a patrol captured two French officers and 27 Dragoons in flight from Salamanca. A trumpet fanfare named *Blasco Sancho* was specially composed by Bandmaster Hurst for the occasion.

Kettle-drums have been of special significance in the cavalry from the earliest times, when it was not unusual for a regiment which had disgraced itself in some way to be forbidden to beat them at its head. They were normally held by the Colonel's Troop and carried by a drum horse, although it was not unknown for a couple of peasants to be used for the purpose when a regiment paraded dismounted. After the use of guidons had been discontinued in Light Cavalry, it was perfectly acceptable for the battle-honours and achievements of a regiment to be displayed on the drum-banners; for a good drum-horse, marching in front of the mounted band or massed trumpeters at the head of a regiment, was a very fine sight indeed, so that a guidon could well be dispensed with. Mechanisation of course put a stop to this, for there was no longer a drum horse and it would not have done, in modern times, to send the Provost Sergeant to collect a couple of peasants to serve instead. By command of Queen Elizabeth II, guidons were therefore restored to the Light Cavalry Regiments.

At the Hohne parade, two old guidons, formerly carried by the 14th and 20th Light Dragoons, were trooped and taken off parade before the presentation of the new guidon. When making the presentation, Field-Marshal Sir Gerald Templer expressed himself as being particularly happy to do so as Colonel of a Regiment of Gurkhas, in view of the close wartime association formed between the 14th/20th King's Hussars and several Gurkha battalions. Having conveyed the warm good wishes of Her

1963

Majesty the Queen, he handed over the Guidon to R.Q.M.S. P. C. Witney, with the words:

'On behalf of Her Majesty the Queen, it is my privilege to commit the Guidon to your keeping, in the full confidence that with God's blessing, you will continue to uphold the great name and traditions of the 14th/20th King's Hussars.'

At this time a Home Headquarters was authorised for each Cavalry Regiment manned by a Retired Officer and a Clerk. Its duties were to provide a secretariat for the Colonel of the Regiment, and to act as the regiment's 'agent' in the U.K. with particular reference to Lancashire. There the regimental recruiting area was situated and also the homes of the majority of soldiers. The H.Q. was established in the Manchester area and a small museum was subsequently set up in the city in 1967. The Home Headquarters was also made responsible for Regimental Association activities and, since 1968, for helping those in difficulties.

In 1961, Colonel Walsh handed over command to Lieut.-Colonel G. A. L. C. Talbot. In this year, with the permission of the Colonel of the Royal Sussex Regiment, official approval was obtained for the *Royal Sussex* to be played as the Regimental March of the 14th/20th King's Hussars. It had in fact been so played ever since 1801, when the 14th Light Dragoons were in Kent and their band discovered to be too drunk to parade, a mishap likely to occur even in the best-ordered regiment in those days. The 35th (Royal Sussex) Regiment came to the rescue and paraded their band at short notice, which resulted in the adoption of the Royal Sussex Regimental March by the 14th Light Dragoons; whether as a compliment to the 35th, or because they liked the tune, it is hard to say. It was to become a subject for periodic comment, during the subsequent history of the 14th, but it was never considered necessary to do anything about it officially until 1961 when, the international situation having become relatively stable, the War Office found time to attend to the regularisation of Regimental Marches. The Colonel of the Royal Sussex, General Sir Lashmer Whistler, who was an old friend of the regiment, kindly presented a pair of menu holders in the form of the Royal Sussex crest to the 14th/20th, to commemorate this unique occurrence. In return the regiment presented to the Royal Sussex a silver port glass for their Bandmaster.

In 1962, the regiment converted to armoured cars. After handing over its tanks to the 11th Hussars, who were kind enough to say it was one of the best handovers they had ever had, it returned to Libya where it was quartered in Benghazi, with 'B' Squadron

The Guidon is marched on parade before being trooped for the first time: the Queen's Birthday Parade, Benghazi, 1963.

'C' Squadron patrol in Cyprus, 1963. The Squadron was 'air portable' – equipped with Ferret scout cars and Landrovers – and was flown from Benghazi to Akrotiri in Cyprus on Boxing Day.

1963

in Tripoli. With 556 rank and file it was somewhat over-strength in spite of the ending of National Service. This was most unusual at the time, especially in a Cavalry regiment, but Lancashire had come up to scratch as anticipated, and the 'Special Recruiters' in Manchester and Preston had been able to get as many good men as they wanted, although there was little unemployment in the area.

The regiment was not sorry to be back in Libya after the somewhat hectic life spent in the Rhine Army. Since the evacuation of the Suez Canal Zone, there were more British troops about, for Great Britain was still in friendly treaty with Libya which had become one of the few parts of the world in which British presence was welcome. The horsemen in the regiment were particularly glad to be back. Thirty horses were found in a stables next to the officers' mess in Benghazi, and although these were the property of the Area Saddle Club, ten others were soon purchased for the regiment at prices between £30 and £50.

At Benghazi, 'C' Squadron became an 'Air Portable' squadron, ready to load its Ferret cars on to Beverley aircraft and dash off at short notice to wherever the authorities required its services. The call came at 5 o'clock on the morning of Boxing Day, 1963, just as the squadron was staggering to bed hoping to be allowed the day off in order to sleep off the customary Christmas hangover. In these unromantic days there was no trumpeter to 'rouse out the soldier 'ere the morning star', with the lively notes of *Boot and Saddle*. The summons came by telephone to the squadron office, and it says a good deal for the discipline of 'C' Squadron that at this hour on Boxing Day morning, there was actually someone there to answer it. In a very short space of time the squadron was airborne, complete with its first-line ammunition and ready for action. Landing at Akrotiri in Cyprus, it pushed on at once to Nicosia.

Up to 1914, Cyprus had been a province of the Turkish Empire, although administered by Great Britain in accordance with a treaty signed in 1878. It was annexed to the British Crown when war with Turkey broke out in 1914. It has a mixed Greek and Turkish population, constantly at enmity, but until the end of the Second World War, the British administration had managed to maintain a reasonable degree of law and order, although a movement for *Enosis*, or union with Greece, began among sections of the Greek population in 1931. This rose again after the war, and a period of Greek guerrilla activity ensued which ended in 1959, when the island became an autonomous republic with a Greek President and a Turkish Vice-President; Great Britain retaining her military bases and a certain responsibility for keeping the peace between the Greek and Turkish communities. It is, in fact, almost impossible to establish friendly relations between Greeks and Turks, who have been at each other's throats for centuries. By Christmas, 1963, the position had so deteriorated that there was a great danger of a Turkish invasion in support of the Turkish Cypriots, who were being cut off from food and water supplies and obliged to defend their lives and property under arms, leading to a series of shocking reprisals between the two communities.

In this kind of situation, armoured cars are of the greatest importance, and those of 'C' Squadron, under Major W. D. Garbutt, were soon actively employed accompanying the Glosters, Rifle Brigade and Sherwood Foresters of the 'Truce Force', in their efforts to restore law and order. Nicosia itself was the chief trouble spot, with fighting going on in the streets and large numbers of houses burnt to the ground. The appearance of the armoured cars proved to be sufficient to separate the combatants, who fled their separate ways, and by the 30th December the city had been cleared without the Truce Force having to fire a shot. The whole island was in a ferment, however, and further anxiety was caused by a Turkish flotilla lying off the coast, following a series of warlike speeches and preparations in Istanbul. 'C' Squadron's armoured cars were soon ranging far and wide over the island, operating in patrols of two cars each, which called for a great deal of enterprise and initiative by the officers and N.C.O.'s each of whom was faced with a grave responsibility. A decision to open fire would have been a most serious one to take, and 'C' Squadron came very near to it on several occasions, but fortunately just managed to avoid it each time. Eventually, Major Garbutt became a kind of senior Intelligence Officer, having to collect and collate the reports on not only his own patrols but those of others in the Truce Force, which were sent to his H.Q. each day. However, this nerve-racking adventure did not last long. At the end of January, 1964, the Life Guards arrived and took over the Union Jacks which 'C' Squadron had been wearing as referee's blazers, draped round the front of the cars. Exactly a month after setting out, the squadron arrived back in Libya.

In 1964, Colonel Talbot handed over command to Lieut.-Colonel S. R. M. Frazer. The regiment at this time could scarcely have been more active. One squadron was just back from Cyprus and the other two changing round between Benghazi and Tripoli. Innumerable major exercises were being carried out, often in collaboration with troops flown out from home. There was a

1965

great deal of liaison with the Royal Navy and there were many enjoyable 'trips in the Skylark', on one of which 'A' Squadron reconnoitred practically the whole of the Mediterranean in H.M.S. *Aisne*. In recent years 'Adventure Training' had become a feature of army life and, as North Africa was just the place for it, the regiment went in for it in the most wholehearted manner.

In the Autumn of 1963, Lieut. Chappell and fourteen members of the regiment had motored across the Sahara from Benghazi to Lagos and back in forty-six days. Dropping in on various French forts en route, they covered over six thousand miles. Some of the three-ton and one-ton vehicles in which they travelled had earlier been declared 'Beyond Economical Repair' and had been obtained from the Local Purchase Dump in Benghazi; they therefore required the full treatment before departure. At Kaduna the party was given hospitality by the Nigerian Army, and at Lagos they appeared on T.V.

Tough going at the best of times, as its name implies, 'Adventure Training' can also be dangerous, and the regiment suffered a sad loss in the lives of Lieut. C. C. Cornish, Cpl. N. W. Kirkham and Tpr. B. L. Bunn, who were killed by a fall of rock while climbing Mount Kenya. They were buried at the foot of the Darwin Glacier, 15,000 feet up, where a service was conducted by Brigadier Blackman, commanding the British rear party in Kenya, and attended by Major Moore, who placed on the grave an ebony cross, bearing the regimental crest. Cornish had been second-in-command of the Air Troop at the time of his death. This troop, led by Captain H. C. Joynson, of the 16th/5th Lancers, who subsequently joined the regiment, was a recent addition to the complex regimental structure, which now consisted of a headquarters and three sabre squadrons (as they continued to be named), a Light Aid Detachment, Signal Troop, Air Troop, Pay Section, Army Catering Corps detachment and, of course, the Band. On the establishment was a vast miscellany of armoured and other vehicles too varied to particularise, and it is safe to say that the regiment could drive anything – including a pair, tandem or four-in-hand – without further instruction. Perhaps it could not claim to be able to do everything, but it could do most things of an active nature, as the variety of duties, exploits and sporting interests clearly showed.

Before the regiment left Libya at the end of 1965 to return home, 'C' Squadron paid another month's visit to Cyprus. This time it was only to take part in an exercise, and there was no shooting going on – or not much. Great Britain had called in the United Nations to keep the peace and the British Garrison had

Her Royal Highness The Princess Anne. Appointed Colonel-in-Chief 14th/20th King's Hussars in 1969.
Oil painting by Bernard Hailstone, 1970.

1968

retired to its base, although a British detachment was serving with the International Force. This detachment, after Easter 1965, included 'A' Squadron of the 14th/20th King's Hussars, commanded by Major R. E. D. Harris. Unlike 'C' Squadron, which went everywhere by air, 'A' Squadron travelled by sea in the comfortable, old-fashioned manner, complete with vehicles, baggage, private cars and horses. Keeping the peace in Cyprus as a unit of the former British Truce Force, the experiences of 'A' Squadron were similar to those of 'C' Squadron which have already been briefly described. A somewhat sore point, which came up later, was that service with the International Force was rewarded with a United Nations Medal, whereas soldiers in the British Garrison were not so favoured, although in fact, they also contributed to keeping the peace at a risk, such as it was, certainly not less than that accepted by those in the International Force.

The beginning of 1966 found the regiment rather more dispersed than usual, with R.H.Q. and 'C' Squadron in Libya, 'A' Squadron in Cyprus, and 'B' Squadron in Perham Down, but by April it was once more united, for the first time in four years. The stay at Perham Down was to be a brief one, just long enough to re-organise and change back into tanks. The regiment was only too well-accustomed to changes in its organisation, but the change this time was rather more emphatic than usual, being based on five squadrons: 'Command', 'A', 'B', 'C', and 'Support'. Before starting, the Guidon was trooped on a parade held on the 28th May, 1966, in commemoration of the 250th anniversary of the raising of the 14th Dragoons. The parade should, of course, have been held in 1965, but had had to be postponed owing to the dispersal of the regiment. On the parade, Colonel R. J. Stephen handed over as Colonel of the Regiment to Colonel B. B. N. Woodd.

In 1966 the Royal approval was given for the affiliation of the 1st/6th Queen Elizabeth's Own Gurkha Rifles whose second battalion was already affiliated to the regiment. The Prussian Eagle was then worn by both battalions which were, however, amalgamated in Hong Kong in 1969.

In December, after Colonel Frazer had handed over command to Lieut.-Colonel P. B. Cavendish, the regiment returned to the Rhine Army and was quartered in Barker Barracks, Paderborn. Reorganisation on the five-squadron basis was completed in July, 1967, with the formation of the Air Troop, and during three months spent out of barracks on exercises, the regiment covered no less than 100,000 miles on the ground in tanks and scout cars, while the Air Troop's helicopters put in over 300 hours in flying

1970

time. In sport, the regiment carried on with its 'you name it, we play it' policy, winning the Royal Armoured Corps Sailing Cup, four cups for ski-ing, the Bren Pairs at Bisley, the Berlin Polo Cup and the Rhine Army Soldier's Polo Cup, in which the regiment was represented by a team found from the grooms, composed of Troopers Broadhurst, Steele, Fenton and Harvey.

The excellence of the reports received for annual inspections was remarkable. In 1968, the Divisional Commander, Major-General Erskine-Crum, congratulated the regiment on its high standard of tactical efficiency, on its achievements during the year, and on the excellent 'Fit for Role' inspection report. The report said, 'They must certainly be one of the best Armoured Regiments in B.A.O.R.'. The Brigadier reported that 'Officers and men have retained their irrepressible good humour, and one could not wish to see a happier or better motivated organisation'.

In the Autumn of 1968 a weekend was organised for the entertainment of parents of soldiers and members of the Regimental Association. They saw the regiment at work and play and were able to inspect the Chieftain tank with which the regiment was in the process of being equipped. The 'Cavendish Arms', the English-style pub in the barracks, open to all ranks and their families, which had previously been opened by the Duke of Devonshire, was also a success with the guests. Several reporters for the Lancashire Press were also invited, a practice which had become customary for such occasions in recent years; the proceedings were therefore fully reported in the regiment's home area in Lancashire.

During the winter of 1968, Captain G. E. Pike took part in the Great Abbai Expedition which made a survey of the upper reaches of the Blue Nile in Ethiopia. This was an ambitious enterprise, for the Nile with its savage cataracts, powerful currents and crocodiles, was a challenge to the small boats in which the expedition travelled. One man, a regular soldier, was drowned, and later the expedition was assailed by armed bandits who, however, failed to inflict any fatal casualties.

In May, 1969, the regiment returned to their old haunts in the Libyan Desert for six weeks training. Before leaving they were warned for service in the Far East starting during the summer of 1970. One squadron was to go to Hong Kong, one to Singapore, and the balance of the regiment initially to Tidworth. This was good news as the regiment had never before served in the Far East. It was destined also to operate in Ulster.

During the training in Libya while the regiment was widely deployed, squadrons and troops received the news by wireless

1970

that the regiment had been honoured by the appointment of H.R.H. the Princess Anne as Colonel-in-Chief of the Regiment.

On the return of the regiment from Libya, Lieut.-Colonel P. B. Cavendish, who received a well-deserved award of the O.B.E. on the completion of his tour of command, handed over command to Lieut.-Colonel J. M. Palmer on 1st July. After the usual hectic B.A.O.R. autumn manoeuvres, the Regiment was honoured by the visit of H.R.H. the Colonel-in-Chief. The Princess stayed at Paderborn from 29th to 31st October and her visit was one of the highlights of the Regiment's post-war history. Whether reviewing her Regiment, dining with her officers, dancing in the Warrant Officers' and Sergeants' Mess or talking with the soldiers and their families, the Princess's charm and youthful vivacity endeared her to everyone.

The appointment of a royal Colonel-in-Chief is an honour to which every regiment aspires, and the 14th/20th King's Hussars are indeed fortunate to achieve it in the person of so charming a lady who will provide so strong an inspiration for the worthy performance of whatever duties may lie ahead. Over two-and-a-half centuries have now passed since Dormer's Dragoons were raised for the defence of their country at a time of peril. The regiment has every reason to be proud of the traditions which it has built up during this long period of service in peace and war, and which it is determined to strengthen and preserve in the future.

H.R.H. Princess Anne, Colonel-in-Chief, during her first visit to the Regiment at Paderborn in 1969.

Regimental Armour 1938/1970

Vickers Mark II

Vickers Mark VI B

Stuart 'Honey'

Top Grant *Bottom left* Sherman *Bottom right* Cromwell

Top Comet *Centre* Conqueror *Bottom* Valentine SP (17 Pdr)

Left Centurion
Centre Saladin
Bottom Chieftain II

The Peninsular and South of France 1808/1814

India 1841/1941

South Africa 1899/1903

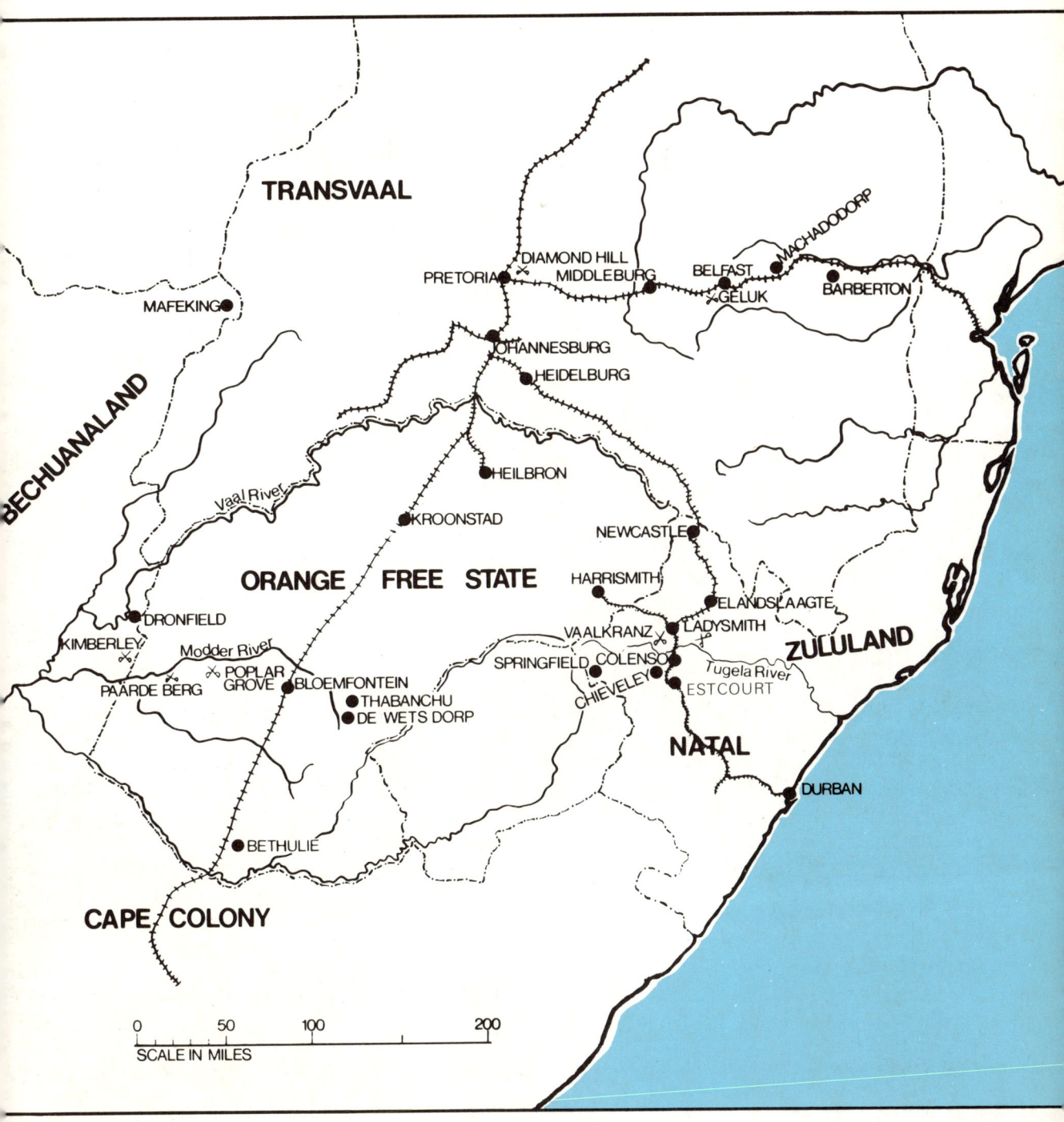

Mesopotamia and Persia 1857/1944

France and Flanders 1914/1918

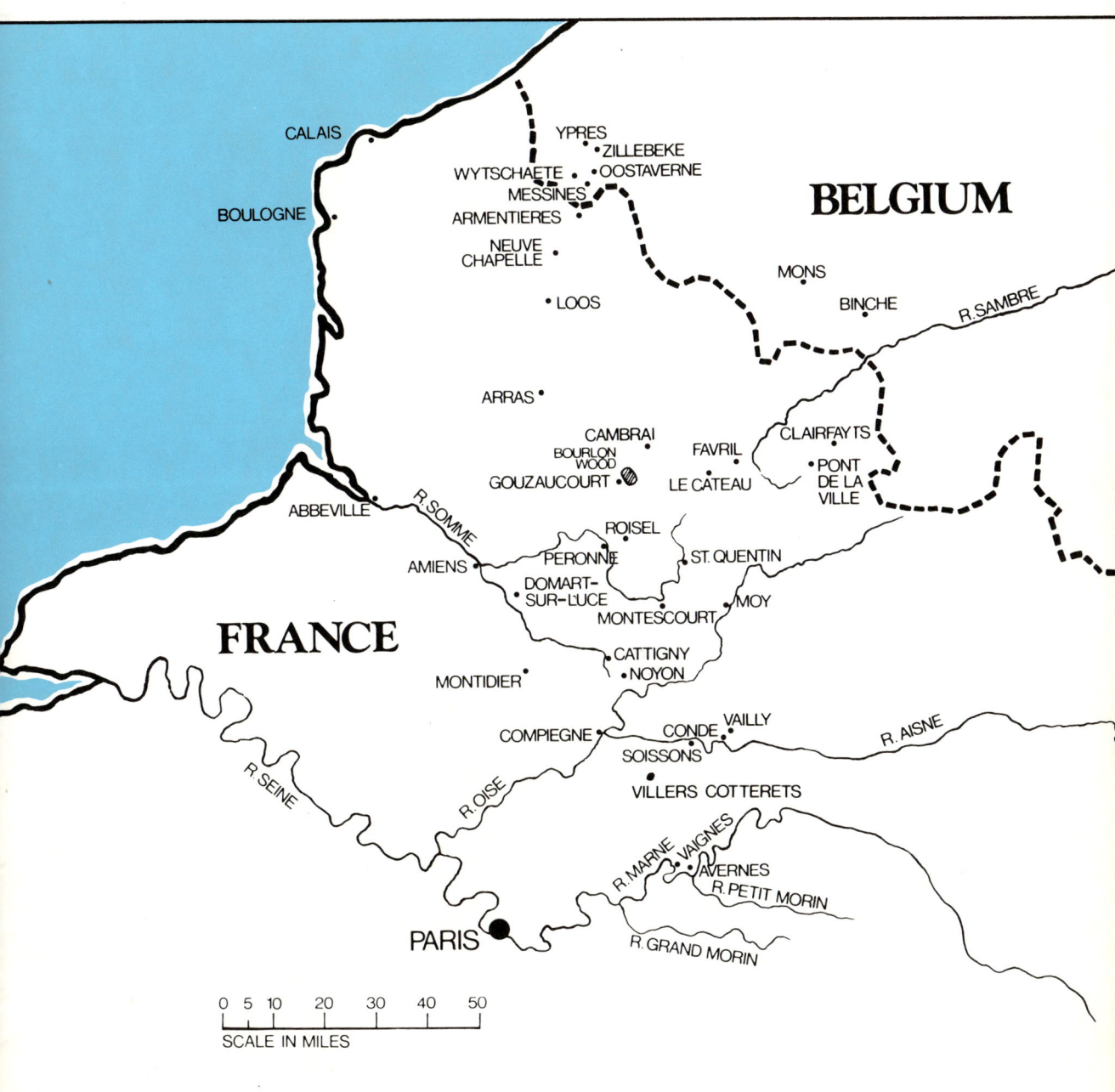

Northern Italy 1945

Major battles and engagements

Jacobite Rebellions

Preston Lancs 12 November 1715

The first engagement fought by the 14th – then Dormer's Dragoons. First Jacobite Rebellion. A fierce engagement took place near the Ribble bridge after which the rebels surrendered. The 14th fought dismounted and suffered the following casualties: Killed: 3 men and 16 horses. Wounded: Brig.-General Dormer and 4 men.

Prestonpans Scotland 21 September 1745

A force, under General Sir John Cope, was surprised by a night advance of the Highland army led by Prince Charles Edward in person. The cavalry were unable to get on the move before being surrounded by Highlanders, who stampeded the horses by cutting at their noses. A party of the 14th, then Hamilton's Dragoons, led by Major Bowles, fought with great distinction before being overwhelmed by the enemy. The life of Major Bowles, who had received eleven wounds, was spared by the intervention of one of the Highland chieftains.

Peninsular War

The Battle of Vimiera 21 August 1808

In August 1808, Wellington made his first landing in Portugal at Mondego Bay and after an engagement at Rolica defeated the French at Vimiera.

The 20th Light Dragoons were the only cavalry available to Wellington. Towards the end of the battle the 20th were committed and they carried out a magnificent charge at a time when our infantry was hard pressed.

At the end of the charge they were nearly cut off in an area surrounded by high hedges but they were able to get clear when our infantry arrived.

Colonel Taylor commanding the 20th was killed during the charge and the total killed and wounded in the regiment was 53.

The Passage of the Douro 12 May 1809

While the main river crossing opposite Oporto was in progress, two squadrons of the 14th under Major Bathurst Hervey, were detached with some infantry three miles up river, and having crossed the river in boats, charged the retreating French army. The charge was initially in column up a track with enemy on either side and in front. This operation cost the two squadrons a total of 36 killed and wounded.

Talavera 20 July 1809

One of Wellington's famous defensive battles. During a crisis in the battle in which the British centre became disorganised, a counter-attack was launched by the 48th Foot (Northamptonshire) supported by Cotton's Light Cavalry Brigade (14th and 16th L.D.). This counter-attack, with the 14th assailing the French flank, restored the situation and contributed to the victory.

Fuentes D'onor 5 May 1811

A hard fought defensive battle aimed at preventing the French relieving the fortress of Almeida. During the battle, Ramsay's Horse Artillery battery was surrounded, but with the help of Brotherton's squadron of the 14th and a squadron of the Royals which charged the enemy, the battery fought its way out with great skill.

The 14th suffered 55 killed, wounded and missing – of which 20 were officers and sergeants.

Salamanca 22 July 1812

An offensive battle in which the Cavalry distinguished itself.

At Castrillos on 18th July the 14th suffered 55 casualties in sharp encounters with French cavalry. On the 22nd at Salamanca, the 14th operated the 3rd Division against the French left flank, but were not heavily engaged and suffered ten casualties only.

The victory of Salamanca led to the occupation of Madrid by Wellington's army.

Vittoria 21 June 1813

The 14th did not take a prominent part in this great victory as the rugged countryside was unsuitable for cavalry. They supported the infantry as and when they could. They took part in the pursuit during which the baggage of the French army and King Joseph's Court fell into British hands, including the silver chamber-pot – now known as 'The Emperor'. This is still a valuable possession of the regiment.

2nd Sikh War

Ramnuggur 22 November 1848

During a reconnaissance of the River Chenab by a British Force, Lord Gough, the Commander-in-Chief, ordered Lieut.-Colonel William Havelock, commanding the 14th, to charge some Sikh cavalry which had crossed over from the far side of the river. This charge was successful in spite of difficulties caused by boggy ground, and large numbers of Sikhs were sabred and the remainder forced to withdraw.

The Sikhs, however, had a main position of great strength concealed in the dry channels of the river backed by artillery. This posed a formidable problem for cavalry on its own but Havelock decided to close this position forthwith.

Re-inforced by another squadron of the 14th and part of the 5th Light Cavalry, Havelock boldly led his troops forward under murderous fire. Savage hand-to-hand fighting took place and Havelock was amongst the slain. Another casualty was the cavalry commander, Brig.-General Cureton – a brilliant leader who had started his service in the ranks of the 14th during the Peninsula War. The casualties of the 14th were 44 killed and wounded.

One squadron was not engaged but formed a base on which the assaulting troops re-formed.

Chillianwallah 14 January 1849

A great day for the British infantry but a sad one for the British and Indian cavalry, whose commander contrived to get them into a position in which they were charged from the rear by the Sikh Horse. Private Tookey of the 14th, whose letters on the campaign have survived, was among the killed.

Indian Mutiny

Jhansi operations 22 March/5 April 1858

The fortress of Jhansi was regarded as the main stronghold of rebel power in Central India and was the scene of a slaughter of English men and women in June 1857.

On the 22nd March, Sir Hugh Rose invested the fortress, deploying the 14th in 'Flying Camps' under Major Gall, to prevent escape by the rebels.

On the 29th March while siege operations were in progress, it was learnt that a strong rebel relief was approaching. While the siege continued, a force under Sir Hugh Rose, including part of the 14th, were detached to where the rebels had crossed the Betwa River. After heavy fighting the rebels were overwhelmed mainly by the 14th, the Nizam's Cavalry and the Gunners. The rebels, who had fought well, were eventually put to flight and many of them perished in the Betwa River, losing all their artillery and much equipment. During the fighting Lieutenant Leith of the 14th greatly distinguished himself and was afterwards awarded the Victoria Cross.

The fortress of Jhansi was finally stormed and taken on the 3rd April. The enemy commander – the Ranee of Jhansi – attired as a cavalry soldier, had however, fled.

The relief of Kimberley 15 February 1900

During the advance of Lord Roberts' army towards Kimberley a cavalry division was formed under General French. This included 'B' Squadron of the 14th (commanded by Major R. M. Richardson), which was detached from the regiment and had landed in Capetown in January.

Having executed an opposed crossing of the Modder River at Klip Drift, French concentrated the Division in close formation, and as a result of the use of boldness, speed and surprise, broke clean through the Boer positions, sustaining only negligible casualties. Following this remarkable operation the Cavalry, with 'B' Squadron leading, advanced the remaining forty miles to Kimberley where they were received by Mr. Cecil Rhodes and the British garrison.

South African War

The battle of Ramadi 28/29 September 1917

On the 28th and 29th September the 15th Indian Division launched attacks on the Turkish stronghold of Ramadi on the Euphrates river.

The 6th Cavalry Brigade were given the task of blocking the Turks' escape route westwards towards Aleppo, and in particular to block the Aleppo road – a task given to the 14th Hussars.

In the early hours of the 29th the 14th – 170 all ranks – were warned by a patrol that the enemy were moving towards them. They were soon visible and fire was opened with rifles and machine guns at close range. The Turks suffered about six hundred killed and wounded within half an hour and the remainder – with the rest of the garrison – surrendered later.

Of 120 men of the 14th actually in the firing line, 27 were killed or wounded including the commanding officer, Lieut.-Colonel R. W. Hewett, DSO, who later died of his wounds.

World War I
Mesopotamia

Rifle Wood 1 April 1918

The attack on Rifle Wood, near Amiens, by a dismounted squadron of the 20th Hussars, commanded by Captain W. D'Arcy Hall, took place during the massive German offensive which started on 21st March 1918.

The Brigade, which was under Canadian Command, was mainly composed of dismounted cavalry units. The 20th Squadron, which was in the second wave, suffered severely from German enfilade fire during their advance, but they closed with the enemy and after hand-to-hand fighting secured their objective at the edge of the wood.

Three out of four of the 20th officers were wounded and the squadron suffered 46 killed and wounded out of a total strength of 138.

Somme 1918

Gebze 13 July 1920

Turkish nationalists had blown up the bridge at Gebze which lay on the communications of the British Force in the Ismid Peninsula. A force, including the 20th Hussars (commanded by Lieut.-Colonel M. C. Richardson), was therefore sent to dislodge them.

Indian infantry, supported by artillery, advanced on the village on the night of 12th/13th July, and at first light the 20th were assembled on the Northern flank facing the Turkish defensive position.

Taking the enemy by surprise, and with completely open ground in front, the 20th charged – swept through the Turkish position – wheeled, and passed through the enemy a second time. About 25 Turks were sabred; the enemy then withdrew, the bridge was secured, and British communications restored.

This operation is thought to have been the last occasion on which a British regiment executed a cavalry charge.

Turkish Nationalist Uprising

2nd World War

Gilan 25 August 1941

During the invasion of Persia, while the 14th/20th with the main body were advancing to the Pai Tak Pass, 'C' Squadron, commanded by Captain P. F. W. Browne, formed the advance guard of a force which was to advance through Gilan in order to outflank the Pass.

Although Gilan was unoccupied, the enemy held a strong position nearby which was assailed by the squadron and part of the Reconnaissance Troop under Lieut. Talbot. The ground was impossible for deployment off the road and when one tank was stuck in a wadi, Captain Browne and SSM Senior recovered it under heavy fire.

As a result of this offensive sweep against a strong prepared position by a handful of tanks, the Persian defence collapsed, and the way was clear for an advance to Shahabad.

Captain Browne received an immediate award of the Military Cross for his fine leadership.

The battle of Medicina (Italy) 16 April 1945

The town of Medicina was held by a force of German paratroops with armoured support and anti-tank guns including '88's'.

After an advance through difficult country and against strong opposition on the 16th, the 43rd Gurkha Lorried Infantry Brigade Group closed on Medicina in the evening led by 'C' Squadron (Shermans) and 2nd Bn. 6th Gurkhas carried in the APC's of 'A' Squadron.

'C' Squadron broke into the town just as it was getting dark, and in conjunction with the Gurkhas, overwhelmed the opposition by the speed and violence of their assault.

Major P. F. W. Browne, MC, commanding 'C' Squadron, who was severely wounded, received an immediate award of the DSO, and five other members of the Squadron received decorations.

Chieftain: the world's most powerful tank in 1970. Crewed by the 14th/20th King's Hussars in B.A.O.R.

Regimental moves and stations 1715-1970

14th King's Hussars

1715/1717	England	**Preston 1715**
1717/1742	Ireland	Mullingar Gort Cavan Sligo Athlone Ballyshannon Castlebar
1742/1745	England	
1745/1747	Scotland	**Prestonpans 1745** *Falkirk 1746*
1747/1795	Ireland	Castlebar Athlone Dublin Kilkenny Clonmel
1794/1795	Holland	2 Troops – Nijmegan Osnabruk Bremen
1795/1797	West Indies	**San Domingo Le Mirebalais 1797**
1797/1808	England	Chelmsford Canterbury Hythe Dorchester
1808/1814	Portugal and Spain	**Douro Talavera Fuentes D'Onor Salamanca Vittoria Pyrenees Orthes**
1814	England	Weymouth
1814/1815	America	**New Orleans**
1815	England	Hounslow
1815/1819	Ireland	Dundalk Dublin
1819/1825	England	Canterbury Dorchester
1825/1828	Ireland	Cork Dublin
1828/1833	England	Lancashire Yorkshire Brighton Midlands Gloucestershire Bristol
1833/1836	Ireland	Dublin Dundalk
1836/1838	Scotland	Edinburgh
1838/1841	England	Hounslow Dorchester
1841/1857	India	2nd Sikh War **Ramnuggur 1848 Chillianwalla 1849 Gujerat**
1857	Persia	
1857/1860	Central India	Indian Mutiny 1857/58 **Jhansi Calpee Gwalior Jowra-Alipore Ranode**
1860/1862	Ireland	Newbridge
1862/1867	England	Lancashire Aldershot Hounslow
1867/1868	Scotland	Edinburgh
1868/1874	Ireland	Curragh
1874/1876	England	Aldershot Colchester
1876/1881	India	Bangalore
1881	South Africa	Natal Ladysmith
1881/1886	India	Secunderabad
1886/1894	England	Shorncliffe Aldershot Brighton Hounslow Midlands Manchester
1894/1899	Ireland	Cahir Dublin Newbridge
1899/1903	South Africa	Boer War **Kimberley Ladysmith Pretoria** *Geluk*
1903/1906	England	Aldershot Shorncliffe
1906/1915	India	Bangalore Mhow Meerut
1915/1919	Mesopotamia and Persia	**Kut Baghdad Khazimain Ramadi Tekrit**
1919/1920	England	Tidworth
1920/1922	Germany	Cologne Rhine Army
1921/1922	Silesia	(One Squadron)
1922/1923		Cologne

14th/20th Hussars

1923/1926	England	Tidworth
1926/1928	England	York
1928/1930	England	Aldershot
1930/1931	England	Hounslow
1931/1933	Egypt	Abbassia
1934/1936	India	Risalpur
1936/1938	India	Lucknow
1938/1939	India	Secunderabad
1939/1941	India	Meerut
1941/1945	Middle East	**Persia 1941** *Gilan Pai-Tak Pass* Hamadan Quayara Mosul Kermanshah Shaiba Quayara Burg-el-Arab Damascus Alexandria Aleppo Sidon Beirut

499

1945	Italy	**Medicina Bologna** Chiavari
1946	Germany	Luneburg
1946/1947	Germany	Wuppertal
1947/1951	England	Catterick
1951/1952	England	Crookham
1952/1955	Libya	Sabratha
1956/1957	Germany	Munster
1957/1960	Germany	RHQ Hohne Squadrons Detmold Berlin Celle
1960/1962	Germany	Hohne
1962/1966	Libya	Benghazi (Squadrons periodically detached at Tripoli and in Cyprus)
1966	England	Tidworth
1967/1970	Germany	Paderborn
1970/	England and Far East	Tidworth: RHQ HQ Squadron Singapore: one Squadron Hong Kong: one Squadron

20th Hussars

1st incarnation
(20th Inniskilling Light Dragoons)

1759/1763	Ireland	

2nd incarnation

1778/1783	England	

3rd incarnation
(Originally 20th Jamaica Light Dragoons)

1792/1803	West Indies	Jamaica
1803/1805	England	

Right Wing

1805/1808	Italy Egypt Sicily England	*Maida 1806* *El Hamid*

Left Wing

1805/1808	South Africa via South America England	Cape of Good Hope *Monte Video* Buenos Aires

United Regiment

1808/1809	Portugal	**Vimiera**
1809/1812	Sicily	
1812/1815	Sicily Spain and Italy	*Castella* **Villa Franca** *Genoa*
1815/1818	England	Hounslow

4th incarnation

1861/1872	India	Campbellpore
1872/1879	England	Brighton Manchester
1879/1884	Ireland	The Curragh
1884/1890	Egypt	*Hasheen Tofrek Toski*
1890/1895	England	Aldershot
1895/1901	India	Mhow
1901/1903	South Africa	Boer War *Harrismith*
1903/1904	Egypt	
1904/1914	England	Canterbury Colchester
1914/1918	France & Flanders	**Mons** *Aisne Ypres* **Somme 1918 Amiens**
1918/1919	Germany	Berg Reuland
1919/1920	Egypt & Turkey	*Ismid*

Colonels of the 14th/20th King's Hussars 1922/1972

General Sir Richard L. McCreery, GCB, KBE, DSO, MC, Colonel 14th/20th King's Hussars 1947/57. He served in the 12th Royal Lancers, was Chief of Staff to the C-in-C Middle East (General Alexander) 1942/3, commanded a Corps in the Italian Campaign and subsequently commanded the 8th Army. He was C-in-C, BAOR, 1946/48.

Left
Major-General Sir Henry W. Hodgson, KCMG, CB, CVO, 1922/30 (14th King's Hussars).

Right
General Sir George De S. Barrow, GCB, KCMG, 1922/37 (20th Hussars).

Left
Brigadier F. B. Hurndall, MC, 1937/47.

Right
Lieut.-Colonel R. J. Stephen, MBE, 1957/66.

Left
Lieut.-Colonel B. B. N. Woodd, 1966/72.

Right
Lieut.-Colonel R. P. D. F. Allen, MBE, designated Colonel 1972.

Succession of Colonels, Commanding Officers, Adjutants, Quartermasters, Band Masters and Regimental Sergeant Majors
1922/1972

Colonels
1922/30	Major General Sir Henry W. Hodgson, KCMG CB CVO, 14th King's Hussars
1922/37	General Sir George de S. Barrow, GCB KCMG, 20th Hussars
1937/47	Brigadier F. B. Hurndall MC
1947/57	General Sir Richard L. McCreery GCB KBE DSO MC
1957/66	Lieut.-Colonel R. J. Stephen MBE
1966/72	Lieut.-Colonel B. B. N. Woodd
1972	Lieut.-Colonel R. P. D. F. Allen MBE

Commanding Officers
1922/25	Lieut.-Colonel J. G. Browne CMG DSO
1925/29	Lieut.-Colonel F. B. Hurndall MC
1929/32	Lieut.-Colonel C. G. Darley DSO
1932/36	Lieut.-Colonel J. A. T. Miller OBE
1936/40	Lieut.-Colonel A. V. Pope
1940/43	Lieut.-Colonel L. H. S. Groves
1941/43	Lieut.-Colonel J. B. Norton 26th Hussars
1946/48	Lieut.-Colonel H. A. R. Tilney OBE (Had previously temporarily commanded from 1943/1945)
1948/51	Lieut.-Colonel R. J. Stephen MBE (Had previously temporarily commanded from 1945/1946)
1951/54	Lieut.-Colonel B. B. N. Woodd
1954/56	Lieut.-Colonel R. P. D. F. Allen MBE
1956/59	Lieut.-Colonel P. F. W. Browne DSO MC
1959/61	Lieut.-Colonel E. G. W. T. Walsh
1961/64	Lieut.-Colonel G. A. L. C. Talbot
1964/66	Lieut.-Colonel S. R. M. Frazer
1966/69	Lieut.-Colonel P. B. Cavendish OBE
1969/72	Lieut.-Colonel J. M. Palmer
1972	Lieut.-Colonel T. G. Williams MBE

Adjutants
1922/25	Captain G. M. Hamer
1925/27	Captain F. P. Macintyre OBE
1927/29	Captain V. H. Jones
1929/32	Captain D. S. Frazer
1932/35	Captain J. D. G. Chaytor
1935/38	Captain B. B. N. Woodd
1938/40	Captain R. P. D. F. Allen
1940/41	Captain R. J. W. McAllen
1941	Captain J. E. Parry-Crooke
1941/44	Captain G. A. L. C. Talbot
1944/46	Captain B. C. L. Tayleur
1947/49	Captain A. R. Sturt
1949/52	Captain W. A. L. Reid MC
1952/53	Captain R. A. McClure
1953/55	Captain J. M. Palmer
1955/56	Captain P. L. J. Groves
1956/57	Captain J. D. Gowlett
1957/59	Captain W. D. Garbutt
1959/61	Captain C. C. G. Ross
1961/63	Captain J. A. Pharo-Tomlin
1963/64	Captain C. A. Park
1964/66	Captain J. V. Eyre
1966/67	Captain R. F. Cornish
1967/68	Captain D. V. F. Chappell
1968/71	Captain J. R. Smales
1971	Captain C. M. J. O'Brien

Quartermasters
1922/26	Captain J. F. Best
1926/41	Major W. J. Smith MM
1941/48	Captain P. T. Drew MBE
1948/56	Captain R. M. Roberts
1956/62	Captain B. E. Moore
1962/64	Captain R. Boulter
1964/70	Captain T. Vale
1970/	Captain E. Sheen

Bandmasters 1862/1969

14th King's Hussars
1862/74	Mr. G. Crowe
1874/83	Mr. A. Sims
1883/87	Mr. R. Foster
1887/1910	Mr. H. Hemsley
1910/22	Mr. W. Robinson LRAM

20th Hussars
1885/98	Mr. J. Hinds
1898/1905	Mr. A. Hendry
1905/10	Mr. R. Collier
1910/20	Mr. C. Hartley
1920/22	Mr. H. Carotti

14th/20th King's Hussars
1922/25	WOI W. Robinson LRAM
1925/41	WOI R. Grimes
1941/55	WOI R. Hurst ARCM
1955/62	WOI R. Mott
1962/69	WOI B. Thomas ARCM
1969/	WOI C. Petherham

Regimental Sergeant Majors

1922/25	RSM J. Goddard MC
1925/26	RSM W. J. Smith MM
1926/31	RSM S. W. Piper
1931/37	RSM L. E. Trueman MM
1937/40	RSM P. T. Drew
1940/41	RSM G. H. Swallow
1941/42	RSM A. E. Crocker
1942/45	RSM A. Slatter MBE
1945/48	RSM C. G. Smith
1948/52	RSM R. Saville
1952/53	RSM L. R. Charlton
1953/54	A/RSM A. E. Le Maitre
1954/55	RSM B. E. Moore
1955/61	RSM A. F. Prevett
1961/62	RSM E. Sheen
1962/64	RSM P. C. Witney
1964/66	RSM T. R. Cripps
1966/69	RSM S. Jude
1969/71	RSM W. J. Bingham
1971	RSM J. Sharp

Regular and Short Service Officers
1922/1970

Name	Final or present rank	Year of joining
Allen, R. P. D. F.	Lieut.-Colonel MBE	1931
Ambler, M. J.	Major	1907
Anderson, S. L.	Captain	1948
Bain, N. E.	Captain	1952
Barnes, C. L. R.	2nd Lieutenant	1969
Barrow, J. D.	Lieutenant	1963
Baxter, R. D.	Captain	1952
Beart, G. R. D.	Major MBE	1951
de Beaujeu, D. L.	Major	1957
Beaumont, J. F.	Captain MC	1945†
Bell-Irving, J.	Captain	1945
Bentley, W. H.	Captain (QM)	1965*
Best, J. F.	Captain (QM)	1917*
Bird, D. H.	Major	1959†
Boulter, R.	Captain (QM)	1960*
Bowles, W. G. C.	Captain	1963
Bridges, A. H. I.	Captain	1951
Bromley, L. P. J. S.	Lieutenant	1949
Brooks, A. B.	Lieutenant	1948
Browne, J. G.	Brigadier CMG, DSO	1900
Browne, P. F. W.	Lieut.-Col. DSO, MC	1933
Browning, P. C.	Lieutenant	1931
Brunton, D. J.	Major (QM)	1941*†
Bullock-Brown, E.	Lieutenant	1917
Burch, N. F. d'E.	Lieutenant	1958
Burnand, P. V.	Lieutenant	1954
Byrde, A. W.	2nd Lieutenant	1970
Caddell, W. M.	Lieut.-Col. (26H)	1941*
Cavendish, P. B.	Brigadier OBE	1965†
Chancellor, J. L. M.	Major	1948†
Chapman, J. P.	Lieutenant	1922
Chappell, D. V. F.	Captain	1960
Charlton, L. R.	Major (QM)	1953*
Chaytor, J. D. G.	Captain	1924
Clarke, A. F. S.	Lieut.-Colonel	1931
Clarke, E. E.	Major (QM)	1940*
Clarke, P. C.	Major CVO	1959†
Clifford, P. F. S.	Major	1934
Clifford, P. R. H.	Captain	1964
Clifton-Bligh, J. R.	Captain	1963
Coates, W. A. E.	Lieutenant	1922

* Previous service in the ranks
† Transferred from other regiment

Colquhoun, T. A.	Captain	1964	Hamilton, B. R.	Lieutenant	1966
Congreve, W. R.	Major	1935	Harman, P.	Major	1960
Cornish, C. C.	Lieutenant	1960	Harris, R. E. D.	Major MBE, MC	1948
Cornish, R. F.	Captain	1962	Hart, I. M. A.	Lieutenant	1948
Cripps, T. R.	Captain	1966*	Hart, T. W.	Lieutenant	1954
Cropper, P. G.	Captain	1912	Haynes, D. W.	Lieutenant	1932
Crotty, W. F.	Major MBE	1948†*	Heath, D. A.	Lieut.-Colonel MC	1942
Cullinan, M. A.	Lieutenant	1966	Henderson, J. A.	Lieutenant	1950
			Hiddingh, A. G.	Major	1933†
Darley, C. G.	Lieut.-Colonel DSO	1907	Hoare, P.	Lieutenant	1966
Darling, J. C.	Major, The Hon. DSO	1922	Hodson, K. M.	Captain	1961
			Holderness-Roddam T. D.	Lieutenant	1961
Dashwood, R. J.	2nd Lieutenant	1969	Hope, J. F. A.	Captain	1963
Davis, M. G. S.	Captain	1965	Hope, M. L. A.	Captain	1962
Dean, C. R. K.	Lieutenant	1966	Hurndall, F. B. (Colonel of the Regiment)	Brigadier MC	1903
Dennistoun, J. D.	Major	1931			
Donovan, J. S. A.	Major	1941*†	Hurndall, J. W. W. (Later Sqn. Ldr. RAF)	Lieutenant DFC	1933
Drew, P. T.	Major (QM) MBE	1941*			
Edge, W. R. T.	Captain	1964	Hyde, J. A. W.	Major	1951
Edwards, M. G.	Lieutenant	1966			
Eliott-Lockhart, P.	Lieutenant	1968	James, M. A.	Lieut.-Colonel MC	1946†
English, R. W.	Major	1954†	Johnston, C. F.	Major	1932
Eyre, J. V.	Major	1962†	Joicey, J.	2nd Lieutenant	1927
			Jones, V. H.	Lieut.-Col. OBE	1917
Fanshawe, E. L.	Lieut.-Colonel	1933†	Joynson, C. H.	Lieutenant	1954
Fenwick, P. T.	Captain	1953	Joynson, H. C. W. G.	Major	1966†
Finneron, J. A.	Captain	1944			
Fletcher, R. W.	Major	1948†*	Keegan, C. F.	Captain	1918
Fooks, O. J. F.	Lieut.-Colonel	1909	Keith, J. R. G.	Lieutenant	1962
Frazer, D. S.	Colonel DSO	1926	Kenward, P. T.	Captain	1928
Frazer, S. R. M.	Lieut.-Colonel	1963†	Kimball, E. R.	Lieutenant	1922
Fuller, P. F.	Lieutenant	1952			
			Lang, T. G.	Lieutenant	1961
Garbutt, W. D.	Major	1948†	Lethbridge, J. C. B.	Major	1923
Goodhart, J. H.	Lieut.-Colonel MC	1913	Loraine-Smith, G. N.	Major	1936
Goodhart, M. H.	Major	1949	Macgregor, J. C. W.	Lieutenant	1967*
Gordon, D. B. M.	Captain	1962	Macintyre, F. P.	Major OBE	1913
Gowlett, J. D.	Captain	1946	Maitland, J. R. B.	Captain	1949
Groves, L. H. S.	Lieut.-Colonel	1917	Mann, J. J.	Major	1938
Groves, P. L. J.	Captain	1945	Mann, C. J.	2nd Lieutenant	1970
Guiseppi, G. St. A.	Lieutenant	1950	Mann, R. J.	Lieutenant	1968
			Marnham, P. H.	Major	1940
Hall, J. R. S.	Lieutenant	1959	McAllen, R. J. W.	Captain	1935
Hamer, G. M.	Lieut.-Colonel	1914	McCallum, A. de S.	Lieutenant	1955
Hannay, R. H.	Captain	1934†	McClure, R. A.	Captain	1942

Name	Final or present rank	Year of joining
Meautys, T. G.	Major	1938
Melitus, P.	Captain	1948†
Micklem, E. J.	Lieutenant	1967
Midwood, T. I.	Lieutenant	1959
Miller, H. D. T.	Lieut.-Colonel	1928
Miller, J. A. T.	Lieut.-Colonel OBE	1908
Mocatta, V. E.	Lieut.-Colonel OBE	1907
Moger, J. M. D.	Lieutenant	1968
Moore, B. E.	Major (QM)	1956*†
Mosse, P. S.	Captain	1945
Moule, G. G.	Captain	1912
Mylchreest, M. D.	Captain	1949†
Nestle, J. F.	2nd Lieutenant	1934
Nicholson, H. R.	Lieutenant	1936
Norton, J. B.	Brigadier	1919
O'Brien, C. M. J.	Captain	1963
Oliver, R. W.	Lieutenant	1966
Osborne, P. J. B.	Lieutenant	1923
Palmer, J. M.	Lieut.-Colonel	1948
Park, C. A.	Major	1956
Parry-Crooke, J. E.	Captain	1938
Patrick, R. A.	Lieutenant	1961
Paul, C. E.	Captain MC	1948
Pearson, J. P. S.	Major	1935
Pemberton, C. A.	Captain	1954
Pemberton, J. B.	Lieut.-Colonel	1923
Petre, A. H. C.	Lieutenant	1917
Pharo-Tomlin, J. A.	Major	1954
Pike, G. E.	Captain	1964
Poole, G. S.	Captain	1924
Pope, A. V.	Lieut.-Colonel	1909
Prevett, A. F.	Captain	1961*
Ramsay, A. G. P.	Lieutenant	1950
Rawlins, J. P.	Captain	1963
Reed, P. G.	Captain	1945†
Reid, W. A. L.	Major MC	1948†
Roberts, R. M.	Lieut.-Col. (QM) OBE	1948*
Ross, C. C. G.	Major	1951
Ross, C. P.	2nd Lieutenant	1970
Russell, R. G.	Lieutenant	1967
Sanders, G. S.	Captain (SRO)	1939
Scarr, D. E. R.	Major	1947†
Scarr, D. P. R.	Major	1947†
Scott, G. L.	Major	1931
Scott, T. P.	Lieutenant	1967
Scott-Dickens, G. L.	Major	1948†
Sheen, E.	Captain (QM)	1962*
Silvertop, D. A. H.	Lieut.-Col. DSO MC	1933
Simmons, M. J.	Lieutenant	1954
Smales, J. R.	Captain	1963
Smith, W. J.	Lieut.-Col. (QM) MM	1926*
Sparrow, R. W.	Major MC	1914
Stanley, D. M.	Major	1915
Stanton, A. J. C.	Captain	1937
Stephen, R. J. (Colonel of the Regiment)	Lieut.-Colonel MBE	1929
Stephens, E. S.	Captain	1922
Stockton, W. J.	Major	1964†
Stopford-Sackville, N. V.	Lieut.-Col. CBE TD	1921
Studd, E. B.	Lieut.-Colonel	1931
Sturt, A. R. (Senior)	Captain	1915*
Sturt, A. R.	Major	1941*†
Sullivan, G. L.	Major MBE MC	1932
Sumner, D. D.	Captain	1942
Swallow, G. H.	Major	1941*
Symons, J. N.	2nd Lieutenant	1970
Talbot, G. A. L. C.	Lieut.-Colonel	1940
Tayleur, B. C. L.	Colonel OBE	1938
Taylor, M. A. B.	Lieutenant	1966
Thomas, J. R.	Captain	1948†
Tilney, H. A. R.	Colonel OBE	1924
Trueman, L. E.	Lieut.-Colonel (QM) MM 2OL (IA)	1937*
Tubbs, V. J.	Major	1957
Tyers, R. F.	Major	1948†
Urban-Smith, M. A.	Major MC	1946†
Valdes-Scott, J. A.	Lieutenant	1966
Vale, T.	Major (QM)	1960*
Vickery, P. R. G.	Captain	1964
Vickery, M. J. H.	Lieutenant	1968
Walker, G. B.	Major	1931
Walsh, E. G. W. T.	Lieut.-Colonel	1948†

* Previous Service in the Ranks
† Transferred from other Regiment

Name	Rank	
de Wend Fenton, J. D. L.	Lieut.-Colonel	1912
West, P. M.	Captain	1949†
Whadcoat, C. C.	Lieutenant	1917
Whittington, P. J.	Captain	1957
Williams, T. G.	Lieut.-Colonel MBE	1967†
Williams, D. A. J.	Captain	1967*
Williams-Wynn, R. W.	2nd Lieutenant	1970
Woodd, B. B. N. (Colonel of the Regiment)	Lieut.-Colonel	1930
Woodhouse, R. A. G.	Lieut.-Colonel	1914
Workman, P. J.	Lieutenant	1959
Wreford, D. E.	Major	1948†
Yorke, S. C. G.	Captain	1943

National Service Officers 1946/1961

Name	Rank	Dates of service
Arnold, J.	2nd Lieutenant	1952/53
Balfour, C. J.	2nd Lieutenant	1953/54
Batty, M. G.	2nd Lieutenant	1953/54
Batty, T. J.	2nd Lieutenant	1951/52
Beck, J.	Lieutenant	1946/47
Blease, C. J. T.	2nd Lieutenant	1958/59
Boddington, R. S.	2nd Lieutenant	1952/53
Bowering, J. A.	2nd Lieutenant	1953/54
Broadbent, G. A.	2nd Lieutenant	1957/58
Brown, N. S.	2nd Lieutenant	1956/57
Burt, D. L.	2nd Lieutenant	1949/51
Chetwynd, T. W.	2nd Lieutenant	1958/59
Cleveland, G. R. N.	2nd Lieutenant	1954/56
Craig, C.	2nd Lieutenant	1948
Cruise, C. R.	2nd Lieutenant	1955/56
Dromgoole, J. M.	Lieutenant	1946/47
Dunn, E. E.	2nd Lieutenant	1947/48
Eardley-Wilmot, C. V.	2nd Lieutenant	1951/52
Evans, N. A. P.	2nd Lieutenant	1955/57
Fooks, M. O. J.	Lieutenant	1946/48
Forgan, C. D.	2nd Lieutenant	1958/59
Fradgley, A. P. H.	2nd Lieutenant	1951/52
Garnett, C. P.	2nd Lieutenant	1951/52
Gilbert, J. S.	2nd Lieutenant	1956/57
Goodhart, J. H.	2nd Lieutenant	1951/52
Gould, P.	2nd Lieutenant	1946/48
Grant, G. I.	2nd Lieutenant	1948/49
Grieve, A. T.	2nd Lieutenant	1949/51
Groves, J. F.	2nd Lieutenant	1951/52
Hazell, C. J.	2nd Lieutenant	1958/59
Hicks, E. J.	2nd Lieutenant	1954/55
Hicks, T. P.	2nd Lieutenant	1952/53
Hill, V. B.	2nd Lieutenant	1956/57
Hinton, D. A.	2nd Lieutenant	1953/54
Horlock, P. M.	2nd Lieutenant	1948/49
Howe, K. G.	Lieutenant	1948/49
Huggan, T.	2nd Lieutenant	1946/47
Hughes, M. C.	2nd Lieutenant	1950/51
Hughes, J.	Lieutenant	1947/48
Hume, D. H.	2nd Lieutenant	1952/53
Hutchison, G. G.	Lieutenant	1947/48
Jameson, R.	2nd Lieutenant	1953/54
Johnson, J. E.	2nd Lieutenant	1954/55
Joss, W. H.	2nd Lieutenant	1946/47
Kampe, A. G.	2nd Lieutenant	1951/52
Kay, R. H.	2nd Lieutenant	1959/60
Kenward, J. T.	2nd Lieutenant	1952/53
Lee, A. J.	2nd Lieutenant	1961
Lewis, L. K.	2nd Lieutenant	1949/50
Ling, R. C.	2nd Lieutenant	1951/52
Ling, R. G.	2nd Lieutenant	1947/48
Long, R. C.	2nd Lieutenant	1950/51
Medwell, J. D.	2nd Lieutenant	1950/51
Mocatta, G. D.	2nd Lieutenant	1956/57
Moody, G. E.	2nd Lieutenant	1956/57
Musker, R. J.	2nd Lieutenant	1955/56
Oakshott, M. A. J.	2nd Lieutenant	1951/52
Patterson, W. M.	2nd Lieutenant	1952/53
Peden, S. H.	2nd Lieutenant	1955/56
Pitcher, J. E.	2nd Lieutenant	1948/49
Pollen, P. L.	2nd Lieutenant	1950/51
Rider, P. L.	Lieutenant	1946/47
Rollinson, P. F.	2nd Lieutenant	1954/55
Sewell, R. G.	2nd Lieutenant	1952/53
Shipton, A. A.	2nd Lieutenant	1948/49
Sidwell, D. A.	2nd Lieutenant	1951/52
Smith, I. D.	2nd Lieutenant	1958/59
Sparrow, D.	2nd Lieutenant	1951/52
Stanton, H.	Lieutenant	1946/47
Stell, L. V.	2nd Lieutenant	1956/57
Stoddart, D. R.	2nd Lieutenant	1958/59
Stoddart, P. L. B.	2nd Lieutenant	1953/54
Stopford-Sackville, L. G.	2nd Lieutenant	1952/53
Tennant, S. J.	2nd Lieutenant	1954/55
Turnbull, M. S.	2nd Lieutenant	1951/52

Name	Rank	Dates of service
Vaughan, D. J.	2nd Lieutenant	1958/59
Vernon, G. T.	2nd Lieutenant	1954/55
Villiers, Smith, T. F.	2nd Lieutenant	1954/55
Warrington, P. B.	2nd Lieutenant	1954/55
Wates, P. C. R.	2nd Lieutenant	1959/60
Wheaton, R. H. S.	2nd Lieutenant	1949/50
Whitwell, W. R.	2nd Lieutenant	1951/52
Willy, C. D.	2nd Lieutenant	1950/51
Winterton, N. R.	2nd Lieutenant	1958/59

Wartime Officers 1940/1946

Adam. M. L. B.	Lieutenant
Andrew, F. A.	Lieutenant
Beatty, J. L.	Lieutenant
Best, P.	Lieutenant
Blowfield, H. H.	Lieutenant
Bottomley, H. C.	Lieutenant MM (SAAC)
Boult, G. F.	Lieutenant
Brailey, K. T.	Captain MC (SAAC)
Brown, H.	Captain*
Burgham, R. C.	Lieutenant
Camburn, G. A.	Captain
Campbell, P. V.	Captain
Clarke, C. H.	Captain
Cornes, R. C. J.	Lieutenant
Court, J.	Lieutenant
Cox, E. J.	Captain
Cunningham, J. D.	Lieutenant
Dodgson, H. C.	Captain
Durnford, A. M.	Lieutenant
Elliott, F. L.	Lieutenant
Fraser, J. W.	Captain
Gill, T. W.	Captain MBE
Goldney, A. B.	Lieutenant
Groundes-Peace, J. V. St. C.	Captain MBE
Hall, R. H. P.	Captain
Hardy, R. McL.	Lieutenant
Harrison, J. E. R.	Lieutenant
Hemy, S. E.	Lieutenant
Henniker-Heaton, C.	Major
Hickmott, E.	Lieutenant
Jackson, O. M. H.	Captain
Jewels, T. S.	Lieutenant
Johnson, R. M.	Lieutenant
Kneller, L. C.	Captain
Lockwood, P.	Lieutenant
Longstaff, C. C.	Captain TD
Loveitt, G. W. M.	Lieutenant
Moffat, P. H. H.	Captain
Myers, C. T.	Lieutenant
Norman, F. R.	Lieutenant
Nottidge, T. W.	Lieutenant
Pickford, A. W.	Lieutenant
Ross, A. A.	Captain
Rough, W. G. S.	Captain
Rutter, J. H.	Captain
Saxon-Harold, D.	Lieutenant
Squiers, H. G.	Lieutenant
Stanley, P. E.	Lieutenant
Stratton, A. E.	Lieutenant
Strover, D. M.	Lieutenant
Taylor, S. T.	Lieutenant
Thompson, R. M.	Captain
Tilke, D. J.	Lieutenant
Vickers, L. H.	Captain
Wardley, W. J.	Lieutenant
Wharton, T. R. B.	Captain
Williams, A. J.	Lieutenant
Williams, J. T.	Lieutenant
Wilson, J. V. T.	Lieutenant
Woodley, B. J.	Captain

Attached Officers 1942/1969

REME

Captain G. D. Rose
Captain P. D. Jackson
2nd Lieutenant K. A. Masser
Captain A. F. Giblett
2nd Lieutenant D. B. Morris
2nd Lieutenant W. A. Allison

2nd Lieutenant I. S. Stark
Captain G. White
Captain R. J. Alexander
Captain R. Mealer
Captain P. R. Hemsley
Captain J. Fettis
2nd Lieutenant A. J. Creep
Captain W. D. Grant
Major W. H. D. Wood
Lieutenant D. Pilgrim
2nd Lieutenant M. A. Humphries
Captain W. Wall
Captain M. R. J. Kelly
2nd Lieutenant K. C. Todd
2nd Lieutenant A. E Sheil
Captain G. T. Ardrey
Captain D. E. King

AAC
Captain M. F. Sumner   DLI
Captain M. P. R. Barnes   WG
Major R. S. Evans RTR.,
Lieutenant D. V. Fortune, BW
Major H. D. E. Boyt, LG
Captain B. H. Poett, 5 DG

RAMC
Captain H. B. Hewitt
Captain R. W. Harvey
Captain J. A. Cooper   MC
Captain P. Blaxter
Captain J. Mathews
Lieutenant E. A. Sieger
Lieutenant G. L. Gibson
Captain J. W. Goodfellow
Captain J. Biggins
Captain J. W. Jerrams
Captain N. H. Munro
Captain A. C. W. Matheson

RAPC
Major E. V. Crombie
Major J. J. Langdon-Mudge

Captain A. E. Bush
Major J. L. Ferguson

RA Ch D
Captain The Rev B. R. Davies
Captain The Rev J. Temple-Bourne
Captain The Rev M. Guthrie   MC
Captain The Rev R. T. Holtby
Captain The Rev B. Howarth
Captain The Rev C. Low
Major The Rev C. King
Captain The Rev C. R. W. Gilbert
Captain The Rev T. J. Morgan
Major The Rev T. R. Jennings
Captain The Rev R. J. Stanley
Captain The Rev I. H. Bull
Captain The Rev J. C. R. Webb

Italian Liaison Officer World War II
Lieutenant Alvise De Robilant

The Regimental Medal

In 1909 Lieutenant-Colonel E. D. Browne-Synge-Hutchinson, VC, Commanding the 14th King's Hussars, instituted 'The 14th King's Hussars Regimental Medal', the old 14th Light Dragoons Regimental Medal having fallen into abeyance. This was to be awarded to any officer, warrant officer, non-commissioned officer or man of the Regiment who contributed in some conspicuous manner to the military efficiency or the military honour of the Regiment; further, it was laid down that length of service or attainment to a certain rank could not in itself be counted as a sufficient qualification. Since 1960, officers and soldiers attached to the Regiment (REME etc.) have also been eligible for the award.

Aldershot 1952: General Sir Richard McCreery, Colonel of the Regiment, being presented with the Regimental Medal by Major-General W. J. Eldridge. The medal was instituted in its present form in 1909.

1909	Colonel E. D. Browne-Synge-Hutchinson, VC, CB
	SSM. L. Dove
	Sgt. J. Goddard
	L/Cpl. H. Asquith
	L/Cpl. F. Crossley
	Pte. W. G. Bye
1910	Saddler Sgt. J. Spring
	Lt.-Col. E. J. Tickell, DSO
	SSM. R. R. C. Carnegie
	Bandmaster H. Helmsley
1912	ORQMS. C. W. Andrews
	SSM. F. Battson
1919	Lt.-Col. E. J. Bridges, MC
	Lt.-Col. H. F. Pridgeon, DSO, DCM
	Captain and Riding Master P. Thwaite
	SSM. J. Mayhew
	FQMS. A. E. Cooper
	SSM. S. J. Gardener
1921	RQMS. R. C. Dutch
1922	Lt. A. R. Sturt
1924	Major V. E. Mocatta OBE
	Sgt. A. Hallard, DCM
1925	Lt.-Col. J. G. Browne, CMG, DSO
1926	SSM. J. Procter
1929	Lt.-col. F. B. Hurndall, MC
	SSM. L. E. Trueman, MM
1930	RSM. S. W. C. Piper
	Major A. V. Pope
1931	Captain D. S. Frazer
1932	Lt.-Col. C. G. Darley, DSO
1933	Major J. D. L. de Wend-Fenton
	QMS. (ORS) D. R. Wilson
	Major G. M. Hamer
	Captain R. A. G. Woodhouse
	Tpr. A. E. Everson
1934	Captain (QM) W. J. Smith, MM
1935	SSM. (RI) H. Brown
1936	SQMS. W. Northam
1937	Lt.-Col. J. A. T. Miller, OBE
	Captain J. B. Pemberton
	SSM. A. E. Crocker
1939	RSM. P. T. Drew
	Sgt. J. Astley
	SSM. C. Waller
1941	Major J. B. Norton
	RSM. G. H. Swallow
	Bandmaster R. E. G. Grimes
	Sgt. (A/SQMS) P. Z. Germains
1943	Lt.-Col. L. H. S. Groves
	Lt. T. W. Gill MBE
	RSM. A. E. Slatter
1944	RQMS. C. G. Smith
	SSM. R. W. Easto
1945	Major R. J. Stephen, MBE
1946	Lt.-Col. H. A. R. Tilney, OBE
	RQMS. R. M. Roberts
	MQMS. C. G. Blacow
	SSM. V. Williamson
	Major G. H. Swallow, Bar
1947	Captain R. A. McClure
	Sgt. F. Winstanley
	Major J. J. Mann
1948	Captain P. T. Drew, MBE, Bar
	Major P. F. W. Browne, DSO, MC
	SSM. L. J. Adams
1949	Major R. P. D. F. Allen, MBE
	Major A. R. Sturt
	RSM. R. Saville
	TQMS. L. R. Charlton
	Sgt. J. W. Walters
1952	General Sir Richard L. McCreery, GCB, KBE, DSO, MC
	Lt.-Col. E. B. Studd
	Captain P. S. Mosse
	SSM. A. Senior
	Cpl. V. C. Coles
1953	Cpl. E. A. N. Holdway
1954	Lt.-Col. B. B. N. Woodd
	Major B. C. L. Tayleur
	Bandmaster R. Hurst
1956	Captain R. A. McClure, Bar
	SQMS. A. E. Cundy
	RSM. A. F. Prevett
	Sgt. J. C. W. Macgregor
	Sgt. G. W. Tasker
	Sgt. D. A. Williams
	Sgt. G. P. Shakespeare
	SSM. A. E. Le Maitre
	SSM. J. A. Reynolds
	AQMS. J. E. Thompson
	Sgt. W. Volley
1958	Major W. D. Garbutt
	RSM. T. Vale
	S/Sgt. J. V. Justin
1959	Tpr. B. Grubb
	Lt.-Col. G. A. L. C. Talbot
	Lt. (QM) R. Boulter
1960	WOI. J. W. Vickers, REME
1961	Lt.-Col. E. G. W. T. Walsh
	RSM. E. Sheen
1962	Major R. W. English
1964	Major C. C. G. Ross
	RSM. P. C. W. Witney
	Sgt. I. R. Rumble, REME
	Lt.-Col. G. A. L. C. Talbot, Bar
1965	Lt.-Col. O. J. F. Fooks
	Captain G. S. Sanders
1966	Major M. A. Urban-Smith, MC
	WOII. D. J. Flowers
	RSM. J. C. W. Macgregor, Bar
	SSM. W. Taylor
	Lt.-Col. S. R. M. Frazer
1967	SQMS. C. Osborne
	Major J. M. Palmer
	Major W. D. Garbutt, Bar
1969	Lt.-Col. P. B. Cavendish, OBE
	ASM. R. Ottaway, REME
	SSM. J. Sharp
	Major M. H. Goodhart
	Major (QM) T. Vale, Bar

1971 Colonel B. B. N. Woodd, Bar
Captain J. J. Escott
Sgt. B. Draper
Sgt. K. Steele

Index

Notes: The rank given against a name is that attributed on first or only mention; a rank subsequently attained may follow in brackets.

For individual engagements, see under Wars, Battles and Skirmishes, arranged in order of mention; also pp. 495–8.

A

Abercromby, Gen., 48
Adams, Lt. (QM) W., 336
Adams, SSM, 405–6
Aix-la-Chapelle, Treaty of, 31, 33
Allen, Maj. (Lt.-Col.) R. P. D. F., 463, 465, 470–72
Ambler, Capt. (Lt.-Col.) M. J., 411, 413
Amiens, Treaty of, 63, 65
Anne, H.R.H. The Princess, 483
Anne, Queen, 15
Anson, Maj.-Gen., 142
Anson, Lt. (Gen. Sir George), 45
Apthorp, Capt. Richard P., 222
Argyll, Duke of, 17, 18
Armitage, Maj. (R.H.A.), 299
Armitage, Tpr. J., 438
Armstrong, Tpr., 454–5
Astley, Capt. A. G. L., 382
Auchmuty, Sir Samuel, 73, 75
Austin, Lt., 401

Babington, Capt., 186
Badcock, Capt. L. B., 135
Baird, Gen. Sir David, 70–72
Baker, Lt.-Col. C. M., 199
Balcarres, Lord, 55–6
Banks, Tpr. V., 458
Barker, Brig. A. R., 454
Barr, Lt., 362
Barrow, Gen. Sir George de S., 427
Bassinthwaite, Sgt., 341

Battle honours: Vimiera, 89; Douro, 97; Talavera, 107; Toulouse, 188; Douro, Talavera, Fuentes D'honor, Salamanca, Vittoria, Pyrenees, Orthes, Peninsula (on Guidon of 14th/20th King's Hussars), 188; Peninsula, 250; Suakin, 255; Vimiera, 255; Marne, 337
Beamish, Cornet (Lt.) William, 241
Beckwith, Maj. William, 211–12
Beresford, Gen., 72–3
Blackford, Cornet Job, 116
Blackman, Brig., 480
Blackwell, L/Cpl., 424
Blake, Maj. (20th Light Dragoons), 95
Blake, Sgt., 425
Bland, Lt. J. Cooper, 401, 406
Blasco Sancho, trumpet fanfare, 475
Blyth, Cornet D'Urban, 222
Bonaparte, Joseph, Napoleon I's eldest brother (1768–1844): as King of Spain (1808–13) chapter 11 *passim*; his carriage and other possessions captured at Vittoria, 167; headquarters at Bayonne, 171
Boreham, L/Cpl., 442
Botha, Christian, 294
Botha, Hans, 303
Botha, Gen. Louis, 280, 285, 287–8, 291–2, 294–5, 297, 309
Bowles, Maj. Richard, 24
Boyle, Capt. William, 16
Brailey, Lt. (Capt.) K. T., 455
Bridges, Capt. (Lt.-Col.) E. J., 382, 396, 410, 413

Broadhurst, Lt., 258
Broadhurst, Tpr. L., 482
Bromley, Lt. L. P. J. S., 468
Brook, Sgt., 405
Brooke, Lt. H. A., 353–4
Brotherton, Capt. (Gen. Sir Thomas), 116, 119, 124–5, 130–32, 134, 147, 155, 158, 169, 172–3, 177–8, 406
Brown, SSM, 425
Brown, Maj. (Col. Browne-Synge-Hutchinson) E. D., 276, 283, 285–6, 299–300, 310, 343, 439
Brown, Capt. Robert J., 237
Browne, Lt. (Brig.) J. G., 300, 419, 437–9, 454–5
Browne, Maj. (Lt.-Col.) P. F. W., 452, 454–5, 472
Bruce, Capt. T. R., 354, 377
Brunton, Lt. (Maj) D. J., 437
Brydges, Lt. J. W. E., 201
Bunn, Tpr. B. L., 480
Burt, Tpr. J., 454
Burt, Lt. R. F., 407
Burton, Lt. R. W., 413
Butler, Maj. the Hon. Charles, 96, 170

C

Calder, Admiral, 68, 70
Caldwell, Lt.-Col. Sir James, Bt., 34
Camburn, Lt. (Capt.) G. A., 453
Cameron of Lochiel, 21
Cameron, Maj., 60
Campbell, Lt., 438–9
Campbell, Gen. Sir Colin, 217, 221
Campbell, Lt.-Col. Francis P., 251
Carew, Lt. S., 341
Carpenter, Gen., 18
Carter, Col. Arthur, 58
Cavendish, Lt.-Col. (Brig.) P. B., 481, 483
Chalmers, Capt. (R.A.M.C.), 299–300
Chamber-pot ('the Emperor'), secured at Vittoria by a patrol of the 14th Light Dragoons, 167–8
Chappell, Lt. (Capt.), 480
Charlotte, Cpl., 340
Chaytor, Capt. J. D. G., 425
Churchill, Brig. (Maj.-Gen.) George, 59–9
Churchill, Winston, war correspondent of the *Morning Post*, 274, 447, 451; quoted: 274, 282, 284–5, 443, 462, 464
Clark, Capt. (R.A.M.C.), 406
Clarke, Mrs Mary Anne, mistress of the Duke of York, 62
Clarke, Capt. (Maj.) William, 216
Clifford, Maj. P. F. S., 459
Collard, SSM, 301
Cook, Sgt., 333
Cook, Lt.-Col. G. T. R., 366, 400, 401
Cooper, Capt. (R.A.M.C.), 459
Cope, Gen. Sir John, 21, 23–5
Cornish, Lt. C. C., 480
Craig, Sir James, 69
Cristy, Capt., 334
Cropper, Lt. P., 398

Cumberland, Duke of, 27–32, 36, 39
Cundy, SQMS, A. E., 470
Cureton, Lt. A. J., 224
Cureton, Brig.-Gen. C. R., 217
Curran, Sgt., 362
Currie, SSM, 269

D

Dalton, Capt., 275
Darley, Lt.-Col. C. G., 422
Darling, Capt. (Maj.), 331
Dawes, Lt. B. M., 269
Dawnay, Lt., 407
Deakin, 2/Lt. C. G., 374–5
Dennistoun, Capt. (Maj.) J. D., 437
Denny, Capt. (King's Dragoon Guards), 282
Doherty, Maj. (Gen.) Henry Edward, 221
Donovan, Lt. (Maj.) J. S. A., 438–9
Doran, Sgt. J., 438
Dormer, Lt., 96
Dormer, Brig.-Gen. (Lt.-Gen.) James, 16
Dove, Cpl. (Sgt.), 285–6, 295
Dragoons, Dormer's, 16
Dragoons, origin of name, 16
Dundee, Viscount (John Graham), 21
D'Urban Blyth, Cornet William, 222
Durnford, Lt. A. M., 436

E

Edwards, Lt.-Col. G. T. G., 323, 332, 334
Ellis, Lt. T., 135
Erle, Lt.-Col. Thomas, 36
Erskine, Sir William, 129
Escott, Lt., 267–8
Evans, Sgt., 454–5

F

Fairbrother, Lt., 401
Fane, Brig., 87
Farquarson of Invercauld, 18
Farrington Gardiner, Lt.-Col. H., 45
Featherstonhaugh, Capt. A. E. H., 411
Fenner, Tpr., 471
Fenton, Tpr., 482
Fenwick, Lt. (Capt.) P. T., 471
Ferdinand, Archduke Franz., 319, 322
Finneron, Lt. (Capt.) J. A., 458
Fitzgerald, Capt. John F., 221
Foster, Lt., 310
4th (Dormer's) Dragoons: 17–25, 28–32, 34–5, 38, 483; in Ireland in 1747, 33; converted to 14th Light Dragoons, 41; changed uniforms in 1784, 43; contributed to recruitment of 20th Light Dragoons, 45; one squadron incorporated with 8th Light Dragoons, 50; in West Indies, 55–62; re-designated 14th (Duchess of York's

Own) Regiment of Light Dragoons, 62; at Chelmsford in 1803, 66; sent to Peninsula in 1808, 92; as part of Light Cavalry Brigade in Portugal, 93; secure chamber-pot ('the Emperor') belonging to (King) Joseph Bonaparte at Battle of Vittoria, 167; earn nickname 'the Emperor's Chambermaids', 168; brigaded with 'their old comrades of the '45' (13th Light Dragoons), 171; part of 'Ragged Brigade', 172; Peninsular War honours on Guidon, 188; land at Dover, July 1814, 199; arrive off New Orleans, 199; return from America in 1815, 202; praised in Gen. Lambert's despatches, 205; posted to Ireland in 1816, 207; open school at Brighton, 208; inspected by William IV, 210; praised as 'the most efficient corps in the British Army', 212; ordered to India, 213; in Persia, 231; become Hussars (1861), 249; *see* 14th Hussars

14th Hussars: sail for South Africa in 1881, 251; in India 1881–6, 257; leave for South Africa in 1899, 265; in action with the 20th, 312; attend coronation of King Edward VII, 314; baboon as mascot, 315; Prussian Eagle crest replaced, 344; other references *passim*; amalgamate with 20th Hussars, 418–19; *see* 14th/20th Hussars

14th/20th Hussars: re-designated 'King's Hussars', 427; mechanised, 428; Kukri badge approved by King George VI, 466; presented with new Guidon by the Queen, 473; presented with a Guidon by Sir Gerald Templer, 473, 476; headquarters established in Manchester area, 476; *Royal Sussex* adopted as regimental march, ibid.; converted to armoured cars, ibid.

Frazer, Lt.-Col. S. R. M., 479, 481
Frederica, the Princess ('Royal Patroness' of 14th Light Dragoons in 1798), 62
French Revolution, the, outbreak of, 43

G

Gage, Maj. A. M. B., 260
Gall, Lt. (Maj.-Gen.) Herbert, 215, 221, 237–8, 240–41, 243–6
Garbutt, Maj. W. D., 479
Gardiner, Col. (13th Dragoons), 23–4
George I, King, Elector of Hanover, 15
George II, King, 19
Giles, Lt. James, 239
Gillespie, Lt. (Lt.-Col.) Rollo, 54, 59–61
Goodhart, Lt. (Lt.-Col.) J. H., 325–6
Goring, Cpl., 336
Gowan, Lt. Lawrence St. P., 241
Gray, Sgt., 362
Greenslade, Lt., 338
Gregory, Cpl., 309

Grey, Lt.-Gen. Sir Charles, 45
Grosvenor, Lt. the Hon. H., 296, 307
Groves, Lt. (Lt.-Col.) L. H. S., 416, 432, 435–7, 445, 465, 468
Guidons, of 14th Dragoons, 36, 38; battle honours borne on, 89, 97, 107
Gwynne, Lt. John, 135

H

Haddon, Cpl. A., 438
Haig, Sir Douglas (Field-Marshal, 1st Earl of Bemersyde), chapters 23–28 *passim*
Hall, Lt. F. (14th Light Dragoons), 139
Hall, Sgt. H. H., 453, 455
Hall, Lt. (Lt.-Col.) W. D'Arcy, 326, 332–3, 340, 399, 401, 407
Hallard, Sgt., 413
Hamilton, Col. (Maj.-Gen.) Archibald, 20
Hamilton, Col. (Brig.-Gen.) G. H. C., 275, 299, 306
Hammond, Cornet R. C., 201
Hanley, Cpl. William, 155, 475
Hannay, Capt. R. H., 425
Hanson, Capt., 197
Harper, Tpr., 455
Harris, Capt. (Maj.) R. E. D., 472, 481
Harvey, Tpr. D. W., 482
Harvey, Lt. J., 301
Harwood, Sgt. John, 221
Hatton, Lt., 367
Havelock, Lt.-Col. William, 216, 220–21, 231
Hawk Dramatic Society, the, 470
Hawk, The, 466
Hawker, Capt. Peter, 96
Hawley, Gen., 28–30
Hayhurst, Pte., 333
Heath, Capt. (Lt.-Col.) D. A., 449, 455
Hersey, Sgt., 300
Hervey, Maj. (Col.) Sir Felton Bathurst, Bt., 97, 115, 135, 140, 155, 158, 169, 199, 205
Hewitt, Maj. (Lt.-Col.) R. W., 348, 350–51, 354, 357, 374, 384, 395
Hicks, Lt. E. J. N., 469
Highlanders, under 'Bonnie Prince Charlie': fighting qualities and reputation of, 22–3
Hill-Whitson, Lt. (Lt.-Col.) T. E. L., 296, 357
Hitler, Adolf, 297, 424, 426–9, 431, 434, 472
Hume, Lt. D. H., 469
Hurndall, Lt.-Col. (Brig.) F. B., 421–2, 464
Hurst, Bandmaster R., 466
Huske, Gen., 29
Hutchinson, Lt. C. G., 274–5

I

Ireland, Sgt., 440
Irish, among original recruits to 14th, 17

515

J

Jacks, Capt., 194
Jacobites and Jacobite Rebellions, 16–32
James II, King, 15
James, Maj., 472 M.A. (Lt.-Col.)
Jeffrey, Lt., 366
Jenkins, Capt., English smuggler, 20
Johnston, Lt. (Maj.) C. F., 425, 437, 440
Joicey, 2/Lt., 423
Jones, Tpr., 438
Joynson, Capt. (Maj.) H. C. W. G., 480

K

Kilmarnock, Lady, 29
King, Maj. (Lt.-Col.) John Wallace, 216, 221, 223
Kirkham, Cpl. N. W., 480
Kneller, Lt. (Capt.) L., 452–3
Knipe, Lt. (Capt.) R., 96, 134
Knox, Col. John H., 258

L

Landsheit, Sgt., 194; quoted, 71, 74–5, 86, 193
Lawrence, Capt. (Maj.) F. R., 275
Lee, Lt. H. R., 311
Legge, Maj. N., 311
Leigh, Trumpeter, 300, 301
Leith, Lt. James, 240
Light Dragoons, introduction of, 34
Little, Capt. (Lt.-Col.) A. C., 341, 390, 400, 401, 406, 417
Lloyd, Lt. Ambrose, 228
Lloyd George of Dwyfor, Earl, 321, 399, 417
Long, SSM, A., 455
Loraine-Smith, Lt. (Maj.) G. N., 425, 463
L'Ouverture, Toussaint, 57–8

M

McAllen, Capt. R. J. W., 435
McConnel, Lt. J. K., 341, 362
McCreery, Gen. Sir Richard L., 463–4, 472
MacDonalds (of Keppoch and Glengarry), 21
McGregor, L/Cpl., 454–5
Macintyre, Lt. F. P., 382
Mackintosh of Borlum ('Old Borlum'), 18
McMahon, Capt. William, 222, 239
Mann, Major J. J., 444
Mar, Earl of, 16, 17
Marlborough, Duke of, 15, 19, 36, 47, 193
Marshall, Cpl. (exploit at Vimiera 1808), 88
Mason, Capt. G. K., 360
Mewburn, Capt. S. W. R., 374
Micholls, Capt. (Col.) W. H., 366
Miller, Lt. (Lt.-Col.) J. A. T., 350, 424
Miller, Capt. Sir James P., 260, 285
Milles, Maj. T. P., 135, 161, 199, 205
Mocatta, Lt.-Col. V. E., 423
Moira, Maj.-Gen. the Earl of, 47–8
Money, Gen., quoted on the use of cavalry, 66
Montrose, James Graham, Marquess of, 21
Moore, Maj. B. E., 480
Moore, Sir John, 85, 91–2
Morrison, Cpl., 313
Moule, Lt., G. G., 383, 395–6
Murray, Lord George, 18, 28
Musgrave, Capt. Christian, 210–12
Mussolini, Benito, 427–8, 431
Mylchreest, Capt. M. D., 469

N

Napoleon I (Bonaparte 1769–1821): chapters 5–14, pp. 65–202 *passim*; 451; quoted, ibid.
Need, Capt. (Lt.-Col.) Arthur, 237, 239–40
Negro's Friends, the (society), 44
Nelson, Horatio, Viscount (1758–1805), 67–70
Newcomin, Capt. Beverly, 16
Ney, Marshal, 116–17, 125, 127–8
Nightingale, Florence, 356
Nixon, Tpr. C., 455
Norton, Lt.-Col. (Brig.) J. B., 432

O

O'Brien, Maj. (Brig.-Gen.) D. J., 275
O'Shaughnessy, Pte., 325

P

Pack, Gen. Sir Denis, 125
Pain, Cpl. William, 227
Palmer, Lt. (Lt.-Col.) J. M., 465, 468, 470–71, 483
Paris, Treaty of, 35
Parry-Crooke, Capt. J. E., 435, 444
Paul, Lt. C. E., 467
Pelham, Capt. Henry, 16
Pellew, Lt. E., 145
Pemberton, Lt. (Lt.-Col.) J. B., 421–3
Percy, Lt.-Col. the Hon. Henry, 205–7
Pichegru, 'Citizen-General', 48
Pike, Capt. G. E., 482
Plumley, Cpl., 455
Pocock, Col., 437–8, 440
Poole, Capt. G. S., 423
Pope, Lt. (Lt.-Col.) A. V., 351, 411–12, 424, 427, 432
Popham, Commodore Sir Home, 70–73
Prettejohn, Capt. (Lt.-Col.) Richard, 231, 239, 248

R

'Ragged Brigade, the', soubriquet of

13th/14th Light Dragoons in Peninsular War, 172, 181–2, 184–6, 189
Ramsay, Capt, Norman, 132
Rapin, Maj. Solomon, 16
Red Indians, 41
Redmayne, Lt. Leonard, 236, 239
Reynolds, SQMS, J., 470
Richardson, Capt. (Maj.) Lionel J., 260
Richardson, Lt.-Col. M. C., 415
Ridgwell, Sgt., 308
Rights of Man, Declaration of, 44
Roberts, RQMS (Lt.-Col.) R. M., 465
Ross, Maj. (R.H.A.), 169
Ross, Capt. Horatio, 467–8
Rumsey, Capt. (Brig.) L. C., 428
Rupert, Prince, 67
Russell, SSM, 300
Russell, Lt.-Col. Sir William, Bt., 251

S

St Vincent, Lord, 43
Sandford, Maj. (Col.) George, 45, 55
Sanford, Capt. (Maj.) G. A., 390, 406
Saxe, Marshal, 20, 31
Scarr, Maj. D. E. R., 472
Scudamore, Capt. (Lt.-Col.) 227, 237–8, 250
Senior, SSM, A., 438–9
Sexton, Pte., 301
Shakespeare, Sgt. G. P., 470
Shard, Lt. C. B., 413
Shenton, Pte., 307
Silvertop, Lt. (Lt.-Col.) D. A. H., 460
Silvertop, Capt. W. A., 390
Slade, Gen., 107
Smith, Tpr. H., 458
Soames, Lt. H. M., 330
Southwell, Lt. the Hon. Arthur, 178
Sparrow, Lt. (Maj.) R. W., 326, 332, 334, 336, 339
Stalin, Joseph Vissarionovich, 442, 464
Stanton, Capt. A. J. C., 432, 461
Steele, Tpr. J., 482
Stephen, Lt.-Col. (Brig.-Gen.) R. C., 343, 355, 465
Stephen, Maj. (Lt.-Col.) R. J., 435, 441–2, 447, 459, 465, 468, 472, 481
Steuart, Maj. (Col.) C., Bombay Army, 224, 236, 238
Stevens, Lt. James, 16
Stewart, WOI, Michael (R.A.E.C.), 447
Stratford, Tp.-Sgt.-Maj. J., 418, 423
Stratton, Lt. A. E. J., 458
Stride, Trumpeter, 299
Stuart, Charles Edward ('Bonnie Prince Charlie', the Young Pretender), 21–4, 27–32
Stuart, Brig. C. S., 235, 239
Stuart, James Francis (the Old Pretender), 16–18
Studd, Lt. (Lt.-Col.) E. B., 425, 435, 437, 444, 449, 465, 473
Sturt, Capt. (Senior) A. R., 420–21

Sturt, Capt. (Maj.) A. R. (Junior), 449
Sullivan, Maj. G. L., 460
Summerill, Mrs. 418
Sutherland, SSM, 310
Swallow, Capt. (Maj.) G. H., 441

T

Talbot, Lt. (Lt.-Col.) G. A. L. C., 437, 439–40, 463, 472, 476, 479
Talbot, Lt.-Col. Neil, 114
Tasker, Sgt. G., 470
Tayleur, Lt. (Col.) B. C. L., 436, 445, 469–70, 473
Taylor, Lt., 401
Taylor, Sgt., 309
Taylor, Col. Charles, 76, 87, 88
Thomson, Lt. R. M., 325–6, 339
Tilney, Lt.-Col. (Col. the Rev.) H. A. R., 445, 451, 454, 459, 463, 465
Tookey, Pte. George, 215–16, 222–4
Tottenham, Capt. (Maj.) C. B., 296, 298, 300, 313
Townsend, Lt. (Col.) John, 134–5, 183, 186
Tremble, Pte., 82
Trueman, SSM (Lt.-Col.) L. E., 421–3
20th Inniskilling Light Dragoons, raised in 1759, 34–5
20th Light Dragoons: resuscitated in 1779, 42; disbanded, 43; resurrected in 1791, 45; in Jamaica, 45, 53–4; at Colchester in 1803, 66; in convoy for Gibraltar, 68–9; land at Saldanha Bay in 1806, 71; in Argentine, 73–5; return home (1807), 76; in Egypt in 1807, 81–2; issued with new arms and uniforms (1808), 84; at Vimiera, 87–9, 95; as part of Light Cavalry Brigade in Portugal, 93; Peninsular War battle honours on Guidon, 188; land in Spain, 191; dispositions of Regiment in January 1813, 192; issued with new uniforms (1812), 193; return to England, September 1815, 198; sent to Ireland in 1817, 207; 'emerge from limbo', 249; other references *passim*; become Hussars (1861), 249; *see* 20th Hussars
20th Hussars: in Egypt and the Sudan, 253; in action with the 14th, 311; send detachment to coronation of King George V, 320; inspected by King George V, 342; their trumpeters sound *Cease Fire* 11 November 1918, 407; ordered to disband, 417; attached to 2nd Life Guards, ibid.; other references *passim*; amalgamate with 14th Hussars, 418–19; see 14th/20th Hussars

U

Utrecht, Treaty of, 15–16

517

V

Vatass, the Rev. Peter, appointed to 14th Dragoons in 1745, 36, 62
Versailles, Treaty of, 42
Villeneuve, Admiral, 68
Vyse, Col., 48

W

Wade, Gen. (Field-Marshal), 25, 27–8
Walker, Lt. (Maj.) G. B., 461
Walmoden, Gen., 50
Walsh, Lt.-Col. E. G. W. T., 472, 476
Warde, Gen. (Col. of 14th Light Dragoons), 43
Wars, Battles and Skirmishes: Spanish Succession, 15; Sheriffmuir, 17; Jenkins' Ear, 20; Austrian Succession, 20, 31, 33; Fontenoy, 21; 'Canter of Coltbridge', 23; Prestonpans, 24, 27–30, 32; Falkirk Muir, 29; Culloden Moor, 30; Minorca, 33, 42; Seven Years' War, 34, 41; American Independence, 41; Gibraltar, 42; Saratoga, 42, Dunkirk, 47; Tourcoing, 47; Valenciennes, 47; Bokstel, 48; Geldermalsen, 50; Tuil, 50; Le Mirebalais and Grand Bois, 58; Trafalgar, 68; Alexandria, 81; Vimiera, 86–9; Oporto, 94–7; Talavera, 98–107; 'Combat of Salinas', 102; Almeida, 117; Busaco, 118–19; Sobral, 123–4; Torres Vedras, 126; Fuentes D'Onor, 131–2, 134–5, 140; Gallegos, 131, 138; Badajoz, 137, 141–4, 146, 159; Ciudad Rodrigo, 138–42, 146, 151–3, 159; Carpio, 139; Llerena, 145; Valmusa, 147; Guarena River, 147, 152; Salamanca, 148, 151, 153, 155, 157, 159–60; Blasco Sancho, 156; Burgos, 160–61; Vittoria, 161–2; 165–70; Pampluna, 167, 169–70, 172; St Pierre, 177; Passage of the Gaves, 181; Orthez, 184; Toulouse, 187–9; Villena, 193–4; Tarragona, 194–8; Villa-Franca, 195–6; Genoa Advance, 198; Nervi, 198; San Martino, 198; Sestri, 198; New Orleans, 200, 201; Waterloo, 205, 207, 225; First Sikh War, 215; Second Sikh War, 216; Ramnuggur, 217, 219–22, 225; Chillianwalla, 223–5, 227; Mons, 225; Gujerat, 226; Crimea, 228–9; Indian Mutiny, chapter 17 *passim*; Jhansi, 238–41, 243; Kunch, 244; Kotah-ki-Serai, 247; First Boer War (1881), 251; Ginnis, 254; Toski, 255; Isandhlwana, 262; Maiwand, 262; Majuba, 262; Second Boer War (1899), 263; First World War, outbreak of, 317, chapters 23–28 *passim*; Second World War, outbreak of, 429, chapters 30, 31 *passim*; Medicina, 453–4
Wash, SQMS, 421
Wellesley, Arthur, *see* Wellington, Arthur Wellesley, 1st Duke of
Wellington, Arthur Wellesley, 1st Duke of (1769–1852): 61; in command of 33rd Foot, 47–8; Peninsular War, 79–202 *passim*
Whadcoat, Lt. C. C., 382
Whidborne, Lt. C. S. L., 397, 413
Whitelock, Gen. (Argentine campaign 1807), 76
Whitney, Lt.-Col. (13th Dragoons), 24
Whyte, Gen., 58
Williamson, Sir Adam, 56
Wills, Gen. (in Jacobite campaign), 17–18
Wilson, Lt.-Col. (Gen. Sir Robert), 192
Witney, RQMS, P. C., 476
Woodd, Maj. (Lt.-Col.) B. B. N., 463, 468, 470–71, 481
Woodhouse, Capt. (Maj.) J. D. F., 395–6, 411
Woodhouse, Lt. (Lt.-Col.) R. A. G., 350, 398
Woodley, Lt. B. J., 442–3
Woolf, Lt. C. N. S., 390
Wright, SSM, 354
Wright, Lt.-Col. William, 20

Y

Yorke, Brig., artillery commander 1806, 71
Youngman, 2/Lt. W. R., 411